THE MAYBRICK MURDER AND THE DIARY OF JACK THE RIPPER: THE END GAME

CHRISTOPHER J. M. JONES
and DANIEL L. DOLGIN Ph.D

'If investigators assume that something is too elaborate to be a fraud, then they are likely to be deceived."

Dr Kenneth W. Rendell,
Forging History (1993)

Brickmay Publishing Ltd

Second edition, 2024

First published by Mango Books, 2022

© Christopher J.M. Jones, 2022 and 2024

The right of Christopher J.M. Jones and Daniel L. Dolgin to be identified as the authors of this work has been asserted in accordance with the Copyright, Designs & Patents Act 1988.

All rights reserved. No part of this book may be reprinted or reproduced or utilised in any form or by any electronic, mechanical or other means, now known or hereafter invented, including photocopying and recording, or in any information storage or retrieval system, without the prior permission in writing of the publishers.

All images from authors' collection unless otherwise stated.

Cover design: Christopher Jones

Published by

Brickmay Publishing Ltd
Liverpool

ISBN 978-1-0687376-1-9

Printed by Ingram Content Group

THE MAYBRICK MURDER AND THE DIARY OF JACK THE RIPPER: THE END GAME

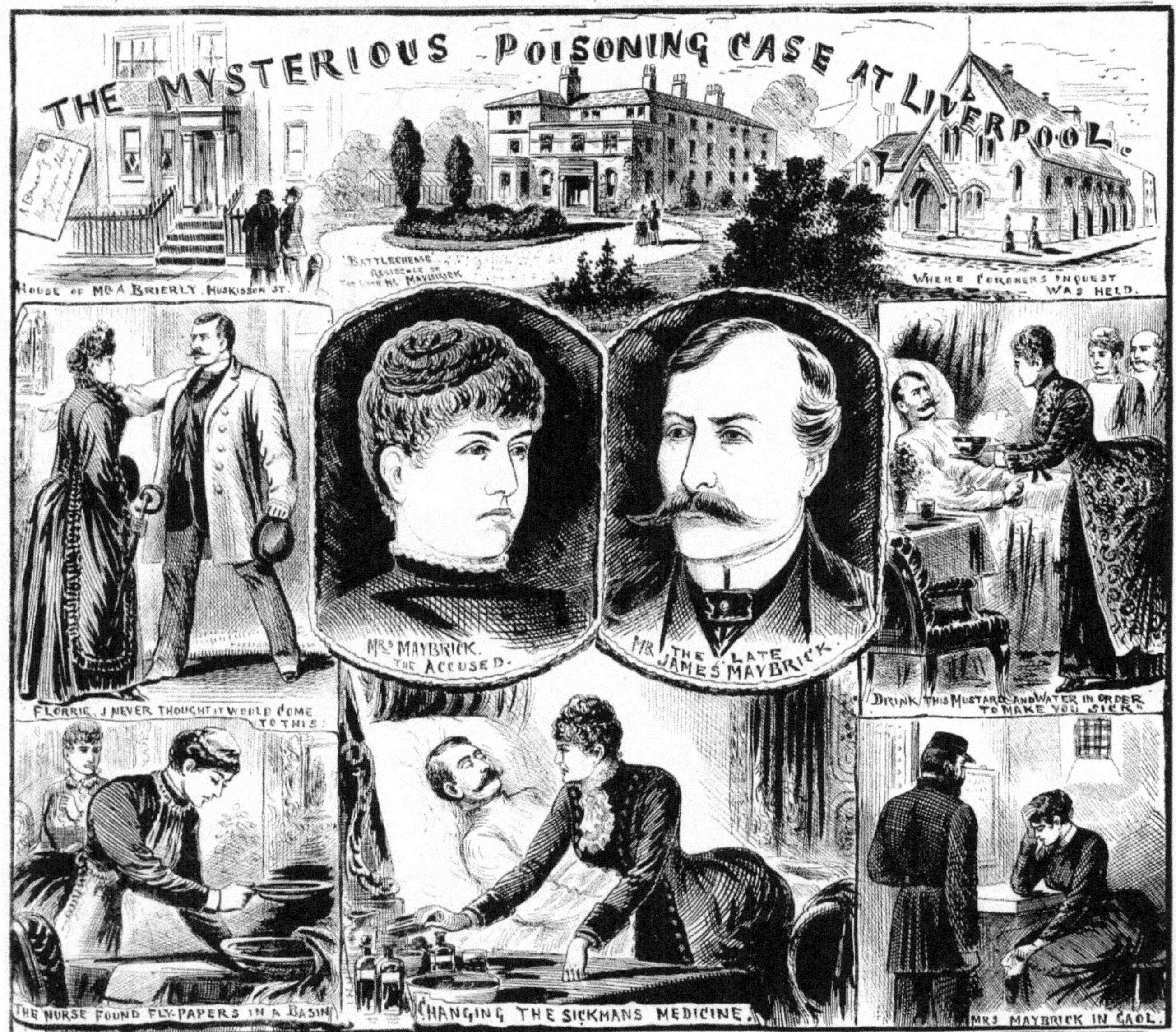

THE ILLUSTRATED POLICE NEWS
LAW COURTS AND WEEKLY RECORD

No. 1,321. SATURDAY, JUNE 8, 1889. Price One Penny.

For three special women:

Sandra Jones,
Nancy McKinnon (6th April 1956 – 30th April 2022),
and Florence Elizabeth Maybrick

JAMES MAYBRICK'S FAMILY TREE

William Maybrick (1772-1843)
m.1791
Sarah Pye (1773-1853)

12 children but only 6 survive into adulthood

John Maybrick (1793-1832) m. 1814 **Sarah Moore** (1794-1855)	**Michael Maybrick** (1799-1846) m. 1825 **Ann Wagstaff** (1803-1877)	**Martha Maybrick** (1802-1851) m. 1820 **John Ellison** (1801-1864)	**Lydia Maybrick** (1811-1850) m. 1832 **Simeon Burton Frankland** (1811-1842)	**Charles Maybrick** (1815-1873) m. 1835 **Ann Jones** (1815-1887)	**William Maybrick** (1815-1870) m.1834 **Susannah Wainwright** (1816-1880)
Ann (1823-1839) **George** (1823-1884) **William** (1824-1851) **Sarah** (1826-1832) **Charles** (1829-1831)	**William** (1826-1888) **Hannah** (1829-1854) **Maria** (1832-1838)	**William** (1820-1887) **Jane** (1824-1911) **Richard** (1827-1892) **John** (1830-1831) **Sarah** (1837-1851)	No children	**John** (1840-1911) **Sarah** (1843-1871) **Mary** (1845-1861) **William** (1847-1861) **Charles** (1849-1924) **Lydia** (1852-1937) **Ann** (1854-1920) **Emma** (1856-1941)	**William** (1835-1915) **James** (1837-1837) **James** (1838-1889) **Michael** (1841-1913) **Alfred** (1844-1848) **Thomas** (1846-1923) **Edwin** (1851-1928)

William Maybrick (1835-1915) m.1854 **Margaret Murdock**	**James Maybrick** (1838-1889) m. 1881 **Florence Maybrick** (1861/62-1941)	**Michael Maybrick** (1841-1913) m. 1893 **Laura Withers**	**Thomas Maybrick** (1846-1923) m. 1879 **Julie Tomlinson**	**Edwin Maybrick** (1851-1928) m. 1892 **Amy Tyrer**
Alfred (1855-1912) **Susannah** (1858-1932) **Mary** (1859-1919)	**James Chandler** (1882-1911) **Gladys Evelyn** (1886-1971)	No children	**Ethel** (1880-1976) **Thomas** (1885-1916)	**Amy Doris** (1894-1988)

ABOUT THE AUTHORS

Christopher Jones is a retired secondary school teacher, though he still works part-time as a mountain leader specialising in supporting DofE expeditions in the hills and mountains of North Wales. Christopher is a graduate in modern history and politics from Liverpool University. He later obtained the PGCE teaching qualification, a Masters in Education and the prestigious NPQH award. He taught in comprehensive schools in Bootle and Liverpool on Merseyside. He was for many years Head of History in a Bootle school before later becoming a Deputy Headteacher in one of Liverpool's largest secondary schools.

The authors next to a statue of Edgar Allan Poe in Baltimore, USA at the Jack the Ripper Conference, April 2018

Christopher has had numerous articles published. He had two published in the History of Education Society Bulletin on the work of 'Rosamond Davenport Hill at the London School Board' (1994) and the 'Hill Family and Hazelwood School in the early nineteenth century' (1996). In 2007, he organised the Trial of James Maybrick at Liverpool Cricket and Sporting Club, an event that was part of Liverpool's Capital of Culture celebrations. He went on to write the highly-praised book *The Maybrick A to Z* (2008), which he plans to update in the near future. He has contributed numerous articles on the Maybricks in various journals, including the excellent *Whitechapel Society Journal*. He has also contributed to two books produced by the Whitechapel Society. In the first, *Jack the Ripper: The Suspects* (2011), he wrote about the credentials of James Maybrick to be the Ripper. In the second, *The Little Book of Jack the Ripper* (2014), he wrote about the Ripper letters. As a person with a historical background, his core aim has always been to develop hypotheses based on the facts rather than to select the facts to support a preconceived theory.

Dr Daniel Dolgin is a licensed psychologist and author residing in the Pensacola, Florida area. He has a daughter, enjoys flying drones and all types of photography. He received his PhD from the Illinois Institute of Technology in Chicago. Subsequently he accepted a commission with the US Navy and completed a six-month Navy Flight Surgeon/Aviation Psychologist training course that included military flight training, ground school, human factors, physiology, and safety. A focus of interest was pilot selection techniques, technology transfer and international collaboration. He was appointed US Navy medical and human factors representative to NATO. As a result, Dr Dolgin facilitated the establishment of international defense exchange agreements with the United Kingdom, the Netherlands, the Czech Republic and Israel.

Commander (ret.) Dolgin is author or co-author of many published articles, textbook chapters and technical reports on personnel selection, pain management, historical non-fiction and cultural issues in psychology. His article 'The Babe of Mobile' appeared in *Ripperologist* magazine (2000). For several years Dr Dolgin was a columnist, photographer and monthly contributor to *Pol0tial Magazine*. A unique and educational coloring book, *Color Me Healthy With Diet and Exercise*, was published in April 2019.

His close collaboration with author Christopher Jones began in 2008, resulting in the publication of an article in the *Whitechapel Society Journal*, 'Florence and the Machine Inventor.' They both share a passion for Florence Maybrick, the world she inhabited and the enduring mystery that surrounds her.

ACKNOWLEDGEMENTS (First edition)

We would like to gratefully acknowledge the following for the assistance they have provided in the production of this book. Firstly, the wonderful and helpful library staff in all the libraries in which we have carried out research. That includes the staff of the Public Records Section at Liverpool Central Library; the staff at Mobile, Alabama; Highland Park, Illinois; Norfolk, Virginia; the National Archives in Kew and the British Library in London; Mobile Presbyterian Church, Government Street, Mobile. A special mention must go to the archivist at the Sonoma County, California Library. The archivist located the relatives of Frederick Cushing's granddaughter, Margot Crossman, who very kindly shared a copy of her grandfather's diary with us. Secondly, those knowledgeable individuals who provided expert help and guidance, especially our genealogically trained research assistant, Lois Marie O'Konek, Roger Wilkes, Derek Warman and Dr David LeMay M.D., who provided medical information about the detrimental physical and cognitive effects of arsenic and strychnine use. Thirdly, thanks to the kind volunteers who agreed to proofread the book: Geoff Poole, Lindsay Rogers, Lisa Wyatt, Dave Bruce, Colin Allen, Anne Navein and Colin Dunn. Finally, a thank you to Adam Wood, who provided some much needed help and advice, and helped facilitate the publication of this book.

ACKNOWLEDGEMENTS (Second edition)

We would again like to thank all the people and organisations listed above who helped us write and produce the first edition of our book. Some of these individuals have again been instrumental in helping us write and produce the second edition, especially Roger Wilkes, who has an endless store of knowledge about the Maybrick case and the Diary of Jack the Ripper. He reread much of the new edition and in so-doing gave numerous helpful pieces of advice. A special thanks must also go to Tom Langford who helped design and produce the cover for the new edition. The second edition includes a section on the Maybrick watch, an issue which was only briefly dealt with in the first edition. Help here was provided by Timothy Dundas who still runs his watch repair business in West Kirby on the Wirral. It is a wonderful establishment and Timothy Dundas is a charming and helpful individual.

THE MAYBRICK MURDER AND THE DIARY OF JACK THE RIPPER: THE END GAME

INTRODUCTION (First Edition)

BY CHRISTOPHER JONES

In 2007 it was the 800th anniversary of the founding of the township of Liverpool by King John. It was also the 200th anniversary of the founding of Liverpool Cricket and Sporting Club in Aigburth, Liverpool. The following year, 2008, Liverpool was to be the European Capital of Culture. To mark all these special occasions, each of the chairpersons of the sporting sections at Liverpool Cricket Club were asked to arrange special events.

Trial of James Maybrick, Liverpool, May 2007.
L-R: Donald Rumbelow, Shirley Harrison, Chris Jones, Keith Skinner, Jeremy Beadle, Robert Smith
(Chris Jones Collection)

As chairman of the Liverpool Collegiate Rugby Club, based at the cricket club, I decided to organise a historical panel discussion based around the lives of James and Florence Maybrick, both of whom had been members of the club in the 1880s. What I didn't know – and didn't suspect – was the widespread interest that would be generated by my idea. The original intention had been to hold a small-scale event one Friday night in the club. Shirley Harrison, author of the book on the Ripper Diary, was contacted and she agreed to attend. I then decided to contact some well-known Ripperologists and local historians and, before I knew it, I had somehow managed to assemble a stellar cast of experts. Keith Skinner, Paul Begg, Donald Rumbelow, Professors Bill Rubinstein and David Canter, and local expert Vincent Burke all agreed to speak. Michael Barrett rang me up out of the blue and demanded that he be allowed to make a contribution. I agreed to his request, though in the end he failed to turn up. One other person who also rang me to ask if he could attend was Jeremy Beadle, TV personality and true crime guru. He agreed to compere the whole programme, which by now had been transformed into a weekend event. As was to be expected from Jeremy, he compered the proceedings with charm and professionalism. Three other people in attendance at the event were Robert Smith, the current owner of the Diary, Albert Johnson, who brought his infamous 'Maybrick watch', and Paul Dodd, owner of the property that was once Battlecrease House, home of the Maybricks.

As a result of the trial event I was suddenly catapulted into the murky world of Ripper and Diary politics. I had seriously underestimated the strength of feeling that existed on both sides of the Diary debate, and was totally under-prepared for the onslaught of opinions that were soon drowning me in a cacophony of noise, not all of it pleasant. I decided that there was an urgent need for an objective review of both the Florence Maybrick murder trial and the authenticity of the Diary. It led me to produce my *Maybrick A to Z* book, which was well received. I tried to present the facts in a balanced manner, leaving the reader with the opportunity to analyse them and reach their own conclusions.

The book led to an unexpected series of beneficial and enjoyable experiences. I got to meet a diverse group of people, and even appeared briefly on TV as an expert on the daytime television programme *Murder, Mystery and My Family*. I met the leading players in the Diary and Watch saga, including Michael Barrett, Anne Graham and Albert Johnson. I know there were times when the relationship between the three of them was extremely poor; however, towards me, they were all courteous, helpful and engaging. On a visit to Barrett's house in Ainsdale, near Southport, he showed me the draft outline of a book he was planning to write. It was immediately obvious from its content and his handwriting style that Barrett did not pen the Ripper Diary, although he could, of course, have contributed in other ways to its construction.

The other great experience resulting from the book was what I came to call the 'Maybrick Odyssey'. As part of the research for my books and articles I travelled around Britain and America following the Maybrick trail. I visited Florence's birthplace in Mobile, Alabama. There I met my co-author, Daniel Dolgin, and we immediately became firm friends. He shares my passion for unearthing the truth about the Maybrick case. I went to the Maybricks' home in Norfolk, Virginia. I spent a wonderful day in Highland Park, a small town near Chicago. The Moraine Hotel, where Florence resided for several years, has long gone but there are still some remains, artifacts and records to be viewed. Perhaps the most poignant trip was to South Kent, Connecticut. I walked down Old Stone Road, and passed the spot where Florence had her simple home built. It was an isolated and rather bleak place, so very different to the grandeur of Battlecrease. I visited her grave in South Kent School, where Tom O'Leary took the time to show me around the school and provided me with a large amount of information.

I am a frequent visitor to Battlecrease – or as it is now simply called, number seven, Riversdale Road. Paul Dodd, the owner of the property, has had much to put up with over the years, but he remains remarkably cheerful and helpful. The outer façade of the building is very similar to when the Maybricks lived there, though the configuration of the rooms inside, especially downstairs, has changed considerably. On the first floor, now a rented apartment, it is still possible to see the room layout as it appeared on the plans drawn for Florence's trial over one hundred years ago. The bedroom in which James died is now a lounge area for the flat. The window still looks out over the cricket field, where occasional rugby matches are now played.

As a result of my travels and research, I amassed a vast amount of new material. I was helped in this quest by Daniel Dolgin and Roger Wilkes. Daniel, based in America, close to Florence's birthplace, was able to pursue leads that were beyond my capabilities. He is a likeable, determined and motivated character, with a long-standing interest in the Maybrick case and Ripper Diary. He met Paul Feldman and Anne Graham long before my interest in the case was sparked. He purchased some important items from Feldman, and has his own rather special collection of Maybrick memorabilia. With his distinctive American perspective, he has written two wonderful articles on Florence's case. His drive and ambition were crucial in the production of this book.

Chris Jones with Anne Graham, August 2021
(Chris Jones Collection)

Roger's interest in the case also long predates mine. As a local journalist with a specialist knowledge of the case, he was one of the first people whom Shirley Harrison contacted when she started writing her own book. He has a private collection of books and materials on the Maybricks that is better than any library. He has contributed many ideas and materials to this book, and we are grateful for his help and kindness.

All the new material we gathered gave us the opportunity to re-evaluate the events surrounding Florence's trial in 1889 and the appearance of the Diary in 1992. It was clear that many things written in the books about both cases were simply inaccurate, or were given an interpretation not warranted by the facts. We decided it was time to write a new book, one that would examine the question of Florence's guilt and the authenticity of the Diary. We believed people wanted facts and objectivity.

In this book we have tried to meet these criteria. We did not just want to produce yet another book on the two interlinked stories; instead, we wanted to produce a book that provided conclusions justified by supporting evidence. People deserve to know if Florence murdered her husband, and if James was Jack the Ripper. **Chris Jones (May 2022)**

INTRODUCTION (Second Edition)

BY CHRISTOPHER JONES

Dan and my myself were delighted by the response to the first edition of our book, especially when it won a Book of the Year Award from a group of distinguished writers and true crime experts. Nevertheless, we knew it could be improved and the second edition has a lot of new material in it. James Maybrick may have died in 1889, but the research into his life continues unabated. There is still new material to be unearthed and this book contains some new insights and information. For example, newly discovered records have shown James' membership details at the Royal Liverpool Golf Club at Hoylake on the Wirral. The course was the venue for the British Open Championship in 2023. We have discovered new details about the Domino Ball attended by Florence and Edwin Maybrick shortly before James' death. We have a new section on the Maybrick watch. Our aim, as in the first edition, was to get to the truth and not to impose our personal beliefs on our research methods or our conclusions. Hypotheses must be based on facts. We hope you enjoy the second edition of the book. **Chris Jones (September 2024)**

1

TWO MYSTERIES

Liverpool's two greatest crime mysteries are entirely separate, yet, paradoxically, totally intertwined stories. The first focuses on a young and attractive American woman, Florence Maybrick, who in 1889 was convicted of the murder of her much older husband, James Maybrick, a Liverpool cotton merchant. Florence's trial in Liverpool was one of the sensations of the late-Victorian period. It attracted worldwide attention, including that of three American Presidents and Queen Victoria. For many, Florence's guilty verdict was one of the greatest miscarriages of justice to have ever occurred in a British criminal court. Such was the outcry at the verdict, that it provoked a far-reaching debate which contributed to the creation of the Court of Appeal. Although sentenced to be hanged, Florence's sentence was commuted by the Home Secretary to life imprisonment. She spent 15 years in prison before being released, though she was never pardoned. Several books have been written about the case, and while most are sympathetic to Florence, they rarely provide a definitive answer to the question of whether she murdered her husband.

The second mystery emerged in 1992, just over one hundred years after Florence's trial. A journal was brought to the public's attention, allegedly written by James Maybrick, in which he supposedly claimed to be Jack the Ripper. The document, dubbed the *Diary of Jack the Ripper*, has proven to be one of the most controversial documents in the annals of crime. For many, it was an obvious fake. Philip Sugden, one of the most respected authors on the Ripper killings, savaged the provenance and credibility of the journal, and branded it a '*transparent hoax*.'[1] There can be no doubt that James Maybrick is the most controversial of all the Ripper suspects. He was a respected cotton merchant who, at the time of the murders, lived in Liverpool, the city of his birth, and not London. He was not considered a suspect at the time of the Ripper killings and is not mentioned in any contemporary police document. Indeed, he was not linked to the murders until the emergence of the Diary. James Maybrick's credibility as a Ripper suspect is therefore intrinsically bound up with the authenticity of this document. Is it possible that James was the most infamous serial killer of all time and that he recorded his innermost thoughts about his murderous deeds in a diary?

THE NINETEENTH CENTURY MYSTERY

For seven days in the summer of 1889, the eyes of the world were focused on a murder trial in Liverpool. Florence Maybrick, an American woman in her mid-twenties, was charged with the murder of her fifty year old husband, James. The case had everything newspaper editors could possibly want to grab the attention of their readers. First and foremost, there was sex, adultery and drugs, a heady mix that was guaranteed to shock the prim and proper mindset of Victorian Britain. Florence, a young and attractive woman, had become disillusioned with her older husband and had started to look elsewhere for romance. Alfred Brierley was her husband's friend and, like James, a cotton merchant on Liverpool's busy Cotton Exchange. Brierley was younger than James and Florence was attracted to him. Florence was also angry with her husband after finding out he was paying money to maintain another woman. In March 1889, Florence and Brierley spent two nights together in a hotel in London. When Addison made his opening speech for the prosecution at Florence's trial, he drew the jury's attention to the event and told them Florence and Brierley had '*lived there together as man and wife, slept together, went out together*.'[2] His tone was slow and measured, but his intention was clear; he wanted to paint a picture of Florence as a fallen woman, a person who was desperate and deprived enough to commit any act – even murder.

One of the elements in the case that caught the public's attention was the alleged use of arsenic to kill the victim. It was the prosecution's view that Florence had poisoned her husband with arsenic extracted from flypapers so she could be with her lover, Brierley. An important piece of evidence against Florence was her purchase of two sets of flypapers. On 30th May 1889, a Liverpool newspaper ran the headline '*The Flypaper Theory – A Reminiscence*.'[3] The flypapers were important, as five years earlier, in 1884, two Liverpool women, Mrs Flanagan and Mrs Higgins, had been convicted of the murder of three people using arsenic extracted from flypapers. Although arsenic was a dangerous poison, it was used in the manufacture of many goods and products that were commonly available in Victorian Britain, including paints, fireworks, paper printing, flint glass, plaster casts, vermin and insect powders, flypapers, clock and compass dials, and Fowler's solution, a medicine used to treat leukaemia and skin conditions.[4] Women used an arsenical-based solution as a cosmetic; they applied it to their faces as it would make them whiter. The widespread use of arsenic led to the passing of the Sale of Arsenic Act in 1851 to try and curb its sale in Britain. In an effort to prevent flypapers being used for '*nefarious purposes, they were made with a little bitter-tasting quassia and a brown colouring agent*.'[5] Therefore, to use an arsenical solution as a murder weapon necessitated disguising its bitterness. This could be done by adding it to something with a strong taste, such as brandy or meat juice. The Maybricks' servants testified at Florence's trial that some of the food in the house tasted differently to how it should have tasted.

---

[1] Sugden P., *The Complete History of Jack the Ripper*, (Robinson, London, 2002) pages 10-11.
[2] Irving H.B., *Trial of Mrs Maybrick*, (William Hodge, London, 1927) page 7.
[3] *Liverpool Daily Post*, 30th May 1889.
[4] *Liverpool Citizen*, 19th June, 1889.
[5] Blake V., *Crime Archive: Mrs Maybrick*, (The National Archives, Kew, 2008) page 29.

James and Florence Maybrick (*The Graphic*, 15th June 1889)

While Florence used arsenic occasionally in solution form as a facial cosmetic, James was a habitual user of the drug. He had first taken arsenic, along with strychnine, when a chemist recommended it to him after he contracted malaria in Norfolk, Virginia, in the 1870s. On his return to Liverpool James continued the habit. The use of arsenic was surprisingly common at that time amongst the more affluent businessmen of Liverpool, who believed it increased their virility. In the weeks before Florence's trial, newspaper stories started to appear about James' use of arsenic. As a result, his character and personality came under scrutiny during the court proceedings. James was a man who appeared to be healthy, sociable, successful and respected, but hidden beneath the surface was a person who could be difficult, aggressive, had hypochondriacal tendencies and was addicted to dangerous drugs. Some of these traits were known to his close friends, but as they gradually leaked out in the press, public opinion started to turn in Florence's favour. It became apparent that it was not just Florence who was hiding illicit secrets; her husband too had a dark side to his character. In June 1889, a month before the trial, a reporter from the *Liverpool Daily Post* tracked down a chemist who said that on many occasions he had sold James a *pick-me-up* tonic that contained arsenic.[6] Other newspaper stories told of his liaisons with women other than his wife. From Norfolk, Virginia, still further stories surfaced about James frequenting a local *sporting-house* or brothel before his marriage. Its owner stated that not only was James a regular visitor, but he also freely used arsenic whilst on the premises.

As more and more sordid stories about James and Florence emerged, public interest in the case grew dramatically and *Maybrick mania* gripped Liverpool. The case became such a *cause célèbre* that it transcended national boundaries. While James had been born and bred in Liverpool, Florence was an American, born in Mobile, Alabama. After the guilty verdict, the American public rallied to her side, led by the formidable campaigner Mary Dodge (who wrote under the pseudonym Gail Hamilton), whom Florence described as '*my most eloquent and steadfast champion in America*.'[7] Mary Dodge had the advantage of being the cousin of Mrs James Blaine, the wife of the Secretary of State in the Benjamin Harrison Presidency, and she was prepared to use this connection to the advantage of Florence's campaign. With Dr Helen Densmore's help, Dodge organised the Women's International Maybrick Association. Its first president was Caroline Harrison, the First Lady. On the committee were many of the leading American suffragettes of the day. Christie wrote about these women, '*No mountain of opposition was too high for these feminine Zolas to scale, no pit of apathy too deep for them to scour in their zeal for their heroine*.'[8]

Maybrick mania was further fuelled by the fact that the drama had a smattering of well-known public figures at the heart of its proceedings. One of the most famous was James' brother, Michael Maybrick (1841-1913), who was England's leading baritone. His music bridged both the operatic world and the field of popular singing, and some of his tunes were the best known of the day, earning him both money and fame. As well as being an outstanding singer, Michael was a prolific composer of popular songs, writing under the name *Stephen Adams*. His first successful song was *A Warrior Bold.* He accepted 5s for it, plus a royalty which amounted to well over a thousand pounds within a few years. With Frederick Weatherly (who wrote the lyrics), he co-wrote a string of best-selling songs, starting with *Nancy Lee* in 1877, which brought him to national prominence and quickly '*netted £1,000' in royalties*.'[9] His next big success was *The Midshipmite*, which he sang at concerts in St James's Hall. Two of his sacred songs, *The Star of Bethlehem* and *The Holy City*, brought him international acclaim and, in 1884 he toured North America. The wealth that Michael earned from his concerts and royalties enabled him to acquire an exclusive flat in Wellington Mansions, near Regent's Park in London, and later a large house on the Isle of Wight.

Florence's trial was also significant because it opened a window on the gender inequalities that were never far from the surface in Victorian Britain. As a woman, Florence faced double standards both in terms of the law and the powerful social norms that governed expected behaviours. Under British divorce laws, a man only had to show that his wife had committed adultery in order to get a legal separation and divorce; whilst a wife, in addition to adultery, also had to prove that she had been subject to cruelty, desertion, or a serious sexual assault such as rape. Even if the woman had the evidence to support her case, the process could be slow and expensive, and she still might lose custody of her children. Even more of a straight-jacket than the legal constraints was the social value system that directed how a woman should behave. Middle class women were expected to be '*strong in the management of their staff but weak and passive as wives*.' Wives who did not

[6] *Liverpool Daily Post*, 15th June 1889.
[7] Maybrick F., *My Fifteen Lost Years*, (Funk and Wagnalls, London, 1905) page 139.
[8] Christie T.L., *Etched in Arsenic*, (Harrap and Co., London, 1969) page 190.
[9] *Edinburgh Evening News*, 17th December 1877.

conform to the prevailing values of '*chastity, philanthropy and morality risked being judged as depraved or even mad.*'[10] While James' adultery might receive looks of disapproval, Florence's behaviour with Brierley shocked the nation. Queen Victoria, influenced by Florence's adultery, believed her to be guilty of murder. Only after the intervention of Henry Matthews, the Home Secretary, did she reluctantly agree to commute the sentence to life in prison. Queen Victoria wrote, '*the only regret that she feels about the decision is that so wicked a woman should escape by a mere legal quibble! The law is not a moral profession, she must say. But she must never be further commuted.*'[11] The Queen was true to her word, and despite numerous representations to her, including those from three different American Presidents, she stubbornly refused to contemplate Florence's early release. It was only after the Queen's death and the accession to the throne of her son, Edward VII, that Florence finally got released from prison.

Was Florence guilty of poisoning James? The jury clearly thought so. Successive Home Secretaries also thought so, as they resisted several well-orchestrated attempts by Florence's supporters to get her pardoned. To answer the question of whether Florence was guilty or not, we must examine the two questions Sir Charles Russell, Florence's defence counsel, posed to the jury at her trial. The first was: '*could it be proved that James died from arsenical poisoning*?' This is an especially pertinent question as the amount of arsenic found in his body after his death was insufficient to kill a normal person, let alone someone who regularly took the drug. The second of Russell's questions was: '*if it was a case of arsenical poisoning, then was the poison administered by Florence*?' Florence had added a mysterious powder, shown later to be arsenic, to a bottle of meat juice that was due to be given to James during his illness. There was, therefore, a case to be answered, but was Florence guilty of the crime for which she was convicted?

THE TWENTIETH CENTURY MYSTERY

In March 1992, Michael Barrett, a retired scrap metal dealer from Liverpool, telephoned Doreen Montgomery, a leading figure in the Rupert Crew Literary Agency in London. He said his name was Williams and that he had Jack the Ripper's Diary. The following month Barrett – using his real name – took the Diary to London and showed it to Montgomery and the writer, Shirley Harrison.

The Diary measured approximately 11 by 8½ inches. It was hardbound in black cloth with black leather quarter binding, with seven bands of gold foil across the two-inch spine. It appeared that it might have originally been a scrapbook or a photograph album. The paper was largely of a good quality, and was well-preserved. The first 48 pages had been cut and torn out; there were 63 pages with handwriting on and 17 blank pages at the end.

The Diary of Jack the Ripper (Chris Jones Collection)

The Diary provided a graphic account of the murders of seven women, including the five canonical Ripper victims. Its author claimed he '*was once a gentle man*' but had been driven to embark on his murderous campaign as a result of anger at his wife who was having an affair. It ended dramatically, with the infamous signature '*Yours truly Jack the Ripper*,' and was dated '*third of May 1889*.' From some of the references in the narrative the supposed author could be identified as James Maybrick, a Liverpool cotton merchant who had died in May 1889, some six months after the murder of Mary Kelly, who is usually regarded as the last of the Ripper's victims.

Michael Barrett (1952-2016) told Montgomery and Harrison his story. He was a Liverpudlian who had held a variety of occupations, including working as a scrap metal dealer. In 1976, he married Anne Graham, and in 1981 they had a daughter named Caroline. Following an accident, Barrett became a house husband, looking after Caroline while Anne went to work as a secretary. In the early 1990s, the Barretts lived in Goldie Street, Kirkdale in Liverpool. Barrett would pick up his daughter from primary school in nearby Fountains Road. On the way he would stop off in the Saddle pub and have a drink with one of his friends, Tony Devereux, who had worked as a compositor on the *Liverpool Echo*. Barrett claimed that in May 1991, while he was visiting Devereux in his house, Tony gave him a brown paper parcel and told him to '*do something with it*.' Barrett opened the parcel at home and found it contained the Diary. He had repeatedly quizzed Devereux about where he got the Diary from, but he would not answer his questions. In August 1991, Devereux died from a heart attack so was unable to substantiate the story told to Doreen Montgomery and Shirley Harrison. One of his daughters, Nancy Steele, said in May 2007 that no-one in her family had ever seen her father with the Diary, and they would have known if he had kept it for any length of time.[12] Harrison listened to Barrett and, '*on the spur of the moment*,' decided to take the Diary to the nearby British Museum so an expert could view it.[13] A manuscript historian studied the document and said it

[10] Colquhoun K., *Did She Kill Him?*, (Little Brown, London, 2014) page 38.
[11] Quoted in Graham A. and Emmas C., *The Last Victim*, (Headline, London, 1999) page 215.
[12] Jones C., *The Maybrick A to Z*, (Countywise, Birkenhead, 2008) pages 122-123.
[13] Harrison S., *The Diary of Jack the Ripper*, (Blake, London, 1998) page 10.

looked authentic, but recommended it be scientifically tested. Harrison then took it to Jarndyce's antiquarian bookshop, where the owner also felt it could be authentic but again recommended it should be scientifically tested. These positive comments on the Diary's authenticity led Montgomery to draw up an agreement of collaboration between Harrison, Michael Barrett and his wife Anne, binding them '*to share the responsibilities, expenses and royalties*' from any future book written about the Diary.[14] In June 1992, Robert Smith of the publishing company Smith Gryphon, made a successful bid to win the publishing rights for the Diary.

The biggest problem in accepting the Diary as the genuine journal of James Maybrick is its poor provenance. Since 1992, Barrett's account of how he acquired the Diary has changed on several occasions. To make matters more confusing, Anne Graham (Barrett's wife was to revert to her maiden name following their divorce) provided a different account of its origins. Their changing versions of events can only be understood by placing them in the context of the bitter breakup of their marriage. Anne had been reluctant in 1992 and 1993 to become involved in any discussions on the Diary's provenance, or the production of Harrison's book. She also refused to accept royalties from the book. She later claimed she had considered burning the Diary. Robert Smith suggests a possible explanation for Anne's behaviour was she believed her husband had stolen the Diary and was '*determined to distance herself from any criminal activity.*'[15] As media speculation on the Diary's origins reached fever pitch, the pressures on Barrett grew to breaking point and he started to drink excessively. This led to violent arguments. On Sunday 2nd January 1994, Anne left Barrett after he had assaulted her and left her unconscious. She took their daughter, Caroline, and never returned to Goldie Street. According to a letter Anne wrote to Paul Feldman in July 1995, she had endured years of abuse due mainly to her husband's alcoholism.[16]

In May 1994, Paul Feldman (1953-2005), who had bought the video rights to the Diary, started to investigate the hypothesis that Anne Graham was a descendant of James Maybrick through his relationship with his long-term mistress, Sarah Ann Robertson. Michael Barrett was furious when he heard Feldman's claims. In June 1994, he gave an interview to a *Liverpool Daily Post* reporter, Harold Brough, in which he claimed he had forged the Diary. Five days later he retracted the confession. His solicitor stated he had not been in full control of his faculties when he made the confession, and that he had gone into the alcohol treatment unit of a local hospital for help with his drinking problems.

Although the relationship between Feldman and Anne Graham had been decidedly frosty, in July 1994 she travelled to London with Caroline and stayed at his house. While there, Anne surprised Feldman by telling him the Diary had been given to her by her father. She claimed to have given it to Devereux so he in turn could give it to her husband, whom she hoped would use it to write a novel. Her father, Billy Graham, supported her account and said he had been given it by his step-mother, Edith Formby, whose own mother, Elizabeth (née Griffiths) Formby, had supposedly been a friend of Nurse Yapp, the Maybricks' nanny. Feldman was delighted with Anne's account as it provided him with an alternative provenance for the Diary, one which allowed him in August 1994, to sign a film deal with New Line Cinema. Feldman then started to pursue a new hypothesis, one that saw Anne being descended not from James but from Florence Maybrick. Without a shred of real evidence, he suggested Anne's grandfather, William Graham, was the illegitimate son of Florence, who had a brief affair when aged just 15, and was brought up by a blacksmith from Hartlepool.

The bitter dispute between Barrett and his estranged wife reached new depths in January 1995 when he signed a five-page affidavit explaining how he, Anne and Tony Devereux had forged the Diary. While the changing stories of Barrett and Graham cast great doubt on the provenance of the Diary, they were not the only problems faced by those who wanted to establish it as an authentic document. A series of scientific tests on the paper, the ink and the handwriting also posed questions about the credibility of the Diary. Probably the least contentious of these were the tests on the journal. The Diary did appear to be a typical Victorian scrapbook. Such scrapbooks were common, and were used to glue in photographs and personal memorabilia. Although the document is probably Victorian, such scrapbooks are easy to come by and one could have been obtained by someone who wanted to produce a forgery.

It is on the issue of the ink that the most controversial scientific results were found. Numerous tests have tried to establish whether its chemical composition is modern, or compatible with inks found in late Victorian England. The results of these tests have been contradictory. In July/August 1992, Dr David Baxendale, a former Home Office scientist, examined the Diary. In his first report of 1st July 1992, he concluded that while the paper was probably late Victorian, the ink was not iron-based, and this was significant as he believed iron was a key constituent in all inks from that period. Shirley Harrison and Robert Smith asked Baxendale to produce a fuller account of his finding. As a result, he produced a second report on 9th July 1992 in which he said he had found a synthetic dye called nigrosine in the ink, and as that had only been in use since the 1940s, the Diary must have been written after 1945. Dr Baxendale's report was, in Shirley Harrison's own words, a '*bombshell*' that had the potential to completely undermine the entire credibility of the Diary.[17]

Baxendale's results were soon contradicted by research findings from Dr Eastaugh, a specialist in dating old manuscripts. He used a proton microprobe to test samples of ink taken from the Diary and some black powder stuck between its pages. His results on the ink contradicted two of Dr Baxendale's findings. Firstly, he found that the composition of the ink did not '*appear to be substantially synthetic.*' Secondly, he found the presence of iron in measurable amounts. His report of June 1993 stated that '*the results of various analyses of ink and paper in the Diary performed so far have not given rise to*

[14] Linder S., Morris C. and Skinner K., *Ripper Diary: The Inside Story*, (Sutton, Stroud, 2003) page 9.
[15] Smith R., *The True History of the Diary of Jack the Ripper*, (Mango Books, London, 2019) page 14.
[16] Taken from an email to the authors of this book by Keith Skinner, 16th June 2020.
[17] Harrison S., op cit., page 15.

any conflict with the date of 1888/9. If the Diary is a forgery then it has 'passed' a range of tests which would have shown up many materials now used in ink and paper manufacture.'[18] Although his findings added support to the view the Diary might be authentic, Eastaugh believed it was still possible for it to be a sophisticated modern forgery.

Despite the contradictions in the reports, none of the tests conducted since 1992 have found anything that could not have been found in ink from the 1880s. A test conducted in 1994 by Analysis for Industry (AFI) for Melvin Harris did indicate the presence of a preservative called chloroacetamide. Harris believed this to be crucial, as this chemical was not produced commercially until 1972. However, the following month Leeds University conducted two tests and concluded that it was *not* present in the ink. Shirley Harrison later ascertained that chloroacetamide had been found in preparations dating from the 1850s. Three independent analyses, in 1992, 1993 and 1994, identified a similar range of chemicals in the ink that effectively ruled out the presence of Diamine. This was the ink that Barrett claimed in his affidavit to have bought from the Bluecoat Chambers in Liverpool and used to forge the Diary. In 1995, Alec Voller, the Chief Chemist for Diamine, examined the ink and stated categorically that it was not Diamine.

The controversy over the results of the scientific tests and the poor provenance of the Diary, have led many to dismiss it as a forgery. However, some research did suggest Maybrick was a credible candidate to be the Whitechapel murderer. James was a frequent visitor to London. Sir Charles Russell, Florence Maybrick's counsel at her trial in 1889, said about James: '*You cannot follow closely the habits of a man who is in Liverpool, London, and other places going about his business.*'[19] Professor Rubinstein argued that the fact that all the Ripper killings took place at the weekend is suggestive. Prostitutes walked the streets every night of the week, so why should someone want to commit murder at the weekend when there are potentially more witnesses around? Rubinstein argues such a pattern: '*is consistent with the lifestyle of a Liverpool cotton broker who spent the weekdays at the Liverpool Cotton Exchange but was free to travel on weekends (as Maybrick was).*'[20] James also had a knowledge of the Whitechapel area. In 1858, he had moved to London and worked for Gustavus Witt, who had his offices off Fenchurch Street, close to Whitechapel. It was also discovered that James regularly used prostitutes. Mary Hogwood, a brothel-keeper in Norfolk, Virginia, stated James frequented her brothel when he was in America. William T. Stead visited Liverpool in the early 1890s to try to establish the truth about Florence's guilty verdict. He was scathing about James' character, and wrote that he maintained '*relations with loose women.*'[21] The Diary has many references to powerful drugs and medications, and James was a regular user of both arsenic and strychnine.

The Diary, the Watch, and the circumstantial evidence surrounding James Maybrick, have convinced some that he was Jack the Ripper. Although Maybrick lived in Liverpool, he did visit London. He was a regular user of prostitutes, and a habitual abuser of dangerous drugs. In the summer of 1888, his health and demeanour were suffering as a result of his unhealthy lifestyle. His personal life was in turmoil and his wife was about to start an adulterous affair. Despite these circumstantial pieces of evidence, James remains a highly controversial candidate to be the notorious serial killer. There are numerous problems with the Diary, not least the fact that it is not in James' handwriting. There is also a serious problem with the inadequate provenance of the Diary. Although dismissed as a hoax, the respected Ripperologists, Begg, Fido and Skinner wrote '*the origin of the journal has never been determined.*'[22]

LINKS TO THE RIPPER DIARY: THE MAYBRICK WATCH

The debate over James Maybrick's credentials to be Jack the Ripper started with the emergence of the Ripper Diary in March 1992. The debate took another twist with the emergence of the Maybrick Watch in 1993. The watch is a small, elaborately engraved gentleman's pocket watch. It has small scratches on the inside cover of the case that can only be properly viewed with a powerful magnifying glass. Around the edge are scratched the five initials of the canonical Jack the Ripper victims; in the middle are the words, '*I am Jack*;' and at the bottom is a signature, '*J. Maybrick*.' On the back of the case, the letters '*J.O.*' have been professionally engraved.

The watch was made around 1846 by Henry Verity of Lancaster and has a London gold hallmark. It has been described as: '*rather unassuming and quite simple. It is a gentleman's dress watch used for social occasions such as balls or dinners. It is smaller than the standard men's pocket watches of the time and slightly larger than a ladies' watch. The initials J.O. are engraved in a cartouche on the outside of the back. The movement is an English lever mechanism.*'[23]

The watch belonged to Albert Johnson (1936-2008), who lived in Wallasey on the Wirral. Johnson had a varied working life. He served in the Merchant Navy and also worked in a local brewery for 25 years. In the early 1980s, he took a redundancy package from the brewery and tried his hand at several self-employed occupations before working part-time at Birkenhead Technical College where he was employed as a security guard. On 2nd July 1992 (the date written on the receipt), after winning some money on the horses, Johnson bought a gold watch for £225 from Stewart's jewellery shop, 34 Seaview Road, Wallasey, as an investment for Daisy, his granddaughter. He had seen the watch in the shop for at least

---

[18] Linder S., Morris C. and Sinner K., op. cit., page 18.
[19] Irving H.B., op cit., page 179.
[20] Rubinstein W.D., 'Hunt for Jack the Ripper' in *History Today*, Vol. 50, May 2000.
[21] Stead W.T., 'Ought Mrs Maybrick to be Tortured to Death?' in *The Review of Reviews*, (Vol. VI, October, 1892).
[22] Begg P., Fido M. and Skinner K., *The Complete Jack the Ripper A to Z*, (Blake, London, 2010) page 346.
[23] www.jayhartley.com

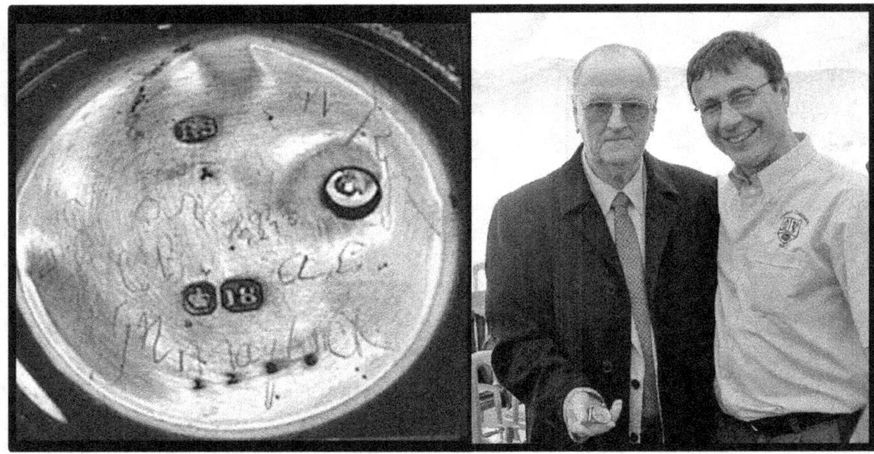

The Maybrick Watch: Left: Inner engravings, and Right: Owner Albert Johnson with author Chris Jones (Chris Jones collection)

one month prior to purchasing it whilst visiting the TSB nearby to withdraw money. Johnson said he put the watch into a drawer in his house where it remained for around 10 months. After the subject of watches came up in a conversation at Johnson's workplace, he told his colleagues he owned a Victorian gold watch and not long afterwards took it into work to show them. When they were inspecting the watch, scratches were noticed on the inside back of the case. To ascertain what the scratches said, they examined it further using a microscope. Although they could not make out all the markings, they could see some initials, the words '*I am Jack*' and a name which looked like '*J. Maybrick*' though the letter '*y*' was not entirely clear. This event occurred not long after an article on James Maybrick and the Diary of Jack the Ripper had appeared in the *Liverpool Daily Post*. Johnson contacted Harold Brough, the reporter who had written the article, but he was very dismissive of Johnson's claim to have Maybrick's watch. Nevertheless, he did give Johnson the contact details of Robert Smith.

On 3rd June 1993, Johnson contacted Smith and told him he thought he had James Maybrick's watch. The next day, Smith received a letter from Johnson in which he described the watch and included a rough drawing of the inside cover showing the scratches. On 14th June 1993, Albert and his younger brother, Robbie, took the watch to London to show it to Smith. He examined it and told the Johnsons the scratches matched up with the narrative of the Diary. Smith also believed, but didn't tell the Johnsons, that the signature on the watch, '*J. Maybrick*,' was similar to James Maybrick's signature.[24] On 26th June 1993, Smith received a written statement from Suzanne Murphy of Stewart's Jewellery Shop in Wallasey, confirming Johnson had bought the watch from their shop and it had been in the Murphys' possession for five years.

When Smith told Shirley Harrison about the watch she experienced a sense of '*near panic*.' She thought it marked the '*first of the bandwagon riders*' who would try to capitalise on the Diary.[25] Despite her doubts, Harrison and her research assistant, Sally Evemy, travelled to Liverpool to meet Albert and his brother and view the watch. Albert told them the story of how he bought the watch and that he had only noticed the scratches at a later date. Harrison and Evemy visited the shop where Albert bought the watch, and the owners – Ron and Suzanne Murphy – confirmed they had sold it to him. Murphy also confirmed his story in a signed statement for Paul Feldman. In the statement, he wrote: '*I sold the MAYBRICK Watch to ALBERT JOHNSON on or about the 14th July 1992 for a sum of £250.00. There is nothing unusual I can recall about the watch, other than the fact that it was hallmarked 1846. I had owned the watch for a couple of years prior to selling it. It had been given to me by my father-in-law, who had a Jewellers Shop in Lancaster. At first it did not work, so I kept it in a draw [sic] and then eventually some time before selling it, I sent it through to MR DUNDAS, a Watch Repairer at The Clock Workshop, 4 Grange Road, West Kirby, Wirral. Mr Dundas fixed the watch and sent it back to me. The watch case was then cleaned and the watch put in the window – and Mr Johnson purchased it. Having now seen the watch for the first time since selling it, I am almost certain that the markings were present when the watch was sold, but they were not markings that I would have taken notice of.*'[26]

On 5th July 1993, Albert and Robbie Johnson, plus their solicitor, Richard Nicholas, took the watch to Paul Feldman's house in Hertfordshire. Feldman wrote: '*Albert was in his late fifties, tall with grey, balding hair. His brother was forty-three, only about five foot six with fair hair. They were like chalk and cheese*.' Feldman noticed the engraved initials *J.O.* on the watch and asked Albert Johnson, '*why O*' if it was James Maybrick's watch? Johnson just shrugged his shoulders and didn't try to explain. Feldman was impressed by his response as he felt if the watch had been a forgery then Johnson would have at least engraved the correct initials on it.[27] Feldman asked Gerald Freed, a jeweller of some 50 years' experience whom he had invited to his house to examine the watch. Freed told Feldman, the scratches are '*very, very old. I'd be astounded if anyone could say different*.'[28]

On 27th June 1993, Robert Smith visited Albert Johnson in Liverpool and offered to pay for the watch to be scientifically tested in return for a 25% share in the watch. Johnson declined the offer and decided to pay for the research himself. Johnson's solicitor, Richard Nicholas, contacted a number of laboratories who told him: '*they did not believe that scratches in metal could be dated accurately, if at all*.'[29] In August 1993, Nicholas contacted Dr Turgoose of the Corrosion and

24 Linder S., Morris C. and Skinner K., op cit., page 41.
25 Harrison S., op. cit., page 239.
26 Feldman P., *Jack the Ripper: The Final Chapter*, (Virgin, London, 1997) page 361.
27 Ibid., page 26.
28 Ibid., page 29.
29 Linder S., Morris C. and Skinner K., op cit., page 42.

Protection Centre at the University of Manchester Institute of Science and Technology (UMIST) which specialised in research on the development, properties, and performance of metals and alloys.[30] Turgoose agreed to proceed with the test using a scanning electron microscope to examine the scratches and Johnson agreed to meet the £400 costs. Nicholas, who believed in the Johnsons' integrity, said it would have been a '*brave act by a forger*' to pay for the testing, as Albert Johnson had done, if such tests '*would in all probability expose the scratches as a recent hoax.*'[31]

Dr Turgoose's first report of 10th August 1993 stated in its introduction that '*it was not expected to be possible to provide definite ages of the engravings;*' however, '*it might be possible to discuss relative ages of the various markings and come to an opinion regarding the likely ages.*' This important admission by Turgoose is often ignored by those who believe the watch to have been once owned by James Maybrick. Despite his misgivings at accurately dating the scratches, Turgoose in the conclusion of his report stated: '*The wear apparent on many of the engravings, evidenced by the rounded edges of the markings and the 'polishing out' in places would indicate a substantial age for the engravings. The actual age would depend on the cleaning or polishing regime employed, and any definition of number of years has a great degree of uncertainty and to some extent must remain speculation. Given these qualifications I would be of the opinion that the engravings are likely to date back more than tens of years, and possibly much longer. However, whilst there is no evidence which would indicate a recent (last few years) origin of the engravings, it must be stressed that there are no features observed which conclusively prove the age of the engravings. They could have been produced recently and deliberately artificially aged by polishing, but this would have been a complex multi-stage process using a variety of different tools, with intermediate polishing or artificial wearing stages. Also, many of the observed features are only resolved by the scanning electron microscope, not being readily apparent in optical microscopy, and so, if they were of recent origin the engraver would have to be aware of the potential evidence available from this technique, indicating a considerable skill and scientific awareness.*'[32]

One of the interesting findings of Turgoose's research was that the markings on the watch had not all been made by the same implement and they had not all been made at the same time. Turgoose found that the '*I am Jack*' and the '*J. Maybrick*' scratches, which he believed to be the earliest markings, '*show no differences*' and therefore had been made with the same inscribing tool. However, some of the other markings, including the initials of the canonical victims, had been made later and had been made using at least three other different inscribing tools. Further, in the '*M.K.*' [Mary Kelly] initials, Turgoose found brass particles that '*appear to have come from the inscribing tool.*' He said one features of these is that they '*appear to have corroded surfaces, and again this may suggest some significant time since they were deposited.*'

Shirley Harrison had at first considered the watch to be a '*potential embarrassment*' but, after the positive report from Dr Turgoose, she felt it might become a '*major plank in the campaign to reinstate the Diary as a genuine article.*'[33] As a result, she encouraged Albert Johnson to have the watch tested for a second time. The new test was carried out by the metallurgist, Dr Robert Wild of the Interface Analysis Centre at Bristol University. Once again, the cost of the testing, £587.50, was paid by Johnson. Wild analysed the scratches on the watch using a technique known as Auger electron spectroscopy in which '*the surface is bombarded with a focused beam of electrons.*' Two approaches were used to try and identify when the engravings had been made. The first involved comparing the composition of the atoms on the engraved surface with the original surface. Wild's tests did '*appear to indicate that the surface composition does indeed vary with depth.*' However, Wild stated that '*more work*' was needed to resolve some of the issues involved in this analytical process. For example, the polishing of the watch which had been carried out some six to ten years prior to the tests, had removed some of the surface layers from the original surface of the watch. Nevertheless, his tests indicated the engravings had been made before the watch surface was polished and that in turn indicated '*the engraving was certainly older than ten years.*'

The second approach involved '*determining the amount of corrosion on the brass particles embedded in the engraved areas*' and using that to try and '*estimate the length of time*' the brass particles from the engraving tool would have to be exposed to give that level of corrosion. The tests found one of the particles to be '*very heavily contaminated and appears to have been considerably corroded.*' This suggested the particle '*has been embedded in the surface for some considerable time.*' However, Wild also said it would require a lot more work and '*a considerable amount of time*' to provide an accurate date for the scratches on the watch. His report concluded: '*From the limited amount of evidence that has been acquired it would appear that the engraving on the back of the watch has not been done recently and it is at least several tens of years old but it is not possible to be more accurate without considerably more work.*'[34]

The two reports gave encouragement to those who believed the Diary might be genuine. Harrison came to believe in both Albert Johnson and the authenticity of his watch. After his death she wrote: '*once my book was published and the world learned of the discovery of the "Maybrick Watch," Albert was subjected to unending and sometimes cruel cross-examination. He bore it all with good humour - always ready to attend functions, meet the press and put the watch through forensic tests. Like the rest of us he wanted to know the truth. He was offered a great deal of money for his watch but only recently, when he was ill, did he seriously consider selling. Together with his devoted wife of 50 years, Val, Albert was welcome wherever he went. Everyone liked and trusted him and our gatherings will just not be the same without his kindly*

[30] www.materials.manchester.ac.uk
[31] Linder S., Morris C. and Skinner K., op cit., page 43.
[32] The full Turgoose report is available to view at: www.casebook.org
[33] Linder S., Morris C. and Skinner K., op. cit., page 70.
[34] Taken from the Wild Report which is available to view at www.casebook.org

genial humour.' Harrison also wrote: '*Together, Albert Johnson's watch and Michael Barrett's Diary present powerful support for my belief that James Maybrick, a man obsessed by time, was indeed Jack the Ripper.*'[35] Another person convinced by the reports was Feldman. He came to believe that Albert Johnson had a Maybrick family connection and that the watch had been in his family's possession for many years.

Although there were sections in the Turgoose Report and the Wild Report that made positive reading for those who believed in the authenticity of the watch, there were also cautionary statements in both reports which meant the test results were far from conclusive. Turgoose admitted that it was simply not possible to provide a definitive age for the engravings on the watch. He also said the engravings could have been produced recently and been artificially aged by polishing. Wild said he only had the watch for a few hours and as a result '*a thorough examination was not possible.*' He said any accurate dating of the engravings would require considerably more work and time. Another problem with the watch was that the scratches did not include the initials of the two Manchester victims whom the diarist claimed to have killed. Those who believe the watch may have belonged to James Maybrick argue that he did not know the names of these two women. Although it is possible he may not have known their names when they were killed, if the diarist had been James, then he would have found out their names from a search of their possessions or by examining newspaper reports about the murders. The missing initials do undermine the credibility of the watch being a genuine item belonging to James. The scratched initials on the watch also do not include Martha Tabram who very probably was a Ripper victim.

One person who wasn't convinced by the watch and the testing regimes it had undergone was Diary-sceptic, Melvin Harris. He argued the embedded brass particles the scientists had found in the engravings could have come from a forger using an old engraving tool. Whilst Turgoose did admit in his report the scratches could be recent, he also said it would take a considerable level of skill and scientific awareness on the part of a would-be forger to produce such a forgery. Those who think the watch is genuine argue the Johnson brothers lacked the skills to have produced such a sophisticated forgery.

Perhaps more damaging to the watch's credibility was an affidavit signed by Timothy Dundas in July 1996. Dundas had been the man who had cleaned and serviced the watch in 1992. In the affidavit he stated: '*I examined this watch and serviced it and I think I fitted a spring and polished the case. The only markings on this watch at that time were repair markings. A month or so later Mr Stewart contacted me and asked me if I had seen any marks on this watch, relevant to Jack the Ripper, and I told Mr Stewart the only marks on the watch were repair marks.*' Dundas felt the watch, because of its size, was a lady's rather than a gentleman's watch. He also had no doubt that any marks relating to Jack the Ripper had been made after he had cleaned it. Those who believe the watch may have belonged to James Maybrick suggest that Dundas was simply mistaken and point to the fact that Ron Murphy, the man who sold the watch, had claimed to have seen some markings on it. The problem with the latter view is that Dundas was a skilled craftsman who worked on the watch with a magnifying eye-glass. If scratches had been present, then he is almost certain to have seen them when he mended and serviced the watch. In August 2024, Dundas confirmed to Christopher Jones in an interview in his shop, that he was '*definite*' there had been no markings relating to Jack the Ripper when he repaired the watch. He was therefore certain that the marks must have been made after he had worked on the watch.

Dundas' shop in West Kirby, Merseyside, 2024 (Chris Jones collection)

For Albert Johnson the results of the tests were conclusive. He said: '*We could go on forever testing but it wouldn't make any difference. People have already made up their minds and those who don't believe the diary won't believe this either. But in my mind, I have absolutely no doubt about who the Ripper was.*'[36] Robert Smith even claimed that privately, Dr Wild had told him the scratches on the watch could possibly date back to 1888 or 1889.[37] Smith wrote the Diary and the watch were '*inextricably linked.*' If the engravings on the watch were '*more than several decades old, the diary itself could not be a modern, post 1987 forgery, as many people had claimed.*'[38]

In September 1993, an article in the *Liverpool Daily Post* suggested the discovery of the watch '*might provide the decisive piece of evidence in establishing James Maybrick as Jack the Ripper.*'[39] That didn't happen; if anything, the watch only increased the controversy surrounding the candidature of Maybrick to be the serial killer. The tests on the watch have not conclusively proved it to be a genuine item once owned by James Maybrick. On the other hand, the tests have also not shown it to be a forgery. As a result, the debate around the credibility of the watch as a genuine item once owned by James Maybrick has, like the debate around the Diary, continued to rumble on unabated.

---

[35] Harrison S., op. cit., page 71.
[36] *Daily Mail*, 23rd November 1994.
[37] Linder S., Morris C. and Skinner K., op. cit., page 71.
[38] Smith R., (2019) op cit., page 35.
[39] *Liverpool Daily Post*, 29th September 1993.

2

THE MAYBRICKS OF LIVERPOOL

The Maybricks were a family of skilled artisans who had lived in Liverpool for several generations before James Maybrick's birth in 1838. James' great-grandfather, Charles Maybrick (born in 1753), had been a glassmaker. George III was on the throne when James' grandfather, William Maybrick (1772-1843), a watch toolmaker and copperplate engraver, diversified into musical instruments, moving his shop – where he specialised in the making of high-quality flutes – to 24 Tarleton Street in the centre of Liverpool in 1816. A little later, he moved his increasingly successful business a little further down the same street to number 3.[40] William was a noted singer, a member of the Liverpool Festival Choral Society, who, as a sideline, sang at private and public dinners.[41]

In 1824, William broke from the Choral Society and set up the Liverpool Musical Society. He acted as conductor, while his son Michael (1799-1846), who was James' uncle, served as organist.[42] Michael was an even more talented musician than his father, and while still a young man became organist at St Peter's, one of Liverpool's most important churches. The organ had been installed in the church in 1764, and the Town Council had agreed to pay the £40 annual salary of the organist.[43] Under the leadership of the Maybricks, the Liverpool Music Society held many successful musical events in the town, such as a sold-out concert in March 1836 at the Music Hall in Bold Street, featuring a selection of sacred music.[44] In 1839, William decided to disband his own musical society and rejoin the Liverpool Festival Choral Society.

In August 1791, William Maybrick (James' grandfather) married Sarah Pye (1773-1853). Together they were to have twelve children, though only six of them were to survive into adulthood. That so many of their children died young is not surprising given the limited wealth of the family and the high infant mortality rate of the early nineteenth century. They were also all born during the Napoleonic Wars, a conflict which had an adverse effect on trade in general and Liverpool in particular. The youngest of William and Sarah's children were twin boys named Charles (1815-1873) and William (1815-1870). It is a sign of the increasing affluence of the family that the twins were to live the longest of all the children and were to have the most children themselves.

William (James' grandfather) was a committed Anglican, who in the 1820s was appointed parish clerk to St Peter's Church, a post he was to hold for 20 years. The church, opened in 1704, was an imposing building but possessed '*few claims to architectural design*.'[45] It was most well-known for its festivals of church music. The parish clerk was an important figure and often deputised for the vicar, signing off the entries in the baptismal and marriage registers. Although the work could be time-consuming, it was a part-time role and not well paid. The annual accounts for the Corporation of Liverpool in 1824/25, show that St Peter's had two parish clerks: Mr E. Coventry, who was paid £8 a year, and Mr Wm. Maybrick, who was paid just £6 for the year.[46] It was this poor financial reward that led some parish clerks to embezzle church funds. Although there is no known case of William acting in a dishonest manner, accusations of wrongdoing were occasionally pointed in his direction. In 1823, he responded to one such accusation with a letter to the local newspaper, in which he stated he was the most '*proper*' person to collect mortality fees, and that he had not the '*smallest idea*' of '*pocketing*' any of the money, though it would not necessarily be illegal if he had done so.[47] William's prominence in local music societies and his

St. PETER'S CHURCH, LIVERPOOL.

[40] *Liverpool Mercury*, 4th January 1822.
[41] *Liverpool Mercury*, 27th June 1823.
[42] *Liverpool Mail*, 5th October 1850.
[43] Picton J.A., *Municipal Archives and Records 1700-1835*, (Gilbert G. Walmsley, Liverpool, 1886) page 278.
[44] *Gore's Liverpool General Advertiser*, 3rd March 1836.
[45] Lewis D., *The Churches of Liverpool*, (Bluecoat Press, Liverpool, 2001) page 9.
[46] *Liverpool Mercury*, 20th January 1826.
[47] *Gore's Liverpool General Advertiser*, 1st May 1823.

role as parish clerk, helped raise his profile in Liverpool. He wasn't above using his influence to benefit his family; in 1836, he placed an advert in the local newspaper to solicit votes for his son-in-law's candidature for the post of Collector of Taxes.[48]

On 9th May 1843, William Maybrick died, aged 71. The *Liverpool Mercury* recorded he had been one of the parish clerks for 20 years, and was '*universally respected and esteemed.*'[49] The following month his son, also called William Maybrick – the father of James – succeeded his father as parish clerk.[50] Three years later he was appointed by the Registrar of the Diocese of Chester to the '*office of apparitor for the Liverpool and Ormskirk districts.*'[51] This was another post his father had held. It made him a church official with the power to summon witnesses and execute the orders of an ecclesiastical court. William was an engraver by trade, but his work for the church began to take up more and more of his time, and at some point the role of the parish clerk became a full-time post. This change reflected the post's increasing workload. The clerk was responsible for the administration of baptisms in the parish. In St Peter's in the early 1850s, the church had an average of 140 baptisms every week, and it could expect to hold 7,000 baptisms every year.[52] For all these baptisms, there was both a religious and a civil dimension as they had to be registered in line with the law. In 1853, the cost of each registration was one shilling, and there was usually an additional cost to pay for the baptism itself. Not everyone was happy with these charges and, like his father, William faced questions over whether he was profiteering from them. One critic, calling himself a '*poor man,*' penned a letter to the *Liverpool Daily Post* attacking the charges. William responded by stating the costs involved were for the registration and not the baptism, and the church always waived the fee when a family had insufficient funds to pay it.

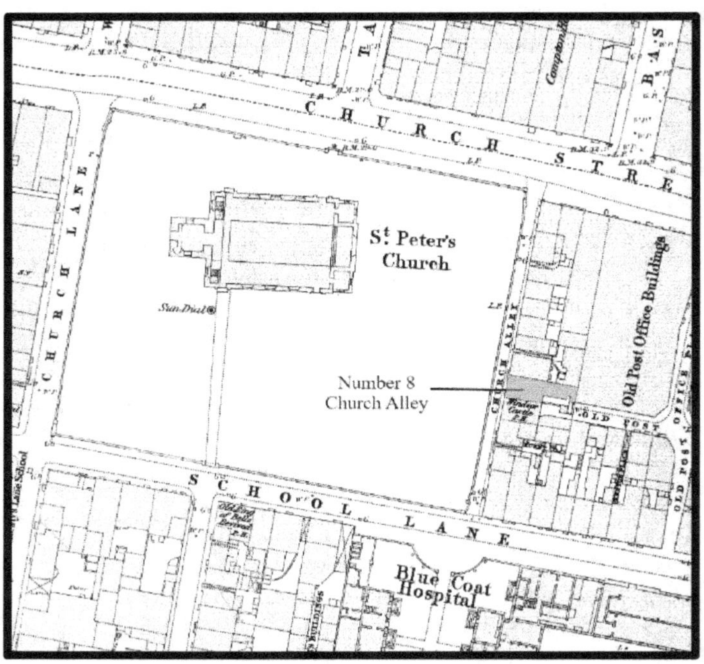

Church Alley in 1848. The Maybricks lived at No. 8

The clerk was also responsible for ensuring the appropriate paperwork was completed for burials in the parish. For that, he received 6d for every burial.[53] Later, this was changed so the clerk received a single payment of £50 a year.[54] In a busy parish, such as St Peter's, the various fees meant the role of the parish clerk could be relatively lucrative. William held the post for almost 27 years. After his death, a local newspaper commented that the role had given him the '*opportunity of being possessed of much valuable information respecting the parish, which no other official connected with it could possibly obtain. Mr Maybrick was, indeed, Rector Campbell's right-hand man, and as such was held in the highest esteem.*'[55]

In 1834, William Maybrick married Susannah Wainwright (1816-1880). The couple were to have seven children, all boys, though two of them died when they were young. The eldest son, William Jr, was born in 1835. A second son, James, was born in 1837 but died when just four months old. When he was born, the family lived in Spring Place off Clare Street, near the town centre, but by the time he was buried, in October 1837, they had moved to Church Alley.[56] The following year, on 24th October 1838, another boy was born, also named James (1838-1889). He was christened on 12th November 1838 in St Peter's Church.

The 1841 Census lists the young family with its four members and no servants living in 8 Church Alley, a narrow street that overlooked St Peter's Church. Later that year, Michael (1841-1913) was born. He was named after his uncle, who, rather appropriately, had been the church organist. Alfred was born in 1844, but died in 1848 after contracting scarlet fever. His early death must have made an impression on James, then aged ten, as when his own son developed the same illness years later he immediately moved his daughter out of the family home to protect her from the deadly disease. Thomas was born in 1846, and the youngest of the Maybrick siblings, Edwin, was born in 1851.

---

48 *Liverpool Standard and General Commercial Advertiser,* 10th May 1836.
49 *Liverpool Mercury*, 12th May 1843.
50 *Liverpool Mercury*, 30th June 1843.
51 *Liverpool Mercury*, 24th April 1846.
52 *Liverpool Standard*, 3rd January 1854.
53 *Northern Times*, 11th June 1856.
54 *Gore's Liverpool and General Advertiser*, 11th April 1850.
55 *Liverpool Daily Post*, 30th June 1870.
56 Baptismal Record, St Peter's, 1837, page 279.

The 1851 Census shows that the Maybricks were still living at 8 Church Alley. William's occupation is recorded as '*parish clerk*' and no longer as an engraver, indicating the full-time nature of the role. His eldest son William, aged 15, is listed as a carpenter and gilder's apprentice. The three other boys, James, Michael and Thomas, are listed as scholars. Edwin was not born until after the Census had been taken.

Little is known about family life in the Maybrick household, but given the stability of William and Susannah's marriage, it is assumed the children had a normal upbringing. It is also not clear which school the Maybrick boys attended. It is possible they were educated at home or attended the Liverpool Collegiate School which had been built to provide an education for middle class students of the Anglican faith. When the foundation stone for the school was laid by Lord Stanley on 22nd October 1840, a special service was held at St Peter's attended by the Bishop of Chester.[57]

James spent his childhood living in Church Alley. It was a narrow road that ran from Church Street down to the Blue Coat (Hospital) School. The Blue Coat, opened in 1718, was built by Bryan Blundell, a sea captain, as a '*residential charity school for poor children.*'[58] The school had a strong connection with St Peter's Church and the education of the boys, and later girls, was based on the principles of the Anglican faith.

Church Street was one of Liverpool's main streets. A visitors' guidebook written in 1886 describes it as '*one of the most central and busy thoroughfares in the city, and is the point where the principal streams of traffic from the southern and eastern portions converge on their way to the Exchange, Landing Stage, and chief offices.*'[59] Although Church Alley was less hectic than Church Street, it was still a busy thoroughfare. In the late 1850s, the street had two public houses, a tea shop, a printers and more than four commercial offices. The Maybricks lived at number eight, and next door to them was a brewhouse named the Windsor Castle. Living in Church Alley had its advantages, especially for William, as it faced the church where he worked. It also had disadvantages, not least from the noise from living in the town centre and right next to a brewhouse.

In 1858, the Maybricks' house and the brewhouse next door were put up for sale. The advert for the buildings showed that William paid an annual rent of £18 for his property.[60] The Maybricks moved from Church Alley to 23 Brunswick Road, where they are listed in the 1860 *Liverpool Street Directory*. They didn't stay there long, as in the 1861 Census the family is shown as living in 77 Mount Pleasant. The Census returns show that William was still the parish clerk. It lists his two youngest sons, Thomas and Edwin, as scholars and Michael as a '*Professor of Music.*'

In the 1860s, Mount Pleasant was an important and busy road climbing up a hill from the town centre. The famous Adelphi Hotel was situated at the bottom and there was a large workhouse at the top. Although many of the houses on the street were boarding houses, the house that the Maybricks occupied would have been larger than their home in Church Alley. A sign of the family's increased affluence was that they were able to afford to pay a servant; the 1861 Census shows that a servant named Mary Smith was living with the family.

The two oldest brothers are no longer living in the household. William was married and living with his own family. James had moved to London. According to a document known as *Russell's Brief*, which had been produced to help provide background details for Florence's defence team at her trial, James left Liverpool when he was 20, which would therefore be sometime in 1858 or 1859, and went to work in a '*Shipbroker's office in London.*'[61] The document states that while James was in London he met '*Sarah Robertson, 18, an assistant in a jewellers shop, she lived with him on and off for 20 years as his wife. Her relatives thought she was married and she passed as Mrs M. with them. They have five children, all now dead.*'

Although there are serious questions over the accuracy of the document – for example, it has Sarah Robertson's age wrong as she would actually have been in early twenties – it is known that around this time James did meet a woman of that name, and he did start an on/off relationship with her. Unfortunately, the details about her are sketchy and contradictory. In the censuses she is listed under three different surnames, and her age in some census listings does not match up with the expected age based on the previous census details. The first problem with trying to track down Sarah Robertson is that while some books state that she was born on 2nd August 1837 in Sunderland, there is no record of any person with that name being born in that year.[62]

The 1841 Census does record a four year old named Sarah Robinson, not Robertson, and her possible brother, George (aged one) as living with Christiana Lindsay Robinson (aged 20) in Flag Lane, Sunderland. Flag Lane was one of a number of run-down back streets that ran off the old High Street near the docks in the east end of Sunderland. That year's Census does not make clear the relationship between Christiana and Sarah; was she her mother, or possibly her aunt? It is likely that the woman registered as Christiana Robinson was the same who had been born Christiana Lindsay Robertson on 8th November 1817, although of course that would have made her 23 and not 20 at

---

57 Wainwright D., *Liverpool Gentlemen*, (Faber and Faber, London, 1960) page 32.
58 Sharples J., *Liverpool*, (Yale University Press, London, 2004) page 177.
59 *Visitor's Illustrated Guide*, (Marples and Co., Liverpool, 1886), page 111.
60 *Liverpool Mercury*, 9th April 1858.
61 Feldman P., op cit., page 109.
62 Graham A. and Emmas C., suggest Sarah Ann Robertson was born on 22nd August 1837; however, most books suggest she was born on 2nd August 1837.

the time of the census in 1841. Christiana's father was given on her birth certificate as Alexander Hay Robertson (1781-1847) and her mother as Sarah Pell. Elsewhere on Flag Lane (no house numbers are provided in the 1841 Census) lived Alexander Robertson, aged 60, described as an '*agent*,' bracketed with Alice Robertson, '*female servant*,' aged 21, and Edward Robertson, aged 11. Christiana's father, Alexander Hay Robertson, was born in 1781 so he could indeed have been 60 in 1841; but whether he is the Alexander Robertson shown in the 1841 Census as living in Flag Lane is unclear. This Alexander Robertson describes himself as '*agent*,' and on her marriage banns Christiana cites her father as a '*general agent*' – so it is possible. But if the 21 year old Alice really was his daughter, why is she not so denoted but instead described as a servant? Furthermore, there is no record of Alexander Hay Robertson having had a son called Edward.

On 14th November 1847, Christiana Robertson married Charles James Chase (1821-1863), a tobacconist living in London. On the marriage certificate she is shown as Robertson and not Robinson. They lived in 40 Mark Lane, Tower Hill, London. The 1851 Census has the couple living in 1 Postern Way, Tower Hill and living with them is Sarah Ann Robertson, who is listed as the niece of Christiana. Sarah's age is given as 15, and her birthplace as Sunderland. There is no mention of George Robinson who, if he was still alive, would have been aged 11.

In the 1861 Census, Charles and Christiana Case are listed as living in 36 Jamaica Street, Mile End, London. In the same census, '*Sarah Robertson*,' aged 25 and born in Sunderland, is recorded as living in 172 Fenchurch Street, London, and working as an '*assistant to a hair jewellers*.' In 1861, the hair jewellery shop was run by Ellen Dewdney, aged 27, and listed in the census as a widow.

In 1858, James moved to London and at some point started working for Gustavus Witt, who had offices in both Liverpool and London. His main office in the capital was in Fen Court, off Fenchurch Street. The evidence therefore suggests that the woman listed as Sarah Robertson and living in 172 Fenchurch Street in the 1861 Census is the same woman mentioned in the *Russell Brief* document who had a relationship with James Maybrick. At that time, she worked as an assistant in a hair jewellery shop (rather than a jewellers), and probably met James as both of them were living and working close to one another in the Fenchurch Street area of London.

Although the relationship between James and Sarah began at some point around 1860, and it is probable the two of them lived together, no record of them co-habiting has been found. Nor has a marriage certificate been discovered. Nevertheless, evidence has been found that suggests a close relationship *did* exist between James and Sarah Ann Robertson. Researcher Keith Skinner found what is believed to be Sarah's Bible, which contained the inscription: '*To my darling Piggy. From her affectionate husband JM. On her birthday August 2nd 1865*.' The Bible was in the possession of the daughter of William and Alice Bills. As Sarah Anne Robertson had been living with the Bills prior to her death, it is likely the book did belong to her. The problem with the inscription is that the handwriting does not match that of James' found on other documents. Perhaps Sarah wrote the inscription herself, in order to give some credibility to her claim that she and James were married.

HAIR MEMENTOS.

DEWDNEY, Designer of every description of HAIR JEWELLERY, begs to inform ladies and gentlemen resident in town, or any part of the kingdom, that he beautifully makes, and elegantly mounts in fine gold, hair bracelets, chains, brooches, rings, pins, &c., and forwards tne same, carefully packed in boxes, at about ONE-HALF the USUAL CHARGE. A book of specimens sent free on receipt of two postage stamps.

DEWDNEY, ARTIST IN HAIR,
(FROM PARIS,)
172, Fenchurch-street, City, London.
N.B. Show-rooms First-floor.
A beautiful collection of specimens, handsomely mounted, kept for inspection.

On 12th February 1863, Charles Case died from diphtheria, aged 42, and in May 1866 Christiana married for a second time, to Thomas David Conconi, at St Peter's Church, Stepney. He was a paymaster in the Royal Navy. Sarah Ann Robertson was one of the witnesses. In 1868, Thomas Conconi added a codicil to his will: '*In case my said wife shall die during my life then I give and bequeath all my household goods, furniture, plate linen and china to my dear friend Sarah Ann Maybrick, the wife of James Maybrick of Old Hall Street, Liverpool, now residing at No 55 Bromley Street, Commercial Road, London*.'

This addition is informative, as it makes clear that while Sarah was living with her relatives in London, James had returned to Liverpool and was living in Old Hall Street, close to where Witt had his Liverpool office in the Knowsley Buildings. This separation is also evident in the Census of 1871, where Thomas and Christiana Conconi are shown as living in 55 Bromley Street, Stepney, London. '*Sarah Maybrick*' is recorded as living with them, but James is listed as living in his family's house in Liverpool. Sarah Maybrick is described as a niece to Christiana, and as a '*merchant's clerk wife*.' As no marriage certificate exists, and James was living some 200 away, one can only assume that Sarah has provided her surname as Maybrick to keep up the pretence that she was married.

On 27th July 1876, Thomas Conconi died from a pulmonary abscess, aged 47, in Sydenham, Kent. The informant was '*S.A. Maybrick, niece*,' living at the same address. The fact that Sarah continued to use the surname Maybrick, even though James at this time was based in Norfolk, Virginia, suggests she still had hopes of rekindling their relationship. James, on the other hand, appears to have left her behind in his quest for self-improvement and advancement.

In the 1881 Census, Christiana is listed as residing at 237 Queen's Road, Deptford in south London. Living in the same house is Sarah A. Robertson, niece to Christiana, who is recorded as being a widow with no occupation, aged 35. Sarah's age is incorrect; if she was 15 in the 1851 Census and 25 in the 1861 Census, then that would make her 45 in 1881. Living in the same house is Gertrude Conconi, aged eight, who is recorded as the daughter of Christiana. If that information is correct, then Christiana (if she had been born in 1817) would have been aged 56 when she gave birth to her daughter. Paul Feldman considered Gertrude to be a '*bit of mystery,*' and wondered whether his research team had '*discovered an illegitimate James and Sarah offspring, born in 1873.*'[63] The mystery deepens even further as there is no official record of Gertrude's birth. Gertrude married George Bridge (1862-1927) in 1895, an '*artist and worker in mosaic.*' At the marriage, Gertrude gave her name as Gertrude Blackiston, '*otherwise Conconi.*' Sarah Maybrick was a witness at the wedding. Why Gertrude should change her name is unknown; it is just another piece of a confusing jigsaw.

The 1891 Census shows that Christiana Conconi was still living in Queen's Road, but had moved from number 237 to 265. This address is significant, as it is the one identified by Alexander MacDougall in 1891 as being the home of the woman who claimed to be the '*real wife*' of James Maybrick. In that year's census, Christiana is described as a widow living on her own means. Four other people are living at the address, including a school board teacher (presumably a lodger); a 13 year old visitor who is listed as a '*scholar*'; Gertrude, aged 18 and daughter to Christiana; and finally Sarah Robertson, who is listed as Christiana's niece and as being single. Sarah's age is again incorrectly recorded as being 44, when she was likely to have been 55. It also means that in the three censuses from 1871 to 1891 Sarah has been listed as being a wife, a widow and single.

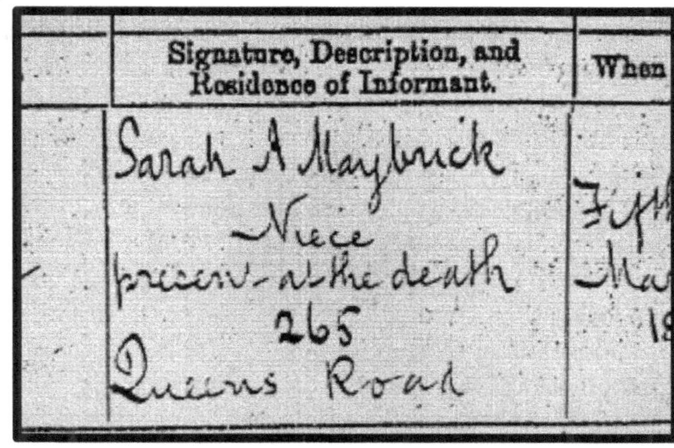
Signature, Description, and Residence of Informant.	When
Sarah A Maybrick Niece present at the death 265 Queens Road	

Extract from the death certificate of Christiana Conconi

Christiana Conconi died in 1895. On the death records Sarah signs herself as '*Sarah Ann Maybrick,*' On 17th January 1927, Sarah Ann Robertson herself died, at Tooting Bec Hospital. The records state that she was '*Sarah Ann Maybrick, otherwise Robertson, spinster of independent means of 24 Cottesbrook Street, New Cross.*' Her age was incorrectly recorded as 72, when in fact she would have been around 90 years old. Sarah was buried in an unmarked grave in Streatham, London. At the time of her death, she was living with William and Alice Bills; it is probable that Alice was a member of the Bills family who, in 1891, were living next door to Christiana Conconi, at 267 Queens Road, New Cross.

The contradictory nature of the evidence makes it difficult to determine many of the key details of Sarah Ann Robertson's life story. We do not know for sure when she was born, though it is likely to have been 1836 or 1837. We do not know who her mother was, though it is possible that it was Christiana Robertson, who is usually recorded as her aunt. We are not certain who Sarah's father was. It is also difficult to define Sarah's relationship with James Maybrick. That they did have a relationship is clear. The document *Russell's Brief* states that they had an on/off relationship for 20 years, and had five children together. It was MacDougall who, in 1891, first revealed Sarah's existence, though he did not refer to her by name. He wrote: '*There is a woman who calls herself Mrs Maybrick and who claims to have been James Maybrick's real wife. She was staying on a visit at a somewhat out of the way place, 8 Dundas Street, Monkwearmouth, Sunderland, during the trial [of Florence]; her usual and present address is 265 Queen's Road, New Cross, London SE.*'[64] Maybe Sarah Ann went to Sunderland to escape press intrusion; it was the place where she was born, so she may still have had relatives there to whom she could turn for help.

Although the contradictory nature of the evidence makes it difficult to determine Sarah's relationship with James, there are sufficient clues to reach some considered conclusions. Firstly, it is clear that James and Sarah did have a relationship, and that it started after 1858, when he moved to London. The relationship was probably at its most intense in the 1860s, but it is likely to have tapered-off in the 1870s when James worked in America. What happened after his marriage is less clear. Some level of contact must have been maintained as James agreed to pay Sarah £100 a year. The writer and campaigner W.T. Stead wrote that James only '*occasionally*' met his abandoned lover after his marriage, although he did give her some of Florence's diamonds '*within the last year of his life.*'[65] If this is true, then perhaps he had started to rekindle his relationship with Sarah after his own marriage had started to crumble. The relationship has been described as '*on/off*' and that does appear to be an apt description of their time together. No record has ever been found of James and Sarah living together. Although Sarah did on occasions refer to herself as

---

[63] Feldman P., op cit., page 111.
[64] MacDougall A.W., (1891) op. cit., pages 20-21.
[65] Stead W.T., 'Ought Mrs Maybrick be tortured to death? in *The Review of Reviews* (Vol. VI, October 1892) pages 390-396.

Mrs Maybrick, no marriage certificate has been discovered. When James married Florence in 1881, his marriage licence described him as a '*bachelor.*' If he had previously been married, then that fact would have emerged.

We are therefore left with the conclusion that James and Sarah never married. That some people *thought* they were married was probably caused by Sarah providing them with false information in order to maintain the pretence that she had married James. Sarah continued to refer to herself as James' wife, even though he had deserted her, which suggests she maintained feelings for him. While James probably did reciprocate some of these feelings, he was socially ambitious and her poor background meant that it is unlikely he saw her as marriage material. He was prepared to abandon her when he had the opportunity to marry someone from a more exclusive background.

Several different sources state that James and Sarah had five children together. As the authors of these sources are so diverse, but consistent, it *is* possible that Sarah was pregnant on five occasions. The more difficult questions are when did these pregnancies occur and what happened to the babies. Two of the modern authors, Nigel Morland and Bernard Ryan, both state that three babies were born before James' marriage to Florence and a further two born afterwards. In both cases, neither author provides any references to substantiate their statements.

What is more credible are the views of writers who were contemporaneous to James and Sarah. *Russell's Brief* states there were five children, but they were all dead in 1889. Stead wrote two articles in 1892 to try and help get Florence released from prison. Although the articles are similar in content, there are some slight but significant differences between them. In the October 1892 article, Stead wrote that Sarah '*bore him [James] five children and then he cast her off without remorse when he saw his chance of marrying poor Florence.*' This makes it clear that all five children were born *before* James' marriage to Florence.

In the article published in the November edition of his journal, Stead wrote that '*the statement that there were five children born of the intimacy was made on the authority of the woman herself. Four of them appear to have died in infancy, and the fifth only survived for a short time.*' This is highly significant, as Stead is claiming that his information came directly from Sarah Ann Robertson herself, and she said all five children died not long after they were born. The fact that he, or one of his staff, spoke directly to her makes his article highly credible. It is a view that is also supported by the fact that none of these births were registered; stillbirths in England and Wales did not have to be legally registered until 1st July 1927. The evidence therefore suggests that Sarah *did* get pregnant; that all the pregnancies occurred before James' marriage to Florence; and that all five babies died either at birth or soon afterwards.

James' move to London around 1858 was a typical characteristic of the Maybrick brothers, as all of them were prepared to take risks in order to improve their social standing. William lived in or near Liverpool all his life. He followed several occupations, including as a bookkeeper and commission agent. Thomas moved to Manchester, where he became a shipping agent; however, hydraulics seems to have been his speciality. In 1894, with William James Ashworth, Thomas patented a new invention – an improved brake apparatus for automatically preventing colliery cages from plunging down pit or lift shafts when ropes or cables broke. In the 1901 Census, he is listed as a master hydraulic packer.

Michael, the middle brother, was the most successful of the Maybricks. From a very early age it was apparent that he possessed great musical abilities. At the age of 14 he was appointed the organist at St Peter's Church, a post he held for eight years. His precocious talent meant that he was soon generating a steady income from his role of parish organist and by teaching the piano and the organ from the family home, which he rather grandiosely called a '*musical academy.*'[66] In 1865, he travelled to Leipzig to study keyboard and harmony with Carl Reinecke, Ignaz Moscheles and Louis Plaidy, and '*he did so with so much success so as to receive an excellent testimonial from Plaidy.*'[67] It was while he was in Leipzig that it was discovered he possessed a fine baritone voice and, as a result, it was decided to focus more on his singing qualities than on his playing abilities. He travelled to Milan to study singing under Gaetano Nava, and quickly established himself as a '*great favourite in private circles. His appearances on the stage in some of the Italian cities also won him a host of admirers.*'[68]

After three years studying abroad Michael returned to Britain as a highly promising singer. His first concert on his return was in November 1868 in Newcastle-upon-Tyne and he received a '*unanimous encore.*'[69] In December 1869, Michael's parents travelled to Chester to see him perform for the first time since his return from Milan.[70] In March 1870, Michael made a triumphant return to Liverpool, making his singing debut in a concert organised by the Philharmonic Society. Despite suffering from a few nerves and a cold, he received '*loud applause.*'[71]

Around 1858, James moved to London where the evidence suggests he started to work for Gustavus Claussen Schutz (1817-1869) a merchant who had an office at 45 Lime Street off Fenchurch Street. Schutz's partner was

---

66 *Liverpool Mercury*, 15th January 1861.
67 *Isle of Wight County Press*, 30th August 1913.
68 *Liverpool Mercury*, 16th March 1870.
69 *Liverpool Mercury*, 16th November 1868.
70 *Cheshire Observer*, 11th December 1869.
71 *Liverpool Mercury*, 16th March 1870.

Gustavus Andreas Witt (1840-1905) a young aspiring merchant from a German background who had become a naturalised British citizen. After Schutz's death in 1869, Witt took over the company, renaming it G.A. Witt & Co.[72] James became a partner in Witt's new company which had an office at 7 Fen Court in Fenchurch Street and another in Liverpool at 28 Knowsley Buildings. In 1872, Witt's bank rated his firm '*very respectable*,' and reported that it was mainly engaged in '*the American produce trade*'. Working for Witt caused James to change his location on several occasions. The *Russell Brief* states he moved to London around 1858/59, and that '*he returned to Liverpool a few years later and they [James and Sarah Ann Robertson] lived in Chester for 3 or 4 years and at Manchester and Liv[erpool].*'

A lack of documented evidence makes it difficult to clearly track James' movements, but some of his activities are recorded in newspapers and other documents. Two of these suggest that his career had progressed extremely well. In the first one, a certain '*James Maybrick of 46 Lime Street, gentleman*,' is listed in February 1866 as one of a number of people who had shares in a venture identified as the English Joint-Stock Bank Limited.[73] Although Lime Street is the name of a well-known street in Liverpool, it is more likely that the address referred to was the Lime Street located off Fenchurch Street in London. The fact that James had shares in such a bank indicates there had been a marked upturn in his personal finances. The second report is an intriguing reference to a '*James Maybrick from London*' who was a guest at a fashionable wedding in Sunderland in August 1866.[74] Although there is an obvious link to Sunderland as it was Sarah Ann Robertson's place of birth, it remains rather a mystery as to why James should be a guest at such a wedding. Sarah is not listed as a guest and it seems unlikely, given her humble background, that the invitation had any connection to her. The groom was George Elliot, later Sir George Elliot, 2nd Baronet, who was a colliery owner and a Conservative MP who sat in the House of Commons for two periods between 1874 and 1895. It is possible that the reference is a coincidence, but records suggest he was the only person with the name James Maybrick in Britain at that time.

Young James Maybrick (Chris Jones collection)

As Witt had offices in both London and Liverpool and had business clients spread over a wide area, it is easy to understand why James may have frequently changed his location whilst working for him. We know from Thomas Conconi's will, that in 1868 James was living in Old Hall Street, Liverpool. Although no address has been found for him living in Chester, there is a reference to a person called '*Maybrick*' being part of a winning crew at an event in 1870 staged by the Royal Chester Rowing Club,[75] and mention of a '*J. Maybrick*' being on the list of subscribers for the Chester Regatta in the same year.[76] There is also a reference to a '*Mr James Maybrick*' playing golf with Mr

[72] *The Scotsman*, 4th November 1875.
[73] *Northampton Mercury*, 17th February 1866.
[74] *Newcastle Journal*, 24th August 1866.
[75] *Cheshire Observer*, 30th April 1870.
[76] *Cheshire Observer*, 30th July 1870.

George Scott in a tournament in August 1872 at Royal Liverpool Golf Club at Hoylake on the Wirral.[77] Club records show that James was a member of the golf club at the time.

These references provide a fascinating glimpse into the life of James in his twenties and thirties. He appears to be a hard-working and ambitious businessman who had become friends with some powerful and influential figures. In his social life, he was an active sportsman who was a member of some high-status sporting clubs. James was also a keen walker, and we know that he went on several walking holidays with his brothers and friends. If music and the church had been the stepping-stones that helped boost the career of James' father, then gentlemen's clubs and networking were to be the stepping-stones for James. Therefore, it is not surprising that James became a Freemason in Liverpool in September 1870 when he was initiated into St George's Lodge of Harmony (No. 32). By joining the Lodge, James was able to come into direct contact with some influential figures. One of its most distinguished members was Frederick Arthur Stanley, 16th Earl of Derby, who was initiated into the Lodge in 1865 and became its Master in 1868. Stanley's father had been Prime Minister, and he himself became an MP and served as Colonial Secretary from 1885-86. He later became Lord Mayor of Liverpool (1895-96) and the first Chancellor of Liverpool University.

Liverpool Cotton Market (*Harper's Weekly*, 5th September 1874)

The year 1870 should have been a special one for the Maybricks. From relatively humble beginnings, the family story had been one of success and upward social mobility. William, James' father, had been a parish clerk in Liverpool for 27 years and was widely respected. James had returned from London as an ambitious and driven man. Michael had returned from his musical studies abroad and was making headlines all around the country with his fine baritone voice. William and Susannah's eldest son, William Jr, was married, and they had three grandchildren, two girls and a boy. In June 1870, William and Susannah went to stay temporarily in New Brighton on the Wirral, because of Susannah's '*delicate state of health.*'[78] On Monday the 27th, William was taken ill with pains in his chest, although the symptoms didn't seem great enough to cause an alarm. The next day he had a second and more severe attack, and died at eleven o'clock at night. Although William had previously suffered from issues with his heart, he appeared to be in good health and his death was a great shock to his family. He was aged just 55.

William's final will of January 1866 contains no surprises. He bequeathed to his '*dear wife Susannah*' all his '*household, furniture, books and plate.*' He also left her the money from his various insurance policies, as well as all the other items of property and income within his *'real and personal Estate and Effects*' for '*her own use without impeachment during the term of her natural life.*' His sons, William, James and Michael, were instructed upon their mother's eventual death to '*sell and dispose of and convert into money the whole*' of his estate, effects and property, and then divide the money raised amongst any of his children who might be surviving on a '*share and share alike*' basis. William's will suggests that the Maybricks were a cohesive family unit. Nobody was left out, and William ensured that his '*dear wife*' was well catered for after his death.

The 1871 Census records six people living in the Maybrick household in 77 Mount Pleasant, Liverpool. Living with Susannah are three of her children, James (aged 31), listed as a '*commercial clerk*;' Thomas (24), listed as a '*cotton salesman*;' and Edwin (20), listed as a '*cotton dealer/merchant.*' Also, in the house was Susan Maybrick, aged 13, who was the daughter of William, the eldest brother, and Mary Webster, aged 23, a servant. Two of the Maybrick brothers were living elsewhere. William, the eldest, was living in Liverpool with his own family. Michael had joined Mr Sims Reeves in an operatic tour of the country. His popularity grew such that he found it '*more profitable to exchange the operatic stage for the concert room.*'[79] In 1873, while ill in bed, he wrote the words and the music to his first big song, *A Warrior Bold*, and within a few years had earned well over a thousand pounds in royalties.

Working for Witt had been a major learning curve for James and he had gained a real understanding of the world of business and trade. His work had taken him to America on several occasions, with his first known voyage being on the *SS China* in January 1869. James' name also appears on a list of the passengers arriving back in Liverpool in

[77] *Liverpool Mail*, 10th August 1872.
[78] *Bolton Evening News*, 30th June 1870.
[79] *Isle of Wight County Press*, 30th August 1913.

August 1871 on the Cunard steamer *Abyssinia*.[80] He is recorded as a guest in the St Charles Hotel in New Orleans in December 1873. Staying with him in the hotel was his great friend, George Davidson.[81] The fact that Witt sent James to America and entrusted him to run the company's office in Liverpool, can only mean he considered him to be a dependable colleague. We know from an affidavit that Witt provided after Florence's trial that he also considered James a personal friend.

The year 1874 was a busy and a pivotal year for James. He spent the first few months of it in America, only arriving back in Britain from New York at the end of April when he sailed into the Mersey aboard the Royal Mail steamer *Cuba*.[82] In July, he gave evidence in the law courts in St George's Hall, Liverpool, in a legal action against his employer brought by a business client. It was a case in which Witt successfully defended a claim for damages.[83] In September, James returned to America on the steamship *City of Chester*, sailing from Liverpool to New York. It was to be only a short stay, as he sailed back from New York for a second time that year on the Royal Mail steamer *The City of Brooklyn*, arriving in Liverpool in mid-November.[84]

In December 1874, Witt and James Maybrick formally dissolved their partnership. James was now ready to fully commit to his own fledgling business venture – *Maybrick and Company, Cotton Merchants* – which he had launched with his youngest brother, Edwin, as his junior partner. The ending of the partnership between Witt and James must have been amicable, as they remained friends and for the next two years James based his own company in Witt's office in the Knowsley Buildings in Tithebarn Street.[85] The timing of the split probably reflected the fact that James was now ready and confident enough to strike out on his own. His years working for Witt had been valuable and profitable. He had learnt the art of buying and selling commodities, and he had acquired sufficient funds to start his own company. This was important, as a cotton merchant sold the cotton that he had personally purchased as opposed to a cotton broker who sold someone else's cotton.

An early sign of the success of James' new business venture came in July 1876, when he and his brothers Edwin and Thomas were all declared Freemen of the Town of Liverpool. Historically, the role had been extremely significant and carried certain privileges including voting at elections and exemption from the town dues. However, by the time James became a freeman, the position was symbolic rather than functional and this once historic office was no longer as exalted as it sounded. According to Picton, admission to the freedom of the borough of Liverpool was obtained by '*birth, servitude, purchase, or gift*.' Under the birth criteria, '*every son of a freeman, born within the borough bounds, was entitled to the privileges of a burgess on attaining the age of twenty-one*.'[86] This meant that James and his brothers, were all eligible to become freemen as their father William had been one. That James waited until his late twenties before pursuing his entitlement was probably because he wanted to use it to enhance his credibility as a businessman. It is not known how much time he expended on his freeman's office, but it is likely to have been minimal. Shortly after his death, the city's revision court went through the formality of removing his name from the list of freemen.[87]

In 1875, James travelled to Norfolk, Virginia, to establish a base to purchase cotton bales. He spent half the year in Norfolk, normally September to March – the cotton-picking season in Virginia – and the other half in Liverpool. Norfolk would have been a natural choice for an ambitious cotton merchant as its railways linked it with the cotton growing areas of the Southern States. Half of all the ships in Norfolk carried their goods to Liverpool. Norfolk had a thriving cotton exchange, and many of its cotton merchants were from Liverpool. One of these was Nicholas Bateson, a friend of James, and the two of them shared a house together on York Street, from 1877 until James' wedding. In the autumn of 1877, James became ill with malaria fever. At Florence's trial, Nicholas Bateson was brought over to Liverpool from Memphis, Tennessee, to testify on behalf of the defence. He told the court that James was treated at first with quinine but it had no effect. As a result, '*he took arsenic and strychnine, by order of Dr Ward*.'[88] Bateson's claims that James had started to take arsenic during his time at Norfolk were supported by statements from Thomas Stansell, an African-American, who acted as James' valet for over four years before his marriage. Stansell was also brought over to Liverpool by Florence's defence team to testify at her trial. In an affidavit he signed prior to sailing from America, Stansell said that three weeks after he started working for him, James had told him that he was feeling '*seedy*,' and wouldn't be going to work that day. He gave Stansell some money and told him, '*Buy me half a dollar's worth of arsenic. If the druggists refuse to sell it to you, come back and I will give you an order*.'[89] Stansell bought the arsenic and gave it to James, who stirred it into some beef tea. Stansell said that he had '*frequently bought arsenic*'

---

[80] *Liverpool Daily Post*, 2nd August 1871.
[81] *Times-Picayune*, 10th December 1873.
[82] *Manchester Courier*, 20th April 1874.
[83] *Liverpool Mercury*, 21st July 1874.
[84] *Manchester Courier and Lancashire General*, 18th November 1874.
[85] *Gore's Directory*, 1876.
[86] Picton J.A., op cit., page 194.
[87] *Liverpool Echo*, 30th September 1889.
[88] Irving H.B., op cit., pages 185-7.
[89] *Norfolk Virginian*, 1st August 1889.

for James, and when he felt unwell he '*quite often*' took arsenic and '*mixed the drug in his soup.*' Stansell said that in addition to arsenic James took all kinds of medicines and that '*his room looked like a drug store.*'

Another person who witnessed James' use of arsenic during his time in Norfolk was Captain R. Thompson, a master mariner who was also to be a defence witness at Florence's trial. He said that in 1880, he had been a second officer on the steamship *Plantain*, and had sailed from Liverpool taking two dogs for Mr Bateson. Thompson said that during his stay in Norfolk he met James almost every day, and had become '*intimate with him.*' He said he accompanied him into a druggist on Main Street and an assistant handed James two powders saying, '*Now Mr Maybrick, be careful.*' Thompson said a day or two later he had been sent to the same druggist on a message by the ship's captain and the assistant told him the nature of the powders he had given James. Thompson said when James came into his cabin he asked him about his habit of '*taking a dangerous and noxious drug.*' James said, '*What is that?*' Thompson replied, '*arsenic.*' James responded, '*Who the devil told you that?*' Thompson said the druggist's assistant had told him, and James replied, '*Damn his impudence.*'[90]

The house James rented on York Street, Norfolk (Chris Jones collection)

Further evidence of James' arsenic habit comes from Franklin George Bancroft, an artist and writer from Columbia, who was a friend of James. In 1894, he provided an affidavit that confirmed James had regularly used arsenic. Bancroft said that between the years of 1874 and 1876, when James had lived in Norfolk, Virginia, he had frequently been in his company. He stated that from time to time he had seen James take a case out of his waistcoat and empty a white powder into a glass of wine. On one occasion, Bancroft had asked James what the powder was and James told him it was '*composed of arsenic among other ingredients.*'[91] He said he took it for '*longevity and fair complexion.*' This affidavit is significant, as it suggests James had started to take arsenic three years before he developed malaria fever in 1877.

James believed that arsenic had aphrodisiacal qualities. For similar reasons, James also visited Charles Edward Brown-Séquard (1817-1894) in New York. Dr Séquard was a neurologist, physiologist and pioneer endocrinologist, who provided James with '*prescriptions of an aphrodisiac kind*' that contained strychnine and nux vomica.[92] Time was to show that James' increasing reliance on these powerful drugs were to keep him neither young nor virile.

During his stay in Norfolk, James threw himself into many aspects of local life. In 1878, he became a member of the Virginia Club, a place where local businessman could relax and socialise in style and comfort.[93] In February 1879, James served on one of the committees organising a special '*Hop*' and dinner at the Atlantic Hotel in honour of the officers of the Navy Yard and United States vessels in the harbour. Two hundred people attended the event, and there was a '*brilliant company of lovely ladies and gallant gentlemen.*'[94] It would have been an occasion that James would have enjoyed as, according to Christie, he '*was for ever falling in and out of love and was entangled in several tentative engagements during his visits to the United States.*'[95] Christie's assertion is supported by an article in a New York newspaper written after James' death. The article quoted an American businessman who said James was well known in the New York business community and was considered a '*good-hearted, genial fellow.*' It went on to state: '*During his many visits to America, Mr Maybrick seems to have fallen in love with at least one young lady on each of his ocean trips. He was ambitious to marry an American heiress. During a voyage to this country he made the acquaintance of a Miss Valentine, to whom he afterwards became engaged; but after some months the engagement was broken and Mr Maybrick returned to his native land. Miss Valentine was a beautiful girl and possessed of considerable property.*'[96]

---

[90] Irving H.B., op cit., page 189.
[91] The affidavit is printed in Maybrick, F., op. cit., pages 391-392.
[92] Irving H.B., op cit., page 35.
[93] www.virginiaclub.com
[94] *Norfolk Landmark*, 1st February 1879.
[95] Christie T.L., op. cit., page 36.
[96] *Evening World, New York*, 30th May 1889.

Julia Devens Valentine (1854-1879)

This article has a great deal of credibility as the unnamed American businessman speaks positively about James and refers to details that were not public knowledge. Julia Devens Valentine (1854-1879) and her maid were passengers on the Cunard Royal Mail steamship *Cuba*, sailing from New York to Liverpool in April 1874. Also on board was James Maybrick.[97] Julia Valentine and her maid are listed as travelling back to America, again on the *Cuba*, arriving in New York on 10th September 1874; James is not recorded as a passenger on that return voyage.[98] Any relationship between Julia Valentine and James must have been short-lived, as in June 1877, she married the famous American sculptor John Quincy Adams Ward, though she sadly died in childbirth just 18 months later. If the report of her engagement to James are accurate, then he had abandoned Sarah Ann Robertson and was actively seeking an American heiress to marry. There are some striking parallels between the experiences of Julia Valentine and Florence Chandler. Both were young American women who were seemingly wealthy. Both were a captive audience on an eleven-day Atlantic voyage, allowing a very debonair English businessman to charm them with his wit and elegance. Their respective pictures also suggests that they were not that dissimilar in their looks.

In March 1879, James collected donations from members of the Portsmouth and Norfolk Cotton Exchange in order to pay for rations to be issued to '*289 white and 287 coloured applicants*' at the local soup-house.[99] Much less salubrious than this act of public spiritedness, were James' regular visits to one of the many brothels in Norfolk. After Florence's arrest, Mrs Mary Hogwood (Howard) gave a lengthy statement to a reporter from the *New York World.* She said that prior to his marriage, James had visited her brothel '*regularly for eighteen months, coming two or three times a week during that time.*' During his visits it was a '*common occurrence for him to take arsenic two or three times an evening.' He used to carry it in 'a small phial, and, putting a small quantity on his tongue, he would slip it down with a sip of wine. Always before taking it he would say, "Well, I am going to take my evening dose!"'* Hogwood said James often arrived at her house intoxicated, and when he did, he was '*reckless in taking the drug.*'[100]

Church and music had helped James' grandfather and father rise from the ranks of skilled artisans to widely respected clerks in one of Liverpool's most important churches that was later to become the Anglican pro-cathedral in the city. Although they never made it to the '*currant jelly set,*' as the top echelon of Liverpool society were called, James' family had nevertheless become one of the more well-known families in the town. James' brother, Michael, was a Victorian success story. His singing and musical prowess earned him fame and fortune and took him into the orbit of royalty. James too had come a long way, partly through hard work but also through his knack of being able to make useful contacts. By 1879, he was a successful and respected cotton merchant, running his own company with offices in Liverpool and Norfolk, Virginia. He was a member of some exclusive clubs both in Britain and America. He was an active and committed Freemason.

Yet despite his success, some of the elements that were later to contribute to his self-destruction were already in play. He had hypochondriacal tendencies and took all kinds of medicines. He drank to excess and was often intoxicated. He had started to take dangerous drugs such as arsenic and strychnine, and had already received warnings about the consequences of this dangerous habit. His friend Nicholas Bateson overheard James' physician in Norfolk, Doctor Ward, telling him that if he continued to take arsenic in such large quantities, he would certainly kill himself.[101] James' use of arsenic had possibly predated the malarial fever he developed in 1877, and he had started to take it for aphrodisiacal purposes. He frequented the brothels of Norfolk which put him at risk of catching sexually transmitted diseases. He had used and left behind a woman in London who probably still loved him. He had had a series of dalliances with rich and younger American women. At some point, the negative elements in his life were almost certain to catch up with him. Perhaps they already had; he told Dr Séquard in the late-1870s, that he was suffering from the effects of '*free living.*'[102]

---

97 *Liverpool Mercury*, 20th April 1874.
98 New York, Passenger and Crew Lists (1820-1957) September 1874 on www.ancestry.com
99 *Norfolk Virginian*, 1st March 1879.
100 *Norfolk Virginian*, 16th August, 1889.
101 *Norfolk Virginian*, 31st May 1889.
102 Christie T. L., op. cit., page 36.

LINKS TO THE RIPPER DIARY: PAUL FELDMAN AND THE SEARCH FOR MISSING MAYBRICKS

Paul Feldman (1953-2005) was a businessman, producer, researcher and author, who decided in 1992 to produce a documentary that would reveal the identity of Jack the Ripper. He originally focussed on Montague Druitt as the prime suspect, but changed the direction of his research after the emergence of the Maybrick Diary. Although initially sceptical of the authenticity of the Diary, he came to believe it was a genuine document and that James Maybrick was the Whitechapel murderer. In the introduction to his book *Jack the Ripper: The Final Chapter*, Feldman wrote: '*I had for some time believed that the diary was genuine. I now know that it is. I also know that I have proved it beyond any reasonable doubt.*'[103]

Feldman's research into the Diary's provenance can only be described as manic. A snapshot of his thinking is revealed in one of the personal notes of researcher Keith Skinner from July 1994. He wrote: '*Paul F believes the Diary to be real and written by James Maybrick. Believes it to be inherited by Mike Barrett, who is not the Mike Barrett in the picture. Believes his identity has been changed – and he has been given either an invented background or someone else's background... Barrett's true identity probably descends from one of the illegitimate children of James and Sarah (Maybrick's mistress).*'[104]

Although Feldman's ideas were to change over time, Skinner's note does provide an insight into some of the wild hypotheses that were directing his thinking. For example, at one point he believed that neither Mike Barrett nor his estranged wife, Anne Graham, were who they claimed to be and that they had been given new identities by the Government. On another occasion, he claimed that Mike Barrett's sisters were not actually his sisters and the Barretts' marriage licence had been forged.

Although these ideas can be easily dismissed, some of his research did unearth new evidence. Feldman believed the Diary to be a genuine historical document; however, he did not believe Barrett's account that it had been given to him by Tony Devereux. As a result, he started to pursue alternative theories for how it may have ended up in Barrett's hands.

One of his early lines of research was that it had been removed from Battlecrease (the Maybricks' home in 1888/89) by electricians doing some rewiring in the house and then sold to Barrett. After speaking to the electricians involved in the work, he concluded that this story was bogus and that they would just '*lie for the right price.*'[105] Instead, Feldman came to believe that, if the Diary had not been removed from Battlecrease, then the only way it could have ended up with Barrett is if it had been a family heirloom which in turn meant that Barrett, or his wife, must be somehow related to the Maybricks. This hypothesis led Feldman and his team to research the detailed background of everyone involved in the Diary story, including James and Florence Maybrick and the families of Michael Barrett, Anne Graham and Tony Devereux.

One group of Maybricks who caught the attention of Feldman and his research team was a branch of the family centred around the Fenland market town of Whittlesey, in Cambridgeshire. Feldman believed he had discovered a line of illegitimate descendants of James Maybrick, stemming from his relationship with his mistress Sarah Ann Robertson. Although there is no official record of Sarah Robertson ever marrying Maybrick, nor of her producing any offspring, legitimate or otherwise, some writers on the case have asserted that Sarah bore James no fewer than five children. In 1892, the journalist W.T. Stead wrote that '*there were five children born of the intimacy*' between James and Sarah and that his information '*was made on the authority of the woman herself.*' Crucially, Stead goes on to add that all five children died when they were young. Despite this serious flaw in his theory, Feldman came to the conclusion that not all of James Maybrick and Sarah Ann Robertson's children had died young, and he '*may have even discovered living descendants*' of the couple.[106]

Feldman identified a woman named Margaret Minetta Edgis, also known as Maybrick (1874-1957) as James and Sarah's illegitimate daughter. She married a man named Mark Woolston(e) and together they had eight children. The problem with Feldman's assertion, apart from the fact there is no evidence to support it, is that the official records of this branch of the family are full of gaps and contradictory information. For example, in 1910, at the birth of Naomi (one of the daughters of Mark and Margaret Woolston), her surname is recorded as '*Woolston,*' but when she died eight months later, her surname is recorded as '*Maybrick*'. Another daughter, Rose Ellen, went on to bear a daughter of her own, Jeanette Grady. In 1994, Grady told Paul Feldman that she believed she was related to James Maybrick through her grandmother, Margaret Minetta, who was also known as Elizabeth. Grady claimed Margaret Minetta had links with Liverpool and was a well-educated, '*proper Victorian lady.*'[107] Peter Jepson, one of Margaret Minetta's

[103] Feldman P., op. cit., page v.
[104] Linder S., Morris C. and Skinner K., op cit., page 103.
[105] Feldman P., op cit., page 135.
[106] Ibid., page 127.
[107] Ibid., page 117.

grandsons, told Feldman that '*everyone in the family knew we were connected to the Maybricks and the Liverpool events.*' Despite this bold assertion, he also added that while he had spent a lot of time with his grandmother, it was '*impossible to question*' her about the past because '*you would get nothing.*'[108] In other words, while there was some family folklore which suggested there might be a connection to James Maybrick, there was no documented evidence to support the claim and, as Feldman himself admitted, they were '*just curious stories.*'[109]

In September 2020, Christopher Jones interviewed Stephen Porter, the grandson of Emily Minetta Woolston (1909-1990), who was the third eldest child of Margaret Minetta Woolston. Porter was extremely helpful and open about his family's history. He said he had been close to his grandmother and had lived with her for three years prior to his marriage. He said his grandmother was '*obsessed*' with Jack the Ripper and would watch every programme on television about the case. One day she told Porter that the media believed the Ripper was either Queen Victoria's doctor or her nephew. Porter asked her whom she thought the killer was, and although she did not reply, she smiled and winked at him. He interpreted her gestures to imply that she knew the identity of Jack the Ripper. Porter also said that one New Year's Eve night, while he was driving Emily Minetta back to her home, they passed the local cemetery where some members of the family were buried. He said to his grandmother that he might carry out research into the family background. She replied: '*Don't do my side as you might not like what you find out.*'

Porter told Jones that he was '*100% certain*' his great-great grandfather was James Maybrick, and that Maybrick was Jack the Ripper. Although there is no doubting the sincerity of his beliefs, Porter did admit his grandmother never once mentioned James Maybrick's name, and he only made the connection to him after the publication of Feldman's book. Jones was left with the impression that while there is undoubtedly some mystery surrounding Margaret Minetta and her early life, and there are some '*curious stories*,' there is simply no proven link to either James Maybrick or Sarah Ann Robertson.

The only evidence that Feldman puts forward to establish a link between the Whittlesey Maybricks and James Maybrick is a photograph he claimed showed Sarah Ann Robertson as an old woman sitting in the garden of 24 Cottisbrook Street with Elizabeth Susannah Woolston (1905-1992). Elizabeth, often called Lizzie, was the eldest of the daughters of Margaret Minetta and Mark Woolston. She died at the home of her niece and her husband, Janice and Paul Roughton. Janice was the daughter of Ann Woolston. Janice showed Feldman many photographs which had once belonged to Aunt Lizzie. In one of them, Lizzie was aged about 20, dating the photograph to the early 1920s. She was sitting in a garden drinking tea with a much older woman whom Janice thought might be a Mrs Read, a lady Lizzie had often visited. Feldman later shared the same photograph with Ethel Hartnett, a cousin of Barbara Bills. Barbara Bills was the woman who owned the Bible that James Maybrick supposedly gave to Sarah Ann Robertson. Her mother, Alice, had been living at the same address as Sarah at the time of her death. When Ethel saw the photograph in 1995, she identified the old woman as Sarah Ann Robertson. She said Sarah had attended her wedding to William Hartnett in September 1923.

To Feldman, this was the proof he needed to claim the connection between Sarah Ann Robertson and the Whittlesey Maybricks was '*now firmly established.*'[110] In fact, like so many of Feldman's assertions, it is unproven and open to debate. It was just one picture; the woman in question was recognised by only one person and it was taken at an event that happened more than 70 years earlier. Even if it was Sarah Ann Robertson, which seems unlikely, that does not prove she was related to the younger woman and it does not provide any evidence to help explain the provenance of the Diary.

The main reason why Feldman was researching the Whittlesey Maybricks was to try and find out if Michael Barrett was related, through the illegitimate children of Sarah Ann Robertson, to James Maybrick. If that was the case, it would explain how Barrett happened to be in possession of Maybrick's journal.

It became obvious to Feldman that there was no link between Barrett and the Whittlesey Maybricks. He therefore decided to look at the possibility that the link was in fact with the family of Barrett's ex-wife, Anne Graham. One of the sons of Margaret Minetta Woolston was named Sheppard Shalgrave Woolston (Maybrick). He was born in 1913, but then records of him disappeared. When the rest of the family entered the workhouse in 1915, he was not recorded as being with them, yet there is no record of his death. Feldman suggested to Anne Graham that Sheppard Shalgrave could actually be her father, William (Billy) Graham, as their dates of birth were similar. That Feldman proposed such a hypothesis without any evidence to support it, shows how desperate he was to establish a Maybrick link.

After listening to Feldman, Anne replied, '*You just might have something here, Paul.*'[111] She then told Feldman that she had first seen the Diary in 1968 or 1969 when she was packing her father's possessions as he was about to move house. Her father told her he had been given the Diary on Christmas Day 1950 by his stepmother Edith, who

[108] Ibid., page 120.
[109] Ibid., page 122.
[110] Ibid., page 127.
[111] Ibid., page 153.

told him that his step-grandmother had left it to him. Anne Graham claimed the Diary had later been passed to her by her own father and she had given it to Devereux to give to her husband.

Feldman's trawling of the Maybrick records had initially been based around his hypothesis that Michael Barrett was related to James Maybrick. He abandoned that idea when no such link could be found. His research then switched to the possibility that Billy Graham – Anne Graham's father – was related to James Maybrick, only for that to be abandoned as well. Finally, his research moved on to the view that Billy Graham was in fact related to Florence and not James Maybrick.

In July 1994, after just two interviews with an elderly and frail Billy Graham, Feldman arrived at the remarkable conclusion that Graham was in fact descended from Florence Maybrick. Graham had therefore inherited the Diary from his own father who, Feldman surmised, must have been an illegitimate child born to Florence in 1879. '*According to rumour,*' Anne Graham wrote: '*It was during one protracted stay in England towards the end of 1879 that Florence embarked on her first love affair. It was even suggested that she gave birth to an illegitimate son as a teenager. The account continues that she placed the child, named William after her father, in the hands of a Hartlepool blacksmith and his wife named Graham and continued to support him financially.*'[112]

William Graham (1979-1950)

In other words, we are expected to believe that Florence, aged around 15, had a brief affair and, in 1879, gave birth to an illegitimate child. She then gave the baby to a blacksmith in Hartlepool whom she didn't know. It was yet another hypothesis floated by Feldman without any evidence to support it. We know from the records of trans-Atlantic voyages that Florence travelled back to America in August 1878 and probably spent most, if not all, of 1879 living in New York. The best Feldman could muster to support his idea was a statement by John Baillie Knight that he had first met Florence '*in or about the year 1879.*' He also pointed to a brief period after Florence left prison in 1904, when she called herself Mrs Graham in an attempt to escape press intrusion, and to the fact that after her death her address book was found with all the 'G's torn out. Even Anne Graham had to admit that she was '*not completely convinced*' by the theory which, if true, meant that Florence was her great-grandmother.[113]

A long-standing Diary sceptic, the journalist Melvin Harris, was totally dismissive. He wrote: '*The Florence fairy tale has her exporting her illegitimate son to Hartlepool and handing it over to a family whose name just happened to resonate with her old family name Ingraham. We are expected to believe that the baby was just dumped and forgotten and only remembered many years later, when it became important to hand on the Diary. Not a scrap of evidence supports this. No document links Florence with the blacksmith in Hartlepool.*'

Despite Anne Graham's assertion that the Ripper Diary had been given to her by her father Billy Graham, no documentary evidence exists to substantiate this claim. Some sceptics have suggested the whole story was concocted just to benefit Paul Feldman, who at the time was negotiating a lucrative Hollywood film deal.

In 1994, Feldman wrote: '*Of course, the Diary is real and there is a growing belief in the media that this is the case. Our research team have uncovered families of illegitimate Maybricks. These revelations have not surprised them whatsoever and most of them believe that this has always been known within the family.*'[114]

Feldman's theories have received little support. Although there is no doubting the scope of his intentions and the vigour in which he pursued them, there is a lot to doubt about the veracity and strength of his conclusions. His work may have led to '*daring speculations,*' but at the same time they '*often produced unconvincing hypotheses.*'[115] Feldman's research marked him out as a man who was bent on trying to prove his hypotheses rather than testing them in an objective manner. This approach cost him a lot of money and led him down a series of blind alleyways.

In the end, for all his passion and zeal, he ended up with an untenable and an unsupported theory that, rather than providing a robust provenance for the Diary, only served to further undermine its credibility as a historical document.

[112] Graham A. and Emmas C., op cit., page 27.
[113] Ibid., page xxi
[114] Wolff C. (compiled), *Who Was Jack the Ripper?* (Grey House Books, London, 1995) page 30.
[115] Begg P., Fido M. and Skinner K., op cit., page 167.

3

THE HOLBROOKS AND THE CHANDLERS

Florence Elizabeth Chandler was born in Mobile, Alabama. The exact year of her birth is unclear. In her autobiography she gives the date as 3rd September 1862; however, on her American passport application – a legal document she signed – the date is stated as 3rd September 1861. Alexander MacDougall, the Scottish lawyer who met Florence's mother and who campaigned for Florence's release from prison, wrote a letter in which he states that Florence's father '*died when she was an infant.*'[116] As her father died in July 1862, this suggests that Florence was born in September 1861.

Florence's father was William Gaines Chandler (1829-1862). He died, aged just 33, following a short illness. Her mother Caroline (Holbrook) Chandler (1839-1910), known as Carrie, faced a daunting future. She was a widow with two young children. To make things worse, she was a mistrusted Northerner, a Yankee living in the Confederacy at the time of the American Civil War of 1861-65. Although in a difficult position, Carrie was a woman of strong character, an attribute that had been demonstrated on numerous previous occasions by generations of her forebearers.

Carrie was born on 4th February 1839, in Dorchester, Massachusetts, USA, the only daughter of Darius Blake Holbrook (1798-1858) and Elizabeth Thurston Ingraham Holbrook (1807-1876). Both sides of Carrie's family were well connected, and her distinguished lineage qualified her to be one of the *Daughters of the American Revolution*. This is an organisation which included women over the age of 18 who had directly descended from an ancestor who had helped achieve American independence.

Darius Blake Holbrook (1798-1858)

Carrie's father, Darius Blake Holbrook, was also been born in Dorchester. His family had originally come to America from Shropshire, in England. His mother's family were Ridgeways, one of whom – Sir Thomas Ridgeway – had been the first Earl of Londonderry in the north of Ireland. The Ridgeways had come to the United States '*on the ship Jacob and Mary in November 1679,*' and had settled in Springfield Township in New Jersey.[117] One of the sisters of Darius' mother, Elizabeth (Ridgeway) Holbrook, had married a Quincy and was an aunt to John Quincy Adams, the sixth President of the United States.

Carrie's mother, Elizabeth Ingraham, was born in Portland, Maine. Her great-great-grandmother, Sarah Phillips, was the sister of John Phillips, who founded Phillip's Academy in Exeter, New Hampshire, one of the oldest secondary schools in the United States. Sarah Philips married the Rev Benjamin Thurston. Their daughter Elizabeth Thurston (1787-1856) married James Milk Ingraham (1781-1856). The Ingraham family were one of the most prominent families in Portland. Another of the Ingrahams was the wife of Philander Chase, the first Bishop of Illinois and uncle to Salmon P. Chase, who was Secretary of the Treasury under Lincoln and Chief Justice of the Supreme Court of the United States.[118]

Darius Blake Holbrook has been described as '*one of the best-known men of his day.*'[119] He was an energetic entrepreneur involved in numerous business undertakings. His admirers described him as '*swashbuckling, shrewd and dynamic.*'[120] His detractors were not so complimentary, especially those who lost money in his ventures. To give some understanding of the diverse scope of his interests, he made his first fortune in the textile industry; he was associated with Cyrus W. Field in the laying of the first Atlantic cable; he was involved in securing the grant for the Illinois Central Railway; and he served as President of the Great Western Railway Company.[121]

In the 1830s, Holbrook bought thousands of acres of land on the lower Mississippi at a bargain rate. His purchases included Cairo, the southernmost town in the state of Illinois. It was situated at the confluence of two of America's greatest rivers, the Mississippi and the Ohio. Although its location gave it the potential to be a commercial hub of significance, the area was prone to flooding. Holbrook believed the solution lay in generating the funds to tackle the

---

[116] *Manchester Courier and Lancashire General Advertiser*, 26th September 1891.
[117] Lansden J.M., *A History of the City of Cairo, Illinois*, (South Illinois University Press, 2009 reprint) page 193.
[118] Maybrick F., op. cit., pages 16-18.
[119] *Pittsburgh Dispatch*, 8th August 1889.
[120] Christie T.L., op. cit., page 24.
[121] Hutto R.J., *A Poisoned Life*, (McFarland and Co., Jefferson, 2018) page 5.

problem. In 1837, he established the Cairo City and Canal Company and set about raising money by selling bonds, primarily in Britain, where investors would have been unlikely to have knowledge of the town's geographical problems. The private banking house, Wright and Company, agreed to take control of the bond sales using optimistic illustrations of the planned development. The advertising campaign boldly described Cairo as the '*Mine of Golden Hope.*'[122] The money generated allowed Holbrook to build '*at vast expense a levee around the place, enclosing one thousand acres of land, foundries, saw mills, a dry dock, a hotel and numerous other buildings and in so doing attracted hither some two thousand people.*' It is estimated that Holbrook spent '*one million and four hundred thousand dollars*' on the project.[123] In 1840, this promising start came to an abrupt end when Wright and Company went bankrupt. The collapse of the bank led to the collapse of Holbrook's own company and the British investors in his scheme lost their money. Within two years, just 50 people remained in Cairo and floods had destroyed much of the town.[124] In 1842, the renowned English novelist, Charles Dickens, visited Cairo and was damning in his verdict, describing it as '*a dismal swamp... a place without a single quality, in earth or air or water to commend it.*'[125] After Dickens returned to England he continued his critique of Cairo and also poked fun at its founder in his novel *Martin Chuzzlewit* (1844). One of the book's characters was Zephaniah Scadder, an unscrupulous operator, who sold swamp land to a young Chuzzlewit. While obvious comparisons can be drawn between Holbrook and the fictional character Scadder, some of these are undeserved. Although it is the case that a large number of investors did lose money, there can be no doubt that Holbrook believed in the project and worked hard to realise his dream for the town.

Elizabeth Thurston Holbrook (1807-1876)

In the late 1850s, the advent of the railways and improved levees finally saw Cairo develop as a commercial centre. By 1858, the population of the town had grown to 2,000 and it had become the county seat of Alexander County. Holbrook did not see the fruit of his labours as he died in 1858; nevertheless, he is still regarded as the Father of Cairo. One local historian wrote that for more than 15 years Holbrook '*never swerved an inch in his devotion to the city of Cairo. The very best years of his life he had put into his attempt to establish it; therefore one must readily agree that the Cairo of today owes its existence more to Darius Blake Holbrook than to any other man.*'[126]

Darius Holbrook married Elizabeth Thurston Ingraham in 1836 and the couple settled in a rather grand house, 17 East Fourteenth Street, New York, when that '*thoroughfare was one of the most fashionable in town.*'[127] Two years later their only child, Caroline, was born.

Carrie was an intelligent and vivacious young woman of strong character. She was considered a '*good conversationalist, handsome and prepossessing.*'[128] She was also a '*wonderful dancer.*'[129] Her outgoing personality made her extremely popular and she had '*many friends in the old Knickerbocker set.*'[130] This was a group that supposedly comprised the descendants of the British and Dutch aristocratic families who had governed the early American colonies or had some links to European aristocratic families. One person who knew Carrie well, described her as a '*little magnetizer*' of the male sex. He wrote that she had '*particular sway over men from her early girlhood. Scarcely accounted beautiful, she could have given "handicap" to any prize beauty after the first half hour.*'[131]

In 1856, Carrie travelled to Mobile, Alabama, to spend the winter months with the Rev Joseph Holt Ingraham, one of her mother's brothers. The Rev Ingraham was a colourful character. Before the age of 17 he had sailed to Buenos Aires.

Rev J. H. Ingraham (1809-1860)

[122] *Cairo Bulletin*, (Cairo, Illinois), 3rd September 1910.
[123] *Cairo Bulletin*, (Cairo, Illinois), 25th September 1877.
[124] *Kansas City Star*, 4th May 1969.
[125] Dickens C., *Boz in Egypt*, located at www.charlesdickenspage.com
[126] Murray J., *Darius Blake Holbrook – Securing a Foundation*, in Alexander County Profiles at alexander.illinoisgenweb.org/1968profiles/hist1968e.htm
[127] *New York Times*, 4th October 1903.
[128] *Pittsburgh Press*, 11th September 1892.
[129] De Leon T.C., *Belles, Beaux and Brains of the 60s*, (T. Fisher Unwin, London, 1909) page 410.
[130] *New York Times*, 4th October 1903.
[131] De Leon T.C., op cit., pages 410 and 408.

While he was in South America he is *'said to have taken part in a native revolution.'*[132] After his return, he attended both Bowdoin and Yale but failed to graduate from either college.

In the early 1830s, Ingraham settled in Mississippi and became a teacher at Jefferson College. In 1832, he married Mary Brooks, the daughter of a wealthy planter. In 1836, he published his first novel, and quickly established himself as a prolific writer of cheap novels. In the 1850s, his life took a change of direction, when he was ordained as a minister in the Episcopal Church. In December 1853, he became the first Rector at St. John's Protestant Episcopal Church, Mobile, a post he held until January 1857.[133] In 1855, he published his most popular novel, *The Prince of the House of David: or Three Years in the Holy City.* The book took the form of a collection of letters from the fictional character, Adina, to her father, whilst she was living in Jerusalem.

Carrie would have been excited about visiting her uncle, not least because he promised to introduce her to the '*exclusive society*' of Mobile.[134] Although much smaller than New York, Mobile was a vibrant city and one of the centres of the Southern social scene. Carrie soon enjoyed the attention of the young men of Mobile. At that time there was a distinct behavioural code for rich, white gentlemen of the South. Historians have argued that it '*emphasised courage, aggression, pride, a disdain for cowardice, and an exaggerated display of masculinity as manifestations of their honour.*'[135]

If the young men of Mobile wanted to impress Carrie, then she in turn wanted to impress them. As well as her confident demeanour, she was 'fair of face, with an unusual charm of manner... Miss Caroline Holbrook possessed exceptional ancestry, as well as the potent power of personal charms.'[136]

Caroline 'Carrie' Holbrook (1839-1910)

The Mobile that Carrie visited in 1856 was a relatively young American town. Although it had been founded by the French in 1702, it did not become part of the United States until 1813, when it was captured from the Spanish by American forces and added to the Mississippi Territory. In 1817, this territory was split into two parts, with Mobile becoming part of the new Alabama Territory. Two years later, in December 1819, the territory was converted into a state and Alabama became the 22nd state of the United States. When Carrie arrived in Mobile, it had a population of almost 30,000. These inhabitants included 20,323 white citizens, 1,041 '*free persons of colour*' and 8,366 slaves.[137]

Mobile was in the middle of the '*Golden Fifties.*' A decade when the city was at the peak of its prosperity. This wealth rested upon the cotton trade. One local described cotton as '*the circulating blood that gives life to the city.*'[138] The land to the north of Mobile contained some of the richest cotton growing areas in the south, and was known as the Black Belt. Cotton was shipped down river from the cotton plantations. The bales were then loaded on to ocean-going ships and transported around the world. Mobile became the second largest cotton exporting seaport in the world; only New Orleans exceeded it in volume of business. The cotton trade brought wealth to the city and its citizens: '*fine horses and beautiful carriages were seen on the streets, and the coffee shops and bars were filled with men in embroidered waistcoats and beaver hats, all talking cotton.*'[139]

One group of Mobile's inhabitants who did not share in the growing wealth of the city, even though they were the very people who made it all possible, were the slaves. It was slaves who worked in the cotton fields. It was also slaves who did the work in the homes of the richer Mobilians. In 1856, slaves made up 28% of the city's population. Most people in Mobile were in favour of slavery. Although the importation of slaves into America had been illegal since 1808, the city still had a slave market on St Louis Street where the plantation owners and Mobilians could buy and sell slaves. It is difficult to know exactly what Carrie thought of slavery, but as some in her own family had embraced it and because her first husband's family owned a large number of slaves, it is probable that she accepted the institution. Daniel Chandler, her soon to be father-in-law, is recorded as owning 26 slaves in 1850, and 10 in 1860.[140]

---

[132] Extract in Mississippi Encyclopedia on John Ingraham at www.ulib.niu.edu/badndp/ingraham_joseph.html
[133] Hutto R.J., op cit., page 8.
[134] *Chicago Inter Ocean*, 31st October 1897.
[135] Goldberg, M. D., *Southern Honour, Confederate Warfare*, (University of Louisville thesis, 2011) accessed at ir.library.louisville.edu
[136] *Sunday Chicago Inter Ocean*, (Chicago, Illinois) part 4, page 29, 31st October 1897.
[137] Based on the Census taken in Fall of 1855 and published in the Mobile City Directory.
[138] Amos H.E., *Cotton City*, (University of Alabama, Alabama, 1985) page 18.
[139] Delaney C., *The Story of Mobile*, (HB Publications, Mobile, 1994) page 92.
[140] U.S. Federal Censuses of 1850 and 1860 (Slave Schedules).

Carrie's uncle, the Rev Ingraham, wrote the book *The Sunny South*, which appeared just three months before his death in 1860. The book provided a strident defence of slavery, the plantation system and the way of life in the Southern States. In one passage which makes shocking reading to the modern mind, he wrote that the Negro slaves in the South were '*happier in bondage than free*.' He described the free Negroes of the Northern States as '*miserable creatures, poor, ragged and often criminal*.'[141]

Carrie's first two husbands – William Chandler and Franklin Du Barry – were both ardent supporters of the Confederate cause during the Civil War. This is particularly notable for Du Barry, as he was born in the North but chose to fight for the South. We also know from William Chandler's probate documents that he and Carrie owned a slave, a Mulatto girl aged about 22, named Mollie.[142] It is not known what her role was, but it was presumably to help with childcare and chores around the house.

Daniel Chandler (1805-1866)

During Carrie's time with her uncle in Mobile she quickly attracted a '*troop of admirers*.'[143] One of these was William Gaines Chandler (1829-1862), a wealthy businessman, who proved to be the '*most ardent*' of her suitors. William was a member of '*an old Southern Family of distinguished connections*.'[144] His father was Daniel Chandler (1805-1866), one of Mobile's most prominent citizens. He had been born in Warrenton, Georgia in December 1805, and was educated at Franklin College before studying law in Winchester, Virginia. After qualifying as a lawyer, he moved to Mobile where he was to live for the rest of his life. He became a partner in a law firm with John A. Campbell (1811-1889), who was to serve as a judge on the US Supreme Court and later became a minister in the Confederate Government during the Civil War. In 1828, Daniel Chandler married John Campbell's sister, Sarah (1809-1887). The couple were to have five children, of which William, born in 1829, was the oldest.

Around 1850, the Chandler family moved into a newly-built Greek-style mansion – complete with Doric columns – at 252 Government Street, in the heart of the city. It was an impressive three-storey building, reflecting Daniel Chandler's status and wealth. In the late 1800s, the building came to be used as a Catholic boys' school, the McGill Institute. It was demolished in 1953 to make room for the Admiral Semmes Motor Hotel, which was also later demolished. Today, the property at 252 Government Street is a parking lot. The base of one of the Doric columns somehow escaped demolition, and remains as a reminder of the once grand mansion that once stood there.

Left: Postcard showing the Chandler mansion on Government Street, Mobile;
and Right: remains of one of the Doric columns from the house. (Chris Jones collection)

Carrie and William Chandler were soon '*mutually taken with one another*.' Although Chandler was ten years older than Carrie, he was considered one of the '*most agreeable of Mobile's young men, educated and refined, and quite*

[141] Ingraham J. H., *The Sunny South or the Southerner at Home*, (G.G. Evans, Philadelphia, 1860) page 59.
[142] Probate document for the estate of William G. Chandler, filed August 30th 1862, and kept in Mobile County Probate Courts.
[143] *Daily Register*, (Mobile, Alabama) 22nd May 1889.
[144] *Sunday Chicago Inter Ocean*, (Chicago, Illinois) part 4, page 29, 31st October 1897.

successful in business.'[145] He had graduated from Yale College in 1848 with distinction. Years later, some of the older residents of New Haven told a newspaper reporter that they remembered William Chandler as a '*tall, handsome young man, a typical Southerner.*' They said he was a '*general favourite with everyone who knew him,*' and moved in the '*highest social circles.*'[146] After he left college, '*contrary to the expectations and advice of his friends, he commenced at once with zeal and ardour in preparing himself for mercantile business.*'[147]

He trained for the world of commerce under the guidance of Newton St John (1810-1876), who was originally from New York State but had settled in Mobile in the 1830s. Newton St John established his own private bank, St John, Powers and Company, and at the time when William Chandler joined it was '*the strongest local private banking firm*' in Mobile.[148] It was for a '*long time agents of Messrs. Baring Bros., London,*' and had '*engagements*' which were of a '*great magnitude.*'[149] Chandler must have impressed Newton St John, because in 1857 he was invited to become one of the partners in the bank. His new role '*opened a large scope for the activity of his mind, his business habits and his varied acquirements. No man of his age in this community was more distinguished for prompt decision, accurate judgement, a well-balanced and self-poised mind.*'[150]

On 12th October 1857, Carrie and William Chandler were married by the Rev Dr George C. Pennell at Trinity Episcopal Church in Carrie's home city of New York.[151] After their honeymoon they returned to Mobile, where '*they lived in good style. Mrs Chandler increased her influence in society and was even as much of a belle as before her marriage.*'[152]

Three months later, in January 1858, Carrie's father died. Under the terms of his will, his property portfolio was left to his widow and to Carrie. This included the house in New York and the land he had purchased in 1838 that stretched over the boundaries of the states of Virginia, West Virginia and Kentucky.

It is highly probable that the early years of Carrie and William's marriage were happy ones. One report stated: '*the promise for their future was one of exceptional blessings. Young, handsome, intelligent and wealthy, they began their married life under social conditions never exceeded in culture of refinement.*'[153] The *Mobile City Directory of 1859*, shows that the couple lived in 13 North Joachim Street, which was only a few hundred yards from the home of William's parents. According to the US Census of August 1860, they were still living in the same house. William is listed as a '*merchant*' and the value of his personal estate was given as $15,000. That was a sizeable amount in 1860, especially when one compares it to his father, whose personal estate in the same census was only $5,000. The key difference between William and Daniel Chandler was that Daniel's real estate was valued at $20,000, while William's was valued at zero. That presumably means that William and Carrie did not own the house in which they lived.

The Census of 1860, also lists the name of the Chandlers' young son, Holbrook St John Campbell Chandler, who was born on 4th November 1859.[154] He was named after Carrie's maiden name, William's senior business partner, and William's mother's surname. In September 1861 (or possibly 1862), the young couple welcomed a second child with the birth of Florence Elizabeth Chandler.

We get some idea of the style in which the family lived from the list of their possessions shown in William Chandler's probate documents. The hallway and main downstairs rooms, apart from the kitchen, had chandeliers; the one in the hall was a gas chandelier. There were pictures, oil paintings and engravings in the dining room. Food was served off silver plate, china and glass. The living rooms and two bedrooms upstairs were carpeted, and there was a wide variety of furnishings including a dining table and eight dining chairs, a sideboard, bookcase, two sofas and two armchairs.[155]

The early promise and positivity of the Chandler marriage was not to last long. On 3rd July 1862, after suffering from a short but severe illness, William Chandler died. According to his obituary, his death was the result of '*close attention to business and over-mental exertion.*' Two days earlier, the notice in the newspaper that provided the details of his internment stated that he died of '*ramollissement of brain [morbid softening].*'[156] Years later, at the time of her daughter's trial in 1889, Carrie's then-solicitor said that William had died from '*inflammation of the brain, caused by the extreme tension and anxiety attendant upon the heavy financial responsibilities of his firm in the midst of the civil war.*'[157]

---

145 *Daily Register*, (Mobile, Alabama) 22nd May 1889.
146 *New Haven Register*, 27th December 1892.
147 *Mobile Advertiser and Register*, 8th July 1862.
148 Amos H.E., op cit., page 38.
149 *Baltimore Sun*, (Baltimore, Maryland), 2nd October 1876.
150 *Mobile Advertiser and Register*, 8th July 1862.
151 *New York Times*, 13th October 1857.
152 *Pittsburgh Press*, 11th September 1892.
153 *Sunday Chicago Inter Ocean*, (Chicago, Illinois) part 4, page 29, 31st October 1897.
154 Name and date shown on Holbrook's passport application of June 1878, found at www.ancestry.com
155 Probate document for the estate of William G. Chandler, filed August 30th 1862, and kept in Mobile County Probate Courts.
156 *Mobile Advertiser and Register*, 6th July 1862.
157 *Evening Express*, (Liverpool, England) 19th June 1889.

William was buried in the Chandler plot in Magnolia Cemetery in Mobile. In 1863, a year after his son's death, Daniel Chandler was struck down by a disease from which he never fully recovered. He died three years later, in 1866, while on a trip to New Orleans and was buried in Magnolia Cemetery, a few metres away from the grave of his son.

The death of William Chandler at a young age and after such a short illness, gave rise to a great deal of malicious gossip, all of it directed at his wife. Carrie was already unpopular with some of the women in Mobile as she had '*executed a matrimonial coup by capturing an extremely eligible man from the Southern Belles.*'[158] The death of William increased these feelings of jealousy and resentment. To some extent this was understandable; she was from the North, against whom the Southern States were in the middle of a brutal civil war. After Chandler's death, stories started to spread that Carrie had prevented William's relatives from visiting him, and that she had also stopped him from receiving the appropriate medical treatment. More alarmingly, there were even suggestions that his death may have been caused by Carrie administering poison to him. One of William's cousins, Mrs Wyatt Randall, stated: '*The entire family was convinced beyond the possibility of doubt that Mrs Chandler poisoned her husband.*'[159]

Chandler family plot in Magnolia Cemetery, Mobile
(Chris Jones collection)

In 1889, in the weeks before Florence's trial, a Mobile newspaper recycled some of these old rumours. They ran a story from a gentleman who said he was '*well acquainted*' with Carrie. He claimed that she had a '*regular mania for collecting all sorts of poisons.*' She obtained them from all around the world, and had them on display in '*a fine cabinet.*'[160] Some days later the same newspaper was forced to retract its story, after people came forward to say that they had been admitted to the sick room and Carrie had nursed her dying husband to the best of her abilities.[161] An explanation for why Carrie possessed a range of potions was provided in her affidavit of 1894, which was part of the Harris submission to Asquith. She wrote it was her '*habit to attend to the ailments of my slaves,*' as was the custom of Southern ladies at that time, and she became '*aware of the preparations and selection of medicines and lotions.*'[162]

The rumour mill was given further oxygen by the presence in Mobile during the time of William's illness of Lieutenant Franklin Du Barry. According to one newspaper report, he was a '*dashing young officer connected with the ordnance department of the Confederacy. He paid devoted attention to Mrs Chandler, and she recklessly encouraged him. The improper conduct of the two became a favourite topic for local gossip.*'[163]

One woman who was familiar with these rumours was Florence Aunspaugh who, as a young teenager, was to stay in Liverpool with James and Florence Maybrick. She wrote: '*In the antebellum days Mobile was a swift place and the women were much swifter... Mrs Chandler would receive young men regardless of whether Mr Chandler was at home or not, would meet them at the door, throw her arms around their necks and kiss them, take them in the parlour and sit down in their laps and continue to pet them... One of the chief recreations and pleasures... was for the towns which were located on the river and had steamboats to have what we call moonlight boat excursions on the river. The gentlemen would charter a boat. The lower deck which was the freight deck was cleared for dancing... Mrs Chandler was right in the midst of all this; would go even if Mr Chandler did not go and she and some of the boys would go off to the passengers cabins alone and stay for an hour or more.*'[164]

---

[158] Christie T.L., op. cit., page 27.
[159] Quoted in Christie T.L., op. cit., page 27.
[160] *Daily Register*, (Mobile, Alabama), 22nd May 1889.
[161] See newspaper report in Hutto R.J., op cit., page 14.
[162] Affidavit of the Baroness von Roques, in Levy J.H., *The Necessity for Criminal Appeal*, (P.S. King and Son, London, 1899) pages 472-473.
[163] *Pittsburgh Press*, 11th September 1892.
[164] Trevor Christie Collection.

It is important to remember that Florence Aunspaugh's correspondence with Christie took place some 80 years after these events, and that she was simply repeating what she had been told by others. While Carrie was probably the subject of malicious rumours, it is unlikely that there was any substance to them. The idea that a young woman from the North could have prevented William's influential family from visiting him when he was seriously ill is simply unbelievable.

It is also clear that William's illness was brought on by the pressures of war. The Confederacy relied for most of its wealth creation on the cotton plantations. The Union naval blockade and loss of control over many of its rivers caused cotton exports to fall by 95%, bringing the economy close to collapse. One of the main ways the government tried to generate revenue was by printing money. This led to hyper-inflation, a disruption to commerce, the collapse of the financial infrastructure and the ruin of many Southern banks.

These pressures were particularly difficult for St John, Powers and Company, because Newton St John had been opposed to the secession of Alabama from the Union. In May 1861, he moved his family to New York. William Chandler and his banking partner, Benjamin Whitaker, attempted to continue the business but the task proved beyond them. Although there was no formal dissolution of their bank, when financial demands were placed upon it by the Planters Bank of Tennessee in February 1862, it was unable to make the necessary payments and it collapsed. The timing of these demands on the bank match the onset of William's illness.

Although it is probable that Carrie found Franklin Du Barry a handsome man, it is not credible to suggest that they had an affair while William was seriously ill and she was herself recovering from her second pregnancy. What makes it even more doubtful is that Du Barry's Confederate Army records reveal that, in March 1861, Daniel Chandler wrote a letter in support of his application to join the Confederate forces.[165] It is unlikely he would have written such a letter if Du Barry had been conducting an affair with his daughter-in-law. Even more significant, is a letter sent in February 1862 to the Confederate Headquarters in Richmond, Virginia which supports the case for Du Barry to be promoted to the rank of captain. The three-page letter outlines Du Barry's family background, his military service, and his commitment to the Confederate cause. It states that he had been on the '*most arduous and active duty*' and he had done all the duties of a '*full captain without rank or pay.*'[166] The letter is on the headed paper of St John, Powers and Company and is signed W.G. Chandler. Such a glowing tribute would not have been written by William if he had any suspicions that his wife was cavorting with Du Barry. Therefore, we can reject the view that William Chandler was poisoned by Carrie. Such stories were based on rumours and jealousy, and they later became exaggerated at the time of Florence's trial.

The months following William's death must have been difficult for Carrie. Apart from the emotional shock and grief she would have been feeling following the sudden death of her husband, she also had to face a range of practical problems. Although the rumours about her behaviour were undeserved, they must have alienated her from at least some of William's family. According to one account, '*so strong and insistent were the suspicions*' that Carrie poisoned her husband that an '*investigation and prosecution of the widow were threatened.*' This supposedly did not occur, as the city authorities were more concerned with tackling the problems of the war.[167]

The problem with this view is that if such evidence had existed, it is certain the Chandler family would have ensured the authorities pursued a prosecution. As there was no prosecution, there can have been no evidence. In 1860, William had written a will in which he bequeathed everything to Carrie. The will had been written in the offices of St John, Powers and Company, and had been witnessed by two of William's friends, Waller Thompson and Enoch Fulford Hellen. His true feelings for Carrie are made quite clear by his references to his '*beloved Wife*' and '*my dear Wife.*' His concern for her is also shown by his suggestion that, after his death, Carrie should return to the North. The reasons he provides are the adverse impact of the Southern climate on Carrie's constitution, and the expense of living in the South.

A month after his death, William's will passed through the Probate Court of Mobile County. The value of his estate, including '*property of all kinds,*' was said '*not to exceed $17,000.*'[168] Rather surprisingly, considering the financial problems of his bank, this figure was in excess of the $15,000 shown in the 1860 Census return. It was a sizeable amount, even after the debts of just over $1,000 had been paid. The document gives a breakdown of the value of each individual item of household property. The most valuable item was the Mulatto slave girl, Mollie, who was valued at $1,000. The next most valuable items were all each worth $200; they included carpets for six rooms, a picture and the two sofas. The document also provides details of two insurance policies that William had taken out in 1859. The first was with the New York Life Insurance Company and was for $6,000, and the second was with the New England Mutual Life Insurance Company and was for $4,000.

---

[165] Letter dated March 20th 1861; and stored in the Confederate Army Records Office in Florida.
[166] Letter from *St. John, Powers and Company*, dated February 18th 1862; and stored in the Confederate Army Records Office in Florida.
[167] Christie T.L., op. cit., page 27.
[168] Probate document for the estate of William G. Chandler, filed August 30th 1862, and kept in Mobile County Probate Courts.

After the death of her husband, Carrie felt isolated. Her uncle, the Rev Ingraham, had moved to a church in Holly Springs, Mississippi. Her mother was in New York and, due to the war, it would have been impossible for Carrie to have travelled to that city. After some deliberation, Carrie decided to move to Macon in Georgia, some 350 miles from Mobile. One reason suggested for this move was because there were '*several of her husband's relatives*' living there, though they '*would have nothing to do with her.*'[169] This seems unlikely, especially if William's relatives were being unfriendly towards her. Another reason suggested as to why she supposedly selected Macon was to be with Captain Du Barry; however, according to his Army records, in November 1862 he was '*ordered to report to General Beauregard in Charleston.*'[170] If Carrie had decided to follow Du Barry, then Charleston and not Macon would have been her chosen destination.

Franklin Bache Du Barry (1837-1864) had a distinguished family background. His paternal grandfather, Jean Baptiste Marie Du Barry (1764-1830), had been born in France. Due to his aristocratic background, in 1791 he fled the country to escape the wrath of the French Revolution. He travelled to Santo Domingo, where he owned sugar plantations, but had to flee from that country as well when a slave uprising occurred in 1793. He travelled to America and settled in Philadelphia. He married twice and had eight children. One of these was Franklin's father, Dr Edmund Louis Du Barry (1797-1853). He was born in Philadelphia and studied medicine before becoming a surgeon in the US Navy. In 1827 he married Emma Duane (1812-1893), and they were to have seven children – six boys and one girl. The Du Barrys lived for a while in Bordentown, New Jersey, where they purchased a house next door to Joseph Bonaparte, the exiled brother of Napoleon Bonaparte, the former Emperor of France. Dr Du Barry was to become a physician and personal friend to Joseph Bonaparte, and named his second eldest son after him.

Franklin Bache Du Barry's two forenames paid homage to the families he was related to through the maternal side of his family. Du Barry's mother, Emma Duane, was the daughter of Colonel William Duane (1760-1835), who had served in the American Army during the War of 1812 and had later become the editor of the *Aurora*, an influential Philadelphian newspaper. One of her half-brothers, William John Duane (1780-1865), served several terms in the Pennsylvania Assembly and was briefly the US Secretary of the Treasury in 1833. In 1805, William John Duane married Deborah Franklin Bache (1781-1863), who was the daughter of Sarah ('Sally') Franklin Bache (1743-1808) and the granddaughter of Benjamin Franklin (1706-1790), who is considered one of the Founding Fathers of the United States. Franklin Du Barry was also related to Benjamin Franklin through another line of his maternal family. Colonel William Duane's second wife, and the mother of Emma Duane, was Margaret Hartman Markoe (1770-1836). She had previously been married to Benjamin Franklin Bache (1769-1798). His father was Richard Bache (1737-1811) who served as US Postmaster General from 1776 to 1782. He had married Sarah (*Sally*) Franklin, the daughter of Benjamin Franklin.

Prior to the American Civil War, Franklin Du Barry served as Second Officer on the *USS Bibb*, a coastal vessel that was carrying out a detailed survey of the Gulf Coast. In March 1861, Du Barry applied to join the Confederate Army. In his letter, he said he had resigned as the *Bibb* was being transferred to the US Navy and it would be '*under orders to proceed against the Confederate States.*'[171] His application was supported by a letter from Daniel Chandler, who wrote that while he had '*not the pleasure of his personal acquaintance*' with Du Barry, he had been referred to him by someone whose judgement he trusted. Why would Franklin Du Barry, born in the North, and whose brother – Beekman Du Barry – was to serve with distinction in the Northern Army, want to fight for the South? One person who knew him was the journalist De Leon, who wrote that Du Barry supported the South '*from conviction.*'[172] Further support for this view comes from one of the letters in his army files, in which he wrote that '*his sympathies were with the South*' and that if the Confederate States faced aggression, then he was prepared '*to fight in their defence.*'[173]

On 25th April 1861, Du Barry was accepted into the Confederate Army and told to report to General Bragg in Pensacola, Florida. He was appointed Second Lieutenant and took up the post of Assistant Chief of Ordinance. It was a role that meant he was responsible for the procurement and issuing of military hardware. Although his Northern background led to some suspicions of him, he quickly acquired a reputation for being a capable officer. In January 1862, Du Barry was promoted to the rank of First Lieutenant and joined Robertson's (later Dent's) Battery of Light Artillery. The unit was sent to Tennessee and became part of the Confederate Army of the Mississippi which fought at Corinth and at the Battle of Shiloh in April 1862.

After Shiloh, Du Barry was promoted to Captain and ordered to report to General Forney in Mobile where he served as Chief of Artillery. Du Barry remained in Mobile until November 1862 when, at his own request, he was ordered to report to General Beauregard in Charleston, South Carolina. The city of Mobile, with its wide bay and important port, was a target for Federal forces for much of the war. The entrance to Mobile Bay was protected by a

---

[169] *Pittsburgh Press*, 11th September 1892.
[170] Letter from *Du Barry*, dated July 10th 1863; and stored in the Confederate Army Records Office in Florida.
[171] Letter from Captain Du Barry, dated 20th March 1861; and stored in the Confederate Army Records Office in Florida.
[172] De Leon T.C., op cit., page 408.
[173] Letter from Daniel Chandler, dated March 18th 1861; and stored in the Confederate Army Records Office in Florida.

series of forts, and it was part of Du Barry's duties to ensure that these forts had sufficient munitions to defeat any assault. In October 1862, the Governor of Alabama wrote a letter to Jefferson Davis, the President of the Confederacy, complaining about the weak state of Mobile's defences. He wrote that General Farney's command was '*widely scattered and with the exception of Colonel Powell, commanding at Fort Morgan, and Captain Du Barry, his Chief of Artillery, he has scarcely another officer upon whom he can rely.*'[174]

After Du Barry's posting to Mobile in April 1862, it would not have been long before he was invited to attend one of the city's social events. Through most of the war, Mobile remained a lively place and '*many dances and parties were given for the soldiers stationed in the city.*'[175] As well as his distinguished family background, Du Barry had an impressive personal presence. The journalist, De Leon, said Du Barry had a '*splendid physique and much personal magnetism,*' and was a '*society favourite.*'[176] According to a report in a Virginian newspaper written in 1889, Du Barry was a '*remarkably handsome man and a dashing officer. He fell in with the Chandlers, and soon there was some talk of his attentions to the lady.*'[177]

The trouble with reports such as this one is that they are written decades later and contain a number of inaccuracies. For example, this particular report gets his name wrong, calling him '*Dubassy*' and describes him as a '*French vicomte,*' which he certainly wasn't. Some important clues that help us gain a true understanding of the relationship between the Chandlers and Du Barry come from two letters sent by William Chandler in early 1862. Both are long and detailed letters written in support of Du Barry being promoted to the rank of captain. Both are written on headed paper belonging to the Office of St John, Powers and Co.; the first is signed by William Chandler, and while the second does not bear his signature it is in identical handwriting to the earlier letter.

The first letter is dated 18th February 1862, and is addressed to Mr E.S. Dargan, a lawyer from Mobile who had been elected as a representative to the Confederate Congress. In the letter, Chandler describes Du Barry as '*my cousin's friend.*' Although this does not necessarily indicate a close friendship, the amount of detail about Du Barry's family and military service, plus the positive manner in which it is written, does suggest a degree of intimacy. The second letter is dated 21st March 1862, and is addressed to George W. Randolph, Secretary of War, Richmond. The content is similar to the first letter, though it is slightly longer and provides even more detail about Du Barry's military service. It states that Du Barry's '*whole heart was with the South,*' and that prior to the war he had been '*passing most of his time in the South.*' In this letter, Chandler wrote that in supporting Du Barry he is pressing the case for a '*friend.*' Crucially, near the end of the letter, Chandler writes that he has '*known Lt. Du Barry so long, I feel so much pride... in his success.*'[178]

From these letters and other verifiable information that is available, it is possible to make some reasonable assumptions about the relationship between Du Barry and the Chandlers. Firstly, if Du Barry had spent '*most of his time in the South*' and William Chandler had known him '*so long,*' it seems safe to assume that William and Carrie knew Du Barry prior to the outbreak of the war. It is possible they met whilst he was serving on the *USS Bibb* in the Gulf region. They may have been introduced by one of William's cousins. When he was based in Pensacola, Du Barry probably visited the Chandlers in Mobile. Du Barry's army records provide details of his travel expense claims, and on at least two occasions while he was in Pensacola he travelled through Mobile on his way to other destinations. He was also entitled to leave during his six-month posting to Pensacola, Florida, and may have taken the opportunity to visit Mobile's busy social scene. After April 1862, when Du Barry had been posted to Mobile, he probably did develop a friendship with the Chandlers and was invited to social events at their house.

Finally, and perhaps most importantly, the notion that Carrie and Du Barry quickly embarked on a sordid affair can be dismissed. Du Barry was a respected army officer who was trying to secure a promotion, and Carrie was the wife of a man who came from one of Mobile's leading families. Carrie and Du Barry probably did strike up a friendship as they were both Northerners who had embraced the cause of the South. On top of that, they were both lively characters known for their conversation. It is likely that if there was any gossip about the two of them at this early stage, it was simply a case of jealousy. It is hard to believe that Carrie, with two young children and nursing a sick husband, would embark on a love affair with a person she barely knew.

Du Barry was also busy helping to organise the defence of Mobile Bay. In July 1862, as William Chandler was being buried, he was at his desk dealing with a report that he was responsible for the loss of a steamer, a charge he firmly denied.[179] It is much more reasonable to assume that the close relationship between Carrie and Du Barry developed after the death of her husband, when Carrie was isolated and needed someone to support and protect her.

---

[174] Referenced in Christie T.L., op cit., page 28.
[175] Delaney C., op cit., page 115.
[176] De Leon T.C., op cit., pages 408 and 409.
[177] *Norfolk Daily Landmark*, (Norfolk, Virginia) 9th August 1889.
[178] Letter from *St. John, Powers and Co.*, dated March 21st 1862; and stored in the Confederate Army Records Office in Florida.
[179] Letter from Captain Du Barry, dated July 5th 1862; and stored in the Confederate Army Records Office in Florida.

In October 1862, three months after her husband's death, Carrie relocated to Macon, Georgia.[180] According to a report in a Macon newspaper, she rented a house in Mulberry Street where she '*lived a life of luxury and ease*.'[181] The same report added that the '*dashing captain [Du Barry] found that his admiration for the lady was greater than ever, and as a natural consequence the Mulberry Street Mansion became his headquarters*.'

It is difficult to believe that Carrie, with her two young children and in the middle of a Civil War, lived a life of luxury. However, she would have had a comfortable existence as she had received a healthy inheritance from her dead husband's estate. When Carrie first moved to Macon, Du Barry was based in Charleston, South Carolina, where he had been posted in November 1862 and was to remain for the next six months. Charleston was about 250 miles from Macon, going by train via the city of Savannah. On 28th November 1862, Du Barry applied for a '*leave of absence for seven days*' in order to visit Macon to carry out some '*private business*.'[182] After his application was approved, Du Barry visited the city and he must have met up with Carrie.

One newspaper report was later to describe Du Barry as a '*brave but weak and erring man*.' He was no longer infatuated with Carrie, but '*conceived himself to be under some obligation to protect her*.'[183] The fact that Du Barry applied for leave and travelled to Macon does suggest that he had genuine feelings towards Carrie. Whether these feelings centred more on concern and protection, rather than love, is open to speculation; nevertheless, one can probably fix the beginning of their romance from this date.

In May 1863, Du Barry was ordered to report to Major Richard Matthaei Cuyler, the Commanding Officer of the Confederate Arsenal at Macon. At the start of the Civil War, Cuyler was given the task of helping to put the Confederate States on an effective war-footing, by building a new armoury at Macon.[184] Du Barry took up his new post at the Macon Arsenal on 29th May 1863, and was to remain there for the next three months. Cuyler intended to put Du Barry '*in charge of the Armoury as soon as he reports for duty*.'[185]

That Cuyler had personally selected Du Barry for such an important role, is a clear sign of the respect that Du Barry's superiors had for his work. We can get an understanding of how highly he was valued by examining some of the tributes paid to him in his army records. In February 1863, the Chief Artillery Officer in Charleston, wrote: '*Du Barry is a tried and thoroughly efficient Artillery and ordnance officer and entirely competent to his charge in either capacity*.' He recommended that he should be '*raised to the rank of Major*.'[186]

On 7th April 1863, a Federal assault on Charleston's harbour defences involving nine ironclads commenced. In the attack Du Barry's role was crucial, as he had to ensure that the harbour's cannons had sufficient ball and powder to be able to fight off the attack. In his dispatches following the conclusion of the assault, Brigadier-General Ripley, Commanding Officer, Charleston, wrote that during the recent military engagement '*Capt. F.B. Du Barry, district ordinance officer, was especially active and energetic in the supply of ammunition and material for the batteries*.'[187] On 4th August 1863, Brigadier-General Ripley sent a letter in which he wrote that '*in consideration of the meritorious services*' of Du Barry, he recommended that he be '*advanced to the rank of Major*.'[188]

On 14th July 1863, six weeks after arriving in Macon, Du Barry married Carrie Chandler. The service took place at Macon's Christ Episcopal Church, and was celebrated by the Church's Rector, the Rev. Henry Kolloch Rees (1822-1893). According to the register, one of the official witnesses was Lewis Whittle, the senior warden at the church. Although a newspaper report written later was to claim that the wedding took place in front of hundreds of guests, it is a view that can be dismissed. Neither Carrie nor her new husband would have known many people in Macon and, due to the problems of war, it is doubtful that any friends would have travelled to the event. It would have been a quiet affair. Also, as Du Barry had only just been appointed to his new role, it is unlikely that he would have had more than a day or two off to celebrate his wedding. News of the marriage would have reached Mobile, and it is likely that some eyebrows were raised when people heard that Carrie had remarried barely a year after the death of her first husband. They may have also been shocked when they heard who her new husband was, and perhaps this was the time when the rumours about her behaviour in Mobile started to circulate.

Du Barry's stay at the Macon Arsenal was to only last three months. On 27th August 1863, Colonel Gorgas (1818-1883), who was Chief of Ordnances for the Confederacy, sent a note to Major Cuyler wanting to know if Du Barry's '*services are particularly required at Macon*' or whether he could be spared. Cuyler must have allowed Du Barry to leave, because at the beginning of September Du Barry was ordered to return to Charleston and '*report to General Beauregard for ordnance duties*.'[189] The special order that instructed Du Barry to '*proceed without delay to*

---

[180] Date fixed by Carrie in an interview after Florence's trial, *Liverpool Echo*, 14th August 1889.
[181] *Macon Telegraph*, 25th May 1889.
[182] Letter from Captain Du Barry to his Commanding Officer in Charleston, dated November 28th 1862; and stored in the Confederate Army Records Office in Florida.
[183] *Pittsburgh Press*, 11th September 1892.
[184] Davis R.S., '*A Cotton Kingdom Retooled for War*' in *The Georgia Historical Quarterly*, Vol. 91, No. 3, (Fall, 2007) page 276.
[185] Quote referenced in Hutto R.J., op cit., page 25.
[186] Letter and note, dated 10th February and 14th March 1863; and stored in the Confederate Army Records Office in Florida.
[187] Official Records of the Union and Confederate Navies in the War of Rebellion; Series 1, Vol.14, page 260.
[188] Letter from Brigadier-General R. S. Ripley, dated August 4th 1863; and stored in the Confederate Army Records Office in Florida.
[189] Letters dated August 27th 1863 and 5th September 1863; and stored in the Confederate Army Records Office in Florida.

Charleston' was signed by no less figure than John Withers, the Assistant Adjutant-General in Richmond. Although the order does not explain the reason for the new posting, it is likely that it was in response to the renewed assault on Charleston that had begun on 10th July 1863. What made this attack more serious than the one three months earlier was that it was a combined naval and land attack rather than just one by the ironclads. Although Charleston was able to repulse the attack, it was to remain under intermittent bombardment from August 1863 until it was evacuated in February 1865.

The needs of war and the growing reputation of Du Barry led to an order on 24th October 1863, directly from General Beauregard himself, that '*specially charged*' Du Barry 'with the duties of Chief of Ordnance' for the 1st, 5th, 6th and 7th Military Districts of South Carolina. The order further stated that '*all requisitions from these Districts will be forwarded through him.*'[190]

Just two weeks later, on 7th November, that order was '*revoked*' by Brigadier-General Thomas Jordan (1819-1895). At first glance this looks like a reduction in Du Barry's responsibilities. Although this view is plausible, it might not be accurate. Under the new order, Du Barry was '*charged with the execution of all orders as to placing in position, ordnance and ordnance stores*' subject to the direction of General Jordan. In other words, rather than being demoted, it appears that Du Barry was being placed in charge of all the ordnance deployment in South Carolina, Florida and Georgia, subject only to the authority of the general in charge.

On 6th December 1863, Du Barry wrote to his superior officer, Brigadier-General Thomas Jordan (1819-1895), Chief of Staff under General Beauregard, and asked him for '*thirty days leave of absence for the purpose of going to Grenada, Miss., and bringing my wife to Georgia.*' The obvious question raised by this letter is, what was Carrie doing in Grenada? The probable answer is that instead of following her husband to Charleston, which was under bombardment, she decided to travel with her two children to Grenada, where she must have had friends. Her uncle, Rev Joseph Ingraham, had moved from Mobile to his new parish in Holly Springs in Mississippi, which was only 80 miles from Grenada. By December 1863, the clouds of defeat were starting to encircle the Confederacy, and Carrie must have sent a telegram to her husband asking him to take her back to Macon. On 5th January 1864, Du Barry sent another letter to General Jordan asking for his leave to be extended by ten days. He wrote that he needed to '*nurse my wife, who is very ill. Her family are in the enemies[sic] lines and I have no one to take care of her.*' The letter demonstrates how isolated Carrie was, and why Du Barry was so keen to go to Grenada to bring her back to Macon.

By Spring 1864, Du Barry was an experienced officer who had the full trust of his superiors. His next promotion, to the rank of Major, was surely only a matter of time; but it was never to happen, as he became seriously ill. The journalist, De Leon, wrote he had received some '*urgent letters*' to try and get Du Barry sent abroad, as the '*doctors said a sea voyage was the sole hope for some mysterious malady that was rapidly ending him.*' With the help of some influential friends, Du Barry managed to obtain '*orders to purchase ammunition abroad.*'

By chance, De Leon met Du Barry as he and his family travelled from Richmond to Wilmington. When he saw him, he was '*shocked to see but a wreck of a brilliant fellow.*' De Leon spent the '*tedious and trying*' journey with young Florence sitting on his lap.[191] Some authors have suggested that the exact nature of Du Barry's illness is unclear. For example, Trevor Christie wrote he '*was either wounded or contracted consumption.*'[192] In fact, his army records provide a clear answer as to the nature of his illness. On 26th April 1864, Du Barry formally applied '*for six months leave of absence for the purpose of visiting Europe for the benefit of my health.*' He included with his letter a recommendation from the Medical Director of the Department of South Carolina and Florida, who stated he had '*fully examined this officer and find him suffering from phthisis pulmonalis [tuberculosis].*'

The Medical Director supported Du Barry's application for leave, stating that in his opinion he would not be able to resume his duties in a '*less period than six months.*' He added that Du Barry needed a '*change of climate*' to help his condition improve.[193] It is evident from De Leon's account, and from the examination of his doctor, that Du Barry was extremely ill in the Spring of 1864, with tuberculosis or – as it was called then – consumption. It is likely he had contracted the disease a few years earlier, and it had slowly but progressively affected his health. His army records show he had periodic bouts of illness. While these records do not signify the exact nature of the complaints, they were probably early warning signs of the inevitable decline in his health that were the direct result of this devasting illness.

Due to the severity of his illness, on 30th May the Adjutant and Inspector General's Office of the Confederate States, in Special Order Number 125/22, granted Du Barry leave to travel overseas. The only safe way to leave the South was on the fast-sailing ships known as blockade runners. These ships were the lifeblood of the Confederacy as they enabled the import and export of goods to continue despite the war; though much of the imported goods were luxury items that made large profits for the ship-owners. The ship that Du Barry was to sail on, the *Fannie*, had

---

[190] Special Order no. 222, by command of General Beauregard, dated 24th October, 1863, and stored in the Confederate Army Records Office in Florida.
[191] De Leon T.C., op cit., page 409.
[192] Christie T.L., op cit., page 29.
[193] Letters from Captain Du Barry and the Medical Director of South Carolina and Florida, 26th April 1864; stored in the Confederate Army Records Office in Florida.

arrived in the South full of such goods, including fancy clothing and shoes, which were auctioned off in Charleston's salerooms.[194] On 26th May 1864, Captain Du Barry and his family boarded the *Fannie* bound for Scotland. It is possible that Du Barry's brother, William, was in the port to see them off.

The *Fannie* was one of the most successful of all the blockade runners. She had been built in Scotland in 1859 by Messrs. Caird and Co. for the coastal trade, and in the previous thirteen months had successfully '*run the blockade no less than twenty-two times.*'[195] The *Fannie*'s captain, Dunning, had made eight successful blockade runs. At 5:15am on the second day of the voyage Du Barry died. He was buried at sea around 12 noon on the same day, about 150 miles from Wilmington. One of the passengers gave an account of the burial which was printed in newspapers in Georgia and South Carolina. In it he wrote: '*In that frail little steamer, quivering with her efforts to escape the relentless fate bearing down on her with frowning guns and the ferocity of a tiger, while every living heart on board was throbbing with anxiety for safety, they were suddenly called upon to render the last and most solemn rites known to our existence. No time to stop in mid-ocean; while words that consigned "dust to dust," "ashes to ashes" went up in presence of the grim destroyer, but still dashing onwards through the waves a short and hurried service.*'[196]

The Southern newspapers that carried the reports of Du Barry's death spoke of him fondly. One described him as '*an efficient and accomplished ordnance officer,*' and that he had served the Confederate Army with '*distinguished zeal and ability in the Virginia and Kentucky campaigns. In his death the service has lost a brave, amiable and conscientious officer.*'[197]

Around the time of Florence Maybrick's trial, the newspapers that suggested Carrie might have had something to do with the death of her first husband hinted she could have also been responsible for the death of her second husband. They said Carrie had insisted on him being buried at sea and refused the captain's suggestion to return the ship to port.[198] Of all the allegations aimed at Carrie, this is the most absurd. There is no evidence to suggest that Du Barry's death was caused by anything other than tuberculosis. It is unlikely the ship's captain would have made the offer to return to port as he was in a desperate race to escape the Union ships that were trying to capture his vessel. Even if he had made the offer, what would have been achieved by returning to port? Charleston was under siege, and Carrie had no family or friends in the city. The burial of Du Barry at sea was the only sensible option.

On 28th June 1864, the *Fannie* sailed into the Clyde flying the Confederate flag. As she berthed at Greenock, Scotland, she was decked out in bunting and '*the officers and crew were given an extra glass of grog to drink the health of Gen. Lee.*'[199] Carrie must have disembarked with a degree of trepidation; she had lost two husbands in under two years, had two young children in tow and much of her money, being Confederate dollars, would have been worthless in Britain. She must have realised that her current predicament was unsustainable, and she needed to return to New York. It is not recorded exactly how long she remained in Britain; but it is known that, by the Summer of 1865, Carrie and her children were back living at the home of her mother.

In 1865, after the many ups and downs in her life, one might have expected that Carrie would have wanted a period of calm; however, that did not happen. She was soon prominent on the New York social scene, often seen in tandem with one of her cousins from Mobile, Miss Frank Crawford, who in 1869 married Commodore Cornelius Vanderbilt, one of America's richest men. Once again Carrie started to attract male admirers, one of whom was Charles Rebello, who claimed to be an Italian count. According to one report, '*during the fall of '65 and the winter and spring of '66 [Rebello] used to call*' at Carrie's house '*frequently, and was entertained in the parlour as any gentleman would be.*'[200]

Carrie's dalliance and marriage to Rebello is one of the oddest episodes in her tumultuous life, not least because it is not clear exactly who he was; although one thing is certain – he was not an Italian count. In her divorce court case of 1868, Carrie claimed Rebello was a British subject. Research has identified a Charles Rebello, who had been British Vice Consul in Cuba in the early 1860s and who later moved to live in the United States; however, he died in New York in 1888 and the Rebello who married Carrie was still alive in 1893.[201] There are some other possible candidates for Carrie's mysterious fiancé, including a man of Cuban descent who was called up to serve in the US Army in May/June 1863, however the exact identity of the Rebello remains a mystery. While it is not certain who Charles Rebello was, there is evidence to support the view that a person of that name married Carrie in a ceremony in Newark, New Jersey in October 1865.[202]

---

[194] *Charleston Daily Courier*, 18th June 1864 and the *Charleston Mercury*, 12th July 1864 for details of auctions and items that were up for sale.
[195] *Greenock Telegraph and Clyde Shipping Gazette*, 28th June 1864.
[196] *Daily Constitutionalist*, (Augusta, Georgia) 13th August 1864.
[197] *Charleston Mercury*, 10th June 1864.
[198] *Pittsburgh Press*, 11th September 1892.
[199] *Greenock Telegraph and Clyde Shipping Gazette*, 2nd July 1864.
[200] *Columbus Daily Times*, (Columbus, Indiana) 18th December 1893.
[201] *Davenport Democrat*, (Davenport, Iowa) 20th December 1893.
[202] *New York Herald*, 7th May 1866.

In December 1893, when Carrie's daughter Florence was attracting headline news, an attorney contacted the County Court in Columbus, Indiana asking about details for any divorce proceedings involving the Baroness (Carrie's then status) and someone with an Italian sounding name. This enquiry alerted the newspapers and soon reporters were delving into this aspect of Carrie's life. One of the most detailed accounts appeared in the *Columbus Daily Times* of December 1893. The paper reported that, on 4th January 1868, '*two strange well-dressed ladies' arrived in the city of Columbus, Indiana. One was small and slender with 'a very beautiful childlike face and fragile form*,' whom they identified as Caroline Rebello. The other was '*an elderly lady, dark complexion*,' who was identified as Elizabeth Holbrook, mother of Caroline Rebello. The women were accompanied by two attorneys. Other newspaper accounts stated they were accompanied by two children, including a young Florence who was '*lionised*' by the local people.[203]

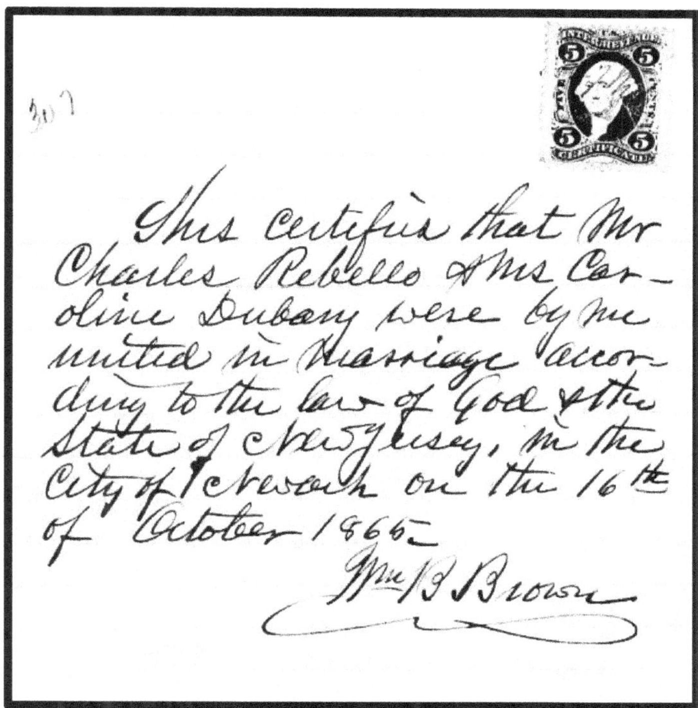
This certifies that Mr Charles Rebello & Mrs Caroline Dubarry were by me united in Marriage according to the law of God & the State of New Jersey, in the City of Newark on the 16th of October 1865.

Wm B Brown

Marriage certificate of Caroline Du Barry and Charles Rebello (Chris Jones collection)

Carrie had chosen to come to Columbus because, under Indiana law, a person only had to be resident in the state for one month before applying for a divorce. Carrie found accommodation at the rather superior boarding house belonging to a Mrs Maynard, where she and her mother and the two children were to stay for the next 30 days. Mrs Maynard was interviewed by a newspaper reporter in 1903 and said she still had a '*strong regard*' for Carrie, and that she also had a trunk of clothes belonging to her which she had left behind in her boarding house.

In petitioning for divorce, Carrie's attorney in Columbus, John A. Keith, provided a detailed statement of her account of the marriage proceedings. In it, he claimed that the '*marriage ceremony was solemnised in the state of New Jersey by a person unknown to [her], and no witnesses were present; that no licence was granted and no record of same was ever filed in the proper office to [her] knowledge.' He went on to add, the 'said marriage was procured through the fraud, false representation and duress of this plaintiff [Carrie] by the said defendant [Charles Rebello].*'

While these details were rather alarming, even more bizarre details were to follow. It was claimed that Rebello disappeared '*immediately after the marriage ceremony*,' and later '*left the United States*.' It was said that the couple had not spent even one day living together as man and wife, and Carrie never took Rebello's name. Various witnesses were called to support the statement, including Florence's mother. She said: '*In March '66 [Carrie] told her... she had been married to Charles Rebello, and that the marriage was a forced one and was by duress and fraud and not properly certified... that she had not seen Rebello since '66, that Rebello never contributed to her [Carrie's] support, and that she existed solely from her father's estate... Rebello was an Englishman, and sailed from New York, about the first of September 1866, on a steamer for Venezuela, South America*.' After listening to all the evidence and to the witness statements, the divorce was granted by the court on 25th March 1868.

Newspaper reports of the divorce proceedings provide more questions than answers. We do not know who Rebello was, or what his motives were in marrying Carrie. We are not sure why Carrie married him. If it was as simple as being forced to marry under duress, why did she not go immediately to the police? What did Rebello do between the date of the wedding in October 1865 and leaving America in September 1866? Did he still visit Carrie's house in Spring 1866? Why did Carrie not tell her mother about the wedding until March 1866? Did Rebello really go to Venezuela?

Despite these unanswered questions, there are some points of interest in the whole affair. Firstly, the fact that Carrie got married in October 1865 suggests that she had arrived back in the United States earlier that year than is usually assumed. Secondly, if it was that case that Carrie lived solely off money from her father's estate, then by inference all the money she had inherited from her husband had gone. Thirdly, as Carrie was a woman of strong character who had survived the death of two husbands and a civil war, she was unlikely to have been easily intimidated into marriage. She must have viewed Rebello, with his supposed title and riches, as potential marriage material, but later came to suspect that he was just an imposter who was after her money.

---

203 *Indianapolis Star*, (Indianapolis, Indiana) 13th July 1903.

As for Rebello, he did not appear at the divorce proceedings in 1868 but did resurface briefly in 1893 when he made an unsuccessful legal claim to try and obtain a share of Carrie's inheritance. His behaviour in 1893 seems to confirm Carrie's opinion that he was '*merely the adventurer she suspected him of being.*'[204]

The mysterious saga with Charles Rebello does not appear to have been the only scandal that engulfed Carrie after her return to America. There were also reports she '*was mixed up in a scandal with an actor.*'[205] Like many reports concerning Carrie, it is difficult to ascertain how much is truth and how much is just gossip. Even if many of the stories written about Carrie have been exaggerated, or based upon unsubstantiated rumours, it does appear she lived a rather care-free existence and the stories, whether true or false, were simply a by-product of this lifestyle.

It is not easy to track down with any certainty all of Carrie's movements from the late 1860s onwards. She appears to have criss-crossed the Atlantic on a number of occasions, spending time in New York, England, France and Germany. One place she lived for a while was at a house called *The Vineyard* in the village of Kempsey, three miles south of Worcester in England. The Vineyard was described as a '*good country residence*' that had an entrance hall, drawing and dining rooms, five bedrooms and dressing rooms and a two-stalled stable.[206]

Evidence for Carrie's stay in the Vineyard comes from a letter written by General Charles Carroll Tevis (1829-1900), an American adventurer and soldier who served in a variety of armies, including the Unites States Army, the Ottoman Army and the French Army. He fought in several wars in the nineteenth century, including the American Civil War and the Franco-Prussian War of 1870-1871. In May 1869, in a letter to a friend in America, he wrote: '*My address after 1st June [1869] will be the Vineyard, Kempsey, Worcester, Worcestershire, England, care of Mrs F. C. Du Barry.*'[207]

Why was Carrie living in Kempsey, and how long did she live there for? The answer to the first question appears to be that the Vineyard had a link to her father's side of the family. In the 1861 Census, the owner of the house was William Wallace Gabriel, aged 42, who was a solicitor. William Gabriel's mother's maiden name was Anna Marie Holbrook. Carrie's family on her father's side – the Holbrooks – had originally come to America from Shropshire, which is one of the counties that has a border with Worcestershire. The answer to the second question is not certain, though a report in a Liverpool newspaper in 1889 stated that Carrie lived there for two years, with a German governess was tutoring her children. The report added that locals remembered Carrie as a '*fine, handsome woman and good company. The house was full of visitors.*'[208] One of those visitors was General Tevis. Like Carrie, he was a Francophile and had volunteered to join the French Army in the Franco-Prussian War. He was also an old friend of Beekman Du Barry, the older brother of her dead second husband.

It is unlikely that Carrie's stay in Kempsey lasted two years. She had been in America in early 1868 to arrange her divorce from Rebello and, we know from the British Census of 1871 that she was no longer at The Vineyard in Kempsey as another family are listed as living in the house. We also have evidence from a picture of Florence printed in the New York newspaper the *World* which was said to be based on a photograph taken in Paris. In the picture, Florence is said to be aged seven. That would mean that at some point in late 1869 Carrie and her two children were living in the French capital. We do know that they were to spend a great deal of time living in France, and that all three of them were fluent French speakers. Holbrook was to study medicine in a Parisian university.

The only odd thing about the move was its timing. In July 1870, the French Government declared war on Prussia, and in early August French forces moved into German territory. The early confidence of the French quickly disappeared as a superior Prussian Army, better trained, equipped and led, invaded north-eastern France and within six months had captured Emperor Napoleon III and totally defeated his French Army. The defeat of Napoleon III did not end the fighting, as a new French Republican Government was set up in Paris and continued the war for another five months. On 19th September, the Prussian Army surrounded Paris and besieged the city until its surrender on 28th January 1871.

According to one report, Carrie had been staying with friends in Paris when the siege started and found herself trapped in the city. The American historian Philip Katz estimated that in 1870, on the eve of war, at least 5,000 Americans called Paris their home.[209] The rapid Prussian advance would have driven nearly all these Americans from the city; however, some did remain and it has been suggested that at the height of the siege around 150 Americans were still in Paris.[210] A detailed list of these was published in the *Anglo-American Times* in January 1871, and neither Carrie or her children are on it.[211] This suggests that if Carrie was in Paris at the onset, then at some point she moved out of the city. At the end of the siege the Prussians entered the city and many of their officers were billeted in

[204] Hutto R.J., op cit., page 37.
[205] *Morning News*, (Savannah, Georgia), 25th May 1889.
[206] *Worcester Journal*, 18th July 1874.
[207] Hutto R.J., op cit., page 47.
[208] *Liverpool Echo, 9th August 1889.*
[209] Katz P.M., *From Appomattox to Montmartre: Americans and the Paris Commune*, (Harvard UP, 1998) page 26.
[210] Dougherty M. P., *American Diplomats and the Franco-Prussian War: Perceptions from Paris and Berlin*, (University of California, 1980) accessed at core.ac.uk/download/pdf/215552817.pdf
[211] *Anglo-American Times*, 14th January 1871.

accommodation that was used by American citizens. Wickman Hoffman, an American diplomat in the city, recorded: '*This [March 1] was a busy day for me. Mr Washburne [US consul-general] was overrun with concierges and servants complaining that the Prussians were occupying American apartments.*'[212]

This suggests that, if Carrie was back in Paris in March 1871, it is likely she would have come into direct contact with Prussian officers staying in her home or in the home of one of her friends. That in turn would explain how, in the turmoil of Paris in the aftermath of a war, Carrie had come to meet a young Prussian cavalry officer named Baron von Roques.

Florence Chandler aged 7, based on an actual photograph taken in Paris, France.
(*New York Herald*, 3rd December 1893)

On 4th April 1872, a new chapter in Carrie's life began with her third marriage (or fourth, if you include the mysterious wedding to Charles Rebello). Her new husband was Baron Heinrich Louis Adolph von Roques, born on 22nd December 1845. He was a Prussian Cavalry Officer in 8th Cuirassier Regiment. They were married in the Evangelical Church, Military Community, Wiesbaden.

Although Carrie was a Francophile, her politics were more about personal survival than international intrigue. She was attracted by the man and his title. As to the Baron, how did he view Carrie? She was older than him; he was 26, she would have been 33 when they married. She had already been married twice, and had two children. She had a love of France, and he was a German soldier who was part of a Prussian Army that had just inflicted a humiliating defeat on France. It is likely that for the Baron, as for Carrie, the marriage was based partly upon a physical attraction and partly on the hope of personal advancement. Marriage offered Carrie the chance of both stability and excitement, and she would have been delighted to have acquired the title of Baroness. She continued to use the title long after her marriage collapsed. There was also a pragmatic strand to the Baron's thinking. Carrie was from a distinguished American family and, on paper at least, was a wealthy heiress. The von Roques family had the title, but not the wealth to go along with it. Marriage to a rich woman would allow him to live the lifestyle he craved.

One newspaper later wrote that the newlyweds were to live in the '*baronial castle*,' however, that was not the case.[213] Carrie's rather nomadic existence continued, though in somewhat grander settings, as her husband's military career led to a series of posting around Europe. They lived in Cologne, then Wiesbaden and finally in St Petersburg, where the Baron was appointed military attaché to the German Embassy.

In 1874, during their time in Wiesbaden, Carrie – now Baroness von Roques – was presented to one of the daughters of Queen Victoria. She was to write about the occasion in 1890, when she sent a letter to the Queen asking for clemency for her daughter.[214] Florence and her brother usually accompanied their mother and their latest stepfather on the Baron's various European postings. In her autobiography, Florence barely mentions these years, and when she does her memories are surprisingly positive. She wrote: '*My life was much the same as that of any other girl who enjoyed the pleasures of youth with a happy heart. I was very fond of tracing intricate designs and copying the old-time churches and cathedrals. My special pastime, however, was riding, and this I could indulge in to my heart's content when residing with my step-father, Baron Adolf von Roques.*'[215]

The marriage between Carrie and the Baron was not a success. The Baron was '*unfaithful and cruel*' to Carrie.[216] As well as being violent, the Baron's expensive tastes, drinking and gambling all placed a strain on the family's finances, much of it sourced from Carrie's income from her father's estate. On 11th March 1875, the Baron and Carrie took out a two-year loan of $6,675, with interest at 6% payable half-yearly, from Richard Cowan of Cairo, Illinois. As security for the loan they granted him a mortgage over seventy-two blocks of land in the city of Cairo.

---

[212] Hoffman W., *A Narrative of Personal Adventure and Observation During Two Wars, 1861-65, 1870-71*, (Sampson Low, London, 1877) accessed at www.gutenberg.org/files/51195/51195-0.txt
[213] *Macon Telegraph*, 25th May 1889.
[214] HO 144/1639/A50678D/667.
[215] Maybrick F., op. cit., page 20.
[216] *Pittsburgh Press*, 11th September 1892.

At some point the Baron and Carrie defaulted on the payments. Although Cowen died in June 1878, George Fisher, who was granted legal title to his estate, sold the plots of land by public auction.[217] In March 1879, a German banker sued the Baroness in the New York courts, claiming that she and the Baron owed him over 13,000 thalers on bills of exchange drawn up by the Baron and endorsed by her.[218] Around the same time, a London wine merchant named John Prosser wrote to Carrie's American lawyer about the money she and her husband owed him. In the letter he said his involvement with the Baroness had caused him to have '*a very heavy loss, a lawsuit, work and anxiety.*'[219]

In 1878, the marriage collapsed and the couple parted, though they were never to divorce. One person who knew Carrie well described Baron von Roques as '*a roué*' [a debauched man]. She said Carrie '*finally gave him an allowance and left him.*'[220] At the time of Florence's trial in 1889, it was necessary to get the Baron's signature on some legal documents to raise income from a land sale. Carrie's attorney, William Potter, located the Baron living in '*a side-street in Vienna.*' He agreed to sign the documents if given 1,500 marks and an assurance that he would never be liable for any of his estranged wife's legal or business dealings.[221]

In the late 1870s, after her marriage had collapsed, it was suggested that Carrie had an affair with the British diplomat, William H. D. Haggard, and that she accompanied him to Tehran, Persia after he obtained a post in the legation in that city.[222] This story about Carrie's alleged affair with Haggard is a good example of how stories about her were exaggerated or simply untrue.

William Henry Doveton Haggard (1846-1926) was a British diplomat and the brother of Sir H. Rider Haggard, author of *King Solomon's Mines*. In December 1875, he married Caroline '*Carrie*' Anna Carroll in Washington DC. She was an American, the daughter of William T. Carroll, the clerk of the Supreme Court. The couple moved to England, but the marriage was not a happy one and they soon split up. In his divorce case against his wife, in 1882, Haggard said the marriage had been brought to breaking point by his wife's constant use of '*violent language against him.*' In 1877, he had the opportunity to become attached to the British Legation in Teheran, and decided to accept the post without informing his wife. He did leave her a letter in which he '*told her he had come to the conclusion that separation between them was inevitable,*' and left her £100 to pay for her passage back to the United States. In 1880, he learned of his wife's application for a divorce in the United States on the grounds of desertion, and as a result returned to London to consult a solicitor. In his divorce proceedings of 1882, Haggard's parents testified about the violent temper of his wife, and that he had gone to Teheran '*for the purpose of separating from his wife.*'[223] Two weeks later the Judge granted the divorce.[224]

The details of the case show that Haggard had not travelled to Persia to be with Carrie, but instead had accepted a post to escape from an unhappy marriage. On top of that, Haggard was in Teheran from 1877 to 1880, and we know that Carrie travelled back to America in August 1878 and was to remain in the country for much, if not all of 1879, contesting a court case. Therefore, we can say with some certainty that there is no basis to the accounts of Carrie and Haggard eloping together to Teheran. The story probably had its roots in journalists searching desperately for sensational stories about Carrie's past. In so doing, she may have become confused with Haggard's first wife, who was an American and also known as Carrie. The whole Haggard saga is a cautionary tale; while Carrie was a woman with a past, it was not as bad a past as was often portrayed in the newspapers.

During the 1870s, Carrie continued to travel back and forth across the Atlantic Ocean. On 6th October 1873, she is listed as arriving at Boston, Massachusetts on the *SS Siberia* which had sailed from Liverpool.[225] The record shows she travelled alone. This would have been the first time she would have seen her mother, Elizabeth Holbrook, since her wedding to the Baron. On 24th November 1873, after a six week stay, she set off on the return journey to Germany and caught the steamer *Parthia*, bound for Liverpool. She was listed on the passenger list as '*Baroness von Roques from Germany.*'[226] Again, she appeared to be travelling alone.

On 24th November 1875, the Baroness and Mrs Von Roques are listed as arriving in Liverpool after travelling across the Atlantic on the *SS Baltic*.[227] It is possible that the reference to '*Mrs*' is a mistake, and it should have read '*Miss*' Von Roques, and that her daughter, Florence, was travelling with her.

In 1876, Carrie's mother, Elizabeth Holbrook, travelled to Germany to see her daughter and grandchildren. Sadly, she never returned to America as she died on 9th May 1876 and was buried in Cologne. Little is known about Elizabeth Holbrook, but she must have been a rock upon whom Carrie depended as she chartered some of the rougher moments of her hectic life. She must have also been important to both Florence and to her brother, Holbrook St John Chandler.

---

217 *Cairo Daily Bulletin*, 14th August 1881.
218 *New York Times*, 12th March 1879.
219 Christie T.L., op cit., page 32.
220 Letter from Veronica Jegethoff to Trevor Christie in the Trevor Christie Collection.
221 Christie T.L., op cit., page 241.
222 *Daily Inter Ocean*, (Chicago, Illinois), 24th May 1889.
223 *Norfolk Chronicle*, (Norfolk, England), 25th March 1882.
224 *Norfolk Chronicle*, (Norfolk, England), 11th April 1882.
225 *Boston Daily Globe*, 7th October 1873.
226 *Boston Daily Globe*, 24th November 1873.
227 *Liverpool Daily Post*, 24th November 1875.

While Carrie was on her travels, the children spent periods of their life under the care of Florence's grandmother. Christie has asserted that Carrie placed her children in '*institutions for long periods.*'[228] There is no evidence to support this view; Carrie may not have been the perfect mother, but she did look after her children, and when they were not with her they were with her own mother in New York. In her autobiography, Florence wrote: '*I was educated partly in Europe and partly in America, under the instruction of masters and governesses. I was too delicate for college life. I lived partly with my maternal grandmother, Elizabeth Holbrook, of New York, and partly with my mother, the Baroness von Roques, whose home was abroad. When not with them, I was visiting or travelling with friends.*'[229]

In 1878, Carrie and her children were living in France. In an affidavit of 1894, the Baroness gave her address at that time as being 58 Avenue Malakoff, Paris. On 17th July 1878, she picked up an arsenical-based face wash from the Parisian chemists of Monsieur L. Brouant. The face wash was required to treat an '*eruption*' on Florence's face caused by '*delicate digestion.*'[230] A month earlier, Holbrook had applied for an American passport as he intended to travel to Italy. He provided a French address on his application, but it was a different one to his mother's Parisian address. He listed his date of birth as 1856 rather than 1859, presumably to appear to be aged over 21.

The Baroness' time in France was to be abruptly interrupted by a court case that caused her to return to America. In 1875, before travelling to Germany, Elizabeth Holbrook delivered a deed to her friend, Annie E. Bennett, in which she left her property on East Fourteenth Street, New York in trust not to Carrie, but to her grandchildren. After she died in Germany in 1876, Elizabeth Holbrook's will was found, in which she left all her property to Carrie.

In March 1879, Isaac Rosenthal, a banker from Weisbaden, Prussia sued the Baron and Baroness von Roques in the Court of Common Pleas in New York to '*recover $13,015, the value of certain bills of exchange alleged to have been executed by the Baron and endorsed by the Baroness.*'[231] In order words, he wanted to recover the money he had lent the Baron and hoped to achieve that in New York where the Baroness now owned her parents' former home. It was this court case that caused the Baroness and Florence to sail back to New York on the steamship *Celtic* in August 1878.[232] As no records exist of the Baroness and Florence sailing back to Europe in 1879, it is probable that they spent the entire year in America contesting the case that lasted from March 1879 to February 1880. There is a reference from John Baillie Knight, a family friend to both the Baroness and Florence, who said he saw them in his aunts' house in England '*in or about the year 1879*;' however, it is likely that he saw them in 1878 rather than 1879.[233]

In the court case of 1879, Rosenthal won an attachment against the rents on the property, which amounted to $5,000 a year. Before the trial started the trust deed that Elizabeth Holbrook had made prior to going to Germany was found among her partly-burned papers. Mrs Bennett tried to establish the legal validity of the trust deed, and so release the property from the attachment. In October 1879, the case was tried before a judge and jury and the latter decided that the trust deed had indeed been executed by Mrs Holbrook, and therefore the grandchildren were entitled to the property. Reports of the trial state that the Baroness and Isaac Rosenthal were '*examined at great length*' during the proceedings.[234] Not surprisingly, Rosenthal appealed the decision and in February 1880 the case was heard by a higher court. The judge, Chief Justice Daly, decided that '*the grandchildren are entitled to the property, and that the creditors of the Baroness von Roques have no claim on the premises, and the attachment is set aside.*'[235] The decision was a significant victory for the Baroness and her children. It meant she did not have to repay the money lent to her husband by Rosenthal from the rents realised on the property in East Fourteenth Street. The case was also significant in that it brought the Baroness and her children back to New York to fight the case. Now that it was won, they could return to France. In March 1880, they booked a passage on the *SS Baltic* sailing from New York to Liverpool.

Trevor Christie wrote that during her youth, Florence had been a tender hostage to '*her mother's emotional instability, financial insecurity, and lack of sound values.*' He said that Carrie handed a '*soiled legacy' down to her.*[236] These are damning words, but are they are accurate? The problem one has in making an objective analysis of Carrie's life is that so much written about is simply inaccurate. Carrie was a flawed character, but many of the flaws attributed to her have been greatly exaggerated. There had been at least three men in Carrie's life, but it is unfair to blame Carrie for Florence's lack of a father-figure. Florence's father had died soon after she was born, and Franklin Du Barry died before she was two years old. Carrie cannot be blamed for leaving Baron von Roques if he was violent towards her.

Did Carrie suffer from emotional instability? No, she was a woman of character; strong, determined and passionate. Did she suffer from financial insecurity? Possibly, but only in so far as anyone else might have done if faced with the same issues that she had to overcome. Did she lack sound values? Here she is open to some of the criticisms

---

228 Christie T.L., op cit., page 32.
229 Maybrick F., op. cit., page 20.
230 Levy J.H., op cit., pages 474-477.
231 *New York World*, 12th March 1879.
232 *New York Weekly World*, 10th August 1878.
233 HO 144/1638/A50678D/24.
234 *New York Herald*, 1st November 1879.
235 *Evening Post*, (New York), 5th February 1880.
236 Christie T.L., op cit., page 33.

levelled against her. She was a young woman when she married, and her vivacious manner and New York lifestyle may have shocked some in the antebellum South, especially those who were jealous of her easy charm. Did she drive her first husband to his death? Absolutely not, he was killed by the stress of the Civil War. Did she kill her second husband? Certainly not, he died from tuberculosis. In the late 1860s, she may have played a little close to the wind with some of her relationships, but that did not make her either a bad person or a bad mother. In 1872, when she married for a third time, she hoped to find love and stability, but sadly was to gain neither. All the evidence suggests that she had a strong loving relationship towards her two children, and that she was fiercely protective of them. When Florence faced the greatest challenge of her life after her conviction for murder, it was her mother who was her strongest and most vehement defender. Carrie was to sacrifice everything in the pursuit of justice for her daughter. That is not a soiled legacy.

LINKS TO THE RIPPER DIARY: THE MYSTERIOUS CASE OF FLORENCE'S INITIALS

In March 1946, the *Mobile Press Register* ran a story which claimed they had found the initials '*FM*' neatly '*cut with a diamond into the pane of a window in McGill Institute.*' The newspaper said it was a '*silent reminder that beautiful Florence Maybrick (née Florence Chandler) once lived in the spacious building on Government St.*'[237]

The article included a picture that did appear to show some initials scratched into the window pane. At the time the article was written, the McGill Institute was a Catholic boys' school, though it had originally been the Greek-style mansion with Doric columns that had been the home to Daniel Chandler and his family. In the late 1800s, the building had become converted into a school before being demolished in 1953.

Trevor Christie picked up on the article in his book, writing that Florence, '*while staying with relatives as a young girl, one day in a dreamy moment, she wistfully etched her name "Florence Chandler" on a windowpane of the old Chandler mansion.*'[238] There is an obvious problem with Christie's account as, according to the newspaper report, only the initials '*FM*' were scratched into the window, and not the name '*Florence Chandler.*' There are also problems with the newspaper story from 1946, not least the fact that Florence never lived in the Chandler mansion and had left Mobile when just a few months old. If she had returned to Mobile as a young girl and scratched her initials then she would have written '*FC*' and not '*FM.*' If the newspaper was accurate in its reporting and the initials scratched in the window were '*FM,*' then that would mean that they had to be made after Florence's wedding, and not when she was a young girl visiting relatives. Would a woman in her twenties commit such an act of vandalism on a window of a building in which she had never even lived? Extremely unlikely. As far as we are aware, the first time Florence visited Mobile after her wedding was in December 1908, when she gave a lecture at the Battle Hotel on prison reform. The mansion then was no longer a home but a school. Would Florence, who would have then been aged 46, scratch her name in the window of a school? Totally unlikely.

We can almost certainly conclude that, if there were scratched initials on the window pane, and they did spell out the letters '*FM,*' then they were not made by Florence, either when she was a young girl or later in life when she was a middle-aged woman.

Although the accuracy of the story about Florence's initials being scratched on a window pane is very doubtful, the fact it appeared in books on Florence's life might have sparked an idea in the mind of a clever forger. Could incriminating letters be found at any of the murder scenes of the Ripper victims? According to the alleged Diary of Jack the Ripper, the answer is *Yes.* Catherine Eddowes (1842-1888) was the fourth canonical Ripper victim, and the second one to be killed on the night of 30th September 1888. Her body was found at 1:45am by Police Constable Edward Watkins in Mitre Square. She had been strangled and then savagely mutilated. Her left kidney and her womb had been removed. The tragedy and brutality of Catherine Eddowes' death is significant as far as the possible candidature of James Maybrick being Jack the Ripper is concerned. A simple sketch of the dead woman's face was published in the 1960s. On both of her cheeks, just below the eyes, two inverted V-shape incisions had been made. The diarist, in his account of the Eddowes' murder, wrote, '*Her nose annoyed me so I cut it off, had a go at her eyes and left my mark.*'

According to Shirley Harrison, the two cuts on the cheek could '*have formed the M that was Maybrick's mark.*'[239] The problem with that statement is the marks simply do not look like the letter M. If the diarist had been the killer and he had indeed left a mark, then the mark he would have made would have been far more obvious than these two incisions. It is a classic case of grasping at straws and finding what you are looking for, even though it does not exist.

The search for non-existent initials is even more apparent in the case of Mary Kelly (1863-1888), who was the last of the canonical Ripper victims and the one to suffer the worst mutilations. She was murdered in the early hours of

[237] *Mobile Press Register*, 3rd March 1946.
[238] Christie T.L., op cit., page 33.
[239] Harrison S., op cit., page 119.

Friday 9th November 1888 in Miller's Court. She was the only Ripper victim to be killed indoors, which is probably the reason why she was so savagely mutilated; the murderer knew there was less chance of him being disturbed as he carried out his gruesome slaughter. The first police officer on the scene the next morning later described the sight of the victim as '*too harrowing to be described.*' Her whole body had been slashed beyond recognition, and many body parts had been removed and placed around the room.

The terrible and brutal murder of Mary Kelly is another issue of contention in the debate over whether James Maybrick was Jack the Ripper. Those who think he was point to a photograph showing bloodstained markings on the wall beside Kelly's bed that supposedly show the letters '*FM*' (Florence Maybrick). The diarist wrote, '*An initial here and an initial there will tell of the whoring mother.*'

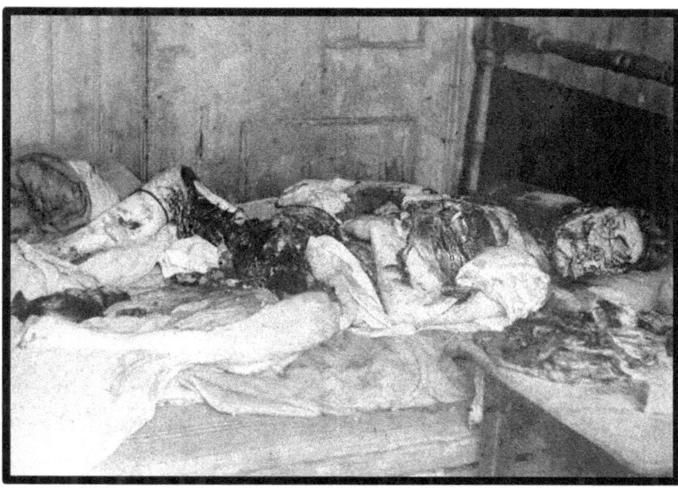
Enhanced picture of Mary Kelly's dead body
(Jay Hartley collection)

Paul Feldman broke down the police photograph of the murder scene into two-inch squares. He then systematically enlarged each of the squares and examined the contents. In one of these enlarged squares he claimed to have found the initials '*FM*' which were '*clear and precise. The initials of Florence Maybrick, the adulterous wife.*'[240] Feldman pointed out that, as the photograph was certainly not a forgery, if the Diary was written by a modern forger then he had '*not just been extremely lucky but remarkably observant.*' Feldman suggests that as Kelly's heart was missing, then James Maybrick (assuming he was the killer) may have used it to scrape the initials of his unfaithful wife on the walls of the room.

Jay Hartley, like Feldman, also believes the initials to be significant. He suggests that as well as there being the letters '*FM*' on the wall, Kelly also had the letter '*F*' carved on her left arm and a crude tattoo of a heart carved close to the '*F.*' He argues the tattoo is significant because Kelly's heart was missing when the coroner made his examination of her body. Hartley links the heart tattoo to a line in the Diary in which its author writes: '*May God forgive me for the deeds I commited [sic] on Kelly, no heart no heart.*' He further argues that if the Diary was a modern forgery, then its author would simply not have known about the various initials and markings and therefore '*if the diarist referred to the carved F on the arm and the initials on the wall, he did so because he was the murderer.*'[241]

Few are convinced by the view that there are clear initials on either the wall or on Kelly's body. Her body was savaged by the killer in what can only be described as a mad frenzy. Not surprisingly, her body was covered in cuts and bruises. Donald Rumbelow argued that if the initials did exist on the wall and they were so obvious as Feldman claims, then they would have been visible to the police, the doctors and the inquest jury, all of whom visited the room following the murder, yet no mention is ever made of them. Rumbelow also points out that the journalist who accompanied the jury describes how the police inspector meticulously pointed out with one hand the bloodstains on the wall and pointed with his other hand to the bloodstains on the mattress. He added the '*fact that nobody mentions such letters is clear evidence that they did not exist. Reading letters into bloodstains is like reading faces into the clouds; we are fooled, as Hamlet would say, to the top of our bent.*'[242] Hartley does try to provide a reason why there is no police reference to any markings or initials by stating the '*room was incredibly dark, and the markings were not noticeable to the naked eye. The flash of the camera brought it to visibility.*' Although the room was probably dark, that does not mean the police did not use some of form lighting to examine the murder scene. The police inspector who pointed out the bloodstains to the jury would not have been able to carry out that task in the dark. The room must have been lit sufficiently well for him to proceed and there are simply no references to any sign of visible initials on the wall or the body.

Although there are blood marks on the wall, what they say – if they say anything at all – is an entirely subjective exercise. They are certainly not, as Feldman claimed, '*clear and precise,*' showing the letters '*FM.*' They only look that clear and precise to those who are determined to find what they are already looking for. In that sense, the bloodstain initials on the wall of Kelly's room closely resemble the findings of the initials '*FM*' on the window pane in the Chandler mansion house, in that they both provide interesting stories but, under closer scrutiny, neither story can be validated by an objective analysis of the facts.

---

240 Feldman P., op cit., page 64.
241 https://jayhartley.com/the-writing-on-the-wall/
242 Rumbelow D., *The Complete Jack the Ripper*, (Penguin Books, London, 2004), page 253.

4

LOVE AND MARRIAGE

On Monday 22nd March 1880, the *SS Baltic* sailed into the Mersey estuary and berthed in the great seaport of Liverpool. It had been an eventful 11 day voyage, with the ship sailing dangerously close to icebergs on the previous Thursday morning.[243] Taking advantage of the excellent First Class facilities on board the White Star liner were a collection of well-to-do passengers. They included Mr G. Walker, the United States Consul-General in Paris, and the famous Irish Nationalist MP Charles Stuart Parnell, who disembarked at Queenstown, Ireland.

Also on board was the American Civil War hero, General John G. Hazard, who had fought for the Union forces in some of the most famous battles of the war. Hazard was travelling to Liverpool with his wife, Adelaide (Eads) Hazard and her maid. They had married just two weeks earlier on 26th February in St Louis, Missouri, in what one American newspaper described as '*the most noteworthy marriage of the season*.'[244] The stepfather of Mrs Adelaide Hazard was the world-renowned American civil engineer and inventor Captain James Buchanan Eads (1820-1887), who had built the first road and rail bridge to cross the Mississippi River at St Louis. Before the Civil War, Hazard had been involved in the cotton business. In 1874, he returned to the trade and based himself in New Orleans. In March 1880, he and his new wife were travelling to Liverpool to '*make their future home*' in the city.[245] Six months later, Hazard would place an announcement in a New Orleans newspaper stating: '*On and after this day the firm name of Hazard & Co. here is changed to Hazard and Scharpe. We will continue our business in Liverpool under the firm name of Hazard & Co*.'[246]

James Maybrick was another of the well-to-do passengers on board the *Baltic*. He and General Hazard were already known to one another. James probably first met Hazard when he '*spent a season*' in New Orleans in the early 1870s.[247] They would have also met in Liverpool. Passenger records for trans-Atlantic voyages show that Hazard spent several months in the city every year from 1876 onwards.[248] On one of those voyages, in August 1878, both James and Hazard are listed as sailing together on the *Baltic* from Liverpool to New York.[249] Hazard became so well established in Liverpool that in July 1879 he was invited to be one of the special guests at a dinner at the Adelphi Hotel hosted by Mr A. B. Forwood, former Mayor of Liverpool, to celebrate American independence.[250] James Maybrick and Hazard may have also met through their Freemasonry connections. Hazard belonged to the Franklin Lodge on Rhode Island, which he had joined in 1860. His grave headstone has a Templar Cross marked on it, showing his Mason affiliation.

SS Baltic by N. Jacobsen (1879)

Also on board the *Baltic* was Baroness von Roques and her two adult children, Holbrook St John and Florence Chandler. The relatively small number of First Class passengers on board the steamship meant that James and Florence would have frequently encountered one another in the state room or the dining room. At the time of Florence's trial, nine years later, a romantic story circulated about how they first met. According to an account in a Liverpool newspaper, Florence: '*stumbled in descending the companion-way leading to the dining saloon. She would have fallen to the bottom but for the fact that Mr James Maybrick was there and caught her in his arms. In doing so he sprained his ankle, and was laid up for some time*.' The newspaper went on to say that the two of them instantly struck up a relationship; it was '*a case of pure love, and the Liverpool cotton merchant felt that he could not do better than marry this young American belle who had so captivated him*.'[251]

---

243 *Liverpool Mercury*, 23rd March 1880.
244 *Boston Globe*, 2nd March 1881.
245 *Cincinnati Star*, 27th February 1880.
246 *Times-Picayune*, 2nd September 1880.
247 *Daily Picayune*, 22nd May 1889.
248 For example: *Liverpool Daily Post*, 18th August 1876; *Liverpool Daily Post*, 10th January 1877.
249 Liverpool to New York Passenger manifest (August 1878) on www.ancestry.com
250 *Liverpool Mercury*, 5th July 1879.
251 *Garston and Woolton Reporter*, 1st June 1889.

A more likely version of events is that the two of them were introduced to one another by Hazard, who knew James, and who may have also known Florence's family as well.[252]

Although Florence was only 18, she was a fine-looking woman with long golden hair and piercing blue eyes. James was on the lookout for a young and attractive American heiress, and he must have thought Florence fit the bill perfectly. He had already allowed one heiress, Julia Devens Valentine, to slip through his fingers, he was not going to let it happen again. Though more than 20 years her senior, James had the confidence and the *bonhomie* that enabled him to converse with Florence in a relaxed manner, and he went out of his way to win her over with a charm offensive. Although in his early forties, '*his worldly position was good*' and '*he carried his years well.*' He was not yet suffering from the obvious physical effects of his drug misuse.[253] He must have appeared to Florence as well-dressed, educated and entertaining, and extremely persistent. Any physical attraction that existed between the two suitors was enhanced by a range of shared interests including a love of horse racing. Ryan suggests that Florence attended the 1879 Grand National in Liverpool, and she asked James if he knew which horse had won the 1880 race.[254] In reality, it is unlikely that Florence did attend the National in March 1879, as she would have been with her mother who was contesting a court case in New York against the claims of Isaac Rosenthal.

Whatever the truth, James and Florence got on so well together that, according to one source, the ship's captain Henry Parsell interrupted the final meal of the voyage to raise a toast to the couple on their impending marriage.[255] Although James and Florence became close during the voyage, it is unlikely they got engaged on the ship. Christie is probably closer to the truth when he wrote the two of them had '*reached an understanding*' during the voyage, a formal engagement coming later.[256]

There are some interesting parallels to be drawn between the courtship and marriage of Hazard and James. Both men married younger women from well-connected and wealthy families. Both marriages started well but developed problems. In both cases, there is evidence that the dissolute lives the two men lived in their pre-marriage days had led them to develop habits they found difficult to break from. In a letter to one of his other daughters, James Eads informs her that Hazard wanted Adelaide to formulate some plan of separation as he was satisfied they '*cannot live together.*' He urged her to write to Adelaide, as she was upset and very '*miserable.*' Eads was scathing about Hazard, describing him as a '*libertine – selfish and dictatorial.*'[257] The term '*libertine*' is telling and, if accurate, paints a picture of man who, although married, continued to have numerous sexual liaisons. Hazard's actions led to a breakdown in his relationship with Adelaide, though they never actually divorced.

General John G. Hazard (1832-1897)

Not long after the *Baltic* berthed in Liverpool, Florence's mother and brother left the city, leaving Florence behind to continue her courtship with James. Hazard and his wife invited Florence to stay with them at the Childwall Abbey Hotel, in an affluent suburb of the city. James visited her almost every day and the budding romance flourished.[258] When Florence rejoined her mother, James followed her and spent time with her in Paris and London, where the Baroness was renting accommodation on Kensington High Street.[259]

In the summer of 1880, Florence was again invited by the Hazards to stay with them in Liverpool. James was a frequent visitor, pursuing Florence with a fervour that must have impressed her. His persistence proved successful and the couple became engaged, the marriage planned for the following summer.

Now engaged to Florence, James returned his focus to the cotton business. He travelled to Norfolk, Virginia, arriving on 7th September 1880, and spent the winter months in America.[260] Five months later he sailed back to Liverpool on the White Star steamer *Adriatic*, arriving home on 8th February, 1881.[261] He needed to return early as he had a wedding to plan. He is recorded in the April 1881 Census as staying in the Adelphi Hotel in Liverpool.

[252] *Liverpool Daily Post*, 30th May 1889.
[253] *Glasgow Herald*, 8th August 1889.
[254] Ryan B., *The Poisoned Life of Mrs Maybrick*, (toExcel Press, London, 2000) page 16.
[255] Ibid., page 15.
[256] Christie T.L., op cit., page 37.
[257] www.ancestry.com
[258] Graham A. and Emmas C., op cit., page 32.
[259] *Commercial Gazette*, (London) 7th October 1880.
[260] *Norfolk Virginian*, 8th September 1880.
[261] *Liverpool Daily Post*, 9th February 1881.

Love and Marriage

Christie suggests that the relationship between James and Florence was founded on '*avarice and deception.*'[262] James was less attracted by Florence's good looks than he was by the possibility of taking ownership of the lands she would inherit from her grandfather's estate. Florence's mother saw an opportunity of gaining a '*seemingly rich son-in-law*' who would be able to provide for her in the later years of her life. For her part, cynics suggest that Florence was merely looking for a way of escaping her overbearing mother. Florence saw James, a successful businessman, as her route to a life of comfort and stability. While James and Florence probably did overestimate each other's wealth, there must have been more to their mutual attraction than just financial gain.

To James, marriage to a much younger American woman meant an entire change in his way of life. His care-free existence would be greatly curtailed, though – as time would show – not entirely ended. For Florence, marriage also meant changes. She would be leaving her small circle of family and friends and moving to a city where she would not know anybody. She would move from dependence upon her mother to dependence on a man she barely knew. Although the change would have frightened her, it probably also excited her. She was a woman who believed herself to be in love.

Did James love Florence? He had previous opportunities to marry but never pursued them. Something must have changed his mindset. There is no doubt that financial betterment was part of his motivation, but it also appears that he was captivated by Florence, otherwise he would not have pursued her in the zealous manner that he did.

One of the important sources of information on the Maybricks is the correspondence from Florence Aunspaugh (1873-1949) to the author Trevor Christie. Florence's father, John Aunspaugh, was a senior figure in the cotton firm Inman Swann and Co. of Atlanta, Georgia, and a business colleague and close friend of James. He attended James' wedding, and his daughter, Florence, stayed in Battlecrease, the Maybrick's home, during the summer of 1888. Florence Aunspaugh provided Christie with detailed recollections of her time in Battlecrease, and also of her father's views of James and Florence. The validity of Florence Aunspaugh's memories has been called into doubt, partly because her critics believe her to have been eight years old when she stayed in Battlecrease – she was in fact 15 – and partly because some of her recollections have been shown to be inaccurate. For example, she wrote that Edwin Maybrick went to South America when Florence was arrested so he wouldn't have to appear at her trial. That was not the case, and he did testify. Although some of her views are not accurate and she was an elderly woman when she corresponded with Christie, she did have first-hand knowledge of the family and received a letter from Florence when she was in Aylesbury Prison. It is also likely that the Maybricks were a frequent topic of conversation in her own household.

In her correspondence with Christie, Florence Aunspaugh stated the Baroness told her father on the day of James and Florence's wedding that she was '*bitterly opposed to the match and did not believe that any good would come of it.*' The Baroness added that James had been very '*persistent,*' and was '*always crowding Florie with engagements.*'[263] Although it is impossible to verify this story, it does appear to have a ring of truth to it. The Baroness would have been conscious of James' age, especially as he was of a similar age to her. It is also likely that James did pursue Florence in a '*persistent*' manner, and probably did crowd her with engagements. This suggests that James was attracted to Florence. In allowing James to court her, Florence was demonstrating a streak of independence, especially if she was going against her mother's declared wishes. She must have been open to James' overtures, but probably needed more convincing before she was finally prepared to commit to marriage.

A few months after James and Florence's wedding, the Baroness wrote to her lawyer in New York and told him that her new son-in-law was prepared to '*assist*' her in the legal fight over the lands in America that had been left to her by her father. In the letter she described James as '*devotedly in love with his wife.*'[264]

What had prompted this change of heart by the Baroness? She may have started to see James' persistence towards Florence in a more positive light, as a sign of genuine affection. There was also probably an element of self-interest. The Baroness was in debt and being pursued by creditors. She may have come to perceive James, with his business contacts in Britain and America, as a useful ally in her ongoing financial struggles.

James' sudden plans to get married to a young American woman must have come as a shock to his family and friends. According to Christie, Michael – James' younger but influential brother – was '*strongly opposed to the union.*' This was partly because the couple had known each other such a short time, but also because he believed that Florence and her mother were '*adventuresses.*' Christie suggests that James' other brothers were also '*not enthusiastic*' about the marriage, apart from Edwin, who was '*more or less neutral*' on the matter.[265]

It is easy to understand this hostility, as the Maybrick brothers were conservative by inclination. For James to be considering marrying someone who was much younger – and from another country – would have certainly surprised

[262] Christie T.L., op cit., page 39.
[263] Trevor Christie Collection. In various documents the abbreviated form of Florence's name is spelt either 'Florie' or "Florrie;' we have retained the spelling as used in each individual example.
[264] Christie T.L., op cit., page 47.
[265] Ibid., 39.

them. They might have liked the fact that Florence's family was well-connected and her mother had the title of Baroness, but this positive feeling would have soon disappeared when they delved a little more into the Baroness' back story. They would have discovered a woman separated from her fourth husband, living a nomadic lifestyle and not being as wealthy as she claimed.

Florence Elizabeth Chandler (1861/1862-1941)

Another family who would have been both surprised and shocked by James' upcoming wedding were the Janions, a Liverpool family with whom James was intimate. Ryan suggests the news had a '*devastating effect*' on three of the Janion sisters, who had hoped that James would have married one of them.[266] Florence Aunspaugh recalled her father told her that when Matilda Janion (later Mrs Briggs) was a younger woman, she had been madly in love with James and had made a '*desperate effort to marry him.*'[267] In later years, it is claimed, she hoped James might marry her younger sister, Gertrude Janion.[268] Although it is impossible to check the veracity of these assertions, it is likely they would have been irritated that James was to marry a stranger, someone he had known for such a short time. This in turn may have led to a feeling of resentment towards Florence.

Despite all the opposition, James was not to be deterred from marrying Florence and he set about making the necessary preparations. On 4th July 1881, two weeks before his wedding, James was granted a coat of arms by the ancient College of Arms in London. It cost him £76 10s, the equivalent of a few thousand pounds today. It depicted a sparrow holding a sprig of hawthorn, often referred to as '*may*' and carried the legend '*Tempus Omnia Revelat*' or '*Time Reveals All.*'

Much has been written into possible meanings of the coat of arms. A simple and obvious view is that James was trying to impress his young bride and her family. He wanted to appear the perfect English gentleman; on his marriage certificate James recorded his profession as '*esquire.*' The coat of arms was all part of the illusion that he was a man of means and substance.

The wedding of James and Florence took place in St James's Church, Piccadilly, London, on 27th July 1881. The church was a very fashionable one. It had been designed by Sir Christopher Wren and consecrated in 1684. Wren thought very highly of it and singled it out for description and commendation in his letter '*Upon the Building of National Churches.*'

At the wedding, Florence wore a long white satin and lace dress. James wore a white satin waistcoat, and his cutaway coat was lined with cream-coloured satin. The service was conducted by the Rev J. Dyer Tovey. The wedding was attended by family members and friends, with Florence given away by her brother, who had come from Paris for the event. At one point during the day, the Baroness put her arms around an embarrassed John Aunspaugh, and reputedly said, '*Oh, here is my long lost love.*'[269] Among the guests from Liverpool were James' brothers and the Janion sisters. James' brother, Michael, was the best man, despite his reservations about the suitability of the couple. Alongside his description of himself as '*esquire,*' James entered his father's profession as '*gentleman.*'

According to Morland, after the ceremony the bride and groom and their guests were transported by carriage to the Globe Theatre in the Strand to watch a production of the play by Meilhac and Halévy entitled *Frou Frou.* If true, one can only assume that it was arranged by Michael, who may have been poking fun at his

St James's Church, Piccadilly, London

[266] Ryan B., op cit., page 19.
[267] Trevor Christie Collection.
[268] *Norfolk Virginian*, 20th August 1889.
[269] Quoted in Graham A. and Emmas C., op cit., page 34.

new in-laws. '*Frou Frou*' was the nickname given to the play's main character, Gilberte, a frivolous wife and a rather indifferent mother, who lived the life of an idle but fashionable wealthy woman. Gilberte elopes with her husband's friend, but her husband tracks them down and kills her lover in a duel. Frou Frou returns home but dies a few months later hoping that her sins will be forgiven. One of the play's main actors was Richard Mansfield, who played the part of Brigard, the father of Frou Frou. In 1888, Mansfield was back in London performing in a play about Dr Jekyll and Mr Hyde. Mansfield's performance was so powerful that some people felt he should be considered a suspect in the Jack the Ripper murders.

DIOCESE OF LONDON. 19th July 1881.

APPEARED PERSONALLY, James Maybrick Esquire, of the Parish of Saint James, Piccadilly, in the County of Middlesex, a Bachelor, of the age of twenty one years and upwards,

and prayed a Licence for the Solemnization of Matrimony in the Parish Church of Saint James Piccadilly, aforesaid,

between him and Florence Elizabeth Chandler of No 18 Avenue d'Antin, in the City of Paris, in the Republic of France, a Spinster, a Minor of the age of Nineteen years and upwards but under the age of twenty one years and made Oath that he believeth that there is no Impediment of Kindred or Alliance, or of any other lawful cause, nor any Suit commenced in any Ecclesiastical Court to bar or hinder the Proceeding of the said Matrimony, according to the tenor of such Licence. And he further made oath, that he the said Appearer hath had his usual Place of abode within the said Parish of Saint James Piccadilly for the space of Fifteen days last past. And he lastly made Oath that the said Minor hath no Father living or Testamentary Guardian to her lawfully appointed or Mother unmarried or Guardian to her appointed by Her Majesty's High Court of Justice Chancery Division having authority to Consent to such intended Marriage

Sworn before me, TS May Surrogate — J Maybrick

One might have expected the wedding of the brother of a well-known celebrity to the daughter of a Baroness from a well-connected American family to have attracted a few column inches in the newspapers, but news of the event was remarkably sparse. Morland has described the wedding as '*quiet; the world did not even know of it until it appeared in the Births, Marriages and Deaths columns of the Liverpool Daily Post and the now defunct Mercury.*'[270] The listing, appearing some three days after the event, gave only the barest of details.

It is possible that James kept the news quiet to prevent his former lover, Sarah Ann Robertson, from hearing about it. Christie asserts that it was only after the event that James told her about his wedding.[271]

After a brief honeymoon, the newlyweds settled into the pattern of life that James had followed prior to his wedding.[272] They spent half the year in Liverpool and the other six months in Norfolk, Virginia. While in Liverpool, they rented a house on Livingston Avenue, which was off Lark Lane, very close to Sefton Park. The house belonged to Mrs Matilda Briggs, one of the Janion sisters. It was in this house that Florence gave birth to her first child, James Chandler Maybrick. He was born prematurely, eight months after the wedding on 24th March 1882. The birth of their first baby so soon after their wedding is an indication that the early years of James and Florence's marriage were happy ones.

One person who kept in close contact with James and Florence at this time was General Hazard. At the time of Florence's trial he told a reporter that he was '*quite intimate with the Maybricks*' during his stay in England and he '*knew of no ill-feeling between them.*' When news broke of Florence's arrest, he said '*the whole matter was a painful surprise to him.*'[273]

The Maybrick baby, James Chandler, was given the affectionate pet name of '*Bobo.*' Sometime later, he was given a second name, '*Sonny.*' In a letter written by Florence Maybrick to Florence Aunspaugh while she was in Aylesbury Prison, she said if the '*old happy days were still in existence*' she would have the '*largest ball*' for her in Battlecrease and she '*would not have to retire when dinner was announced, as you and Sonny had to do when you were here before.*'[274] Florence Aunspaugh uses the name Sonny on several occasions in her account of her stay in Battlecrease

[270] Morland N., *This Friendless Lady*, (Frederick Muller, London, 1927) page 9.
[271] Christie T.L., op cit., page 40.
[272] Morland N., op cit., page 9.
[273] *Daily Picayune (New Orleans)*, 22nd May 1889.
[274] Trevor Christie Collection.

in 1888; for example, she wrote '*the little boy whom they called Sonny.*' The evidence therefore suggests that James had two pet names: Bobo and Sonny. It is likely Bobo came first, and was given to him when he was a baby, with Sonny coming a little later, presumably after the birth of his sister, when he was no longer a baby but a young boy. At no point in her correspondence with Christie does Florence Aunspaugh use the name Bobo; she only ever uses Sonny. Nevertheless, his earlier pet name was still used by some people and never died out. Even after his death some newspapers referred to him as Bobo; one report led with '*Death of Bobo, Mrs Maybrick's son.*'[275]

In the 1880s, Norfolk, Virginia was a typical city of what Mark Twain called the '*American Gilded Age*'. This was the period of rapid industrialisation and economic growth in the northern states of America in the late nineteenth century. The industry that grew the most was the railways, and its expansion was to transform Norfolk from a relatively unimportant town into a major port. The railways linked Norfolk to the coalfields, and these provided it with vast amounts of cheap coal which made it an attractive port for refuelling steamships. The railways also linked the city to the cotton growing areas of the southern states. Cotton bales, which had traditionally been transported south by river to the coastal ports, now travelled east by railways to the eastern seaports such as Norfolk. A deep-water channel meant the port of Norfolk was '*open to vessels of the largest size*' and remained open all year round.[276] This suited the cotton growers, and cotton quickly became the most important commodity of Norfolk's foreign trade. In 1865, Norfolk handled only 59,000 cotton bales, most of which came from nearby plantations; by 1880, it handled almost 600,000 bales, a ten-fold increase. It was cotton that was the single most important element that linked the two great seaports of Liverpool and Norfolk.

While railways and cotton drove the economic expansion of Norfolk, the continuing success of its traditional industries remained important. These older enterprises included the harvesting of strawberries and oysters. More than 500 local boats were involved in harvesting local oysters. The success of both its new and traditional industries led to the population of the city growing from 22,000 in 1880 to over 35,000 a decade later. The expansion of the town meant that '*Gilded Age Norfolkians could choose among nearly five hundred places of business within the city limits, including twenty-six restaurants and saloons and eleven banks.*'[277] The busiest part of Norfolk was the Market Square, where a daily food market was held featuring fresh fish, oysters, seasonal fruit and vegetables.

The railways also linked Norfolk to nearby Virginia Beach. In 1882, the Seaside Hotel and Land Company bought five miles of the Virginia Beach waterfront, and it was not long before it became one of the great seaside resorts of the South. Florence would have found the female fashions of Norfolk to have been in marked contrast to the stuffy norms of Victorian Liverpool. The new dress style in Norfolk was called '*Henry II,*' and garments were worn as '*tight as human nature can endure.*'[278]

If the house that the Maybricks rented in Liverpool was large but not grand, then the house they rented in Norfolk was palatial and refined. Freemason Street was then, and still is, one the city's finest residential neighbourhoods. The street still retains many of its features from the late nineteenth century, including cobblestone paving, granite curbs, cast iron fences and brick sidewalks. The house the Maybricks rented was typical of the homes being built at that time to accommodate the growing middle classes. It had many features associated with the Federal houses that were so popular on the eastern seaboard in that period, including a symmetrical design and arched windows. Inside, it was bright and airy. It was a home that showcased James Maybrick as a successful businessman.

Thomas Stansell, who had been James' body servant before his marriage to Florence, continued to be employed by him during the Maybricks' stay in Norfolk. He told a local newspaper the couple '*lived in fine style and had a great deal of company.' He said he 'used to superintend all their dinners and receptions, which there were many.*' He added that during his time working for the couple he '*never heard an unpleasant word pass between them.*'[279]

Although the early years of the Maybrick marriage appear to be happy, one potential problem was James' use of arsenic. Stansell said James continued to use arsenic after his marriage, and '*his doses of arsenic grew larger.*' Stansell continued, '*Mrs Maybrick used to give him a white powder at his request, but I don't think she knew it was arsenic.*' Stansell's statement is supported by John Fleming, a master mariner from Halifax, Ontario, who sent an affidavit to Asquith after Florence's trial. Fleming said he had known James when he lived in Norfolk, sometime between 1882 and 1884. He recalled seeing him put a grey powder on his food and asked him what it was. James had replied it was arsenic. Fleming was shocked, and said to him, '*Good God, man, that is a deadly poison.*' James replied, '*We all take some poison more or less; for instance, I am now taking enough arsenic to kill you.*' James said he took arsenic occasionally as it '*strengthens*' him.[280] If James had started his arsenic habit as a means of treating the symptoms of malaria, he was now using it primarily as an aphrodisiac. He had a young wife and he needed to prove his virility.

---

[275] *Dundee Courier*, 9th April 1911.
[276] Jones C. W., *Norfolk as a Business Centre, Its Principal Industries and Trades* (Virginian Press, Norfolk, 1881) page 8.
[277] Parramore T. C., et al., *Norfolk – the First Four Centuries*, (University Press of Virginia, Charlottesville, 1995) page 247.
[278] Ibid., page 245.
[279] *Norfolk Virginian*, 24th August 1889.
[280] Irving H.B., op cit., page xlii.

During his time in Norfolk, James appears to have been successful in his business dealings. The local newspapers mention his activities on several occasions. For example, in December 1881 he is recorded as having purchased 131 bales of cotton.[281] This was one of the biggest consignments listed, and it would have produced a healthy profit once the bales had been shipped to England. On another occasion, in 1884 James is listed as having purchased 97 bales of cotton.[282] Once again this was one of the largest consignments. To have been able to purchase such large amounts of cotton demonstrates that James must have been making a sizeable profit, and that his business had a healthy cash-flow. Another example of the success of James' business is that he came to be seen as an active and valuable member of the Norfolk and Portsmouth Cotton Exchange. In October 1882, at the first meeting of the new Directory of the Cotton Exchange, James was appointed to the Exchange's Committee on Membership.[283]

The house the Maybricks rented on Freemason Street, Norfolk. (Chris Jones collection)

The following year, in September 1883, James attended an '*enthusiastic joint meeting*' of the Cotton Exchange and the local manufacturers' association at the Atlantic Hotel in Norfolk. The meeting was called to listen to a joint report from the two bodies that outlined proposals to further improve trains links between Norfolk and its hinterland.[284] The following month James was elected one of the Directors of the Cotton Exchange. The local newspaper records that there was a '*large vote*,' and '*much interest*' was '*manifested in the balloting*.'[285] The fact that James triumphed in such a large vote indicates the esteem in which he was held by his fellow cotton brokers. John Aunspaugh is reputed to have said of James that he was '*one of the straightest, most upright and honourable man in a business transaction I have ever known*.'[286]

Morland wrote that James' office was in downtown Norfolk and '*he stayed there all day as a rule*,' and '*frequently prepared a scratch meal in a room off his own office*.'[287] We know from local directories that James was originally based in the Cotton Exchange, and that meant he probably used one of the rolltop desks that were provided for the cotton merchants.[288] It was only later, as he became more successful, that he seems to have had his own office with a private telephone.

It is likely he returned home for a leisurely lunch, as that was the common practice for the cotton merchants. It was also not far for James to walk, being only a ten-minute stroll from his house on Freemason Street to the Cotton Exchange building. Ryan wrote that James arrived at the Exchange at around eight o'clock, and went through his mail and cables from Liverpool at his desk. He would then move to the Exchange floor, where he would note the daily cotton prices and converse with his fellow cotton merchants.[289] These would have included both Nicholas Bateson, with whom he had previously shared a house in Norfolk, and Morden Rigg, a fellow Liverpudlian and another successful cotton merchant. James would have then walked the short distance to the cotton warehouses and made the appropriate purchases. After lunch, he would have returned to the Exchange building to make the necessary shipping arrangements for his purchases. Sometime after four or five o'clock, James and his fellow traders would head off to one of the gentlemen's clubs, such as the Virginian Club, for drinks and relaxation. At around seven

---

[281] *Norfolk Landmark*, 10th December 1881.
[282] *Norfolk Landmark*, 19th January 1884.
[283] *Norfolk Landmark*, 27th October 1882.
[284] *Norfolk Virginian*, 14th September 1883.
[285] *Norfolk Virginian*, 11th October 1883.
[286] Quoted in Graham A. and Emmas C., op cit., page 28.
[287] Morland N., op cit., pages 12-13.
[288] Chataigne J. H., *Directory of Norfolk and Portsmouth 1882-83*, (Chataigne, Norfolk, 1883)
[289] Ryan B., op cit., pages 23-24.

o'clock, he would return home for an evening meal and drinks on the veranda. Later in the evening, the Maybricks may have entertained guests at their home or gone out for the evening to the theatre.

James appears to have been popular. After his death, a Norfolk newspaper stated he had been '*much liked by those in contact with him.*' It also said that he '*moved in fashionable circles,*' and was '*a great club man.*'[290] James had retained his membership of the Virginian Club from his pre-marriage days. He may also have attended the monthly meetings of the Freemasons. Florence, too, made a favourable impression. She gained the reputation of being a '*highly cultured and refined woman; exquisitely sensitive, and expressive in her kindly grace, manner and speech.*'[291]

Although the Maybricks enjoyed their time in Norfolk, in 1884 James resigned from the Norfolk Cotton Exchange and the couple moved to live in Liverpool on a permanent basis. The reasons for this move were probably both business-based and personal. Other Eastern seaports were starting to effectively compete with Norfolk for the cotton trade, and the main element of Norfolk's trade was soon to be the export of coal. James may have also tired of the upheaval of moving across the Atlantic twice a year. He wanted a permanent home for his family, and he wanted it in his home city.

There is a tendency to take a cynical view of the Maybrick marriage and suggest it was doomed from the start; however, such a view would be inaccurate. The evidence suggests the early years of the marriage were both happy and successful. Nowhere is this more evident than in the time the couple spent in Norfolk, between 1881 and 1884. They lived in fine style in a large house with a very fashionable address.[292] They held many dinners and receptions, and their contemporaries – such as Stansell and General Hazard – never heard the couple disagree. James' business was flourishing, and he was well respected by his fellow cotton merchants. He was a member of Norfolk's finest and most prestigious clubs.

Despite this happiness and success, there were two potential clouds on the horizon; James' continued use of arsenic and the presence, back in England, of a woman who felt that she should have been his wife.

LINKS TO THE RIPPER DIARY: WAS JAMES MAYBRICK THE AUSTIN AXE MURDERER?

In the edition of her book about James Maybrick and the Diary of Jack the Ripper published in 2003, Shirley Harrison suggested a link between James and a serial killer who terrorised Austin, Texas between December 1884 and December 1885. The eight axe murders were referred to by contemporaries as the '*Servant Girl Annihilator*' or the '*Austin Axe Murders.*' Seven of the victims were women (five black and two white), and one was a black man. On top of that, at least two other women and two other men were seriously injured in attacks by the killer.

All the victims were attacked in their beds with an axe as they slept; five of the women were dragged outside and raped, mutilated and killed. Six of the murdered women had a railway coupling pin driven into their ears. An axe was left behind at the scene of the murder. Also left behind were some footprints made by the killer, who had removed his boots – possibly so he could quietly exit the crime scene. An examination of these footprints revealed that he appeared to be missing a toe from his right foot.

When it was first suggested to Shirley Harrison that there might be a link between the Austin and Ripper killings, her reaction was one of '*curiosity but detachment.*'[293] That initial feeling should have warned her not to proceed any further with the dubious hypothesis. Although Harrison is a respected author, she provides absolutely no evidence for James Maybrick being the Austin serial killer; all she does provide are a few extremely tenuous connections. The first of these is that she has '*no diary dates for him [James Maybrick] in Liverpool that clash with the killings.*'

That is hardly a surprise as James was a Liverpool cotton merchant and not a high-profile celebrity. Apart from certain dates that came to light as a result of Florence's trial, it is very difficult to identify what James did on a day-to-day basis. Even his wedding only attracted a few lines in the newspapers. It is known that in 1884 he resigned as a member of the Norfolk and Portsmouth Cotton Exchange in Virginia and, with his wife Florence, decided to permanently settle in Liverpool, England. Therefore, at the time of the Austin murders James was living in Liverpool and not America. There are two verifiable dates that identify James' movements in April 1885. On 1st April he signed an application form to become a member of Liverpool Cricket Club, and on 16th April he was in Paris to attend the funeral of his brother-in-law, Holbrook Chandler. While neither date provides him with an alibi, they both place him a long distance away from the Texas murders.

[290] *Norfolk Virginian*, 22nd May 1889.
[291] *Virginian-Pilot, The Ledger Star*, 27th July 1986.
[292] *Norfolk Virginian*, 21st October 1882.
[293] Harrison S., *Jack the Ripper: The American Connection*, (Blake, London, 2003) page 72.

Love and Marriage

Harrison tries to support her assertion that James is a serious candidate to be the Austin serial killer by attacking his *character*. She describes him as a '*secret womanising, arsenic-driven, cotton merchant*' who was '*leading a double life*' during his time in Virginia. On the surface, he was a respectable businessman, yet underneath this façade he was a regular user of both drugs and prostitutes. It is certainly the case that, during his pre-marriage days in Norfolk, he frequented the brothel that was run by Mary Hogwood (Howard); however, there is no evidence that he continued to go to her brothel after his marriage. In her own statement, Hogwood states that '*up to the time of his marriage, he called at my house when in Norfolk at least three times a week.*'

Harrison argues that around the period of the Austin murders, James was becoming '*increasingly unwell*;' that his marriage was beginning to crumble, and that it was therefore '*very likely that he was, indeed, often away from home.*' This argument has no substance. The overwhelming consensus is that the problems in the Maybrick marriage did not appear until 1887 when Florence found out that James was paying money to another woman. The Maybricks had a second child in 1886, which strongly suggests that their marriage was still strong and robust at the time of the Austin murders.

In December 1884, the world's largest ever International Cotton Exposition opened in New Orleans, and Harrison suggests that '*it seems unlikely that Maybrick would have missed such an important business opportunity.*' The biggest problem with this proposition is that there is no evidence that James attended the event. His name has not been found in any article that covers the event. He is not listed as staying in any of the hotels during the period of the Exposition, or during the time that the murders occurred.

Even if James *had* attended the event, it does not mean that he dashed to Austin, savagely murdered a woman and then dashed back to New Orleans without anyone realising he had gone. The distance between Austin and New Orleans is over 500 miles.

For James to have committed the Austin murders, he would have needed to have been away from home for substantial periods of time. He would have criss-crossed the Atlantic (a six- to ten-day voyage each way), travelled by train to Austin and then back to New York. At the least, a four-week period away from home for each attack and murder was required. Multiply that by at least seven (because on one occasion two murders were committed on the same night), and James would have been away from home for a minimum of seven months during a one-year period. He would have also had to have been away from home over two consecutive Christmas holiday periods. Such a hectic schedule – repeatedly criss-crossing the Atlantic and committing several violent murders – is not a realistic suggestion.

No evidence exists that James crossed the Atlantic Ocean *once* in 1885, let alone on numerous occasions. He is not listed as a passenger on any trans-Atlantic steamships, he is not shown on immigration records, and he is not recorded in any newspaper as a passenger arriving at an American port or returning to Liverpool. Such records would exist if he had made these journeys.

Between 1869 and 1884, James made numerous voyages, and his name repeatedly appears in passenger manifests and/or in newspaper reports. For example, in March 1879, James is listed as a cabin passenger arriving on the steamship *City of Berlin*, arriving in Liverpool having sailed from New York. In February 1881, he is listed as arriving in Liverpool on the White Star steamer *Adriatic*, which set out from New York. The chances of James travelling incognito on Atlantic steamships was impossible. He was a frequent traveller, well-known to ship captains and crews.

Finally, if James Maybrick is accepted as the Austin serial killer, then you also have to accept that he was probably the same person who murdered women in London in 1888.

A possible link between the Texas and Whitechapel serial killings was proposed in 1888 by the American newspapers, the *Austin Daily Statesman* and the *Atlantic Constitution*. In September 1888, the *Statesman* noted a '*striking similarity*' between the Austin and Whitechapel murders, though it did add that this similarity must be just a '*mere coincidence.*' The *Statesman* stated that what made this coincidence '*more singular*' was the view that the Austin murderer, who was seen on one occasion, was '*like the Leather Apron, a short, heavy-set personage.*'[294]

In October 1888, the same newspaper again drew its readers attention to possible parallels between the two serial killings in an article under the headline, '*Thrilling co-incidents.*' These links included the fact that in both sets of murders the victims were women, and that all of the victims had received serious injuries to their head. However, the newspaper added that these were just a '*coincidence*', and that the London and Austin women had not been killed by the same person.[295] The *Atlanta Constitution* went further than the *Statesman* and wrote, without any evidence to support the statement, that in Texas '*people firmly believe that the London Murderer of women is the man who killed so many women in Austin a couple of years ago.*'[296] The suggestion was that the Texas killings had abruptly ended, so perhaps the murderer had travelled to England where a year or so later he restarted his murderous campaign. If this unlikely scenario is accepted, there remains the obstacle that the modus operandi of the Austin serial killer and

---

[294] *Austin Daily Statesman*, 5th September 1888.
[295] *Austin Daily Statesman*, 5th October 1888.
[296] *Atlanta Constitution*, 14th October 1888.

Jack the Ripper were very different. Even Harrison admitted that there is '*no obvious similarity between the methods of the Austin killer and those of Jack the Ripper. The Ripper strangled and disemboweled his victims, with no apparent sexual motive; the Austin women were battered, a railway coupling pin driven into their brains.*'[297]

It is the case that Scotland Yard did at certain points in the Ripper investigations pursue the idea that the Ripper may have been an American. For example, it was suggested that the infamous *Dear Boss* letter (dated 27th September 1888) was penned by an American, as the term '*Boss*' is an American word. Also, Francis Tumblety, the Irish-born American, has been proposed as a credible candidate to be Jack the Ripper. He did live in Whitechapel at the time of the murders, and fled to America on 20th November 1888, not long after the Mary Kelly murder, to escape from a police charge of gross indecency.

Another possible American link surfaced after Matthew Packer, a potential witness of the Whitechapel murderer, provided a statement that on the night of the Elizabeth Stride murder he saw someone wearing an American hat and speaking with Yankee twang buy Stride grapes. As a result, suspicion began to fall on any Americans who were then in London, and the police even questioned three cowboys who were working at the American Exhibition in the city.[298]

In all these cases, the hypotheses were based around the premise that the Ripper was actually an American who travelled to Britain and committed the murders. In the case of James, the opposite would have had to be true.

There are so many insurmountable problems with the proposition that James Maybrick was the notorious axe murdering serial killer of Austin – not least that there is absolutely no evidence that he was in America at the time of the killings – that the hypothesis can be dismissed out of hand. James was not the Texas serial killer; indeed, he is not even remotely credible as a suspect for the killings.

On the other hand, there are some suspects who make much more likely candidates to be the serial killer. One of these is Nathan Elgin. In February 1886, while in a drunken and wild state, he dragged a girl from a saloon to a nearby house and started to savagely beat her. Her screams alerted the neighbourhood, and two police officers arrived on the scene. When they tried to arrest Elgin, he pulled out a knife and they shot him. He died the next day. At his autopsy it was found that that he was missing a toe from his right foot. This detail, and the end to similar-style murders, led many to believe that Elgin was the notorious serial killer. Not everyone is convinced of his guilt; the investigation into the Austin serial murders continues to this day.

[297] Harrison S., op cit., (2003) pages 71-72.
[298] Sugden P., op cit., page 303.

5

A LIVERPOOL FAMILY

In February 1884, James and Florence left Norfolk for the last time and made Liverpool their permanent home. They arrived back into a city that was in the midst of dramatic change. In 1880, two charters recognised the new status of Liverpool. One raised Liverpool to a city, and the other created a bishopric. St Peter's Church, where James' father had served as parish clerk, had become Liverpool's Pro-Cathedral, and plans were put in place to build a cathedral. Although it was to be many years before work on the Anglican Cathedral was to start, several other buildings and institutions were established that were considered to be characteristic of the great Victorian cities. The Philharmonic Hall was built between 1846 and 1849. It was to be the home of the Liverpool (later the Royal Liverpool) Philharmonic Orchestra. The famous Adelphi Hotel was built between 1868 and 1869. Charles Dickens described it as the finest hotel in the world. The hotel was rebuilt in 1912 on the same site and was designed to be even grander than the one it replaced. The Victoria Building on Brownlow Hill was built between 1887 and 1892. It became the home of the new University College of Liverpool.

In January 1886, the new railway tunnel under the Mersey linking Liverpool and Birkenhead was opened by the Prince of Wales. It was a magnificent feat of engineering, and typified Liverpool's drive and ambition. The growing prosperity of Liverpool led to the steady development of the city's suburbs. This process was aided by the improvement in local transport. A network of horse-drawn omnibuses to districts such as Aigburth and Garston first appeared in 1831. An Act of Parliament in 1868 gave the Liverpool Tramways Company permission to establish a tramway system. In 1869, the service started with 16 horse-drawn cars. These cars, built in New York by John Stevenson, were double-deckers seating 46 passengers. The first tram left Dingle in November 1869 and about 7,000 passengers were carried on the first day of service. New routes soon appeared, including a one-hourly service to Aigburth and Garston where the Maybricks were to establish their new home.

If Liverpool was changing as a place in which to live and work, Florence was changing as a person. When she had first arrived in the city she was a teenager and an outsider; she was now a mother in her twenties and the wife of a successful cotton merchant. Compared to the early days of her marriage, she would have been more confident and far more prepared for the challenges that lay ahead. Nevertheless, she would still have had some misgivings about the move. She knew she would be in frequent contact with her husband's old friends and was aware some of them probably still had doubts about her as a suitable wife for James.

Beechville, Liverpool (Chris Jones collection)

One thing that would have pleased Florence was her new home. When the Maybricks returned to Liverpool they rented a house named Beechville in Grassendale Park, which was about five miles from the city centre. Grassendale was an area of riverside land, some 20 acres in size, located between Aigburth and Garston. It was bought from John Woollright, a wealthy Liverpool silk mercer, by a group of Liverpool businessmen in the 1840s and was, according to the contract that they signed, '*divided for the purpose of the erection thereon by such persons respectively for moderate sized villas for their own residences.*'[299] Although the contract was signed by 54 subscribers, building work began slowly. According to the 1881 Census, there were only 22

[299] George S., *Liverpool Park Estates*, (Liverpool University Press, Liverpool, 2000) page 91.

occupied households in Grassendale. The adjoining Cressington Park, which was developed slightly later, had 55 households in 1881, creating a thriving community.[300]

Both parks benefited from the development of the horse-drawn tram system and the building of the railway line to Liverpool Central by the Cheshire Lines Committee. One of the railway stations on the new line was Cressington Park Station. It was just a five-minute walk from Beechville and it allowed James to get into his office easily and quickly. Renting a house was not unusual in Victorian England, even for the aspiring middle classes. Colquhoun has pointed out that for most '*middle class Victorians, house ownership was less important than occupying the sort of property that signalled status, so that only around ten per cent actually bought their homes.*'[301]

On his return to Liverpool, one of James' first steps was to become a member of the influential Liverpool Cotton Association, which had been formed in 1882 with the amalgamation of Cotton Brokers Association and the Liverpool Cotton Exchange. The Association had the task of ensuring the trade in cotton was properly regulated.[302] It had some 600 members who each paid an annual fee of £3 3s.

In June 1884, James applied to become a member of the association. Richard Hobson, his good friend, seconded the application. Hobson was a successful and influential cotton merchant, and his support for the application would have given it much gravitas. James' application was approved at a meeting of the Directors of the association on 30th June 1884. The association minutes show that James was based in Rumford Place and had not yet moved to the Knowsley Buildings.[303] As a member of the association, James was able to participate in all aspects of its running, including its weekly meetings and organisational structures. Membership of the Association also enhanced his status as an accredited cotton merchant.

On 1st March 1886, the Board of the Cotton Association again discussed an issue relating to James. This time it concerned a dispute that he was involved in with another Liverpool firm, the Coddington Brothers. The firm at this time was headed by John Shaw Bradbury as the two Coddington brothers who had originally founded the firm were both dead. The minutes do not record the exact nature of the dispute, only that the board declined to intervene and instead stated that the matter should go to arbitration.

Cotton was Liverpool's largest and most important trade in the nineteenth century. Vast quantities of raw cotton were imported through Liverpool and taken to the Lancashire cotton mills. The finished goods were then taken back to Liverpool and exported all around the world. This maritime mercantile economy was '*by definition a flexible, deal-making and credit-based environment, in which personal interactions connected buyers with sellers.*'[304] The intermediaries who connected the buyers with the sellers were Liverpool's cotton merchants and brokers. They originally conducted their business outdoors on the quayside of the Old Dock. In 1808, a new Exchange Building was opened at the back of the Town Hall; however, the cotton merchants and brokers continued to conduct their business on the paved area outside known as *the flags*. Although working outside had its obvious disadvantages, it did mean they could keep up to date with the latest news about shipments and prices. This news was crucial, as changes in supply and demand caused constant fluctuations in the price of cotton. Big commissions and profits could be made by those who could accurately predict the market, while major losses could be sustained by those who made an error of judgement.

By the mid-1880s, James was an experienced and successful cotton merchant. His company had offices in Liverpool and in America. Edwin, his brother and business partner, had relocated the company's American base from Norfolk, Virginia, to Galveston in Texas.[305] James even appears on Galveston's tax roll in 1885 for tax assessment for the previous year. It was Edwin and not James who now spent half the year in America and half the year in Liverpool. Edwin is regularly listed in the Galveston newspapers as being amongst the returning cotton buyers to the city. In August 1887, a Texas newspaper stated that these buyers returned every cotton season with '*as much regularity as do the migratory birds flock to this section in their regular season.*'[306] With his numerous contacts on both sides of the Atlantic, James must have looked forward confidently to the future.

One of the organisations of which James was a member that had helped him in his early business career was Freemasonry. On his return to Liverpool in 1884, James continued to be an active Freemason. In both October 1886 and October 1887, he attended meetings of the St George's Lodge of Harmony in Liverpool. The records list him on both occasions as a '*visitor*' at the meetings.[307] That means two things: firstly, James had to still be a Freemason otherwise he would not have been allowed to have attended the meetings; and secondly, James must have been a member of a lodge other than the St George's Lodge of Harmony. It is possible that he was a member of the Orpheus

---

300 Ibid., page 94.
301 Colquhoun K., op cit., page 20.
302 Taylor S., *Bulls and Bears*, (C. Tinling and Co., London, 1908)
303 Liverpool Cotton Association Ltd., *Board Minute Book, Vol.1* (Sept 1882-Dec 1888).
304 Belchem J., (ed.) *Liverpool 800: Culture, Character & History*, (Liverpool Univ. Press, Liverpool, 2006) page 290.
305 Morrison and Fourmy's, *General Directory of the City of Galveston, 1886-1887*, page 265, accessed at www.ancestry.com
306 *Galveston Daily News*, 21st August 1887.
307 Robinson B., *They all love Jack*, (Fourth Estate, London, 2015) page 495.

Lodge which was based in London. There is a record that shows a person named '*J. Maybrick*' as a member of Orpheus Lodge, attending a meeting of another London lodge as a visitor.[308] Orpheus was the lodge his brother, Michael, was a member. As the lodge met on Saturday, it would have been possible for James to have attended meetings when he was visiting his brother. Apart from James and Michael, another member of the Maybrick family who was an active Freemason was their first cousin, John Maybrick, the river boat pilot. A newspaper report of February 1884, lists John as attending the funeral of a prominent Liverpool Freemason, who like him, was a member of the Walton Lodge 1086.

One of the clubs that James joined was Liverpool Cricket Club which was less than a ten minute walk from Beechville and directly opposite Battlecrease House, the home to which the Maybricks would move in 1888. James joined the club in April 1885, while Florence joined in 1888 as one of the '*lady subscribers*' with no voting rights. As women were not allowed into the main pavilion, a Lady's Pavilion was built on the eastern side of the ground.[309] The club's membership was decidedly upper-middle class in character, and joining it would have certainly appealed to the socially-aspiring Maybricks. It has been suggested that James was very active in the cricket club; for example, Morland states that James was an '*ardent member*' of the club.[310] However, there is little evidence to support this view and it is known that '*he scarcely ever participated in sports*' at the club.[311] Although he may not have played cricket, we know that he was a frequent visitor to the club. One newspaper after his death described him as a '*familiar figure on the grounds of Liverpool Cricket Club at Aigburth, near to where he lived.*'[312]

The club would have provided James with opportunities to rub shoulders with other businessmen and civic leaders. One of these was Alfred Brierley, another cotton merchant, whose family was well known and respected in Liverpool. James' last entry in the club archives sees his name crossed out and the word '*dead*' written next to it. In 1892, James' brother, Edwin, joined the club.

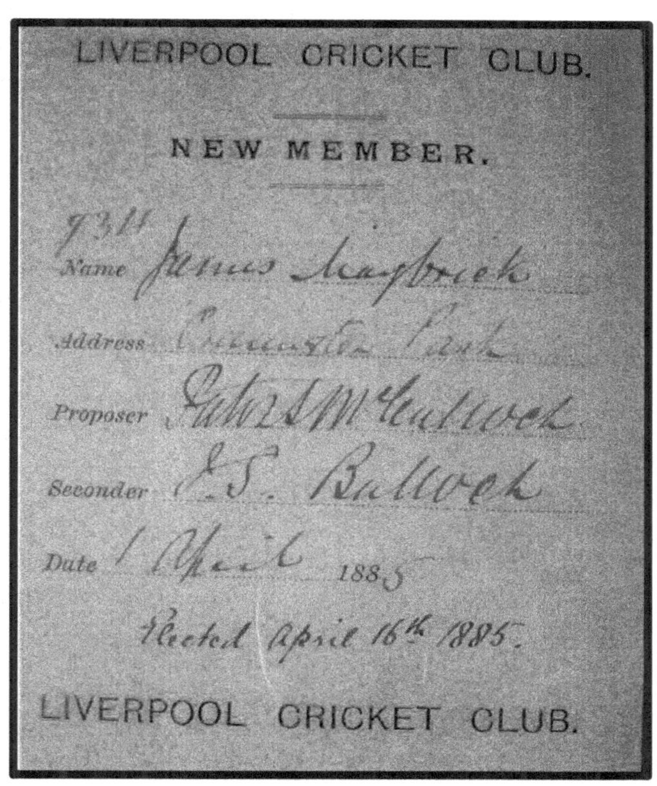

LIVERPOOL CRICKET CLUB.

NEW MEMBER.

[illegible]

Name James Maybrick

Address [illegible] Park

Proposer [illegible]

Seconder [illegible]

Date 1 April 1885

Elected April 16th 1885.

LIVERPOOL CRICKET CLUB.

James Maybrick's application to join Liverpool Cricket Club in 1885. (Chris Jones collection)

Another club that James belonged to was the exclusive Palatine Club, situated in Bold Street in Liverpool's city centre. It is not known exactly when James joined the club, but we do know that on occasions he used the club as his postal address. In a letter to David Armstrong, an attorney at law based in Louisville and New York, dated 23rd February 1881, James said that he would be shortly sailing to England from America, and gave his postal address as the Palatine Club.[313] Interestingly, a letter he received from Alfred Roe, the Baroness' New York lawyer in March 1885, had also been addressed to the Palatine Club. It is therefore likely that James used the club as a postal address to keep some of his correspondence secret from Florence.

It is little surprise that James joined the club because it was a place in which important business contacts could be made. Picton wrote that the club was a '*handsome structure in Bath Stone. Club life is not indigenous in this ancient and loyal borough. Liverpool is a place to make money in, not to spend it.*'[314] The *Visitors' Guide to Liverpool* of 1886, stated that until the establishment of political clubs in Liverpool, the Palatine Club '*was the only institution of the kind in the city, the conditions of Liverpool life being adverse to the growth and maintenance of this special product of civilisation.*'[315]

It is difficult to ascertain exactly how happy Florence was in the years after the Maybricks decided to live in Liverpool on a permanent basis. Levy wrote she was '*a foreigner and stranger in Liverpool, where she had scarcely a friend.*'[316] When Florence first arrived in Liverpool she did not know anyone in the city but, as the years passed, her easy charm allowed her to gradually acquire a circle of friends. As one American newspaper put it, the Maybricks

[308] Ibid., page 503.
[309] Onslow T., and Sturgeon J., *Dogs and Ladies Not Allowed: The 200 Year History of Liverpool Cricket Club*, (Countryvise, Birkenhead, 2007) page 48.
[310] Morland N., op cit., page 14.
[311] *The Pall Mall Gazette*, 9th August 1889.
[312] *Liverpool Citizen*, 15th May 1889.
[313] Copy of letter stored in the Richmond Chancery.
[314] Picton J.A., (with illustrations by Stephen Amer), *Memorials of Liverpool, Historical and Topographical* (Birkenhead, 1873).
[315] *Visitors' Illustrated Guide*, op. cit., page 68.
[316] Levy J.H., op cit., page 19.

were soon '*deep in the social swim of the city'* and a *'bright and charming*' Florence '*became very popular.*'[317] A Liverpool newspaper wrote that Florence moved '*somewhat extensively in society in the southern suburbs of the city and had a large circle of acquaintances. At social gatherings, and bazaars she was exceedingly popular and often seen.*' It added that in the summer Florence was a '*frequent visitor at the fine lawn-tennis ground at Cressington,*' which was very close to Beechville.[318] Christie perhaps summed up the situation best when he wrote Florence had '*many ostensible friends but no intimates.*'[319]

Despite this lack of a close female confidante, it is likely that Florence was content with the state of her marriage. She lived a comfortable existence in an exclusive Liverpool suburb. Her husband appeared to be making good money and they could entertain friends on a regular basis and in some style. Florence liked to be the centre of attention, and took pleasure when complimented on her looks and fine clothes. She had a good-natured charm, and her friends called her '*Birdie*' after her favourite song.[320]

Palatine Club, Bold Street, Liverpool

Like other middle-class Victorian women, Florence lived a life of enforced leisure. Whilst this existence was an anathema to many women, it suited Florence. In Beechville, the Maybricks had three servants.[321] They freed her from the daily grind of household and maternal chores and this allowed Florence to indulge in her passion for the arts and her love of shopping. Her husband appeared devoted to her and happy to indulge her every whim. His affectionate nickname for her was '*Bunny*' and, despite their age difference, they still enjoyed things in common, including entertaining, cards, horse riding and horse racing. To friends of the Maybricks, they must have appeared an almost perfect couple.

Although none of the serious issues that were to take the Maybrick marriage to breaking point had yet emerged, there was one matter that was a constant cause of friction between James and his wife and, more significantly, between James and the Baroness. This issue stemmed back to 1879, when the Baroness had agreed to a proposal from David Armstrong, a lawyer from Kentucky with offices in Louisville and New York. He offered to sell the lands she owned in Kentucky and Virginia and split the profits from the sale in half. Armstrong later described it as the worst decision he had ever made as it was to end up involving him in many years of constant wrangling with the Baroness. In 1881, not long after his marriage to Florence, the Baroness asked James to get involved in her ongoing legal battle over her land claims in America. The Baroness wrote to her lawyer in New York describing her new son-in-law as a businessman of '*high standing,*' saying he was prepared to '*assist*' her as he was devotedly in love with Florence.[322]

James wrote twice to David Armstrong but received no reply. This prompted Florence to write a letter to Armstrong on 1st November 1881, stating that her mother was '*very anxious*' he should communicate with her husband '*with regard to the Virginia property*' and she hoped to hear from him shortly. Florence added a rather telling final paragraph to the letter, stating '*the Baroness trusts to your honour and discretion with regard to any private matters [*originally she had written affairs, but changed the word to matters*] she may have confided with you... as my husband is quite ignorant of her personal affairs.*'[323]

What was it that James was '*quite ignorant*' about? It is likely that he did not know the full story of the Baroness' colourful social and love life. Perhaps that was the reason why Florence had altered the word '*affairs*' to '*matters*' in her letter. It is also likely that James had little knowledge of the true state of the Baroness' finances. On paper she

---

317 *Columbus Enquirer Sun* (Columbus, Georgia) 10th August 1889.
318 *Liverpool Courier*, 31st May 1889.
319 Christie T.L., op cit., page 43.
320 *Liverpool Review*, 6th July 1889.
321 *Liverpool Weekly Courier*, 25th January 1890.
322 Christie T.L., op cit., page 47.
323 Copy of letter stored in the Richmond Chancery dated 1st November 1881.

appeared to be a wealthy woman, owning a high-value house in New York and vast tracts of lands in the Southern States. However, the reality was very different. The house in New York was heavily mortgaged; her ownership of the lands was disputed; she was deeply in debt and was being pursued by creditors in both Europe and America. It is little wonder, therefore, that Florence did not want James to know the full extent of her mother's financial affairs.

Armstrong replied to Florence's letter and in December 1881, James sent him a communication in which he tried to fix a time and date for a meeting, in either New York or Louisville.[324] After receiving a telegram back from Armstrong, James arranged to meet him in early January 1882 in the Hoffman Hotel in New York.[325] On 16th January 1882, the Baroness signed a document that gave Florence a one-third interest in the lands or proceeds of the Virginia and Kentucky properties.[326]

The fact that the Baroness signed such a document shows that relations between her and James were positive, and she must have been optimistic that a potential buyer could be found for the lands. On 19th January 1882, James sent another message to Armstrong asking him to clarify the exact whereabouts of the land that the Baroness claimed to own as she had indicated to him that most of it was in Virginia and West Virginia, yet Armstrong had told him that over half the land was actually in Kentucky. James also said the Baroness had been approached by some unknown party in Paris who was interested in buying the property.

The paper trail between James and Armstrong sheds a little light on the rather murky world of the Baroness' land claims. It also shows that James became increasingly aware the Baroness hadn't told him the full truth about her dealings, and that much of her land claims were tenuous at best. At some point, Armstrong had made James aware of the Baroness' debts and the relationship between James and the Baroness started to deteriorate.

The Baroness' main income was the relatively small allowance of $800 a year that was provided jointly by Florence and her brother Holbrook, which was derived from the rent they received from the family home in East Fourteenth Street, New York. This flow of income was crucial to both the Baroness and her children. At one point, James wrote to the family's lawyers in New York as he was '*anxious to hear*' whether they had been able to re-rent the house. He added it was '*essential*' that the house '*does not remain empty even for a day.*'[327] While the Baroness' financial plight made her vulnerable, her own actions did little to help her cause. She left a trail of debts and broken promises, and was less than honest and transparent in many of her dealings. During the bitter court case between the Baroness and Armstrong in 1906, Armstrong said the Baroness '*victimised and defrauded all who dealt with her.*' The author, Trevor Christie, in a letter to Florence Aunspaugh dated 1942, described the Baroness as a '*ruthless, grasping old harridan who violated her pledged word time and time again and destroyed the faith of her closest friends.*'[328]

The deteriorating relationship between the Baroness and James is clearly evident in a series of letters that the Baroness wrote to Armstrong in the 1880s. In one of them, she wrote that James was a '*man who judges everything by its money value and expresses no belief in sentiment of any kind.*' She described her finances as '*desperate*' and that James '*did not approve*' of the money sent to her by her daughter. On another occasion, she wrote that she didn't want '*one word of any kind said to the Maybricks about my affairs. Their conduct to me has been of a nature to force me to decide for some time past to keep my affairs to myself and for myself. I have up till now treated them with love and frankness. I have been cast off, insulted, doubted and treated with utter disregard.*'

In yet another letter she wrote, '*Maybrick expressed the opinion and caused my poor child to write "that I best allow my home to be sold. I ought to take an attic room and do my own work; it was absurd to keep a servant or a little dog" (my only companion). I need never expect any help or aid from them.*'[329]

As feelings of animosity increased between the James and the Baroness, Florence's brother Holbrook Chandler, who was studying medicine in Paris, became involved in the dispute. In 1884, in a letter to his mother, he wrote: '*I don't pretend to know his [James Maybrick] tricks, but he has forbidden Florie telling us a word of his affairs and has completely thrown dust in her eyes. We unfortunately cannot write to her or hear from her except through him, and he dictates her letters. I greatly regret this most unexpected attitude of Maybrick's, turning out to be such a bully and brute, but such being the fact we have to protect ourselves as far as practicable.*'[330]

The letter has been interpreted in various ways; in particular, the phrase '*bully and brute*' has clear connotations of domestic violence. One is left with the distinct impression that James was bullying his wife so that she wouldn't make good on her financial commitment to her mother. In isolation, this letter does appear quite damning, but it needs to be seen in the context of two years of increasingly bitter communications between James and the Baroness. There were wrongs on both sides. James' efforts to help the Baroness had come to nothing, and he was left feeling

---

[324] Copy of memorandum stored in the Richmond Chancery dated 28th December 1881.
[325] Copy of memorandum stored in the Richmond Chancery dated 9th January 1882.
[326] Documents from the *Baroness von Roques versus David Armstrong case* (1906) stored in the Richmond Chancery.
[327] Copy of letter stored in the Richmond Chancery dated 27th November 1884.
[328] Trevor Christie Collection.
[329] Documents from the *Baroness von Roques versus David Armstrong case* (1906) stored in the Richmond Chancery.
[330] Christie T.L., op cit., page 48.

angry and exasperated by the experience. He wrote, '*unfortunately my past experiences has taught me that I cannot rely upon the verbal promises of the Baroness.*'[331]

James had tried to help expedite the Baroness' land claims, but in so doing he had found not pots of gold but debts and deceit. It had made him bitter and hostile towards his mother-in-law, and he directed Florence to cut her mother's allowance. His actions made the Baroness' already precarious financial position even worse. They also had an impact on Holbrook. He was struggling to pay his way through medical school, and he would not have wanted the extra burden of finding additional money to help keep his mother. In that context, one can more easily understand the anger that he directed towards James, and why he called him a '*bully and a brute.*' It must have been a difficult time for Florence, caught in the middle of a dispute between her husband and her mother and brother.

The financial troubles of Holbrook were the least of his problems. He had been seriously ill for some time, suffering from consumption (tuberculosis). The Baroness would have known the illness was almost always fatal, and that Holbrook faced an early death. In a letter to Armstrong she expressed the view that if she had '*the means his life could have been prolonged. The expenses of the illness are very great and I am in great distress and need.*'[332]

Holbrook died in Paris in April 1885, and was buried in one of the city's graveyards. James, but not Florence, travelled to Paris for the funeral. Florence probably did not attend due to concerns about her own health. In March 1885, in a letter James wrote to Alfred Roe in New York, he added the final line '*with kind regards from my wife who I am glad to say is improving in health.*'[333] The Baroness later wrote that Florence had '*the same bronchial affliction as that of which my son died two years ago, and physicians have told me that if ever settled down on her lungs, it would be fatal.*'[334] The funeral card sent to Holbrook's friends listed many of his relatives but, surprisingly, there was no mention of Florence. Perhaps her mother was still angry with her over money issues, and may have blamed her for her brother's early death.

Holbrook Chandler had made his final will and testament in New York in March 1880. There are two significant aspects to the will. Firstly, Holbrook left his gold watch and jewellery to his godson, young William Chandler of Mobile Alabama. The fact that he was the child's godfather demonstrates that he and Florence, if not the Baroness, had rebuilt their relationship with the Chandler side of the family. Secondly, he left his estate in the first instance to his mother. The key element of that estate would have been the income from renting the property on East Fourteenth Street in New York. Although this income went to his mother, he ensured that it was managed by the family's lawyer in New York. He may have loved his mother, but he probably didn't trust her to effectively manage any property assets, especially if she was residing in France.

This income would have been extremely welcome to the Baroness, as she would no longer have to survive on an allowance provided by her children. The income derived from Holbrook's estate only passed to Florence (or her children if Florence had herself died) after the death of her mother. In the years immediately prior to his death, Holbrook would have been pleased that he had sequenced his will in this particular manner as he would not have wanted the income from his estate to have fallen into the hands of James.

Although Florence was no doubt badly shaken by the death of her brother, her life in Liverpool appeared to get back to normal fairly quickly, and by the autumn of 1885 she was pregnant again. On 3rd April 1886, the Maybricks, along with young James (Bobo) and their nursemaid, signed in as guests at the Hand Hotel in Llangollen, North Wales. Unfortunately, the register does not provide dates for the departure of the guests. A week later, on 10th April, Miss Gertrude Janion, the youngest of the Janion daughters, signed into the same hotel. Gertrude, who was a similar age to Florence, had possibly gone to keep Florence company while her husband went out walking or had returned to work in Liverpool.

The Hand Hotel seems to have been a favourite of the Maybricks and other Liverpool cotton merchants. Hotel records show that James stayed in the hotel on a couple of occasions. After his death, the Liverpool police visited Llangollen because a medicine bottle found at Battlecrease had the name of Mr Humphrey Jones, the local chemist, on the label. They also checked the Hand Hotel register, but could find no mention of Florence and Brierley staying together at the same time in the hotel. According to the hotel register, while Florence had not appeared to stay in the hotel after April 1886, Brierley had stayed there in January 1888, but he had been '*accompanied by a gentleman.*'[335]

On 20th July 1886, Florence gave birth to a daughter, who they named Gladys Evelyn, at her home. Dr Hopper from Rodney Street and Mrs Howell, a private nurse from Hale, were in attendance at the birth. It had been a difficult labour, and it took Florence some months to recover her strength. James wrote to her mother in Paris that '*the doctors made a fine mess of Florie's case, but thank God she is getting on alright.*'[336]

[331] Letter from James Maybrick to Mr Potter, dated 6th December 1887 and stored in the Richmond Chancery.
[332] Christie T.L., op cit., page 48.
[333] Copy of letter stored in the Richmond Chancery dated 17th March 1885.
[334] *Liverpool Echo*, 14th August 1889.
[335] *Liverpool Daily Post*, 15th June 1889.
[336] Graham A. and Emmas C., op cit., page 39.

Not long after the birth a serious scarlet fever epidemic hit Liverpool. According to an interview given by the Baroness in August 1889, young James – who would have been aged around five – was '*seized*' with the illness, and as a result, '*Mr Maybrick, the baby, and the nurse, immediately went away to Wales.*'[337] The Baroness fixed the date as being two years earlier, placing it in 1887; but she also said that her '*daughter had not recovered from the effects of the baby's birth, and had been severely ill with an attack of bronchitis.*' The fact that Florence was still suffering the effects of childbirth would suggest that the incident occurred in 1886.

Scarlet fever is a highly infectious disease and was, until the discovery of antibiotics, a potential killer. Florence decided to take no chances. According to her mother, while James and Gladys headed off to Wales, Florence remained in Beechville with her son. She was: '*determined to stay alone and nurse her boy. She was six weeks in that house alone. There was no other person there except the cook. The cook prepared her food and set it on the floor outside the door. A disinfected curtain hung in front of the door. There was nobody to change the linen or do anything except my daughter. After her meals she washed the plates clean and put them outside the door. For six weeks she sat by the bedside of her little boy and saved his life.*'[338]

Robert Janion (1816-1881) and Domitila Janion (1830-1911)

The whole episode is revealing, as it demonstrates that while Florence could be lazy and frivolous, there was another side to her; she could also show resolve and determination. James has been criticised for running off to Wales at the first sign of danger; however, his actions were a sensible precaution. Gladys was at risk of infection. He would have also remembered his brother Alfred who died from scarlet fever when he was four years old.

On 14th September 1886, the christening of Gladys took place in the Anglican church of St Nicholas in Halewood, just outside Liverpool. The happy event occurred in the same church in which James had been christened on 29th May 1882. The church was chosen because it was the parish church of Domitila Janion, the godmother of both children. Her husband, Robert Janion, who had died in 1881, had been a trusted friend of James even though he was some 20 years older than him. One of the Janion daughters, Mrs Briggs, said in an interview she gave after Florence's trial, '*Mr Maybrick, long before his marriage, was a friend of my father and visited our house frequently. On several occasions he gave little presents to myself and my sisters.*'[339]

Robert Cheshyre Janion (1816-1881) was born in Cheshire but emigrated as a young man to the Sandwich Islands, where he became a merchant specialising in beef exports. In 1845, he formed a business partnership with a pair of Liverpool merchants, James and John Starkey, and they established the trading firm of Starkey, Janion and Co. They built up a fleet of sailing ships in which to export Hawaiian sugar and products of the island's whaling fishery in a triangular trade between Honolulu, the city of Victoria in British Columbia and Liverpool. Having made a sizeable fortune, Robert Janion returned to Liverpool in 1851, having two years earlier married Domitila Rodriques, a noted beauty and daughter of the Chilean consul to the Sandwich Islands. In Liverpool, the family settled at Woolton Grove in Gateacre, a 12 bedroomed mansion set in 15 acres of grounds. At some point, James was introduced to the Janion's good-looking daughters Matilda, Gertrude, Ellen, Vida, Minnie and Constance (known as Martha). He may have even been engaged to Matilda, the eldest daughter, but she eventually married an Indian Army captain, Thomas Briggs, in 1871. Matilda's marriage was not a success; the couple split up and Thomas Briggs died in March 1893. In 1882, Martha wed a stockbroker named Charles Hughes, who lived across the road from Woolton Grove.

The nature of the relationship between the Maybricks and the Janions has been much scrutinised. The fact that Domitila Janion was chosen to be godmother to both the Maybrick children demonstrates that James (and probably

[337] *Liverpool Echo*, 14th August 1889.
[338] *Liverpool Echo*, 14th August 1889.
[339] *Evening Express*, 15th August 1889.

Florence) thought highly of the family. The more problematic relationship seems to have been with the Janion daughters. It has been argued that the guilty verdict at Florence's trial was in part due to the role played by two of the sisters, Mrs Briggs and Mrs Hughes, both of whom gave evidence for the prosecution at the trial. In his book, Christie, refers to the two sisters, plus Nurse Yapp, as a '*deadly cabal.*' He quotes from a contemporary newspaper that commented that, if Florence was executed, '*she will have been done to death by women.*'[340]

Florence Aunspaugh wrote that Mrs Briggs despised Florence. If this was true, perhaps she was jealous at seeing the younger woman in the role she once coveted. Another accusation made against Mrs Briggs was that she was often in the Maybrick home, and exercised great influence over the household staff. After the trial she flatly denied this saying: '*I never went to the house except by Mrs Maybrick's invitation. I never spoke to her husband against her in my life. We were on good terms with her, and it is cruel to impute malicious motives to us. I never interfered in any way. I was always sent for if there was trouble or sickness, and I did my best for them both. Whenever Mrs Maybrick was ill, I helped her as a friend and neighbour.*'[341]

On the positive side, Mrs Briggs did provide the Maybricks with accommodation on two separate occasions. James and Florence occasionally borrowed money from her. Florence borrowed £100 from Mrs Briggs around the time of her brother's death in 1885, paying it back in instalments.[342] It is therefore likely, that after a frosty start, the relationship between Florence and Mrs Briggs thawed and they became more friendly towards one another, without ever becoming intimate.

LINKS TO THE RIPPER DIARY: FREEMASONRY AND THE MAYBRICKS

In his book *Jack the Ripper: The Final Solution*, published in 1976, Stephen Knight proposed a highly controversial theory involving the British Royal Family, the British Government and leading Freemasons as being the perpetrators of the Whitechapel murders. In simple terms, he suggested that the five canonical victims were all murdered to cover up a secret marriage between Prince Albert Victor, Duke of Clarence and Avondale, who was second in line to the throne, and Annie Elizabeth Crook, a working-class woman and a Catholic.

According to the theory, the Government was worried that if news of this marriage reached the public, it would discredit the Royal Family and help ferment a revolution. To prevent this from happening, it was necessary to kill four prostitutes who were trying to blackmail the authorities about the secret wedding. A fifth prostitute was killed in error as a result of mistaken identity.

The murders themselves were carried out not by a single person, but involved three people; '*two killers and an accomplice.*'[343] A crucial element of the theory was that the murderous conspiracy was secretly '*carried out by and on behalf of*' the country's most influential Freemasons, who were the '*real power behind the Throne and the Government.*' These men were concerned that '*if the Throne went, and Britain became a republic, the Masons went too.*'[344]

The main source for Knight's book was a man named Joseph Gorman Sickert (1925-2003), an artist and picture restorer, who claimed to be the illegitimate son of the well-known artist Walter Sickert and Alice Margaret Crook. He in turn claimed that he had been told the account by his own father, Walter Sickert. He said Alice Crook was the daughter of Annie Crook, the woman who had supposedly secretly married Prince Albert Victor. His story was first aired in a 1973 BBC documentary on Jack the Ripper before being investigated by Stephen Knight.

Prince Albert Victor was the eldest son of Prince Edward (later Edward VII) and Princess Alexandra. According to Gorman Sickert, Princess Alexandra was concerned about her son's '*personal development,*' so introduced him to the famous painter Walter Sickert, in the hope that he might teach him about art and, in so doing, encourage the Prince's personality to grow. As a result of this decision, Prince Albert Victor met Annie Crook, a young shop-girl who was one of Sickert's models, at the artist's studio in Cleveland Street, London.

Gorman Sickert said the Prince and Annie Crook had an affair, and then married in secret. The two witnesses were Walter Sickert and Mary Kelly, who was to be the final Ripper victim. Gorman Sickert told Knight that the Prince and Annie Crook had a daughter, Alice Crook, born on 18th April 1885, and that the child and her mother lived in a basement apartment on Cleveland Street. An Irish Catholic woman named Mary Kelly was paid by Sickert to move into the basement apartment and act as nanny to the young girl.

In early 1888, Queen Victoria and the British Prime Minister, Lord Salisbury, found out about the secret marriage and the child. Salisbury ordered a police raid on the premises in Cleveland Street and two people were taken away.

---

[340] Christie T.L., op cit., page 57.
[341] *Evening Express*, 15th August 1889.
[342] Morland N., op cit., page 17.
[343] Knight, S., *Jack the Ripper: The Final Solution*, (Chancellor Press, London, 2003) page 13.
[344] Ibid., page 28.

The first was Prince Albert, who was returned to Court and '*placed under strict supervision.*' The second was Annie Crook. She was confined for 156 days at Guy's Hospital, and later at various other institutions, before dying 32 years later, certified insane. Somehow, Mary Kelly and the baby managed to avoid being seized by the police. Kelly gave the child back to Sickert and he took her to Dieppe, France, where she spent the rest of her childhood.[345]

After giving up the child Mary Kelly turned to prostitution to fight off poverty and starvation. With the help of three fellow prostitutes she decided, in July or August 1888, to blackmail the authorities in a desperate effort to raise funds. Although it was only for a '*paltry*' amount, it frightened Salisbury and his fellow Freemasons into drastic action. It was decided that Kelly and the three other women involved in her scheme – Mary Ann Nichols, Annie Chapman and Elizabeth Stride – had to be '*rendered harmless.*'

Sir William Gull (1816-1890), the Queen's physician and a leading Freemason, was '*entrusted with the mission.*' Gull was the man who had institutionalised Annie Crook with a bogus certificate on insanity. What Salisbury did not take into account was Gull's '*highly developed sense of the bizarre*', and his determination to '*eliminate the women strictly according to Masonic tradition.*'[346] Gull was driven to Whitechapel by the coachman John Netley, the man who had supposedly driven Prince Albert Victor to Cleveland Street. Netley tracked down the women and then lured them into the carriage. He also assisted Gull in the murder and mutilation of the women. The third person involved was none other than Sir Robert Anderson, Assistant Commissioner of Scotland Yard. He was another high-ranking Freemason, and belonged to the same lodge as Salisbury and Gull. His main role was to prevent the murders from being properly investigated by the police.

Sir William Gull (1816-1890)

The first two victims, Nichols and Chapman, were killed inside the carriage and their dead bodies were placed by Netley where they were later found. The attempt to lure Stride into the carriage failed as she was too drunk, so Netley followed her and killed her by Berner Street while Sir Robert Anderson kept watch. Catherine Eddowes was killed in the carriage on the same night as Stride's death. Her death was a case of mistaken identity, because she used the alias Mary Ann Kelly and was therefore confused with Mary Jane Kelly. The last victim, Mary Jane Kelly, was the only victim to be killed inside her own home.

The fact that all the women involved in the blackmail scheme were dead caused the killings to stop. Netley twice tried to kill the child, Alice Crook, but failed in both attempts. According to Gorman Sickert, after Netley's second failure he was chased by an angry crowd and threw himself into the Thames, where he drowned. The child lived into adulthood and married a man called Gorman, who turned out to be impotent. She then became Sickert's mistress, which she remained for 12 years. They had one son, Joseph Gorman, who later changed his name to Joseph Gorman Sickert. Walter Sickert died in 1942 and Alice in 1950.

When Joseph Gorman Sickert first told Knight his account, the author had the '*growing conviction that his story was not – could not – be true.*'[347] Despite these doubts, Knight was sufficiently intrigued by Gorman Sickert's account to interview him further and investigate his allegations. After unearthing some interesting but entirely circumstantial evidence – such as the fact that both Albert Victor's mother and Alice Crook were deaf, there was widespread anti-Catholic sentiment at the time of the Ripper murders, and Prince Albert Victor was linked to a scandal in Cleveland Street – Knight became convinced that Gorman Sickert's story was true.

Knight supported the idea that there was a Masonic conspiracy at the heart of the murders by pointing to what he considered to be similarities between the Ripper killings and certain Masonic rituals. For example, relying on evidence from noted Ripperologist Donald Rumbelow he said all the victims were strangled before being mutilated. As they were dead, the cutting of the throat served no practical purpose; however, the act was significant because it was '*a sacred part of Freemason ritual.*' Both Chapman and Eddowes were left with their intestines deliberately placed on their shoulders, an act that Knight said was '*definitely Masonic.*' Chapman had rings and farthings placed at her feet, another Masonic ritual. Eddowes had triangular flaps of skin cut on both of her cheeks. According to

---

[345] Ibid., pages 27-28.
[346] Ibid., pages 34-35.
[347] Ibid., page 30.

Knight, this had a '*precise Masonic relevance*' as a sacred sign of Masonry is two triangles, which '*represents the altar top of the Holy Royal Arch.*'[348]

To Knight, the most conclusive proof that the murders were part of a Masonic conspiracy was the decision of Sir Charles Warren, Commissioner of Police and a leading Freemason, to order the removal of the chalk writing on the wall in Goulston Street. Warren even forbade the taking of pictures of the graffito before it was removed. The words on the wall were: '*The Juwes are the men That Will not be Blamed for nothing.*' As this was possibly the only real clue ever left by the Ripper, alongside the scrap of Eddowes' apron found on the ground underneath the writing, Warren's decision was astonishing. He later excused his behaviour of the grounds that the words might have inspired anti-Jewish riots. Knight argues that the key word in the writing was '*Juwes*,' which is not a misspelling of Jews but instead refers to the three apprentice Masons, Jubela, Jubelo and Jebelum, who killed Hiram Abiff, the Grand Master who was in charge of the building of Solomon's Temple. Warren wanted to destroy the writing as he was alarmed that it would reveal that the murderer was a Freemason.

Sir Charles Warren, Commissioner of the Metropolitan Police

Although Knight's book was a bestseller, his ideas received a battery of criticisms from experts on the Ripper murders. Paul Begg wrote that the entire story '*collapses through lack of support.*'[349] Begg pointed out elements of the account that were inaccurate. For example, Walter Sickert isn't known to have had a studio in Cleveland Street, and although Annie Crook – who wasn't actually a Catholic – was eventually committed to a lunacy ward, she enjoyed many years of liberty before that happened. It is also the case that John Netley did not die in the Thames, but was killed in a traffic accident in 1903.

In echoes of Michael Barrett's behaviour years later, in 1978 Gorman Sickert confessed to the *Sunday Times* that his story of the Masonic conspiracy was a hoax. After Knight's death in 1985, Gorman Sickert retracted his confession and claimed he had only said it was a hoax to protect the reputation of Walter Sickert. For those who had always doubted his original account, Gorman Sickert's confession and retraction only confirmed their rejection of his story. According to the authors of the *Jack the Ripper A to Z*, '*No part of Joseph Gorman Sickert's story, as allegedly told him by Walter Sickert, has ever been substantiated by concrete evidence and many details of Stephen Knight's representation of the story have been completely disproved.*'[350]

Despite the criticisms of Knight's book, some Ripper authors have recycled certain of his ideas. Paul Feldman latched on to a suggestion by Nigel Morland that the woman who was imprisoned against her will might have actually been Florence Maybrick rather than Annie Crook. Feldman also refers to that fact that Netley's fatal traffic accident occurred very close to the London home of Michael Maybrick, a leading Freemason.[351]

Bruce Robinson, in his 2015 book *They All Love Jack*, also revisited some of the ideas proposed by Knight. In particular, he resurrected the notion of a direct link between the murders and Freemasonry. He wrote, '*Masonry permeates every fibre of this conundrum.*' There was, he wrote, a great cover-up by the police and the Establishment, and this concealment was '*a conspiracy of HM executive, who almost without exception were Freemasons.*'[352] Robinson argues that it became apparent to the senior police officers leading the Ripper investigations that the perpetrator was a Freemason, and therefore '*to protect itself, the System was obliged to protect him – and that's about the size of the mystery.*'[353] Robinson also agreed with Knight's assertion that the mutilated bodies showed signs of

[348] Ibid., pages 168-170.
[349] Begg, P., *Jack the Ripper: The Facts*, (Robson Books, London, 2004) page 400.
[350] Begg P., Fido M. and Skinner K., op cit., (2010) page 467.
[351] Feldman P., op cit., page 313.
[352] Robinson B., op cit., page 59.
[353] Ibid., page 130.

Masonic rituals. Leading figures, including Sir Charles Warren, recognised these rituals and therefore became determined to cover-up key incidents. In so doing, Warren and his fellow Freemasons were '*actually covering up the murderer's tracks*' and that made them '*accessories to murder.*'[354]

Knight, Feldman and Robinson all target Freemasons to be Jack the Ripper, though they all have different candidates. Knight suggests that three people were involved in the killings rather than just one person; Feldman focuses on James Maybrick, whom he believes was the author of the Ripper Diary; while Robinson suggests that the real culprit was not James, but his brother, Michael Maybrick. Robinson wrote that Michael's '*primary motive*' for the murders '*was a hatred of women, and whores in particular.*'[355] Robinson also argues that Michael had another motive that drove him to commit the Ripper murders and additional murders, and this motive was his hatred of Freemasonry, which he hated no less than the women he killed. Robinson wrote, '*what motivated him [Michael] was ritual. He wanted body parts, trophies, wanted to leave his mark.*'[356] Robinson suggests that Michael's decision to kill the prostitutes in Whitechapel was '*purely opportunistic. The logistics were crude, and apart from the ridicule of Freemasonry, and Warren along with it, there was no master plan.*'[357]

It is a verifiable fact that both James and Michael Maybrick were Freemasons. Records exist showing that James was initiated into the St George's Lodge of Harmony (No. 32) in Liverpool in September 1870.[358] James probably saw Freemasonry as a useful stepping-stone to help boost his career ambitions. James wasn't just a Freemason; he was an active and enthusiastic Freemason. Evidence to support this view is provided by a document which records that, in January 1877, he was nominated by the Worshipful Master of the St George's Lodge No. 32 to become its secretary for the following year. As this was a prestigious post, it demonstrates James must have been well respected within the ranks of Liverpool Freemasonry. He would have played a pivotal role in the life of the Lodge, and would have had a key responsibility for communications between the provincial and national arms of the organisation.

Michael was initiated into Freemasonry in May 1876. He was to be a leading Freemason, becoming one of its national officers. All the evidence points to the fact that, rather than hating Freemasonry as Robinson suggests, Michael revelled in his membership of the organisation. Michael loved being a leading Freemason as it brought him into the orbit of the Prince of Wales, who was the most important Freemason in the country. He also came into contact with many members of the government, who were also Freemasons. Michael attended and helped organise many high-profile Freemason events. Michael was also a member of the Savage Club, a gentlemen's club in London whose membership included leading figures in the fields of music, the arts, law, literature and science. In April 1882, the Prince of Wales was invited to become an honorary member of the club, and at a dinner and gala night to celebrate the occasion Michael was one of the performers selected to entertain the Prince. Michael was also a member of Britain's military reserve. In February 1886, he joined the Artists' Corps (20th Middlesex). In March 1889, he performed in front of the Prince of Wales and his family at an event to mark the opening of the Corps' new headquarters. Michael Maybrick was not an anti-establishment or an anti-Freemasonry figure; he was a conservative, a royalist, and a Freemason to the very core of his being.

According to Bruce Robinson, James Maybrick was '*an active Freemason until the day of his death.*'[359] Robinson argues that the Maybrick family crest that James had commissioned just prior to his wedding had a Masonic symbol on it. It featured a falcon, representing Horus the ancient Egyptian god, in '*deference to the memory of Masonry's first Grand Master, Hiram Abiff.*'[360] In both October 1886 and October 1887, James attended meetings of Lodge 32 in Liverpool; however, as he was listed as a visitor at these meetings, he must have then been a member of a different lodge. Robinson suggests that both he and his brother Michael were members of the Orpheus Lodge based in London. One of the two ministers at James' funeral in May 1889 was the Rev. Dr Hyde, a long-standing friend and another active Freemason. Therefore, while it might be the case that the mutilated bodies of the Ripper murders did exhibit certain Masonic rituals, there is no evidence to link either James or Michael to the killings. There is also no evidence to suggest that either James or Michael hated Freemasonry; in fact, the evidence that does exist suggests that their support for the organisation was active, enthusiastic and complete.

Intriguingly, Bruce Robinson argues that attempts have been made to try and remove James' name from the list of Freemason members. According to the official Freemason records stored at Freemasons' Hall in London, James was never a member of the organisation; although one document that Robinson did receive from the Freemasons suggested that James was briefly a member of the organisation from January 1873 to his resignation in 1874. This particular document cannot be accurate as several other documents exist that show James remained a Freemason until

[354] Ibid., pages 146 and 337.
[355] Ibid., page 496.
[356] Ibid., page 119.
[357] Ibid., page 572.
[358] www.ancestry.com
[359] Robinson B., op cit., page 492.
[360] Ibid., page 759.

his death in 1889. For example, there is an entry in the official Freemason yearbook of 1888 that lists both James and Michael Maybrick as eighteenth-degree Freemasons.[361]

Robinson suggests that the attempts to remove all traces of James from Freemason records were motivated by the belief, promoted by his brother Michael, that James was Jack the Ripper. The organisation wanted to distance itself from James to try and avoid any potential scandal if his name came into the public domain as the notorious serial killer.

If an effort was made to try and remove James' name from the world of Freemasonry then it was not a very good attempt, as there are several examples of documents recording James' involvement in the organisation still in existence. In some cases, these documents are not too difficult to find. The book outlining the history of Lodge 32, written by two Freemasons from it, not only lists James Maybrick as being a member of the Lodge but even includes a paragraph about him stating that he has been identified as a possible candidate to be Jack the Ripper.[362] That book was published in 2005, ten years before Robinson's book was published.

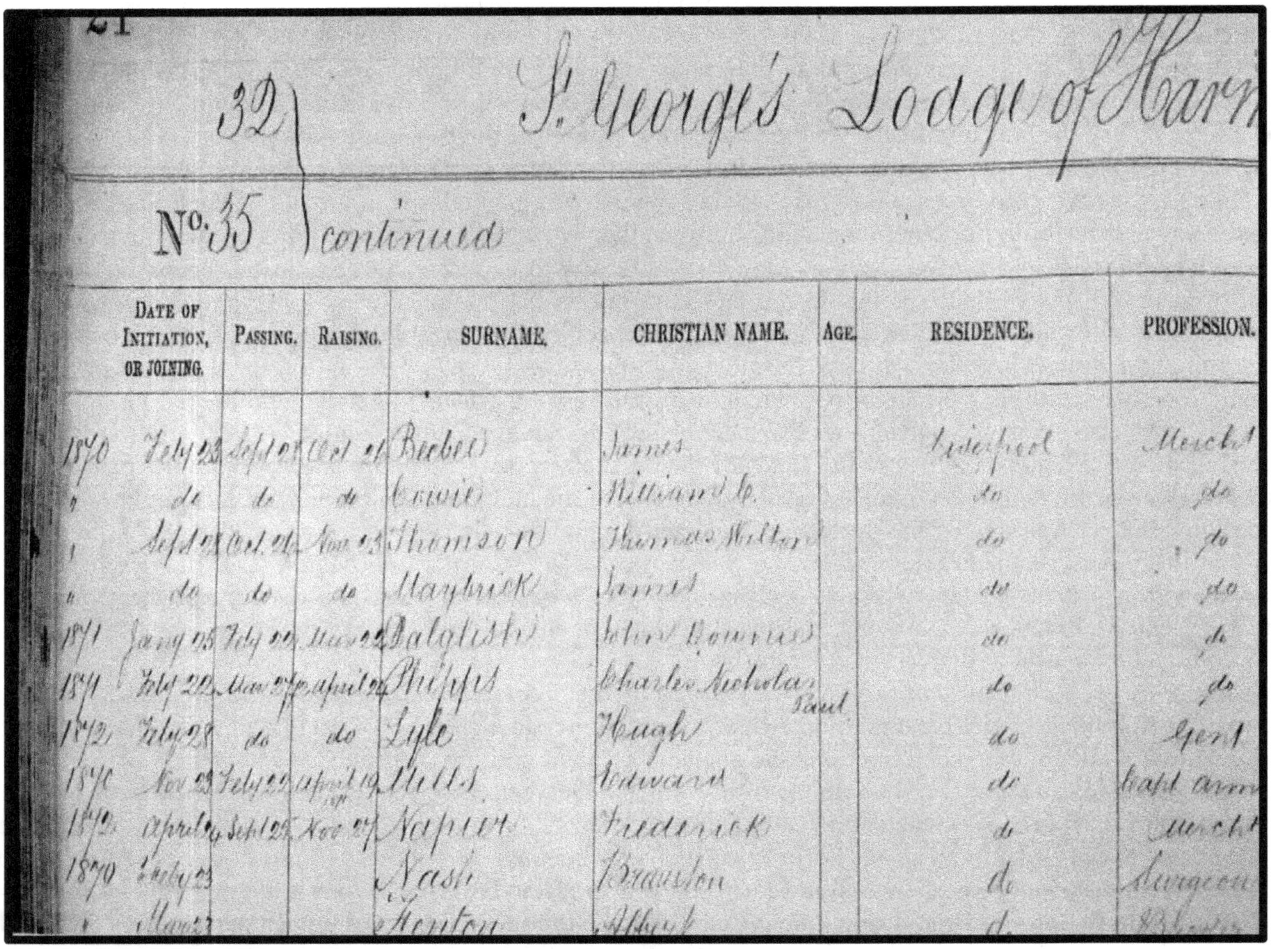

32 St. George's Lodge of Harm[ony]

No. 35 continued

Date of Initiation, or Joining.	Passing.	Raising.	Surname.	Christian Name.	Age.	Residence.	Profession.
1870 Feby 23	[illegible]	[illegible]	[illegible]	James		Liverpool	Mercht
do	do	do	Cowie	William C.		do	do
Sept [illegible]	[illegible]	[illegible]	Thomson	Thomas Walter		do	do
do	do	do	Maybrick	James		do	do
1871 Jany [illegible]	Feby [illegible]	[illegible]	Dalglish	John Bowness		do	do
1871 Feby 22	[illegible]	April [illegible]	[illegible]	Charles Nicholas Paul		do	do
1872 Feby 28	do	do	Lyle	Hugh		do	Gent
1870 Nov [illegible]	Feby [illegible]	April [illegible]	[illegible]	Edward		do	[illegible]
1872 April [illegible]	Sept [illegible]	Nov [illegible]	Napier	Frederick		do	Mercht
1870 Feby 23			Nash	[illegible]		do	Surgeon
[illegible]			Fenton	Albert		do	[illegible]

Record of James Maybrick's membership of the Freemason's St George's Lodge of Harmony (Chris Jones collection)

The fact that such documents exist undermines Robinson's hypothesis that there was a secret Masonic conspiracy that tried to destroy all traces of James being a Freemason. Also, if some records did get deliberately destroyed at Freemason Hall, then a more likely motive would have been to distance the Freemasons from a man who was shown to be a serial adulterer, drug abuser and whose reputation had been badly damaged from the evidence provided by the defence team at his wife's trial for murder. Damage limitation by Freemasonry, possibly; great conspiracy to protect the ruling elite, extremely unlikely.

[361] Ibid., pages 504-5.
[362] Hill M. and Griffiths B., *32 CCL*, (published by the Freemasons, 2005) page 52.

6

MARITAL STRIFE

The year 1887 should have been a good one for the Maybricks. The couple had been back in Liverpool for three years and they lived in some style in an affluent suburb of the city. In July 1886, a second child had been born. It had been a difficult labour for Florence and she took a while to fully recover, but she was finally getting back to full health. The Maybricks were a sociable couple and they could be seen at some of the city's premier social events. On Wednesday 31st August 1887, James was one of a group of leading Liverpool citizens who had been invited to attend a banquet at the Town Hall for the Officers of the Fleet.[363] A few days later, on 3rd September, James and Florence attended a Garden Party in the Botanic Gardens in Wavertree Park, Liverpool. The event was organised by the Mayor, Sir James Poole – whom James knew – for prominent Liverpool families to meet the admiral and officers of the Channel Fleet currently anchored in Liverpool. There were numerous other notable guests at the occasion including several representatives of the Janion family, as well as Mr and Mrs Richard Hobson, who lived on the Wirral and who were good friends of the Maybricks. Sadly, the event was spoilt by heavy rain which turned the park into a soggy state.[364]

To their many friends, the Maybricks must have seemed the perfect couple. One person who knew them well was Morden Rigg (1852-1936), another successful cotton merchant who had conducted business in Norfolk, Virginia, at the same time James and Florence lived in the city. Like them, Rigg moved back to England and settled with his wife on the Wirral peninsula in Cheshire. At the time of Florence's trial, he made a statement to Mr Cleaver, her solicitor, in which he stated that he and his wife had '*stayed with the Maybricks at Grassendale [Beechville] and also on one occasion at Battlecrease, and they stayed with us at Bromborough. I never had any reason to think that there was any domestic unhappiness between them.*'[365]

It wasn't just their friends who thought the Maybricks were perfectly happy – it was a view shared by their servants. Emma Parker, the children's nanny, commented that they were '*always affectionate to one another.*' Two of their servants at Battlecrease, Elizabeth Humphreys and Mary Cadwallader, described the Maybricks' life as a '*thoroughly ordinary domestic life.*' Cadwallader went further, and said she '*never saw any quarrelling, at any time, between Mr and Mrs Maybrick, except little differences of opinion, when she used to think Mrs Maybrick was not always conciliatory.*'[366]

While the Maybricks' life at Beechville appeared to be happy, below the surface it was not so tranquil and three major events were to shake the marriage to its core. Firstly, James' continued use of arsenic and other poisonous substances were to have a marked and detrimental effect on his physical health. Secondly, financial troubles, which periodically plagued James and Florence, were to place further stresses on the marriage. Thirdly, and most importantly, at some point in 1887, Florence found out that James was paying money to another woman. In an interview given by the Baroness in 1904, she described James as a '*debauchee.*' She said, '*some of James Maybrick's intrigues with other women came to the attention of his wife, though in an accidental way. She saw in his office books where he paid out a large sum of money to a woman in Liverpool, who together with her children, he was supporting in splendid style.*'[367]

In August 1889, Mr Macklin, of Roe and Macklin, Florence's New York lawyers, gave an interview in which he said: '*Only a few days after Maybrick's death, a bill was received from a dressmaker who wanted £10 for dresses that were not made for Mrs Maybrick. Investigation showed that the dresses had been made for a woman who had been Maybrick's mistress for twenty years. In her possession also were found family jewels which had been missing for a long time, and which the woman said were left with her by Maybrick as security for money loaned him.*'[368]

If this woman had been James' mistress for 20 years, it is likely that Macklin was referring to Sarah Ann Robertson, the woman he had known long before he married. She was upset when she heard James was to marry Florence and he agreed to pay her an annual sum of money. One of the problems with fixing on Robertson is that she normally lived in London and not Liverpool. MacDougall, in his 1891 book, wrote that the woman who claimed to be James' '*real wife*' lived in 265 Queen's Road, New Cross. This was an address at which Robertson did live for a while. Confusingly, in the same book MacDougall also wrote: '*The woman about whom Mrs Maybrick and Mrs Briggs did*

---

[363] *Liverpool Daily Post*, 1st September 1887.
[364] *Liverpool Mercury*, 3rd September 1881.
[365] MacDougall A.W., *The Maybrick Case: A Statement of the Case as a Whole*, (Bailliere Tyndall and Cox, London, 1896) page 22.
[366] MacDougall A.W., *The Maybrick Case: A Treatise*, (Bailliere Tyndall and Cox, London, 1891) page 69.
[367] *Sunday Oregonian, Portland*, 20th November 1904
[368] *Norfolk Virginian*, 11th August 1889.

consult Mr Donnison [Mrs Briggs' lawyer] was some Mrs Samuelson, to whom James Maybrick was paying a yearly sum of money.'[369]

Did MacDougall make a mistake with the name, or was James involved with a second woman? There was a Mrs Christine Samuelson who accompanied the Maybricks on trips in 1889, but she makes an unlikely candidate to be one of James' lovers. She was in her twenties and recently married, and therefore could not have been James' mistress for 20 years. At the inquest into James' death, Christine Samuelson provided evidence but then disappeared. Perhaps she was made aware that a member of her family had been involved with James and decided to move away to prevent any embarrassment to that woman.

Whoever she was, it must have been a devastating blow to Florence to discover that James was paying money to another woman. In 1889, Mr Macklin said, '*nearly two years ago*' [i.e. in 1887], Florence '*commenced proceedings to procure a separation.*'[370] Unfortunately, there is no information on how far she progressed along this path. It is likely that she soon realised it was a complex route to pursue.

Florence was in a difficult position. Although she was angry with her husband, she also recognised her relative powerlessness. It is probable that Florence's moves towards separation did not proceed very far. Ryan wrote that, faced with this drastic situation and with no intimate friends to consult, Florence '*consulted her own self-reliance*' and decided she '*would no longer sleep*' with James.[371] Although it is possible that for a period of time, Florence did refuse to sleep with her husband, it is not the case that this situation existed for the rest of their marriage.

At some point she did consent to share a bed again with her husband. Mrs Briggs said she had been told by Florence that, '*sometimes she and her husband occupied the same bedroom and that sometimes one occupied the bedroom and the other the adjoining bedroom.*'[372] James told Dr Hopper he had slept with Florence in December 1888. Therefore, although Florence's discovery that James was paying money to another woman was a serious blow to the marriage, it was not the knock-out blow that it has sometimes been described.

If James' marital problems were self-inflicted, so too were his health problems. Florence Aunspaugh wrote that James '*was always taking strychnine tablets and was great on beef broth and arsenic. My father one said: "Maybrick has a dozen drug stores in his stomach."*'[373]

By 1887, James' excessive drug use was having a marked effect on him, a fact that was obvious to those friends who only saw him from time to time. According to Florence Aunspaugh: '*In 1885 my father was in England, in 1887 Mr Maybrick came to the US and the moment my father looked at him he noticed and was astonished how much he had broken and aged in those two years. In 1888 when I was with my father in England, he said it was very perceptible that Mr Maybrick had again failed very much in that one year. When my father came home he told my mother, "She would hardly know Maybrick, he had aged so much, and he did not believe he would be here very much longer."*'[374]

While some of the Maybricks' marital problems were a direct result of James' behaviour, the financial issues they faced were more to do with a downturn in the cotton market. The extent of his business problems is revealed in a letter Florence wrote to her mother in October 1887 in which she said her husband's assets were reduced to just £1,500 of which some £500 was in the bank and the rest was with Edwin in Galveston, Texas, so he could purchase cotton bales. She said James had made just £125 profit in the last five years and as a result they had been living off the company's capital.[375]

The Maybricks' financial issues were exacerbated by both James and Florence's inability to live within their means. John Aunspaugh once said to James, '*Well, Maybrick, you surely do spend a lot of money for one who is always expecting a great calamity.*'[376] Florence was a spendthrift, who purchased exquisite furnishings for the house and who had an expensive taste in clothes. Florence Aunspaugh wrote that James bought his wife '*beautiful handsome clothes for every occasion, both indoors and out.*' She owned '*one of the most beautiful dresses*' young Florence Aunspaugh had ever seen. It was '*a very light grey or fawn coloured silk of a very heavy rich quality, trimmed in dark purple velvet and ecru Brussels lace. The back of the skirt was unusually attractive. It was in three large puffs, one below the other, the last terminating in a long train. At the side of the pleated skirt in front were panels of purple velvet. The waist was especially pretty... Over this was a purple velvet zouave jacket, edged with the Brussels lace. Low neck, back and front, short sleeves with velvet cuffs and edged with the lace.*'[377]

With such expensive tastes, it would have come as a real blow to Florence when James decided they had to economise and he cut back on the money he provided her to pay the household bills. He reduced Florence's allowance to just £7 a week, and that had to cover all the food for the family and staff, plus the servants' wages and other

---

369 MacDougall A.W., (1891) op. cit., page 506.
370 *Norfolk Virginian*, 11th August 1889.
371 Ryan B., op cit., page 28.
372 *Evening Express*, 12th June 1889.
373 Trevor Christie Collection.
374 Trevor Christie Collection.
375 Christie T.L., op. cit., page 44.
376 Trevor Christie Collection.
377 Trevor Christie Collection.

household costs. Faced with such a situation, Florence started to accumulate substantial debts. Often, and without her husband's knowledge, she used to borrow money from friends such as Mrs Briggs, and family members such as Michael Maybrick. She also pawned some of her jewellery and borrowed from money-lenders, sometimes at high rates of interest.

In October 1887, a distraught Florence wrote to her mother about the perilous state of her own debts and also about the financial problems facing James' cotton business. She said: '*I am utterly worn out and in such a state of overstrained nervousness I am hardly fit for anything. Whenever the doorbell rings I feel ready to faint for fear it is someone coming to have an account paid, and when Jim comes home at night it is with fear and trembling that I look into his face to see whether anyone has been to the office about any of my bills... My life is a continual state of fear of something or somebody... Is life worth living? I would gladly give up the house tomorrow and move somewhere else, but Jim says it would ruin him outright, for we must keep up appearances until he has more capital to fall back upon and to meet his liabilities, since the least suspicion aroused all claims would pour in at once, and how could Jim settle with what he has now.*'[378]

The great hope the Maybricks always clung to when it came to solving their perennial financial problems was that there would be a successful resolution to the land claims of Florence's family in America. In 1879, the Baroness had signed an agreement with David Armstrong; if he could sell the land, then they would divide the income derived from it on a fifty-fifty basis. In 1887, Armstrong approached the Baroness with a modified proposal. He offered to pay her a one-off lump sum of $10,000 if she agreed to sell him all her lands and waive any claims she might have to the properties.

As the Baroness was in her usual state of financial hardship, she decided to accept Armstrong's offer. Although this transaction appears to be a relatively straightforward one, it was, in fact, fraught with all sort of potential problems which later led to a bitter court case in 1909. In 1887, the most immediate problem faced by the Baroness was a document she had signed in January 1882 giving Florence a one-third interest in the Virginian and Kentucky properties. For the agreement between Armstrong and the Baroness to proceed smoothly, this issue needed to be resolved.

On 2nd December 1887, James and Florence received a letter from Mr Potter, the Baroness' attorney, which asked Florence to renounce all claims she had to any portion of the money generated by Mr Armstrong selling the Virginia and Kentucky lands.

James was not prepared to accept such an idea. On 6th December 1887, he replied to Potter, stating: '*It is scarcely likely that I as her husband and a man of business will consent to renounce, or allow her to renounce, all claim upon the land now. Unless we have a solid guarantee that the proportion due to her will be paid.*' He added that while he did '*not wish to appear discourteous*' to his mother-in-law, '*past experiences have taught me that I cannot rely upon the verbal promises of the Baroness.*'

Potter replied almost immediately to James and assured him he would use his moral influences upon the Baroness to fulfil her agreement to pay out one-third of the $10,000. As a result, James sent a cable back on 12th December in which he wrote: '*In consideration of your assurances that you will exercise your moral influences upon the Baroness to fulfil her contract and pay out one third of the $10,000 to be reinvested through yourself, I unhesitatingly consent to allow my wife to sign the deed of renunciation.*'[379] Despite this, the deal was not finally completed until almost the end of Florence's trial in 1889, when there was a desperate need to get her signature on the document.

Another event in 1887 that was to have an impact upon the Maybrick household was the resignation of the children's nanny, Emma Parker. She had been with them for five years and had travelled to America on two occasions.[380] Parker told the Maybricks she was leaving as she was getting married for the second time. On 19th September 1887, she married John Charles Over, a joiner, at Edge Hill in Liverpool.

Although the nanny's resignation surprised the Maybricks, Florence was not too unhappy. She wrote to her mother saying: '*Nurse is quite changed since baby's birth. Poor little mite: it gets neither petting or coaxing when I am not with it and yet it is such a loving little thing, and ready for a smile for every cross word that nurse says to her. I cannot understand why she does not take to the child... I am afraid she is getting too old for a young baby and has not the forbearance and patience to look after Gladys as when she had Bobo. With him it was a labour of love – with poor little Gladys it is a labour of duty only.*'[381]

There was probably some truth in Florence's criticism of Emma Parker who, in 1887, was in her early forties and had a teenage son from her first marriage to Samuel Powell. It could not have been easy for her looking after the two Maybrick children, especially as Florence had been ill on several occasions.

---

378 Florence's letter was given to the newspapers by Alexander MacDougall. See *Liverpool Weekly Courier*, 25th January 1890.
379 Documents from the *Baroness von Roques versus David Armstrong case* (1906) stored in the Richmond Chancery.
380 *Cheshire Observer*, 8th August 1936.
381 Florence's letter was printed in the *Liverpool Weekly Courier*, 25th January 1890.

Although Florence gave a somewhat bitter final comment on her, Emma Parker was more complimentary about the Maybricks. In an interview given in 1889, she said James and Florence were '*always affectionate to one another*' and Florence was '*devotedly attached to her two children.*'[382]

With Emma Parker, leaving the Maybricks needed a new nanny and in September 1887, Nurse Alice Yapp was recruited to join the household. Yapp was originally from Ludlow in Shropshire where her parents had run an inn called the Nag's Head. Prior to joining the Maybricks, she had worked for six years for Mr and Mrs Gibson, who lived in Fairfield in Liverpool and then Birkdale, a small town just north of Liverpool.[383] James had travelled alone to Birkdale to engage her. This was unusual, as this task was normally considered to be the role of the mistress of the household. Morland describes it as '*almost revolutionary*' by the standards of the day.[384]

After Florence's trial, stories appeared in American newspapers which claimed that three years earlier, Yapp had been the main witness in a court case in Canada in which a husband had brought an action against his wife for separation. The suggestion was that Yapp had to leave Montreal quickly to '*escape the possibility of being indicted for perjury.*'[385] Although this story was widely reported, no evidence has ever been found that Yapp visited Canada. Prior to working for the Gibsons, she worked for a lady in Oxton, Birkenhead for 18 months and then for two years for a Mr Caleb Smith Jnr., a shipbuilder who lived near Sefton Park.[386] According to a letter she wrote to the *Liverpool Echo*, she had been '*living in or near Liverpool for twelve years.*'[387]

Nurse Yapp's time working for the Maybricks is full of controversy. Florence Aunspaugh described her as a '*very efficient capable woman,*' but also as a '*most deceitful and treacherous one.*' She said Yapp '*despised and hated Mrs Maybrick.*'[388] Yapp had been due to get married to a man from a watchmaker's shop in Lord Street, Liverpool; however, the relationship ended when he had to move to Scotland. According to Christie, this left her an '*embittered*' woman who was jealous of Florence. Emma Parker accused Yapp of having an '*exceedingly prying nature,*' and as soon as Florence's back was turned she would open letters and was '*prying about in her room.*'[389]

The *New York Herald* carried a story in August 1889 in which a Liverpool man, Mr Levi of Everton Road, accused Nurse Yapp of spying on him as he wrote a letter. According to the report, he said: '*Last October [1888] I went to Battlecrease to see Mrs Maybrick, and found she had gone to Southport. I asked if I might write a letter to her, and was shown into a room for that purpose. I wrote the letter supposing that I was alone in the room. Just as I finished, something caused me to turn, and I found Alice Yapp leaning over my shoulder and perusing the letter. It made me so angry that I struck her.*'[390]

One story, if true, may account for some of the apparent bitterness that Nurse Yapp showed towards Florence. The Baroness said in early 1889 she received a letter from her daughter in which she said she had returned home earlier than expected from an evening out. Although she had '*given strict orders to Yapp*' that on no account was she to leave the children alone in the night nursery, she found upon her return that the children were on their own. She '*found her little boy out of bed trying to find some matches, while the baby, the girl, was screaming at the top of her voice.*' Florence '*had reprimanded Miss Yapp severely.*' She added that the nurse's behaviour was at serious fault and she could '*no longer trust her.*' She thought she might have to '*discharge*' Yapp from her post as nanny. The Baroness felt this episode was important as it turned Yapp against her daughter and pushed her into the arms of Mrs Briggs who, due to her long friendship with James, was '*a greater power in the house*' than Florence.[391]

Although the year 1887 seemed to mark something of a downturn in James' health, it would be wrong to see him as being on an inevitable path to physical decline. James may have been a hypochondriac and a regular user of dangerous medications, but he was also a man who enjoyed physical exercise, including long walks with his friends in the nearby Welsh mountains. It is also believed he owned a Humber safety bicycle.[392]

To many of his friends, James appeared to be a healthy man. Mr McGuffie, the chemist in Liverpool who had been making up some of James' prescriptions for 15 years, described him as a '*strong, broad-shouldered, healthy man.*'[393] According to Florence Aunspaugh, James: '*was a man somewhat above medium height. While you would not term him a handsome man as to features, yet he had a fine forehead, a very pleasant intellectual face and an open and honest countenance. Was well educated, well informed and a very interesting conversationalist. Light sandy coloured hair, grey eyes and the florid English expression. He had none of that blunt abrupt manner, so characteristic of the*

[382] *York Herald*, 18th August 1889.
[383] Letter from Alice Yapp in *Liverpool Echo*, 22nd August 1889.
[384] Morland N., op cit., page 18.
[385] *Norfolk Landmark*, 16th August 1889.
[386] *York Herald*, 18th August 1889.
[387] Letter from Alice Yapp in *Liverpool Echo*, 22nd August 1889.
[388] Trevor Christie Collection.
[389] *New York Herald*, 18th August, 1889.
[390] *New York Herald*, 14th August 1889.
[391] *South Wales Echo*, 14th August 1889.
[392] Morland N., op cit., page 16.
[393] *Evening Express*, 15th August 1889.

English, but was exceedingly cultured, polished and refined in his manners; and was a superb host... was always immaculate in his person and well groomed.'[394]

James had many friends, both male and female, and some of these – such as George Davidson and Mrs Briggs – were long-standing. Captain Irving, a man who knew James well, described him as '*a mighty good fellow.*' Morland wrote that '*James was convivial, a jovial drinker with a knack for making friends. He was always "hail fellow well met" and both a ladies man and a good companion.*'[395]

Although James could be sociable, kind and generous, he could also be morose, pessimistic and quick tempered. He appeared to be fond and loving towards his wife, yet he also seems to have had a jealous and controlling nature. It was these contradictory traits that led people to view James in very contrasting ways. Florence Aunspaugh said there were '*two unfortunate features in Mr Maybrick's "make-up." That was his morose, gloomy disposition and his extremely high temper.*'[396]

These views about the negative aspects of James' personality were not shared by everyone. One newspaper reporter who knew James said he was '*always impressed by his calm and gentle manner*' and that he had '*been falsely spoken of outside as morose and austere.*'[397] After Florence's trial, during which James' reputation had been badly tarnished, some of his friends tried to portray him in a more positive light. They described him as '*a particularly domestic man, spending a remarkable proportion of his time at home*' and that he '*was a great reader and extremely fond of music.*'[398]

In early 1888, the Maybricks moved from Beechville to a much larger house less than half a mile away, taking out a five-year lease on the property. The building was located on Riversdale Road in Aigburth, directly opposite Liverpool Cricket Club where James and Florence were both members. Before the Maybricks moved in, the house was simply numbered 6A. Florence decided to name it *Battlecrease House*, a title said to be derived from an agricultural term.[399]

Battlecrease House (*Liverpool Echo*, 9th August 1889)

In the summer of 1886, two years before the Maybricks moved into the house, the premises had been converted into a suburban club for gentlemen. It was the idea of Philip Eberle, a well-known hotelier and caterer, who was '*notable in the public life of Liverpool for close upon half a century.*'[400] Eberle believed the County Club, as he called it, would meet the needs of the growing number of cotton merchants and other businessmen wanting somewhere to relax and unwind after work. The club was not just for men; ladies, too, were eligible to join. Eberle had the house redecorated from top to bottom, and engaged Messrs Cook and Townshend, the nearest thing to Harrods in Liverpool, to furnish it in luxurious style. In the '*expensive pleasure grounds*' he installed a bowling green and tennis lawn, and announced plans for a large billiard room which could also be used as a ballroom. He built stables for members who wanted to keep their horses on the premises. The finest silver, china and glass were purchased, and several pianos installed.

Unfortunately for Eberle, the venture swiftly failed. At Eberle's bankruptcy hearing in 1888, he explained he gave it up because the agreement he thought he had reached with the freeholder had not been adhered to. His admission that only one member had actually stayed there overnight drew laughter, and pointed to the fact that the club was never a success – probably as there was already a gentlemen's club on the other side of the road in the shape of Liverpool Cricket Club.[401]

---

394 Trevor Christie Collection.
395 Morland N., op cit., page 8.
396 Trevor Christie Collection.
397 Peregrine in the *Prescot Reporter*, June 1889.
398 *Sheffield Evening Telegraph*, 10th August 1889.
399 *Liverpool Citizen*, 21st August 1889.
400 *Liverpool Echo*, 20th February 1906.
401 *Liverpool Mercury*, 1st June 1889

Following the collapse of Eberle's club, the building went out to rental as two private homes.[402] The work carried out by Eberle on both the building and the gardens would have made the two properties very desirable residences, and they must have caught the eye of the Maybricks. According to one report, they moved there from nearby Grassendale '*at the suggestion and urgent request*' of Florence. James '*considered it too large for their wants, but Mrs Maybrick seemed to have set her heart upon it, and he yielded to her wishes.*'[403]

The Maybricks occupied the southerly half of the house (the side closest to the railway and river); the other half was occupied by Mr Douglas Steel, a local lawyer.

It is very easy to understand why Florence wanted to move to Battlecrease, as the house had extensive grounds, including an orchard which had a variety of different fruit trees, stables and dog kennels. A newspaper reporter in May 1889, described it as a '*house of considerable dimensions, situated in the midst of a very pleasant residential neighbourhood... about five minutes walk from Mersey-road Railway Station. Sheltered from the roadway by a high ivy-clad wall with an extensive piece of well laid out and tree-skirted grounds extends in front, whilst a serpentine carriage drive leads from the double gate to the principal entrance of the house. On the northerly side lies an orchard, fresh with the foliage and bloom of spring.*'[404]

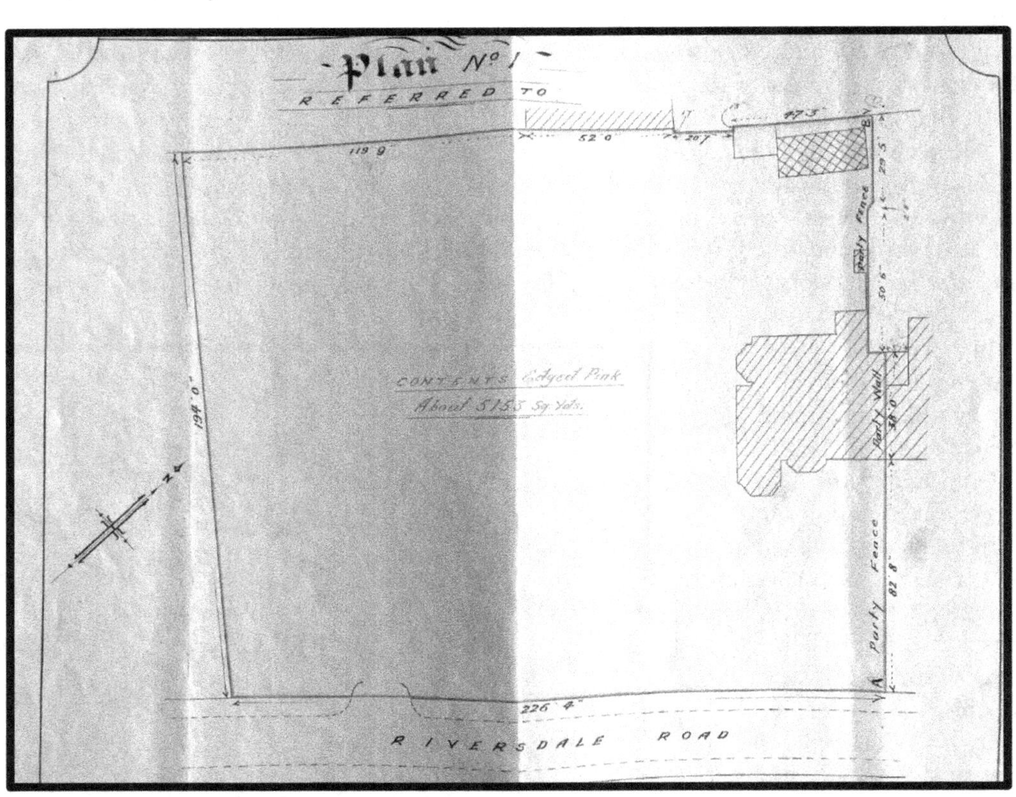

Plan of Battlecrease House and its grounds taken from its title deeds (Courtesy of Paul Dodd)

Further evidence of the splendour of Battlecrease comes from Florence Aunspaugh, who stayed in the house in the summer of 1888. She recalled that it was '*a palatial home. The grounds must have consisted of five or six acres and were given most excellent care. There were large trees, luxuriant shrubbery and flowerbeds... A conservatory was near the house and a pair of peacocks roamed the grounds.*' The house also benefitted from the installation of an early form of central heating, probably the idea of Eberle, but the large rooms, with their high ceilings, could still feel cold in winter and they needed additional heating from coal fires.

We know quite a lot about the interior décor of Battlecrease from the list of items that belonged to the Maybricks that were sold in auction in early July 1889. The list shows the Maybricks' home was that of an upper middle-class family and '*had been furnished with refined taste and elegance.*'[405]

As one entered, there was an old oak settee in the hallway. Downstairs there were Turkish carpets in the dining room and the library, and a Persian carpet in the drawing room. There was a pair of Dresden candelabra hanging in the lounge and the dining room. Also in the dining room was a beautiful large oak dining table with pillars and leaves. There were six Chippendale chairs and a pair of matching elbow chairs, plus a further four mahogany Chippendale chairs. There was a large amount of silverware, including a silver tea service and a beautiful dessert service of Parisian china. Some of these would have been on display in the beautiful sideboards, including one of early English design and a Queen Anne display cabinet. Some items, such as a serving dish which can still be viewed, carried the Maybrick coat of arms. Such an extravagance was clearly designed to impress their guests. Downstairs, a Collard & Collard cottage piano forte occupied a prominent position. There was an old oak bureau and a pedestal-writing table in solid

---

[402] *Liverpool Mercury*, 20th May 1889.
[403] *Liverpool Citizen*, 21st August 1889.
[404] *Liverpool Mercury*, 5th May 1888.
[405] *Garston and Woolton Reporter*, 13th July 1889.

oak. There was a quaint bracket table with '*negro supports*,' undoubtedly a reminder of Florence's childhood. There was a Sheraton card table, and one can easily imagine James, Florence – and maybe Edwin Maybrick and Alfred Brierley – playing a game of whist.

All around the house there were beautiful clocks, ornaments and paintings. The clocks included a Viennese regulator clock and an old-fashioned eight-day clock. There were Japanese and Chinese vases and ornaments and a pair of bronze statuettes.

Original serving dish with the Maybrick coat of arms (Chris Jones collection)

James had an interest in the Arts, and was a frequent visitor to the Walker Art Gallery in Liverpool. At an exhibition in the gallery in 1886, he bought two paintings on angling by Mr J. T. Steadman, and some watercolours by Mr James S. Crompton and Mr R. Rutherford.[406] These paintings, plus other oil and watercolour drawings, were displayed throughout the house. The water colours included '*A Ferry Boat on the Rhine*' attributed to F. Goodall, two landscapes by E.J. Duval, and '*The Village School*' by J. Fabius. The Maybricks also owned two engravings by Watson Nichol, entitled '*When a man's single he lives at his ease,' and 'When a man's married his troubles begin.*'

In one of the rooms downstairs, an oak bureau and writing table were to be found. One thing the room didn't have too many of was books. Only about 35 books were lots at the auction, and most of those were the '*usual common-place books of reference and dictionaries, with the addition of a few encyclopedias, reviews and novels. There was nothing of special interest in them.*'[407]

The original main entrance to Battlecrease House (Chris Jones collection)

One of the more interesting downstairs rooms was James' small study, which was always kept locked with a Yale key which only he possessed. This room was never cleaned unless he was in it. It was here that James kept valuable items and documents he didn't want his wife to view. After her trial, while she was in prison waiting for news of a possible commutation of her sentence, Florence told her mother that James had a '*black box in which he kept a lot of things.*' Florence said that she was not allowed to examine inside it, but James told her that the box contained her wedding certificate and '*some burial certificates or some papers relating to cemetery lots. There were all sorts of things there which I knew nothing about.*'[408]

A locked box in a locked room is an obvious indication that James had items he did not wish Florence to examine. It is likely that much of this material was fairly mundane, relating to his work. Florence was very open in her letters to her mother, and James would not have wanted her to have kept the Baroness informed about the state of his business. It is also likely that some of the hidden items related to his personal vices, the heavy cost of his club memberships, his drug purchases and maybe even his financial dealings with his long-term mistress.

The opulence of downstairs was replicated in the first-floor bedrooms, where French and Arabian bedsteads, expensive curtains and other quality furnishings could be found. The master bedroom was really two rooms, comprising a large room and a smaller room, which could only be accessed off the larger one. This room is usually described as the inner-dressing room. In it, there was only space for a single bed and some basic furniture. James

[406] 'Notes Here and There' by Peregrine in *The Prescot Reporter*, 8th June 1889.
[407] *Garston and Woolton Reporter*, 13th July 1889.
[408] *Evening Express*, 22nd August 1889.

slept in this smaller room on occasion. In the larger room there was a suite of American walnut furniture. Another bedroom, used by guests, had a suite of mountain ash furniture.

The children's nursery was also located on the first floor, and there were the '*familiar Christmas pictures from the illustrated weeklies*' hung on the walls of the room.[409] One of the most poignant items that went up for auction was a child's folding hammock cot and hair mattress, which sold for 14 shillings. Other rooms on the first floor included a dressing room (where Nurse Yapp often slept), located through the night nursery, a linen closet, a bathroom and a toilet featuring a new flush mechanism. On the second floor could be found two bedrooms used by the servants, and an additional guest room.

Given the financial difficulties the Maybricks had faced in 1887, it is rather a surprise that the following year they moved into Battlecrease, a much larger house which would have been more expensive to run. Such a move could have only been possible if, at some point in 1888, James had come into a sizeable sum of money. One possibility was his involvement in the Electric Sugar Refining Company. The company had been founded in the United States in 1884, to commercialise a sugar refining process supposedly invented by '*Professor*' Henry Friend, who claimed to be a German professor of chemistry but, in reality, he was none of these things; his invention was little more than an elaborate scam for swindling investors. James was one of the '*original investors*' in the company, and it was partly due to him that '*the stock was so eagerly bought up in Liverpool.*'[410]

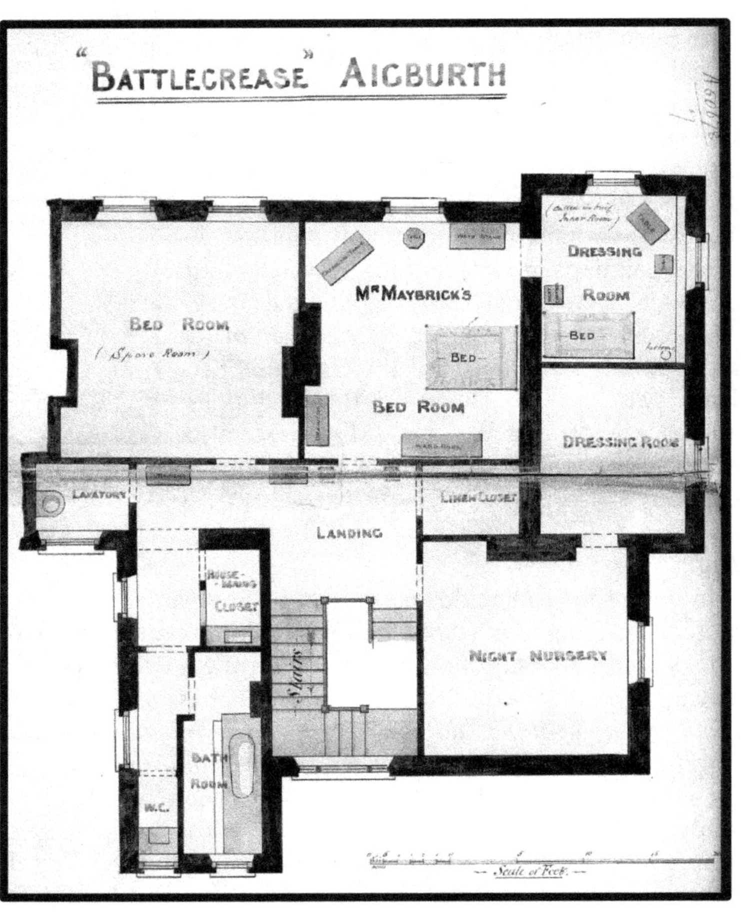

First floor plan of Battlecrease House drawn up for Florence's trial

Staged small-scale demonstrations of the process gave the false impression that the machinery was a major break-through in refining sugar, and the company's stock price rose from $100 per share in 1884 to $625 per share in 1888. In March 1888, J. B. Wallace, a sugar dealer from Liverpool, visited New York on business and asked repeatedly to view the machinery, but had all his requests cancelled. As a result, he informed his friends that Electric Sugar was '*very fishy*' and urged them to sell their holdings. His advice '*soon got abroad in Liverpool*' and many Liverpool investors immediately sold their shares.[411] In 1889, Friend died, and the company collapsed after it was revealed that his process was a complete fabrication. If James had invested heavily in the Electric Sugar Company, but sold all his shares in early 1888 (around the time he moved into Battlecrease) when the shares were at their peak price, then he would have achieved a sizeable return on his investment. It was also the case that James' business portfolio stretched beyond his interests in the cotton trade. He continued to look after Gustavus Witt's business concerns in Liverpool and had investments in other business ventures including *The Carnarvon Freehold Copper Mining Company (Limited)* in North Wales. In July 1889, George Smith, James' bookkeeper, described James' business as being in '*prosperous circumstances.*'[412]

One of the consequences of having a larger house was that it needed to be staffed by a team of servants. During their stay at Battlecrease, five, possibly six, servants were employed. Two of these were men; one was the gardener named James Grant. He rarely came inside the house, and was not called to testify at Florence's trial. He married a former housemaid at the house, Alice Jones. Friction between Florence and the gardener was caused by the three cats Florence kept; Grant would complain they damaged his flowerbeds. His wife was a friend of Nurse Yapp, and seemed to share her dislike of Florence. She referred to her as '*an old cat, always sticking indoors.*'[413] The second man, supposedly named Alan, was a combination of butler and coachman; however, he is only referred to in Florence Aunspaugh's account and is not mentioned in any other contemporary document. It is known that the Maybricks kept

[409] *Porcupine*, 6th July 1889.
[410] *New York Times*, 30th May 1889.
[411] *New York Times*, 10th January 1889.
[412] Smith's Additional Statement, July 1889; HO 144/1639/A50678/D26
[413] Trevor Christie Collection.

a carriage and horses and that they also frequently entertained guests, so it is possible that such a person did play a role at Battlecrease, if only on an irregular or part-time basis.

The four female servants were to play prominent roles in the unfolding drama that was to engulf the house in 1889. One of these was Nurse Yapp, the children's nanny, who moved with the Maybricks from Beechville. According to Christie, she was a '*domineering type*' and '*ruled the servants' hall with a tight rein.*' She also liked to try and ensure that if new staff were taken on they were her friends.[414]

Although Yapp's age, experience and status would have allowed her to have a degree of influence over the younger staff, it is unlikely she could have dominated Elizabeth Humphreys, the cook. Humphreys was the oldest of the four female servants and joined the staff in late 1888, though she had previously worked for the Maybricks when they lived in Beechville. Her home was in Frodsham, on the Cheshire side of the Mersey.[415] She was a confident, attractive, friendly and independently-minded woman. As she had a friendly demeanour, Florence would confide in her. The *Liverpool Daily Post* described her as the '*best and kindliest friend Mrs Maybrick had got amid these extraordinary surroundings.*'[416] After the trial, Humphreys signed a petition calling for the commutation of Florence's sentence.[417]

Mary Cadwallader was the waitress at Battlecrease. She served the food and helped out in the kitchen. She also ran errands for the family. Nicknamed '*Gentle Mary,*' she grew up on a large farm in Shropshire and was the eldest of 14 children. She shared the Maybricks' love of horses. At the time of the trial, she lived with her parents in the north-end of Liverpool. According to Christie, she was of '*cadaverous appearance,*' very pale and thin.[418]

Elizabeth (Bessie) Brierley was the housemaid at Battlecrease. Like Humphreys, she started to work for the Maybricks in late 1888.[419] She was unmarried, and lived off Lark Lane by Sefton Park, about one mile from Battlecrease. Brierley had a range of tasks around the house, including cleaning, making the beds, clearing the slops from the bedroom and brushing the clothes.

Florence Aunspaugh commented that Battlecrease had '*an air of secrecy.*' Nurse Yapp and the gardener would converse '*in low suppressed tones*' and would stop abruptly if anyone approached. The other servants acted in a similar manner. Florence Aunspaugh added that both Yapp and Mrs Briggs '*despised and hated*' Florence, but she did not have the intelligence to recognise the fact. She said Mrs Briggs was constantly interfering in the running of the house and giving advice to James, such as what to eat and what to wear. She could not recall '*one instance where Mrs Maybrick gave an order or instruction to a servant. I've heard Mr Maybrick give quite a few and when he did the servants stood to attention.*' Florence Aunspaugh was probably quite perceptive in her view that the servants could be dismissive of Florence; and it is the case that, after James' death, some of them treated her with both disdain and hostility. Nevertheless, Florence was not the passive figure she is often accused of being. We know from her mother that Florence gave Nurse Yapp a severe telling off when she found that she was not looking after her children when she returned home early from a night out. We also know that during the early stages of James' illness, Florence was in full charge of running the household, giving clear instructions on what her husband could eat and drink.

It is likely that Mrs Briggs did at times interfere in the running of Battlecrease, but probably not to the extent that has been suggested by her critics. It is also likely that Yapp thought herself to be rather superior to Florence and was prepared to articulate her opinions, but she too could be put in her place by both Florence and James. Florence Aunspaugh recalled an incident in which she had tried to lift baby Gladys out of her cradle. Yapp was extremely angry with her, and threatened to slap her '*back and blue.*' James happened to be passing the nursery and heard Yapp's remarks, and angrily warned the nanny that if she spoke to young Florence like that again, he would '*kick her down the steps and break every damn bone*' in her body.

Apart from the extensive grounds, Battlecrease had a couple of key advantages over Beechville. One of these was its facilities for keeping animals, having both kennels and stables. If Florence loved her cats, then James loved his dogs and he kept a few of them, including some hunting dogs. Both James and Florence loved horse riding. Florence Aunspaugh said she '*saw six horses – a pair of handsome-looking blacks, which were always hitched to the carriage; a pair of greys, which were hitched to what they called the trap, and two bay saddle horses, one Mr Maybrick used the other Mrs Maybrick. When they had a Tally Ho party all six of these horses were hitched to the Tally Ho.*'[420] The Maybricks also owned a fashionable three-seated phaeton carriage, which had two side seats facing each other for the passengers and one high seat for the coachman. According to Ryan, every Sunday morning James and Florence would go out riding. On their return, they would walk, hand in hand, and then Florence might sit on James' lap and tease him about his grey hairs.

[414] Christie T.L., op cit., page 42.
[415] *Liverpool Mercury*, 29th May 1889.
[416] *Liverpool Daily Post*, 2nd August 1889.
[417] *Liverpool Echo*, 17th August 1889
[418] Christie T.L., op cit., page 92.
[419] *Garston and Woolton Reporter*, 1st June 1889.
[420] Trevor Christie Collection.

The second big advantage of the move to Battlecrease was the opportunity to entertain friends in a more lavish setting. Florence Aunspaugh said the Maybricks '*rarely spent more than one or two nights a week at home alone. Two or three times a week they would have company for dinner, or company would come in after dinner.*' The grandeur of the ballroom made it the perfect room for hosting a dance or a special meal. The Maybricks had a long table which was positioned in the middle of the room and could accommodate 20 guests at a formal dinner. One such dinner was held in 1888 in honour of John Aunspaugh on one of his visits to Liverpool. James, Florence and Aunspaugh stood at the entrance of the room in order to receive the guests as they filed in to dinner. According to Florence Aunspaugh, every single guest commented on Florence's beauty. She heard remarks such as '*Mrs Maybrick, how beautiful you are this evening, you look like a Greek statue, you look stunning, you look like a goddess. Maybrick has got the prettiest wife in England.*'

Florence lived a pampered existence in Battlecrease. If she had not been up late the previous night she would join James for breakfast around nine o'clock before he caught the train to his office. If she had been up late she might stay in bed until eleven-thirty, and then eat her breakfast in her bedroom or the dining room. It was the nanny's job to get the children up, dressed and fed. When the weather was good, Nurse Yapp would take the children outside and Florence might join them for a while. Florence would then read, paint or write a letter to her mother or one of her friends. In the afternoon, she might take the carriage to Liverpool to visit the shops or to meet up with her husband. Florence loved to be flattered and admired, and could be easily upset by the slightest indiscretion in her appearance. One day, whilst walking in Liverpool, Florence became upset when she discovered she had a hole in her stocking. She became even more upset and began to cry when James started to tease her about it.

After the anguish of 1887, the move to Battlecrease seems to have restored at least some stability to the Maybrick marriage. Several of the people who visited the house during this period, from Dr Hopper to friends such as Mr and Mrs Morden Rigg and Mr and Mrs Nicholas Bateson, saw a couple who appeared to be at ease with one another. Florence Aunspaugh stayed in the house for several weeks in 1888 and wrote that the relations between Florence and James always seemed '*very amicable. He called her Bunny. He would always kiss her goodbye with the rest of us when he left in the morning if she was up, but if she was still in bed he would go to her room before leaving.*'

Not all of their friends shared the view that James and Florence were in a happy relationship. In June 1888, the couple visited the London home of James' former business partner Gustavus Witt, who felt that the marriage was in an '*unsatisfactory state of affairs.*' Witt, as James' friend, blamed the troubles on Florence and felt that James was always trying to '*take a generous view of his wife's shortcomings.*' Although Witt was undoubtedly biased in his viewpoint, he was probably correct in his assessment that the marriage was not as stable as others felt it to be.

Despite this undercurrent of friction, Florence did appear to be enjoying her life and was taking '*great delight in teas, card-parties and balls.*'[421] James and Florence attended various social events including those at the Wellington Rooms in Mount Pleasant, which had a large ballroom and '*played an important part in the life of the city as a place of fashionable assembly.*'[422]

In October 1887, Florence had informed her mother that she found even the simple exercise of walking to be '*so painful*;'[423] as 1888 progressed, she became physically stronger and healthier. She also became increasingly confident and out-going. Edwin, James' brother, noticed the difference in Florence's attitude. He told the Baroness when she arrived at Battlecrease after James' death that Florence had been very '*quiet and domestic... but this winter she was changed and would go out to dances.*'[424] In a letter to the Home Secretary in August 1892, the Baroness wrote that in her early years of marriage, Florence was '*a delicate invalid, nursing little children, attending to the house – painting her only recreation – studious, quiet and modest... The December of 1888 was the first time during her married life she had been able to dance or had been out in society; and her health was then stronger.*'[425]

If 1887 was in many ways the nadir of James and Florence's relationship, the following year saw some signs of recovery. In agreeing to the move to Battlecrease, James was probably trying to win back his wife's affection. Florence loved her new home and the style of living it brought with it. It appealed to her vanity, and she loved being the belle of the ball. It is possible that in time the marriage might have recovered, but that didn't happen. As 1888 unfolded, Florence became more confident and stronger, and started to develop a taste for a more active social life.

As this was happening James was moving in the opposite direction. His age, drug-taking and hypochondriac tendencies, were all having a detrimental effect upon his health. The sturdy and confident man whom Florence had encountered back in 1880 was now a shadow of his former self.

In July 1888, things got so bad that he was '*ordered to Harrogate for his health.*'[426] James booked himself into the Queen's Hotel in the town, and spent four nights taking in the waters of the Harrogate Spa. At Florence's trial, Dr

[421] Christie T.L., op cit., page 42.
[422] *Visitors' Illustrated Guide to Liverpool*, op. cit., pages 81-82.
[423] Letter from Florence to her mother printed in the *Liverpool Weekly Courier*, 25th January 1890.
[424] MacDougall A.W., (1891) op cit., page 10.
[425] HO 144/1639/A50678D/99.
[426] Irving H.B., op cit., page 69.

Hopper, James' doctor, testified that between June and September 1888 he had seen him '*perhaps twenty*' times.[427] In the summer of 1888, while Florence was being treated by Dr Hopper, she told him that her husband was '*in the habit of taking some very strong medicine which had a bad influence on him; for he always seemed worse after each dose*.' Florence asked Dr Hopper to '*remonstrate*' with James, as he was '*very reticent*' to discuss the matter with her. As a result, on his next visit to Battlecrease, Dr Hopper searched James' dressing room but couldn't find any poisonous medicines.[428] To keep up his sexual appetite James increased his daily drug intake, but this was neither a sensible nor a long-term solution to his problems.

James had developed – as Dr Hopper had clearly warned him – '*dangerous habits*' and these were only to get worse. To that extent, the beginning of the end of the Maybrick marriage can be dated to the latter part of 1888 rather than the turmoil of the previous year. Florence wanted love, affection and excitement, and if she couldn't get it from James, then she was prepared to look for someone else to provide her with what she wanted.

LINKS TO THE RIPPER DIARY: DID THE DIARIST HAVE AN INTIMATE KNOWLEDGE OF THE MAYBRICK FAMILY?

People who argue that the Diary is an old document and that it was written by James Maybrick, support their proposition by stating the author of the document had an intimate knowledge of the Maybricks' family life. Robert Smith, who currently owns the Diary, wrote: '*those who claim that the diary relies on modern published sources are very wide of the mark. There is far too much personal knowledge and experience contained within its pages to suggest that is other than an historic document, completely originated by its author*.'[429] He cites a few lines extracted from the Diary to try and support his claim. For example, the diarist wrote, '*My dearest Gladys is unwell yet again*.' Robert Smith draws attention to this line, especially the word '*again*.' He argues the diarist's mention of Gladys' '*recurrent ill-health*' strongly indicates its author '*possessed first-hand intimate knowledge of the Maybrick family*.'[430]

Shirley Harrison also argues the word '*again*' is of '*crucial*' significance.[431] She suggests this particular phrase supports the view that the author had '*intimate personal knowledge of the family*,' as none of the various books written about the Maybricks suggested Gladys was often unwell.

There are several things wrong with these assertions. Firstly, the idea that a young child might be '*unwell yet again*' is hardly a great surprise. In fact, it would be more of a surprise if the child hadn't been ill on more than one occasion. Maybe if the diarist had mentioned some specific illnesses, such as whooping cough, it would have added some credibility to the statement.

Secondly, references to Gladys' health *can* be found in contemporary accounts. A letter from Margaret Baillie, a friend of Florence's mother, contains the line that she is feeling '*sorry*' for Gladys; this quote can be found in Levy's book on Florence's trial published in 1899.[432] Although it does not contain the phrase '*unwell again*,' it does imply there was something medically wrong with Gladys. This latter view is reinforced by Dr Humphreys' testimony at Florence's trial. He told the court he treated both the Maybrick children for whooping-cough in the early months of 1887. He also said he had '*attended the children*' in the early part of March 1889.[433] Therefore, the children were unwell again.

Thirdly, it is easy to identify how such a line could be taken from a modern book on the Maybricks. Ryan, in his 1977 book on Florence Maybrick, wrote that in March 1888, Dr Richard Humphreys was summoned to Battlecrease; it was a house he knew well, as '*he had often attended the Maybrick children*.'[434] If, as Ryan states, Dr Humphreys had often attended the Maybrick children, then it is easy to conclude they must have been frequently ill. No intimate knowledge is required, only the ability to lift a line and place it in the narrative of the Diary.

The diarist misses a clear opportunity to demonstrate personal knowledge of the Maybrick family when he refers to James Chandler Maybrick, James and Florence's son, as '*Bobo*.' In one passage the diarist writes, '*I worry so over Bobo and Gladys, no others matter*.' Although it is the case that James Jr was given this nickname when he was a baby, as a young boy he was given the second nickname of '*Sonny*.'

In 1888, the year of the Ripper murders, Florence Aunspaugh stayed with the Maybricks and spent much of her time playing with young James. In her correspondence with Trevor Christie, she writes about James and uses the

[427] Ibid., pages 32-33.
[428] Ibid., page 35.
[429] Smith R., "*The Maybrick Diary: A New Edition*" in the *Journal of the Whitechapel Society*, June 2019, page 25.
[430] Smith R., op cit., pages 138-139.
[431] Harrison S., op cit., page 169.
[432] Levy J.H., op cit., page 29.
[433] Irving H.B., op cit., page 87.
[434] Ryan B., op cit., page 32.

nickname *Sonny* on several occasions, for example: '*One evening Sonny and I were trying to find some way to interest ourselves and I found one of Mrs Maybrick's books in a nook.*' If the Diary was written over the period 1888/89, why does only the nickname '*Bobo*' appear, whilst '*Sonny*' never appears?

Perhaps it is because the nickname Bobo is referenced in all the books, yet Sonny does not appear until after 1992 when the Diary surfaced. In Ryan's 1977 book, he refers to the nickname saying Mrs Howell had attended Florence '*when Bobo and Gladys were born.*'[435] On the other hand, the reference to '*Sonny*' only came to light after Florence Aunspaugh's correspondence with Christie was made readily available after the Diary had already appeared. The Bobo reference is not a mistake, but it shows no personal insight into the Maybricks; however, a reference to the nickname Sonny by the diarist would have shown real insight. But that did not happen.

James Chandler Maybrick known as *Bobo* and *Sonny*

The diarist mentions James' brothers on numerous occasions. This again is supposed to show he had some great insight into the Maybrick family. However, not only does the diarist not produce any material other than information that can easily be sourced from modern books, he also makes some crucial mistakes that demonstrate a lack of knowledge about family relationships. This is clearly revealed by the diarist's failure to refer to some of the family's nicknames. The Maybricks had a penchant for using nicknames or abbreviated forms. Michael was referred to as *Blucher*; James as *Jim*; Thomas as *Tom*; and William, the older brother, as *Will.* A postcard exists in which Michael directly refers to William as '*Will.*' The diarist fails to mention any version of a name other than those that featured in the books.

Crucially, when the diarist refers to Thomas, he always calls him '*Thomas,*' while his family and close friends always (other than in official documents) called him '*Tom.*' This is made clear in a number of contemporary sources. In the letter from Charles Ratcliffe to John Aunspaugh, Ratcliffe wrote that just after James' death, Michael Maybrick forced Florence to '*get up and go with Tom to Liverpool.*' Florence Aunspaugh recalls that whilst she was staying with the Maybricks in Liverpool, James took her, his two children and Nurse Yapp to Manchester to '*spend the day with Tom.*' She also refers to the brother's wife as '*Mrs Tom Maybrick.*'[436] In correspondence from Amy Main, Edwin Maybrick's daughter, to family friend Derek Warman, she refers to Thomas as *Tom* on multiple occasions. This is highly significant, as she met him many times. The fact that the diarist on every occasion calls him Thomas and not Tom reveals that he was not privy to first-hand family knowledge, and that in turns means it cannot have been James who wrote the Diary. It also means that it cannot have been Michael Maybrick who wrote the Diary, as he too would have referred to his brother as Tom and not Thomas.

The diarist makes another mistake when he refers to Thomas Maybrick and James in terms of their business ventures. The diarist wrote, '*Thomas has invited me to visit him. I know him well.*' He also wrote, '*Business is flourishing.*' A little later in the Diary he wrote, '*Thomas has requested that we meet as soon as possible. Business is flourishing.*'

Those who suggest the Diary is genuine point to these extracts and argue they show an intimate knowledge of family life. But is this the case? Once again strikingly similar lines can be found in the Ryan book of 1977. Ryan wrote, '*Thomas Maybrick, who dined frequently with James and Florence when his business brought him the twenty miles from Manchester to Liverpool, was cordial enough.*'[437] Ryan also wrote, '*Maybrick's cotton brokerage flourished.*'[438]

If the diarist did use the Ryan book to help source some of his material, then there is a problem; for although the Ryan book is excellent in many ways, it does contain some mistakes. For example, it is unlikely the two brothers did frequently dine with one another. They did meet occasionally, as Florence Aunspaugh's correspondence to Christie demonstrates; but MacDougall, who examined the relationship between the two brothers soon after James' death, wrote that, as far as he could ascertain, Thomas '*had not visited his brother for some years and there was very little communication with him.*'[439]

---

[435] Ibid., page 55.
[436] Trevor Christie Collection.
[437] Ryan B., op cit., page 22.
[438] Ibid., page 26.
[439] MacDougall A.W., (1891) op cit., page 62

Also significant is the use of the word '*flourishing*' in terms of the state of James' business. This is important because the evidence suggests that in 1887, James' business had been struggling badly. We know from a letter written by Florence in late 1887 to her mother, that James' financial assets had been greatly reduced and he had made only £125 profit in the past five years. Florence suggested they move to a smaller and cheaper house, but James was concerned if that happened then all his creditors would be at his door. Around the time of Florence's trial in July 1889, George Smith, James' bookkeeper, said James' business was in '*prosperous circumstances.*'[440] Something had changed and it may well have been due to James' business concerns beyond the cotton trade. For example, he probably made a lot of money by cashing in the shares he almost certainly owned in the Electric Sugar Refining Company. The diarist provides no additional details. This lack of knowledge and detailed information suggests the diarist merely copied certain words from modern books on the Maybricks.

Michael Maybrick (*Illustrated Sporting and Dramatic News*, 20th October 1877)

It is noticeable that the diarist says hardly anything about James' eldest brother William, other than the line, '*I cannot understand why William will not accept my offer to dine. He is not unlike me, he hates the bitch.*' There is an obvious reason for the scarcity of information here; the author knew practically nothing about William as he barely gets a mention in any of the books on the case. Ryan touches upon William very briefly, stating, '*Maybrick's fourth brother, William, who lived in Liverpool, scarcely seemed interested to learn of the proposed marriage.*'[441] Ryan also wrote the '*Maybricks were in full attendance at the funeral. Even William, who dwelt in Liverpool but who had never entered Battlecrease House, came to say farewell to his brother.*'[442] Once again we can trace back a supposedly intimate snippet of family knowledge to a modern source.

There are frequent references to Michael, another of James' brothers. The diarist writes on a few occasions that he would travel to London and stay with him; for example, he wrote '*I will visit Michael this coming June.*' No intimate knowledge on display, as all the books state that James stayed with Michael in his apartments in London. Maybe, if the diarist had said something particular about the apartment not mentioned in any books, that would have demonstrated some intimate knowledge, but it never occurs. Michael was the most well-known of the Maybrick brothers, a famous composer who performed under the stage name of *Stephen Adams*. The diarist wrote, '*if Michael can succeed in rhyming verse, then I can do better.*' The problem with this line is that Michael composed the music and practically never wrote the words to his songs. He usually collaborated with a lyrist, such as Fred Weatherly. In fact, there is only one song, *A Warrior Bold*, that it is known that Michael actually wrote the words for. In 1911, he said he wrote both the music and words for that particular song while he was ill in bed.[443] A person with intimate family knowledge would have known that fact, and also known that Michael gave the name of the lyrist as '*Edwin Thomas*'. That was a name constructed from the Christian names of two of the Maybrick brothers. That is a clever use of words, but it is not referred to by the diarist, undoubtedly because he did not know that story.

One passage in the Diary that did seemingly provide some support for the notion that it might be authentic, is the diarist referring to himself as '*Sir Jim.*' For example, in one passage when the diarist is boasting that as a result of his crimes his name will be on '*every person's lips*,' he suggests that Her Gracious Majesty might honour him with a knighthood. He writes, '*I deserve at least an honour so all for a whim, I can now arise Sir Jim.*'

This is important, because in June 1993 (after the Diary had been brought to the public's attention), Keith Skinner accessed the Christie archive and found a piece of correspondence from Florence Aunspaugh in which she wrote, '*She [Nurse Yapp] did not see why Sir James [James Maybrick] ever brought me there anyway.*'[444] Paul Feldman, Shirley Harrison and Robert Smith all believe this reference to be extremely important. Robert Smith argues that, as the name '*Sir James*' can only be found in the Christie archives and not in any modern books, that can only mean that the diarist had '*first-hand knowledge of James Maybrick's unusual affectation within the family.*'[445]

---

440 Smith's Additional Statement, July 1889; HO 144/1639/A50678/D26
441 Ryan B., op cit., page 20.
442 Ibid., page 81.
443 *Isle of Wight County Press*, 30th August 1913.
444 Trevor Christie Collection.
445 Smith R., op cit., pages 35-36.

The problem with this assertion is if James did have an affectation to be called '*Sir James*,' then why did he not actually write that particular name in the Diary if he was in fact the author of the document? The diarist uses the name '*Sir Jim*' and *not* '*Sir James.*' Modern books provide many references to the fact that James was on occasions called Jim; for example, Ryan wrote about the nurse who attended Florence after her children were born that '*Jim knew her and liked her.*'[446]

If one employs a parallel comparison technique, comparing references from the Diary with extracts from modern books on James and Florence Maybrick, it is easy to identify where all the factual references in the Diary may have been sourced. The table below provides just some examples of this analysis to show how a clever forger might have written the Diary cherry-picking phrases and then incorporating them into the Diary's text.

DIARY REFERENCES	**EXTRACTS FROM BERNARD RYAN'S 1977 BOOK**
*Business is **flourishing.***	*Maybrick's cotton brokerage **flourished.***
*My medicine will **give me strength.***	*I take this arsenic once in a while because I find it **strengthens me.***
*I am in the **habit of taking strong medicine.***	*For some time he had had a **habit of taking a strong medicine.***
*I feel a **numbness** in my body.*	*James complained to his brother [Michael] of his persistent symptoms: pains in the head and **numbness** of the limbs.*
*Fuller believes there is **very matter with me.***	*[Fuller said] that he could find **very little the little the matter with him.***

A detailed analysis of the Diary makes it clear its author did not have an intimate knowledge of the Maybricks. Every single piece of information found in the Diary can be easily sourced from a limited number of modern books. The 1977 Ryan book, in particular, has sentences that seem to directly correspond with some of the passages contained within the text of the Diary.

In fact, not only does the Diary not show any intimate knowledge, it actually contains several mistakes in its references to the lives of James and Florence and their family. Some of these are relatively minor, some are of much greater significance; however, cumulatively, they add up and point directly at the Diary being a modern hoax constructed from a few modern books.

[446] Ryan B., op cit., page 55.

7

DANGEROUS LIAISONS

The *Liverpool Mercury*, somewhat surprisingly, considering the murderous deeds of Jack the Ripper, described 1888 as '*not a particularly eventful*' year. The same could not be said for the Maybrick household, where emotions were running high and actions were already in play that were to plunge the family into scandal and destruction.

The age gap between James and Florence was becoming increasingly apparent, and nobody was more aware of this than James himself. It was this realisation that drove him to change doctors from Dr Hopper to Dr Drysdale, an elderly Scotsman, who practiced medicine at Rodney Street, Liverpool.

Dr Drysdale (1817-1892) was a pioneering homeopath, who had earned a national reputation for his new approach to tackling ill-health. Having established a practice in Liverpool at 18 Rodney Street in 1841, Drysdale founded the first homeopathic dispensary in Benson Street and, from its inception, was closely associated with the homeopathic Hahnemann Hospital in Hope Street, a gift to the city from the sugar magnate Sir Henry Tate in 1887.

Dr Drysdale (1817-1892)

James turned to Dr Drysdale for help because he was '*noted for his skill in treating nervous dyspepsia*.'[447] James had six consultations with Dr Drysdale: on 19th, 22nd and 26th November, 5th and 10th December 1888, and 7th March 1889. At the first meeting, James described his symptoms to the doctor. He told him that for three months he had been: '*suffering from attack of pains from side to side of the head and a creeping all over his head, preceded by pains on the right side of the head and a dull headache. He was never free from pain except in the early morning and possibly in the forenoon... After smoking much or taking too much wine he became numb down the left leg and hand and liable to eruption upon the skin*.'[448]

During the consultations, Dr Drysdale quizzed James about the medications he had been taking, and he replied, '*nitro-hydrochloric acid, strychnine, and hydrate of potash and several others*.' Dr Drysdale believed that James was suffering from '*nervous dyspepsia*' and that he was a hypochondriac.[449] He prescribed a range of homeopathic remedies. It has been suggested that these homeopathic remedies led to a marked improvement in James' condition.[450] This is not the case.

During his consultations with Dr Drysdale, James was honest about his symptoms but he was less honest about the range of drugs he was taking, or that he was a regular user of arsenic. He did mention he used strychnine, but it is doubtful he would have told the doctor the extent to which he was using the drug. As a result, the remedies that Dr Drysdale prescribed could have only ever be partially successful. During his last consultation in March 1889, James told the doctor that most of his symptoms were better; however, he had never been more than two or three days free from a headache, though the headaches were not as bad as they had previously been. He said there was still pain and numbness in his left leg and hand, but that too was not as bad as it had been in the previous year. James, at best, may have lessened his acute condition, but he was still in the chronic stage and any sudden increase in his use of powerful drugs would have almost certainly caused his health to take a dangerous turn for the worse.

While James was suffering bouts of illness in 1888, Florence's health had improved. It is likely that during this period her appearance was at its most striking. She was no longer a shy and rather demur teenager, but a confident and attractive woman in her mid-twenties. She was 5 feet 3 inches tall, and her weight would have been around 112 pounds.[451]

The Baroness believed the pictures of her daughter that were in circulation around the time of her trial provided an inaccurate presentation of the way she appeared in real life. She especially hated the picture of the waxwork model

---

[447] Ryan B., op cit., page 29.
[448] Irving H.B., op cit., page 195.
[449] Ibid., page 196.
[450] Rubinstein W. D., 'Hunt for Jack the Ripper' in *History Today*, Vol. 50, May 2000.
[451] The figures come from when she entered Woking Prison in August 1889, shown in Maybrick F., op cit., page 64.

of Florence that had been constructed after her conviction. She felt the shape of its face and eyes gave it a misleading impression of her character. Instead, the Baroness always felt the photographs taken of her daughter by Medrington's in Liverpool in 1887 provided the most accurate picture of Florence's appearance.[452]

Florence Maybrick (Photograph taken by Medrington's, Bold Street, Liverpool in 1887)

[452] *Liverpool Echo*, 30th September 1889.

According to Florence Aunspaugh, Florence was a '*beautiful and attractive woman.*' She had a '*rounded figure, well developed bust and hips, slender waist, tapering arms and legs, small wrists and ankles, small feet and hands with rather long tapering fingers.*' The '*crowning glory*' of her appearance was the hair; blonde with a tinge of red, and '*inclined to be curly and always arranged in a becoming style.*' She was also struck by Florence's eyes, which she described as '*the most beautiful blue I have ever seen,*' though she added, '*they would appear to be entirely without life, or expression, as if you were gazing into the eyes of a corpse.*'

Not all commentators agreed that Florence was beautiful; a reporter from the *Porcupine* described her as '*not at all handsome*' and her complexion as '*swarthy or voluptuous.*'[453] Other reporters were more generous. A reporter from the *Liverpool Daily Post* wrote she '*was homely and pleasant looking. She is altogether younger and more attractive in feature and in her slight but well-proportioned figure, than many of her portraits make her out to be.*'[454] Another reporter echoed these sentiments, commenting that her '*dark brown hair is curled in clusters around her forehead, and without being what is regarded as classically handsome, her features are regular and pleasing and her figure is petite and elegant.*'[455]

Florence is often described as being not very clever. Florence Aunspaugh wrote that Florence '*fell far below her husband in intellect and had nothing like the intelligent mind her mother the Baroness von Roques had. My father often remarked, "Mrs Maybrick could hardly reach the standard of mediocrity."*'

Charles Ratcliffe, who was a friend to both James and Florence, said of Florence when some of her love letters were discovered after James' death: '*I always knew she was dumb... but I did not consider her that dumb to leave her affairs accessible to any who chose to penetrate.*' Even the Baroness said, '*my daughter is not a woman of very much penetration. If you could see her you would not wonder at the ease with which she has been deceived.*'[456]

Although Florence could be naïve, she was more intelligent than she is usually given credit for. She was fluent in two, possibly three languages; she was an avid letter writer; she was articulate; and she had a reputation for being an entertaining conversationalist. After her prison years, she wrote a book and embarked on a nationwide lecture tour of America. In Mobile, Alabama, in December 1908, she spoke to an audience of 800 people for two hours about her life and her time in prison.

In the early years of her marriage, Florence had been an innocent abroad. By late 1888, this was no longer the case. Although still naïve in many ways, Florence had become more confident and she was learning to become almost as calculating as her husband. She had an increasing longing to get greater enjoyment out of her life. She started to attend more dances and she began to look at men, other than her husband, with more than just an admiring eye.

According to Aunspaugh, Florence '*began her lapses soon after her first child was born; the cotton brokers and their wives knew this, yet they received her hospitality and extended their hospitality.*'[457] Considering her age at that time, her physical health and the fact that she was living in cities that were unknown to her, this statement is extremely unlikely. It is possible that Florence had already developed a flirtatious manner, and that may have had led to some idle gossiping, but the idea she had sexual '*lapses*' in the early years of her marriage can be dismissed as unrealistic. What *is* true, is that after James' death, Battlecrease was searched by the Maybrick brothers and two of the married Janion sisters, and they found '*thirteen love letters from Edwin, seven from Alfred Brierley and five from Williams.*'[458] Very little is known about Williams and there is no evidence that he had a sexual relationship with Florence. It is assumed that he was a London solicitor, though he may have been from Liverpool. According to Florence Aunspaugh, '*Williams gave three hundred dollars*' towards Florence's defence costs at her trial, and he also '*advised*' her defence team, though '*on the quiet.*' As Williams' name comes from two separate sources – Florence Aunspaugh and Charles Ratcliffe – we have to assume that the letters from him to Florence did exist, though they were never presented as evidence at her trial.

The fact that there were affectionate letters to Florence from Edwin, James' youngest brother, is even more intriguing. As these letters were destroyed, it is very difficult to gauge the exact state of the relationship between Florence and Edwin. Nevertheless, there are some clues that the two of them may have indeed been quite close. John Aunspaugh told a story about an incident that occurred at a dinner held at Battlecrease at which he was the guest of honour. Some 20 couples were sitting around a long table; Aunspaugh and James were sitting next to each other at the top of the table, while Edwin was sitting near Florence at the other end. Aunspaugh happened to be looking at James when he heard Florence say to Edwin with a laugh: '*If I had met you first things might have been different.*' James reacted very angrily to the words, dropping his knife and clenching his fist, while his eyes glared and his face '*flushed the colour of fire.*' Nothing came of the incident, and James quickly regained his composure and picked up his knife. Aunspaugh later asked another guest at the dinner for an explanation about what had happened, and was

---

453 *Porcupine*, 1st June 1889.
454 *Liverpool Daily Post*, 1st August 1889.
455 *Liverpool Mercury*, 1st August 1889.
456 *Liverpool Echo*, 14th August, 1889.
457 Trevor Christie Collection.
458 Feldman P., op. cit., page 410.

told, '*Why, Edwin and Mrs James have been sweet on each other for quite a while.' Although the rest of the evening passed smoothly, Florence Aunspaugh said that the incident had 'made somewhat of an impression on my father at the time but he soon forgot all about it.*'[459]

Some on the Liverpool Cotton Exchange felt that Florence and Edwin might have had an affair, though there is little evidence to support such a view. As Edwin and Florence were close, it is something of a surprise to find his cold attitude to her at the time of her trial. Maybe his attitude reflected an attempt to protect himself, as he certainly would not have wanted his love letters to Florence to have been read out in court. Ratcliffe, in a letter to John Aunspaugh, wrote that around the time of James' death, Edwin was '*deep in the mire himself*' and was suffering from '*nervous prostration.*' This suggests the relationship between Edwin and Florence was more than just platonic in nature. Perhaps Edwin was jealous of Florence's relationship with Alfred Brierley. He did tell Florence's mother, when she arrived at Battlecrease after James' death, that he was '*very fond of Florence*' and he '*would have never believed anything wrong about her... until a letter to a man was found. I wish I could meet Brierley.*'[460] Florence clearly felt disappointed and betrayed by Edwin. In a letter she wrote to her mother from prison whilst awaiting her trial, she said: '*I did think Edwin was true and returned some of the trust and affection I have thrown on him for so many years. His day of retribution will come, for God is just.*'[461]

While it is difficult to ascertain whether Florence had a love affair with either Williams or Edwin Maybrick – although in both cases it seems unlikely – there is no doubt that she had an affair with Alfred Brierley (1851-1923). Brierley was born in Rochdale in 1851, one of ten children. His family, who were well known and respected in Liverpool, had made their money in the Lancashire cotton industry. His grandfather Abraham Brierley (1793-1864) had established four large and successful cotton mills. His father Joseph Brierley (1817-1896) ran the Holland Street Mill in Rochdale which, with the others at College Street, Brimrod and Lowerhey, boasted 1,900 looms and 100,000 spindles. Joseph Brierley was said to have been '*completely broken down*' by his son's involvement in the Maybrick case.[462]

Alfred Brierley (*The Chronicle*, 9th August 1889)

Alfred Brierley lived in 60 Huskisson Street, Liverpool and, like James, was a cotton trader. His company, Brierley, Wood and Co., was based in 4 Old Hall Street in Liverpool, just around the corner from James' offices in the Knowsley Buildings. Brierley probably met James through work, though they may have met at Liverpool Cricket Club where they were both members.

When Brierley first met Florence is not entirely clear. In a newspaper interview Brierley gave in August 1889, he stated that prior to November 1888 he and Florence were '*merely distant acquaintances.*'[463] This view is supported by Edwin's comments to the Baroness that Florence only met Brierley '*this winter at some dances.*'[464] If this is the case, then Brierley met Florence at a time when she was disillusioned with her marriage and looking for some alternative male company. As a tall and handsome bachelor, Brierley caught Florence's eye and there can be no doubt that she was attracted to him.

Not all the women of Liverpool shared Florence's view of Brierley's good looks. At James' inquest, a female spectator complained that Brierley was '*not all my fancy painted.*' The scribe from the *Porcupine* also found him a disappointment. '*Figure to yourself,' one woman remarked to another, 'a medium-sized man verging on middle age [he was thirty-eight], with a fresh, freckled complexion, flowing red whiskers and beard, and light brown hair parted down the middle. His expression, I should say, is not intellectual, and a simpering smile which hovers round his*

[459] Quoted in Harrison S., op. cit., page 70.
[460] Quoted in Graham A. and Emmas C., op. cit., page 129.
[461] Quoted in Christie T.L., op. cit., page 70.
[462] *Liverpool Review*, 3rd August 1889.
[463] *Garston and Woolton Reporter*, 17th August 1889.
[464] MacDougall A.W., (1891) op cit., page 10.

features makes him look finnikin. Oh, not at all my beau-ideal of a hero. What could little Mrs Maybrick be thinking of to run after such a very undistinguished man?"'[465]

It was at a ball at Battlecrease in November 1888, that a '*mutual attraction apparently blossomed*' between Florence and Brierley.[466] The chemistry between them was noticed by a few of the guests and Charles Ratcliffe wrote a letter to John Aunspaugh in America, which included the line, '*Think Alf is getting the inside track with Mrs James' affection.*' Another person at the ball who noticed the attention Brierley was giving Florence was Miss Gertrude Janion, one of the younger Janion sisters. She was also attracted to Brierley, and was irritated by the attention he was giving to Florence. As Florence and Gertrude were of a similar age and relatively close, Florence would often confide in Gertrude. In so doing, she was putting herself in a potentially risky situation, as Gertrude might tell her older sister, Mrs Briggs, what Florence was up to.

The Christmas period 1888, must have been a difficult time in Battlecrease. The relationship between Florence and James was getting close to breaking point. He was struggling with his health and was increasingly irritable, while she was beginning to look elsewhere for love. To make the tension even greater, Michael Maybrick came to stay for Christmas. Relations between Florence and her brother-in-law were polite and cordial rather than warm and friendly. Florence's mother claimed that before the bitterness that developed between Florence and Michael during James' illness, Michael had shown nothing but '*kindly intentions*' towards her daughter. The Baroness said such was Michael's friendly regard for Florence that she had been the first person to hear '*the strains of The Holy City, which was sung to her by the composer*' on board his yacht. It was a story Florence later said was untrue. In an interview she gave in 1904, Florence said she had only met Michael and Edwin once before her wedding to James, and '*they were guests at my home, not oftener than once a year.*'[467] As Edwin stayed in Liverpool for half the year, and because he was in business with James, he must have visited the house more frequently than once a year; however, it is probable that Michael was a very infrequent visitor to Liverpool.

There was probably a diplomatic truce between Florence and James while Michael stayed with them. James would have been embarrassed if his brother had seen him and Florence arguing. After he departed, the rows started to break out again. One argument on New Year's Eve was especially heated and James, in a furious fit of temper, ripped up his will. Florence wrote to her mother informing her of what happened: '*In his fury he tore up the will this morning as he had made me sole legatee and trustee in it. Now he proposes to settle everything he can on the children alone, allowing me only the one-third by law. I am sure it matters little to me as long as the children are provided for. A pleasant way of commencing the New Year.*'[468] Although Florence's letter doesn't say what caused the argument, the fact James acted in the manner he did, suggests that he was very angry with his wife and had become suspicious of her behaviour. James' intention is clear; he did not want Florence to take control of the family's wealth when he died.

James' mood swings could be very dramatic; one moment he was loud and aggressive to his wife, yet within a short time he could be caring and generous in his attitude. This is demonstrated by the fact he took out additional insurance policies to protect his wife and children at the same time that he ripped up his will.

Prior to 1888, James had taken out an insurance policy for £500 in his wife's name with the Scottish and Widows' Fund. In October 1888, he decided that this policy was insufficient to protect his family, so he took out a new policy with the Mutual Reserve Fund Life Association of New York in their Liverpool office. The policy was for £2,000, and the beneficiary was his wife. In January 1889, he took out a second policy with the same company, this time for £3,000 and the beneficiary was his estate. Although the latter policy was not in his wife's name, she would have directly benefitted from its provision. The timing of these policies coincides with his persistent headaches and his frequent visits to Dr Drysdale. It is probable he did have concerns about his health and realised he needed to do something to protect his family. Interestingly, he had a medical for each of the new two new policies, and on both occasions he was given a clean bill of health. One can only assume he did not tell the doctors either about his headaches or his use of dangerous drugs.

One characteristic more than any other that defined James' lifestyle during this period was his incessant drive to obtain different medications to feed his insatiable drug appetite and his chronic hypochondriac tendencies. In the last year of his life, James visited Dr Hopper on 20 occasions, Dr Drysdale on six occasions and Dr Fuller on two occasions. That means he visited a doctor on average once every fortnight.

On top of that, he visited numerous chemists up and down the land. The list of the medicine bottles found in Battlecrease and James' office prior to Florence's trial, shows that they had come from over 20 different chemists. As labels had been removed from other medicine bottles, it is likely that James had visited even more chemists than the list appears to show. While some of these medicines were no doubt sourced for Florence and the children, there is clear evidence of James' excessive drug use. Whenever James visited a new town he saw an opportunity to acquire

[465] *Porcupine*, 1st June 1889.
[466] Christie T.L., op. cit., page 50.
[467] *The Sunday Oregonian (Portland)*, 20th November 1904.
[468] Christie T.L., op. cit., page 51.

additional medicines. For example, one of his medicine bottles came from Humphrey Jones, a chemist in Llangollen, North Wales. In February 1889, James stayed in Llangollen whilst on a walking holiday with some of his friends, including George Davidson, George Holt Jnr., a well-known Liverpool merchant, and Harold Gibbons, another cotton trader. One report states the group walked for up to 20 miles a day while on the trip.[469] It appears that James' healthy habit of outdoor walking was coupled with his unhealthy habit of attempting to source new medications. Just prior to Florence's trial, the police interviewed Mr Humphrey Jones over the medicine bottle found in Battlecrease. He said that any bottles containing arsenic left his chemists with a red label and were clearly marked '*Poison,*' and the '*bottle in question bears a white label, showing that an ordinary article was purchased.*'[470]

At least six of the chemists in which James had bought medicines were in London; a couple were located close to Regent's Park where James' brother Michael lived. In addition, it is possible James visited an unknown London doctor as he may have been suffering from psoriasis of the feet. Psoriasis is an autoimmune condition in which white blood cells attack the skin cells. This can lead to new skin cells developing too quickly causing them to pile up on the skin's surface. Although this is usually an inherited condition, it can be caused by external factors including stress, heavy use of alcohol, high blood pressure medication and antimalarial medication. As all these factors applied to James, it is plausible he suffered from psoriasis.

The evidence for this was provided by Dr Forbes Winslow, a British psychiatrist, who was involved in the running of lunatic asylums. In August 1889, Forbes Winslow was active in the campaign in London to get Florence's trial verdict overturned. At a public meeting in the Cannon Street Hotel in London, he read out a letter from a doctor who claimed that not only had James consulted him over his psoriasis, but that he had prescribed a treatment involving a solution of arsenic.[471] Although it is possible to dismiss the letter, it is clear that Dr Forbes Winslow took it seriously and even referred to it when he wrote his memoirs in 1910.

Although it is not certain James visited a doctor in London for a possible psoriasis condition, he did manage to find a new source for his arsenic needs. In January 1889, he met Valentine Charles Blake (1844-1921), a man who was involved in the campaign to launch Ramie Grass as a substitute for cotton on the British market. James met Blake in his office in the Knowsley Buildings, and was delighted to hear that arsenic was used in the manufacture of the product.

In an affidavit of 1894, Blake stated that James had asked him if he knew about the Austrian peasants of Styria who ate arsenic, or if he had read De Quincey's *Confessions of an English Opium-eater.* James then said to him: '*One man's poison is another man's meat, and there is a so-called poison which is meat and liquor to me whenever I feel weak and depressed. It makes me stronger in mind and in body at once. I don't tell everybody and wouldn't tell you only you mentioned arsenic. It is arsenic. I take it when I can get it, but doctors won't put any in my medicine except now and then a trifle that only tantalises me. Since you use arsenic can you let me have some? I find difficulty in getting it here.*'

Blake said he had no licence to sell arsenic, but agreed to provide James with the drug providing that, in return, James would help him in promoting the grass seed. A month later, Blake returned to Liverpool and gave James about 150 grains of arsenic in three packets: one packet of white and two packets of black arsenic (mixed with charcoal). When Blake gave James the arsenic, he warned him: '*Be careful, you have almost enough to kill a regiment.*'[472]

James took the arsenic and invited Blake to Battlecrease for a meal. Blake turned down the offer as he had to return to London, but said that he would dine with James the next time he came to Liverpool. He never saw James again.

Unfortunately for Florence, Blake did not give evidence for the defence at her trial. In his affidavit, he claimed that he had written to Florence's lawyers before her trial had started but never received a reply. He did not pursue the matter as at that time he was more concerned about his only son who was missing and presumed drowned.

Blake's evidence could have been crucial at the trial as it would have explained why there was so much arsenic in Battlecrease when the house was searched after James' death. It may also have explained the presence of the black arsenic that was found in the *Arsenic - Poison for Cats* package.

The reliability of Blake's affidavit has been questioned. He has been described as a person with a chequered personal history, who was '*not entirely honest.*' Blake's father was Sir Valentine John Blake, the 12th Baronet of Menlough in Ireland. After his father's death, Valentine Blake hoped to inherit the title and the wealth of the estate; however, as he was the son of the Baronet's second marriage, his claim was weak and everything was inherited by the eldest son of the first marriage. Blake was so angry at the decision that he started a lengthy court case to try and get his father's first marriage declared null and void. In 1878, the case was dismissed by the courts, leaving him with expensive legal costs. It has been claimed that his failed law suit turned him into an '*embittered man who throughout his life made poor choices, had a drink problem and found it difficult to form relationships.*' As a result of his debts

[469] *Liverpool Courier*, 1st June 1889.
[470] *Liverpool Daily Post*, 15th June 1889.
[471] *St James's Gazette*, 16th August 1889.
[472] HO 144/1639/A50678D/702.

and poor decision-making, it has been suggested that Blake might have concocted the story about providing James with arsenic in the hope of receiving money from the Baroness in return for evidence that could secure Florence's release.[473]

Whilst it is true that Blake did make some poor choices in his life, and that he was often in debt, the main details of his affidavit were all fully supported in a separate affidavit signed by William B. Nation, Blake's employer. Nation described himself as a '*manufacturing chemist*.' He declared that Blake's statements '*as to my having employed him in the capacities he describes are quite correct, as is also his description of the manufacturing carried on by me at my premises, the Atlantic Works, Abbey Road, West Ham, and the fact of arsenic and soot being mixed with the chemical manure*.'

Nation stated that in early 1889, he '*twice sent him [Blake] to Liverpool to see Mr James Maybrick*.' He added: '*It is correct that the said Mr Blake had access to and (with my full permission) possession of arsenic manufactured by me, some white, some mixed with soot and some with charcoal, as described in his said declaration*.' The source and strength of Nation's affidavit means that, for all Blake's faults, his statement that he provided James with arsenic is almost certainly true.

James' heavy drug use had been affecting him adversely for some time, but by 1889 the effects were becoming more visible. Florence had observed her husband taking a white powder. Every time he took it he became more nervous and irritable. Florence believed the powder to be strychnine as she '*never had the slightest idea*' that James was taking arsenic.[474] When Florence tried to question James about his use of the powder, he flew into a rage and refused to answer any of her questions. She had already spoken to Dr Hopper about her concerns in the summer of 1888; he had searched James' dressing room, but had been unable to find the powder.

In March 1889, Florence again raised the issue, this time with Dr Humphreys, the local doctor who had been treating the children. In his testimony at Florence's trial, he said that while he was treating the Maybrick children, he had a conversation with Florence about her husband's health. According to Dr Humphreys, '*she said he was taking some white powder, which she thought was strychnine, and she asked what was likely to be the result. I said that if he took a large enough dose, he would die... I said to Mrs Maybrick, not meaningly, however, "Well, if he should ever die suddenly call me, and I can say you have had some conversation with me about it*."[475]

As well as mentioning the powder to Dr Humphreys, Florence carried out a search of the house, but she could not find where James had hidden it. He had probably kept it in the black box which was located in his study that was always locked. When James took the powder out with him it was kept in a sachet hidden in his clothes, as he had a '*fad for secret pockets*.'[476]

As James was refusing to answer her questions, in early March 1889, Florence decided to inform someone whom she knew James would take notice of, namely his brother Michael. At Florence's trial, Michael admitted under questioning from Sir Charles Russell that he had received a letter from Florence, which he had subsequently destroyed. In the letter, Florence '*stated that she had found my brother taking a white powder, and that she thought that it might have something to do with the pains in his head*.' He said when James had next come to London he questioned him about the matter, but James had called it '*a damned lie*.' As a result, he said he had not pursued the issue any further.[477]

The month of March 1889, is one of the most pivotal in the whole Maybrick drama. The start of the month saw Dr Humphreys, the young local doctor who lived in Garston Old Road less than half a mile from Battlecrease, treat the Maybrick children. He had first visited the house in early 1887, when the children were suffering from whooping cough, and since then '*had often attended the Maybrick children*.'[478] The illness the children suffered from in March doesn't appear to have been too serious, as they both recovered quite quickly.

Despite the illness of the children and the clear discord between husband and wife, James and Florence decided to stay overnight at the Palace Hotel in Birkdale, near Southport. Staying in the same hotel as the Maybricks were a young couple, Charles and Christine Samuelson, and Alfred Brierley. According to evidence that Christine gave at James' inquest, they stayed at the hotel '*about a fortnight or three weeks before the Grand National*.'[479] As the Grand National took place on Friday 29th March, possible dates for the Palace Hotel trip are a fortnight earlier (the weekend of 16/17th March) and three weeks earlier (the weekend of 9/10th March). As it is believed that James visited London on 16th March, that leaves the previous weekend, 9/10th as the obvious date for the Palace trip. Some sources suggest the Maybricks stayed overnight in the hotel after attending a race meeting, but that is unlikely as there were no such

---

473 Parry S., 'Valentine's Days' in the *Journal of the Whitechapel Society*, October 2021, pages 26-31.
474 *Evening Express*, 22nd August 1889.
475 Irving H.B., op cit., page 87.
476 *Pall Mall Gazette*, 13th August 1889.
477 Irving H.B., op cit., page 30.
478 Ryan B., op cit., page 32.
479 *Liverpool Courier*, 31st May 1889.

meetings occurring anywhere near Birkdale over that period. There had also been a severe snowstorm on Friday 8th March which had disrupted sporting events and had led to major floods as the snow melted.

Palace Hotel, Birkdale

The most obvious explanation for the trip is that the Maybricks decided to spoil themselves and visit one of the finest hotels in the north of England. One contemporary guidebook commented that '*the cuisine and cellars of the Palace are a fit subject for the praise of the most fastidious gastronome.*' In 1881, after going into liquidation, the Palace had been relaunched as a hydropathic hotel, pandering to the Victorian fad of combining a holiday with water-based health cures. A new wing was added, the bathrooms were equipped with modern suites and hot and cold water. Electric lighting was produced by a steam-driven generator. Tennis-courts and pavilions, croquet, bowling, archery, walks, horse-riding, billiards and dancing – in the finest and largest hotel ballroom on the coast – ensured that the Palace appealed to the rich and famous. There was midweek dancing, Saturday dinner-dances and, on Sundays, orchestral teas and evening concerts.

The Samuelsons were a young, wealthy and prominent Liverpool couple. Charles' father was a successful tobacco merchant who had served as Mayor of Liverpool in the 1870s. Christine's father was William Steenstrand, a well-known and successful figure on the Liverpool Cotton Exchange. Their marriage in February 1886 had been a significant social event and the Mayor of Liverpool had '*placed two carriages at the disposal of the wedding party.*'[480]

The Samuelsons had befriended the Maybricks in December 1888, and the two couples had met on several occasions in early 1889. Florence would have enjoyed the company of Christine, who was the same age as her and had a reputation as being '*very gay*' and liking '*parties and every possible social occasion.*'[481] It was during this stay at the Palace Hotel that an incident occurred that was to take on a much greater significance than it merited. According to testimony given by Christine at the inquest into James' death, Florence told her that '*she hated her husband.*' Christine was briefly questioned about Florence's words by Mr Pickford, who had been employed by Florence's solicitors to look after her interests. In response, Christine admitted the words '*were part of a conversation and not an isolated remark.*' Pickford did not press Christine any further, so the wider context that caused Florence to utter the words was not provided. This was a mistake by Pickford. When Florence was in Walton Gaol awaiting her trial, she gave her mother an account of what had happened in the Palace Hotel. She said: '*I remember perfectly well saying I hate Jim. It was on an occasion when we were all playing cards, and there was a row between Mrs Samuelson*

[480] *Liverpool Mercury*, 26th February 1889.
[481] Morland N., op cit., pages 24-25.

and her husband, and Mrs Samuelson said to her husband, "I hate you." I went into the bedroom to mediate between them, and I said to Mr Samuelson, "You must not take serious notice of that, I often say I hate Jim."'[482]

If Florence's account is accurate, then Christine did not tell the full truth and gave the misleading impression that Florence had said the fateful words to her when in fact she had made them to Charles, her husband. Christine also failed to provide any context for how and why the remark was made. When questioned by Pickford, she was provided with an opportunity to give the background context but failed to do so other than to say it was part of a wider conversation. As a result, an innocent statement came to be twisted and given a meaning that was never intended. Why did Christine act in such a manner? Was she just distancing herself from a former friend who was being accused of murder, or was there more to her actions? To make her actions even more questionable, Christine disappeared after the inquest and did not appear as a witness at Florence's trial. This situation was not lost on MacDougall, who wrote that Christine's disappearance was presumably due to the fact that '*otherwise she would have found it necessary to say a little more than she did about her acquaintance with the Maybricks, which she said only lasted from December to March.*'[483]

While one can understand why the Maybricks decided to go to the Palace Hotel with their new friends the Samuelsons, the presence of Alfred Brierley in the hotel is more puzzling. It is unlikely that he, as a single man, would have chosen to go there with two married couples. It seems more likely that he just happened to be staying there. Records show that he did stay at the hotel from time to time.[484] Maybe Florence picked the hotel and the dates of the visit after hearing that Brierley was going to be staying there; if that was the case, then she was playing a dangerous game.

One newspaper article provides an even more sensational reason for the hotel trip. According to this report, Brierley claimed that '*throughout the intrigue with Mrs Maybrick he was little more than passive. At first when she made violent love to him at Southport under her irate husband's eyes he responded as most men would have done, quite without arrière-pensée [ulterior motive].*'[485]

It seems extremely unlikely that Florence and Brierley had a sexual encounter at the Palace Hotel, especially as Brierley would have realised that it would have provoked a violent response from James if he had found out what had happened.

Whatever the nature of encounter, it seems to have galvanised Florence to want to pursue a course of action that was ultimately to lead to her conviction. She had decided that brief moments with Brierley were no longer enough, she wanted to spend some quality time with the man that she had almost certainly fallen in love with.

The following weekend, Saturday and Sunday 16th/17th March, James travelled to London to visit Michael. This was the occasion when his brother questioned him about Florence's assertion that he was using a white powder.

Arthur and Suzanna Flatman

With James away, Florence had an opportunity to plan her own visit to London to meet Brierley. On Saturday 16th March, she sent a telegraph to Mr Arthur Flatman (1849-1913), who ran a private hotel in Henrietta Street, Cavendish Square, saying she wanted to book a sitting-room and bedroom. As she had not received a reply, the following day, 17th March, she sent another telegraph to the hotel saying the rooms were to be engaged for a Mr and Mrs Thomas Maybrick of Manchester, and provided details of the sort of dinner they would like to have. She added that she '*had taken it upon herself to make the arrangements*' because her sister-in-law was '*not very experienced*' in such matters.[486] On Monday 18th March, Florence telegraphed the hotel again, informing them that Mr and Mrs Maybrick would arrive on Thursday 21st March, and would stay for one week and that they were '*not particular as to the price.*'

Flatman finally replied to Florence, but his response implied he was expecting two couples to stay at his hotel. As a result, on Wednesday 20th March, Florence sent yet another telegraph, in which she said: '*Mrs Maybrick hopes she had not confused Mr Flatman by writing for her sister as his letter gives her the impression that he expects both her and Mrs T. Maybrick, whereas it is only the lady and her husband who are coming to town.*'[487]

[482] MacDougall A.W., (1891) op. cit., page 499.
[483] Ibid., page 499.
[484] *Southport Visiter*, 21st March 1889.
[485] *The South Australian Chronicle*, 3rd August 1889.
[486] Irving H.B., op cit., page 262.
[487] Trial exhibit L, HO 144/1638/A50678.

The series of messages reveal Florence's determination to meet Brierley. They also make clear the steps she took to try and hide her actions; however, the choice of both hotel and name under which she made the booking showed a lack of clear thinking. The hotel was popular with cotton merchants, while Thomas was the name of one of James' brothers; both choices, therefore, reduced her chances of keeping her stay a secret. It has been suggested that Florence was '*going out of her way to provide her husband with evidence for a divorce. Otherwise, she was either acting out of sheer unthinking stupidity or striking out blindly in an effort to hurt him publicly.*'[488] A simpler explanation is that she selected the hotel as she had stayed there with her mother some nine years earlier.[489] She knew the hotel to be comfortable and quieter than the bigger London hotels.

Flatman's Hotel at the turn of the twentieth century by which time it had been renamed the Dysart

On Thursday, 21st March, Florence took the morning train to London. She told James she was going to visit an old family friend, Margaret Baillie, who was not very well. She instructed the servants to redirect her mail to the Grand Hotel in London, where she would be staying.

On her arrival at Euston Station, Florence took a cab to Flatman's hotel, arriving at about 1:30pm. She registered and was shown up to the hotel's finest suite, which had a bedroom and an adjoining sitting/dining room, by Mr Alfred Schweisso, the head waiter. That evening, Florence had arranged to meet John Baillie Knight, the nephew of Margaret Baillie and a long-time friend to both Florence and to her brother, Holbrook, to whom he had been an '*intimate friend.*'[490] Some weeks prior to her trip to London, Florence had written and asked him to meet her as she needed his advice.

On Thursday evening, John Baillie Knight arrived at the hotel at 6:30pm and took Florence out for dinner at the Grand Hotel and then on to a performance at the Gaiety Theatre. Over dinner she told him all about her problems, saying she was '*in some great trouble.*' She had come to London to see a solicitor as she wanted to separate from her husband as '*she could not live with him any more on account of him keeping this woman... that he was cruel to her and had struck her.*' At the end of the night, Baillie Knight dropped Florence back at the hotel.

At 9:30am on Friday 22nd March, Schweisso took a single breakfast up to Florence's room. Later, at James' inquest and at Florence's trial, the waiter said that when he took the breakfast into her room he saw a man in the sitting room. He noticed that this man was not the same person who had taken Florence out to dinner the previous evening.

Intriguingly, Schweisso's evidence changed between the inquest and trial as to the identity of this man. At the inquest, he stated that Brierley and Florence, '*stayed at the hotel as man and wife*' from Thursday to Sunday.[491] That implies it was Brierley that he saw on Friday morning; however, police inquiries later established that Brierley spent Thursday night in Liverpool, and took the Friday afternoon train to London. The police must have informed Schweisso, so at the trial – while he still states that he saw someone with Florence who wasn't the man she had been out with the night before – he went on to say that he did not see Florence with Brierley together until '*half-past seven*' on Friday evening. MacDougall, the Scottish lawyer who took up Florence's cause, wrote to Schweisso in 1890 to

---

[488] Jones F., *Murderous Women*, (Headline, London, 1991) pages 160-161.
[489] *New York Herald (London edition)*, 14th August 1889.
[490] *Pall Mall Gazette*, 13th August 1889.
[491] *Liverpool Mercury*, 6th June 1889.

try and clarify exactly what happened on Friday morning. Schweisso replied that he could '*scarcely recollect anything*' about events that morning and he may have made a '*mistake*.'[492]

It is likely that on the Friday morning, Florence was alone in her room when the waiter brought her breakfast, and that Schweisso was either confused at the inquest or had been pressured by the police to claim that he had seen Brierley with her. Brierley arrived at Flatman's Hotel early Friday evening, and had dinner with Florence in her hotel sitting-room that night. According to Schweisso's trial evidence, Brierley '*occupied the same bedroom in the hotel as Mrs Maybrick... up to Sunday*.'[493]

Just after noon on Sunday, 24th March, Florence and Brierley checked out of the hotel. The manager expressed his surprise as the room had been booked for the week. Brierley apologised, and provided the rather vague excuse that he had received a telegram from his brother. At the inquest, Schweisso said Brierley had settled the bill, but at Florence's trial he said *she* had paid. It had in fact been Brierley who had settled the hotel bill of two pounds and thirteen shillings.

Brierley and Florence at Flatman's Hotel
(*Illustrated Police News*, 17th August 1889)

The two nights that Florence spent with Brierley at Flatman's Hotel were to be one of the main reasons why Florence was convicted at her trial. To the police, it provided a motive for wanting to murder her husband. So why did she do it? Florence provided an answer in comments she made to Sir Charles Russell, telling him: '*He piqued my vanity and resisted my efforts to please him. I told him I was going to London and taunted him with being a coward. And afraid to meet me and willing to let such a chance slip by. I was, however, momentarily infatuated. Before we parted he gave me to understand that he cared for somebody else and could not marry me, and that rather than face the disgrace of discovery he would blow his brains out. I then had such a revulsion of feeling I said that we must end our intimacy at once*.'[494]

Florence's account supports the view that it was she who took the lead in arranging her liaison with Brierley in London, and that Brierley, as his friends suggested, was more passive in his attitude to Florence. In an interview with a reporter from the *New York Herald,* when asked who suggested the London trip, he replied: '*I decline to state*.' He did add that when they parted on the Sunday morning, they had a '*distinct understanding*' that '*nothing of the sort, by that I mean a meeting in London or any other place other than home, was ever to occur again*.' This prompted the reporter to ask if they had the intentions therefore of meeting at home; to which Brierley replied, '*None whatever. On the contrary, we parted in London as if we were never to meet again*.' Further, he said that he and Florence agreed not to correspond '*unless she got in some complications in consequence of our journey*.'[495]

After leaving Flatman's Hotel on Sunday morning, Florence travelled to Margaret Baillie's house, where she stayed the rest of the week.[496] In an attempt to cover her tracks, Florence told her aunt that she had been staying in the Grand Hotel. It was a lie that came back to haunt her. At some point over the next couple of days, Florence visited Markby and Stewart, the solicitors recommended to her by John Baillie Knight, and told them of her husband's cruelty and that he was maintaining another woman. They, in turn, provided her with clear instructions about the contents of any letter she should write to James if she wanted to pursue a separation from him. They stressed that it was important for her to follow this route if she wanted to continue living in the house with her two children.

On Saturday night, as Florence and Brierley were spending the night together at Flatman's Hotel, Michael Maybrick was compering and performing at a Smoking Concert at the Beaufort Club in Dover Street, London. The Duke of Beaufort, the President of the Club, attended the event, as did HRH Prince Albert Victor. Michael sang the *Sentry*

492 MacDougall A.W., (1891) op cit., pages 16-17.
493 Irving H.B., op cit., page 157.
494 Trevor Christie Collection.
495 *Garston and Woolton Reporter*, 17th August 1889.
496 *Pall Mall Gazette*, 13th August 1889.

Song, a Gilbert and Sullivan tune and, at the conclusion of the concert, spoke '*some well-chosen words*;' proposing a vote of thanks to the Duke and thanking the Prince for his presence at the event.[497]

Two days later, on Monday 25th March, Michael sang the same song '*with great effect*' at another event he had organised, a concert to mark the opening of the new headquarters of the Artists' Corps (20th Middlesex). The Artists' Corps, as the name suggests, was comprised of artists, musicians and entertainers. Its honorary colonel was Sir Frederick Leighton, one of the greatest painters of his day. Michael had joined the corps in February 1886, stating his profession as '*musician*' and his height as six feet one and half inches.[498] At the time of the concert in 1889, he held the rank of lieutenant. It was a very special event as the new headquarters was being opened by the Prince of Wales who attended it with his wife and three daughters. On the same evening, Michael organised a '*most enjoyable smoking concert*' for his comrades and again he entertained those present with a few songs.[499]

The night after he had entertained royalty, Michael took Florence out to dine at the Café Royal in Regent Street and then on to the theatre. Michael referred to the occasion after Florence's trial when the newspapers carried stories that he had always disliked her and had avoided her company. Michael claimed such reports were untrue and his relations with Florence were '*always pleasant.*' He said Florence had come to him '*time and time again for money and one thing and another, and she always got it.*'[500]

The fact that Florence could stay overnight with Brierley and then, within a day or two, be happy for James' brother to entertain her in such style, tells us a little about her as a person, and that she was capable of manipulating people to her advantage. Before she returned to Liverpool, John Baillie Knight took Florence out to dinner and the theatre for a second time. She showed him the draft letter of separation that had been prepared by the solicitors. It was a letter she never sent. Perhaps, if Brierley had made a firm commitment to her, she might have proceeded with the legal separation.

On Thursday 28th March, Florence boarded the train and headed home to Liverpool. According to Morland, she brought back far more luggage than she had taken to London. She was loaded down with a whole range of accessories from the shops of the capital, including '*silk and velvet bags with beetle-wing embroidery of iridescent green spangles... a matinee bag of leather fitted with scent bottle, opera glasses and biscuit case; and the new parasols which, she discovered, were longer and slimmer than last year's.*'[501]

Florence's week in London had been truly eventful. She had spent two nights with her lover. She had been taken out to dinner and the theatre on at least three occasions, including once by her famous brother-in-law who had spent the previous day hobnobbing with the heir to the throne. She had spent four nights with an old family friend. She had been to a solicitor about arranging a separation from her husband. She had been shopping.

And, in between all these activities, she had told countless lies.

There is also a possibility she was being secretly observed. After her trial, the *New York Herald* claimed Florence had been '*watched by the police*' throughout her stay in London, and they had taken photographs of the people she had met.[502] Christie called this report '*one of the strangest features of this strange case.*' He wrote that, if it were true, it would suggest James was in search of evidence that his wife was cavorting with Brierley.[503]

It is extremely unlikely that the story is accurate. It seems improbable that the police would be diverting their finite resources to follow Florence around the streets of the capital. In the same edition that the *Herald* had reported the story about Florence being watched, there was another article stating there were rumours the police had been '*constantly shadowing*' Brierley, but added, these rumours had '*no foundation.*' It is very likely that the story about the police secretly following Florence in London were also based on little more than unfounded rumours.

LINKS TO THE RIPPER DIARY: DID THE DIARIST DEMONSTRATE AN IN-DEPTH KNOWLEDGE OF THE RIPPER MURDERS?

Much of the debate about the Diary of Jack the Ripper focuses on the poor provenance of the document, or on the conflicting scientific results about the composition of the ink. One of the more interesting areas of debate focuses on the narrative itself; does it provide a unique insight into the mind of the killer, or can all the information in the journal be readily sourced from modern books?

The diarist claims to have killed seven women, two in Manchester and the five who are identified as being the canonical victims of the Whitechapel serial killer. Although the diarist only mentions one of the canonical victims

[497] *Monmouthshire Beacon*, 30th March 1889.
[498] Robinson B., op cit., page 329.
[499] *The Era*, 30th March 1889.
[500] *Evening Express*, 21st August 1889.
[501] Morland N., op cit., page 36.
[502] *New York Herald* (London edition), 14th August 1889.
[503] Christie T.L., op. cit., page 51.

by name, Mary Kelly, it is apparent from the descriptions he provides about the murders that he is referring to the Ripper victims.

Robert Smith suggests that the diarist provides a unique insight into the murders when he wrote, '*Kelly, no heart no heart.*' He argues that no-one knew until 1989 that the Ripper had removed Mary Kelly's heart from her body, and therefore the author must have had first-hand knowledge of the killing. However, this is not the case; Stephen Knight, in his book on the Ripper murders published in 1976, wrote that '*Kelly's heart was also cut out.*'[504] Martin Fido's book (1987) also mentions that the heart had been removed from the body.[505]

Indeed, what is striking about the Diary is how little detail is provided on any of the murders. The supposed two murders in Manchester are described in the briefest of details, making it impossible for any person reading the accounts to try and identify whom the victims might have been and when the murders may have occurred. This lack of detail is suggestive – it implies that the main concern of the author was to be as vague as possible so as to avoid writing something that could later be shown to be inaccurate.

The diarist is not only vague about the two supposed murders in Manchester, he also fails to provide many details about the Ripper murders. For example, the killing of Polly Nichols is covered in just one short paragraph that outlines only the most basic of facts, all of which are very easily accessible from modern books. The diarist writes about the killing: '*There was no scream when I cut. I was more than vexed when the head would not come off. I believe I will need more strength next time. I struck deep into her.*'

Does this statement show any in-depth knowledge? Absolutely not. Martin Fido, in his 1987 book on the murders, wrote of Nichols' killing: '*Dr Llewellyn pronounced her dead. Not a difficult diagnosis as the murderer had slashed her jugular veins, windpipe and half her spinal column; in truth, he had almost cut her head off.*' He also wrote that the killer '*seems to have attempted decapitation at first, but abandoned it as too difficult.*'[506]

If the diarist really had been Jack the Ripper, and the Polly Nichols killing was his first Whitechapel murder, then surely he would have gloated in some depth about the event. There would have been an out-pouring of emotion. There would have been an abundance of graphic details. Yet all we get are a few short and rather tame sentences providing only the briefest of details.

The same pattern can be seen in the diarist's accounts of the other Ripper murders – basic facts easily obtainable from modern books. To try and divert attention away from the paucity of information, these details are sometimes placed into a rhyme. When one recognises this trick for what it is – a diversion – and makes an analysis of the factual content, it is easy to identify that the narrative contains no new information.

This is illustrated by analysing the second Ripper victim, Annie Chapman (1841-1888). Her body was found at approximately 6:00am on Saturday 8th September 1888, in the backyard of 29 Hanbury Street, Spitalfields. The *Liverpool Courier* carried the story under the headline '*Another Fiendish Murder in London*' and went on to state that the new murder was '*far more diabolical*' than even that of Polly Nichols.[507] As well as having her throat cut and her face and body slashed, she had been disembowelled. The diarist wrote that he '*ripped open*' the victim and took '*some of it away with me.*' He claimed he later ate the body part removed from Chapman, and it tasted like '*fresh fried bacon.*'

A police search of the crime scene led to the discovery of a torn piece of envelope and two pills wrapped in a piece of paper. On the back of the envelope was the seal of the Sussex Regiment and on the other side was the letter '*M.*' The divisional police surgeon, Dr George Bagster Phillips, arrived around thirty minutes later. He examined the body and sent it to the mortuary. He searched the yard and found some items that had presumably been the contents of Chapman's pocket, which had been cut open. In his evidence at the inquest, he said the items included '*a small piece of coarse muslin, a small tooth comb, and a pocket comb in a paper case lying at the feet of the woman.' He believed that they had apparently been 'arranged there in order.*'

When Philips carried out the autopsy he noticed that there was '*an abrasion over the bend of the first joint of the ring finger. There were distinct markings of a ring or rings, probably the latter.*'[508] The rings appeared to have been ripped off her fingers, presumably by her murderer. One set of items Phillips did not mention in his evidence was two farthings. This is significant, as the diarist does refer to a '*farthing one and two*' in his account of the murder.

Those who believe that the Diary is genuine, argue the diarist had not made a mistake, and point to a statement made by Inspector Edmund Reid, a leading CID officer in Whitechapel, at the inquest into the death of Alice McKenzie in July 1889. He said that the coins found under McKenzie's body were similar to the ones found under Chapman's body.

---

504 Knight S., op cit., page 170.
505 Fido M., *The Crimes, Detection and Death of Jack the Ripper*, (Weidenfeld and Nicholson, London, 1987) page 92.
506 Ibid., pages 23 and 98.
507 *Liverpool Courier*, 10th September 1888.
508 *London Evening Standard*, 13th September 1888.

The problem with this remark is that Reid was on leave at the time of the Chapman murder. Reid believed that there were nine Ripper murders not five. He also believed, incorrectly, that no body parts were removed from any of the victims.[509] If Reid was correct, and there were nine Ripper victims, then the diarist could not have been the killer as he claimed to have stopped his Whitechapel murders after the killing of Mary Kelly. Also, James Maybrick could not have been the killer as he was dead before the murders of Alice McKenzie and Frances Coles.

The diarist's account of Annie Chapman's murder is almost as brief as the Nichols' murder. There are no details on how he met Chapman, or how he murdered her. There are no details on how the mutilation process was carried out, even though this was the essential part of the killing. According to Dr Phillips, it would have taken at least 15 minutes to complete and required a degree of skill. Coroner Baxter, during his summing up of the evidence at the end of the inquest, stated that the dissection of Chapman's body could have only been done by someone with anatomical skill and knowledge.

The absence of any detail by the diarist again suggests a lack of knowledge about the killing and dissection process. Modern books provide very few details on exactly how the mutilations had been completed, so the diarist had little he could copy into his narrative.

The only points of interest in the diarist's account of the murder of Annie Chapman are his references to the rings and the farthings. The diarist says that he took the rings because they reminded him '*too much of the whore,*' a supposed reference by James to his wife Florence. The diarist refers to the items in a rhyme: '*One ring, two rings, a farthing, one and two, Along with M ha ha Will catch clever Jim, its true. No pill, left but two.*'

There is a dispute over the number of rings worn by Annie Chapman at the time of her death. At the inquest, one witness – Eliza Cooper – said Chapman had been wearing three rings; while Edward Stanley said she wore two rings. A police report later seemed to confirm that it had been two brass rings; a wedding ring and a keeper ring, to prevent it from slipping off the finger. Paul Feldman argued the diarist's accurate reference to there being two rings and two farthings indicated that he had first-hand knowledge of the killing.

In fact, the reference is not in the least bit significant. The presence of two rings and two farthings is mentioned in several books written in the 1970s and 1980s. Stephen Knight, in his 1976 book, quotes a source who wrote, '*a curious detail that seems inexplicable, though I cannot help feeling that it has significance: two brass rings, two new farthings, and a few coins were laid out neatly around the feet of the corpse.*'[510] On top of that, the diarist's references are vague and provide no specific details, such as where the farthings had been placed. The diarist's account would have been significant if details had been provided that weren't known at the time and were later shown to be accurate, such as the design of the rings. That doesn't happen.

Although the diarist's vagueness about Chapman's murder indicates that the Diary is a forgery, the document does contain some clever elements. One of these is the reference to a cartoon that was printed in the satirical magazine *Punch* in September 1888. It was entitled '*Blind-Man's Buff*' and showed a policeman wearing a blindfold and being laughed at while having his pockets picked by some unsavoury-looking characters. The cartoon was an obvious criticism of the police's failure to catch Jack the Ripper. Below the cartoon was the caption '*Turn round three times, And catch whom you May.*' The diarist refers directly to the cartoon, saying that he could not stop laughing when he read it as it contained the first three letters of his surname. The cartoon featured prominently on the dust jacket of the Fido 1987 book on the Ripper murders, and was therefore easy to find by a clever forger who used it to try and provide some credibility to his otherwise limited and erroneous narrative about the Chapman murder.

The murder of Elizabeth Stride is yet another murder covered by the diarist in a short paragraph. He wrote he had nearly been caught after killing the victim, and therefore '*had no time to rip the bitch wide.*' In his brief account he mentions a horse, and appears to be referring to Louis Diemschitz, who drove his horse into Dutfield's Yard at the time of the murder. As he entered the yard, Diemschitz discovered a woman, whom he thought was drunk, lying on the ground. He then went inside the International Working Men's Educational Club, where he was the steward, to get help. It is at this point that the murderer probably managed to slip away from the scene of the crime.

The only other details that the diarist adds are references to a red rose and '*sweet scented breath.*' At Stride's inquest, a local resident testified that he had seen a red and white flower pinned to Stride's jacket. Also at the inquest, Dr Phillips said he had found a packet of cachous in Stride's hand. These were lozenges used by smokers to sweeten their breath.

The diarist has provided two factually correct pieces of information, but once again they are details that are well documented and easy to source. What the diarist fails to mention is that the knife used to kill Stride was short and broad, unlike the long narrow-bladed knife that had been used to kill the other victims. The lack of the abdominal mutilations and the use of a different type of knife has led some to suggest that Stride may not have been a Ripper

[509] Begg P., Fido M. and Skinner K., op cit., pages 430-431.
[510] Knight S., op cit., page 170.

victim. The use of a different murder weapon is significant. The diarist's failure to mention it is also significant. The diarist could not explain the change of knife, so he just ignored it.

The use of modern sources to construct the narrative is illustrated by examining the fourth victim, Catherine Eddowes, who was killed in the early hours of 30th September 1888 in Mitre Square. She had been strangled and then savagely mutilated. Her left kidney and her womb had been removed. If one compares what the diarist wrote with the account of the murder in the Fido book, one can easily identify from where the material may have been sourced.

One particular sentence is highly suggestive; the reference to the '*tin match box empty.*' The empty tin match box was not known to the general public until 1987, when a police list of Catherine Eddowes' possessions was first published. The wording in the Diary is almost identical to the wording on the police list, suggesting that the author of the Diary was either really the Ripper or, far more likely, simply copied from the list. Also, would the killer really have had the inclination or the time to have sorted through Eddowes' possessions in the dark in a public place, and then have put them all back in her pockets?

Those who believe that the Diary is a forgery point to factual errors made in the narrative concerning the murder of the last victim, Mary Kelly (c1863-1888). The diarist wrote that he cut the breasts off and '*left them on the table with some of the other stuff.*' However, according to a report by Dr Thomas Bond (1841-1901), Scotland Yard's divisional surgeon who conducted an examination of Kelly's body, the breasts had been left '*one under the head and the other by the right foot.*'[511] This report was not released until 1987.

It is argued that the forger made a mistake by copying inaccurate information that had been written in some contemporary newspapers. For example, the *Liverpool Weekly Mercury* reported that '*The breasts were cut off, evidently with a sharp knife, and placed on the table near the bed.*'[512] The Fido book refers to an agency report used by various newspapers in 1888 that stated, '*The kidneys and the heart had also been removed from the body and placed on the table by the side of the breasts.*'[513]

Shirley Harrison recognised that the diarist had made a mistake when referring to the position of Kelly's excised breasts, but went on to write that nobody who had committed the savage acts of barbarism could have possibly remembered accurately everything that they did that night. She suggests that the diarist may have accepted contemporary newspaper accounts as the true version of what had happened. The problem with her view is that she argues the exact opposite when it comes to the diarist's recall of the smallest detail when recounting what he had done to other mutilated victims such as Catherine Eddowes.

The Diary exhibits no new material; all the factual information has been taken from modern books. Some of this material has been reworked or turned into rhymes, but none of it shows any great insight into the killings.

This process is made obvious when factual errors from modern sources are replicated into the narrative of the Diary. They are also obvious when whole lines, such as the reference to the '*tin match box, empty,*' have been copied into the narrative. Another such example is when the diarist wrote: '*One whore in heaven, Two whores side by side. Three whores have died.*' These lines look remarkably similar to the lines in a poem entitled '*Eight Little Whores*' that featured in a book on the murders by Donald McCormick published in 1959. This poem was reprinted in the Fido book in 1987. Like so much else, this piece of Diary text appears to have been based on information that the forger extracted from Fido's work on Jack the Ripper.

An analysis of the Diary's account of the Ripper murders reveals that it is a modern forgery constructed from a few modern sources, most notably Stephen Knight's book and Martin Fido's book. In parts, it has been cleverly done; in other parts, it has been poorly done, revealing errors, historical inaccuracies and a basic lack of knowledge about the murders.

---

511 Sugden P., op cit., page 315.
512 *Liverpool Weekly Mercury*, 10th November 1888.
513 Fido M., op cit., page 92.

8

SCANDAL AND INTRIGUE

One of the interests that was close to the hearts of both James and Florence was horse racing. The *Liverpool Courier* reported that Florence was '*desirous of attending race meetings. She was present not only at those in Cheshire and Aintree, but at others.*' The same report stated that, like many other ladies, she '*risked a little on the result of the races.*'[514] Levy wrote that James was a '*confirmed race-goer.*'[515]

To the Maybricks, the Grand National held annually at Aintree Racecourse in Liverpool was one of the highlights of both the racing and social calendar. They would have been especially keen to attend the National held in March 1889 as it was the fiftieth anniversary race and the Prince of Wales was to attend the event to mark the occasion.

The *Liverpool Echo* reported: '*Fortunately, for the many thousands of people who make their way to Liverpool for the express purpose of witnessing the struggle for the Grand National, the weather was charmingly fine. The attendance was, perhaps the largest ever seen on the Aintree course. His Royal Highness the Prince of Wales, who is the guest of the Earl of Sefton, was present, and Prince Albert Victor was amongst the company.*'[516]

Florence was so determined not to miss the Grand National, that she returned from London the day before the event. On the morning of the race, James left early for his office. Florence left Battlecrease between nine and ten o'clock with her friend, Mrs Holden.[517] They took a cab into the city centre. James had organised a hired omnibus to take his party to the races, which departed from outside his office in the Knowsley Buildings. Many years later, a Mr F.E. Carroll wrote to the *Liverpool Daily Post* saying he could vividly remember the Maybrick party leaving for the races on '*Myles Mason's Bus.*'[518]

It was just as well the Maybricks had their own omnibus as huge numbers travelled by train to the races and there was chaos at the stations. The *Liverpool Courier* wrote it was '*impossible to deny that the arrangements at the Exchange and Aintree Stations were not of a very satisfactory nature.*'[519] Despite barriers being erected at Exchange Station to control the crowds, the crushing was '*something frightful.*'

Just before the first race, the Royal party arrived at the course, and in front of cheering onlookers, they made their way to the Royal stand. Included in the party was Lord Sefton, the Lord-Lieutenant of the County, who was also the President of Liverpool Cricket Club where both James and Florence were members. Also in the party was Nott Bower, the Chief Constable of Liverpool, who was to become convinced of Florence's guilt. Another present, who was to become closely associated with the Maybrick case, was Superintendent Bryning. He was one of three superintendents at Aintree who were in charge of nearly 500 police officers from the county constabulary.

The large police presence was required due to the widespread interest in the race. The organising committee had increased the winning money to 1,500 sovereigns, attracting a field of 20 runners considered to be the '*finest chasers to be found anywhere.*'[520] The Prince of Wales had two horses in the field, but much of the interest focused on an Irish horse named Frigate, which had finished second in the National on three previous occasions, in 1884, 1885 and 1888. The race, helped by the fine weather, was fast and exciting, won by Frigate by just a length.

During the afternoon, Alfred Brierley bought grandstand tickets so that members of the Maybrick party could catch a glimpse of the Royal princes. Some accounts suggest the two older Janion sisters, Mrs Briggs and Mrs Hughes, made their way to the Royal stand, closely followed by Mrs Samuelson accompanied by two gentlemen. Alfred Brierley asked Florence if she would like to accompany him, a request she gladly accepted. James did not join the group, and was left angry and brooding, supposedly with Miss Gertrude Janion, who was irritated as she had set her sights on Brierley herself.[521]

The stories that the Janion sisters were part of the Maybrick party were later strongly denied by Matilda Briggs. After Florence's trial, she told a Liverpool newspaper that '*neither herself or any of my sisters, were present at the races.*' She added her sister Gertrude had not seen James '*for some weeks before that event, and never saw him again.*'[522]

---

[514] *Liverpool Courier*, 31st May 1889.
[515] Levy J.H., op cit., page 6.
[516] *Liverpool Echo*, 29th March 1889.
[517] Details provided by Elizabeth Brierley at the inquest, *Liverpool Echo*, 28th May 1889.
[518] *Liverpool Daily Post*, 29th October 1941.
[519] *Liverpool Daily Courier*, 30th March 1889.
[520] Green, R., *National Heroes – The Aintree Legend*, (Mainstream Publishing, Edinburgh, 1999) page 72.
[521] Ryan B., op cit., page 36
[522] *Evening Express*, 15th August 1889.

What is definitely true, is that Florence accompanied Brierley despite her husband's clear instructions to the contrary, and James was greatly annoyed by her behaviour. His mood darkened even further when he saw his returning wife walking hand in hand with Brierley. He believed that Florence had been '*flirting*' with Brierley and he was upset and angry.[523] As soon as she was near, James loudly told Florence off in front of a rather embarrassed party.[524] James' verbal assault on his wife made Florence visibly irritated and as she got on the omnibus to return home, she turned to Christine Samuelson and said: '*I will give it to him hot and heavy for speaking to me like that in public.*'[525]

Florence returned to Battlecrease at around 6:50pm. She went straight to the nursery, where Nurse Yapp was getting the children ready for bed. James arrived home at 7:10pm. He too went to the nursery, where he completely ignored his wife and played with Gladys. Ten minutes later Yapp put the children to bed.[526]

James and Florence moved into their bedroom, and almost immediately a loud argument broke out that could be heard all over the house. Yapp, who was standing on the first-floor landing near the nursery door, heard James say to Florence: '*This scandal will be all over town tomorrow.*'

Mrs Briggs with a younger relative in Cromer (circa 1904)

The bedroom bell rang out and Bessie Brierley, the maid, hurried to the room and was told to summon a cab. There is a disagreement amongst the servants about who called the cab; Yapp felt Florence had called for it as she had decided to leave her husband, while Brierley and Humphreys thought it had been James who had called for the cab as he was ordering his wife to leave the house. Either way, a cab was called and Florence came down the stairs followed by her extremely angry husband.

Elizabeth Humphreys, the cook, was summoned to the hallway by Mary Cadwallader and witnessed the whole scene. She later told MacDougall that James followed Florence down the stairs raving and stamping like a madman. She said the buttonholes on Florence's dress had been '*torn with the way he had pulled her about.*'[527] James demanded that his wife remove her fur cape which he had bought for her to wear in London. Yapp heard James say: '*Florie, I never thought you could come to this.*'[528]

With tensions running high, the servants intervened to try and calm the situation. Humphreys said to James, '*Oh master, please don't go on like this, the neighbours will hear you.*' James responded by telling the cook to leave him alone, and that she didn't know anything about the situation. Humphreys persevered and asked James not to send Florence away that night, saying she had nowhere to go and asking for her to stay until the morning. Both Humphreys and Yapp heard James say to Florence. '*If you once cross this threshold, you shall never enter these doors again.*'[529]

It was at this point that James collapsed in a drunken stupor on the oak couch in the hallway. He was so stiff that Humphreys did not know if he was drunk or in a fit. James' collapse gave the servants the opportunity to intervene more decisively. Humphreys told Brierley to send the cab away. Yapp went downstairs, put her arm around Florence's waist and, by talking about her children, managed to persuade her to go upstairs. She then made a bed for

---

523 *Liverpool Mercury*, 6th June 1889.
524 *Liverpool Mercury*, 6th June 1889.
525 *Liverpool Mercury*, 29th May 1889.
526 Timings come from Nurse Yapp's testimony at the inquest, see *Liverpool Echo*, 28th May 1889.
527 MacDougall A.W., (1891) op cit., page 68.
528 Irving H.B., op cit., page 64.
529 Ibid., page 64.

Florence in the larger dressing-room, which was off the nursery. It was the room in which Yapp usually slept. James stayed downstairs, where he was to remain the rest of the night. At one point Humphreys saw him walking up and down the hall, '*very upset and crying.*'[530] At 11:30pm, Yapp went downstairs and told James that Florence was sleeping in the dressing-room, and he replied, '*Very well.*'

The next morning, James knocked on the night nursery door where Yapp had spent the night. He told the nurse to inform Florence he had lit a fire for her in the inner-dressing room off the main bedroom.[531] If the act had been designed by James to be an apology for his violence of the previous night, then it singularly failed to placate his wife's anger. When Florence awoke, she was sporting a black eye and had decided to separate from her husband.

Nurse Alice Yapp (*Liverpool Echo*, 1st August 1889)

This course of action may have already been in her mind, but James' aggression had been the final straw. Florence realised she needed advice, and turned to Matilda Briggs as she had successfully managed to arrange a separation from her own husband.

As a long-standing friend of James, it is often assumed that Mrs Briggs disliked Florence and therefore she was rather naïve in approaching her for help. While Mrs Briggs did later come to blame Florence for James' death, it is likely that when Florence knocked on her door on the Sunday morning after the Grand National, she was probably sympathetic in her feelings towards her. Mrs Briggs would have been shocked by the sight of Florence's black eye and, having been through a difficult separation herself, would have had some empathy for her plight.

Although Mrs Briggs was not in favour of the separation, she did agree to accompany Florence when she visited Mrs Briggs' own lawyers, plus Dr Hopper and the General Post Office in Liverpool.[532] Mrs Briggs' solicitors were Thomas and Donnison, with offices on Lord Street in the city centre. They had helped Matilda Briggs arrange her own separation and were therefore well qualified to help Florence if she decided to pursue the same course of action.[533]

Florence moved from the solicitors to Dr Hopper, the Maybricks' family doctor, at his offices in Rodney Street, also in the city centre. Dr Hopper recalled the meeting in his testimony at Florence's trial. He said Florence had told him: '*she was very unwell, that she had been up all night, had taken very little food, and was out of sorts, and she asked my advice. I saw that she had a black eye. She said that her husband had been very unkind to her, that they had had a serious quarrel the night before, and he had beaten her. The quarrel she explained was the outcome of a disagreement at the Grand National, but I do not think she told me at that time what that disagreement was about. She said that she had a very strong feeling against him, and could not bear him to come near her. She also said that it was her intention to go to a lawyer and ask for a separation to be arranged.*'[534]

Dr Hopper must have been shocked by Florence's account and her black eye. He had known the couple since 1881 and had always assumed they had a happy marriage. He advised Florence to try and avoid a separation as it was a path that was fraught with problems. He promised to visit her and her husband to see if he could bridge the gap between them.

Florence's final stop of the morning was at the General Post Office. She wanted to obtain a private mailbox so that she could receive her letters from her mother (and possibly Brierley as well) without her husband's interference. Unfortunately for her, no mailboxes were available.

Dr Hopper visited Battlecrease at around 3:00pm. He spoke to Florence first, and then to the couple together. He said they both stated '*their respective complaints against one another in my presence, as to her repugnance for him, and as to the quarrel the night before. Mr Maybrick said that his wife had annoyed him very much at the Grand National, that she had gone off with a gentleman and walked up the course although he had distinctly told her not to do so. I do not think there was any other grievance. In the course of a conversation with Mrs Maybrick she told me*

[530] *Liverpool Mercury*, 29th May 1889.
[531] Ibid., page 64.
[532] Levy J.H., op cit., page 59.
[533] Morland N., op cit., page 34.
[534] Irving H.B., op cit., pages 32-33.

she was very much in debt, and that was the great obstacle to reconciliation. I told her I did not think it would be a serious obstacle, and I strongly recommended her to make a clean breast of it, and to get her husband's forgiveness for the debts, and then everything would be right.'[535]

Although he did not state it in his evidence at Florence's trial, Hopper did say in his testimony at James' inquest that he felt the reconciliation he had brokered had been successful. He said although Florence at first was '*quite unwilling to be reconciled,*' he did feel by the end of his stay that he had enabled '*what appeared to be a perfect reconciliation.*' He also told the inquest that James had later called at his rooms to '*thank me for reconciling them.*' Sometime later, he saw James in Liverpool's Princes Road and asked him if he was happy at home. James had replied '*that they were and he was very much obliged to me.*'[536]

While Hopper believed he had engineered a perfect reconciliation, the truth may have been different. James was still angry at his wife's behaviour at the Grand National and he was suspicious of Brierley's intentions. He told Florence that he intended to place adverts in newspapers asking for information about where she stayed in London, and with whom. As no such adverts have been found, it is unlikely James carried out his threat and it is probable that he was simply trying to scare Florence in an effort to get her to confess.

Florence was also unlikely to have been reconciled after the beating she had suffered and may have hoped for further clandestine meetings with Brierley.

Of the two, it is likely that James was the most-keen on rebuilding the marriage. The cook had seen him visibly upset after his row with Florence. In an honest admission during his talk with Hopper on the Sunday when the doctor tried to broker the reconciliation, not reported at the inquest or trial, he told him that he and Florence had not had sexual relations for three months.[537] This admission, if true, is important for a variety of reasons. Firstly, it shows that although James and Florence's marriage had entered a troubled period in 1887, the couple still had a sexual relationship up until late 1888. We know from a statement made by Dr Humphreys to Mr Justice Stephen after Florence's trial, that Florence suffered a miscarriage in early spring 1889. On being told of the miscarriage, James wanted to know '*how old is the thing,*' so he could be certain he was the father.[538]

If James and Florence had maintained a sexual relationship up until December 1888, as James told Hopper, then it is likely that James was the father. Secondly, it means if they stopped intimacy around December 1888, this coincides with the time period when Florence and Brierley started to get closer to one another. This, in turn means, that if Florence believed herself to be pregnant in April/May 1889, then she would have known that Brierley was almost certainly the father of the unborn child.

At the trial, Mrs Briggs told the court that Florence visited her the day after the Grand National and she didn't see her again until Friday 3rd May. However, Elizabeth Humphreys and Mary Cadwallader both told MacDougall that Mrs Briggs visited Battlecrease on Sunday, 31st March. As Florence was upstairs, James sent the maid to fetch her. After she did, some '*quarrelling and shouting*' occurred and both Florence and Mrs Briggs appeared to be '*very much excited.*' The cause of the row was an insinuation by Mrs Briggs that Florence had invited someone, presumably Alfred Brierley, around to the house without her husband's knowledge. Florence denied the accusation and retreated upstairs again.

At 6:00pm, Mary Cadwallader took a cup of tea to Florence, and found her '*lying on the sofa in a faint.*' After being told this, James rushed upstairs. He became very affectionate, and said: '*Bunny, Bunny, here's your hubby.*' James sent the cook to get Dr Humphreys. The condition of Florence must have been of concern to James and the servants as they '*were all frightened and thought her dead. Dr Humphreys came backwards and forwards four or five times during the night, and as soon as he went away Mr Maybrick sent for him back again.*'

Mrs Briggs stayed the night at Battlecrease. She must not have originally intended to stay as she had not brought her own nightdress and gown. According to Elizabeth Humphreys, '*Mrs Briggs kept coming down to the kitchen to me for beer, and said she was put out about the quarrel and must have something to keep her up. At about nine o'clock she was half-undressed, and had put on a gown of Mrs Maybrick's which was much too small for her, and was standing in this condition when Dr Humphreys came; and he asked me who that woman was.*'[539]

Florence spent the next few days ill in bed. At the end of the week, Florence summoned the cook to her bedroom. She told her the cause of her trouble was that she was in debt, and while she was in London, some '*kind friend*' had '*made mischief between her husband and herself about it.*' Florence said James' income was not sufficient to pay all the bills, and asked the cook to do her best to economise '*without stinting.*'

Some observers believe the torn relationship between James and Florence had been repaired after their bitter row on the day of the Grand National. Dr Hopper thought the couple had been reconciled. MacDougall wrote that '*the*

---

535 Ibid., page 33.
536 *Liverpool Mercury*, 6th June, 1889.
537 Colquhoun, K., op cit., page 50.
538 Letter from Justice Stephen to the Home Secretary (14th August 1889) HO 144/1638/A50678
539 MacDougall A.W., (1891) op cit., pages 68-69.

reconciliation was evidently complete... both Elizabeth Humphreys and Mary Cadwallader...say they [James and Florence] continued to live on perfectly good terms.'[540]

However, beneath the surface tensions continued to bubble away. James instructed Mary Cadwallader to take his wife's letters to him for inspection before she was permitted to take them to Florence. James didn't open the letters, but he did check where they were from and who had sent them.[541]

Dr Hopper advised Florence to send Brierley a letter informing him that she and her husband had reconciled. Florence did send Brierley two letters, but it is unlikely that she mentioned the supposed reconciliation between her and James. Instead, she informed Brierley of her warm feelings towards him and her strong desire to meet him again. As Brierley didn't respond to the letters, on 6th April, Florence secretly visited him at his Liverpool home at 60 Huskisson Street, near the city centre. She told Brierley about her unhappiness at home and her love for him. Brierley coldly informed her that they should no longer meet or write to one another again for the foreseeable future. These words must have been a hammer-blow to Florence.

To make matters even worse, she now faced problems and criticism from yet another source. Margaret Baillie had written to the Baroness, as she believed Florence had not told her the truth about staying in the Grand Hotel during her recent London visit. This prompted Florence's mother to send a letter of reproach to her daughter, demanding a full explanation for her behaviour. The Baroness wrote: '*I cannot understand your movements. I thought you were there with MB. It was ridiculous to have your letters addressed to the Grand when you were not there.*'

John Baillie Knight also sent Florence a letter of reproach. He wrote: '*You certainly did make a mess of it when you were last in London, and really it was quite unnecessary, and still worse to tell so many fibs.*'[542]

To compound her difficulties, the letter from the Baroness to Florence may have been read by James before he passed it on to his wife. Following the rumours, reading this letter would have confirmed his suspicions about Florence and Brierley.

Although James must have been reeling from the rumours about the true nature of Florence's visit to London, he travelled to the capital on Saturday 13th April to pay Florence's considerable debts. Levy fixed the amount she owed to be £1,200, though he said that the exact figure was not proved.[543]

James Maybrick (*The Graphic*, 24th August 1889)

According to a report in the *Liverpool Courier*, '*Mrs Maybrick had frequent transactions with private loan offices. Some of these date as far back as 1887, and although at first they represented only moderate amounts, they were, it is alleged, gradually increased until they involved considerable sums.*'[544]

While he was in London, James stayed with his brother Michael in his Regent's Park apartments. Michael arranged for James to be examined by Dr Fuller, his personal physician. Dr Charles Chinner Fuller (1831-1902) had been educated at University College, London, and practised at 160 Albany Street and at 29 Albany Street, Regent's Park, London. He was Surgeon to the North-West London Free Dispensary for Sick Children. Dr Fuller was to examine James on two occasions. The first of these was on Sunday, 14th April. Fuller said James '*complained of pains in his head and of numbness, and said he was apprehensive of being paralysed.*'[545] After examining him for over an hour, Dr Fuller could not find anything the matter with James apart from indigestion. He told James that he should have no fear of paralysis, which seemed to make him more cheerful. Fuller then prescribed two prescriptions; one was an aperient and the other a tonic, with liver pills.

The following weekend James returned to London, and on Saturday 20th April he visited Dr Fuller at his house and told him that he felt much better. Dr Fuller examined him again and found him improved: '*The dyspeptic symptoms of which he complained had partially disappeared. I thereupon slightly altered the prescriptions and wrote another.*

540 Ibid., page 69.
541 Ibid., page 69.
542 Christie T.L., op cit., page 52.
543 Levy J.H., op cit., page 27
544 *Liverpool Courier*, 1st June 1889.
545 Irving H.B., op cit., page 58.

In it compound sulphur lozenges were substituted for pills, and a little sweet spirit of nitre added. The third prescription I would describe as a nerve tonic.'[546]

The nerve tonic prescribed by Dr Fuller was nux vomica. Although popular as a homeopathic remedy for a wide variety of ailments, nux vomica (literally 'poison nut') was also the main source of strychnine in Victorian Britain. Most of it came from India, where the thorny tree, Strychnos nux vomica, flourished in the wild, producing bright-looking, brownish-yellow berries the size of a small orange. These contained a gelatinous pulp in which were embedded button-shaped seeds. The pulp was washed and the seeds were spread on mats in the sun to dry. After further washing and sorting, the seeds were packed into large bags, most of which were exported to the UK and America. Despite the cleansing process, the seeds contained several toxic alkaloids including strychnine and brucine, a lethal dose for adults being anything between 30 and 120mg.

Although the drug could be highly toxic and had long been used to make rat poisons, in his *Pocket Manual of Homeopathic Materia Medica* (1901) the Austrian-born American homeopathic physician William Boericke (1849-1929) described nux vomica as '*the remedy for many of the conditions incident to modern life.*'

In terms of mood, sufferers were typically sullen and fault-finding – both traits of James. As for physical symptoms reported by the use of nux vomica, Boericke noted that it particularly affected the tongue; although the front would be clean, further back it would be covered with deep fur, as in James' case, white and yellow, with cracked edges. Just as James was to complain of sensing a hair in his throat, Boericke reported sufferers describing a tickling in the throat on waking. Patients reported their stomach would be highly sensitive to pressure, with nausea and vomiting, accompanied by constipation and painful, ineffectual '*straining at stool,*' exactly as James experienced. In men, Boericke reported '*easily excited desire... and emissions from high living,*' accompanied by constrictive pain in the testicles. As in James' case, hands and legs felt numb or even paralysed, with cramps to the calves and soles of the feet.

While James was in London, Florence's life was still in a state of turmoil. Margaret Baillie had not been satisfied by the letter she had received from the Baroness that had attempted to explain her daughter's recent movements and she wrote Florence a letter which expressed her frustrations. In it, she said Florence had told so many lies that she was '*doubtful of the truth of anything that you had said when circumstances looked adverse to you.*'[547]

It was a remark that must have hit home. Florence realised the truth of her stay in London was about to break through the tissues of lies she had created to keep it hidden. She went into panic mode. Abandoned by Brierley, she needed desperately to win back her husband's sympathies, even if only temporarily, while he sorted out her debts. More importantly, if she believed she was pregnant with Brierley's baby, she needed to sleep with her husband again, '*in order to provide the baby with a legitimate father should Brierley not come up to scratch.*'[548]

On 14th April, she wrote the most grovelling of letters to James while he was in London. She started the letter, '*My own darling hubby*!' It was a phrase in stark contrast to her words only a week earlier, when she had told Dr Hopper about the repugnance she felt towards her husband. She continued: '*I have not sufficient self-respect left to lift me above the depth of disgrace to which I have fallen, for now that I am down I can judge better how very far above me others must be morally. I despair of ever reaching that standard again although I may receive some of your confidence by living a life of atonement for yours and the children's sake alone. Nothing you can say can make me look at my actions but in the most degrading light, and the more you impress the enormity of my crimes upon me the more hopeless I feel of ever regaining my position...Darling, try and be as lenient towards me as you can. For notwithstanding all your generous and tender loving kindness, my burden is almost more than I can bear. My remorse and self-contempt is eating my heart out and if I did not believe my love for you and my dutifulness may prove some slight atonement for the past I should give up the struggle to keep brave! Forgive me if you can dearest and think less poorly of your loving wifey, Bunny.*'

She then added a little postscript, '*The children are well. I have been nowhere and seen no-one.*'[549]

Two things are obvious from the letter. Firstly, Florence realised she was in a precarious situation and needed to pacify her husband. Secondly, James probably knew that Florence had met Brierley in London, though he was probably not aware they spent the night together. Michael Maybrick stated at Florence's trial that James had died in complete ignorance of his wife's '*guilty meeting in London.*' That remark is unlikely to be true. The word '*atonement*' implies that Florence needed to make amends for a serious wrongdoing which in turn implies that James knew about her meeting with Brierley.

James returned from London on Monday, 22nd April and normality appeared to return to Battlecrease. James' demeanour seemed to have improved, and he withdrew his instruction to Mary Cadwallader to see all of Florence's letters. James visited Clay and Abraham's, chemists in Liverpool to get Dr Fuller's prescriptions made up for him.

---

546 Ibid., page 58.
547 HO 144/1638/A50678.
548 Graham A. and Emmas C., op cit., page 82.
549 HO 144/1639/A50678.

On Thursday, 25th April, Edwin Maybrick returned to Liverpool from America, where he had been working since August 1888. Her husband's better mood and the arrival of Edwin raised Florence's spirits. She may have felt that the tide of good fortune was beginning to turn her way.

If that was the case, she was mistaken. The true reality of the situation is shown by the new will that James had drawn up at this time. It was dated 25th April 1889, and was witnessed by his good friend George Davidson and his book-keeper, George Smith. The will replaced the one that James had ripped up after his row with Florence at Christmas 1888.

The full text of the will was published in the *Liverpool Daily Post* as Florence's trial was about to commence. The newspaper stated that it was a verbatim copy, which had been extracted in due form from the District Registry attached to the Probate Division of her Majesty's High Court of Justice at Liverpool. The will stated:

> *In case I die before having made a regular and proper will in legal form, I wish this to be taken as my last will and testament. I leave and bequeath all my worldly possessions of whatever kind or description, including furniture, picture, wines, linen and plate, life insurances, cash, shares, property, in fact, everything I possess, in trust with my brothers Michael Maybrick and Thomas Maybrick for my two children James Chandler Maybrick and Gladys Evelyn Maybrick. The furniture I desire to remain intact, and to be used in furnishing a home which can be shared by my widow and children, but the furniture is to be the children's. I further desire that all moneys be invested in the names of the above trustees (Michael and Thomas Maybrick), and the income of same used for the children's benefit and education, such education to be left to the discretion of said trustees. My widow will have for her portion of my estate the policies on my life, say £500, with the Scottish Widows' Fund, and £2,000 with the Mutual Reserve Fund Life Association of New York, both policies being made out in her name. The interest on this £2,500, together with the £125 a year which she receives from her New York property, will make a provision of about £125 a year – a sum which, although small, will yet be the means of keeping her respectably. It is also my desire that my widow shall live under the same roof with the children so long as she remains my widow. If it is legally possible, I wish the £2,500 of life insurance on my life in my wife's name to be invested in the names of the said trustees, but that she should have the sole use of the interest thereof during her lifetime, but at her death the principal to revert to my said children James Chandler and Gladys Evelyn Maybrick.*[550]

The will has proved to be a controversial document. Doubts on its validity were first cast in 1891 by Alexander MacDougall. He said that it was '*inconceivable*' that James could have been in '*sober senses*' when he signed the will as it gave total control of his estate and the well-being of his children to Michael and Thomas Maybrick, while Florence was to have '*neither bed nor blanket.*'[551]

Despite this allegation, it is almost certain that the will is the actual one signed by James on 25th April and witnessed by Davidson and Smith. James had destroyed his previous will at Christmas 1888 after a serious row with his wife, so needed to make a new one. This need had become more pressing in April as he was worried about his health. He was angry with Florence, and may have wanted to punish her. Further, he made the new will just three days after returning from London where he had repaid Florence's substantial debts to moneylenders.

The terms of the will, as published in the *Liverpool Daily Post,* are identical to the one originally stored at Somerset House (with the one possible exception of the spelling mistake of Evelyn). Both George Smith and George Davidson would have seen the will in the newspaper, and if there had been a problem they would have spoken out at the time. The harsh terms towards Florence reflected James' feelings and attitude to her at that moment in time.

LINKS TO THE RIPPER DIARY: THE DIARY AND THE GRAND NATIONAL OF 1889

The diarist refers to the 1889 Grand National race very specifically in one passage, writing: '*Did not the whore see her whore master in front of all, true the race was the fastest I have seen, but the thrill of seeing the whore with the bastard thrilled me more so than knowing his Royal Highness was but a few feet away from yours truly ha ha what a laugh, if the greedy bastard would have known he was less than a few feet away from the name all England was talking about he would have died there and then.*'

What makes this passage interesting is that the race *had* been extremely fast. The winning horse, Frigate, was owned and trained by Mr M.A. Maher and ridden by Tommy Beasley. Frigate is considered to have been the '*best mare to have won the National.*'[552]

---

550 *Liverpool Daily Post*, 31st July 1889.

551 MacDougall A.W., (1891) op. cit., page 206.

552 King P., *The Grand National, Anyone's Race*, (Quartet Books, London, 1983) page 40.

Paul Feldman argued that the reference to the race being the '*fastest*' the diarist had ever seen, is highly significant in the attempt to determine the authenticity of the Diary. He wrote that his Liverpool researcher, Carol Emmas, '*scoured magazines and newspapers for days on end*' before finding only one reference to all the race times and that was in an obscure magazine entitled the *Liverpolitan*, dated March 1939.[553] He argues a potential forger would have found it difficult to have located this reference, and suggests the person who wrote the line must have attended the race. Shirley Harrison makes a similar point, writing the fact the race was '*the fastest on record*' (it wasn't – the 1871 race had been faster) had only been confirmed '*after a great deal of probing in the race archives and local papers. Once again an obscure but accurate detail makes nonsense of the crude modern forgery theory.*'[554]

Despite Feldman's and Harrison's assertions, the details of this race are not as obscure as has been suggested. Frigate is considered one of the great Grand National horses, running the race seven times between 1884 and 1890, winning once and being narrowly defeated on three occasions. Her victory in 1889 is well documented and earned her a '*revered place in racing history.*'[555] The winning jockey, Thomas Beasley, won the National three times and is rated as one of the best jockeys of all time.[556] He came from a famous racing family of four brothers, who between them rode four winners, six seconds and two thirds from 34 rides in the Grand National.

More importantly, any potential forger who carried out his research post-1987 would have found it exceedingly easy to establish the winning times if they had looked in just one or two well-known and easily accessible books. Finch Mason, in his book on the history of the Grand National published in 1911, provides a detailed account of every race, including the winning times, from 1839 to 1911. It would be an easy task to simply check the time for each race and see if the 1889 time actually was a fast one. A second book, *A Race Apart* by Reg Green, published in 1988, provides winning times for every race between 1839 and 1987. The Reg Green book was available in Liverpool Central Library and could therefore have been easily accessed by anyone in that city with an interest in the 1889 race and the times of other Grand National races.

In actual fact, the winning time in 1889 – ten minutes and one-and-a-half seconds – was not that much faster than the races of the previous six years; for example, the winning time in 1884 had been ten minutes and five seconds, less than four seconds slower than 1889.

What would have been far more noticeable to an observer who attended the race and who had been to previous ones was the closeness of the finish and the sheer size of the crowds. The *Liverpool Daily Courier* produced a detailed account of the race, and called it one of the: '*hottest and best-contested Grand Nationals ever run, Frigate won in the gamest manner, and evidently with something to spare.*'[557] After jumping the final fence, Frigate had a lead of three lengths over her nearest challenger, Why Not. This lead was gradually eroded as the two horses approached the finishing-line and, in the end, Frigate won an exciting race by just one length. As Frigate was led back to the winner's enclosure she was greeted with tumultuous cheers and applause from all around the racecourse.

As to the numbers attending the event, the *Liverpool Daily Courier* estimated that there were 20,000 more people present at Aintree than had ever previously attended the race. The crowds arriving by train were so great that barricades had to be placed at Exchange Railway Station as the crushing at the narrow entrance was '*something frightful.*'

The diarist fails to mention either of these two noticeable events, even though the Maybricks' omnibus departed from very near Exchange Station and the scenes would have been clearly visible to all on board the vehicle.

The reference to the Prince of Wales is not as significant as some pro-Diary supporters have made out. The Prince did attend the 1889 Grand National, as did his son, Prince Albert Victor; however, the Prince had attended previous Grand Nationals, including the one held the previous year in 1888. One of the reasons he attended was because he had horses entered for the race. In the 1889 race, the Prince of Wales had two entries: Magic, who finished fifth, and Hettie, who was a faller at the third fence. Therefore, there was plenty of scope for the diarist to make additional fun at the Prince's expense by referring to the failure of his horses. The fact this is not mentioned in the Diary is again suggestive that its author was not actually at the race at all.

In truth, the reference to the 1889 Grand National in the Diary is neither the work of a person who attended the event nor the work of a very clever forger who managed to find out a very obscure detail about relative race times. The 1889 race is mentioned because it is the only race that the person who wrote the Diary knew for a fact had been attended by both James and Florence Maybrick.

All the books on the Maybricks and all the court reports of Florence's trial, make it clear beyond any doubt that the couple attended the event. The reference to the race being the '*fastest*' he had witnessed was deliberately vague because the forger did not know what other Grand National races James had actually attended. Indeed, he could have

[553] Feldman P., op cit., page 296.
[554] Harrison S., op cit., page 174.
[555] Green R., (1999) op cit., page 73.
[556] Green R., *Race Apart – The History of the Grand National*, (Hodder and Stoughton, London, 1988) pages 118-119.
[557] *Liverpool Daily Courier*, 30th March 1889.

attended the much faster 1871 race. As to the problem of obtaining the information about race times, there was no difficulty; a brief look at one easily accessible book would have very quickly provided all the details required to produce the Diary narrative.

As far as the references to events back in Battlecrease after the Grand National are concerned, a modern forger would have had no problems in extracting the relevant details from any of the books on the Maybrick case. They all go into some detail about the bitter exchanges between Florence and James. The diarist gives only a very limited account of the incident despite it being such a pivotal point in the couple's relationship. One would imagine that, had James really written the Diary, he would have said far more about his violent attack on his wife, especially as it is the only documented episode of him using physical violence against Florence.

It is also the case that the assault on Florence that followed the Grand National seriously undermines the motivation provided by the diarist for why he had earlier murdered prostitutes in Manchester and London. The diarist suggests that his wife's affair was the crucial factor in turning a once '*gentle man born*' into a sadistic killer. He repeatedly refers to his wife as the '*whore*' and her male lover as the '*whoremaster*.' According to the diarist, his '*disire [sic] for revenge is overwhelming. The whore has destroyed my life*.'

If James was the diarist, and the whore referred to in the Diary is Florence, one is left with the rather obvious question as to why James didn't take out his revenge on Florence and her lover. They are the obvious targets of his anger, so therefore they would be the obvious subjects for his violence.

If the diarist is to believed, James does not take his anger out on Florence and her lover but instead savagely kills random women in Manchester and London. What makes this even harder to believe is the diarist suggests that he was fully aware of his wife's affair and did nothing to stop it. At one point, the diarist writes: '*The thought of him taking her is beginning to thrill me, perhaps I will allow her to continue, some of my thoughts are indeed beginning to give me pleasure*.'

Does this picture of a passive response to his wife's affair equate with James' violent reaction after the Grand National? The answer is definitely *No*. At the race course, James gave his wife strict instructions not to go walking with Brierley, and he was extremely angry when she disobeyed him. Later that night, he assaulted her, and almost threw her out of the house.

James' friend, Charles Ratcliffe, wrote that James had '*gotten wise to the Flatman Hotel affair*,' and he was '*expecting him to plug Brierley at any time*.'[558] Brierley also believed that James was capable of violence against him. He wrote to Florence saying that any possible future meeting would be '*very dangerous*' and that he was planning to take a '*round trip to the Mediterranean, which will take 6 or 7 weeks*.'[559]

We have a clear picture of James as a man who was jealous of his wife. He simply would not have stood idly by and allowed her to conduct an affair.

James was capable of violence, but he was not Jack the Ripper.

[558] Letter from Charles Ratcliffe to John Aunspaugh, 7th June 1889, in the Trevor Christie Collection.
[559] HO 144/1638/A50678.

9
MEDICINES AND POISONS

It was an important part of the prosecution's case at Florence's trial that although her husband '*complained very much about his liver and his nerves,*' he was on the whole a '*strong and healthy man, going regularly to his office every day.*'[560] If, as the prosecution alleged, James was a healthy man, then something must have happened to have caused his unexpected death.

When Dr Carter, one of James' doctors, was questioned at the trial, he said James had suffered from two illnesses. The first one dated from the time of the Wirral races on 27th April. James had partially recovered from this and had returned to work. He then had a second illness, caused by being given a fatal dose of poison sometime around 3rd May.[561]

The cause of James' first serious illness is easy to identify; it was not any poisonous substance administered by Florence, but a powerful dose of medication that was ordered and self-administered by James himself. The bottle of medicine arrived in the post at Battlecrease at 8:30am on the morning of Friday, 26th April and, because of the postmark, it is usually referred to as the '*London medicine.*' Mary Cadwallader, the maid, accepted the package from the postman and took it straight to James. He told her that he had been '*expecting the medicine for a day or two.*'[562] The package was a small box made of pasteboard and, due to its shape, the maid could tell it contained a bottle. Cadwallader '*believed*' the medicine had been sent by Dr Fuller, though she had not heard his name mentioned.[563]

One thing is certain; the bottle was not one of the medicines prescribed by Dr Fuller following James' recent consultation with him in London. James had taken Fuller's prescriptions to Clay and Abraham's chemists in Liverpool, where they had been compounded. Two assistant chemists, Christopher Robinson and Frederick Tozer, testified at the trial that they had made up the medicines '*in the ordinary way*' and they didn't contain arsenic.

The most obvious possibility is that the London medicine had been sourced by James himself during his recent visit to the capital. A cursory glance through the list of bottles found in Battlecrease and James' office, shows he frequented numerous chemists, including several London chemists. One item on the list, a small bottle containing pills and labelled '*poison,*' was from H. T. Kirby of Newton Street, Oxford Street, London.[564] In an interview given by Michael Maybrick after Florence's trial, he stated that James used to buy medicines from a few different chemists, including '*John Bell in Oxford Street, in London.*'[565] Therefore, it is likely that while James was in London in April 1889, he visited one of the chemists and placed an order for some powerful medication. He then returned to Liverpool, where he awaited its arrival in the post.

If the origin of the London medicine is somewhat of a puzzle, then the exact nature of the medicine is not a mystery at all. We know from both James' own words and his physical response to taking it, that it was a powerful strychnine compound. He first took the medicine on the morning of Saturday, 27th April, and shortly afterwards became very ill. He spent an hour in the toilet being violently sick and experiencing severe numbness in his legs. He attributed his sickness to the London medicine. According to Mary Cadwallader, '*Mr Maybrick said to me that he had had an overdose of medicine from London... Mr Maybrick said he felt very dizzy.*'[566]

Florence also attributed James' sickness to the London medicine. At Florence's trial, Nurse Yapp told the court that about 10:00am on the morning of the Wirral races, Florence spoke to her as James was leaving to go to his office. According to Yapp, Florence said '*Mr Maybrick had taken an overdose of medicine. I asked what kind of medicine, and she said, "Some ordered him by a doctor in London. He was very sick and in great pain."*'[567]

Despite feeling unwell, James decided to go to his office. When James arrived, between 10:30am and 11:00am, both his bookkeepers – Thomas Lowry and George Smith – noticed he was far from his normal self. At Florence's trial, Lowry said, '*James was not looking well*' and Smith said James '*made complaint of stiffness in his limbs.*'[568]

What is of even greater significance are the statements made by the two office workers at the earlier hearings into James' death. They said James had told them that, on the day of the Wirral races, he had a '*strange experience that morning*' and that he had taken '*an overdose of medicine and there was strychnine in it, that he was on the WC for an hour and all his limbs were stiff and he could not move.*'[569]

---

560 Irving H.B., op cit., page 5.
561 Ibid., page 122.
562 Ibid., page 76.
563 Ibid., page 76
564 MacDougall A.W., (1891) op cit., page 587.
565 *Evening Post*, 21st August 1889.
566 Irving H.B., op cit., pages 74-75.
567 Ibid., page 65.
568 Ibid., pages 55-56.
569 HO 144/1639 A50678/442.

Morden Rigg

Despite the numbness in his limbs, James left his office and travelled to the Wirral for the afternoon races. The races in question were the Wirral Hunt Club Steeplechases held in Parkgate. The meeting took place on a '*charmingly situated course overlooking the banks of the Dee, and in full view of the grand panorama of the Welsh hills.*'[570] The *Liverpool Daily Courier* reported the event had been well attended and the '*sport proved very interesting.*'[571] There were seven races that day, including the Hooton Steeplechase and the Wirral Farmers' Steeplechase.

One of the reasons James was determined to attend the event, apart from his love of horseracing, was that it attracted many of Liverpool's and Cheshire's more prominent citizens, including '*a sprinkling of aristocracy.*'[572] The event also attracted some of James' closest friends and colleagues from the cotton trading community, including Morden Rigg and his wife. Rigg was later to say that during the day James had '*turned around to my wife's carriage and told her he had taken an overdose of strychnine that morning and that his limbs were quite rigid. She is prepared to testify to this if necessary.*'[573]

William Thomson (1840-1915) was another friend of James who was at the races. Thomson was a copper smelter from St Helens, a town some 15 miles to the east of Liverpool. Thomson noticed James was having trouble riding his horse and was '*shaking about.*' When he questioned him about what was wrong, James replied that he was not feeling well. Later, James told Thomson he had taken a '*double dose*' of his medicine that morning.[574]

Further evidence of James' use of strychnine on the day of the Wirral races is provided by events that occurred in the evening. James did not return straight to Battlecrease, but instead went to the home of Richard Hobson (1836-1909), another trader on the Liverpool Cotton Exchange. Hobson lived at *The Marfords*, a large Gothic-style house at Bromborough, not far from the race course at Parkgate. He was a close friend of James and it is possible they first met in New Orleans, where Hobson had built up his cotton business before returning to Liverpool and setting up an office at 54 Brown's Buildings near Exchange Flags. Hobson was genial, generous and kindly. '*Though not a public man in the sense of civic effort or political striving,*' the *Liverpool Echo* recalled, '*he was one of Liverpool's prominent citizens by reason of his numerous commercial activities.*'[575]

Richard Hobson

During the meal at Hobson's James' '*hands were so unsteady and twitching' that he spilt his wine and broke the glass. James was 'greatly distressed lest his friends would think he was drunk.*'[576] In an effort to cover his embarrassment, James blamed his symptoms on a '*strong cup of tea;*' however, he must have known that the real cause was the double dose of the London medicine he had taken in the morning. Following the dinner James returned home, arriving after the servants had gone to bed.

It was a part of the defence's case at Florence's trial, that James' medical condition had been made even worse by the soaking he had received on the day of the races. According to one account, the weather had been '*perfectly characteristic of the month, sunshine and showers alternating throughout the afternoon.*'[577] Another account stated there had been a '*few typical April showers of short duration.*'[578] Thus, although the rain may have only been intermittent, it was certainly sufficient to get James wet.

One would have assumed that the powerful side effects from the London medicine on Saturday morning would have warned James of its toxic nature, and he would have avoided taking any more of the mixture. However, such was his craving for

[570] *Liverpool Daily Post*, 29th April 1889.
[571] *Liverpool Daily Courier*, 29th April 1889.
[572] *Birkenhead and Cheshire Advertiser* 4th May 1889.
[573] MacDougall A.W., (1896) op cit., page 23.
[574] Irving H.B., op cit., page 197.
[575] *Liverpool Echo*, 21st January 1909.
[576] Irving H.B., op cit., page 88.
[577] *Liverpool Daily Post*, 29th April 1889.
[578] *Birkenhead and Cheshire Advertiser*, 4th May 1889.

strychnine, that when he woke on Sunday morning he decided to take another big hit of the medicine. Alexander MacDougall believed that James' reaction to the medicine was even worse on Sunday morning than it had been on Saturday morning. Perhaps this was because he was still weak from the previous day, or possibly because he had taken an even bigger dose of the medicine. Whatever the reason, the effects were the same and he almost immediately became ill. The situation must have been serious, as Florence – who was well used to James' constant hypochondriacal complaints – became extremely worried about her husband's condition. She went into the night nursery and asked Nurse Yapp to sit with James in the bedroom while she went downstairs in search of the cook. Florence asked Elizabeth Humphreys to immediately prepare a mustard and water solution, as James '*had taken another dose of that horrid medicine.*' Humphreys said Florence prepared the first cup herself, mixing it with her finger and '*not waiting for a spoon to be got.*'[579]

Yapp was present when Florence returned to the bedroom and said to James, '*do take this mustard and water; it will remove the brandy and make you sick again if nothing else.*'[580] Moments later, Humphreys followed Florence up the stairs; she did not enter the bedroom, but gave a second cup of the solution to Florence on the landing. Humphreys said that while she did not actually see James, she did hear him vomiting. The mustard and water emetic made James sick, but it did not relieve the intense pain he was suffering.

At 10:30am, the bell in the main bedroom rang violently. Before anyone could answer it, Florence ran down the stairs and instructed Mary Cadwallader to go immediately and fetch the local doctor, Dr Humphreys, as James was sick again.

Dr Richard Humphreys

Dr Richard Humphreys (1860-1932) was an inexperienced young doctor when the Maybrick case unfolded. Humphreys, and his twin sister Margaret were born at Llanfair Talhaiarn, near Abergele, Denbighshire in 1860. Their father, Humphrey Humphreys (1826-81), kept the Black Lion Inn in the village. Richard Humphreys was educated at Chester and graduated in medicine from Edinburgh University in 1882. In 1884, aged just 24, he joined a medical practice with premises at 9 Aigburth Road and 4 St Mary's Terrace, Garston Old Road, belonging to Dr Thomas Cayzer. Later, he built up his own successful practice.

Humphreys had previously visited Battlecrease when he treated the Maybrick children; however, he had only treated James on one occasion for a slight nose injury. This lack of detailed knowledge about James' health was to be important, as Humphreys had no knowledge of the extent of his new patient's misuse of drugs. Humphreys arrived at the house just before 11:00am and was taken upstairs to see James in his bedroom. He interviewed James, who was lying on his bed in his dressing gown, while Florence was in the room. James complained about his chest and his heart, that he had a '*feeling of nervousness*' and '*was afraid of being paralysed.*' He said the symptoms had come on that morning and were the '*result of a strong cup of tea.*' He said tea had produced similar symptoms in the past. James complained about the state of his tongue, which he said had '*been furred for a long time, and that he could not get it clean.*' He also complained about a long-standing headache that he had suffered from since as far back as the Ascot races in the previous year.

James told Humphreys about events of the previous day, saying he had been in a '*peculiar state*' at the Wirral races. His legs felt very stiff, and he had been in a '*dazed condition.*' He mentioned his unsteadiness and the uncontrollable twitching of his arm at Hobson's house in the evening, and how he had knocked over a glass of wine.[581] Humphreys was very doubtful about James' tea theory, but he did examine the patient's chest, liver and tongue and quizzed him about any medicines he was taking. In reply, James completely failed to mention the London medicine. He did show Humphreys the prescriptions from Dr Fuller and told him he thought his stiffness of the previous morning was caused by the nux vomica that Fuller had prescribed for him. He informed Humphreys that he was a man who '*prided himself on his knowledge of medicine*' and had read a '*good deal*' around the subject. He admitted some of his friends felt he was a hypochondriac, but denied being one, saying he knew how he felt.

Humphreys stayed for around an hour. Before leaving, he directed James to rest and told him to discontinue taking Fuller's prescriptions. In their place, Humphreys gave him a new prescription for some dilute prussic acid to aid his digestion, and advised him to drink nothing but soda water and milk that day.

---

579 *Liverpool Mercury*, 29th May 1889.
580 Irving H.B., op cit., page 66.
581 Ibid., page 88.

After Dr Humphreys left, James got out of bed, dressed and moved downstairs to rest on the couch. The cook prepared him some bread and milk and Mary Cadwallader took it to the dining room, sounded the gong, and then left the room. Later in the day, Edwin Maybrick visited Battlecrease and found James '*lying on the sofa unable to walk about the room.*'[582] James told Edwin of his illness of the previous day, and the numbness in his legs and hands. Edwin decided to stay in the house for the rest of the day.

As it was Nurse Yapp's day-off, Elizabeth Humphreys was helping to mind the two Maybrick children. During the afternoon she took them into the breakfast room to see the two brothers. In the evening for dinner, Florence asked the cook to prepare oxtail soup for Edwin and herself, and an arrowroot gruel for James. For supper, James had more arrowroot gruel. This time, Mary Cadwallader rather than the cook started to prepare the meal, but the task was taken off her by Florence who finished the preparation and put it in a jug. Cadwallader noticed that when the jug was given to her there was '*something dark in it. Up to the time that I left off making the arrowroot I had not put anything dark into it.*'[583] The fact that the food seemed to have been adulterated was later to assume sinister overtones, but there was in fact a very simple explanation for the change in colour. The cook found a new bottle of vanilla had been opened and some vanilla had been added to the gruel.[584]

James retired to bed about 8:00pm and Florence and Edwin spent nearly an hour talking in the breakfast room. At 9:30pm, the chamber bell rang in James' bedroom. Mary Cadwallader answered it, and James told her to fetch his wife. Florence and Edwin went upstairs and found James lying in bed. He told them he had '*almost lost the use of both legs and his right hand.*'

For the second time that day, Florence sent Cadwallader to fetch Dr Humphreys. James asked Edwin and Florence to rub his legs, which they did until Humphreys arrived.[585] Humphreys listened patiently as James complained about stiffness in both his legs. Once again, he blamed his symptoms on the nux vomica prescribed by Dr Fuller. Humphreys rubbed the muscles in James' legs, and after a few minutes the symptoms seemed to ease. Humphreys prescribed bromide of potassium and tincture of henbane. As he left, he promised to call again in the morning. After Humphreys had gone, James urged Edwin to stay the night, which he did, sleeping in the spare bedroom.

As the London medicine had such a detrimental effect on James' health, it is important to try and ascertain what it was. There are some clues that help in this process. James told Morden Rigg's wife that he had taken an overdose of '*strychnine.*' We also know that it was in a medicine bottle and that the bottle had the name of an unknown chemist printed on the label. Nurse Yapp testified that Florence said James had taken an overdose of medicine, and that it was '*some ordered him by a doctor in London.*'[586] Therefore, it seems likely that the medicine was of a legitimate nature and had been prescribed for James by a doctor or chemist, other than Dr Fuller, while he had been in London.

One of the most common Victorian strychnine-based medicines was strychnine sulphate. The strychnine in this medicine was extracted from the bean of the St Ignatius tree. Although it was similar to the strychnine extracted from the bean of the nux vomica tree, it was much stronger and more potent in its side effects. According to one medical source, exposure to strychnine sulphate can cause '*muscle cramps, stiffness or twitching, vision disturbances and feeling restless or anxious.*'[587] All these symptoms were clearly evident in James' case. For example, he experienced twitching at Hobson's house and this caused him to spill his glass of wine. He experienced stiffness on Sunday when he said that he could not move his legs. He experienced vision disturbances at the Wirral races, and the next day told Dr Humphreys he was in a '*dazed condition.*' He also told Humphreys he had felt anxious, and had an '*indescribable feeling of nervousness.*'[588] Therefore, it seems likely that the London medicine was strychnine sulphate.

On Monday morning 29th April, Edwin found his brother to be feeling rather better. After breakfast, he set off to the office. Shortly after 10:00am, Dr Humphreys called at Battlecrease. James, who was in bed, told the doctor that he was much better, and that '*all the symptoms had disappeared except the furred tongue.*' Humphreys examined James and concluded he was '*a chronic dyspeptic.*' He prescribed a special dietary regime that '*consisted of coffee, toast, and some bacon for breakfast, some Revalenta food and tea for luncheon, and for dinner he was to take alternate meals of fish and bacon.*' He also prescribed '*Seymour's preparation of papaine and iridin. The papaine was a vegetable digestive, and the iridin a slight laxative to act on the liver.*'[589] Papaine is an enzyme extracted from the papaya plant. It helps break down proteins into smaller fragments and thus aids digestion. Although in small doses the preparation is perfectly safe, if taken in large doses it could cause serious irritation and ulcers in the esophagus (the tube connecting the throat with the stomach). Humphreys promised to return to Battlecrease on Wednesday evening.

---

582 *Liverpool Mercury*, 7th June 1889.
583 Irving H.B., op cit., page 74.
584 Ibid., page 76.
585 Ibid., page 47.
586 Ibid., page 65.
587 New Jersey Department of Health and Senior Services, *Hazardous Substance Fact Sheet: Strychnine Sulphate*, (New Jersey, 2002).
588 Irving H.B., op cit., page 100.
589 Ibid., page 89.

On Monday morning, James penned a letter to his brother Michael. In it, he recounted the events of the Wirral races and his subsequent illness. He blamed his illness on the nux vomica prescribed by Dr Fuller, and made no mention of the London medicine. Permeating the letter is a tone of hopelessness and he asks, '*what is the matter with me*?' He hints that his death might be imminent, and that only through a post-mortem would the doctors come to understand what was wrong with him. To a modern psychologist, the letter seems to suggest the onset of clinical depression. Further evidence of this interpretation is evident in his profile; financial stresses and the impact of trying to come to terms with his ageing and physical decline. The medications he was taking are known to cause depression and brain dysfunction. In simple terms, James' life was beginning to unravel in front of him. His use of drugs was an attempt to reverse this process, and for a while they may have helped slow down his decline; however, by April 1889 his chronic drug use was in fact only speeding up the process. It may not have been obvious to his wife, friends and servants – or even to himself – but James was a man who needed real medical help.

LETTER FROM JAMES TO MICHAEL (written on 29th April)[590]

My Dear ~~Michael~~ Blucher,

I have been very very seedy indeed. On Saturday morning I found my legs getting stiff and useless, but by sheer strength of will shook off the feeling and went down on horseback to Wirral Races and dined with the Hobsons. Yesterday morning I felt more like dying than living so much so that Florry called in another doctor who said it was an acute attack of indigestion and gave me something to relieve the alarming symptoms, so all went well until about eight o'clock. I went to bed and had lain there an hour by myself and was reading on my back. Many times I felt a twitching but took little notice of it thinking it would pass away but instead of doing so I got worse and worse and in trying to move round to ring the bell I found I could not do so but finally managed it, but by the time Florry and Edwin could get upstairs, was stiff and for two mortal hours my legs were like bars of iron stacked out to the fullest extent, but as rigid as steel. The Doctor came finally again but could not make it indigestion this time and the conclusion he came to was the Nuxvomica I had been taking. Dr Fuller had poisoned me as all the symptoms warranted such a conclusion. I know I am today sore from head to foot and played out completely.

What is the matter with me none of the Doctors so far can make out and I suppose never will until I am stretched out and cold and then future generations may profit by it if they hold a post mortem which I am quite willing they should do.

I don't think I shall come up to London this week as I don't feel much like travelling and cannot go on with Fuller's physic yet a while but I shall come up again and see him again shortly. Edwin does not join you just yet but he will write you himself. I suppose you go to your country quarters on Wednesday.

I have not seen Dickinson yet.

With love. Your affectionate brother Jim.

James and Florence had been invited to attend a domino ball on Tuesday 30th April, in Wavertree, a suburb of Liverpool, two miles from Battlecrease. Florence was determined to look her best for the event. As she was '*suffering from slight eruption of the face*,' she made herself a face wash, based upon a prescription given to her in America by Dr Greggs of Brooklyn.[591] This wash included in its ingredients a mild arsenic solution. To obtain the arsenic necessary for the face wash, Florence purchased two sets of flypapers. She made the first purchase from a chemist in Aigburth that was very close to her house. The chemist, Thomas Wokes, knew Florence well, and recognised her immediately she entered his shop which served as both a chemist and the local post office.

Wokes' Chemists (*Daily Mirror*, 27th July 1904)

Wokes was questioned about the sale at Florence's trial and he said he wasn't exactly sure of the date of the purchase, but thought it was around 24th April. He said Florence told him that '*the flies were beginning to get troublesome in the kitchen*.' He also said that although the Maybricks had an account in his shop, Florence paid for the flypapers in cash. Later in the day, he sent his '*boy with the flypapers*

[590] HO 144/1639/A50678/29.

[591] Taken from Florence's statement at her trial.

to the house.'[592] The parcel containing the flypapers was taken off the delivery boy at Battlecrease by Mary Cadwallader and placed on a downstairs table. She witnessed James pick up the parcel and inspect it before putting it back down on the table.[593]

A few days later on 29th April, Florence purchased two dozen more flypapers from Hanson's chemists in Cressington, which was also quite close to Battlecrease. As at Wokes' chemist, Florence paid for the flypapers in cash, though she did put the purchase of a lotion on the account the Maybricks had in the chemists.[594]

Florence's purchase of the flypapers was to become a key piece of evidence at her trial. The issue was important, because five years earlier two Liverpool women, Flanagan and Higgins, had been convicted of murder using arsenic extracted from flypapers. Elizabeth Brierley, the housemaid, noticed the flypapers soaking in a '*small sponge basin on the washstand*' in James and Florence's bedroom, and she '*called the attention*' of Nurse Yapp to them. The next morning she '*found some traces of the flypapers afterwards in the slop pail.*' She said that she was surprised, because '*flies were not troublesome at that time.*'[595]

At Florence's trial, Mary Cadwallader admitted the servants had talked about the presence of flypapers in the house and their possible usage. Significantly, in her evidence, Elizabeth Humphreys said she had noticed some flypapers '*on the window-sill in the kitchen*' when she started working for the Maybricks in October 1888. She said there was about half a dozen of them, and they '*lay there a long time.*' She said she destroyed them shortly before Mr Maybrick's death.[596] Humphreys' answer shows Florence had purchased flypapers on previous occasions, and this added credence to her claims she was using the arsenic extracted from the flypapers for cosmetic purposes.

On Monday 29th April, James made a brief visit to his office. Both George Smith and Thomas Lowry remembered James' visit, and they both felt he looked unwell.[597] At Battlecrease, Florence gave Elizabeth Humphreys an unopened tin of Du Barry's Revalenta Arabica and asked her to prepare it for James' lunch. She also gave the cook a little Wigtownshire brown cream jug to put the prepared food in so that James could take it to his office.[598]

Du Barry's food was supposed to be highly nutritious, and have restorative powers. It was prepared by mixing a flour-like powder with water, milk or cream to make a kind of gruel. The Du Barry Company, of New Bond Street, London, claimed their product could cure maladies as diverse as indigestion, constipation, cramps, spasms, fits, heartburn, diarrhea, nervousness, biliousness, liver and kidney problems.

The cook said she prepared the Revalenta on '*about four occasions*' during the week for James to take to his office.[599] On each occasion, Humphreys put the prepared food in the jug and Mary Cadwallader took it upstairs to Florence, who wrapped it up in paper and string and gave it to James. Although the cook prepared the food on four occasions, it was only on Wednesday, 1st May and Thursday, 2nd May that the food was eaten in the office.[600]

On Tuesday 30th April, James was beginning to feel a little better. After getting dressed he went down to the breakfast room, where Mary Cadwallader served him some bread and milk which had been prepared by the cook. James tasted the food and asked Cadwallader if the cook had sweetened it. As the food was not to James' taste, he barely touched his breakfast. When Cadwallader returned to the kitchen she told the cook what James had said, and Humphreys put her finger in it to taste it. She found that it had indeed been sweetened with sugar. Humphreys was asked at Florence's trial if she had sweetened the food, and she replied, '*No.*' She was also asked if she knew who had sweetened the food, and again denied any knowledge.[601]

Around midday, James went to his office. Smith remembered him arriving at around 1:00pm, and Lowry recalled him staying only about half an hour. James sent Lowry out on some errands, including posting some letters and taking a parcel that contained some of the Du Barry's food from the '*office to the house.*'[602] Presumably this means that, while James did take the Revalenta to the office that day, he did not eat any of it.

Despite the slight improvement in his health, James did not feel up to attending the domino ball being held in Wavertree that night. As Florence was still eager to go, Edwin agreed to accompany her. In a letter to her mother written prior to the ball, Florence wrote: '*We are asked to a 'bal masque' which, being in Liverpool and the people provincials, I hardly think likely to be a success. A certain amount of 'diablerie' wit and life is always required at an entertainment of this sort; and as it will be a novel innovation people will hardly know what is expected of them. However, we are requested to come in 'dominoes and masks', and I should like to know how the former is made and*

592 Ibid., pages 52-53.
593 Ibid., page 77.
594 Ibid., page 53.
595 Ibid., page 72.
596 Ibid., page 80.
597 Ibid., page 55.
598 MacDougall A.W., (1896) op cit., page 86.
599 Irving H.B., op cit., page 81.
600 Ibid., page 51.
601 Ibid., page 85.
602 Ibid., page 56.

if the latter are not procurable in gauze instead of papier mache. I think I read something of the kind in an article about the 'bal masque' at the opera in Paris.'[603]

Although Florence may have had doubts about how successful the ball would be, she was still keen to go and wanted to make a big impression. It was reported that she wore a '*very brilliant costume*' to the event.[604]

On Wednesday 1st May, James arrived at his office at around 11:00am. He told George Smith he '*was very seedy.*'[605] James had forgotten to bring the brown jug containing the Revalenta; however, the jug which had again been packaged by Florence was later brought in from Battlecrease by Edwin. James sent Thomas Lowry out to buy a saucepan, a basin and a spoon. He then heated the food up on the fire in the office and ate it. As he was consuming the food, James remarked to Edwin that '*the cook has put some of that —— sherry into it, and she knows I don't like it.*' Later he told Edwin that '*he had not felt so well since his lunch.*'[606]

Later in the afternoon, Captain Irving arrived at the office to meet James and Edwin. Irving was the captain of the Royal Mail steamship *Germanic*, and had been a good friend of James since 1878. After Florence's trial, a reporter from the *Liverpool Daily Post* interviewed Irving about the events of that particular day. He described Irving as '*a tall, well-made, rather good-looking man, with a bronzed face, dark curly hair, whiskers and moustache of the same colour.*' Irving said James had told him that he was feeling unwell after eating his lunch. He blamed his sickness on some bad wine in the soup.

Later, Irving saw James take a small packet from his breast pocket and empty the contents of it into a glass of water and drink it. Edwin asked James what the '*stuff*' was that he had put in the glass, and he replied it was some prescription made up for him by the chemists, Clay and Abraham's. He said James seemed to improve after taking the medicine. Irving said he did not know what the '*stuff*' was that James had taken, but he '*positively asserted that it was not a white powder.*' Irving was not surprised to see James take the medicine. He remarked that James' office was '*more like a chemist's shop that anything else. You saw almost nothing else but medicine bottles.*'

James, Edwin and Captain Irving then took a train from Central Station to Aigburth and the three of them ate a meal at Battlecrease with Florence. Irving said James had fish and soup, which he appeared to enjoy. A short time after the meal, the captain met Edwin and asked him what was wrong with James. Edwin replied, '*Oh he's killing himself with that damned strychnine.*' Captain Irving said it was well known that James had been in the habit of taking strychnine for years.[607]

At some point on Wednesday evening, Dr Humphreys visited Battlecrease to check up on his patient's progress. Humphreys found James to be '*much better*' and advised him to '*continue the same treatment.*' James, for his part, told the doctor that he '*need not call again*;' instead, he would call upon the doctor if any further treatment was required.[608]

The next morning, Thursday 2nd May, James went to his office and again he took the lunch prepared by the cook, which he heated up and ate.

LINKS WITH THE RIPPER DIARY: ARE THE LONDON MEDICINE AND THE *DEAR BLUCHER* LETTER CLUES TO THE RIPPER'S IDENTITY?

Those who believe the Diary to be an authentic document have linked the London medicine to a sinister plot that was supposedly being masterminded by James' brother, Michael. Graham and Emmas wrote that James' friends on the Liverpool Cotton Exchange had seen him '*taking some pills around that time, and they had made him ill.*' They suggest Michael had been '*feeding his brother pills*' and only Michael could have sent him the London medicine, writing, '*Who else but Michael could have sent it from London and given James the impression that it had been prescribed by Fuller?*'[609]

Dr Fuller testified at Florence's trial that James told him he had been taking a pill the doctor had prescribed for Michael. Fuller denied prescribing the pill. He described it in some detail, saying it '*contained powdered rhubarb, extract of aloes, and extract of camomile flowers, and was a mild aperient.*'[610] Therefore, the pill is neither a mystery nor a danger. An obvious explanation is that James was simply helping himself to somebody else's medication; something he was known for doing.

As to the London medicine, why could only Michael have sent it? It could have been sent by several people; or, more likely, it was ordered by James himself from a doctor or chemist in London, who then had it compounded and

[603] MacDougall A.W., (1896) op cit., page 74.
[604] *Liverpool Daily Post*, 30th May 1889.
[605] Irving H.B., op cit., page 55.
[606] Ibid., page 47.
[607] *Liverpool Daily Post*, 9th September 1889.
[608] Irving H.B., op cit., page 89.
[609] Graham A. and Emmas C., op cit., page 93.
[610] Irving H.B., op cit., page 58.

sent in the post to Liverpool. It is known James frequented several London chemists. We also know from the symptoms James suffered after taking the London medicine, that the drug was likely to have been strychnine-based. Therefore, the London medicine was not part of some sinister conspiracy it was just James doing what he always did, buying and taking potentially harmful medicines in dangerous doses.

Bruce Robinson goes a step further than Graham and Emmas. He suggests that Michael was providing James with pills – which he claimed had been provided by Dr Fuller – with the sole intent of trying to kill him. He also suggests the *Dear Blucher* letter was actually written by Michael so as to provide him with an alibi or, alternatively, as a means of incriminating Dr Fuller, or even Florence. Robinson wrote: '*No way did he [James] write this letter. It was faked by a man with 'many pens' [Michael] who was proficient in various schools of handwriting. Michael Maybrick had been systematically poisoning James with pills he claimed were from Dr Fuller, but which in fact had no more to do with him than the postal hotshot of strychnine. The so called 'Blucher' letter was composed to validate a variety of intentions. In the first place, it's probable that Michael thought his mystery brew might actually kill James, and this letter would then serve as his alibi; and second, had 'the London medicine' done the trick, the letter would have vanished, and Florence would have been accused of murdering her husband with strychnine.*'[611]

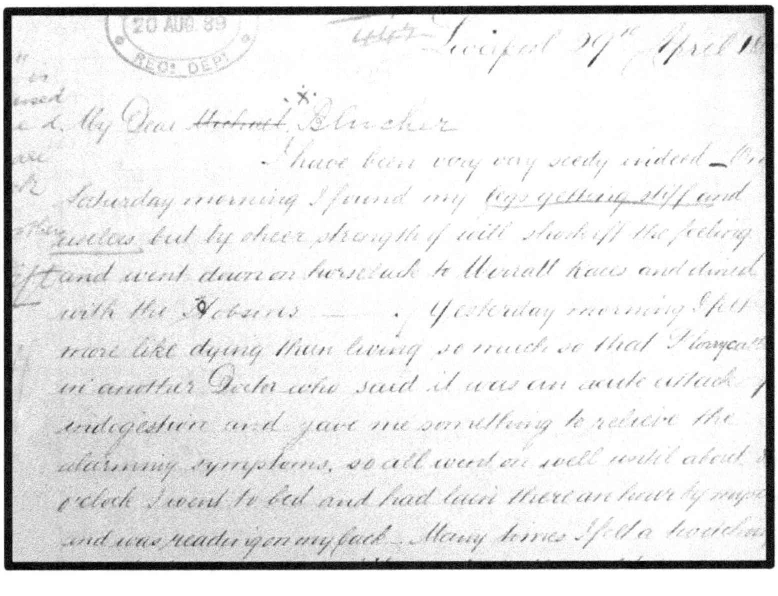
20 AUG. 89
REGD. DEPT
Liverpool 29th April
My Dear ~~Michael~~ Blucher
I have been very very seedy indeed
Saturday morning I found my legs getting stiff and useless but by sheer strength of will shook off the feeling and went down on horseback to Wirrall Races and dined with the Hobsons — Yesterday morning I felt more like dying than living so much so that I [illegible] in another Doctor who said it was an acute attack of indigestion and gave me something to relieve the alarming symptoms, so all went on well until about [illegible] o'clock I went to bed and had lain there an hour by myself and was reading on my back. Many times I felt a [illegible]

A copy of James' *Dear Blucher* letter sent to his brother, Michael (HO 144/1639/A50678/D29)

Like several of Robinson's hypotheses, it is high on speculation and low on facts. To accept this view, you would also have to buy into several other unlikely scenarios. You would have to believe that Michael was Jack the Ripper, and he wanted to incriminate James for the murders. You would also have to believe that Michael wanted to kill his own brother and that he was assisted in this murderous act by his other brother, Edwin, some of James' best friends and even some of the servants at Battlecrease.

Apart from the fact that there is no evidence to support any of these outlandish suggestions, they do not match up with the known circumstances. Firstly, the idea that Michael could feed James – the man who prided himself on his medical knowledge – with a mysterious and poisonous pill without his knowing, is absurd. Secondly, we actually know exactly what Fuller's '*mystery*' pill was; it was just a mild aperient. Thirdly, we know the London medicine was prescribed by a doctor or chemist and therefore must have been a legitimate form of medication. We also know that James sourced medicines from various London doctors and chemists. Fourthly, we know the key details in the *Dear Blucher* letter are all verifiable and match events exactly. Some of these details would not have been known to Michael, who was not present at Battlecrease at the time when they occurred. Therefore, the *Dear Blucher* letter was not written by Michael; it was written by James, and it provides a real insight into his turbulent mindset in the weeks before his death.

The London medicine episode is not referred to in the Diary. This is a surprising omission if the author had indeed been James Maybrick, as the medicine had such a detrimental impact upon his health. One is drawn to the conclusion that the author did not write about it as he did not know what the medicine was or where it came from. This, in turn, implies the diarist could not have been James Maybrick.

In fact, the diarist never refers to specific drugs or named medicines in the Ripper Diary. Instead, he uses the simple generic phrase '*my medicine*.' For example, near the beginning of the journal the diarist appears to be planning a murder in Manchester, and writes, '*Will take some of my medicine and think hard on the matter*.' Further on in the text, after he has supposedly murdered the first Ripper victim (presumably Polly Nichols), he writes, '*My medicine will give me strength and the thought of the whore and her whoring master will spur me on no end*.' Thus, if the diarist is to be believed, his prime motivation for the murders was Florence's adultery, but his drug use was also important as it gave him the necessary strength to carry out the fiendish deeds.

What is very noticeable about the diarist's references to his drug use are how vague they are. They provide no insight or new information and are short on detail. Some basic details are provided, such as his '*hands are cold*,' and he feels a '*numbness*' in his body. There are also some brief references to actual events, such as James' consultations

---

[611] Robinson B., op cit., page 642.

with Dr Hopper and Dr Fuller, though interestingly Dr Drysdale – who had a positive impact upon James' health – is not mentioned. There is also a brief passage in which the diarist states he had '*found a new source for my medicine.*' This is clearly a reference to Maybrick obtaining arsenic off Valentine Blake. All these details are easily obtained from any book on the Florence Maybrick trial.

One of the references to medicines in the Diary is particularly illuminating. It appears very near the end and states: '*I no longer take the dreaded stuff.*' This quote has been seized upon by several authors who believe the Diary is a genuine document. Paul Feldman argues the quote signified that '*James Maybrick had stopped taking arsenic.*'[612] He supports this statement by pointing out that, at James' post-mortem, the doctors found only small traces of arsenic in his body.

Professor Rubinstein argues the reason why the Ripper killings stopped after the Mary Kelly murder in November 1888 (if in fact they did stop) was that on 19th November James changed doctors from Dr Hopper to Dr Drysdale, who treated him with homeopathic remedies. This led to an improvement in James' health, which presumably meant he stopped taking arsenic and '*lost interest in further killings, feeling considerable remorse just before his death.*'[613]

The fundamental weakness with this line of argument is that James did not stop taking dangerous drugs prior to his death. If anything, his intake actually increased. In January 1889, he acquired a new source for arsenic from his association with Valentine Blake. The 150 grains of arsenic that Blake gave him would have provided James with more arsenic than he probably ever had in his life. James' post-mortem may have only revealed small traces of arsenic, but it did, nevertheless, reveal arsenic. If James wasn't taking the '*dreaded stuff,*' then it wouldn't have revealed any arsenic. We also know from various sources, including from James' own statements, that he was, in addition to taking arsenic, also using other dangerous drugs such as strychnine. Indeed, James was taking strychnine in such dangerous amounts that Edwin Maybrick told Captain Irving that he was killing himself with the drug.

Therefore, to argue that James stopped taking arsenic or strychnine just before his death is incorrect. The fact that it is incorrect, points very clearly to the view that the diarist was not James Maybrick.

[612] Feldman P., op cit., page 316.
[613] Rubinstein W. D., 'Hunt for Jack the Ripper' in *History Today*, Vol. 50, May 2000.

10

SECOND ILLNESS AND DEATH

Friday 3rd May, was an important day in the Maybrick case. This was the day Dr Carter claimed the fatal dose of arsenic was administered to James.

The morning got off to a slow start as James was feeling ill again. He sent a message to Dr Humphreys asking him to visit. The doctor arrived at 10:00am and found James sitting in the downstairs morning room. James said he had not been well since yesterday and did not think his medicine agreed with him. Florence, who was also in the room, said to James: '*You always say the same thing about anybody's medicine after you have taken it two or three days.*'[614]

Humphreys examined James, but could not find anything wrong with him other than his tongue was not as clean as it should have been. He advised him to continue with the medicine for the next two or three weeks as it wasn't making him ill and, if anything, assisted his digestion. As the doctor was leaving, James asked if he could have a Turkish bath, to which Humphreys replied in the affirmative.

Later in the morning, James headed to his office. Both Lowry and Smith remembered him attending that day. Smith said James '*did not seem at all well. He was very pale. He left, and never came again.*'[615] After spending a couple of hours at work, James went for a Turkish bath. When he returned to Battlecrease he had terrible pains in both legs and was sick on at least two occasions. Florence told Bessie Brierley to '*prepare the bedroom at once, as the master was going to bed.*'[616] Brierley filled a hot-water bottle for James and he retired to bed in much discomfort. In the evening, Florence took the children to see him. Nurse Yapp accompanied them into the bedroom and she heard James tell Florence he had been sick again. After they left the room, the nurse said to Florence it was strange that James had been ill for so long. She advised her to get a second opinion from another doctor. Florence replied that Dr Humphreys said it was only James' liver that was the problem, but added '*all doctors are fools. They say that because it covers a multitude of sins.*'[617]

As the evening turned into night, the pain in James' legs grew steadily worse. To alleviate his suffering, Florence rubbed his inner thighs with turpentine. As there was no improvement, she sent for Dr Humphreys. The doctor arrived around midnight and saw James in his bed. James told him he had a terrible gnawing pain that '*extended from the hips down to the joints, and was more particularly located in the back aspect of the joint.*' James thought the pain might have been caused by '*excessive towelling and rubbing*' during his Turkish bath. He told the doctor he had been sick twice since returning home and thought '*it was due to some inferior sherry having been put into Du Barry's Revalenta food.*'[618] Humphreys gave James a morphine suppository to reduce the pain and allow him to sleep. The suppository consisted of small capsules of gelatine mixed with morphia that had originally been prescribed for Florence.

Dr Humphreys was back early on Saturday morning, 4th May, to check on his patient. James told him that while the pain had gone, he had vomited and '*could retain nothing on his stomach.*' Humphreys said the vomiting was a common side-effect of taking morphia. As a result, he told James to eat nothing at all and to quench his thirst by washing his mouth out with water or by '*sucking ice or a damp cloth.*' Humphreys prescribed ipecacuanha wine to stop the vomiting.

Ipecacuanha wine was used to tackle gastro-intestinal problems, such as bronchitis and pneumonia. In very small doses, it could be stimulating to the stomach, intestines and liver, exciting appetite and facilitating digestion. In large doses, it was an emetic and caused vomiting. What Humphreys didn't know – or didn't tell James – was that ipecacuanha wine was dangerous when taken in large doses, or when used in conjunction with certain other drugs such as strychnine. As James had a tendency to take large doses, and was also taking strychnine, the medicine so innocently prescribed by the doctor had the potential to do James great harm. Humphreys saw James again later on Saturday, but little must have changed with his condition because the doctor could '*not recollect the visit.*'[619]

---

[614] Irving H.B., op cit., page 89.
[615] Ibid., page 55.
[616] Ibid., page 73.
[617] Ibid., page 66.
[618] Ibid., page 90.
[619] Ibid., page 91.

On Saturday morning, the chemist's lad delivered a bottle of medicine to Battlecrease. Elizabeth Humphreys accepted it and took it straight to James' bedroom. When the cook told Florence what she had done, Florence reacted angrily as she had given instructions that nothing was to be taken into the sick room unless she checked it first.

Later in the day, the cook again saw Florence and asked about James' health. Florence replied that he '*was no better.*' Florence then told her about the '*horrid*' medicine James had been taking. She remarked that '*if he had taken that much more (pointing to her finger) he would have been a dead man.*' She told the cook she had thrown what remained of the medicine down the sink.

At Florence's trial, Elizabeth Humphreys was asked whether this medicine was the London medicine. Humphreys replied, '*I thought she meant the London medicine. She said that "horrid" medicine.*'[620] Therefore, at the point when James became seriously ill for a second time, he had again taken the same London medicine containing strychnine that he had taken the first time he was ill. What made it even more dangerous, was that James had taken it in a weakened physical state, and at the same time as he was taking ipecacuanha wine. He was also taking it on an empty stomach.

Under advice from Dr Humphreys, and because he couldn't retain anything in his stomach, James ate hardly anything at all on Saturday. Elizabeth Brierley, the housemaid, said she did not take any food to James apart from a glass of milk, which she took up to him in the evening.[621]

On Saturday, a story circulated that Mary Cadwallader had been sent by Florence to Wokes' Chemists with a prescription the chemist refused to make up on the grounds it contained a poisonous drug. The story was not just mischievous, it was also grossly inaccurate.

In an interview given by Cadwallader after the trial, she explained what had happened. She said Dr Humphreys was in James' bedroom writing out a prescription for him, but '*he put it on one side before completing it; and Mrs Maybrick, in her excitement and hurry, I suppose, handed it to me with instructions to go to the nearest chemists for a bottle of meat juice.*'[622]

Cadwallader went to Wokes' Chemists at around 7:00pm. The chemist said he could not make up the prescription as it was incomplete. He sent Cadwallader back to Battlecrease to find Dr Humphreys, but on her return she found he had gone. Florence informed Cadwallader that in her hurry she had given the maid the wrong piece of paper. According to Cadwallader, Florence then '*passed me the right slip of paper, and on going again to the chemist that same evening I presented it and received a bottle of Valentine's juice. On the following Monday, I believe. Dr Humphreys called at Mr Wokes' and finished the prescription that I had taken there on the Saturday night.*' Cadwallader denied emphatically that the chemist had refused to make up the prescription on the grounds that it contained a poisonous drug. She said the chemist '*could not make it up unless the doctor came and signed it.*'

Cadwallader also denied passing on this story to Nurse Yapp. She said it had probably come from some person who happened to be in the chemists when she had been refused the medicine and that person passed it on to Grant, the gardener at Battlecrease. She said the gardener asked her about the incident, and she explained to him it had been a simple mistake involving an unsigned prescription. The police did investigate the matter and concluded that nothing untoward happened. Although Florence's action was just an accident, it was soon caught up in the swirl of ill-founded rumour that was starting to engulf her at that time.

On Sunday morning 5th May, James was no better. As Florence was coming down the stairs she met the cook, who again asked about James' condition. Florence told her he was in a much worse condition and '*had been ill all night.*' Humphreys suggested to Florence that she could '*look after the master.*' Florence responded by telling her that James was so bad he simply wouldn't recognise her.[623]

Dr Humphreys visited on Sunday morning and found that James was hawking rather than vomiting, and that he '*complained of his mouth being very dirty, and his throat was troubling him. His throat showed a slight redness, but his tongue was very dirty and furred.*'[624] Unlike Florence, the doctor felt James' condition had slightly improved, although he had not made the progress he would have expected. The doctor prescribed prussic acid from the bottle which James had not finished the previous week. He also told James to take Valentine's meat juice and wash his mouth with Condy's fluid.

Valentine's meat juice was an American health tonic made from pure beef extract. It was the brainchild of Mann S. Valentine Jnr (1824-1893), a merchant and inventor, who was desperate to cure his dying wife of '*a severe and protracted derangement of the organs of digestion.*' After a series of experiments, Valentine devised a process of rendering all the goodness of raw meat into a highly condensed form. It worked and his wife recovered. Valentine's

[620] Ibid., page 81.
[621] Ibid., page 73.
[622] *Liverpool Echo*, 21st August 1889.
[623] Irving H.B., op cit., page 81.
[624] Ibid., page 91.

meat juice became popular with orthodox physicians, and was advertised in professional publications including the *British Medical Journal.*

As he was leaving Battlecrease, Dr Humphreys asked Florence if she would like to have a second medical opinion. Florence declined, telling him it wasn't necessary as James had seen many doctors in the past and they '*have done him so little good.*'

On Sunday afternoon, around 2:00pm, Edwin arrived at Battlecrease and went upstairs to see his brother, who was still in bed. James told him that '*he had been very sick, and that he vomited, and could not retain anything in his stomach.*'[625] To try and quench his thirst and remove the '*dirty*' taste from his mouth, James asked Edwin to give him a brandy and soda. Although Edwin must have realised he was going against the advice of James' doctor, he gave him the brandy. Half an hour later, James vomited and remained sick all that afternoon. When Dr Humphreys returned in the evening he told James he had better not eat or drink anything and, if he was thirsty, he should have a '*wet towel put to his mouth.*' James asked Edwin to stay the night, which he agreed to do.

On Sunday evening, the cook went upstairs to find out what Florence wanted prepared for dinner. Florence, who was on the landing near James' bedroom, ordered the food and the cook then followed Florence into the bedroom. James told her he was '*very sick and wanted a drink of something.*' He asked Humphreys to make him some lemonade with a little sugar in it. He gave precise instructions on how it was to be made, saying he wanted her '*to make it as you would for any poor man dying of thirst.*' Florence intervened and offered him lemon juice; however, James insisted that he wanted freshly-made lemonade from the kitchen. Florence said he could have it, but only as '*a gargle.*' The cook asked James if, as well as the lemonade, would he like any lemon jelly or barley-water. He replied that he would '*like something, anything of that sort.*' The cook went downstairs and prepared the lemonade, on her return placing it on the right-side of the bed. Florence picked up the glass of lemonade and placed it on the washstand which was on the left-side of the bed. She said to James, '*You can't have it, dear, except as a gargle.*' He replied, '*Very well.*' The cook said James looked '*very wistfully*' as Florence removed the glass of lemonade from his reach.

It was later to be suggested that Florence had acted in a cruel manner when she refused to allow James to drink the lemonade. In fact, she was just following the doctor's instructions. Edwin ignored the doctor's advice and gave James a brandy and soda; half an hour later James was sick. Ironically, while Edwin's behaviour was not questioned, Florence's behaviour was used by some to portray her as an uncaring and spiteful wife.

On Monday morning 6th May, Dr Humphreys was back at Battlecrease. Although James '*still complained of his tongue very much,*' the doctor found '*he was better able to retain a little food.*'[626] James had a tickling sensation in his throat which he found very uncomfortable and caused him to retch, though he was more inclined to hawk rather than actually vomit. As the Valentine's meat juice did not seem to agree with James, Humphreys told him to stop taking it. Humphreys also stopped his other medicines and personally made up for him some Fowler's solution, which was a '*mixture of white arsenic, carbonate of potash, and lavender water.*'

At Florence's trial, Humphreys was asked about the quantity of arsenic that was in the solution. He replied: '*one per cent. I gave the deceased four drops in about five tablespoonfuls of water. He was to have a few drops of that in less than half a teaspoonful every hour. I made the medicine myself while I was there. It was put into a medicine glass, which contained about sixty or eighty doses. In the whole of the doses there was about 1-25th of a grain. I showed him how to take it, and gave it to him myself. He took three doses altogether.*'

Fowler's Solution had been developed in the late eighteenth century by a Staffordshire physician, Thomas Fowler, in order to treat malaria, then rife in the Fens of East Anglia. It later acquired a reputation as a cure-all for a range of ailments, most notably asthma.

At around 11:00am on Monday, Elizabeth Brierley went upstairs and asked Florence if she wanted James' bedclothes changed. She replied that his '*bed had better not be disturbed.*'[627] Afterwards, Florence placed the dirty bedclothes outside the bedroom door. At this point James was well enough to sit up in bed, and Mary Cadwallader saw him reading the papers, writing letters and even sending off some telegrams.[628]

The slight improvement in James' condition allowed Florence to go out shopping. While she was out Nurse Yapp heard James moaning, so she entered the bedroom. At Florence's trial, she said James '*seemed flushed and hot, and was moving from one side of the pillow to the other. He asked me if I would rub his hands as he complained of numbness. I did this, and I stayed with him, I should think, for ten minutes.*'[629]

In the afternoon, after Florence returned home, Nurse Yapp spoke to her about James' condition and suggested Florence should send for Dr Hopper. Florence replied she did not think James would see him even if he came to the house. Dr Humphreys returned to Battlecrease in the evening and ordered James some '*Brand's beef tea, some*

---

[625] Ibid., page 47.
[626] Ibid., page 91.
[627] Ibid., page 73.
[628] Ibid., page 77.
[629] Ibid., page 66.

chicken broth, Neave's food, and some milk and water.'[630] In an attempt to bring a complete end to his vomiting, Humphreys recommended the application of a blister to the stomach. At this point, James was not complaining of any pain in his stomach and had no itching or pain in his eyes or eyelids. This is important, as they are signs of arsenical poisoning.[631]

In the late afternoon post on Monday, Florence received a letter from Alfred Brierley, whom she hadn't seen since she went to his house on 6th April. He had written the letter in response to a telegram from Florence, which he described as '*a staggerer.*' As this telegram has disappeared, one can only speculate on what she had told him. As he wrote in his reply that he could not find '*an advertisement in any London papers,*' it is likely Florence had informed him of James' threat to place adverts asking about her movements in London.

The overall tone of the letter has been interpreted in different ways. Christie believed it implied that both Florence and Brierley still '*cherished hopes of future idylls.*'[632] The difficulty with this view is that Brierley refers to the liaison as an '*unhappy business.*' He is clearly alarmed that James would find out about the affair, and was planning to leave the country for six to seven weeks until things settled down. It is the letter of a man running scared, and although he writes that he is prepared to meet Florence, he is vague about how and when that might happen. Brierley's reference to the '*D and D*' is unclear, though Christie suggests it might stand for '*dinner and dance.*' If true, it suggests rumours were in circulation about the two of them.

Letter from Alfred Brierley to Florence Maybrick
(Chris Jones collection - HO 144/1640/A50678)

LETTER FROM BRIERLEY TO FLORENCE
(received 6th May, 1889)

My dear Florie, I suppose now you have gone I am safe in writing to you. I don't quite understand what you mean in you last about explaining my line of action. You know I could not write, and was willing to meet you, although it would have been very dangerous. Most certainly your telegram yesterday was a staggerer, and it looks as if the result was certain, but as yet I cannot find an advertisement in any London paper. I should like to see you, but at present dare not move, and we had better not meet until late in the Autumn. I am going to try and get away in about a fortnight and think I should take a round trip to the Mediterranean, which will take six or seven weeks, unless you wish me to stay in England. Supposing the rooms are found, I think both you and I would be better away as the man's memory would be doubted after three months. I shall write and tell you when I go. I cannot trust myself at the present to write about my feelings on this unhappy business, but I do hope that sometime hence I shall be able to show you that I do not quite the deserve the strictures contained in you last two letters. I went to the D and D and of course heard some tales, but myself knew nothing about anything. And now dear, goodbye, hoping we shall meet again in the autumn. I shall write about sending letters before I go. A.B.

In an effort to prevent James from intercepting her correspondence, Florence had arranged for her letters from Brierley to come to her via her friend, John Baillie Knight, who lived in London. He was far from happy with this situation. He wrote a long letter to her remonstrating about her behaviour in London and all the lies she told to cover up her meeting with Brierley. He told Florence that he was '*not going to be led into telling any more lies or doing any underhand or dangerous missions.*' He also objected to receiving letters that were intended for Florence. He asked her: '*Why can't they be sent to your own house now? I am obliged to speak what I think because I am tired of all this scheming which only seems to me to endanger your reputation at a most critical time and not to serve any further end.*'[633]

---

[630] Ibid., page 92.
[631] Ibid., page 102.
[632] Christie T.L., op cit., page 59.
[633] HO/144/1638 A50678/D13.

Dr William Carter

On Tuesday morning 7th May, Dr Humphreys was again at Battlecrease. James, who appeared rather better, told the doctor he was '*quite a different man altogether today after you put on that blister last night.*'[634] Although James was able to retain a tablespoon of food every hour, he was still '*constantly complaining of the offensive feeling of his mouth.*' Humphreys advised him to wash his mouth with Sanitas to try and clear it.

Florence was not convinced by James' assertion that he was feeling better. She believed the time had now come for a second medical opinion. Her decision was probably also influenced by the fatigue she was starting to feel from being constantly at her husband's sickbed. She sent a telegram to Edwin asking him to contact Dr McCheane (1820-1889), a respected surgeon at Liverpool Lock Hospital and a friend of Edwin. Edwin did contact the doctor, but as he was not well himself and, as he rarely went out on visits, he recommended Edwin contact Dr William Carter at the Royal Southern Hospital in Liverpool.

Early in the afternoon, Edwin telephoned Dr Carter, a man he had never previously met, and asked him to go immediately to see his sick brother. As Dr Carter was still seeing patients, he told Edwin that he could not go until later in the afternoon. The two of them arranged to meet at Battlecrease at 5:30pm. Edwin telegraphed Dr Humphreys and asked him to join them at the house at the appointed time.

Edwin took the 4:45pm train to Aigburth and met the two doctors at Battlecrease. As Dr Carter had never treated James, Edwin and Dr Humphreys informed him of the history of the case. Edwin did not tell the doctor of his brother's chronic use of different drugs. Carter later recalled a small incident that indicated to him James' '*thoughtful kindness of character.*' He said that while he was visiting Battlecrease it started to rain heavily. His wife had been waiting outside in an open carriage. When James was told there was a woman in the rain, he absolutely insisted that she be '*conveyed*' into the house to take shelter in the drawing room.

Carter then examined James who was in bed and extremely restless. Carter described James as a '*somewhat fair-complexioned man of about fifty years of age, of slight but muscular build.*'[635] James told Carter he had suffered greatly from vomiting, though that was getting less severe. He said his most distressing symptom was: '*an intense thirst, a sensation as of a hair in his throat, which he was compelled to make incessant efforts to get rid of, and a bad taste in his mouth, which he more than once described as being as foul as a midden.*' Carter examined James' tongue and found it quite furred, though the breath was sweet. As Carter referred out-loud to the contrasting nature of James' tongue and breath, a young woman sitting at the window in the bedroom remarked, '*It was so; that his breath was quite sweet, though his tongue was so bad.*' Dr Carter turned around to see Florence sitting in the window. Neither Edwin nor Humphreys had thought to introduce her to the new doctor who was examining her husband. It was a foretaste of things to come. Carter checked James' throat, which he found to be '*red, dry and glazed.*' He then checked the main organs, which he found to be healthy. As he carried out his checks, James continually complained of the uncomfortable sensation in his throat. The doctor checked James' urine, which appeared '*normal.*' He then retired to the bathroom to examine a motion which had been retained for his inspection. It was '*copious, loose*' but contained '*neither blood nor mucus.*'

Florence followed Carter into the bathroom and they had a conversation about the possible cause of James' illness. She suggested that James' '*constitution might have been injured by indiscretions as to food before his marriage.*'[636] Although it is not clear what she meant, it is possible she was referring to James' habit of taking mysterious powders. Either way, Carter dismissed the suggestion as not relevant. After examining James and consulting Humphreys, Carter concluded that he was suffering from '*acute dyspepsia, resulting from indiscretion of food, or drink, or both.*'[637] In other words, the acute dyspepsia had been caused by James taking some irritant that had adversely affected his stomach but not his other organs. Humphreys threw away the remainder of the Fowler's solution and the two doctors prescribed small doses of antipyrine and a small dose of tincture of jaborandi. The antipyrine was to allay James' restlessness and the pain in his throat. The jaborandi was given to increase the saliva and to relieve the throat. They also gave James a mouthwash of diluted chlorodyne (chlorine water) to relieve the feeling of foulness in his mouth. In addition to the medicines, Carter recommended that James continue with the diet of Neave's food, chicken broth, milk and lime water prescribed by Humphreys the previous day. Importantly, both doctors agreed that

---

[634] Irving H.B., op cit., page 92.
[635] Carter W., 'Notes on the Maybrick Trial' in *Liverpool Medico-Chirurgical Journal*, (no.18, Jan 1890) page 120.
[636] Irving H.B., op cit., page 113.
[637] Ibid., page 113.

James '*was going on very favourably, and would be well in a few days.*' Humphreys told James of his positive diagnosis and that he '*would soon recover.*'[638]

Carter was a distinguished, respected and experienced physician. Humphreys, who was struggling to improve James' medical condition, must have welcomed the older doctor's assistance. Carter came to the correct diagnosis, that James' illness had been caused by him taking some irritant which had adversely affected his stomach. He changed James' medication and also gave advice on his diet. Therefore, in the due course of time, James should have gradually returned to full health. However, that did not happen, and four days later James was dead. What went wrong?

One possibility is that James didn't improve because Florence had already given him the fatal dose of arsenic. That was the view later accepted by Humphreys and Carter, and afterwards by the police. Another, more likely possibility, is that despite his best intentions Carter was unable to help James because he did not realise the full extent of James' condition. Carter, like Humphreys before him, was not told about James' dangerous use of powerful drugs. Another problem faced by Carter, was that although he had handled cases of people who had overdosed medicinally with arsenic, he had never previously dealt with anyone who had actually died from arsenical poisoning.[639]

Tuesday saw another of the minor incidents that were later to take on a more sinister connotation. Nurse Yapp witnessed Florence pouring something out of one medicine bottle into another. The incident took place on the landing outside James' bedroom, where there was a table with several medicine bottles on it. Nurse Yapp recalled the incident at Florence's trial. When cross-examined by Sir Charles Russell, the counsel for the defence, she was forced to admit that Florence's actions had occurred in a place which would have been in full view of anyone who was going up and down the stairs and she had not attributed anything of importance to it at the time.[640] As was the case with several of Florence's other behaviours, a simple and rather sensible action, reorganising and tidying up the half empty medicine bottles that littered the house, came to be viewed with suspicion.

According to Christie, Wednesday 8th May was the '*fateful day*' in the history of the Maybrick case.[641] Although James had a restless night, he did feel slightly better in the morning. Edwin went in to see him before he headed into the city and asked if he would like him to contact his brother, Michael, and tell him to come to Liverpool. James told him that he did not think it was necessary. James asked Edwin if he thought they should send for a professional nurse. He said Florence had suggested sending to Halewood for Mrs Howell, the nurse who had attended her in the past. Both James and Florence knew the nurse well and liked her. Edwin said he would ask the doctor for his opinion on the matter. As usual, Dr Humphreys arrived early in the morning and examined James. As he believed James was a little better, he made no changes to his treatment. After having a brief conversation with Florence, who told the doctor how tired she was getting, Humphreys went to the telegraph office and, at 9:00am, sent a message to Mrs Howell informing her that Florence would like a nurse sent to Battlecrease.

James' continued illness was the talk of the servants. Nurse Yapp was on the landing near James' bedroom, when she saw Florence and asked her how the master was. Florence replied, '*about the same.*' Yapp then heard James ask Florence to rub his hands. She said, '*you are always wanting your hands rubbed; it does you no good.*'[642] Due to her increasing fatigue, Florence asked Mary Cadwallader to come into the main bedroom and help her wash James. Cadwallader witnessed Florence give James some medicine.

At 9:37am, Florence sent a telegram to her mother in Paris that simply said, '*Jim very ill again.*' Later in the morning, Edwin left his office and went to Rodney Street to call on Dr Carter who told him that although his brother was very ill, both he and Dr Humphreys '*trusted that he would recover.*'[643] After hearing this, Edwin decided he did not need to telegraph Michael and ask him to come to Liverpool.

At mid-morning, Mrs Briggs and Mrs Hughes arrived at Battlecrease in response to a telegram Mrs Briggs had received the previous day from Michael, asking her to visit his brother. As they arrived at the house, they were met on the lawn by a clearly agitated Nurse Yapp who said: '*Thank God, Mrs Briggs, you have come, for the mistress is poisoning the master. For goodness sake go and see him for yourselves.*' Mrs Hughes asked Yapp what reasons she had for making such a terrible accusation. Yapp told them about the flypapers, the incident in which the chemist had refused to make up a medicine and about how '*the food intended for Mr Maybrick had been tampered with by his wife.*'[644] The two sisters were so shocked that they did not bother with the usual formalities, but instead went straight upstairs to see James in his bedroom. They were immediately followed by an angry Florence who told them they had no right to be there. Mrs Briggs' role in the Maybrick affair has been criticised; however, there is no doubt she was genuinely concerned when she saw James' condition and considered him to be in '*serious peril.*'[645] Mrs Briggs asked

---

[638] Ibid., page 92.
[639] Ibid., page 119.
[640] Ibid., page 70.
[641] Christie T.L., op cit., page 59.
[642] Irving H.B., op cit., page 67.
[643] Carter W., op cit., page 124.
[644] *Evening Express*, 15th August 1889.
[645] Irving H.B., op cit., page 40.

James about his symptoms and he told her he was very weary and restless. At that point, Florence firmly intervened and said James needed complete rest and she would explain everything downstairs. According to Mrs Briggs, James did not want her to leave the room and begged her to stay. She remembered him saying, '*I will let you go if you will come back in an hour.*'[646]

After Mrs Briggs and Mrs Hughes had gone downstairs, Florence informed them of James' symptoms and the views of his doctors. Mrs Briggs suggested that Florence should send for a nurse. Florence disagreed, saying there was '*no occasion for one, as she could nurse him herself.*' She added this view was also shared by the doctor. What Mrs Briggs didn't know, and for some reason Florence didn't tell her, was a telegraph had already been sent to Hale to ask for a nurse. Florence probably resented the interference by Mrs Briggs and wanted to show that she was the mistress of the house; however, her apparent hostility to the request to call for a professional nurse made her look callous. As a result of Mrs Briggs' continued insistence, Florence eventually agreed to send for a nurse. Mrs Briggs then wrote out a telegram to the Nurses' Institute in Liverpool and Florence gave her the money to pay for it. At around 12noon, Mrs Briggs and Mrs Hughes left the house and headed for the telegraph office. While at the office, Mrs Briggs sent a second telegraph to Michael in London stating, '*Come at once; strange things going on here.*' After the sisters left Battlecrease, Florence sent a telegram to Edwin, who received it in his office after returning from his visit to Dr Carter. In the telegram, Florence wrote, '*Jim worse again; have wired for a nurse.*' Edwin immediately telegraphed his brother, Michael, telling him to come to Liverpool. He then headed off to Battlecrease by the 12:40pm train. On his way from the station to Battlecrease, he met Mrs Briggs and Mrs Hughes who told him what happened in the house that morning. As a consequence, Edwin headed straight to the Nurses' Institute but found, on his arrival, that Nurse Gore had already been sent to Battlecrease.

At 2:15pm, Nurse Ellen Ann Gore arrived at Battlecrease. She was a professionally trained private care nurse from the Nurses' Institute in Dover Street, Liverpool. The Institute was one of the first of its kind in the country and had a reputation for excellence. It provided the nurse trainees with a highly practical year-long course. The nurses were trained to: '*study the art of patience, to be quiet, watchful, methodical and cheerful, and were trained both to ensure that the sickroom was well aired and perfectly clean and the patient was given medicine or food with strict accuracy and punctuality.*'[647] The more formal manner of nursing promoted by the Institute was very different from the style that Florence had experienced with Mrs Howell. Instead of a friendly face, Florence now encountered a pale, thin, ghostly-looking woman.[648] Although Florence would have preferred Mrs Howell, she would have initially welcomed the arrival of Nurse Gore as she was getting increasingly tired and her husband's health was getting worse rather than better. As the nurse seemed to be taking a long time to change into her working clothes, Florence went to her '*several times and asked her to hurry.*'[649] Nurse Gore described James' condition as fully conscious, but '*very ill indeed, and in bed.*'[650] His feet and legs were very cold and he had recently vomited. James told her that the doctors did not know what was wrong with him but they believed there was something wrong with his liver and stomach. Florence took the nurse some medicine from the medicine box in the lavatory and she gave it to James.

FLORENCE'S LETTER TO BRIERLEY (written on Wednesday 8th May)

Dearest, Your letter undercover to John K. came to hand just after I had written to you on Monday. I did not expect to hear from you so soon, and had delayed in giving him the necessary instructions. Since my return I have been nursing M. day and night. He is sick unto death. The doctors held a consultation yesterday, and now all depends upon how long his strength will hold out. Both my brothers-in-law are here, and we are terribly anxious. I cannot answer your letter fully today, my darling, but relieve your mind of all fear of discovery now and in the future. M. has been delirious since Sunday, and I know that he is perfectly ignorant of everything, even of the name of the street, and also that he has not been making any inquiries whatever. The tale he told me was a pure fabrication, and only intended to frighten the truth out of me. In fact he believes my statement, although he will not admit it. You need not therefore go abroad on that account dearest; but, in any case, please don't leave England until I have seen you once again. You must feel that those two letters of mine were written under circumstances which must even excuse their injustice in your eyes. Do you suppose that I could act as I am doing if I really felt and meant what I inferred then? If you wish to write to me about anything do so now, as all letters pass through my hands at present. Excuse this scrawl, my own darling, but I dare not leave the room for a moment and I do not know when I shall be able to write to you again. In haste, yours ever, Florie.[651]

646 *Evening Express*, 15th August 1889.
647 Colquhoun K., op cit., pages 84-85.
648 Graham A. and Emmas C., op cit., page 103.
649 HO 144/1640/A50678D/279 page 44.
650 Irving H.B., op cit., page 141.
651 Ibid., page 17.

With Nurse Gore in the house, Florence had some free time and she decided to respond to the letter received from Brierley on Monday. She quickly wrote in pencil a two-sided letter on a sheet of her mother's stationery headed with a crown and the initial 'R' (for Roque). She could have posted the letter herself as the post box was less than a five-minute walk from the house; however, due to fatigue, she made the fateful decision of asking Nurse Yapp to post it.

Picture of Florence Maybrick stored in the National Archives (Chris Jones collection)

Yapp was at the garden gate with Gladys. At 3:00pm, Florence gave Yapp the letter and asked her to take it to the post box at Wokes' in time to catch the 3:45pm post. The letter never made it into the post box. Yapp claimed Gladys accidentally dropped it as they crossed the road near the post office, so she opened it in order to place it in a clean envelope. Later, she said that as she did so she saw the words, '*Mr darling*' [actually '*Dearest*']. She then read the letter '*twice*' on the step of the post office.[652] Yapp's account of events is hard to believe. A more likely explanation is that when she saw to whom the letter was addressed, she manufactured an excuse to open and read it.

When Yapp opened Florence's letter she changed the whole dynamic of the case. To James' family and friends, and later to the police, the letter provided the motive for murder. The language of the letter also raised concerns. When Florence addressed Brierley as '*Dearest,*' she shocked Michael and Edwin as much as she had astounded Yapp. When she described James as being '*sick unto death,*' she set alarm bells ringing, as only the day before his doctors had indicated his condition was improving.

Shocked by its contents, Yapp decided not to post it, but instead give it to Edwin. When he entered the driveway to the house at around 5:00pm, she took him to a seat in the garden, out of sight of the house, and gave him the letter. After Edwin had spoken to Nurse Yapp and read Florence's letter, he went straight to see Nurse Gore, whom he had not met. He made it clear that the professional nurses were responsible for James' food and medicines and that '*nobody was to attend to him at all except the nurses.*'[653] Edwin did not mention Florence by name, but his intention was clear: the nurses and not Florence were now in charge of James' care.

A little after 6:00pm, Nurse Gore wanted to give James some food so she looked for the medicine glass in the bedroom. As she could not find it, she went to look for Florence to ask her where it was. Florence replied she had seen it in the bedroom, so Nurse Gore returned to the bedroom to look for it again. As she was still unable to locate it, she went to the lavatory where she saw Florence had mixed some medicine with water in the medicine glass to try and prevent it burning James' throat. Nurse Gore threw the medicine away and put the meat juice into the glass which she then gave to James. Around 7:00pm, Dr Humphreys arrived at Battlecrease and was surprised to find Nurse Gore rather than Mrs Howell attending the patient. He later remarked that he was never informed why Mrs Howell did not turn up at house.[654] As Humphreys found James to be no worse, he made no changes to his medicine or treatment.

At around 9:00pm, Michael Maybrick arrived at Edgehill station in Liverpool, in response to the telegrams he had received earlier in the day. He was met by Edwin who, on the cab journey back to Battlecrease, brought him up to date with the events of the day and the worrying state of James' illness. On arrival at the house at 9:30pm, Edwin showed Michael the letter from Florence to Brierley. Michael went upstairs to James' bedroom where Florence was waiting at the bedroom door. When he looked at James, he '*was very much shocked to see the state he was in, he being only semi-conscious.*'[655] Michael went downstairs and spoke to Florence in the morning-room, telling her that he was not satisfied with his brother's treatment. Florence questioned what he meant and Michael said she should have called in a professional nurse and another doctor at an earlier stage in James' illness. Florence responded by saying that no one '*had a better right to nurse the husband than his wife.*' Although Michael agreed with her comment, he reiterated his view that he was not at all happy with his brother's treatment.

At 10:30pm, Michael went to Dr Humphreys' house, where he had a lengthy conversation with the doctor about James' '*health and prospects.*'[656] He mentioned to the doctor that he had suspicions about the case. When he returned to Battlecrease, he spoke to Nurse Gore and told her the same thing that Edwin had said several hours earlier, that only she and the other professional nurses could administer food and medicine to James. From this moment onwards, Michael was in full control and Florence had little say over events in Battlecrease. Following his conversation with Nurse Gore, Michael went to the guest's bedroom on the second floor of the house to spend the night.

Thursday 9th May, was yet another pivotal day at Battlecrease. James had a very restless night, but when Edwin checked on him early in the morning, he told him he was feeling a little better.[657] Edwin reminded Nurse Gore, who had remained all night with James, that she was responsible for all his food and medication. He then went into town to arrange for additional nurses to attend his brother. Not long after Edwin left, Dr Humphreys called to see James. Unlike Edwin, Humphreys believed James' condition to be '*not so favourable*' compared to the previous day. James was complaining of great pain in his rectum and there had been '*considerable straining*' and '*diarrhoea.*' Humphreys gave James a suppository to alleviate the pain. At about 11:30am, Nurse Callery arrived at Battlecrease to replace Nurse Gore, who had been on duty for more than twenty hours. Like Gore, Callery was a professionally trained nurse from the Dover Street Institute. She found James to be '*very much exhausted, and complained of a burning sensation in his throat and pains in his abdomen.*'[658] Gore informed Callery of the instructions she had been given by the

[652] Nurse Yapp's testimony at the inquest, see *Liverpool Echo*, 28th May 1889.
[653] Irving H.B., op cit., pages 50-51.
[654] Ibid., page 93.
[655] Ibid., page 24.
[656] Ibid., page 93.
[657] Ibid., page 48.
[658] Ibid., page 151.

Maybrick brothers with regard to James' care and told her everything she needed was already in the sick room. During the next twelve hours, Callery gave James '*some peptonised Neave's food, champagne, chicken broth, brandy and medicine ordered by Dr Humphreys.*' She also gave him some ice for his throat. On the one occasion when the nurse left the bedroom to fetch ice, Florence was not left on her own with James as Michael was in the room.

Early in the afternoon, Dr Humphreys returned to Battlecrease to check on James' condition. James told him he would like to see Dr Carter, so Humphreys sent a telegram to Carter asking him to come to Battlecrease. At 4:30pm, in response to the telegram, Dr Carter arrived at the house where Humphreys, Nurse Callery and Michael, were all waiting for him. As soon he arrived, before he had even seen James, Michael abruptly asked Carter to tell him what was wrong with his brother. Carter said James was suffering from dyspepsia. Michael, still in an abrupt manner, asked him, '*but what is the cause of it?*' Carter replied that the exact cause was unclear to them, but that he and Humphreys believed James '*must have committed a grave error of diet by taking some irritant food or drink, or both, and so have set up inflammation.*'[659] Michael then turned sharply towards Humphreys and asked him if had mentioned to Carter the conversation that had taken place between them the previous night about his suspicions. Humphreys said he had not mentioned it. Carter was greatly surprised by the turn in the conversation and wondered what was going to be said next. An emotive Michael said to him: '*God forbid that I should unjustly suspect anyone, but do you not think if I have serious grounds for fearing that all might not be right, that it is my duty to say so to you.*' Both Humphreys and Carter agreed, if Michael had concerns, then he should tell the two of them. Michael said that until mid-April, James had been able to eat any ordinary food, but that he had been subject to sick attacks since he had returned home. He said there appeared to be a '*contrast between the condition of James' health while at and away from home respectively.*' There had been a most '*serious estrangement between husband and wife; that the wife had been known to be unfaithful; and that just before the commencement of the illness she was known to have procured many flypapers.*'

Michael's statement placed the two doctors in somewhat of a dilemma; although they felt it pointed towards a '*terrible possibility,*' they also believed that the accusation was '*quite unjustifiable.*' After a period of anxious deliberation, Humphreys and Carter decided that their duty was to: '*surround the patient with such absolute safeguards as would prevent anyone from tampering with him, and to maintain an attitude of great vigilance.*'[660]

The group then moved into James' bedroom where Dr Carter started to examine the clearly distressed patient. Carter found James to be in practically the same state he had been when he examined him on Tuesday, with the addition of tenesmus (continual diarrhoea), which was causing him a great deal of discomfort. Carter tried to carry out an examination of James' lower bowel, but had to abandon it because it caused him great pain. The doctor was puzzled by the appearance of tenesmus, but thought it indicated that the irritation had spread from the stomach into the large bowel. This meant that James was now in a serious condition. Carter spoke to Humphreys and found he had ordered bismuth, which was an astringent causing contraction of skin cells and other body tissues, as well as being a stomach sedative. The two doctors agreed that if James' illness continued he should receive his medicine in double doses and, if necessary, to add diluted brandy. Due to the concerns raised by Michael, the two doctors also carried out some additional tests. Dr Humphreys checked James' faeces and urine in the bathroom. He boiled about a tablespoon of the faeces in copper with a little hydrochloric acid testing for some metal, such as arsenic or mercury, but found no deposits of any metal. He carried out a similar test on James' urine and again the results were negative.

As well as these tests, Michael gave Carter some of James' Neave's food and brandy, asking him to carry out tests on them. Although Carter arrived in Battlecrease in the late afternoon, by the time he had spoken to Michael, examined James and consulted with Humphreys, it was early evening before he left. Carter took with him the two items given to him by Michael carrying out tests on them when he arrived home. He found nothing wrong with either the food or the brandy. On Thursday evening, Humphreys returned to Battlecrease for the fourth time that day. He found that James was in: '*a state of restlessness, complaining of his tongue and his throat and his bowels, but his strength was maintained pretty well, and he could take nutriment to swallow.*'[661] Humphreys checked James' pulse and though it was quicker than it had been at the start of the week, he did not think it was in anyway alarming. He also checked his temperature and found it to be normal. Although it was obvious that James was in pain and discomfort, he did not '*apprehend any serious results.*'

After James' death, Carter was to provide details on how he treated his patient on four separate occasions: at the inquest, at the magisterial hearing, at Florence's trial and also in a written account he produced a year after the trial. His comments are all consistent with one notable exception, his reference as to whether James had diarrhoea or not. In his evidence at the inquest, Carter stated James told him that he had been '*suffering from diarrhoea and vomiting for some days.*'[662] At the magisterial hearing, Carter said '*the patient complained of having suffered from vomiting*

[659] Carter W., op cit., page 124.
[660] Ibid., page 126.
[661] Irving H.B., op cit., page 94.
[662] *Liverpool Mercury*, 6th June 1889.

and diarrhoea.'[663] At the trial, Carter said something rather different; he stated James had been '*suffering for some days from vomiting*' but added that '*diarrhoea was just appearing.*'[664] Carter's remarks on this crucial point are not only inconsistent, they are also inaccurate. Humphreys, who saw James almost every single day during his final illness, was quite clear that James did not suffer from '*excessive purging or diarrhoea*' until Thursday 9th May.[665] MacDougall, in his account of the case, highlights this inconsistency and inaccuracy in Carter's statements about the onset of diarrhoea and points out that '*diarrhoea is one of the most important symptoms of arsenical poisoning.*'[666] If James received the fatal dose of arsenic on 3rd May, as Carter alleged, one is left wondering why the first signs of diarrhoea did not appear until five days later.

Michael Maybrick

The arrival of Michael at Battlecrease and the employment of the professional nurses, had changed Florence's role to that of virtual bystander. Although she continued to spend most of her time in the bedroom with James, she was never left alone with him and was barred from providing him with any of his food or medicine. Florence was becoming increasingly conscious of the suspicious looks she was receiving and feelings of isolation and powerlessness were beginning to overwhelm her. On Thursday morning, she saw Nurse Yapp in the night nursery and told her that Michael was blaming her '*for Mr Maybrick's illness*' because she had not sent for another doctor or nurse.[667] Not surprisingly, since Yapp was one of Florence's chief accusers, she received little sympathy from her. Yapp reminded Florence that she had suggested to her on two or three occasions the need to send for another doctor.[668] By Thursday evening, Florence's feelings of frustration had reached boiling point. When Elizabeth Humphreys returned downstairs after being up to James' bedroom, she found that Florence had followed her into the kitchen. Florence ordered some dinner and then began to complain to the cook, telling her, '*I am blamed for all this.*' Humphreys asked her in what way, and Florence replied, '*In not getting other nurses and doctors.*' Humphreys said Florence then went into the servants' hall and started to cry. Humphreys said that Florence was: '*very much put out, and added that her position in the house was not worth anything. Mrs Maybrick said, 'This is all through Mr Michael Maybrick.' Florence said that he had always had a spite against her since her marriage. Mrs Maybrick told me that she had been turned out of the master's bedroom, and not allowed to give him his medicines. In speaking about Mr Michael Maybrick, I remember her saying that if he went out of the house she should not allow him to enter it again.*'[669] Humphreys asked Florence about James' health; she replied that he '*was no better*' and '*inflammation had set in.*' Later in the day, Florence told Humphreys that James '*would never pull through.*'[670] At Florence's trial, when Sir Charles Russell cross-examined Humphreys, he asked her if she sympathised with Florence. She replied, '*I did, certainly.*' She said she told her mistress that she would rather be in her own shoes than Florence's.

Valentine's meat juice bottle which was an exhibit at Florence's trial (Chris Jones collection)

The incident that made Thursday 9th such a pivotal day took place late in the evening. At 11:00pm, Nurse Gore returned to Battlecrease to replace Nurse Callery. She was followed into James' bedroom by Florence. Not long after that, Gore opened a fresh bottle of Valentine's meat juice, one given to her by Edwin on Wednesday night. She tasted it first and then gave James one or two spoonfuls of the juice diluted in a little water. Florence mentioned to the nurse that the meat juice had previously made James sick; but she did not reply. James was to be sick on two occasions in the night. As well as the meat juice, Gore gave James some champagne every 15 minutes. She also cleaned his tongue with glycerine and borax. Sometime later, Gore witnessed Florence picking up the opened bottle of meat juice from the chest of drawers and taking it into the inner-dressing room. The door was pushed to so the nurse couldn't see what

[663] *Liverpool Daily Post*, 14th June 1889.
[664] Irving H.B., op cit., page 113.
[665] Ibid., page 103.
[666] MacDougall A.W., (1891) op cit., page 86.
[667] Irving H.B., op cit., page 67.
[668] *Liverpool Courier*, 29th May 1889.
[669] Irving H.B., op cit., page 83.
[670] *The Times*, 29th May 1889.

Florence was doing. Florence returned about two minutes later and placed the bottle on the round table near the window. Gore had become suspicious due to the manner in which Florence moved the bottle. At the trial, she said Florence did not take the bottle openly, instead she '*took it from the table in her left hand, and covered it with her right hand.*'[671] After putting the bottle down, Florence asked Gore to get some ice. This would have involved her leaving the room and going to the lavatory on the landing where the ice was kept. Gore refused and told Florence, '*the patient is sleeping and I'll do it when he awakes.*'[672] Florence went to lie down in the dressing room. She returned when James woke from a restless sleep. As she did, she moved the bottle from the round table and placed it on the washstand.

The incident with the Valentine's meat juice bottle is the single most important event that nearly took Florence to the gallows. When the bottle was later tested it was found to contain half a grain of arsenic. Florence explained her actions on three separate occasions: before the trial to her solicitor, Richard Cleaver; in her statement at the trial; and in her autobiography. The accounts are very similar, but there is one noticeable inconsistency. She told Cleaver, that for a long time, her husband had been in the habit of taking a white powder, possibly '*bromide or strychnine,*' as they '*were only things which relieved his head.*'[673] At around 5:00pm on Thursday, James had asked her to give him some of his powder, but she refused. Later in the evening, after Gore had given him the meat juice, James again asked Florence to give him some powder as he was feeling very sick and depressed. At her trial, Florence said: '*I was overwrought, terribly anxious. Miserably unhappy, and his evident distress utterly unnerved me. He had told me that the powder would not harm him, and that I could put it in his food. I then consented.*'[674] In her autobiography, Florence provided some more details. She wrote that as she carried the bottle through to the inner-dressing room, she upset it and in order to make up the quantity of fluid spilt, she topped it up with a considerable quantity of water. After adding the powder to the bottle, she returned to the bedroom and placed it on the small round table. When her husband awoke, he was sick. As he did not ask for the powder, she moved the bottle to the top of the washstand where he could not see it.[675]

The notable discrepancy in the accounts comes from where the white powder was located. In her autobiography, Florence said she took the powder from '*a pocket in James' vest, hanging in the adjoining room*' [the inner-dressing room]. However, she told Cleaver the powder was in '*ordinary packet tied with string,*' that was '*among the books*' on the table by the bed in the main bedroom. She said there was very little powder in the packet, '*about as much as would lie on a threepenny bit,*' and she put it all in. She threw the paper, which contained the powder, on to the floor of the dressing room. It is likely that Florence's account to Cleaver is the accurate version of events as this conversation occurred just weeks after the incident. In her autobiography, she may have become confused as James was known for hiding his various drugs in secret pockets in his clothes. Florence's account has its compelling features. James did habitually use drugs. As he was bed-bound he would have been unable to have accessed them. He needed someone to supply him with his fix. As he knew the professional nurses would not give him such drugs, he turned to the only other person who was a constant in the bedroom, Florence. As Florence was banned from giving James any food or medicine, the only way she could give him the powder was by some covert method. She probably thought she was giving him strychnine, a drug he regularly used, rather than arsenic. Florence's account may have been accepted if it had not been for all the other accusations that were levelled at her.

On Friday morning 10th May, Dr Humphreys was back again early at Battlecrease to visit his increasingly distressed patient. Although there was '*hardly any sickness*' and James' bowels had '*not moved so frequently*' as Thursday, the doctor still believed him to be in a '*worse*' condition. He was weaker and had a more rapid pulse.[676] As he inspected James, Nurse Gore looked on but did not mention anything about the meat juice incident that occurred during the night. At 11:00am, Nurse Callery arrived to relieve Gore. Before she left, Gore spoke to Callery about the meat juice bottle that Florence had moved. She told Callery to take a sample from the bottle, which Callery did, pouring some of the juice into an old medicine bottle. Apart from that, the bottle remained untouched, presumably on the washstand. On her way out of the house, Gore spoke to Michael and told him she had concerns about the half-full bottle of brandy in the sick room. Michael went straight upstairs and removed the brandy. He later gave it to Dr Carter. Curiously, Gore did not speak to Michael about the meat juice bottle. Instead, she went to the Nurses' Institute in Liverpool to inform the Lady Superintendent about what had happened and consult with her on how to proceed.[677]

Nurse Callery took control of the sickroom and was responsible for administering all of James' food and medicine. Everything she needed was already in the room, apart from some milk, which was brought by one of the servants. Florence remained in the bedroom, but was frozen out of all tasks relating to the care of her husband. She did at one

671 Irving H.B., op cit., page 150.
672 *Liverpool Courier*, 29th May 1889.
673 Levy J.H., op cit., pages 435-436.
674 Irving H.B., op cit., page 228.
675 Maybrick F., op cit., pages 367-370.
676 Irving H.B., op cit., page 94.
677 MacDougall A.W., (1891) op cit., page 108.

stage suggest James might like a hot water bottle, but even that needed the nurse's approval. Callery remained in Battlecrease until 4:30pm. During that time she found James to be in a '*very exhausted condition*,' continually complaining of '*pain in his throat and tongue.*' As she tried to give James his bismuth medicine, he refused to take it. Florence intervened to encourage James to take it. He said to her: '*You have given me the wrong medicine again.*' Florence replied, '*What are you talking about? You never had wrong medicine.*'[678] This conversation was to be another of the incidents that were to be given a sensational slant when it appeared in the press; yet once again, it was an unimportant event. All that happened was that Florence was simply trying to help the nurse administer the medicine to James.

At 1:30pm, Gore returned to Battlecrease following her meeting with the Lady Superintendent. She passed on an instruction for Callery to throw away the sample taken from the meat juice bottle and Callery poured it into the slop-can in the bedroom. Gore then told Michael what happened. He immediately went upstairs and removed a meat juice bottle from the bedroom. Questions were later asked about whether he removed the actual bottle moved by Florence the previous night. At around 2:00pm, when Michael was on his way up the stairs to see James, he saw Florence changing medicine from one bottle to another. He angrily shouted at her, '*Florie, how dare you tamper with the medicine.*' Florence replied that the smaller bottle was full of sediment and she was just pouring the medicine into a larger bottle to make it easier to dissolve. Michael was not satisfied by her reply and told her he would have the '*prescription immediately remade.*' He took the bottle that Florence had been mixing and later gave it to Dr Humphreys. At Florence's trial, Michael told the court that his brother, '*grew gradually worse from that time, and at six o'clock he was highly delirious.*'[679] Not long after 3:00pm, Florence was in the garden taking a break from the sickroom. She had a conversation with Michael asking him why Dr Fuller had not been brought in to help treat James. Michael brushed aside her comment stating he believed, '*Dr Carter fully understood the case, and that it was rather late in the day to send for Dr Fuller.*'[680]

At around 4:30pm, both Drs Humphreys and Carter arrived back at Battlecrease. James was sitting up in bed, and told the doctors he was '*much better*' and '*only wanting sleep to make him quite well.*' The doctors disagreed, and '*considered him much worse.*'[681] James' pulse was still rapid, being for the first time over 100, while his right hand was very white. His tongue was '*simply filthy*' and he was '*very restless, having no sleep.*' The doctors ordered some sulphonal in the form of a powder to help him sleep, one nitro-glycerine tablet for his hand, and some phosphoric acid for his mouth. They told him he was to continue the cocaine for his throat, plus the brandy and champagne.

On Friday afternoon, for the first time, the two doctors considered James' condition to be serious and they started to think that the suggestion made to them by Michael the previous day '*might have some grounds.*'[682] These suspicions became stronger when Michael told them about the incident with the meat juice. He gave Carter the bottles of meat juice and brandy he had removed from the bedroom, and asked him to check them for any poisonous element they might contain.

Illustrated Police News, 17th August 1889

At 4:30pm, Nurse Wilson took over from Nurse Callery, and remained on duty until 11:00pm the same night. Florence remained in the sick room most of the time Wilson was on duty, but the nurse administered all the food and medicine. During the evening, at around 6:00pm, Wilson heard James say to Florence on three occasions, '*Oh, Bunny, Bunny, how could you do it? I did not think it of you.*' She heard Florence reply, '*You silly old darling, don't trouble your head about things.*' Florence also told James '*he could not tell what was the matter with him, or what had brought his illness on.*'[683] At Florence's trial, Wilson stated James was '*quite conscious*' when he made these remarks. If that is the case, what was he referring to when he scolded his wife? There are three possible answers. Firstly, he could have been just referring to the suggestion he had made earlier in the day that he had been given the wrong medicine. Secondly, James could have been told by one of his brothers that they suspected Florence may have administered some poisonous substance to him, even though at this stage all the tests for arsenic had come back

678 Irving H.B., page 152.
679 Ibid., page 25.
680 Ibid., page 25.
681 Carter W., op cit., page 126.
682 Irving H.B., op cit., page 94.
683 Ibid., page 155.

negative. Thirdly, he could have been referring to Florence's relationship with Brierley. Florence did say she made a full confession to James just before he died, and this may have been the occasion when it happened. Under such circumstances, James would have been upset with his wife. Whatever the truth, the remarks by James were to be used against Florence at her trial. They became twisted to imply that she had been acting in a suspicious and harmful manner towards her husband.

At 7:00pm, just before dinner was served, James' office clerks, Thomas Lowry and George Smith, arrived at Battlecrease with some papers. Michael and Edwin took them to James' bedroom. Not long after they had entered the room James shouted out in a very loud and angry voice, '*Oh Lord, if I am to die, why am I to be worried like this?' Let me die properly.*' According to MacDougall, both Mary Cadwallader and Elizabeth Humphreys heard James shout out, and both saw Edwin leave the bedroom with a paper in his hand. They said they had been informed by Nurse Yapp, whom they described as '*knowing and hearing everything*,' that the Maybrick brothers had been trying to get James to sign a copy of his will as they could not find the one he had made a few weeks earlier.[684] MacDougall describes this incident as '*rather remarkable*' and felt it needed to be '*thoroughly investigated.*' Although MacDougall sees it as remarkable, if Michael suspected Florence had poisoned James then the last thing he would have wanted is for all his brother's wealth and possessions to fall into her hands. Not being able to find a signed copy of James' will would have put him into a panic. James was understandably frustrated that he was getting bothered by such a matter when he was in great pain.

At about 9:00pm, Florence went down to the kitchen and asked Elizabeth Humphreys to prepare her some sandwiches and a glass of milk. As Florence was leaving she told the cook to prepare her some soup and another sandwich for the night. She thanked the cook for her kindness, and gave her a kiss. Humphreys asked her how the master was, and she replied that he was '*sinking very fast.*' The cook asked her if there was any hope for him. Florence shook her head and said, '*There was no hope.*' The cook said Florence was '*very much distressed.*'[685]

At 10:30pm, Dr Humphreys was back at Battlecrease for a third time that day. He found James to be '*very ill*' and '*getting weaker*,' his pulse being '*almost uncountable.*' Due to the state of James' throat, it had been extremely difficult to give him any food, so they tried giving him a nutritive suppository. The doctor now '*apprehended danger*' and he warned Michael about his brother's perilous condition. He told him a solicitor was needed to see to James' affairs.[686]

Very late that night, after he had finished his other professional duties, Dr Carter carried out tests on the bottles of brandy and the meat juice. The method he employed was called the Reinsch test, which was used to detect the presence of arsenic, antimony, bismuth and mercury. The test was named after its inventor, a German chemist named Hugo Reinsch, who had developed it in 1841. It was relatively quick and simple to perform. The sample was boiled with hydrochloric acid, and then a copper strip was inserted into the solution. If a deposit started to appear on the copper strip, it indicated the presence of a heavy metal. If it had a silvery coating, it indicated the presence of mercury; if it was dark or grey, it indicated the presence of arsenic. Although the test was straightforward, errors could be made if any of the reagents were contaminated in any way and, as a result, Carter worked slowly and with the '*extreme caution required to avoid mistake.*'[687]

It was midnight before he had his results. The test on the bottle of brandy proved negative; but the test on the meat juice produced a '*marked deposit on the copper foil*,' which meant '*there was some metallic substance in the sample.*'[688] Although the test had identified '*some metallic substance*' and further tests would be required to conclusively prove exactly what the metallic substance was, Carter would have been fairly certain by the colouring of the deposit on the copper strip that he had found arsenic. Despite making this startling discovery, Carter decided to do nothing else that night. He didn't immediately inform Dr Humphreys and he didn't try to warn Michael or the professional nurses at Battlecrease.

His response has been criticised by both his contemporaries and modern authors. Morland wrote that '*nothing is quite so peculiar in the Maybrick case as the behaviour of Dr Carter.*' He suggests that the most obvious thing for Carter to have done was to have gone straight to Battlecrease and administered a suitable antidote to James. Carter responded to the criticisms of him by arguing the fact that '*the irritant had been detected*' proved to him that the safeguards he and Dr Humphreys had introduced to protect James '*were efficient.*'[689] It was rather a lame excuse from an eminent doctor, and his lack of action on that Friday night is a blot on his distinguished career.

During the night of Friday 10th and Saturday 11th May, James' condition got steadily worse. He moved in and out of consciousness, and spent much of the night in a '*delirious*' state.[690] When he was awake and lucid he was extremely

[684] MacDougall A.W., (1891) op cit., page 109.
[685] Irving H.B., op cit., page 83.
[686] Ibid., page 95.
[687] Carter W., op cit., page 127.
[688] Irving H.B., op cit., page 115.
[689] Carter W., op cit., page 127.
[690] Irving H.B., op cit., page 115.

weak. At about 3:00am, Nurse Gore, who had come on duty at 11:00pm on Friday night, warned Florence that her husband was getting close to death. Florence knocked on Michael's bedroom door to wake him up. Michael and Edwin went to the sick room and found James to be '*very ill indeed.*'[691]

After waking Michael, Florence then knocked on Elizabeth Humphreys' bedroom door and told her that James was dying, and she wanted one of the servants to fetch Mrs Briggs. The cook woke up Elizabeth Brierley and Mary Cadwallader, and they went together to inform Mrs Briggs. She said she would inform her sister, Mrs Hughes, and the two of them would go to Battlecrease. At about 5:00am, the children were taken to see their dying father. On Saturday morning 11th May, Dr Humphreys arrived at Battlecrease at his usual time of 8:30am. He examined James and came to the opinion he '*was then dying.*'[692]

At 12:30pm, Dr Carter arrived at the house and spoke with Michael and Dr Humphreys, who had returned to Battlecrease. Carter told them the results of the test on the meat juice and showed them the copper strips coated with the metallic deposits. He said he needed to obtain an unopened bottle of the meat juice to carry out a further test, as the sample used might have had some impurities and provided a false positive. Carter told Michael that if '*the matter turned out to be so bad*' as he feared, then it would be taken out of the '*doctors' hands entirely.*' Carter examined James, who was very weak. He found it difficult to make him understand what was being said to him, and he could not retain any suppositories. It was then '*evident*' to Carter that James '*could not live.*' Drs Carter and Humphreys conferred together and agreed the case was now hopeless; James was dying. They told Michael there was nothing further they could do to save the patient.[693]

LETTER FROM FLORENCE TO Dr HOPPER (Written early on 11th May)

Dear Dr Hopper, I am sure you must have heard of Jim's dangerous illness, and no doubt feel that I ought to have called you in to see him. My misery is great and my position such a painful one that when I tell you that both my brothers-in-law are here and have taken the nursing of Jim and the management of my house completely out of my hands, you will understand how powerless I am to assert myself. I am in great need of a friend. Michael, whom Jim informed of the unhappiness existing between us last month, now accuses me as being the primary cause of Jim's present critical state, to which want of proper care from me as regards his nourishment and medical attention may be added. Michael hardly speaks to me. I am neither cheered or told the worst. I am a mere cipher in my own house, ignored and overlooked. I am too utterly brokenhearted to struggle against myself or anyone else; all I want to do is die, too. I should like to see you as a medical attendant. Could you not call as a friend and ask to see me? I have not been to bed since last Sunday, for although I may not nurse Jim, I will at least be near him to see what is done. It is terrible. How shall I bear it? I have no one to turn to and my husband's brothers are cold-hearted and brutal men. Because I have sinned once, must I be misjudged always? Yours distractedly. F. E. Maybrick

With her world collapsing around her, Florence felt isolated, powerless and friendless. In desperation she wrote a letter to Dr Hopper and asked him to visit her as a '*medical attendant*' and as a '*friend.*' Christie called the letter a '*cry from the heart*' and '*probably one of the most honest communications she ever made.*'[694] The letter makes it clear that Michael and Edwin had taken the management of the house and the care of her husband completely out of Florence's hands. The brothers blamed Florence for being the '*primary cause of Jim's present critical state.*'

Florence was upset and totally despondent. She was also extremely tired. There are two other notable sentences in the letter; the first of these states James had told Michael of the '*unhappiness existing between us last month.*' Presumably that was in April when James had stayed with Michael. Exactly how much he told him is not clear, but it is unlikely he specifically referred to Brierley. The second notable sentence is the one that states '*I have sinned once.*' This is an obvious reference to her stay in Flatman's Hotel with Brierley. It is significant in that while she admits to an adulterous relationship, she is making it clear it was the only time in her married life that she was unfaithful to her husband.

Not long after writing the letter to Dr Hopper, Florence passed out and remained in a state of virtual unconsciousness for the next 24 hours. Christie suggests Florence's swoon may have been '*induced by a dose of chloral.*'[695] More likely, it was brought on by sheer exhaustion. Florence had not slept in her own bed since the previous Sunday and, during the five nights since Sunday, she had only managed a few hours of broken sleep on the bed in the inner-dressing room. She had been up all Friday night and had not had any sleep at all. On top of that, she was under enormous pressure. She was being blamed for her husband's illness and had been excluded from all his care. She faced hostility from all quarters and had no-one to turn to for support. By Saturday afternoon, the exhaustion

[691] Ibid., page 25.
[692] Ibid., page 95.
[693] Ibid., pages 115-116.
[694] Christie T.L., op cit., page 62.
[695] Ibid., page 63.

and stress totally overwhelmed Florence and she simply collapsed. She was carried to the spare bedroom and was oblivious to the unfolding drama in the rest of the house.

As Florence lay prostrate in a dead swoon, James' friends and relatives gathered in Battlecrease for his final hours. Three of his brothers were there: Michael, Edwin and Thomas, who had been summoned from his home in Manchester. Mrs Briggs and Mrs Hughes were there, having remained in the house all day. Drs Humphreys and Carter were also both in the house, though neither of them were in James' bedroom when he actually died.

At 8:30pm Nurse Gore arrived at Battlecrease and replaced Nurse Wilson. Ten minutes later, at 8:40pm, James Maybrick died in the arms of his best friend, George Davidson. He was 50 years old.

LINKS WITH THE RIPPER DIARY: DID JAMES MAYBRICK HIDE A DIARY UNDER THE FLOORBOARDS AT BATTLECREASE?

The last entries in the Diary of Jack the Ripper are the signature and the date of when it was supposedly finished, 3rd May 1889. The date is significant, as it is extremely unlikely on that particular day that James would have had either the time, or the opportunity, to complete the Diary and successfully hide it in his house. James started the day feeling unwell and a message was sent to Dr Humphreys asking him to visit the house. Later in the morning, he headed to his office. After spending a couple of hours at work he went for a Turkish bath. On his return to Battlecrease, James had terrible pains in both his legs and was sick on at least two occasions. He retired to bed in great discomfort. In the evening, Florence brought the children up to see him. Nurse Yapp accompanied the children into the bedroom and she heard James tell Florence he had been sick again. As the evening turned into night, the pain in James' legs grew steadily worse. Florence spent some time with him, rubbing his inner thighs with turpentine. As there was no improvement in his condition, Florence sent a servant to fetch Dr Humphreys. The doctor arrived at Battlecrease at around midnight.

Therefore, it was a busy and painful day for James. On top of that, he had spent much of it with family members, servants, work colleagues and his doctor. Such a schedule makes it impossible to believe that he was able to sit down somewhere private and put his inner-most thoughts down on paper.

The 3rd May date is also significant as it was the last day that James went into his office. If James *had* written a diary entry that day, he would have completed it either in his office or his house. The office is an unlikely location, as he was only there a couple of hours and both his clerks were present. After that day, James never returned to his office. If he had left a diary at work it would have been discovered a long time ago. This means that if he did write any diary entries, he must have completed them at home. If that is the case, where did he hide it? The most obvious place was in his private study on the ground floor in Battlecrease. This room was always kept locked, and only James had a key to the door. After his death, his study was thoroughly searched, and no reference is made by anyone to the discovery of a hidden diary.

There is one other place in Battlecrease where it is suggested that the Diary might have been placed. That location is under the floorboards in the Maybricks' master bedroom, or perhaps the inner-dressing room, the small room off the master bedroom. This hypothesis tries to explain not only where the Diary was placed, but also why it remained hidden until 1992. According to Robert Smith, a space under the floorboards in '*James Maybrick's bedroom was the hidey-hole of this highly secretive, paranoid and manipulative man.*'[696] Smith argues that after writing his final entry James placed the Diary under the floorboards in the bedroom. Eight days later James died, so the Diary remained where he had placed it until it was accidentally discovered a hundred years later by a group of electricians who were completing some work in the house for the owner, Paul Dodd.

In order for this hypothesis to be credible, one has to accept a long list of rather dubious propositions. Firstly, James needed to have written his final entry on 3rd May. For all the reasons given earlier, this is extremely unlikely. Secondly, on his own James would have needed to have lifted heavy wooden floorboards, fixed with brass nails, without anyone else in the house hearing any noise. Such a task would have been very difficult for a fit young builder; it would have been virtually impossible for a sick older man with terrible pains in his legs, who also had the added distraction of people continually popping in and out of his bedroom. The brass nails would have broken; to refit the boards, new brass nails would have been required and they would have needed to have been hammered into place. A great deal of force would have been required. It was an activity that would have generated a lot of noise.

Robert Smith tries to get around these difficulties by suggesting James could have '*created his hidey-hole at any time in 1888 or 1889.*'[697] If there was such a hidey-hole, why was it never discovered? Servants were continually going into the room, cleaning it, making beds, lighting the fire. This scenario paints a picture of a sick man who was

---

[696] Smith R., 'The Maybrick Diary: A New Edition', in the *Journal of the Whitechapel Society*, (June, 2019) page 22.
[697] Ibid., page 22.

barely able to move his legs popping out of his sick bed, releasing floorboards, placing his Diary in the space below and then re-fixing the floorboards in such a solid manner that they were to remain in place for the next one hundred years; and doing all this without anyone in the house hearing anything.

If such an unlikely series of events had happened, the hidey-hole would have quickly been discovered. Battlecrease was emptied of its furniture soon after James' death, but no journal was unearthed. The new occupants of the house would have thoroughly cleaned the bedroom, yet they found no journal. Over the years substantial work has been carried out on the house, including in James' bedroom and the inner-dressing room, and nothing was ever found. In the 1920s the house was converted from gas to electricity, which involved lifting floorboards; it was rewired in 1946, and again in 1977, when Paul Dodd '*gutted the place and lifted the floorboards.*' Dodd told Shirley Harrison in 1997 that if '*anything had been hidden, he was sure that he would have found it.*'[698]

The possibility that electricians had discovered the Diary under the floorboards in Battlecrease was investigated by Paul Feldman when he was writing his book, *The Final Chapter*. On a visit to the house he was told by Paul Dodd that new storage heaters had been installed on the first floor of the house in 1988 or 1989. Feldman contacted Colin Rhodes, the owner of contractors Portus and Rhodes who had carried out the electrical work. He said he had not heard about an item being removed from the house by any of his employees. Feldman then telephoned the electricians who had been involved in the work, and asked them if they remembered anything being found in the house. Once again, he received a negative response. A short time later, after receiving a tip-off from one of the electricians, Feldman tried to contact two other electricians, who had supposedly removed something from Battlecrease after the item had been thrown into a skip. One of these lived around the corner from the Saddle Inn in Kirkdale, where Michael Barrett and Tony Devereux both drank. Feldman started to wonder if the Diary had been taken from Battlecrease by an electrician, who subsequently sold it to Devereux in the Saddle Inn. A few weeks later, Feldman managed to speak to the electrician, who lived in Kirkdale, and asked him if he had taken the Diary. Feldman wrote that the man would not admit it or deny it, but instead asked '*What is my confession worth*?' Feldman became convinced the story was completely bogus, and that the electricians '*would lie for the right price.*'[699]

In 1997, another possible lead involving the electricians was pursued by Robert Smith and Shirley Harrison. Smith had been told by a business friend that one of his clients, Tim Martin-Wright – who ran a business selling domestic alarm systems in Bootle on Merseyside – had been offered an old diary for sale by some electricians in Liverpool. Smith travelled to Liverpool and spoke to Alan Dodgson, the manager of Martin-Wright's shop in Bootle. Dodgson said one of his customers, Alan Davies, who was an electrician who had previously worked for Portus and Rhodes, had told him that one of his former electrician colleagues had removed something from Battlecrease while doing a rewiring job. He claimed they had taken a biscuit tin from under the floorboards that contained a leather-bound diary and a gold ring. Davies told Dodgson that the diary was available for sale at the price of £25. Dodgson passed on the information to Martin-Wright, because he knew he had an interest in purchasing old books. The exact date when this happened is unclear, but Martin-Wright believed that it had occurred '*a month or two*' after his shop opened in October 1991.[700]

Smith and Harrison next spoke to Alan Davies, who confirmed Dodgson's account, and recommended that they speak to another electrician named Brian Rawes. In June 1997, Smith interviewed Brian Rawes, who told him that on a Friday morning in July 1992, he was asked by Colin Rhodes to go to Battlecrease and pick up the firm's van and take it to another one of the company's jobs in Halewood. Rawes said he was dropped off outside the house by Arthur Rigby and went inside, where Eddie Lyons and Graham Rhodes, Colin's son, were working on a rewiring job on the ground floor. As Rawes had never driven the van before, he asked Lyons to guide him as he reversed down the drive and through the gates. Rawes claimed that as he was about to drive off Eddie Lyons told him, '*I've found something under the floorboards. I think it could be important.*'[701]

In 2018, Rawes reconfirmed that story to Keith Skinner, James Johnston and Christopher Jones when they spoke to him in his house in Liverpool.[702] Although there is no reason to doubt Rawes' honesty, there are problems with his story as far as the provenance of the Diary is concerned. He places the date as being in July 1992, which was four months after Barrett contacted London about the Diary. The work on that day was being completed downstairs in Battlecrease and not on the first floor, where the Maybricks' bedroom was situated, and no floorboards were lifted. Harrison and Smith contacted the two electricians, Eddie Lyons and Arthur Rigby, who had been there when the item was supposedly taken, but they both refused to be interviewed.

For a second time, investigations into a possible link to the electricians had produced nothing tangible. It is also worth noting that Brian Rawes, Alan Davies and Tim Martin-Wright never actually saw a diary or any other item

---

698 Harrison S., (1998) op cit., page 309.
699 Feldman P., op cit., page 135.
700 Harrison S., op cit., page 308.
701 Ibid., page 308.
702 Notes taken by Christopher Jones from a meeting with Brian Rawes, 11th June 2018.

that was allegedly taken from Battlecrease. Tim Martin-Wright did ask for a description of the diary on the phone and he did make an offer of £25; however, he didn't hear anything for several weeks and was later told the item had been sold to someone in a pub in Anfield, an area of Liverpool close to Kirkdale.

New life was brought into the electricians' hypothesis as a result of the detailed research of Keith Skinner, who was collecting material for Bruce Robinson's book, *They All Love Jack.* In 2004, Colin Rhodes provided Skinner with timesheets for some electrical work completed at Paul Dodd's house in March 1992. The timesheets showed that on Monday 9th March 1992, Arthur Rigby worked for eight hours installing storage heaters in the house, assisted by the much younger James Coufopoulos, who worked for just two hours. The next day, Tuesday 10th March, Arthur Rigby returned to the house to work for a further four hours to complete the job. This work involved lifting some of the floorboards so that electrical wires could be chased under the boards to the location of the new heaters.

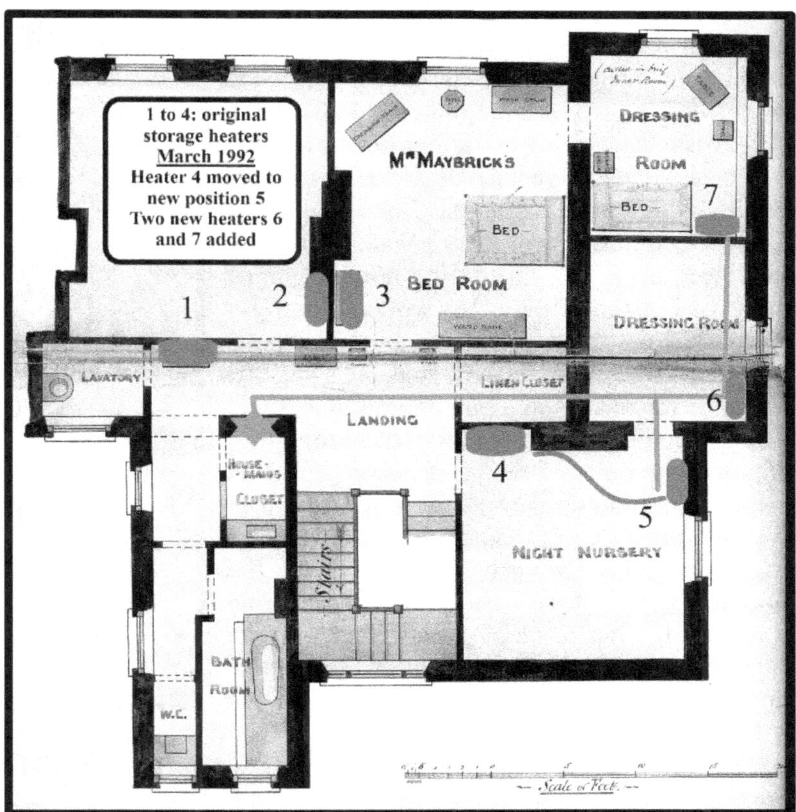

Storage heaters installed by electricians in number 7 Riversdale Road, formerly Battlecrease House (Chris Jones collection)

What makes the date of this work so significant is that on the afternoon of Monday, 9th March 1992 Michael Barrett (using the name of Williams) rang Doreen Montgomery at Rupert Crew Ltd to inform her that he had the Diary of Jack the Ripper. Could this date be just a coincidence, or was the Diary removed from the house on that Monday morning?

Robert Smith has provided a possible reconstruction for what might have happened. He wrote: '*One certain fact is that the diary was found in Battlecrease on 9th March 1992.*' This happened when the electricians were lifting floorboards at the house so that they could install new storage heaters. Smith argues the discovery of the Diary could not have occurred before that date, as the electricians had not worked at the house for at least six months prior to March 1992. Smith then suggests that one of the electricians, Eddie Lyons, who lived in Fountains Road, Kirkdale, and who occasionally drank in the Saddle Inn, took the Diary to the pub and sold it to Barrett. He chose Barrett as he may have heard his '*frequent boasts of being a writer who knows about publishers.*' The '*highly impetuous Barrett goes immediately into action*' and telephones Pan Books because he has some Pan paperbacks at home. They suggest he rings Doreen Montgomery, which he does, using a false name. He then waits five weeks before going to Montgomery's office, in April 1992, as he '*needs the time to research the diary and (with his wife's help) produce a typed transcript.*'[703]

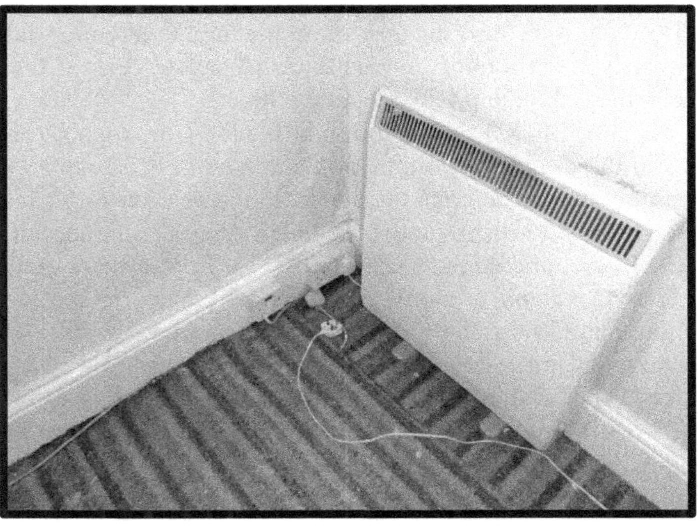

Storage heater fitted on 9th March 1992 in the room that had been the Maybricks' inner-dressing room. The heater was originally placed on the wall on the left before being moved to its current position. (Chris Jones collection)

The fact that electrical work did take place on 9th and 10th March is not in doubt. Paul Dodd has confirmed with Christopher Jones the exact details of the work on two occasions. Prior to 1992, there were four storage heaters on the first-floor of the house. They were placed in the hallway and in three rooms that had been, at the time of the Maybricks' occupancy, the spare bedroom, the main bedroom and the night nursery. As the rooms at the far-end of the house were still cold in winter,

[703] Smith R., (2017) op cit., page 22.

Dodd decided to add two further storage heaters and move one of the existing heaters to a new position. This was the work that was completed on the 9th and 10th March.

In the room that had once been the Maybricks' night nursery, the location of the heater was moved across the room to be close to the window on the outside wall, and the small heater was replaced with a larger one. Two new heaters were added; one in what had been the dressing room, next to the night nursery, and one in what had been the inner-dressing room. No work was completed in the Maybricks' main bedroom. There was no need to complete any work in that room as there was already a storage heater in place. The wires were chased down the hallway and through the dressing room. Even in the inner-bedroom, the work completed was minimal, as the heater was placed in the corner of the room next to the wall with the dressing room. As a result, few floorboards would have been disturbed in that particular room, and the ones which were moved were floorboards that had already been previously lifted by Paul Dodd when he had completed some earlier work. The actual storage heater is still in place, although Dodd has moved its position a few feet from one wall to the adjoining wall. As the work involved was relatively straightforward with little waste, no skip was required for the task.

Electrician Eddie Lyons (left) with Christopher Jones outside Battlecrease House, June 2018 (Chris Jones collection)

The next question that needs addressing is was Eddie Lyons working at the house on these days? The timesheet for the 9th March lists only two electricians working at the house. One of these was Arthur Rigby. He worked for eight hours that day, and therefore could not have travelled across the city and sold the Diary (if indeed it was taken) in a pub around lunchtime. The second electrician, James Coufopoulos, only worked for two hours and, according to his own account, these were likely to have been in the afternoon. Coufopoulos told Christopher Jones that when he arrived at the house the floorboards had already been lifted and his role was to drill holes through the joists and put the electrical cables through them.[704] It is also impossible to believe that a junior electrician would have taken an item, let alone sold it to a person he didn't know. There was also the problem that he didn't drive at the time, and therefore would have needed to travel across the city by public transport in a direction away from his home. We can therefore exclude both Rigby and Coufopoulos as culprits for taking the Diary and selling it in Kirkdale.

Another possibility is Eddie Lyons. The Portus and Rhodes timesheets show that on this day Eddie Lyons and Jim Bowring were working on a sewerage farm in Skelmersdale in Lancashire. However, the work on the site was delayed as they were waiting for materials to arrive. As was the practice at Portus and Rhodes, the two electricians were redeployed to help with existing jobs.

In June 2018, Eddie Lyons admitted to Christopher Jones and three other witnesses, that he had been sent to help with the electrical work at Battlecrease on 9th March 1992. What is significant about this is that Lyons could have simply denied being at the house; in the absence of his name appearing on the timesheet, it would have been almost impossible to disprove his statement. It is also important to state that he emphatically denied taking anything from the house, and added that nobody else from Portus and Rhodes took anything. Lyons added that he did not know Tony Devereux, and only met Michael Barrett on one occasion. Around the spring of 1993, Barrett had come to his house and said to him: '*You are the famous Eddie Lyons that found my diary.*' Lyons invited Barrett into his house and made him a cup of tea. He said Barrett was '*okay*' at first, but later started to threaten him with a solicitor. Lyons then asked Barrett to leave. He described Barrett as a '*weirdo.*'[705]

Robert Smith argues that the '*timesheets provide the strongest possible evidence that the diary came out of Battlecrease on Monday, 9th March 1992.*'[706] While it is true the timesheets, and the admission from Eddie Lyons that he was at the house on 9th March, mean there is a possibility that one or more of the electricians were involved in taking an item from Battlecrease, to describe it as the '*strongest possible evidence*' is a gross overstatement of the case. If we are to accept the hypothesis that the electricians found the Diary, one also has to accept a long list of improbable assertions:

---

[704] Notes taken by Christopher Jones from a meeting with James Coufopolous, 13th June 2018.
[705] Notes taken by Christopher Jones from a meeting with Eddie Lyons, 13th June 2018.
[706] Smith R., (2017) op cit., page 22.

Assertion:
The final entry of the Diary was made on 3rd May 1889.
Verdict:
The idea that James could have sat down and calmly, eloquently and passionately completed his journal on this day is *virtually impossible*. He spent much of the day either with people, or in bed extremely ill.

Assertion:
The Diary was secretly hidden under the floorboards on 3rd May 1889.
Verdict:
The idea that James, who was very sick on that day and returned home from work barely able to move his limbs could somehow have lifted heavy wooden floorboards, fixed with brass nails, on his own, without anyone else in the house hearing any noise, is also *virtually impossible*.

Assertion:
The Diary remained undiscovered until March 1992.
Verdict:
This would mean that James had fixed the floorboards in such a manner that anything he had hidden underneath would remain hidden for over one hundred years. This is yet another *virtually impossible* scenario. He was too ill to fix floorboards that securely, and the house was emptied soon after he died. Any loose boards would have quickly been spotted. On top of that, the floorboards were lifted in the house on four occasions before the electricians did it again in March 1992.

Assertion:
Electricians discovered the Diary on 9th March 1992 when working at Battlecrease.
Verdict:
This is a possible but *unlikely* occurrence. Most of the floorboards that were lifted on that day were in the hallway. The rest were located in rooms that had once been the night nursery or the dressing room next to the night nursery. No floorboards were lifted in the main bedroom and only a small number were moved in the inner-bedroom, and these had all been lifted before.

Assertion:
An electrician sold the Diary to Barrett in the Saddle Inn in Kirkdale.
Verdict:
This is another possible but *unlikely* occurrence. Eddie Lyons did work at Battlecrease on that day. He did live on Fountains Road at that time, and he did visit the Saddle Inn. However, Lyons openly admitted to working at the house on 9th March when he could have easily denied it. He also absolutely and firmly denies taking anything from the house.

On top of all the circumstances that must be in play to accept the hypothesis that the electricians removed the Diary on 9th March, there are numerous other problems with this viewpoint. The July 1992 date, provided by Brian Rawes for the day when Eddie Lyons had told him he had found something important under the floorboards, does not match up with the March date when Barrett contacted London. None of the work on 9th March took place in the Maybricks' main bedroom. There is repeated reference to the Diary being placed in a skip outside Battlecrease, but there was no skip.

Some of the key players, who have provided accounts of a mysterious Diary, never actually saw such an item; they were providing second-hand information of what they had been told by others.

On top of that are the contradictory and continually changing stories from some of the electricians who were supposedly involved in the removal of the Diary. One is left with the same very distinct impression that Feldman reached back in early 1990s – that the electricians' story was completely bogus, and that some of them '*would lie for the right price*.'

If we accept that the Diary is a modern forgery, then we have to address the fact that electrical work was carried out on 9th March at Battlecrease and that Barrett did contact London about a diary on the very same day. There are three possibilities. Firstly, it is nothing more than a coincidence. Such things happen, and the very tight timeline of the day makes it very difficult to accept the electricians' hypothesis. It would mean that floorboards were lifted, the Diary was found and then transported across the city, sold in a pub to Barrett who then contacted London, all in the space of a few hours. The timeline becomes even more unlikely when one factors into it another storyline that was fed to Feldman, that the electricians took the Diary to Liverpool University in an attempt to try and authenticate it as a genuine document.[707]

A second possibility is that Barrett already had possession of the Diary, perhaps given to him by someone else such as Tony Devereux. He is unsure what to do with it, but after talking to Eddie Lyons, who has been at Battlecrease that day, decides it's time to bite the bullet and contact a publisher in London.

Michael Barrett in 1999 (Courtesy of David McCleave)

A third possibility is that Barrett had been working on his own, or with others, to produce a forged diary for some time. This is something he actually admitted in one of his sworn statements. By 9th March 1992, the task of finishing the forgery had been completed, or almost completed; however, it was still a big step to contact a publisher in London as it would mean taking part in a criminal offence. On 9th March, Eddie Lyons enters the Saddle Inn and says he had been working in Battlecrease. This gives Barrett the necessary impetus to go ahead with the next stage of his plan; however, he is still cautious so when he rings London he uses an assumed name. Over the next five weeks, Barrett and his co-conspirators set about fine-tuning their forgery. They clearly have some concerns about it, as Barrett places an advert in the *Bookdealer* of 19th March, in which he attempts to purchase a Victorian diary. A company in Weston-super-Mare responded to Barrett's advert and sent him a small and unused appointments diary with a red cover (which is currently in the possession of Keith Skinner). As the diary was too small and suitable for Barrett's needs, he never used it; however, it clearly shows his intent. He wanted to produce a clever and sophisticated forgery, one that would hopefully hold up under intense scrutiny.

[707] Feldman P., op cit., page 134.

11

SURROUNDED BY ENEMIES

As her husband died in the main bedroom, Florence lay fast asleep in the spare bedroom where she had been carried by Edwin around midday. She was to remain in this unconscious state for more than 24 hours, largely oblivious to the activities that were soon to engulf the house.

For a while after James' death little happened in Battlecrease as Edwin, Michael, and the two married Janion sisters tried to come to terms with his unexpected demise. They must have been in shock; however, shock soon turned to anger. How could it have happened? It was only just over a week ago that he had been at work. Throughout his illness, almost right up to the very end, his doctors had believed he would recover. In their minds, something untoward must have happened.

In such a toxic atmosphere, all eyes focused on Florence. She was the one who had, until recently, controlled all James' food and medicines, and she was the one who had an adulterous affair. The news Dr Carter had provided earlier in the day – that the bottle of meat juice Florence had moved '*suspiciously*' contained traces of arsenic – was the final straw. Michael felt he had no alternative but to take decisive action. Around 10:00pm, he ordered Nurse Yapp to make preparations for the two Maybrick children to be removed from Battlecrease. They were to be taken to the home of Mrs Janion, the children's godmother, the next day.

This act illustrates the power Michael had assumed over the house; he was denying the mother the right to have control over her own children. Yapp and Bessie Brierley went to the linen cupboard on the landing and took out a trunk that was marked with Florence's initials, *F.E.M.*, on its sides. The two of them carried it into the night nursery so it could be used to pack the children's clothes. As Yapp collected the clothing, Brierley went back downstairs. Around midnight, Yapp opened the trunk, which wasn't locked, while Nurse Wilson looked on. Inside the trunk, wrapped up in a sheet, were a chocolate box and a small brown paper parcel. When Yapp and Wilson opened the chocolate box, they found it contained a packet, two bottles and a handkerchief.

The packet was labelled *Arsenic - Poison for Cats*, with a poison sticker on it. This packet was later found to contain 65.2 grains of arsenic mixed with charcoal.[708] The two bottles both contained a white fluid. One bottle was labelled *Solution of Morphia*, while the other had no label. The parcel was opened at one end and some yellow powder was spilling out. Yapp took both the chocolate box and the parcel downstairs to Michael, who was in the breakfast room with Edwin. Michael immediately realised the significance of the discoveries and decided he needed proper legal advice. He went next door and consulted Mr Douglas Quintin Steel (1856-1933), a solicitor with Messrs Layton, Steel and Springman in Birkenhead, who lived there with his wife Maud. Steel was one of seven cricketing brothers, four of whom – including Douglas himself – were to play first class cricket for Lancashire. Steel advised Michael to secure the items with sealing wax and place them in a secure and locked place. Michael returned to the house and locked all the items in the wine cellar.

Once again, a discovery made by Nurse Yapp had changed the dynamics of the household. Her interception of Florence's letter to Brierley had set the wheels of suspicion in motion; now her discovery of the arsenic in Florence's trunk solidified these feelings.

Early on Sunday morning 12th May, the two children were taken in the family carriage to the home of Mrs Janion. With Florence still asleep, Michael ordered a search of the house. The justification was the need to find the keys to the safe. Mrs Briggs and Mrs Hughes, who had stayed the night at Battlecrease, started off in the main bedroom and then moved to the inner-dressing room. In the middle drawer of Florence's dressing table in the main bedroom, under paper lining, Mrs Hughes found '*some*' of Florence's private letters and gave them to Michael, who was in the dressing room at the time.[709]

At the trial, three letters and a draft telegram were produced in court as evidence.[710] Two of the letters were from Alfred Brierley, and the third was the one that Florence had tried to send Brierley but was intercepted. From the Charles Ratcliffe letter, we know that more letters were found in the house. There were thirteen letters from Edwin, seven from Brierley and five from Williams. It is likely that all of these letters would have been in the same place and therefore discovered at the same time. The letters, especially the ones from Edwin, must have come as a shock

---

[708] The amount of arsenic found in the package is taken from Mr Davies' testimony at Florence's trial. See Irving H.B., op cit., page 131.
[709] *Liverpool Mercury*, 7th June 1889.
[710] Levy J.H., op cit., page 65.

to Michael. He would have realised that they had the potential to embarrass the whole family. As these other letters disappeared, one can only assume they were destroyed by the Maybrick brothers.

Mrs Briggs, with Edwin's help, made a search of the inner-dressing room. In her testimony at Florence's trial, she said in the writing table she found a '*small bottle containing fluid and a handkerchief.*' She also found '*a small blue box in an ordinary hatbox in the same room. The hatbox contained a man's hat, and the smaller box contained three bottles. In addition, there was on the top of the box a bottle that had contained Valentine's extract. There was also a tumbler in another hatbox. In that tumbler there was a rag soaking in a whitish fluid, which looked like milk.*'[711] She left the items as she had found them, and later that night they were retrieved by Inspector Baxendale and taken to Mr Davies, the County Analyst. One thing that hadn't yet been found were the keys to the safe. Michael sent Edwin into Florence's room and told him to wake her and get her to tell him where the keys had been placed. Florence later recalled the incident in a poignant passage in her autobiography:

> '*Slowly consciousness returned. I opened my eyes. The room was in darkness. All was still. Suddenly the silence was broken by the bang of a closing door which startled me out of my stupor. Where was I? Why was I alone? What awful thing had happened? A flash of memory! My husband was dead! I drifted once more away from the things of sense. Then a voice, as if a long way off, spoke. A feeling of pain and distress shot through my body. I opened my eyes in terror. Edwin Maybrick was bending over me as I lay upon my bed. He had my arms tightly gripped, and was shaking me violently. "I want your keys – do you hear? Where are your keys?" he exclaimed harshly. I tried to form a reply, but the words choked me, and once more I passed into unconsciousness.*'[712]

Michael's plan after his arrival at Battlecrease was to limit Florence's responsibility for the medical care of James by placing him under the direction of professional nurses. If possible, he also wanted to remove her altogether by sending her to her mother in Paris but without the children, who were to remain in Liverpool. To Michael's great alarm, as more and more suspicious discoveries were made around the house, events were threatening to spiral out of control. His priority now became trying to avoid a public scandal.

To achieve this goal he needed the doctors to produce a death certificate for James in order to prevent the involvement of the coroner and the police. Michael and his brother Thomas visited Dr Carter to ask him to issue a death certificate. He spoke to Carter about the importance of the future welfare of the couple's children and even of the needs of Florence, whom he referred to as that '*unhappy woman.*'[713] If Michael was fully convinced of Florence's guilt he would never have acted in this manner.

Michael's intervention was too late; by raising suspicions with Drs Humphreys and Carter earlier in the case, he had set in motion a chain of events over which he now had no control. In June 1889, Charles Ratcliffe wrote to John Aunspaugh about James' death and the events in Battlecrease, commenting:

> '*Old Dr Humphreys made a jackass of himself. After James died he and Dr Carter expected to make out the death certificate as acute inflammation of the stomach. After Humphreys had a conversation with Michael he refused to make a certificate to that effect, but said there was strong symptoms of arsenic poisoning, though Dr Carter still insisted that it should be inflation of the stomach. Now wouldn't that cork you? A musical composer instructing a physician how to diagnose his case.*'

Charles Ratcliffe is correct in his assertion that Dr Humphreys would have probably issued a death certificate if it hadn't been for Michael's intervention, but once that happened and arsenic had been found in the meat juice, the doctors were left with no choice. They were unable to issue a death certificate and they had to inform the coroner that the death was suspicious.

As Michael was visiting Dr Carter, Florence continued to drift in and out of consciousness. She was in a very forlorn state, unwashed and in the same clothes she had worn when she was placed on the bed by Edwin the previous day. She had not eaten since breakfast on Saturday morning. At some point on Sunday afternoon Dr Hopper called at Battlecrease and asked to see Florence; he was responding to the letter she had sent him on Saturday morning. Although the servants were reluctant to let him into the house, the doctor insisted on seeing Florence. He found that she was suffering from a '*sanguineous discharge which might have been a threatened miscarriage.*'[714]

If Florence was indeed pregnant, and had or was about to suffer a miscarriage, then that would help explain her extremely exhausted physical state. Unsubstantiated rumours were later to circulate that Florence had a miscarriage

---

[711] Irving H.B., op cit., pages 39-40.
[712] Maybrick F., op. cit., page 23.
[713] Carter Dr W., Post-trial transcript notes, New Scotland Yard Crime Museum.
[714] Dr Hopper's assizes statement in Colquhoun K., op cit., page 125.

while in Walton Gaol. Although it is difficult to get to the full truth, it is possible that Florence did lose a baby around this time. If that was the case, then it is almost certain that Brierley would have been the father of the unborn child.

Dr Hopper had not long left the house when Michael returned from his visit to Dr Carter. He entered Florence's bedroom, and said to the professional nurse supervising her: '*Nurse, I am going up to London. Mrs Maybrick is no longer mistress of this house. As one of the executors I forbid you to allow her to leave this room. I hold you responsible in my absence.*'

Florence's humiliation was not yet complete. That evening, as she was starting to come out of her deep sleep, she asked the nurse if she could see her children. The nurse walked up to the bed, and said to her in a cold voice: '*You cannot see Master James and Miss Gladys. Mr Michael Maybrick gave orders that they were to leave the house without seeing you.*'

The reply hit Florence like a thunderbolt, and in her own words left her feeling '*dazed and stricken, weak, helpless, and impotent. Why was I treated thus? My brain reeled in seeking a reply to this query. At last, I could bear it no longer, and my soul cried out to God to let me die.*'[715]

The Baroness later outlined Florence's terrible predicament at that time in a letter she sent to MacDougall, the Scottish lawyer. In it she wrote that while her daughter lay ill in bed, '*prostrated and helpless,*' she was '*surrounded by enemies whose bitterness I need not call your attention to, for it is in evidence, who had prejudiced her, condemned her in their own minds as a murderess, without even telling her their conclusion, and who were boldly ransacking her house – a house in which they had no legal right or other right, to obtain evidence in support of the conviction which they had chosen to entertain.*'[716]

The actions of Michael, Edwin and the married Janion sisters – the searching of the house, removing the children and the manner in which they marginalised a bewildered and distraught Florence – can be viewed in two very contrasting ways. Firstly, they were clearly upset at the unexpected death of someone they loved. If they believed something suspicious, maybe even criminal, had occurred, then one can understand their anger. If they felt that Florence had a hand in that suspicious death, then one can also comprehend the contempt they showed towards her. They wanted to gather evidence and the children needed to be protected.

On the other hand, there is a second way in which their actions can be viewed. It can be seen as an attempt to blacken Florence's character and undermine her in every way possible on the basis of rumour and innuendo. Yes, some suspicious items had been found, but they knew about James' habit of taking all manner of drugs, often in large doses. Edwin, in particular, was aware of his brother's strychnine use. They searched the house without any legal right to do so. *They* may have found some incriminating evidence, but they also hid other evidence such as Edwin's letters to Florence. It is possible that other items were moved or removed. For example, Florence was always insistent that the hat boxes, in which items containing arsenic were found, must have been moved as they were usually kept in the wardrobes in the spare room as there was too little space in the inner-dressing room to store them.[717] In this process, it is the women who are often singled out for blame – the '*female serpents*' as Ratcliffe was to call them – but the real architect was Michael. Edwin was in a panic and incapable of taking a lead. Mrs Briggs would never have acted in the manner she did unless it had been sanctioned by Michael. The professional nurses also followed Michael's directions. Michael now needed the police to follow his cues.

The first police officer to visit Battlecrease after James' passing was Inspector Richard Baxendale (1839-1918). He was to become responsible for most of the routine investigation into the death. Born at Hambleton, a village near Poulton-le-Fylde, Lancashire in 1839, he began his working life as a farm labourer. He joined the police in 1863 at Ashton-under-Lyne, later serving at Barrow-in-Furness, where he was noted for catching sheep stealers. In 1871, Sergeant Baxendale, as he then was, first crossed paths with John Addison QC, who would lead the prosecution against Florence 18 years later. Baxendale gave evidence of arrest at Lancaster quarter sessions in the case against a farmer who had stolen nine sheep for their skins as well as their carcasses. The hides were produced in court, and the farmer was sentenced to seven years' penal servitude. Baxendale encountered the barrister again in his first murder trial in 1876, when Addison defended Joseph Pugh, a slagger at Barrow Iron Works, accused at Lancaster of strangling his wife.

Promoted to the rank of inspector and transferred to Garston, Baxendale was aged 49 at the time of the Maybrick case. He was 5 ft 8¾ ins in height, dark haired and weather-beaten; a legacy perhaps of his previous work on the land. At Florence's trial, Baxendale stated he visited Battlecrease on three separate occasions.[718] The first time was on the evening of Sunday, 12th May, after James' death had been reported to the police as being suspicious. He viewed James' body. He then spoke to Edwin, who took him into James' inner-dressing room and showed him some of the

---

[715] Maybrick F., op. cit., pages 24-25.
[716] Interview in the *New York Herald* and quoted in *The Halfpenny Weekly*, 17th August 1889.
[717] Levy J.H., op cit., page 152.
[718] Irving H.B., op cit., page 128.

things found earlier that day. He took away several items, including some bottles and the hat boxes.[719] Baxendale returned to Battlecrease the next day, Monday 13th May, this time accompanied by Superintendent Isaac Bryning of the County Police, who was to take overall control of the case. A contemporary newspaper described Bryning as a '*stout, elderly man, with a fresh complexion and a bald head, fringe of grey hair and grey whiskers.*'[720] Bryning talked to Edwin, questioned the servants and asked Dr Humphreys to take some samples from the pipes and the drains. The sediment was placed in earthenware jars and taken to Mr Davies, the County Analyst. Other items taken by Baxendale for analysis were bedding from the bedroom in which James had died, a flannel shirt worn two or three days before his death, and Florence's dressing gown, apron and a handkerchief that was in the dressing gown.

On Monday 13th May, a post-mortem was conducted on James in his bedroom, which Bryning attended. Three doctors were involved in the post-mortem: Drs Humphreys and Carter, plus Dr Alexander Barron, who hadn't previously been involved in the case. Dr Barron was Professor of Pathology at University College and a member of the Royal College of Surgeons. He also practised as a physician in Liverpool and had been pathologist to the Royal Infirmary for four years. He had attended about five hundred post-mortem examinations. At James' inquest, Dr Barron said he '*assisted Drs Carter and Humphreys to make a post-mortem examination of the late Mr Maybrick's body. Dr Humphreys telephoned me to assist.*'[721] At Florence's trial, Dr Barron told the court he '*attended the post-mortem on Mrs Maybrick's behalf.*'

The post-mortem commenced at 5:00pm. Dr Barron carried out most of the dissection helped by Dr Humphreys. The only part of the dissection in which Dr Carter was directly involved was the start of the process required for removing the brain. The rest of the time Dr Carter took down the notes, which were chiefly dictated by Dr Barron. The doctors removed various parts of the body, which were placed in sealed glass jars. Jar one had bits of the intestines; jar two had the contents of the stomach; and jar three had a section of the liver. Two small bottles were used to hold the fluid which had flowed from the mouth and the bile. These samples were taken by the police to the analyst for testing.

On Monday evening, Michael, who had returned from his visit to London, handed Inspector Baxendale the chocolate box that contained the packet labelled *Arsenic - Poison for Cats*. He also gave him three of Florence's letters: two sent from Alfred Brierley, the letter she tried to send to Brierley which was intercepted by Nurse Yapp, and a draft of a telegram that was in Florence's handwriting.[722]

Aigburth Hotel, venue for the first day of the inquest into James Maybrick' death, on Tuesday 14th May 1889

On Tuesday 14th May, the inquest into James' death opened at the Aigburth Hotel, which was situated on Aigburth Road, less than 800 metres from Battlecrease. The hotel was known for hosting '*meetings, inquests and parties.*'[723] Samuel Brighouse, the coroner of South West Lancashire, had become involved in the Maybrick case after the police had reported to him that James appeared to have died in suspicious circumstances. It was he who had ordered the post-mortem.

Brighouse (1849-1940) had been born in Lathom in Lancashire and educated at Ormskirk Grammar School. He was admitted a solicitor in 1871 and founded the firm of Brighouse, Brighouse and Jones, of which he remained the head for the rest of his life. This dapper young country solicitor with a military bearing had become coroner for South-West Lancashire in 1884, at the age of just 34, and was to hold the post for 54 years. Tall, bearded and bronzed, his no-nonsense air masked an underlying sense of humour and no shortage of Lancashire common sense. But there was a notable gaping hole in his professional knowledge: Brighouse was a lawyer and, as a result, had no medical qualifications, knowledge or training.

The opening of the inquest was a brief affair. According to a local newspaper, '*the only witness was Mr Michael Maybrick, of London,*' who had been called to identify the deceased.[724] Another local paper reported:

[719] Ibid., page 128.
[720] *Liverpool Review*, 8th June 1889.
[721] *Liverpool Weekly News*, 8th June 1889.
[722] *Liverpool Courier*, 29th May 1889.
[723] Burns P., *Grassendale: Birth of a Suburb*, (Green Hey Press, Liverpool, 2021) page 210.
[724] *Liverpool Mercury*, 15th May 1889.

'The coroner explained that there were suspicions that the deceased had died from poisoning, and looking at what was mentioned in the report of the police he had considered it desirable to order a post-mortem to be made. The primary cause of death was congestion of the stomach, which in a man of the deceased's state of health was at least strange, but all he could then say was that as a result of the examination of the body it was necessary that after hearing sufficient evidence to enable the internment to take place, an adjournment should be made so that the stomach and its contents might be scientifically tested and analysed.'[725]

Sir Samuel Brighouse (1849-1940)
Coroner for South-West Lancashire

James' body was then released for burial.

After the inquest was adjourned, an important event occurred that reveals the manner in which the investigation into James' death was to be conducted. Coroner Brighouse asked the members of the jury if they wished to make the short walk to Battlecrease to view James' dead body. For the foreman of the inquest jury, Mr Dalgleish (or Daglish), this process must have been traumatic as he was to recognise James. After viewing the body, he informed the coroner of an incident that happened on a train just prior to the Wirral races. He said he had seen James remove some powder out of his waistcoat pocket and take it. When Dalgleish asked him what the powder was, James had replied '*strychnine.*' Coroner Brighouse spoke to Superintendent Bryning and Mr Steel, the solicitor acting on behalf of the Maybrick brothers, about Dalgleish's statement. It was agreed to release Dalgleish from jury duty in case he was later to be called as a witness.

In fact, the latter was never to happen. Evidence helpful to the defence's case was being airbrushed out of existence. As MacDougall wrote: '*Mr Dalgleish's statement that the man [James] was physicking himself up with strychnine immediately before his illness was, of course, not likely to be useful to the police, or to Mr Michael Maybrick, who were setting up a case against Mrs Maybrick that James Maybrick's death was due to arsenic administered by her.*'[726]

On 14th May, Superintendent Bryning believed he had enough evidence against Florence to formally caution her. Florence described the event in her autobiography. Dr Humphreys entered her bedroom, took her pulse and then left without saying a word. A few minutes later she heard the '*tramp of many feet coming up-stairs*' and a '*crowd of men*' entered her bedroom. One of these men was Bryning, who stopped at the foot of Florence's bed and said:

'Mrs Maybrick, I am superintendent of the police, and I am about to say something to you. After I have said what I intend to say, if you reply be careful how you reply, because whatever you say may be used as evidence against you. Mrs Maybrick, you are in custody on suspicion of causing the death of your late husband, James Maybrick, on the eleventh instant.'

Florence wrote that in response she '*made no reply, and the crowd passed out.*'[727] A totally bemused Florence felt she was going mad. Why hadn't James' brothers told the police he was an arsenic eater? She had nursed James night and day, and had even employed trained nurses to help look after him during his illness. She wrote:

'I lay ill and confined to my bed, with two professional nurses attending me, and with a policeman stationed in my room, although there was not and could not be the slightest chance of my escaping. The officer would not permit the door to be closed day or night, and I was denied in my own house, even before the inquest, the privacy accorded to a convicted prisoner.'

Realising she desperately needed help, that afternoon Florence spoke to Mrs Briggs, who was still staying in the house with her sister, and asked her for some money so she could send letters and telegrams to her family and the family's solicitors in New York. In a sarcastic tone of voice, Mrs Briggs suggested that Florence should write to Mr Brierley if she needed help. Mistaking Mrs Briggs' reply as a helpful comment, Florence wrote a short note to Brierley asking him for money to cover her '*present needs.*' She warned him the '*truth is known*' about their meeting in London. She gave the note to Mrs Briggs to post, but she gave it to the policeman who was on duty just outside the room.

---

[725] *Liverpool Courier*, 15th May 1889.
[726] MacDougall A.W., (1896) op cit., page 27.
[727] Maybrick F., op. cit., pages 25-26.

This incident shows how friendless Florence was at this time. While Michael was the main architect of events, Mrs Briggs was an able lieutenant and her suggestion to Florence that she should write to Brierley was seen by many as a cynical act designed to get Florence into even more trouble. Florence's isolation became even more complete, when some of her friends called at Battlecrease to see her but were denied entry to the house. Charles Ratcliffe wrote that Michael had put Mrs Briggs in charge of the house, and when he and his wife called around to see Florence they were '*told by Mrs Briggs that Mrs Maybrick was too sick to receive any company. Sutton and his wife called, Holloway and his wife, Hienes and his wife and numerous others. They were all told the same thing. No-one could see Mrs Maybrick.*'

After Florence was cautioned by the police, Mr Steel told Michael that she was in urgent need of independent legal advice and recommended he contact the Liverpool law firm of Cleaver, Holden, Garnett and Cleaver. Michael asked Dr Humphreys to help and, at midday on 14th May, the doctor called at the firm's offices in North John Street in the city centre. Levy refers to Dr Humphreys as a '*kind-hearted and honest man,*' who seems to have been the only person who '*made the slightest effort, at this juncture, to procure fair-play for the accused. It was he who gave her a few shillings, when he found that she had been left penniless and unable to communicate with her friends.*'[728]

Richard Cleaver, the senior member of the firm, was out when Dr Humphreys called so he left a message in which he asked for a member of the firm to go immediately to the house of the late Mr Maybrick for the purpose of advising Mrs Maybrick, who was in custody facing a serious charge. Prior to 14th May, the Cleavers had no business or connection with either James or Florence. Arnold Cleaver, Richard's brother and partner, proceeded to Battlecrease later in the day but was unable to obtain access to the house as he had no permit from the superintendent of police. After being refused entry, he went to see Dr Humphreys, who explained to him why he had not provided a death certificate. He also gave him a draft copy of the post-mortem results, and told him about the allegation that arsenic had been found in a bottle of meat juice that Florence had handled.

The following day, 15th May, Mr Steel called at the Cleavers' office and spoke to Richard Cleaver. He repeated the information given the previous day by Dr Humphreys, though he added details about the intercepted letter from Florence to Brierley. In the afternoon, Arnold Cleaver returned to Battlecrease and for the first time was able to speak to Florence. As he was going up the stairs Mrs Hughes shouted out, '*Go up and see her. She is the greatest liar on earth.*'[729]

Richard Cleaver (1843-1919)

The interview between Arnold Cleaver and Florence took place in her bedroom. As a nurse and a policeman were in the room, the two were forced to speak quietly to prevent being overheard. Florence provided him with her account of events and stressed her innocence. Arnold Cleaver took no notes, as he would have been forced to hand them over to the policeman on duty. That this unsatisfactory interview took place after she had already been cautioned, shows the manner in which Florence's case was being handled by the police.

On 15th May, the first stories of the Maybrick case appeared. *The Liverpool Mercury* provided a short article under the title: '*The Death of Mr James Maybrick.*' It mentioned the opening of the inquest at the Aigburth Hotel, and that a post-mortem had been carried out, but merely added that the results of the investigations had not yet been made known.

In contrast, both the *Liverpool Courier* and the *Liverpool Citizen* carried more dramatic headlines and more punchy accounts. The *Citizen's* headline was '*Suspected Murder of a Liverpool Merchant.*' The newspaper said that from what they had been able to learn about the matter, '*there appears little doubt that Mr James Maybrick came to an untimely end through arsenic poisoning. But the most painful part of the case is that suspicion has fallen on his wife.*' Thus, with only a limited amount of information available, the newspaper was already suggesting that James had been murdered by Florence through the use of arsenic. However, the final part of the report did state that they hoped the '*rumours afloat*' would be '*without foundation,*' and the '*absolute innocence of Mrs Maybrick, who is at present under house arrest in her own home, will be proved.*'

The headline of the *Liverpool Courier* was '*Alleged poisoning of a Liverpool Merchant.*' The story reported the '*examination of the body confirmed the external symptoms of the presence of poisoning – either strychnine or arsenic – and that there is no evidence to show that it was taken accidentally.*' It also said '*extraordinary allegations are afloat*' and the matter had created a '*very painful sensation*' in the local area.

---

728 Levy J.H., op. cit., page 433.

729 Quoted in the Ryan B., op cit., page 77.

James' funeral took place on Thursday 16th May 1889. Florence was only informed of it on the day of the event. In the days beforehand she had spent much of her time in the spare bedroom, depressed and ill. She had been the subject of a great deal of insults from both the servants and James' bothers. Nevertheless, she insisted on seeing her husband's coffin before it left Battlecrease. It had been placed on his bed and covered with white flowers. She knelt before it and prayed, and then began to cry.

She later wrote of her thoughts at that time: '*Death had wiped out the memory of many things. I was thankful to remember that I had stopped divorce proceedings and that we had become reconciled for the children's sake.*'[730]

James' coffin was carried from the house and placed in a large ornate hearse pulled by four large black horses. It left Battlecrease, accompanied by nine other carriages. As the hearse moved away from Battlecrease, Florence watched from a window. When it had moved out of sight she collapsed in a dead faint. The hearse wound its way to Anfield cemetery. It was a large cemetery, created to cope with the rapid growth of Liverpool in the nineteenth century. It had its first internment on 5th May 1863, and came to include four blocks of Romanesque-style catacombs some 25 feet below ground level. The funeral service was held in the Anglican chapel at Anfield Cemetery. It was led by the parish priest from St Mary's, Grassendale, Rev Fred Barker, and by the Rev Dr Charles Hyde of St Matthew's Church, Scotland Road, Liverpool. Dr Hyde had been '*on terms of intimacy with the deceased from his youth up.*'[731] He was a fellow Freemason, and had for a while been the parish priest at St Peter's Church, where James' father had been the parish clerk.

James was buried in the grave where his parents had been laid to rest. The *Liverpool Courier* carried a report of the funeral, stating:

The Maybrick family grave in Anfield Cemetery, Liverpool (Chris Jones collection)

> *The remains of Mr James Maybrick, of the firm of Messrs. Maybrick and Co., merchants, Knowsley-buildings, Tithebarn-street, who died on Saturday at his Aigburth residence, were yesterday afternoon, in the presence of a large assembly of relatives and friends, interred at the Anfield Cemetery. The service in the church and at the graveside was conducted by the Rev. Dr. Hyde and the Rev. F. Barker. The chief mourners were Mr Michael Maybrick, Mr William Maybrick, Mr Thos. Maybrick and Mr Edwin Maybrick (brothers), Mr Alfred Maybrick (nephew), the Rev. F. Barker (Grassendale), Dr Humphreys and Messrs. Henry Coke, H. A. Watson, James Mackee, T.A. Woolley, G.R. Davidson and R. Hobson.*'[732]

The report went on to list the other mourners at the graveside and those who sent wreaths.

On Wednesday 15th May, Michael finally sent a telegram to Florence's mother in Paris. It read: '*Florie ill and in awful trouble. Do not delay.*' On the same day Florence was able, with the money from Dr Humphreys, to send two telegrams to her mother. The first read, '*Jim passed away on Monday,*' while the second pleaded: '*Come at once. Serious charges against me.*'

The telegrams shocked the Baroness, and she caught the first boat train to leave Paris. On Friday 17th May, the Baroness arrived in Liverpool, and by chance met Michael at Liverpool Edge Hill railway station. He told her: '*Florrie is very ill; Edwin will tell you everything. It is a case of murder, and there is a man in the case.*' Michael's statement is unequivocal; he was accusing Florence of causing James' death.

The Baroness was stunned and made her way to Battlecrease, a place she had never visited, in a state of shock. At the house she was met by an agitated Edwin who took her into the morning room. She criticised Edwin for not sending for her sooner, and demanded to see her daughter. He told her the police were in the house. When the Baroness asked why they were there, he replied, '*I suppose you know it is said Jim was poisoned.*' Edwin then explained to the Baroness, in what she later described as a '*broken manner,*' some of the events that had taken place prior to James' death. The Baroness again demanded to know why she had not been summoned sooner, and why Florence had been delivered to the police without a friend on hand to help her. Edwin told her: '*I can assure you we had no idea matters would result in this way. I would rather cut my hand off than have had it so.*'

---

730 Maybrick F., op. cit., page 29.
731 *Liverpool Mercury*, 17th May 1889.
732 *Liverpool Courier*, 17th May 1889.

Edwin's dramatic – and probably untrue – remark did little to dampen the Baroness' ire. She demanded to know what was going to happen to the children, and why they were pursuing her daughter in the manner they were. Edwin tried to justify his actions, saying: '*I have been very fond of Florrie. I would never have believed anything wrong of her. I would have stood by her, and I did until the letter to the man was found.*' The Baroness asked him who this man was, at which Edwin told her it was Brierley. The Baroness replied that her daughter had never once mentioned his name. Edwin told her: '*she met him this winter at some dances, and she was always so quiet and domestic before, I would never have believed it of Florrie, but this winter she was changed and would go out to dances.*'

The Baroness, in a state of despair, went to see her daughter. There were two policemen in the hallway upstairs; she ignored them and went through the open bedroom door and saw Florence '*lying on a sofa, deadly pale.*' Inspector Baxendale was sitting on a chair near the sofa and Nurse Wilson was sitting on a chair next to her. Despite some protests from the nurse, she kissed Florence and then spoke to her in French, asking her what the other people were doing in the room. The nurse told her to only speak in English. The inspector said, '*I warn you madam, I shall write down what you say.*' The Baroness was not put-off by his tone, and told him, '*You may write as much as you like my friend. I have nothing wrong to say; but it strikes me as very strange to see you in this room.*' Florence interjected, and told her mother not to get too excited as the inspector was only doing his duty.

The Baroness asked Florence what was going on, and she replied, '*They think I have poisoned Jim.*' In response, the Baroness said, '*Why if he is poisoned, he poisoned himself – he made a perfect apothecary's shop of himself, as we all know.*' Florence told her mother to go and see her solicitor, Mr Cleaver, as he would explain everything. Before leaving the room, the Baroness sat down next to Florence and asked her a few more questions. Florence said, '*Dr Hopper and Mrs Briggs and Michael believe me guilty; but mammy, I am innocent.*'[733]

The Baroness went downstairs and again spoke to Edwin. He told her that after they had found out about Florence's intrigue with another man they had wanted an excuse to send her back to the Baroness but keep the children in Liverpool. To '*clinch matters*' they had called in Dr Carter, and told him of their suspicions that Florence had put something in the medicine. He had then refused to give a certificate of death.

Late on Friday night, Florence had '*a violent fit of crying and hysteria.*' The Baroness was shocked to find that during this episode her daughter was held down on her bed by four policemen and two nurses. She was especially angry as the policemen were holding her daughter's arms and legs. The Baroness told Nurse Wilson that the policemen had no right to be in a lady's room and, if they just let her hold her hand, she would be calm. Wilson replied in a manner the Baroness felt to be very insolent, saying she had been left in charge and she would act as she thought best. The Baroness, feeling totally impotent, angrily left the room saying on her way out, '*Better death than such dishonour.*' It was a remark she later regretted as it was interpreted to mean she was prepared to poison her own daughter to help her escape any further scandal. It was also used as a reason to justify taking Florence into custody.

The Baroness stayed overnight in the house. The next morning, Saturday, 18th May, at around 10:00am, she saw Nurse Yapp, who had come back to Battlecrease to get more clothes for the children. After asking her about the children, she enquired whether she was the person who '*caused additional trouble to that poor young thing by showing letters you find*?' Yapp replied, '*She wasn't a poor young thing then.*' The Baroness responded by calling her an '*ungrateful, disloyal servant.*'

The Baroness went up to Florence's bedroom to get the address of her solicitors. Nurse Gore wrote the Cleavers' address on a piece of paper. The Baroness left the room and saw Mrs Humphreys, the cook, for the first time. Humphreys said, '*I wish I could help missus – Baroness.*' The Baroness found it impossible to have a proper conversation with the cook as all the nurses and police officers were busy recording everything said. On top of that, most of the rooms in the house were locked; the only rooms upstairs left unlocked were the two bedrooms used by Florence and her mother; the only rooms unlocked downstairs were the dining and morning rooms.

Before leaving for the Cleavers, the Baroness went back again to her daughter's room and asked her about the flypapers and what they were for. Florence replied, '*Why, for cosmetics.*' The Baroness then asked Florence, in French, if she had in fact done anything wrong to her husband. Florence replied, '*No mamma, I swear to you that I am innocent. I did put a powder he asked for in the meat juice, but he did not have it.*'

The Baroness then set off for the Cleavers' offices in town. Her stay with the solicitors was only to be a short one. At noon, Richard Cleaver received information from the police that a magistrate would be attending Battlecrease at 2:00pm for the purpose of hearing some evidence against Florence and formally remanding her. Richard Cleaver told the Baroness that, if she wanted to see her daughter again, then she better hurry back to the house. Although the Baroness didn't fully understand the meaning of the remark, she did nevertheless rush back to Battlecrease.

Earlier that morning, Superintendent Bryning had gone to the County Magistrates Court at Islington, Liverpool and consulted Mr Swift, one of the clerks to the justices. Bryning believed he had collected sufficient evidence to bring a formal charge against Florence for murder. The magistrates agreed, and it was decided to charge Florence at her

733 MacDougall A.W., (1891) op cit., pages 9-12.

house rather than wait until she was fit enough to be taken to a court. Colonel Bidwell JP, one of the county magistrates, and Mr Swift then travelled to Battlecrease with Bryning. They waited at the gates until the Cleavers arrived at the house. Richard Cleaver later wrote in an affidavit: '*The prisoner had been all that week, and was still, in bed in a feeble condition, and in charge of nurses. Having regard to her state of health, and to my opinion on the information then before me that the evidence in the possession of the police was such as to justify further inquiry, I consented to a remand without any evidence being formally given.*'[734]

After a meeting on the lawn of Battlecrease, the party of officials moved into the house and up to Florence's bedroom. Bryning stood at the foot of the bed and said: '*This person is Mrs Maybrick, wife of the late James Maybrick. She is charged with having caused his death by administering poison to him. I understand consent is given to a remand, and therefore I need not introduce any evidence.*' Mr Swift said, '*You ask for a remand of eight days?*' Bryning replied, '*Yes, that is so.*' Mr Arnold Cleaver then said, '*I appear for the prisoner, and consent to a remand.*' Finally, Colonel Bidwell said, '*Very well. That is all.*'

After Florence was charged, police officers placed her in a hall armchair and carried her out to a cab that was waiting in the drive. Bryning, Nurse Wilson and Dr Humphreys also got into the cab, and Florence was taken to prison. She didn't realise it at the time, but she was never to return to Battlecrease.

The Baroness, who had rushed back from the Cleavers, was not allowed into Florence's bedroom while her daughter was being charged. Dr Hopper told her the reason they were moving her daughter was because of her remark of the previous night about death being better than dishonour. The Baroness asked the magistrate if she could speak to her daughter before they removed her, but was refused. As a result, the Baroness went into the bedroom that overlooked the front of the house so she could see what was happening. After entering the room the key was turned, and she found herself locked inside. When the cab had taken Florence away, the Baroness banged on the door and was eventually let out by a policeman.

A contemporary sketch showing Florence Maybrick at the door of Battlecrease House

The harsh treatment of Florence has led to criticisms of Bryning's attitude and methods. Florence was removed from Battlecrease with such haste that she was forced to leave with no toiletries, and without her mother being able to say goodbye. A more serious criticism of the police is that Bryning's first caution of Florence took place on 14th May, just three days after James' death and just the day after he had first visited Battlecrease. He could not have made a thorough review of all the evidence, and must have been influenced by the views of James' family and friends.

On her arrival at Walton Gaol, Florence was met by the prison governor and taken by a female warder down a narrow passageway to a gloomy reception room. She had her valuables taken off her – a watch, two diamond rings and a brooch – was made to wear a blue prison dress, and was measured and weighed. Due to her ill-health, she was taken to a cell that was set aside for sick prisoners. After being locked in the room she sank upon the stone floor in a state of total exhaustion and despair. The cell was small and dark, being lit only by the light that was able to make its way through a dirty, barred window. Apart from the bed, the only other furniture was a chair which had a china cup containing milk and a plate with bread on it.

Florence felt '*numbed*' and a '*sense of terrible oppression*' weighed her down. She remained in the cell for three days. Due to her illness, the first time her solicitor, Richard Cleaver, was permitted by the prison medical officer to see her was Thursday, 23rd May. That visit was the first time he had been alone with Florence. He arranged for her, at the cost of five shillings a week, to be moved to one of the so-called association cells for prisoners on remand. These cells were slightly larger than those for the convicted prisoners. Although they were still very basic, they did have a table, an armchair and a washstand.

---

[734] Levy J.H., op. cit., page 434.

The Cleavers have been criticised for the manner in which they handled Florence's case; in particular, for the way in which they '*complaisantly consented*' to Florence's remand.[735] This criticism fails to take into account the lack of knowledge they had about the case. Prior to 18th May, there had been just one meeting between Florence and Arnold Cleaver, and that had taken place in a bedroom surrounded by police officers who were trying to hear what was being said. The only detailed information that had so far been provided for the Cleavers had come from Dr Humphreys, Mr Steel and the police. With such a one-sided flow of information, it was simply impossible for them to have taken a more holistic view of Florence's situation. Richard Cleaver stated that the '*prominent matters*' within his knowledge prior to his meeting with Florence on 23rd May were '*the intercepted letter to Brierley, the alleged discovery of arsenic in the meat juice, and a statement that the post-mortem appearances were consistent with arsenical poisoning, and that the analyst had found traces of arsenic in the viscera.*'[736]

The meeting in Walton Gaol finally allowed Richard Cleaver to question Florence in some depth. She told him of her husband's habits of taking all kinds of medicines, plus some mysterious powders. She had written to Michael and spoken to Dr Hopper about her concerns. She also told him her version of the story concerning the meat juice; James asked her to add some powder and she had reluctantly done so. Cleaver also quizzed Florence about the flypapers, and she explained they had been bought for cosmetic purposes. As the Cleavers became acquainted with the full range of facts, they began to understand the case against Florence was largely circumstantial. As this happened, they adopted a more proactive stance in a desire to get a fair trial for their client. In Florence's eyes, the Cleaver brothers were heroes rather than villains. She later wrote about Richard Cleaver's '*unwavering faith and kindness,*' saying she owed him a debt which she could '*never hope to repay.*'[737]

During her time at Walton Gaol, Florence was locked in her cell for 22 hours out of every 24. The only time she could leave was when she went to the prison chapel in the morning and an hour's exercise in the afternoon in the prison yard. One of the things she found hardest to deal with was the '*stillness.*' She described the situation in which she was unable to speak to anyone as a form of torture.

Six days after her arrival in Walton Gaol she was visited by Charles Ratcliffe, his wife and two other friends. They were shocked by what they saw. Ratcliffe wrote: '*Mrs Maybrick presented a most pitiful and deplorable picture. She showed that she had been very ill and was yet a sick woman, eyes were sunken, hair dishevelled, dirty and filthy.*' Florence explained that since the death of her husband she had been a prisoner in her own house, and had been subject to abuse by Mrs Briggs and the servants. She spent much of the time in bed lying in her own filth.

Walton Gaol

Ratcliffe continued:

> '*Mrs Sutton went home at once, got a tub and some clean clothes. She and my wife gave Mrs Maybrick a good hot bath and put clean clothes on her. We got her a good soft mattress for the jail bunk and clean bed clothes. The cotton brokers' wives take it turn about to go every day to the jail, carry her a good meal and see that she is kept clean.*'[738]

The remand granted by Colonel Bidwell and issued at Battlecrease on 18th May was only valid for eight days. As a result, on 26th May Superintendent Bryning, local magistrate Mr Barrett, Mr Swift (one of his clerks), the prison governor and Richard Cleaver met in Florence's cell. Bryning again formally charged Florence with the murder of her husband. Florence did not reply, and once again her solicitor Richard Cleaver consented to her being charged without any attempt to prevent it.

As Florence languished in Walton Gaol, the police investigation gathered pace. Even before she had been taken to the prison, further items had been removed from Battlecrease. On 17th May, Sergeant Davenport, who was stationed at Garston Police Station, had been given the duty of ensuring Florence did not leave the house. While he was there,

---

735 MacDougall A.W., (1891) op cit., page 126.
736 Levy J.H., op cit., page 435.
737 Maybrick F., op. cit., page 223.
738 Letter is in Feldman P., op. cit., page 364.

he examined a linen closet and discovered a dressing-bag that belonged to Florence. Within it, he found a selection of powders and pills. Nearby, he also found a small round bottle that contained a white liquid. He gave all the items to Inspector Baxendale, who praised him for his alertness.[739] These items were taken to Mr Davies for analysis. During her trial, Florence wrote, on a list of police exhibits, next to the small round bottle the words *'face wash.'*[740]

On 18th May, Inspector Baxendale, with the help of Nurse Yapp and Edwin, conducted another search of Battlecrease. Altogether they found 117 items from 29 different chemists in Liverpool, Manchester, London and Wales.[741] From the sitting room came six bottles of pills, including two bottles of nux vomica pills (which James had said he could not tolerate) and an empty blue bottle from Hanson's chemist, which was labelled *'Not to be taken.'* Nurse Yapp found 22 items from various places, including bottles of glycerine lotion, pepsin wine and ipecacuanha wine; a bottle from Hansons labelled *'Carbolic Acid: Poison,'* and a box of insect powder. Eight items were found in Florence's bedroom and dressing room, including a bottle of elderflower water and a bottle of white powder labelled *'Antipyrin, Symes and Co., Liverpool.'* The most items by far – some 51 – were found in James' inner-dressing room. These items ranged enormously in type and description. Most were prescription drugs, but the list also included things such as soda mint tablets, Parisian polish and an empty toothpaste pot. A couple of the bottles were marked with the word *'Poison'* on them, such as a small blue bottle from Clay and Abraham's purchased on 27th April 1888.

All the items were sent to Mr Davies for testing. Later, Edwin took Inspector Baxendale to James' offices in the Knowsley Buildings. They removed 27 sets of items, including more than 20 medicine and pill bottles from five different chemists in Liverpool and London. Some of these items had been locked in James' private desk, such as a wine bottle, a brandy bottle, numerous medicines and a small bottle containing pills labelled *'Poison'* from a chemist in Oxford Street, London. Other items found around the office included medicines prescribed by the chemists Clay and Abraham's, and by Thompson and Clapper. Baxendale also took away the pan, basin and jug that had been used to heat the food that James had eaten in his office at the beginning of May. These items were also taken to Mr Davies for analysis.

Inspector Baxendale was back at Battlecrease once again on 20th May. The police records show that Baxendale actually visited Battlecrease on four occasions, and not the three he mentioned at Florence's trial. He was there on 12th, 13th, 18th and 20th May. He collected items from the *'lavatory, the house-maid's closet, the butler's pantry, and the area.'*[742] He also took away five items that were found in a small drawer in James' inner-dressing room, including a box of corn plasters, yet another box of pills, a small bottle of white powder, a small green bottle of pills and a small box of potash tablets.[743]All these items went to the analyst. Other items obtained by Inspector Baxendale around this time included the correspondence between Florence and Mr Flatman. He also visited the chemists of Wokes and Hanson, and bought several flypapers from each establishment. He gave most of the flypapers to Mr Davies for analysing, but kept three sets back from each chemist to present as evidence at the trial. The final item received by Mr Davies from Baxendale was on 1st June, when the inspector gave him a spoon to analyse.

Stories about the Maybrick case had started to dominate the newspapers. In such a climate, it was not too surprising that some of these storylines were based purely on gossip, such as a rumour which featured in an article in the *Liverpool Weekly Courier* that there was going to a second arrest in the Maybrick case. The article didn't identify the person, but as the rumour was being circulated at the Liverpool Cotton Exchange it was presumably Alfred Brierley whom the gossips had it mind. The article did go on to state, with a degree of certainty, that the rumour was incorrect.

Stories were also beginning to appear about James' health and drug-taking habits. One such story featured in the *Liverpool Daily Post,* under the headline: *'The True Story of Mr Maybrick's Medicine.'* The article was clearly well-sourced, as it had some accurate references to recent real events. It mentioned the fact that James had told a friend he had taken an overdose of medicine which contained poison. This presumably referred to events at the time of the Wirral races. It also stated that James had visited a leading physician in London; another accurate statement, as James had visited Dr Fuller on two occasions. It reported that many of James' friends on the 'Change felt he had appeared *'seriously ill'* for *'many weeks.'* He had been *'petulant in his manner and very delicate in appearance as compared with his usual robust state of health.'*[744]

The newspaper accounts of events in Battlecrease soon spread way beyond the confines of Liverpool. Within a week it became a national story and, a little later, an international story. The fact that Florence was so much younger than her husband and was American, made it one of the murder sensations of the late-Victorian period. As Colquhoun pointed out, female murderers were rare, and middle-class female murderers were almost non-existent.[745]

---

739 Irving H.B., op cit., page 128.
740 MacDougall A.W., (1891) op cit., page 587.
741 Ryan B., op. cit., page 88.
742 Irving H.B., op cit., page 128.
743 Ibid., pages 89-90.
744 *Liverpool Daily Post*, 21st May 1889.
745 Colquhoun K., op cit., page 146.

Surrounded by Enemies

Not long after James' death, a dressmaker came to Battlecrease to try and get a bill paid for a garment that had not been intended for Florence. Also around this time, Thomas and Michael Maybrick visited a woman who possessed some of Florence's clothes and jewellery, and who claimed that they had been given to her by James as part-payment for money lent.[746] If this woman was, as most people believe, Sarah Ann Robertson, perhaps James gave her the jewellery as part of the financial allowance he had promised her. The presence of Sarah Ann Robertson is important for another reason, as it provides a motive for murder for people other than Florence. There is an upset and angry mistress. There is a celebrity brother, who liked to control his family, facing potential embarrassment over the actions of one of his wayward family members. There is another brother, Edwin, who was close to James' wife and who may have seen an opportunity to remove him from the scene. Edwin arguably had motive, opportunity and means. For example, he was the one who carried James' food to his office and therefore he could have easily added some poison into the gruel.

Although it is highly unlikely that Sarah Ann Robertson or James' brothers were responsible for his death, an open-minded police investigation would have needed to assess the motives and actions of all the leading characters, but that never happened. If the police had acted in a more impartial manner they may still have come to the view that Florence was their prime suspect, but at least the decision would have been reached after a more objective process.

Florence's treatment after her arrest was nothing short of scandalous. She was effectively a prisoner in her own home, surrounded by former friends who were bent on her conviction. In her ill and isolated state, she had no way of effectively countering the onslaught that was about to come her way.

How had this been allowed to happen? Four key events helped shape the situation in which Florence was to find herself. The discovery of the flypapers sparked the initial suspicions amongst some of the servants, most notably Nurse Yapp. These flypapers were undoubtedly a red-herring, but following the infamous trial of the *Liverpool black widows* they got tongues wagging and created idle and potentially damaging rumours. The interception of the Brierley letter had provided the motive, and had turned her few allies in Battlecrease against her.

There can be no doubt that Edwin was shocked by Florence's actions, and was possibly jealous of Brierley. He could and should have done more to help Florence in her hour of need. He knew the truth about James' drug use, especially strychnine, and his mistress; however, after reading the Brierley letter, he turned against Florence and left her to face her situation alone. The finding of arsenic in the meat juice provided the smoking gun. Florence could have denied adding any powder, but she didn't. Once the arsenic had been found in the meat juice the involvement of the police became inevitable. Finally, the discovery of the package labelled *Arsenic - Poison for Cats* in Florence's trunk cemented her guilt in the minds of many of James' relatives and friends.

LINKS TO THE RIPPER DIARY: DOES THE CHRONOLOGY OF EVENTS MATCH THE NARRATIVE OF THE DIARY?

The rationale given by the diarist for his killing spree is his anger at his wife, whom he refers to as the '*whore*,' because she is having an affair with an unnamed man, whom he refers to as the '*whoremaster*.' The diarist said he would not get '*peace of mind*' until he had sought his '*revenge on the whore and the whoremaster*.' If the diarist's wife was having an affair, then one could understand his anger; however, he turns his anger not on his wife, or her lover, but on the down-at-heel women of London. The diarist claims, whilst drinking in the Poste House, that '*London it shall be*' and all those '*who sell their dirty wares shall pay*.' There are obvious problems with this statement. Firstly, why kill prostitutes in a different city to the one in which you live as opposed to killing the wayward wife and her lover. Secondly, it is unlikely that James would have just stood by and allowed his wife to have had an affair. Charles Ratcliffe, in his letter to John Aunspaugh in June 1889, wrote that James had found out about Florence's fling in Flatman's Hotel and he was '*expecting him to plug Brierley at any time*.' If James was thinking of killing Brierley after just one adulterous episode, it is extremely unlikely he would have allowed his wife to have continued an adulterous affair over several months.

Another big problem is the issue of chronology. Although we do not know for certain how many women were killed by Jack the Ripper, most Ripperologists accept that there were at least five murders. These murders are referred to as the five canonical killings, and start with Polly Nichols on Friday, 31st August 1888 and end with Mary Kelly on Friday, 9th November 1888.

These murder dates present a real problem for those who believe the Diary was written by James Maybrick and he started his murderous campaign after discovering his wife was having an affair. It is usually assumed that the '*whoremaster*' is Alfred Brierley, with whom Florence did have an intimate relationship in March 1889. In a

[746] *Norfolk Virginian*, 11th August 1889.

newspaper interview, Brierley stated that prior to November 1888 he and Florence were '*merely distant acquaintances.*'[747] In other words, the Ripper killings took place before Florence's affair with Brierley and not after it. This view is supported by other eye-witnesses. Edwin, James's brother, told Florence's mother, when she arrived at Battlecrease after James' death, that Florence met Brierley '*this winter at some dances, and she was always so quiet and domestic before, I would never have believed it of Florrie, but this winter she was changed and would go out to dances.*'[748]

The Baroness, in a letter to the Home Secretary in August 1892, wrote in the early years of her marriage Florence was '*a delicate invalid, nursing little children, attending to the house... the December of 1888 was the first time during her married life she had been able to dance or had been out in society; and her health was then stronger.*'[749]

Florence, in a letter to Dr Hopper on the day that James died, wrote, '*because I have sinned once, must I be misjudged always.*' In the letter, which Christie refers to as '*one of the most honest communications she ever made,*' Florence admits to adultery, but is adamant that it only happened once.[750] This relationship with Brierley happened in March 1889, some four months after what is considered to be the final Ripper murder.

Those who believe the Diary is genuine try to reconcile the problems with chronology in two different ways: either by arguing that Florence's affair with Brierley started before November 1888, or by suggesting that Florence must have had other lovers before she started her affair with Brierley. The trouble with both of these views is there is no evidence to support them. Florence did know Brierley before August 1888, but until November 1888, they were, in Brierley's own words, '*merely distant acquaintances.*' At the end of November 1888, Charles Ratcliffe wrote, '*Think Alf is getting the inside track with Mrs M's affections.*' This observation is significant, not only because of the date, 22nd November, but also because it shows the transparency of Florence's feelings towards Brierley. She was incapable of hiding the way she felt, so if the affair had started earlier people would have noticed it.

People who suggest that Florence might have had other lovers, point to a reference in the Ratcliffe letter that states Florence received letters not just from Brierley, but also from Edwin Maybrick and the mysterious Williams. The letters from Edwin probably did show affection, but that does not mean he had an affair with Florence. The Maybricks, like many people at that time, were prolific letter writers and it would have been more of a shock if Florence had not received letters from Edwin. That she decided to keep some letters, indicates they may have been close, but it does not prove they were lovers. It is impossible to conceive of James allowing his brother to have an adulterous affair with his wife. It is also impossible to believe that Edwin, who was dominated by his brothers, would have had the audacity to have embarked upon such an affair.

One final problem facing those who believe the Diary is genuine, is that the diarist admits to the killing of only the five canonical victims in Whitechapel, though he implies he also killed two women in Manchester. That means Mary Kelly was his last London murder in early November 1888, but James Maybrick lived for another six months. Is it possible to believe that the man who savagely mutilated Mary Kelly could have gone back to living a normal life? Rubinstein has argued the reason why the Ripper murders stopped after 9th November 1888, was that James changed doctors and started seeing Dr Drysdale. He treated him on five occasions with homeopathic remedies, and there was a gradual improvement in his health.[751] In other words, a brutal, sadistic killer was changed into a decent human being after taking a few herbal remedies. That is a view that is neither likely nor credible.

[747] *Garston and Woolton Reporter*, 17th August 1889.
[748] MacDougall A.W., (1891) op cit., page 10.
[749] HO 144/1639/A50678D/99.
[750] Christie T.L., op cit., page 62.
[751] Rubinstein W.D., *'Hunt for Jack the Ripper'* in *History Today*, Vol. 50, May 2000.

12

CORONER'S INQUEST

The Reading Room, Garston, the venue for the inquest into James Maybricks' death

The reconvened inquest into James' death opened on Tuesday, 28th May 1889. The venue was the Reading Room in Wellington Street, Garston, one mile from Battlecrease. The brick building, with its sharply sloping roof, resembled a small chapel and stood at the end of a row of terraced houses. It was selected as the venue for the inquest as it was the largest public building in Garston, though its poor acoustics were to provide problems throughout the proceedings. The Reading Room, opened it 1861, was a multi-purpose venue. [752] It was so-named as one of its roles was to serve as a lending library. In August 1889, 343 books were issued. One of the new books acquired that month was the aptly entitled *A Troublesome Girl.*[753] As well as a library, the building served as a place of worship for the local Baptist community and also as an entertainment venue. A newspaper described the interior of the building as being a '*large oblong room – is not quite so puritanical looking as the outside, some attempt having been made at a cheap kind of decoration.*'[754]

The great interest in the Maybrick case ensured that a large crowd assembled outside the building on the morning of the inquest. At 9:30am, the police opened the doors to those directly connected with the case, such as relatives and anyone called to give evidence. It was sometime later before the general public was admitted, and the police took '*considerable care and discrimination*' in deciding who was going to be allowed into the building.[755]

The seating arrangements had been determined by the coroner himself. At the far end of the building was a raised platform upon which the witnesses and relatives of the deceased sat. All the Maybrick brothers were to attend: Michael and Edwin were there every day and sat on the platform; Thomas and William were only occasional attendees. When William was present he sat in a '*remote corner*' of the room.[756] In front of the stage, in the middle of the room, a series of tables had been arranged in a horseshoe shape. The coroner sat in a commanding position in the centre of a cross table with his back to the stage. Alongside him, on his left, were Mr Carr, his clerk, then Superintendent Bryning, and then finally Inspector Baxendale. Two sets of tables were arranged at right angles to the main cross table. On one set, to the right of the coroner, sat the jurors, whilst on the opposite side sat the various counsels who were representing the interested parties. There was William Pickford QC, who had been appointed by Florence's solicitors to represent the defence, and Allan Gibson Steel (1858-1914), who represented the Maybrick brothers. Steel was the brother of Douglas Quintin Steel, James' neighbour. A. G. Steel (the brothers were usually known by their initials) was an outstanding cricketer who captained England between 1886 and 1888. In 1884, he scored the first ever test century at Lords, and his name still heads the Honours Board.

Also in attendance, was Alfred Brierley's barrister, William Mulholland (1843-1927), who was instructed by Brierley's solicitors, Messrs. Banks and Kendall. Brierley was present, but was never called to give evidence. On either side of these tables were further tables for the press. The general public were squashed into an area that

[752] For an account of the official opening of the Reading Room see: *Liverpool Mercury*, 29th January 1861.
[753] *Garston and Woolton Reporter*, 21st September 1889.
[754] *Liverpool Review*, 8th June 1889.
[755] *Liverpool Citizen*, 29th May 1889.
[756] *The Adelaide Express and Telegraph*, 11th July 1889.

stretched from the tables to the doorway and also onto a small gallery that ran above the entrance. In one corner of the room, next to the stage, were the various items of evidence that were to be presented at the inquest. One newspaper commented: '*several tin trunks, suggestive of an opera troupe en voyage, but which proved later on to contain boxes, phials, bottles, papers, letters, flypapers, packets of poison, and such like links to be used in forming the chain of circumstantial evidence, whose weakness or strength will be pregnant with liberty or death.*'[757]

Alan Gibson Steel (1858-1914) barrister and former captain of the England Cricket Team.

At 10:00am, Coroner Brighouse got proceedings underway. The jury consisted of local well-to-do businessmen, some of whom were acquainted with the Maybricks and, according to Florence, had '*at one time had been guests*' at Battlecrease.[758] Two of them, Mr T. Case-Morris and Mr Henry Leyland, had attended James' funeral. The foreman was Fletcher Rogers (1823-1891). Like James, he was a cotton merchant and was the senior partner in the firm of Rogers and Calder, based in Tithebarn Street. He had been the President of the Cotton Brokers' Association, and at the time of his death, in 1891, held the important position of Chairman of the Appeals Committee of the Cotton Association. At the end of August 1889, Fletcher Rogers was to move his family into Battlecrease. It is therefore clear that some of the jurors would have viewed James as a friend and a colleague, and must have been shocked by his sudden death.

Although the composition of the jury does appear to be flawed, it drew little criticism at the time. One local newspaper commented that '*the composition of the jury is of a character commensurate with the gravity of the case, the position of the persons more immediately concerned, and the intricacies of the fact to be investigated and solved.*'[759] The main questioning of the witnesses was carried out by Superintendent Bryning, the senior police officer on the Maybrick case. One person who was not at the inquest when it reconvened was Florence. She remained in Walton Gaol, considered too ill to attend.

After the jury had been sworn in, Coroner Brighouse told them it was their duty, after hearing the evidence, to '*say whether she [Florence] is criminally responsible for the death of her husband.*'[760] The coroner made it clear that, at some point, he would have to adjourn the inquest in order to allow the analysis of the deceased's viscera by Mr Davies to be completed.

Following the presentation of plans of Battlecrease drawn by the surveyor Mr Clemmey, the inquest was ready to hear from the first witness – Michael Maybrick. His background as a public performer allowed him to give his evidence in a calm and composed manner. Under the gentle questioning of Superintendent Bryning, Michael ran through the events prior to his brother's death. He said that after receiving a telegram he travelled to Liverpool on 8th May, and on his arrival was shown the letter Florence had written to Brierley. He visited his sick brother and then spoke to Dr Humphreys. That evening he told Florence he was not happy with his brother's treatment, and a professional nurse and a second doctor should have been brought in earlier. Michael told the inquest about how, after speaking to Nurse Gore, he had given a bottle of brandy and a bottle of Valentine's meat juice to Dr Carter for testing. He had angrily reprimanded Florence after seeing her pour James' medicine from one bottle to another. He told the inquest of the various items found around the house, including the package labelled *Arsenic - Poison for Cats*. The package was presented to the jury for viewing. Michael then answered some questions on James' will and insurance policies. Surprisingly, Pickford asked very few questions of this key witness, and the ones he did ask were of little significance. Steel put the final question to Michael, asking him whether he had called the police. This was the only moment when Michael became slightly agitated. He said that had been the sole responsibility of the doctors, who had refused to issue a death certificate.

Nurse Yapp was the second witness. One newspaper report described her as a '*tall, prepossessing young lady, fashionably though neatly clad, she sustained a long and tedious examination with admirable self-possession.*' Another report described her as '*an intelligent woman apparently about the same age as Mrs Maybrick.*'[761] Yapp spoke about the row between James and Florence after the Grand National and the discovery of the flypapers. She

757 *Liverpool Citizen*, 29th May 1889.
758 Maybrick F., op cit., page 39.
759 *Liverpool Mercury*, 29th May 1889.
760 *Liverpool Courier*, 29th May 1889.
761 *Liverpool Courier*, 29th May 1889.

said that prior to the Wirral races she had never known her master to be ill. She spoke about the increasingly serious nature of James' illness, and implied Florence had stopped Dr Hopper from visiting him during his illness. Yapp also recounted the incident when she had seen Florence pour the contents from one medicine bottle into another one.

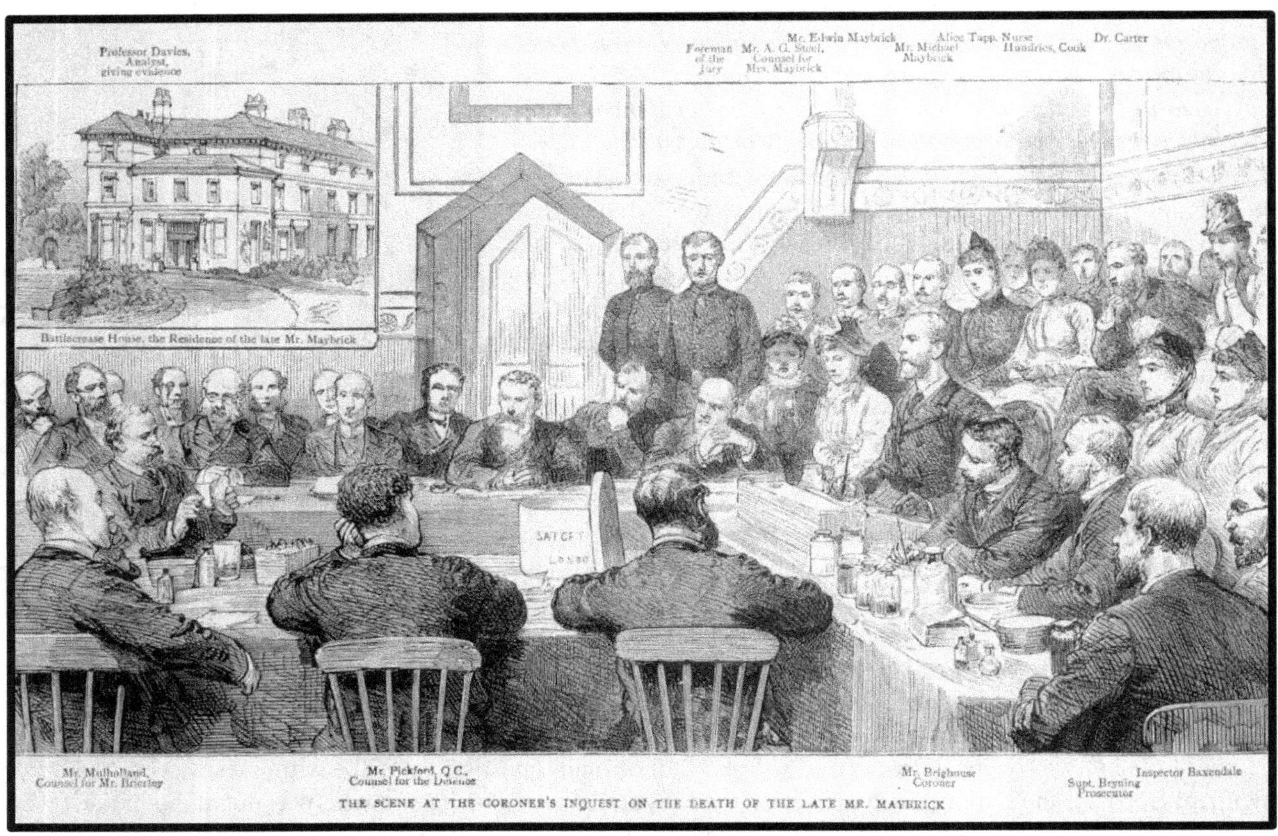

The Coroner's Inquest (*The Graphic*, 15th June 1889)

The crucial moment in her evidence came when she described how she had opened and read the letter that Florence had written to Brierley. Although this act had been widely criticised, the same reporter who praised her self-possession commented '*her act in retaining the letter and handing it to Mr Edwin Maybrick must be commended.*'[762] When the coroner read the letter out loud it created a sensation in the room.

While neither Steel nor Mulholland asked the witness any questions, Pickford quizzed her over some of her statements. He asked if she had seen any medicine bottles, and she answered, '*only malt and cod liver oil, and those kinds of things*.' He then asked her if James had really been in perfect health up to 27th April. Yapp replied, '*No*; *he did not look well for some time, but I did not hear him complain.*'[763] Yapp's statement was important. James may not have complained about feeling ill, but that did not mean he was in full health, as had been implied by Yapp's earlier answers.

After a 30 minute break for lunch, the inquest resumed around 2:15pm. At this point, one of the jurors, Mr W.B. Bowring, told the coroner he was having the greatest difficulty in hearing the exchanges between Bryning and the witnesses. It was a view strongly endorsed by the reporters, who were even further away, and they also asked for the witnesses to speak more loudly.

The first witness after lunch was the housemaid, Elizabeth Brierley. She gave her evidence clearly and concisely, despite appearing to be extremely nervous. She referred to the quarrel after the Grand National and the discovery of the flypapers. Brierley said that prior to James' illness she had completed all the normal duties of a housemaid, but during his illness she only made his bed once and emptied the slops twice. All her usual tasks had been completed by Florence, and she had not been allowed to enter the bedroom.

Brierley was followed by the chemists, Thomas Wokes and Christopher Hanson, both of whom testified to selling Florence flypapers, though only Hanson could remember the exact date of the purchase.

Elizabeth Humphreys, the cook, was next to give evidence. According to one report, she had '*much to say and said it to the point. The appearance of this witness quite belied her profession, for whilst certainly fair, she was neither*

---

762 *Liverpool Citizen*, 29th May 1889.
763 *Liverpool Echo*, 28th May 1889.

fat nor forty.'[764] She said on Tuesday, 30th April, she prepared a basin of bread and milk for James' breakfast. The waitress brought it back to the kitchen and, after listening to her comments, she tasted the food and found it tasted much sweeter compared to how she had originally made it. Humphreys said on Saturday, 4th May she had taken a bottle of medicine, delivered by the chemist's boy, directly to James in his bedroom. She had been sharply told off by Florence, who said all the medicine had to be given to her. Humphreys said she was annoyed at the manner in which Florence had spoken to her. On another occasion, she had made some lemonade as James had particularly asked her to make it as he was so thirsty. When she brought the lemonade to him, Florence had taken it off her hands and told him he couldn't have it. Later the same day, Humphreys returned to the bedroom and asked James how he was feeling. He told her he felt very '*seedy,*' and that '*there are some strange things knocking about.*' Humphreys said she dismissed his comments as she believed him to be '*delirious.*'[765] She also told the inquest about the time Florence had cried in the kitchen, and told her Michael and Edwin Maybrick were blaming her for James' illness.

Mary Cadwallader, the waitress at Battlecrease, also referred in her evidence to the incident about the altered taste of the milk and bread. She told the inquest that James had asked her who had put sugar in the food as it tasted sweet. Cadwallader said she had taken the Du Barry food, that had been prepared by the cook for James, to Florence. She said Florence told her to go downstairs while she wrapped the food in paper and string.

Nurse Gore was the first of the three professional nurses to give evidence. She recalled in detail the incident in which she had witnessed Florence take an opened bottle of meat juice into the inner-dressing room. She said that after Florence returned and put the bottle down, she had asked her to get some ice. As this would have involved her leaving the room, Gore said she refused to do it. The next day the bottle was removed by Michael and given to Dr Carter for analysis. Pickford asked Gore whether, while she was in charge, had anybody but herself given the patient any medicine or food? She replied, '*Not as far as I know.*'

Gore was followed by Nurse Callery. Bryning asked if James said anything to his wife, and she replied he had said, '*Don't give me the wrong medicine again.*'

Nurse Wilson, in her evidence, recalled the time when James said to his wife three times: '*Oh, Florrie, how could you do it; I did not think it of you.*' [Wilson used the pet name *Bunny* and not *Florrie* at the trial.] Wilson said she did not think James was delirious when he made these remarks.

Michael Maybrick was then recalled and produced James' will, which was given to the coroner. Steel explained the will had recently been rewritten, and that Florence would only receive the relatively small sum of £2,000 after James' death. This point should have counted in Florence's favour; however, unfortunately for her, the coroner pointed out that as the seal on the will had not been broken, Florence would not necessarily have known what its contents were. Therefore, the coroner decided not to show it to the jury. Steel then took the opportunity to criticise some of the comments Florence had made to Elizabeth Humphreys about Michael Maybrick hating her. He said the opposite was in fact the case, and Michael had done everything he possibly could to assist her during her married life in order to make her happy.

Christine Samuelson was the last witness of the day. She recounted the events of March 1889, when the Maybricks and the Samuelsons had been at the Palace Hotel, Birkdale. Mrs Samuelson said she had a conversation with Florence in which she said '*she hated her husband.*'[766] This was the remark that Florence was later to say had actually been spoken to Mr Samuelson, and not his wife. Christine Samuelson also accompanied the Maybricks on the trip to the Grand National in April 1889. She told the inquest that on the omnibus on the way home, Florence told her, referring to James, '*I will give him hot and strong for speaking to me like that in public.*' The coroner asked her if Florence was very angry. She replied: '*She was; but I heard no words pass between them.*' The coroner also asked if she was on friendly terms with Florence. Her answer was rather ambiguous: '*I think so.*' Asked by the coroner to clarify what she meant, Mrs Samuelson replied '*Well, I haven't seen her since March.*'[767]

Following her evidence at almost 9:00pm, the coroner adjourned the inquest for a second time so the scientific tests being carried out by Mr Davies could be completed.

It had been a long day and a very bad day for Florence. The prosecution's case had been made thoroughly, whilst the defence team had produced little in the way of counter-arguments. Pickford asked very few questions, and most of them had simply been aimed at clarifying points made by the witnesses. The defence's strategy has been described as a '*policy of close watchfulness,*' with the key aim of trying to '*feel the strength of the case for the prosecution.*'[768]

No questions had been asked about James' heavy use of prescription and non-prescription drugs. The jurors were left with the inaccurate picture that he had been in good health, and therefore his sudden death could well have had criminal causes. In this context, Florence's purchase of flypapers and the discovery of the poison in her personal

[764] *Liverpool Citizen*, 29th May 1889.
[765] *Liverpool Courier* 29th May 1889.
[766] *Liverpool Courier* 29th May 1889.
[767] *Liverpool Mercury*, 29th May 1889.
[768] *Liverpool Daily Post*, 29th May 1889.

trunk must have counted against her. The accounts by the servants that the food tasted differently, and that Florence had been seen pouring medicine from one bottle to another, also counted against her. Nurse Gore's story of how Florence had moved a bottle of Valentine's meat juice added to this narrative of criminal intrigue. Finally, a clear motive had been prescribed to Florence as a result of the letter she had tried to send to Brierley and by the evidence of Christine Samuelson that Florence hated her husband.

In order to obtain the scientific evidence that the prosecution believed would be crucial in securing a guilty verdict, Inspector Baxendale and Coroner Brighouse successfully applied to the Home Secretary for permission to exhume James' body. The exhumation occurred on the night of 30th May. At 11:10pm, vehicles containing two police officers and four doctors arrived at the gates of Anfield cemetery. At the gate, Baxendale showed the paperwork from the Home Office to Mr William Wortley, superintendent of the cemetery, and Mr Roberts, the clerk to the Anfield Burial Board. They opened the gates and the vehicles moved slowly through the cemetery, followed by the cemetery officials and the gravediggers. At the church, some hundred yards from James' grave, the police inspectors and doctors alighted from the vehicles and walked up to his grave. The five cemetery workmen lit their naphtha (an inflammable liquid) lamps and set to work. The lamps '*cast a faint and sickly glow*' over the surrounding tombstones.[769] The gravediggers quickly removed the two cross-flags, and then climbed down into the vault. They fastened ropes to the coffin and proceeded to raise it above ground level. The coffin was then placed with its ends on two garden benches. The screws were undone and the lid removed.

The *Liverpool Daily Post* carried a detailed account of proceedings the next day. Its reporter wrote that there was '*scarcely anyone present who did not feel an involuntary shudder as the pale worn features of the dead appeared in the flickering rays of the lamp held over the coffin by one of the medical men.*'[770] Although James had been in the ground for two weeks, there were few obvious signs of corruption of the body, though most of it – with the exception of the hands and feet – had turned a dark blue. Dr Barron skilfully set to work with his dissecting knife although the body was not taken out of the coffin the doctor removed various parts, including one half of the brain, and placed them in a large stone jar. The coffin was then re-sealed, and the grave was again covered over. Another graphic account of the events was provided by a reporter from the *Liverpool Mercury*. He wrote the:

> *'ghastly process commenced in the presence of Dr Carter, Dr Barron, Dr Humphreys, Mr Wortley, Mr Roberts, Superintendent Bryning, Inspector Baxendale and a police constable. The lid was quickly lifted, the linen shroud torn clear from the corpse, and in a moment the sharp blade of steel deftly directed by Dr Barron, had passed down the centre of the body. The lungs, the heart, the kidneys, a piece of the lower thigh bone were removed, and a moment later the scalp plate had been cleared away and the brain extracted... It was midnight when the solemn stillness of the cemetery was disturbed by the rattle of a couple of cabs making down the central avenue for Walton Lane.*'[771]

James' remains were taken to the laboratory of Mr Davies, at the Royal Institute in Colquitt Street in Liverpool. He carried out his tests behind closed doors in an effort to prevent any of his findings leaking to the press. The exhumation of James' body shows the lengths the police were prepared to go to secure Florence's guilt. If the exhumation had been designed to provide the prosecution with the *coup de grace*, its results were to be rather mixed. Traces of arsenic were found in James' body, but they were well below the levels you would expect to find in the body of a person who had been murdered by arsenic. Although these results were disappointing to the police, they still believed they had sufficient material to obtain a guilty verdict. On the other hand, the lack of arsenic in James' body also provided material for the defence's case that his death had not been caused by arsenical poisoning, but by gastro-enteritis brought upon himself by his drug-fuelled lifestyle.

While the prosecution team was actively pursuing Florence's guilt, the newspapers were beginning to provide details of the defence's case. The *Liverpool Courier* ran a story under the headline, '*The Probable Defence – a new flypaper and poison theory*.' The newspaper wrote that while suspicion pointed at Florence, their readers would be best served by suspending their judgement as the defence team was confident that they could answer all the terrible accusations faced by their client. The article pointed out that some of the medicines taken by James could have produced not only the symptoms he suffered from, but also the viscera traces that were believed to have been discovered by the analysis of his body. The fact that Florence had left the flypapers to soak in an open way '*showed that she had not intended to extract the arsenic for criminal uses.*'[772] The article went on to explain that it was not uncommon for American ladies to use arsenic for cosmetic purposes, and it was certainly common in Germany.

[769] *Liverpool Courier*, 1st June 1889.
[770] *Liverpool Daily Post*, 30th May 1889.
[771] *Liverpool Mercury*, 1st June 1889.
[772] *Liverpool Courier*, 31st May 1889.

The *Liverpool Mercury* ran a story that suggested the case against Florence was a '*weak one.*'[773] It pointed out that the accused had bought the flypapers openly, and only paid cash to avoid the embarrassment of people knowing she was using them for cosmetic purposes. Another account described Florence as being '*popular in society*,' and the '*life and soul*' of a dinner she had attended. Some of the gentlemen present at that event were incredulous she should be accused of murder.[774]

Other articles spoke of how the servants considered her to be a good mistress. Even Nurse Yapp said Florence had '*always been kind to those she employed in domestic duties.*'[775]

Although the course of events were beginning to show some signs of hope for Florence, she remained psychologically and physically shell-shocked in Walton Gaol. Her health had partially recovered, but the news given to her by her solicitor, Richard Cleaver, of events at the inquest and that James' body had been exhumed sent her into a hysterical fit.

On Monday 3rd June, Florence underwent a second formal remand in the prison. At 11:10am a cab from town arrived outside the gaol containing Mr W.S. Barrett, JP, Mr William Swift, the magistrates' clerk, and Superintendent Bryning. They entered the prison and, after consulting with Deputy Governor Mr Gibson they agreed to allow one representative of the press – decided by lot – to witness proceedings.

Although it was a sunny day, the mood inside the prison was decidedly gloomy. The party assembled in the magistrates' room, which was a large, low room, poorly lit by small ground glass windows at one end. Barrett and Swift sat at the head of a long table, whilst Gibson and Bryning sat to one side. A door opened and a large, bearded prison officer entered the room and announced to the deputy governor that the prisoner was outside. In response, Swift requested that Florence should enter the room.

According to the reporter present, '*she appeared quite composed, and evidently half-consciously greeted the gentlemen present with a faint smile. Her dress was deep mourning, with a widow's bonnet, and a long widow's veil which was thrown aside and hung down behind.*'[776] After Florence was seated, Bryning read out the charge against her and asked the magistrates that she be held on remand until the following Wednesday. Swift said Florence's solicitor, Mr Cleaver, had sent a note agreeing to the remand, and Barrett signed the document. Florence was then returned to her cell.

The inquest resumed again on Wednesday 5th June, and was to last for a further two days. This time Florence did attend, and she was moved from Walton Gaol to the Reading Room amid '*a flutter of excitement.*' To avoid the attention of the large crowd of onlookers, Florence entered the building quietly through an entrance at the rear. She was taken to an ante-room that normally served as a library, where she was '*free from the gaze of those desperately eager to see her.*'[777] Florence was to remain in the room for the rest of the day, guarded by two police officers. As a result she would have heard little, if anything, of the unfolding events in the main hall. According to a local reporter, Florence's '*demeanour was one of outward composure and indifference. Her black costume, bonnet and veil were in contrast to her pale face, overcast in spite of its apparent calmness with the shadow of anxiety.*'[778]

Immediately before proceedings commenced at 9:30am, the general public was allowed into the building, and they took up their seats in the gallery over the entrance and at the lower end of the building. The building was soon full, and it was noticeable that the majority of the spectators '*were fashionably dressed ladies, many of them young. Even clergymen found time to be present and share in the general excitement.*'[779] Other newspaper reports agreed, one stating: '*the great majority of the sensation-hunters are of the fair sex and they seem highly satisfied with their privilege of being present. Grey-headed old dames in sombre black, and bright young girls in still brighter summer costume rub shoulders gleefully and ultimately settle down for a day's fill of sensationalism. Many of them prattle and giggle, as though waiting for a curtain to be rung up in a theatre.*'[780]

The proceedings began with the formality of calling the roll of the jurors, which was carried out by Inspector Baxendale. That was immediately followed by an intervention from Florence's counsel, Mr Pickford. He made an application that before they proceeded any further with the evidence of motive, they should deal with the evidence as to the cause of death. Bryning said he had no objection as he wanted an '*exhaustive inquiry.*' Although Bryning was amenable to the request, the coroner was less than pleased and said it was '*a pity that the application was not made before.*' The coroner argued that to listen to the medical witnesses at this stage would '*break the story*' of the eyewitnesses' accounts from Battlecrease. Pickford persisted, arguing that evidence of motive would be irrelevant if it was shown the deceased had not died from arsenical poisoning. After some further discussion, the coroner agreed

---

773 *Liverpool Mercury*, 1st June 1889.
774 *Liverpool Courier*, 1st June 1889.
775 *Liverpool Courier*, 31st May 1889.
776 *Liverpool Courier*, 4th June 1889.
777 *Garston and Woolton Reporter*, 8th June 1889.
778 *Liverpool Courier*, 6th June 1889.
779 *Liverpool Courier*, 6th June 1889.
780 *Liverpool Review*, 8th June 1889.

to accept Pickford's application. This episode shows that the defence team were going to take a more active role in the inquest. If they could prove James' death was not due to arsenical poisoning, then Florence had no case to answer.

The first witness was Dr Hopper, who was described as being a '*rather sparely built elderly man, with sharp features and short black hair just on the turn.*' He faced questions from Bryning, who '*demonstrated much tact and ability, and good method in his questioning... He began rather slowly but soon warmed to his task.*'[781] Hopper said he had been the Maybricks' family doctor since 1881 and knew both James and Florence well, though he was not on '*more intimate terms*' with the couple '*than an ordinary medical man might be expected to be.*' He had treated James for deranged digestion and nervous disorders, and prescribed strychnine and nux vomica but never arsenic.

He believed the Maybricks lived happily, but on 30th March Florence had visited him with a black eye and said she wanted a separation. He tried, at the deceased's request, to bring about a reconciliation. He had a conversation with Florence, who expressed her repugnance for her husband. He said James later told him the two were now happy at home, and he was much obliged to him for his intervention.

In his cross-examination, Pickford quizzed Hopper about James' drug taking. He replied the deceased was in the habit of taking almost any medicines recommended to him by friends, and that he sometimes took double doses. Pickford asked Hopper if it was his impression that James used arsenic as an antiperiodic, and he replied, '*Yes.*' Pickford then asked if, in June 1888, had Florence told him about the deceased's habit of taking all kinds of things, and had asked him to speak to her husband about his habits. Once again, Dr Hopper replied, '*Yes.*' Finally, after hearing his evidence read out, Dr Hopper said he '*was not certain he never prescribed arsenic for the deceased. His impression was that he never prescribed it, but he might have done so, years ago.*'[782]

Dr Richard Humphreys was the next witness. He painstakingly went through all his visits to Battlecrease, outlining James' changing condition and the different treatments he had prescribed. During his testimony the atmosphere of the room became '*exceedingly oppressive, and the coroner, much to the relief of all concerned, permitted an adjournment of a few minutes, which were spent in the sunshine, which made even grimy Garston look bright.*'[783]

When he resumed his evidence, Humphreys said he did not '*anticipate a fatal result*' until Friday, the day before James died. Bryning pressed him whether he was sure that, until that Friday, he had not told anyone that the '*deceased was sick unto death.*' This was a clear reference to a line in the infamous letter that Florence had written to Brierley. Bryning then questioned Humphreys about his knowledge of arsenic and arsenical poisoning. Tellingly, Humphreys said his knowledge of the symptoms of arsenical poisoning only came from books. He said the symptoms would depend entirely upon the amount taken. He continued: '*If a large dose is taken then you will have all symptoms of cholera; then if a moderate dose is taken you will have a diminished degree of this.*'[784] Bryning asked Humphreys what he considered to be the cause of death; he replied, '*They are all consistent with some irritant poison.*'[785]

Not surprisingly, his answers caused a sensation in the courtroom. Humphreys was asked when he first thought the deceased was suffering from the effects of some irritant poison. He replied that he became a little suspicious on the Wednesday prior to James' death, when he started to suffer from diarrhoea and problems with his heart. Coroner Brighouse intervened and asked Humphreys if he could say that, on the Friday, he thought James was suffering from some irritant poison. He replied: '*You see I was under the impression that he might be, so that I cannot say exactly. I was put in a peculiar position, because it had been suggested to me. That strengthened my opinion after the suggestion.*' Humphreys admitted that if the suggestion of arsenical poisoning had not been made to him, then he could not say what conclusions he might have reached about the cause of death. He continued, '*Before the suggestion was made, the symptoms were explainable by what he conceived to be acute congestion of the stomach. I thought the symptoms arose from that cause until the suggestion was made to me. I am of the opinion now that the deceased died from exhaustion consequent on the taking of an irritant poisoning.*'

After a half-hour break for lunch, Humphreys was cross-examined by Pickford, and he was forced to admit that he had no experience of arsenical poisoning or of any irritant poisoning. He was also forced to admit that, prior to the suggestion being made to him, he did not suspect the symptoms were the result of irritant poisoning. Fletcher Rogers, the foreman of the jury, asked Humphreys what ailment he believed James was suffering from when he was first called to the house. He replied that, from the condition of his tongue, Maybrick was suffering from dyspepsia. The rather inconsistent nature of Humphreys' evidence is illustrated yet further by another answer he gave to the foreman of the jury near the end of his testimony. Fletcher Rogers asked whether he would have given an antidote three days prior to James' death if he had suspected the use of arsenic. Humphreys replied, '*No,*' as the deceased had never led him to believe he was suffering from arsenical poisoning. He had no abdominal pain, and had never complained of any pain except in his limbs.

---

781 *Liverpool Review*, 8th June 1889.
782 *Liverpool Mercury*, 6th June 1889.
783 *Liverpool Mercury*, 6th June 1889
784 *The Times (London)* 6th June 1889.
785 *Liverpool Mercury*, 6th June 1889.

Fletcher Rogers (1823-1891)
Foreman of the inquest jury

Next to give evidence was Dr Carter, who in contrast to Humphreys was more concise and consistent in his responses. He outlined his visits to the patient, referred to James' changing condition and to the treatments he had prescribed. He said that on 9th May, Michael Maybrick gave him a small bottle of Neave's food, and the following day he gave him a bottle which was two-thirds full of Valentine's meat juice. When he tested the bottles he found that '*arsenic was present in considerable quantity*' in the meat juice bottle.

When asked what in his opinion was the cause of death, he replied '*irritant poisoning, most probably arsenic.*' Carter said he had formed his opinion prior to the patient's death due to the range of symptoms James had suffered from, of which his '*early death was the crowning symptom, which in the absence of any disease of the heart, lungs or brain, showed strongly there must have been something introduced.*'[786]

Under questioning from Pickford, Carter said that when he first examined James he had not suspected a case of wilful poisoning, but assumed the illness to be caused by '*some grave error of diet.*' He said he had never told Florence, on 7th or 8th May, that her husband was sick unto death as he believed he would recover. Dr Barron, who was present at the post-mortem and exhumation, then gave evidence. He said he had also arrived at the conclusion that death was caused by an irritant poison. Importantly, he added he could not say from the results of the post-mortem examination alone that James had died by arsenical poisoning, but only by '*coupling*' the results with an examination of the history of the case.

Arthur Flatman, the owner of the hotel in London where Florence had stayed two nights with Brierley, was the next witness. He was described as '*a portly, important-looking personage.*' He said he '*had received letters and a telegram from Mrs Maybrick, engaging rooms.*'[787] The essence of these communications was Mrs Maybrick, the wife of the deceased, asked for rooms for her brother-in-law and his wife, Mr and Mrs T. Maybrick. Mr Flatman was asked if a lady, on 21st March, had presented herself at his hotel. He replied he presumed that she had done, as the hotel ledger, which he produced, showed an entry to that effect. He added he did not know anything else about the lady in question, or about any person who may have joined her, and that he would not recognise her if he saw her.

Flatman was followed by Alfred Schweisso, the head waiter at the hotel. His evidence was described as the '*sensation of the day.*' He said he remembered a lady, whom he understood to be Mrs Maybrick, coming to the hotel on the afternoon of 21st March. Schweisso was then taken by Inspector Baxendale into the library where Florence was sitting and, on returning, stated she was the woman who had come to the hotel. He said that about 6:30pm on the day that Mrs Maybrick arrived, a young gentleman took her out. He did not see her return to the hotel as he had gone to bed. The next morning Mrs Maybrick had been joined by another person, whom he presumed was her husband. They stayed at the hotel as '*man and wife*' from Thursday night to Sunday morning. [Brierley actually stayed just two nights, Friday and Saturday.] Superintendent Bryning asked Schweisso if he could recognise the gentleman, and when he pointed at Brierley hissing broke out in court, causing the coroner to threaten to clear the room if it happened again. Not surprisingly, Brierley, '*who had looked anxious all day, was now hot and confused.*'[788] He didn't turn up at the inquest the following day. In January 1890, Schweisso wrote to the Scottish lawyer, MacDougall, stating that he had only been able to recognise Florence at the inquest after a police inspector had twice pointed her out. He also said that he would not have recognised Brierley at all '*if it had not been for the police.*'[789]

Although the main dramatic events of the day were over, three more witnesses gave evidence before the inquest was adjourned. Thomas Lowry, the clerk employed by James, said he had seen him eat food in his office on two occasions. Pickford asked him if James had medicine bottles in his office; receiving the reply Lowry '*did not think there were so many as 27 to 28, but Mr Maybrick did take medicine down to his office.*'

Eliza Busher, the charwoman who cleaned James' office, said she had washed a dirty saucepan, basin and jug – which were produced in court – on 2nd and 3rd May.

The final witness was Mrs Briggs, who described herself as an intimate friend of both Mr and Mrs Maybrick, and had often visited them in their home. She recalled the events that had followed the Grand National in March, and said the couple had later resolved their difficulties. She visited Battlecrease on Wednesday, 8th May and, after being told something by Nurse Yapp, went upstairs into James' bedroom. Before he could say anything to her, she was told

---

[786] *Liverpool Mercury*, 6th June 1889.
[787] *Liverpool Review*, 8th June 1889.
[788] *Liverpool Review*, 8th June 1889.
[789] MacDougall A.W., (1891) op. cit., pages 16-17.

by Florence to go back downstairs. It was after that episode that she sent a wire to Michael Maybrick telling him to come to Liverpool.

Mrs Briggs told the inquest that she was in Battlecrease when James died, and was involved in the search of the house. On 14th May, she was present when Florence wrote a letter to Brierley asking him for money. Florence had asked her to post it, but instead she gave the letter to the police. The coroner then read the letter out in court.

In response to a question from Pickford, Mrs Briggs did say that she might have suggested to Florence that she should write to Brierley if she needed money. Mulholland, representing Alfred Brierley, asked her whether, when she had suggested to Florence that she should write to Brierley, she had warned her that she would show any correspondence to the police, she replied, '*Yes.*'

Mrs Briggs also testified to the finding of several bottles and letters which were in Mrs Maybrick's room. The inquest was then adjourned and Mrs Maybrick was taken to the police station in Lark Lane. A large crowd outside the Reading Room watched as Florence left the building but order was maintained by a strong force of police.

It had been another dramatic day at the inquest, and yet another bad day for Florence. The three doctors had provided much of the evidence. While Humphreys and Carter said they did not suspect arsenical poisoning until it was suggested to them, the fact that all three said that James' death had been caused by some irritant poisoning, probably arsenic, was a strong argument in favour of the prosecution's case. The evidence of Albert Schweisso was another key moment. It was fortunate for Florence that she was in the library and couldn't hear the uproar the head waiter's remarks produced in court.

One other significant event had taken place on that day. At about 2:45pm, Florence had again been formally remanded to remain in custody by a local magistrate. This legal process had taken place in the library, where Florence had spent the whole day. Inspector Baxendale made the request, and once again Florence's solicitor made no objections. One reporter said Florence's demeanour '*betrayed little or no agitation*' as she was remanded. The same reporter wrote that Mrs Maybrick looked much better than she had in Walton Gaol on Monday, and there was more colour in her cheeks.[790]

Florence spent the night in a cell in the nearby police station in Lark Lane, Aigburth, rather than being transported all the way back to Walton. In her autobiography, Florence described the experience:

Lark Lane Police Station (Chris Jones collection)

> '*I passed the night in a cell which contained only a plank board for a bed. It was dark, damp, dirty and horrible. A policeman taking pity on me brought me a blanket to lie on. In an adjoining cell, in a state of intoxication two men were raving and cursing throughout the night.*'[791]

The next day, Thursday, 6th June, the inquest resumed for the final time. The crowd of onlookers that gathered outside the building was considerable, but not as large as the previous day. In the morning, spare seats could be found inside the room. What was more noticeable, was that the overall mood had changed from excitement to tension, as all present were aware that there would be a verdict at the end of the day. The first witness to be called was Edwin Maybrick, who was described in one newspaper as a '*slightly-built gentleman with a light moustache – not unlike portraits of his dead brother... He described the various findings of the incriminating items such as the meat-juice bottles. As he did so he sat with a pencil in his hand, and illustrated his remarks by drawing these articles of furniture with courtesy but almost sang froid.*' He said Florence's dressing table contained just '*odds and ends. For instance, in the drawer there was nothing but paints. She painted a little.*'[792]

Edwin said that on Wednesday 1st May, he had been given a parcel tied up in brown paper by Florence, who told him it was his brother's luncheon. He later saw his brother heat up the food in his office and eat it. In response to a question asked by Steel, he replied he '*was not aware that his brother took arsenic. He knew that he used to take certain medicines occasionally, principally medicines for the liver.*'[793] This reply was, at best, economical with the

---

[790] *Liverpool Mercury*, 6th June 1889.
[791] Maybrick F., op cit., page 38.
[792] *Liverpool Echo*, 6th June 1889.
[793] *Liverpool Mercury*, 7th June 1889.

truth and, at worst, a downright lie. Edwin knew James took strychnine. It is likely he also knew of his brother's arsenic habit. Pickford did not question Edwin about that response, but he did question him about the searches of Battlecrease. In reply, Edwin admitted that '*none of the boxes, bottles and things which he found or saw found, were in places that were locked up.*'[794]

Frederick Tozer, the next witness, said he was a chemist and a druggist who was employed by Messrs. Clay & Abraham's of Castle Street, Liverpool. He said that on 24th April he had made up two bottles of medicine for James, and '*there was no arsenic in either bottle.*'[795]

The next witnesses were the police officers charged who investigated the case. Inspector Baxendale told the inquest of his various visits to Battlecrease and James' office, and the many items he had removed for analysis. Baxendale said he had visited the two chemists belonging to Wokes and Hanson, and had purchased a dozen flypapers from each. He produced some of the flypapers in court as exhibits; the rest he had taken to Mr Davies for analysis.

Sergeant Davenport, a police officer stationed at Garston, said he had examined a linen closet in Battlecrease House and had discovered a dressing case that belonged to Florence. Within it he discovered a selection of powders and pills. Nearby, he also found a small round bottle that contained a white liquid. A Liverpool newspaper provided a graphic description of Davenport's evidence at the inquest: '*Sergeant Davenport on being sworn in took the witness chair with complacency of an old hand, and answered the few questions put to him in the usual official tone and official phraseology. Davenport has a red face and well-oiled black hair. His evidence had presumably been lying heavily on his chest for some time and he got it out as if by rote.*'[796]

The police officers were followed by Edward Davies, the county chemist, who was to be the most important witness to give evidence that day. A contemporary newspaper described him as '*a methodical looking elderly man, not very unlike the late Lord Beaconsfield [Benjamin Disraeli] in appearance.*'[797] Davies, a Fellow of the Pharmaceutical Society and of the Institute of Chemists, was the man who carried out the tests to ascertain whether arsenic could be found in James' body or in the numerous items that had been removed from Battlecrease and James' office.

He said his first involvement in the case came on Saturday, 11th May, the day James died, when Dr Carter asked him to test the bottle of Valentine meat juice moved by Florence. He confirmed Carter's finding that the bottle contained about half a grain of arsenic. He said Inspector Baxendale later brought him a large number of other items for testing. These included parts of James' body, various medicines and bottles taken from Battlecrease and James' office, a pan used to heat food from James' office, deposits from the sinks and lavatory of Battlecrease, and one of Florence's dressing gowns and handkerchiefs. Many of these items had been numbered and been taken to the courtroom so that they could be referred to in a systematic manner.

Davies went slowly and methodically through each one in turn, outlining exactly what he had found and, in some cases, the methods he used to ascertain his results. Important as these findings were, many in the courtroom considered his delivery to be extremely '*dull*' and found it difficult to maintain their interest in his testimony.[798] Davies stated that while not *all* the items contained arsenic, some of them did and, in some cases, in large amounts. For example, arsenic had been found on Florence's handkerchief (distinct crystals of arsenic); the flypapers (two and a half grains on each sheet); the glass and rag found in the hatbox (twenty grains of arsenic); the packet labelled *Arsenic - Poison for Cats* (which he estimated to contain about 109 grains) and in the brown jug that Florence had tied up in brown paper to deliver James' lunch to the office (some distinct traces of arsenic).

Surprisingly, while so much arsenic had been found all around the house, very little had actually been found in James' body. From the parts of the body selected for removal at the post-mortem and at the exhumation, Davies had found just '*1-50th of a grain of arsenic in part of the liver, nothing in the stomach or its contents, but traces, not weighable however, in the intestines.*'[799] Although these levels were very low, Davies did add that '*to his mind it was not absolutely necessary to find a fatal dose in the body in order to arrive at the conclusion that the deceased died from arsenical poisoning.*'[800] Not too surprisingly, Pickford focused much of his questioning on the low levels of arsenic found in James' body. In his final question, he asked if it was the case that only half the quantity of arsenic had been found compared to the amount found in other fatal cases. Davies replied, '*Yes.*' Although this was an important point in favour of the defence, it was not enough on its own to counteract all the other arguments that had been raised by the various medical witnesses during the inquest.

Just before the final witness of the inquest gave her evidence, a significant event occurred. Mr Pickford said to the coroner, '*I understand, Sir, that a communication was made to you at the first sitting by the gentleman who was sworn foreman of the jury. I should like to know whether it is proposed to call him.*' The coroner simply replied,

---

794 *Liverpool Mercury*, 7th June 1889.
795 *Liverpool Daily Courier*, 14th June 1889.
796 *Liverpool Review*, 8th June 1889.
797 *Liverpool Review*, 8th June 1889.
798 *Liverpool Weekly Post*, 8th June 1889.
799 MacDougall A.W., (1891) op cit., page 163.
800 *Liverpool Mercury*, 7th June 1889.

'*No.*' Mr Pickford then said the communication was considered so important the gentleman concerned felt he should no longer continue as the foreman of the jury. Coroner Brighouse said he believed the communication to be '*not relevant,' although he also went on to say that he had informed Mr Steel and Superintendent Bryning about the communication and had discharged the person from serving on the jury.*[801]

This rather cryptic exchange concerned Mr Dalgleish (or Daglish), the original foreman of the jury at the very first sitting of the inquest on 14th May. He had met James on a train around the time of the Wirral races and had seen him take a powder out of his waistcoat pocket. When he asked him what it was, James replied it was strychnine. Dalgleish had provided the coroner with a personal statement informing him of the encounter. The coroner had chosen to inform the police and Mr Steel, the solicitor of the Maybrick brothers about the statement, but had noticeably failed to inform Florence's solicitors, despite the information being so clearly helpful for the defence of their client. MacDougall finds the actions of the coroner in this matter to be '*deplorable.*' He is also critical of Pickford, because he failed to pursue the matter with any vigour and rather meekly said to the coroner, '*I say no more about it, if you do not think it right to go before the jury.*'[802]

The final witness of the day, and of the inquest, was Mrs Hughes. After her testimony Coroner Brighouse commenced his final remarks to the jury '*amid breathless silence. He had his speech prepared, and read it in an earnest, emphatic tone to the jury, laying effective stress on particular words... His lucid and comprehensive review of the of the evidence was very masterful, and he had the whole attention of the court.*'[803]

At the end of his summing up, which lasted about 45 minutes, he asked the jury to consider three key questions: did they believe that death resulted from the administration of an irritant poison? If so, by whom was the irritant poison administered? And if it was administered by Florence, was it administered by her with an intent to take away life? Although the coroner asked the jury to consider these questions, it was the view of at least one newspaper reporter that he had presented the '*ugly facts*' of the case in such a way that '*there was little doubt as to the finding of the jury.*'[804]

The jury moved to Reading Room library, where Florence had been sitting, to discuss the evidence and reach their decisions. Florence was moved, under police escort, to the nearby police station in Garston. Thirty minutes later, at around 5:25pm, the jury returned to the main courtroom prompting the public to scramble '*over seats and tables in the wildest fashion, forming a solid mass around the counsel table.*' The foreman, Mr Fletcher Rogers, said that they were unanimously in the opinion that death had resulted from the administration of an irritant poison. He said that 13 of the 14 jurors had decided that the irritant poison had been administered by Mrs Maybrick, and 12 of the 14 jurors believed that she had administered the poison with intent to take his life.

There was a short delay as a policeman went to collect Florence from the police station and bring her back to the courtroom. According to one eye-witness, '*she was dressed in black, a fall half hiding her face, and a long veil flowing at the back. She braced her shoulders to receive the verdict, but made no reply, seeming to take the whole ghastly matter in a perfectly cool manner.*' She was directly addressed by the coroner, who said: '*Florence Elizabeth Maybrick, the jury have inquired into the circumstances attending the death of your husband, and they have come to the conclusion that he has been wilfully murdered by you. I therefore commit you to the next Assizes to be held at Liverpool, there to take your trial upon that charge.*'

Florence was taken back to the library, and asked by the coroner's clerk if she had anything to say in answer to the charge. She replied that she had been advised by Mr Pickford to say nothing and reserve her defence. She was then driven by cab to Lark Lane police station, where she had spent the previous night. Back in the main room, the coroner turned to the jury and thanked them for their '*invariable courtesy all through this painful inquiry.*'

Outside the building there was a mad scramble by the 50 reporters who had attended the inquest to get their stories to press. Messengers were waiting inside hansom cabs to get the copy as quickly as possible from the courtroom to Garston railway station, while in Liverpool other messengers were awaiting to pick up the copy upon its arrival in the city centre.

Coroner Brighouse's handling of the inquest has been criticised by some modern writers; however, that was not the view of his contemporaries. One local newspaper commented Brighouse had '*regulated the proceedings with great care, legal acumen and judicial dignity.*'[805] It is easy, with the benefit of hindsight, to criticise the verdicts of the jury at the inquest; however, that would be a mistake. While the prosecution had provided a wide range of witnesses, the defence team provided only a few counter-arguments and not a single witness to support their case. All three doctors stated with some certainty that James had been killed by an irritant poisoning, as did Mr Davies, the analyst.

---

801 *The Times (London)*, 7th June 1889.
802 MacDougall A.W., (1896) op cit., pages 26-27.
803 *Liverpool Review*, 8th June 1889.
804 *Liverpool Review*, 8th June 1889.
805 *Liverpool Mercury*, 29th May 1889.

Coroner's Inquest

The facts of the case, as presented to the jury, pointed – as the editorial in the *Evening Express* suggested – with an '*irresistible force*' at a guilty verdict. Florence seemed to have had the motive, the opportunity and the means to have murdered her husband. As the jury was only provided with a rather one-sided view of events, it is perhaps easy to understand why they reached the verdict that they did.

The fact the evidence was so skewed to the prosecution's case means that one has to be critical of certain aspects of the manner in which the inquest was conducted by the police, the coroner and, to some extent, by Florence's own defence team. From the start, the police viewed Florence as the only suspect and assumed that most, if not all, the arsenic in Battlecrease could be traced back to her. Bryning had placed great emphasis on her purchase of the flypapers, yet no fibres from these papers had been found in the various arsenical solutions in the house. The police had taken away many items of her clothing, yet had tested none of James' clothes. The pockets of his jackets must have contained many traces of poisonous drugs.

Illustrated Police News, 15th June 1889

The conduct of the coroner at the inquest can also be criticised. Brighouse was a lawyer by background, with a limited knowledge of toxicology. At the inquest, his ordering of the witnesses' appearances meant he was trying to establish a motive before even establishing that James' death had been suspicious. He said of the statement by Mr Dalgleish – that he had seen James take strychnine just prior to his illness – was '*not relevant.*' In fact it was highly relevant, and the jury should have been made aware of it. The inquest jury was comprised of many of James' friends and colleagues.

It is also possible to be critical of Florence's own defence team. Apart from Dalgleish, they must have known the names of several other potential witnesses who could have testified to James' habit of taking poisonous drugs. Why were they not called to provide evidence? Pickford's decision to reserve his defence at the inquest has been called a '*pragmatic and common-sense attitude*,' because he felt the case was certain to go to trial by jury, and '*he did not want to waste time.*'[806] However, this pragmatic approach could only end in failure.

To Florence, the whole inquest process must have seemed grossly unfair, leaving her with the feeling that she was surrounded by people who were bent on her conviction. In such a climate, she wanted to personally answer some of the criticisms, mistruths and charges made against her. Pickford was very much opposed to her making a personal statement to the court, and strongly advised her not to do so at both the inquest and later at the magistrates' hearing. Florence, though frustrated by this decision, agreed to abide by his advice. Bearing in mind what later happened at her trial when she did make a statement to the court, it was probably a wise decision by her to follow her counsel's instruction.

Perhaps the biggest surprise with regard to the jury's verdicts is that while they were unanimous that James' death was caused by an irritant poison, one member of the jury voted against the motion that the poison had been administered by Florence, and two had voted against the motion the poison had been administered to take James'

[806] Hall J. G. and Martin D. F., *A Perfect Judge*, (Barry Rose Law Publishers, London, 1999) page 98.

life. Unfortunately, the reports do not record who these jurors were, but one can speculate that they were people who knew James and his drug-taking habits well. It had to be the hope of the defence team that if they could provide more details on James' lifestyle, then they might be able to persuade a majority of the jurors of her innocence at Florence's upcoming trial.

LINKS TO THE RIPPER DIARY: WAS MICHAEL MAYBRICK JACK THE RIPPER?

In his book *They All Love Jack: Busting the Ripper* (2015), Bruce Robinson makes some sweeping claims about the Jack the Ripper murders. He argues there was a Masonic backdrop to certain key incidents in the Ripper killings; for example, Sir Charles Warren wanted to quickly remove the graffito left on the wall at Goulston Street after the murder of Catherine Eddowes because it had Masonic overtones.

Robinson makes the case that the country's political elite knew far more about the murders than they admitted and were keen to cover up certain key events and details, for example the truncated manner in which the coroner's inquest into the death of Mary Kelly was conducted. Robinson also made a detailed analysis of the Ripper letters sent to the police, and concluded that some of them came from the murderer and that they provide an insight into the person behind the brutal killings. As well as his account of the canonical murders, he also suggested there were other killings that were perpetrated by the Whitechapel killer, including children, such as the murder of young Johnny Gill in Bradford in December 1888.

Robinson identified James Maybrick's brother Michael as Jack the Ripper, but provides little real evidence to justify his choice. He does point to a composite sketch of the killer that appeared in the *Daily Telegraph* in October 1888, suggesting it bears a close resemblance to Michael. The same picture has also been used to suggest the killer looked like James Maybrick. He argues that there were clues to the Ripper's identity in some of the letters sent to the police, and claims a '*substantial number of these so-called hoaxes were in fact penned by the Ripper.*'[807] Crucially, he suggests that rituals associated with Freemasonry can be seen in the Ripper letters, in the manner in which the victims were killed and in the ways in which their bodies were deliberately left after the murders. According to Robinson, '*Masonry permeates every fibre*' of the murders.[808] The leading figures in the police and government were nearly all Freemasons, and they recognised the Masonic rituals in the murders. To prevent any scandal falling on their organisation, they were forced into a massive conspiracy designed to bury evidence and conceal the truth. Robinson wrote that Sir Charles Warren was a '*transfixed Commissioner of Police*,' and this led him to cover up '*the murderer's tracks.*'[809]

Robinson accepts the view of most Ripperologists and psychologists that the Ripper's '*primary motive*' in committing the murders '*was a hatred of women, and whores in particular.*'[810] He describes the Ripper as a '*recreational killer in the literal sense of the word: a totally sane, highly-intelligent psychopath whose sense of fun animated in some esoteric area of his thinking where humour and homicide collide.*'[811] Therefore, according to Robinson, if you are looking for a '*plausible candidate*' to be the serial killer then you are looking for someone with a big ego, and '*Michael Maybrick had an ego the size of a house.*'[812] As well as his ego, Robinson suggests that Michael '*hated authority almost as much as he hated women.*'[813] On top of that, '*he hated Freemasonry no less than he hated the women he killed.*'[814] As to the children, whom Robinson argues were killed by the Ripper, he suggests that these '*were in some way connected in his head with Florie's kids, surrogates for them just as the Whitechapel scum were surrogates for their mother.*'[815]

Although it was undoubtedly the case that Michael had a large personality, there is absolutely no evidence to suggest he had psychopathic tendencies and hated women. He appears to have been happily married for many years, and we know from the recollections of Amy Main, the daughter of Edwin Maybrick, that Michael's nephews and nieces, including James Chandler (Bobo) and Gladys, were regular visitors to his home on the Isle of Wight.

As to Robinson's assertion that Michael hated authority and Freemasonry, the exact opposite is very much the case. Michael was a leading Freemason, and a passionate supporter of the monarchy. He was a staunch Conservative, and served as a magistrate and as Chairman of the Conservative Association in Ryde on the Isle of Wight. He was to be

807 Robinson B., op cit., page 359.
808 Ibid., page 59.
809 Ibid., page 146.
810 Ibid., page 496.
811 Ibid., page 157.
812 Ibid., page 333.
813 Ibid., page 361.
814 Ibid., pages 534-5.
815 Ibid., page 569.

elected Mayor of Ryde on no less than five occasions. He was also an active member in Britain's military reserve. Michael was an establishment figure to the very core of his being.

Robinson argues that because Michael was a member of several male clubs and organisations, such as the Freemasons and the Volunteer Army, and because he had a '*lungful of bracing male air on the Isle of Wight,*' he was probably a homosexual. He uses the phrase, '*If it walks like a duck, etc., he was probably a bit ducky.*'[816] It is yet another of the unsupported assertions that permeate his book. If being a Freemason and an army volunteer made you a homosexual, then much of England at that time must have been homosexual. If breathing the Isle of Wight air made you gay, then the island must have been some sort of gay paradise.

Michael Maybrick (*Dundee Evening Telegraph*, 9th February 1891)

Michael's brother, James, was a member of numerous male clubs. He was also a Freemason, yet he was a heterosexual. All-male clubs were simply the norm of the nineteenth century. There is absolutely no evidence that Michael Maybrick was a homosexual, and even Robinson admits that he '*doesn't actually know*' that he was one. Robinson also alleges that Michael's musical writing partner Fred Weatherly had homosexual tendencies because they had a personal close relationship. Once again, there is no evidence to support the statement.

According to Robinson, to help cover up his murdering ways Michael needed an alternative Ripper suspect. Therefore, he '*framed his brother James as Jack, offed him with a hotshot of poison, then framed Florence for the murder. I do not doubt that at the time of the outrage Michael's ruse was believed, and the authorities willingly bought into the revelations that his fucked-up brother James was Jack.*'[817]

Robinson adds: '*Moving in the society he did, it wouldn't have been too much of a challenge for Michael to float a whisper that possibly, just possibly, it was his brother who hated his harlot wife enough to kill whores as her surrogate. After all, James was a junkie, much as it pained Michael to say it, already half insane with his addiction and as about as stable as a snake when intoxicated.*'[818] Once again Robinson, has employed sweeping statements, unsupported by evidence, to guide his thinking in the wrong direction.

The evidence suggests that James did not hate his wife. After the bitter quarrel between James and Florence that occurred after the Grand National meeting at the end of March 1889, James asked Dr Hopper to try and broker a reconciliation between himself and his wife. James then went off to London to settle all her debts. While James did undoubtedly take drugs, such as strychnine, the notion that he was half insane from the habit is complete nonsense. His physical health had suffered from the impact of his drug use, but he remained mentally alert, and still visited his office until the very last week of his life.

Robinson argues that Michael was assisted in his plot to kill his own brother, and frame Florence for the murder, by a formidable team he had assembled, each of whom had their '*individual motives for animosity towards Florence.' This team was 'Yapp for her spite, Briggs for her jealously and Edwin for his greed. Michael Maybrick himself constituted the binding ingredient, which was non-negotiable HATE.*'[819]

Robinson argues it was Edwin, not Florence, who put the arsenic into the jug that was used to transport James' food that he ate for lunch in his office on 1st May. Edwin was acting under Michael's direction, and he was a willing accomplice as he was angry at being jilted by Florence in favour of Brierley.

Such a view, that this disparate group could all conspire together to kill someone they loved, is simply not credible. The most likely view is that James slowly but surely killed himself with his excessive use of legal and illegal drugs. Edwin admitted as much, when in May 1889 he told Captain Irving, '*Oh he's killing himself with that damned strychnine.*'

Robinson suggests that the so-called Ripper Diary was actually penned by Michael as part of the process of framing his brother. Once again this is a view that is simply not credible. Robinson describes Michael as a '*man with many pens, who was proficient in various schools of handwriting.*'[820] According to Robinson, Michael was so proficient at copying the handwriting of others that it was he who had actually written the *Dear Blucher* letter and not James. If that is the case, why didn't he write the Diary in James' handwriting? He would have known his handwriting style

[816] Ibid., page 328.
[817] Ibid., page 493.
[818] Ibid., page 497.
[819] Ibid., page 649.
[820] Ibid., page 642.

well, and could have easily made an attempt to replicate it. The fact is the handwriting in the Diary bears no resemblance to James' handwriting. Neither does it bear any resemblance to Michael's handwriting.

Also, why did Michael not provide more intimate and obscure details about James' life? All the details about the Maybrick household are fairly easy to obtain from contemporary or modern sources.

Finally, if Michael wanted the Diary to be found, why did he hide it in such a manner that it did not surface until 1992?

Any objective analysis takes you to three certain conclusions: Michael Maybrick *did not* write the Ripper Diary; he *did not* murder his brother; he *was not* Jack the Ripper.

The final section of Robinson's book is devoted to his view that Freemasonry and the establishment tried to airbrush Michael Maybrick out of history to cover up any involvement or link to his crimes. In 1892, Michael composed the music for the song *The Holy City*, which was to become one of the most popular songs of the nineteenth century. He was at the height of his fame; yet within a couple of years he had, according to Robinson, been transformed from a famous celebrity, a leading Freemason, and a member of some of the most prestigious clubs in England into an '*anonymous recluse married to a fat woman on the Isle of Wight.*'[821] There can be no doubt that Michael did step away from the national limelight. Nevertheless, he did not completely disappear off the public scene, as he went on to be elected Mayor of Ryde, on the Isle of Wight, on no less than five occasions. The local newspaper wrote about him following his death that '*to the people of Ryde the loss will be irreparable, and to very many of them life cannot be exactly the same again since so true a friend, so strikingly endowed and so unique a man has gone where beyond these voices there is peace.*'[822] His funeral in 1913 was one of the biggest ever seen on the island.

It is also not the case, as Robinson asserts, that Fred Weatherly, his old musical partner, largely ignored him in his autobiography. Weatherly refers to Michael on several occasions, calling him '*one of my best friends.*'[823] Shortly before Michael's death in 1913, Weatherly penned the words for the song *Friend o' Mine*, which he dedicated to Stephen Adams, Michael Maybrick's stage name.

If James is an unlikely and implausible candidate to Jack the Ripper, then his brother Michael is an even more implausible one. If Robinson is to believed, then Michael murdered a large number of men, women and children over many years. He even killed James, his own brother, with the help of another brother and some of James' best friends. He wrote many of the letters received by the police around the time of the Ripper killings. The government elite and the country's top police officers were aware that was a Freemasonry link to the crimes, and they did everything they could to cover them up. Michael's motives were a hatred of women and a hatred of Freemasonry.

Every element of this hypothesis is absurd; there is no evidence to support his ideas. Indeed, the evidence that does exist demonstrates that many of his key assertions are inaccurate, and based upon faulty interpretations. This can be clearly seen in his deeply flawed account of Florence's trial, which he claims was rigged by the Freemasons to ensure that Florence was found guilty and hanged. Florence *was* found guilty, but she was never hanged because her sentence was commuted by the Home Secretary – a pivotal member of that governmental elite. He also acted against the preferred wishes of the Queen. According to Robertson, Sir Charles Russell was the architect of Florence's guilty verdict. In fact, Russell wrote a lengthy submission to the Home Office to try and get Florence's sentence commuted. He then spent the rest of his life pleading her case.

These are just a few of the numerous facts that totally and completely destroy the illogical and unsustainable view that Michael Maybrick was Jack the Ripper.

[821] Ibid., page 744.

[822] *Isle of Wight County Press*, 30th August 1913.

[823] Weatherly F.E., *Piano and Gown* (Putnam and Sons, London, 1926) page 276.

13

ROAD TO CONVICTION

Following the guilty verdict at the inquest, Florence was returned to the police cells at Lark Lane where she was to spend several nights waiting for the magisterial hearing. Her first night in the holding cell had been extremely unpleasant, with just a plank for a bed and constant noise from drunken inmates housed in the five neighbouring cells.[824]

Her next few nights were spent under better conditions. Although she remained in an ordinary cell, it had been furnished with a bed and one or two articles of furniture. As no other prisoners were in custody at the building, she '*was allowed to leave her cell and promenade the corridor. This is strongly secured and gives the prisoner the advantage of a little necessary exercise. She passes a good deal of time in this way.*'[825] Despite this small element of freedom, Florence was closely watched by Sergeant Hodgson, the police officer resident in the police station, and was not allowed to eat any food without an officer being present. Mrs Pretty, a local greengrocer from whom Florence had occasionally ordered fruit, sent her '*a daily gift of her best with a note of sympathy.*' Florence commented that this deed was '*all the more striking in its generosity and nobleness, since the charity of none other of my own sex had reached to that degree of justice to regard me as innocent until proven guilty.*'[826] She received her meals from a nearby hotel. Florence was allowed to read the newspapers and took an avid interest in articles about her own case.

She met regularly with Mr Cleaver to discuss her strategy. Although there was a lull between the inquest and the magistrates' hearing, the '*universal interest in the proceedings shows no sign of abatement, and stories of a sensation character are still actively circulated in the city.*'[827] One article concerned a rumour that Florence was suffering from '*some mania.*' This view originated from one of the jury members at the inquest, who was '*intimate*' with the Maybrick family. He said there is '*something wrong with Mrs Maybrick.*'[828]

The magistrates' hearing commenced on Wednesday, 12th June 1889 and lasted two days. It was held in the County Sessions Court at the bottom of Islington, Liverpool opposite St George's Hall. In her autobiography, Florence wrote that she had been taken to the court from Lark Lane Police Station the night before the hearing, but this was not the case.[829] Most contemporary newspapers suggest she was taken to the court very earlier on the morning of the hearing. According to a report in the *Liverpool Daily Courier*, she was taken from Lark Lane just after 5:00am on Wednesday morning in a '*brougham driven by a coachman in livery.*' She was in the custody of Police Sergeant McKeand, Police Constable Hammond and a female warder. The *Courier*, which was rarely sympathetic to Florence's plight, commented that it was yet '*another instance of the great consideration which has been extended to Mrs Maybrick.*'[830] In reality, the police

The County Sessions Court, Islington, Liverpool
(Chris Jones collection)

[824] Maybrick F., op cit., pages 38-39.
[825] *Liverpool Courier*, 10th June 1889.
[826] Maybrick F., op cit., pages 38-39.
[827] *Liverpool Daily Courier*, 10th June 1889.
[828] *Liverpool Weekly News*, 8th June 1889.
[829] Maybrick F., op. cit., page 42.
[830] *Liverpool Courier*, 13th June 1889.

were just taking a sensible precaution, as they wanted to avoid a scene outside the courthouse. Their actions were justified, as a large crowd did build up later in the day but by then Florence was already safely inside.

The court itself was relatively small, and could only hold about 200 people including the spectators, barristers and all others involved in the legal proceedings. Sir William Bower Forwood (1840-1928) was the chairman of the bench, and at one time was assisted by as many as ten other magistrates. Some reporters speculated that many of them had only turned up to '*get a good view of an interesting prisoner*.' Like the inquest, most of those in court were women; one estimate suggested they outnumbered men by two to one. Many of them '*glared persistently and shamelessly at the unfortunate creature in the dock.*'

The hearing was similar to the inquest, in that nearly all the witnesses, with the notable exception of Mrs Samuelson, who had disappeared, were the same. Florence Maybrick sat in the dock in a large and comfortable armchair. Next to her sat an official attendant, also dressed in black but without a veil. A reporter wrote that Florence was:

> '*An extremely slight young woman of middle height and, apparently, of somewhat elegant but rather underdeveloped figure. She wore, of course, the sombre garments of widowhood, which were trimmed with the deepest crape, her crape bonnet and veil met so closely at the forehead that only a few specks of the edge of the widow's white cap could be seen, and her hair was entirely hidden. Her carriage in entering the dock and her conduct while there was graceful and calm, being just, in fact, what one would expect from a woman of first-class training.*'[831]

The first person to give evidence was Superintendent Bryning. He said it was duty, before calling any witnesses, to run through '*the salient points of the case.*'[832] It took him 25 minutes to complete his statement. He spoke about the flypapers, saying that '*a servant named Brierley... found a number of flypapers steeping in a basin on one of the tables in the [bed]room... What became of the flypapers and the liquid in which they were seen there is absolutely no trace. But it may be remembered that about this time... Mr Maybrick's health became unsatisfactory.*'

Bryning spoke about the food James heated up in his office and ate. He said the pan, basin and jug were '*found to contain arsenic. It was remarkable that these were the only things in the office which contained arsenic – those which had warmed the things which had undoubtedly come through Mrs Maybrick's hands. On Saturday the 4th May, Mr Maybrick took to his bed, and from that date to the 8th May, he was attended solely by the prisoner, who forbade the servants to go near him, and directed that medicines or foods which were to be given to the deceased should be given to him from her hands only.*'

He then moved on to what he termed the '*letter incident*,' saying it was '*exceedingly remarkable*' that Florence referred to her husband as '*being 'sick unto death.*' Bryning then focused on the incident in which Nurse Gore had seen Florence move the meat juice. He said Dr Carter tested the bottle, and '*found the contents mixed with arsenic.*'

Bryning finished by speaking about all the arsenic that had been discovered in Battlecrease after James' death.

The witnesses on the first day included Mrs Briggs, Alfred Schweisso and the servants from Battlecrease. MacDougall has argued the police were repeating the tactics that had served them well at the inquest, in that they were putting the '*cart before the horse.*' In other words, they were focusing on motive before they had established that a murder had actually occurred.[833]

Nurse Yapp was called to the witness box after lunch and, due to the slow questioning of Mr Swift, clerk to the magistrates, her evidence took over two and a half hours to complete. Many in the court found the proceedings extremely monotonous, and the number of magistrates on the bench dwindled to three. The loss of interest was partly the result of few new facts emerging about events, and also because the room had become extremely hot. Some of the ladies in the courtroom started to fan themselves with newspapers which they had pleated. A further problem was that many of the witnesses spoke quietly, and their responses were barely audible in the room.

Even Florence seemed to lose interest in the testimonies of the witnesses. One eye-witness wrote: '*Mrs Maybrick sat without moving, her gloved hands folded before her, and holding between her fingers the piece of lead pencil and a folded sheet of note-paper. She did not, however, take any notes. Indeed, it is doubtful if she heard much of the evidence at all. Her manner was now of one who having got into a situation where further effort is futile, is content to allow stronger forces to take their course. Compared with the female attendant beside her in the dock, she looked pallid and bloodless.*'[834]

It was only when Nurse Yapp spoke of finding arsenic in her trunk that Florence appeared to take any real notice of the proceedings. She made a few notes, and passed them to her solicitor. Under cross-examination by Mr Pickford, Nurse Yapp stated that the trunk in which the arsenic was found was in ordinary use as a children's trunk.

[831] *Liverpool Review*, 15th June 1889.
[832] *Garston and Woolton Reporter*, 15th June 1889.
[833] MacDougall A.W., (1891) op cit., page 167.
[834] *Liverpool Daily Courier*, 13th June 1889.

Edwin Maybrick was the last witness of the first day. He recounted the story of how James had eaten the Du Barry food in his office that Florence had packaged. As he was about to leave the witness box, Bryning put to him what many considered to be the most pertinent question of the day: '*Did he know whether his brother took arsenic as a medicine*?' According to one report, Edwin's answer was a '*decided one – the deceased never did.*'[835]

The Magistrates' Hearing (Evening Express, 14th June 1889)

After Edwin left the witness box, the court adjourned for the day and Florence was escorted out of the room. As she did so, some of the female spectators at the rear of the room began to hiss. This demonstration of disapproval was quickly suppressed by the magistrates. Florence did not return to Lark Lane Police Station, instead spending the night in '*one of the retiring rooms at the top of the courthouse, where a luxurious couch had been specially provided for her. A female attendant stopped with her, and Sergeant Hodgson kept guard outside the door, his weary vigil being relieved by another officer at eight o'clock in the morning, when Mrs Maybrick rose after a good night's rest.*'[836] Florence spent some of the time talking to the daughter of the police sergeant, who was very friendly and sympathetic, and this helped to raise her spirits.

At precisely 10:00am on Thursday, Florence entered the courtroom again and proceedings recommenced. Crowds outside were smaller, and even inside the court was only half full, which meant the room was much cooler than it had been on the first day. Once again most of the onlookers were female, including a '*remarkable*' number of young girls who scrutinised Florence with opera glasses, an '*act which betrayed remarkable rudeness.*'[837]

The witnesses on the second day included Michael Maybrick. He was described as a '*tall, good-looking person with a moustache and a bronzed complexion which gives him more the appearance of a sea captain than that of a composer.*'[838] He provided similar evidence to his testimony at inquest, though one new piece of information did come to light during Pickford's cross-examination of him. Michael admitted he had received a letter from Florence early in March, in which she had asked him to speak to James about some medicine he was taking. He said he had not kept the letter.

Under cross-examination, Dr Humphreys said that sometime in early March Florence had asked him to speak to James to try and stop him taking some white powder which was badly affecting him. He also admitted that Florence had spoken to him again about this mysterious white powder when he had first treated James on 28th April.

As at the inquest, the evidence of the analyst Mr Davies was to be a crucial element of the prosecution's case. Probably as a result of Davies' methodical but rather rambling presentation at the inquest, Sir William Forwood told him that the bench only wanted to know his results and not the methods he had employed to obtain them. This instruction not only helped speed up Davies' presentation, but it also led to greater clarity for the non-scientific observers. Davies said he had tested every item he had been given which it was possible or reasonable to analyse. For example, he said the '*Parisian boot polish and insect* powder' were two items he had been given that were impossible to properly test.[839] Davies then ran through the various bottles and vessels in which arsenic or traces of arsenic had been found.

As at the inquest, Pickford focused much of his cross-examination on the low levels of arsenic found in James' body. Pickford asked Davies if it was in the liver that the largest amount of arsenic in cases of poisoning was usually to be found. Davies replied, '*Yes.*' Pickford then asked that if it was the case that only half the quantity of arsenic had been found in James' body compared to other fatal cases. Davies replied, '*Yes, exactly half.*'

Pickford then took his line of questioning to an area he had not explored at the inquest. He wanted to know if any traces of vegetable fibres had been found in the Valentine meat juice bottle. Davies replied he had not found any fibre that he could be sure came from flypapers. His answer indicated that the flypapers, which the police and the prosecution had made so much of, were not the source of the arsenic in the meat juice.

---

835 *Liverpool Daily Courier*, 13th June 1889.
836 *Liverpool Weekly News*, 15th June 1889.
837 *Liverpool Mercury*, 14th June 1889.
838 *Liverpool Review*, 15th June 1889.
839 *Liverpool Mercury*, 14th June 1889.

The magisterial hearing finished at 6:30pm on Thursday evening. Pickford asked the magistrates if they had decided to send the case for trial before a jury at the Assizes, because if they had he would not proceed with a defence. Sir William Forwood and Mr Barrett retired from the bench for a short time. When they returned they said they had decided to send the case for trial. Sir William then asked Florence to stand, and he formally told her that she was committed to the Assizes on the charge of murdering her husband.

Florence did not say anything. As she walked out of court some of the onlookers rushed to try and get close to her, but the police held them back. A reporter wrote: '*It was a curious and pitiful spectacle to behold this fragile looking young widow in her sombre but elegant attire disappearing from a court full of hungry sensation-mongers.*'[840]

The magistrates' hearing had been virtually a re-run of the inquest. The evidence was the same, the witnesses were almost the same, and the verdict was identical. It is easy to be critical of the magistrates' decision, but it is difficult to see how else they could have acted on the basis of the evidence that had been presented to them.

Following the magistrates' decision, Florence was returned to Walton Gaol where she was to remain for the next six weeks while she awaited her trial. She wrote that this '*very terrible. The mental strain was incessant, and I suffered much insomnia. The stress and confinement was telling on my health, as was the separation from my children.*'[841] When she first returned to Walton Gaol following the magistrates' hearing she was in a state of complete nervous exhaustion, and spent some time in the prison hospital under the supervision of Dr Beamish, the prison doctor. When she had recovered she was moved to a cell in the female quarter of the goal.

Although prison life must have been a major shock to Florence, as a prisoner on remand she did enjoy certain privileges that were not open to the convicted felons inside the jail. By paying a small weekly sum, a prisoner could get a larger cell and extra bedding. Florence was able to wear her own clothes and have her food brought into the prison. She was also allowed to receive books and newspapers, and she avidly read all the stories about herself and her deceased husband. Some reports even suggest that she was allowed extra furniture in her cell. Florence was able to see her friends twice a week, on Tuesdays and Fridays. As well as her mother and solicitor, who were regular visitors, Florence received support from some American residents in Liverpool, including the American consul, the Hon. Charles T. Russell, and from some American friends of the family who lived in London. One group of people who gave her limited support were the cotton merchants and brokers on the Exchange. The Maybrick case remained the '*main topic of conversation*' on the 'Change, and the feeling there was '*generally adverse*' towards Florence.[842] Nevertheless, we know from the Charles Ratcliffe letter that some members of the 'Change were sympathetic and supportive of Florence at this time.

Although Florence was incarcerated back in Walton Gaol there was to be no let-up in the Maybrick hysteria that was still engulfing the city. A columnist in the *Liverpool Citizen* wrote:

> *'It is useless to write or talk of any other subject at present in Liverpool than the Maybrick tragedy. A few weeks ago, the time-honoured shake of the hands with "A fine day isn't it?" or "Wretched weather eh?" were the fashionable terms of greeting, but these have entirely been wiped away by the Maybrick business. Everyone you meet now shakes you by the hand, and in the same breath as the familiar "Haw! How d'ye do?" gasps out "And what do you think of Mrs Maybrick?"'*[843]

An enlarged picture of Florence was put on display in a photography shop in Bold Street, Liverpool, drew large crowds. Sightseers still flocked to Battlecrease, even though it had been boarded up and was guarded by the police. Some of the curious onlookers took away plants as souvenirs, or in the hope they could be sold at an opportune moment.[844] Nowhere was the interest greater than at the 'Change. When an itinerant street singer appeared one lunchtime on Rumford Street, near the 'Change, and started to sing some '*doggerel lines on the Maybrick tragedy,*' he was immediately surrounded by a '*crowd of brokers, merchants and others who eagerly listened to his rhymes and purchased the small leaflet on which the words were printed.*' The leaflet, which originally cost a penny, sold so fast that its price rose to sixpence as copies became scarce. The incident provided '*striking proof of the all-absorbing interest which is felt on the Maybrick case on 'Change.*'[845] As well as songs, scurrilous leaflets also appeared. When one man was charged with selling indecent material about the Maybricks, he angrily told the magistrates that he didn't think it was fair he should be singled out when so many other people were doing the same thing.

The Maybrick mania engulfing the city did not just focus on Florence; her dead husband, her mother and Alfred Brierley were also the subject of sensational rumours and newspaper storylines. Mr J. Treeve Edgcome, a lawyer and advisor to Baroness von Roques, had the task of trying to counter the '*many absurd and idle rumours*' that were

---

840 *Liverpool Review*, 15th June 1889.
841 Maybrick F., op cit., page 46.
842 *Liverpool Weekly Courier*, 15th June 1889.
843 *Liverpool Citizen*, 12th June 1889.
844 *Liverpool Mercury*, 22nd June 1889.
845 *Liverpool Daily Post*, 21st June 1889.

circulating about the Baroness in the run-up to Florence's trial. One of the most persistent of these rumours was that the Baroness' first two husbands had died under suspicious circumstances. On 19th June he had a letter printed in several Liverpool newspapers. In it, he wrote that the Baroness' first husband died from '*inflammation of the brain caused by the extreme tension and anxiety*' as a result of severe financial difficulties faced in the American Civil War, while her second husband died as the result of a '*mortal wound*' that he sustained in action. [Du Barry had in fact died from consumption.] He said the rumours concerning the Baroness had only one object, to '*prejudice*' the approaching trial of her daughter. He finished by stating that he hoped his letter would have the effect of '*stopping all the tittle-tattle and the foulest and most unfounded rumours that have reached her ears.*'[846]

One of the oddest stories was a rumour that James had poisoned two dogs belonging to a certain Mr Ernest Tinne, who lived in Mersey Road, Aigburth because their barking had annoyed him. Mersey Road was close to Battlecrease, and James would have regularly walked up the road as it was the location of the railway station. The local newspaper, the *Garston and Woolton Reporter*, investigated the story and concluded that it was untrue. Their report pointed out that not only was there '*considerable distance*' between Battlecrease and the residence at which the dogs lived, there were also dogs in other residences much closer to Battlecrease. The report stated:

> '*The dogs in question died suddenly, and one was buried without examination, but a chemist who was not an analyst examined, it is said, the intestines of the other. From what the gardener told him and what he saw, he formed the opinion that the dog died of arsenical poisoning, but the supposition lacks scientific proof. A further statement was made to the effect that Inspector Baxendale examined the boots of the late Mr Maybrick, and found that they corresponded with footmarks near the dog kennels. The truth is that the inspector made no examination of boots and found no bootmarks. As the field adjoining Mr Tinne's residence is ploughed, he would, had there been any marks, have experienced no difficulty in finding them.*'[847]

The report must be taken as authoritative, as the newspaper covered the area which included both Battlecrease and Garston Police Station. If the report had been inaccurate the newspaper would have been forced to publish a retraction, however, no such retraction ever appeared. The newspaper explains the false allegation as an '*effort to educate the jury who are to try the case.*'[848] Although the stories about James poisoning the two dogs were untrue, some of the stories that appeared in the press at this time about his habit of taking arsenic were accurate. A reporter from the *Liverpool Daily Post* set about trying to discover how widespread James' use of arsenic had been. He spoke to several Liverpool chemists, including Mr Edwin Garnet Heaton, who had kept a shop in Exchange Street East for seventeen years. In June 1889, Heaton told the journalist:

> '*Yes; I knew the late Mr James Maybrick. He was for a long time a pretty regular customer of mine though, singularly enough, he never gave me his name. I recognised him immediately when I saw his photograph. He constantly used arsenic... He was extremely reserved in making his purchases, which he always paid for, and always refused to have booked.*'[849]

This interview is significant, as not only does it confirm that James was a regular user of arsenic, but it also shows he tried to hide the fact that he used the drug.

The *Liverpool Mercury* ran a story that had originally featured in an American newspaper. In the story, Nicholas Bateson – James' friend with whom he had shared lodgings in Norfolk, Virginia – stated James was in the habit of taking arsenic. He was prepared to give evidence at Florence's trial, and referred to a conversation that had taken place between James and the late Dr Ward, in which Dr Ward had told James that if he continued to take the drug in such large quantities, he would certainly kill himself.[850] Arnold Cleaver, Florence's solicitor, travelled to America to find witnesses such as Bateson so that they would have evidence in the trial of James' arsenic habit.

Back in Liverpool, the *Weekly Courier* printed a letter from a Liverpool chemist on the topic of arsenic eaters. He said there were people who regularly took arsenic, but added it was difficult to provide exact numbers as most arsenic-eaters conceal their drug use. He wrote the '*principal reason alleged for eating arsenic is that it protects from disease... and as a remedy against difficulty of breathing and as an aid to the digestion of food.*'[851]

In a letter from Florence to a friend, written in Walton Gaol just prior to her trial, she wrote: '*I hear the police are untiring and getting up the case against me regardless of expense.*'[852] The catalyst for the extra police activity was

---

846 *Liverpool Mercury*, 19th June 1889.
847 *Garston and Woolton Reporter* 22nd June 1889.
848 *Liverpool Weekly Post*, 8th August 1889.
849 *Liverpool Daily Post*, 15th June 1889.
850 *Liverpool Mercury*, 29th June 1889.
851 *Liverpool Weekly Courier*, 22nd June 1889.
852 Maybrick F., op. cit. page 47.

probably the stories that were beginning to appear in the press about James' arsenic habits. They must have been concerned that these stories could undermine their case. Key witnesses were re-interviewed, including the chemists who had sold Florence the flypapers and some of the Maybrick servants. James Grant, the gardener at Battlecrease, was interviewed for the first time. Alfred Brierley had to face the embarrassment of being subpoenaed and was instructed to provide the police with any letters or documents he had in his possession that were relevant to the case. His solicitors responded by telling the police their client had no relevant letters, and that he was not able to make any further statements as he had '*made arrangements to go away.*'[853] Perhaps the one important action taken by the police at this time was sending parts of James' internal organs, removed at exhumation, down to London to be retested by a Home Office scientific expert. On 22nd July, Inspector Baxendale took eleven jars containing James' body parts down to London for Dr Stevenson to analyse.

On 8th and 9th July 1889, at the gallery of Mr Leete and Mr Branch of Hanover Street, Liverpool, the furnishings and effects of Battlecrease were auctioned. The decision to auction all of the Maybricks' furniture, plus many of their personal items, was taken by Thomas and Michael Maybrick, the trustees of James' estate. This decision seemed to be contrary to the terms of James' will, which specified that the '*furniture should remain intact, and to be used in furnishing a home which can be shared by my widow and children, but the furniture is to be the children's.*'[854]

It is unlikely the Maybrick brothers consulted Florence before selling. Not surprisingly, they have been criticised for what seems to be a high-handed decision. On the other hand, the decision to auction the items did make sense. Battlecrease was an expensive luxury that could no longer be afforded. No-one had lived in the house for almost two months and the servants, with the exception of the gardener, had been released. Florence was desperate for money for her defence, and it made sense to auction the furniture to try and capitalise on the Maybrick hysteria engulfing the city. The latter was shown by the '*crowded state*' of the auction room during the two days of the sale, which showed '*the enormous amount of interest which is centred in anything connected with the Maybrick mystery.*'[855]

Mr Leete, a friend of the Maybricks, conducted the auction himself. Interestingly, he is listed as one of those who attended the Wirral races in April 1889. He told the expectant bidders at the start of proceedings that it was:

> '*his painful duty to offer the furniture of the late Mr Maybrick, whom he knew very well. He knew both the dead and the living, and while they must all have profound sympathy at the sad event, he hoped they would all withhold their judgment as Englishmen ought to do, for events might yet tend to exculpate the accused from this most stupendous and terrible charge. The surroundings of that room would indicate to those present the social rank of the family and the beauty and artistic taste displayed in the home. He hoped, at all events, that they all would be anxious that justice should be done according to the laws of England, as doubtless it would be done when the case for the defence was presented. Meanwhile, without feeling or prejudice, he asked his audience to enter into the business of the sale.*'[856]

Mr Leete's opening address, which was apparently met with a murmur of approval, is of interest as it indicates that some sympathy for Florence's plight existed in Liverpool, even amongst James' friends and acquaintances. Further, if he did know James '*very well,*' then he probably also knew a little about his drug-taking habits and that is presumably why he was prepared to withhold his judgement until after the full facts had emerged. A great range of items went on auction over the two days. The items that attracted the most bids were a Collard & Collard cottage piano-forte which sold for 38 guineas, the Maybricks' bedroom suite of American walnut for 36 guineas, and a Queen Anne display cabinet for 22½ guineas. As well as these, other items sold included oak tables, Chippendale chairs, silver plate, clocks, Japanese and Chinese ornaments, blankets, curtains, Turkish and Persian carpets, two Dresden candelabra and a pair of bronze statuettes. Several oil and water paintings and some engravings were also sold. Despite the morbid curiosity that the auction attracted, a local newspaper still commented that the sale was '*conducted throughout with admirable good taste and consideration by this experienced auctioneer.*'[857] Another newspaper described the purchasers as '*chiefly connoisseurs and friends, and it was noticeable that the brokers had very few opportunities of buying against bids that were in many instances more than the market value of the articles offered.*'

A couple of days later a separate auction took place of all the wines in James' cellar at Battlecrease. It was conducted at the public saleroom run by Messrs Unwin and Jackson, and '*realised very good prices.*'[858] When the bills and commission had been paid from both auctions, Michael Maybrick paid £300 – half of the total amount of money raised by the sale – to Florence's defence fund. Not all of Florence's possessions had been sold at the auction; her clothes and some small items that belonged to her were sent to her solicitor.

---

853 HO 144/1638/A50678.
854 Ryan B., op cit., page 112.
855 *Liverpool Citizen*, 10th July 1889.
856 *Garston and Woolton Reporter*, 13th July 1889.
857 *Liverpool Citizen*, 10th July 1889.
858 *Liverpool Weekly Courier*, 13th July 1889.

Two weeks before the trial the composition of the prosecution team was finalised. Mr John Addison, QC, MP (1838-1907), was appointed lead counsel. He was an Irish Roman Catholic who had made a name for himself as a prominent barrister in England on the Northern Circuit. He had served as the Recorder of Preston from 1874 to 1890, and was also, since 1885, Conservative MP for Ashton-under-Lyme. Physically he was a heavyset man, but he possessed a clear, logical mind, and he was not going to be overawed by the defence lawyers at the trial, no matter who was selected.

Mr William McConnell (1837-1906) was appointed junior counsel for the Crown. Like Addison, McConnell was from an Irish Roman Catholic family. His father was a magistrate of County Down. McConnell had been educated in Belfast and London University and was called to the bar in 1862, joining the Northern Circuit where he was soon recognised as one of the leading juniors. He was made revising barrister for Liverpool in 1868, and assisted in the prosecution of Mrs Flannagan and Mrs Higgins in Liverpool in 1884. At Florence's trial, although Addison led the prosecution and made the key opening and closing speeches, McConnell led the examination of some of the important witnesses.

John E. W. Addison QC, MP
(1838-1907)

Sir Charles Russell (1832-1900) was appointed to be Florence's counsel. An Irish Roman Catholic, Russell grew up in Ulster. He became a solicitor in Ireland in 1854, moving to England in 1859 and joining the Northern Circuit. He soon acquired a considerable reputation, and was made a Queen's Counsel in 1872. In 1882, Russell became an MP, representing the constituency of Dundalk. In 1885 he was elected the member for South Hackney, and served for a short time as Attorney General in Gladstone's Liberal Government.

Although Russell was undoubtedly a brilliant lawyer, he had, prior to Florence's trial, a poor recent record of defending people at murder trials. He arrived at the trial exhausted after successfully defending the Irish Nationalist Charles Stewart Parnell from the charge of sedition. He had questioned more than 340 witnesses, often in a bitter atmosphere, and his final speech in defence of Parnell had lasted six days. The case had made Russell something of a celebrity, especially in Liverpool, where there was a large Irish population. Lord Rosebery, a future Liberal Prime Minister, wrote to Russell after his closing speech at the Parnell case, saying '*You have at a bound passed from solid reputation to supreme eminence.*'[859]

Sir Charles Russell QC, MP
(1832-1900)

Given Russell's status and reputation, his appointment as defence counsel was seen as something of a coup for Florence's solicitors, and it gave a real boost to her supporters who believed that Russell could provide the magic that would help deliver a Not Guilty verdict. William Pickford, who had acted as Florence's counsel at both James' inquest and at the magisterial hearing, was appointed as the junior counsel to Russell. Pickford attended the Liverpool Collegiate School and Oxford University. Prior to Florence's trial, he had worked as a barrister on the Northern Circuit for almost 15 years, though much of his work had been in commercial and shipping cases. He had become recognised as one of Liverpool's most prominent legal figures, and a contemporary local newspaper described him as a '*very fine man and his tall straight figure and handsome face are well known. He is one of the ablest counsels in this part of the country.*'[860]

The cost of Florence's defence was substantial. The Baroness managed to raise a few thousand pounds by contacting family relatives and friends in Britain and America. Alfred Brierley, in an interview after the trial, claimed he had '*spent £6,000 on the defence of Mrs Maybrick.*'[861] This is an extremely large amount, and it is more likely that he only contributed a couple of hundred pounds. Michael Maybrick handed over £300, representing Florence's share of proceeds from the auction of the items from Battlecrease.

Another source of Florence's income was a partial pay out on the insurance policy that James had taken out in October 1888. The policy was with the Mutual Reserve Fund Life Association of New York and was for £2,000, payable to his wife. The company had offices in North John Street, Liverpool and had a policy of making advanced payments to clients who faced a pressing financial need. In line with this policy, in early July 1889 they sent a payment of £200 to Florence's solicitors. The Cleaver Brothers sent a cable to the company to acknowledge the receipt of the money, and to thank them because the advanced payment '*was of additional value under the present*

[859] Quoted in O'Brien R. B., op. cit., page 256.
[860] *Liverpool Review*, 15th June 1889.
[861] *Garston and Woolton Reporter*, 7th September 1889.

circumstances.'[862] Due to the guilty verdict at the trial, Florence eventually only received around half of the money that was due to her if the policy had been paid out in full.

One of the key decisions that Florence's defence team had to make was whether to ask for the trial to be moved from Liverpool. In her autobiography, Florence wrote:

> '*The press had for two months supplied nourishment in the form of the most sensational stories about me, to feed the morbid appetite of the public. The excitement ran so high that the Liverpool crowds even hissed me as I was driven through the streets. It was a mockery of justice to hold such a trial in such a place as Liverpool, at such a time, by a common jury; and it was a mockery of common sense to expect that any Liverpool common jury could, when they got into the jury-box, dismiss from their minds all they had heard and seen. In a letter which I wrote to my mother, when in Walton Jail, on the 28th of June, about a month before the trial, I said: "I sincerely hope Messrs. Cleaver will arrange for my trial to take place in London. I shall receive an impartial verdict there, which I cannot expect from a jury in Liverpool, whose minds will virtually be made up before any evidence is heard.*'[863]

Mr Justice Stephen (1829-1894)

In the end, Florence's solicitors decided not to ask for the trial to be moved. They were concerned at the cost of any possible move and, more importantly, they had come to believe that Florence could obtain a fair trial in Liverpool.

Throughout May and June the Maybrick children remained at the home of Mrs Janion, their godmother, under the care of Nurse Yapp. On 21st June, Florence wrote a letter to her mother saying she was concerned about her children's welfare. She suggested that on the days when Nurse Yapp had to attend court, Edwin Maybrick should arrange for the children's former nurse, now Mrs John Over, to look after them.[864] Needless to say, Florence's views were ignored.

In early July, to get the children away from the media frenzy Mrs Domitila Janion sent them away with Nurse Yapp for a three-week holiday to Betws-y-Coed in North Wales. Yapp brought them back on 25th July, and met Edwin Maybrick at Lime Street Station. In a later newspaper interview, Yapp said she never saw the children again. Both children knew their father was dead, and young James '*took on terribly about it,*' but Gladys was '*too young a child to understand.*' The children did not know where their mother was or what had happened. When they asked Yapp, she '*put the little things off*' as best she could.[865]

Friday 26th July, saw the opening of the Assizes at Liverpool. The grand jury was composed of twenty-one well-to-do men drawn from around Liverpool and south Lancashire. The foreman of the jury was Mr H.B. Gilmour of Underlea, Aigburth. The judge appointed to preside over the case was Mr Justice James Fitzjames Stephen (1829-1894). He came from an aristocratic background, and was educated at Eton, London University and Cambridge. He was called to the Bar in 1854, made a Queen's Counsel in 1868 and was called to the bench in 1879.

In 1889, at the time of Florence's trial, he was reaching the end of a long and distinguished career. Two of his works – *General View of the Criminal Law of England* and *History of the Criminal Law of England* – are still considered classical texts by legal scholars. Mr Justice Stephen had an immense presence in court. This came partly from his reputation as one of Britain's leading judges, and partly from his physical attributes. He was six feet tall, with a broad and powerful stature. His size, coupled with a booming voice, commanded the attention of the courtroom. Despite this, there is evidence to suggest that at the time of Florence's trial this once formidable judge was no longer at the peak of his powers. An article in the *Liverpool Citizen* just before the trial began stated:

> '*Mr Justice James Fitzjames Stephen, before whom Mrs Maybrick is to be tried next week, or the week after, has fallen off greatly from a physical point of view. I was present in the Manchester Assizes Court during his famous summing-up against O'Brien, and I could not help remarking how feeble was his once powerful voice and how mumbling were his words.*'[866]

---

[862] *Liverpool Weekly Courier*, 13th July 1889.
[863] Maybrick F., op. cit. page 51.
[864] MacDougall A.W., (1891) op cit., pages 175-177.
[865] *Northern Weekly Gazette*, 24th August 1889.
[866] *Liverpool Citizen*, 24th July 1889.

The conduct and role of Mr Justice Stephen in the Florence Maybrick trial have been much criticised. For example, he made mistakes over exact dates, names and events. A more serious charge levelled at the judge was that he imposed his own rather strict moral views on the case. This is clear in some of the remarks he made both before and during the trial. When he charged the grand jury at the opening of the Liverpool Assizes in July 1889 he placed great stress on Florence's adulterous relationship with Brierley. He told the jury that the case had '*excited very great attention in the country, and certainly, if the prisoner is guilty of the crime alleged to her in the charge, it was the most cruel and horrible murder that could be committed.*'

Stephen then ran through what he described as the '*very bare outline*' of the case. As he did so, he placed great stress on Florence's relationship with Brierley. He described James as a man '*unhappy enough to have had an unfaithful wife,*' and said that '*if a woman does carry on an adulterous intrigue with another man, it may supply every sort of motive... It certainly might quite supply – I won't go further – a very strong motive why she should wish to get rid of her husband.*' He spoke about the flypapers, the letter intercepted by Nurse Yapp, and the phrase '*sick unto death.*' He finished by telling the jury about all the arsenic that was found in the house including the *Arsenic - Poison for Cats* packet, which he said '*appears to be found in a box over which Mrs Maybrick had charge.*'[867] He told the jury they did not have to consider whether Florence was Guilty or not, but whether there was sufficient evidence to put her on trial. Not too surprisingly, following his rather skewed outline of the case the grand jury returned a true bill. Immediately after that Stephen was asked to fix the date for the trial, and he replied, '*But Sir Charles Russell may plead Guilty.*'[868] It has been suggested that the latter remark was an attempt at humour; if that is the case, it was an inappropriate and insensitive comment from an experienced judge.

Mr Justice Stephen's remarks must have rung alarm bells for Florence's hopes to have a fair trial. In a letter to a friend, she wrote:

> '*I have made my peace with God. I have forgiven unreservedly all those who have ruined and forsaken me. To-morrow I partake of the Holy Communion with a clear conscience, and I place my faith in God's mercy. God give me strength is my constant prayer. I feel so lonely – as if every hand were against me. To think that for three or four days I must be unveiled before all those uncharitable eyes. You cannot think how awful it appears to me. So far the ordeal has been all anticipation; then it will be stern reality – which always braces the nerves and courage. I have seen in the Liverpool Post the judge's address on the prosecution to the jury, and it is enough to appal the stoutest heart.*'[869]

On 29th July, in the offices of the Mr T.E. Paget, the District Registrar of Liverpool, probate was granted for James' will. His brothers Thomas and Michael were granted administration of his estate as '*the universal legatees in trust named in the said will.*'[870] The estate was valued at £5,016 1s 0d (gross) or £3,770 16s 6d (net). Therefore, '*contrary to speculation, he had not been poor: in fact after deductions, James's estate was valued at... close to a quarter of a million pounds in today's terms.*'[871]

Although Florence was to see only a small portion of this money, a way had been found to pay for her escalating defence costs. With the approval of Florence's mother, a mortgage for $5,000 had been drawn on the house in New York. The lease had been obtained by the Baroness some ten years earlier and had been made over to her daughter. Florence signed the mortgage, and it was made over to '*Richard Stewart Cleaver of the city of Liverpool, gentleman.*'[872]

The money was desperately needed to pay for the cost of hiring Sir Charles Russell. His usual fees were £500, with a daily cost of £100, though he did accept a lower level of remuneration when Pickford informed him of Florence's limited financial resources. Sir Charles Russell did not arrive in Liverpool until 30th July, a day before the trial was due to start. After speaking with the Cleaver Brothers at their offices, he headed straight to Walton Gaol to speak to Florence. Although this was considered an '*unusual step,*' he felt it was necessary as he was '*perplexed with the instructions in the brief.*' His intention was simple; he wanted to question Florence for the '*purpose of getting the truth out of her.*' Florence's answers must have impressed him. He later stated that he had decided in his own mind that '*it never entered her [Florence's] mind to do any bodily injury to her husband.*'[873]

From the moment Florence had been arrested the defence team had been on the back foot and forced to play catch up. The authorities had unleashed the full power of the police against her, and she had been totally overwhelmed under such a fierce onslaught. When she did manage to get solicitors to represent her, they too easily allowed her to

[867] *Liverpool Echo*, 26th July 1889.
[868] Irving H.B., op cit., page xxiv.
[869] Maybrick F., op. cit. page 47.
[870] *Liverpool Mercury*, 30th July 1889.
[871] Colquhoun K., op cit., page 205.
[872] Ryan, B. op cit., page 117.
[873] Maybrick F., op. cit. page 48.

be taken into custody. At both the inquest into her husband's death and at the magistrates' hearing her defence team played a minimal role, asking few searching questions of the witnesses. Crucially, her solicitors had not deployed any witnesses to speak in her favour.

Finally, as the trial was about to begin, the defence team appeared to have a strategy in place to defend their client. A top barrister had been employed. Witnesses had been brought in from America. Medical experts were lying in wait to challenge the prosecution's experts, and to provide an alternative narrative for why James had died so unexpectedly. Then, just when it appeared the tide was beginning to turn in Florence's favour, Mr Justice Stephen was appointed to preside over her trial. The writer Maurice Moiseiwitsch (1914-1972), in his account of the trial, wrote: '*In charging the grand jury at the trial, Mr Justice Stephen rattled all the weapons in the prosecution's armoury – the flypapers, the letter to Brierley in which she had said that her husband was sick unto death, the arsenic in the body and so on... Thus, from the outset, it was made plain that the judge allied himself with the popular condemnation of the young woman.*'[874]

The judge's pre-trial comments had to be of serious concern to Florence as she faced the toughest week of her entire life. Failure at this point could lead to the gallows. Although Florence's life hung in the balance, she wrote that the day before the trial was due to commence, she was:

> '*calm in spirit, and in a measure prepared for the awful ordeal before me. Up to that time I had shown a composure that astonished everyone. Indeed, some went so far as to say I was without feeling. Perhaps I was toward their kind. I would have responded to sympathy, but never to distrust. At that time, I was suspected by all — or, rather, people were not sufficiently just to content themselves with suspicions; they condemned me outright, and, unheard, struck at a weak, defenceless woman; and this upon what is now generally admitted to have been insufficient evidence to sustain the indictment.*'[875]

LINKS TO THE RIPPER DIARY: DID THE RIPPER MURDERS STOP AFTER THE DEATH OF JAMES MAYBRICK?

At around 1:00am on 17th July 1889, more than two months after James Maybrick's death, another Ripper-style murder took place in London's East End. The victim was Alice McKenzie (1849-1889), known as *Clay Pipe Alice* due to her habit of smoking a pipe. Her body was discovered by Police Constable Walter Andrews in Castle Alley, which was 'one of the more disreputable thoroughfares in the neighbourhood north of Whitechapel High Street.'[876] She was found lying on the pavement on her right side, with her clothes pulled up almost to her waist, and there was a noticeable pool of blood under her head. Two doctors were involved in the post-mortem on McKenzie's dead body.

One of these was Dr Thomas Bond (1841-1901), the police surgeon for Scotland Yard. In October 1888 he had been asked to assist in the police investigations into the Ripper murders by Robert Anderson (1841-1918), the Assistant Commissioner of the Metropolitan Police. Bond had reviewed the inquest accounts of the first four canonical victims, and also examined the dead body of Mary Kelly. He submitted a report to Anderson, which has been called the first ever criminal profile.[877]

After later examining McKenzie's body, Bond concluded:

> '*I see in this murder evidence of similar design to the former Whitechapel murders, viz. sudden onslaught on the prostrate woman, the throat skilfully and resolutely cut with subsequent mutilation, each mutilation indicating sexual thoughts and a desire to mutilate the abdomen and sexual organs. I am of the opinion that the murder was performed by the same person who committed the former series of Whitechapel murders.*'[878]

Not everyone agreed with Bond's findings. Dr George Bagster Phillips, who had carried out the initial post-mortem on McKenzie's body, took a different opinion. His view of the murder is important, as he had also been involved in the post-mortems of Chapman, Eddowes and Kelly. He concluded: '*After careful and long deliberation, I cannot satisfy myself, on purely anatomical and professional grounds that the perpetrator of all the "Wh Ch. Murders" is our man. I am on the contrary impelled to a contrary conclusion in this noting of the mode of practice and the character of the mutilations and judging of motive in connection with the latter.*'

At 2:20am, on 13th February 1891, Police Constable Ernest Thompson turned into Swallow Gardens, a narrow alley in Whitechapel, and discovered the body of Frances Coles (1865-1891). Her throat had been cut seconds before the

874 Moiseiwitsch M., *5 Famous Trials*, (Heinemann, London, 1962) pages 72-73.
875 Maybrick F., op. cit. page 49.
876 Begg P. and Bennett J., *Jack the Ripper*, (Carlton Books, London, 2017) page 192.
877 Begg P., Fido M. and Skinner K., op cit., page 61.
878 Quoted in Rumbelow D., op cit., page 131.

officer had entered the alley; she was bleeding profusely, but was still alive. She was to die on her way to hospital. Like several of the other Ripper victims, she was a prostitute and had a drink problem. A ship's fireman, James Sadler, was arrested for her murder. He seemed a likely suspect as he had a violent temper, had bought a knife on the day of the murder and had spent the evening drinking with Coles. Sadler was to be released before the case went to court. The knife he owned did '*not appear sharp enough to commit the injuries to Cole's throat*,' and he was so drunk at the time of the murder it was felt '*he could not have coordinated such an attack effectively*.'[879] Importantly, it was found that Sadler had been away at sea when the canonical Ripper murders had been committed. As a result of Sadler's release, Coles' death – as with the deaths of the canonical victims – was officially labelled as a case of murder by person or persons unknown. Whether Coles was murdered by Jack the Ripper is not certain. She had not been mutilated like the other victims, though it is possible the approach of PC Thompson scared away the killer before he had set about his savage butchery of the body.

If Alice McKenzie and Frances Coles were Ripper victims, then James Maybrick could not possibly have been Jack the Ripper as he was dead when their murders occurred. The respected Ripperologist Philip Sugden wrote it was '*entirely possible that the Ripper slew both Alice McKenzie and Frances Coles. Their injuries were similar, though not identical, to those of the canonical victims*.'[880] Sugden went on to make the point that the differences in the injuries may be more significant than the similarities because, by the time of their deaths, the modus operandi of the Ripper was well known and had inspired a spate of imitative attacks.

Police mortuary photograph of Frances Coles

One writer who definitively believes that McKenzie and Coles were Ripper victims is Bruce Robinson. He argues that after the death of Mary Kelly in November 1888 the murders did not stop; the only thing that stopped was '*the police associating him with his crimes*.' Robinson claims that the Ripper was in fact Michael Maybrick and, as well as the canonical murders, he also killed Johnny Gill (December 1888), James Maybrick (May 1889), Alice McKenzie (July 1889), the woman whose torso was found at Pinchin Street (September 1889), Frances Coles (February 1891) and '*likely many more*.'[881] Robinson explains the difference of opinion between Drs Phillips and Bond over the question of whether McKenzie's death was a Ripper murder by pointing out that Phillips was a Freemason, while Bond was not. He suggests that Phillips had recognised certain Masonic markings on the victim's body, and therefore was keen to bury the evidence and undermine the view the Ripper had struck again in Whitechapel.

Although Robinson believes there were numerous Ripper murders, the fact that Jack the Ripper was never caught means it is not certain how many women were murdered. It is generally accepted that he killed five, though Philip Sugden wrote that he killed '*at least four, probably six, just possibly eight*.'[882] The five victims regarded as the work of the Ripper are Mary Ann (Polly) Nichols, murdered on Friday, 31st August 1888; Annie Chapman, murdered on Saturday, 8th September 1888; Elizabeth Stride, murdered on Sunday, 30th September 1888; Catharine Eddowes, also murdered on 30th September; and Mary Kelly, murdered on Friday, 9th November 1888. In Sugden's list of possible victims, the sixth woman would have been Martha Tabram, murdered on 7th August 1888. Eight victims would include Tabram, McKenzie and Coles.

There are some similarities to be found amongst the Ripper's canonical victims. All five were probably prostitutes to some degree; all the murders occurred in the Whitechapel area, and all the victims were residents of the East End. Most were drunk or thought to be drunk at the time they were killed. All of them were estranged from their husbands, or families, due to their excessive drinking habits. Every murder took place at the weekend, suggesting the murderer had regular employment and possibly worked elsewhere during the week. The murders were committed between midnight and 6:00am. All of the victims except Mary Kelly were killed outdoors, and were probably killed in the same manner. The fact that Mary Kelly was killed indoors was probably the reason why she was so savagely mutilated; the murderer knew there was less chance of him being disturbed as he carried out his gruesome slaughter.

Stephen Knight, in his 1976 book on the murders, suggested that all the victims knew one another; however, there is no hard evidence to support his view other than the fact that they all lived in one small part of Spitalfields, where

---

[879] Begg P. and Bennett J., op cit., page 207.
[880] Sugden P., op cit., page 359.
[881] Robinson B., op cit., pages 473-474.
[882] Sugden P., op cit., page 359.

the casual lodging houses were most densely concentrated. Also, there is no clear or apparent motive for any of the killings. The fact that they were all prostitutes makes them '*too poor to be worth robbing.*'[883] Further, there is no evidence the killer had sexual intercourse with the victims.

Sir Melville Macnaghten (1853-1921), who had been Assistant Chief Constable of CID from June 1889 and then Chief Constable from 1890, made a report on the killings in 1894 that was not to enter the public domain until many years later. His prime purpose in writing the notes, which became known as the MacNaghten Memorandum, was to exonerate a suspect, Thomas Cutbush, who had been accused in a national newspaper story of being Jack the Ripper. Macnaghten identified three named individuals as being stronger candidates to be the serial killer. They were Kosminski, a Polish Jew who '*became insane due to many years indulgence in solitary devices*;' Michael Ostrog, a '*Russian doctor and convict,*' and Montague Druitt, a '*sexually insane*' school teacher who committed suicide by drowning himself in the Thames in December 1888. As to the murders, he wrote that there '*were five victims and five victims only.*' He then went on to list the five victims, who were to become identified as the canonical victims: Nichols, Chapman, Stride, Eddowes and Kelly. Macnaghten wrote that the '*fury of the mutilations increased in each case, and seemingly, the appetite only became sharpened by indulgence. It seems then highly improbable that the murderer would have suddenly stopped in November '88 and been content to recommence operations by merely prodding a girl behind [Cutbush's crime] some 2 years and 4 months afterwards.*'

Macnaghten suggests a '*much more rational theory*' is that after the terrible murder of Mary Kelly in November 1888, the killer's brain '*gave way*' and he '*immediately committed suicide*' or, because he was '*hopelessly mad,*' was placed in an asylum by his relatives.[884]

Macnaghten makes an important point about the violence and brutality of the Kelly murder. Is it conceivable that, after such a horrific act, the murderer could have calmly returned to normal everyday life? If you accept that James Maybrick was the serial killer, then you also have to accept that after the Kelly murder he somehow managed to slip back seamlessly into normality and decided never to kill again. Further, you have to accept that a crazed and demented psychopath would have been happy to idly standby and allow his wife to have an affair with another man. It is a hypothesis that is bereft of credibility and flies in the face of everything we know about psychopaths.

Whether there were more Ripper victims after Mary Kelly is uncertain, although it is possible. However, the chances of James Maybrick being the notorious Whitechapel serial killer are very unlikely.

---

[883] Rumbelow D., op cit., page 66.

[884] The Macnaghten Memorandum is shown in many books; for example, see Begg P., Fido M. and Skinner K., op cit., pages 323-327.

14

THE PROSECUTION OPENS ITS CASE

St George's Hall, Liverpool circa 1900

The trial of Florence Maybrick for the murder of her husband opened on Wednesday, 31st July 1889, and lasted for one week. The venue was St George's Hall in Liverpool, a magnificent neo-classical building described by Queen Victoria as *'worthy of ancient Athens.'*[885]

The Great Hall dominated the interior of the building. It was lit by chandeliers suspended from the ceiling by representations of the prows of Greek ships. Granite columns along the length of the hall divided it into bays featuring statues of Liverpool's most famous citizens. The impressive floor consisted of 30,000 Minton tiles featuring heraldic and maritime designs. Another one of the Hall's impressive features was its heating and ventilation system which made it the first air-conditioned public building in Britain. During Florence's trial, one local newspaper commented that *'fortunately the ventilation of the building is adequate and not withstanding the thronged state of the court and the heat outside, the atmosphere was wholesome.'*[886]

St George's Hall was a multi-purpose venue. At the south end of the building there were two courts, one for civil cases and one for criminal cases, both chambers being about 60 square feet. One of the biggest problems with the design of the criminal court was its extremely poor acoustic properties and, despite attempts to remedy the defect, the issue was never satisfactorily resolved. During Florence's trial, both the prosecution and defence counsels had to repeatedly ask witnesses to speak louder as their answers could not be clearly heard. The spectators were forced to '*strain their ears*' in order to catch what was being said in court.[887]

Florence's trial attracted a great deal of attention both in Liverpool and throughout the rest of the country. Mr Jennings, who was the Keeper of St George's Hall, said he had been in charge of the Hall for five years and had dealt with notorious cases, but that they all sank '*into total insignificance beside the Maybrick trial.*'[888] He guessed that the total number of people who were admitted into the court during the seven days of the trial was about 7,000. That included about 400 people every day that wanted '*just a peep*' at events inside. A large proportion of these, similar to the inquest and magisterial hearing, were women, mostly younger in years. Jennings said the men were keen to look at Sir Charles Russell, and the women at Mrs Maybrick.

---

885 Aughton P., *Liverpool – A People's History*, (Carnegie Press, Preston, 1990) page 163.
886 *Liverpool Mercury*, 1st August 1889.
887 *Liverpool Daily Post*, 1st August 1889.
888 The full interview is in the *Liverpool Review*, 17th August 1889.

The Prosecution Opens its Case

The Friday, the third day of the trial, was the busiest. On that day alone, Jennings received no fewer than 72 letters applying for admission. The crowds were so great inside the court that the refreshment contractors, Galt and Capper, '*never did such a business in the hall before.*' The crowds outside the Hall were also extremely large.[889]

One of Jennings' key duties was looking after the witnesses. The Grand Jury room was made available for prosecution witnesses. Another room was also made available to them so the '*gentlemen were able to have a smoke if they wanted.*' The defence witnesses were accommodated in the Sheriff's Court. One of the problems the witnesses faced while they gave their evidence was the use of opera glasses by the spectators in court. One lady had brought such a large opera glass to '*bear fully upon the witnesses*' that Jennings had to go to her and '*desired her to discontinue her objectionable scrutiny.*'[890]

At 8:35am on Wednesday 31st July, Florence was brought out of Walton Gaol in a horse-drawn prison van. The prison warden himself took charge of the van, helped by two of his assistants. Florence was accompanied inside the van by two female warders. Just before 9:00am, the prison van was driven through the tunnel door entrance of St George's Hall that led to the holding cells under the courtroom.

When it was clear Florence's cell was fully prepared, the two female warders escorted her from the prison van down a corridor and into the cell. As she did so, she '*walked bravely and uprightly*' and was '*entirely unsupported by the female warders accompanying her. And a glimpse of her face showed that she was almost entirely unmoved by any thoughts of the terrible ordeal she was about to pass through and that she was quite determined to pass through that ordeal with courage and calmness.*'[891]

Florence's arrival at St George's Hall went largely unnoticed on the first day of the trial; however, when she was spotted she was greeted with some abuse from the crowds outside the court. As the trial progressed, the mood gradually changed and by the end, most people cheered her arrival as they had started to believe in her innocence.

One of Florence's biggest pre-trial concerns was whether she would get a fair hearing in Liverpool. As it turned out, none of the jury came from Liverpool, or had a background in the cotton industry. They were mainly skilled artisans drawn from Lancashire towns. The foreman of the jury, Timothy Wainwright, was typical of the social background of most of the jury, being a plumber from Southport. The twelve men were Timothy Wainwright (plumber, Southport), T. Ball (plumber, Ormskirk), A. Harrison (woodturner, Bootle), W. Walmsley (provision dealer, North Meols), W.H. Gaskell (plumber, North Meols), J. Taylor (farmer, Melling), G.H. Welsby (grocer, St Helens), R.G. Brook (ironmonger, St Helens), J.W. Sutton (milliner, North Meols), J. Tyrer (painter, Wigan), J. Bryers (farmer, Scarth Hill, Bickerstaffe), and J. Thierens (baker, Ormskirk).

The main criticism of the jury was not that they were biased, but that due to their social background, they were intellectually incapable of understanding the complexities of the case, especially the medical evidence. Florence later wrote: '*The jury belonged to a class of men who were not competent to weigh technical evidence, and no doubt attached great weight to the opinions of the local physicians, one of whom was somewhat of a celebrity.*'[892]

MacDougall wrote that one of the jurymen had, not long before the trial started, so '*brutally mistreated his own wife*' that he had been ordered by the magistrates to pay her money every week to '*enable her to live separately.*'[893]

The Liverpool Citizen, in a powerful article, posed the question:

> '*Is it just or reasonable that a trial which has agitated the whole country and has involved such delicate issues that the most experienced and learned scientific men are utterly unable to agree upon its merits, should be decided by a dozen plumbers, glaziers and grocers from county villages? The thing's a farce!*'[894]

Not all Liverpool newspapers agreed with the views of the *Citizen.* A reporter from the *Liverpool Review* wrote:

> '*Judging, as well as I could by appearances, I calculated the average age of the jurymen was about thirty-eight years each. Their aspect was that of decent, good-natured fellows, and their faces showed nothing beyond interest in the case – one had no fear that they were stubborn pragmatic men who would decide the issue in advance.*'[895]

At 9:30am, the High Sheriff left the North-Western Hotel opposite St George's Hall, where he was staying, and walked to the Judge's Lodgings to escort Mr Justice Stephen to the courts. Just before 10:00am, Sir Charles Russell, accompanied by his junior William Pickford, entered the courtroom. Russell's appearance instantly grabbed the

---

889 *Evening Express*, 1st August 1889.
890 *Evening Express*, 1st August 1889.
891 *Evening Express*, 31st July 1889.
892 Maybrick F., op cit., pages 236-237.
893 MacDougall A.W., (1891) op cit., page 553.
894 *Liverpool Citizen*, 10th July 1889.
895 *Liverpool Review*, 10th July 1889.

attention of the spectators, and '*every eye was immediately turned towards the clear-cut features of the famous advocate... Of late years he has aged somewhat in appearance, being now quite grey, but the bright and vigorous manner remains.*'[896] The prosecution team, Mr Addison, Mr McConnell and Mr Swift were the next to arrive. A few minutes after 10:00am, a fanfare of trumpets announced Mr Justice Stephen's entry into the court. After the jury was sworn in, Florence was called up from the holding cell below the court. All eyes turned towards her as she entered the dock. According to a local reporter, she wore:

William Robert McConnell (1837-1906)

> '*a neatly-fitting crape costume, with a crape pointed bonnet and "weepers" covering the back of her dress. Instead of the thick impenetrable veil which covered the whole of her face on the previous occasions, she wore only a very thin black "fall" reaching to her lips, and her face was plainly discernible. Her light brown hair was brushed back from her forehead, and her face, though pale and thin, was homely and pleasant looking. She is altogether younger and more attractive in feature and in her slight but well-proportioned figure than many of her portraits make her out to be.*'[897]

Florence later wrote that when she entered the dock her manner was '*calm and collected,*' as she knew she was innocent and because she had a '*strong faith in Divine support.*'[898] As she took her place, she was flanked on one side by the Governor of Walton Gaol, and on the other by a female warder. Some of the spectators in the seats behind spoke words of encouragement to her. Later, such actions caused Mr Jennings to leave these seats empty. The murder charge was read out and Florence pleaded '*Not Guilty.*'

At 10:08am, Mr Addison launched the case for the prosecution with an opening address that lasted almost two hours. He had not proceeded far when he was interrupted by Sir Charles Russell, who leant across and whispered something to him. Addison said, '*It has been suggested to me, and probably it is right, that, except the scientific witnesses, all the witnesses be requested to leave the court.*'[899] The witnesses then withdrew, with the exception of Michael Maybrick, who was allowed to stay. Addison then resumed his address. Step by step he ran though the events from Florence's stay in Flatman's Hotel to James' death.

One newspaper commented that Addison possessed a '*clear, pleasing, resonant voice,*' but went on to say he '*led off proceedings in a very moderate speech, extending over a couple of hours, during which one heard the now familiar story of the case all retold.*'[900] Another newspaper wrote that Addison, who was a '*well-known and good-tempered barrister,*' made a '*singularly unbiased and fair, though somewhat prosy opening speech.*' It also commented that if there if there was any indication of feeling from the '*good-natured cherubic counsel for the prosecution, it was one rather of sympathy than of severity.*'[901]

Addison's manner was calm and deliberate as he tried to establish a clear chain of events that would link together all the facts as he saw them. His style may have lacked the eloquence of Russell, but it was effective. It was also perhaps more suited to the practical men who sat on the jury. Addison's case was based around the notion that James, although a hypochondriac, was a healthy man who was gradually poisoned by his wife, who had a clear motive for the crime. He referred to the time that Florence and Brierley spent together in Flatman's Hotel where '*they lived there together as man and wife, slept together and went out together.*' Addison spoke about what had happened at the Grand National, and the row between James and Florence that followed it. He described Florence's purchase of the flypapers, and posed the question: '*One asks what she wanted them for and what became of them*?' He brought in the exchange of letters between Florence and Brierley, and heavily emphasised one of Florence's phrases, '*He is sick unto death.*' He referred to Florence's actions in removing a bottle of meat juice in a '*concealed manner.*' He ended by talking about James' death and the discovery of large amounts of arsenic around the house. He directly addressed the jury, saying:

> '*Gentlemen, there is no reason to doubt that James Maybrick died by arsenic, and arsenic given to him by repeated doses. Who did it? I shall be compelled and am compelled to submit there is very cogent and powerful evidence to show that it was his wife who administered it.*'[902]

---

896 *Liverpool Mercury*, 1st August 1889.
897 *Liverpool Daily Post*, 1st August 1889.
898 Maybrick F., op cit., pages 52-53.
899 Irving H.B., op cit., page 3.
900 *Liverpool Review*, 3rd August 1889.
901 *Liverpool Daily Post*, 2nd August 1889.
902 Irving H.B., op cit., pages 22-23.

The first person to give evidence was the surveyor, Mr Clemmey, but he only testified to the accuracy of the plans he had drawn up of the interior of Battlecrease. His work didn't impress Mr Justice Stephen, who *'did not consider them as of much if any service.'*[903]

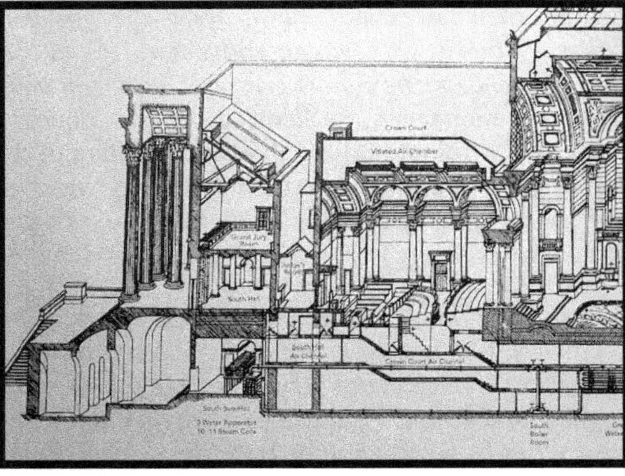

Diagram showing the Crown Court at St George's Hall (Taken from Dr D.B. Reid's original plans for the warming and ventilation system for the Hall.

After Clemmey had presented his plans Michael Maybrick entered the witness box, where he was examined by Mr McConnell. Michael said that after receiving three telegrams on Wednesday, 8th May he left London for Liverpool. His brother Edwin met him at Edgehill Railway Station. When they arrived at the house, Edwin showed him Florence's letter to Brierley. He said that when he saw James, he was *'very much shocked to see the state he was in, being only semi-conscious. Shortly afterwards I saw Mrs Maybrick... and I said to her that I was not satisfied with my brother's treatment. She asked me what I meant, and I said that she ought to have called in professional nurses, and also another doctor earlier.'*[904] He said he voiced his concerns to Dr Humphreys later that night, and to Dr Carter the next day. Michael said on Friday morning, following a conversation with Nurse Gore, he went into the sick room and *'took away about half a bottle of brandy. I again saw Nurse Gore in the afternoon, and following our conversation I took from the washstand in the bedroom part of a bottle of Valentine's meat juice, which I gave precisely as I found it, to Dr Carter.'*

Michael told the court about the incident on Friday afternoon when he had spoken angrily to Florence. He had said to her, *'Florie, how dare you tamper with the medicine.'* Michael said Florence explained her actions by saying *'there was so much sediment in the smaller bottle that it was impossible to dissolve it,'* and therefore she was putting *'it into the larger bottle so that the medicine might be more easily shaken.'*[905] Michael said he was *'much annoyed and dissatisfied'* by Florence's actions, and had the prescription remade. He said at about 11:30pm on the evening of the day James had died, *'Nurse Yapp brought me a chocolate box containing several small bottles and a small parcel labelled with a long red label, "Arsenic - Poison."'* He gave the box to Inspector Baxendale, along with some letters he and Edwin had found on Sunday morning when they searched the bedroom.

A few minutes before 1:00pm, Sir Charles Russell started his cross-examination of Michael Maybrick. Looking *'rather pale and haggard-looking,'* Russell put his questions *'quietly and leisurely'* in a manner designed to disarm the witness.[906] He asked if James' condition had gradually deteriorated from Wednesday, 8th May onwards, to which Michael replied there had been a *'decided improvement up to Friday morning' in James' condition, but after that he 'collapsed hour by hour.'*[907] Michael told Russell that he had *'from the first a strong suspicion in the case.'*

Under questioning, he admitted the bottle of medicine that he had seen Florence *'tamper'* with, had been tested and found to contain no arsenic. Michael also agreed that Florence had not tried to conceal her actions. Russell asked him if he was aware that on the Wednesday, Florence had telegraphed for a nurse. Michael replied, *'I learnt it subsequently.'* Russell then asked Michael if James was a man given to dosing himself; Michael replied, *'Not that I am aware of. I never saw him. At times he took a little phosphorus, I know.'* Russell continued by asking Michael if he had ever been told about James dosing himself. He replied he had never heard it apart from in Florence's letter, which he had received in early March and had destroyed. He said that when James next came to London he had questioned him about the matter, but his brother had called the suggestion *'a damned lie.'* As a result, he said he had not pursued the issue any further. Russell asked Michael if James had died in ignorance of Florence's *'guilty meeting in London'* with Brierley. He replied, *'Yes, I am convinced of it.'* Russell followed that question by asking Michael if he was aware that there were *'complaints on both sides.'* He replied, *'Yes.'*

Michael Maybrick's evidence had proved to be something of an anti-climax. The spectators in court who had expected some form of gladiatorial struggle between the famous composer and the equally famous defence counsel were disappointed. Instead, Sir Charles Russell had begun the process of quietly chipping away at the prosecution's case, and in that he had scored some minor successes. Under cross-examination, Michael admitted that Florence had telegraphed for a nurse and had urged Edwin to call an additional doctor. He also admitted that some of the items he had removed for testing, such as the brandy bottle, had contained no arsenic. The infamous tampering with the

903 *Liverpool Daily Post,* 1st August 1889.
904 Irving H.B., op cit., page 24.
905 Ibid., page 25.
906 *Liverpool Echo,* 31st July, 1889.
907 Irving H.B., op cit., pages 26-27.

medicine bottle had been shown to be an innocent act. Russell managed to get Michael to admit that Florence had warned him of his brother's fondness for a mysterious white powder presumed to be strychnine. He also admitted that James had a mistress, though the defence didn't make any use of this information. But the admission showed that if Florence had some guilty secrets, then so did James.

The next witness was Dr Hopper, the physician who had cared for the Maybricks for seven years, although he did not treat James during his final illness. Under examination from Mr Addison, he said that James:

> '*was a very healthy man, but he complained from time to time of symptoms which in my mind were not very serious; slight dyspepsia and nervousness, which I thought to be exaggerated. After June, 1888, he complained more than formerly. I usually prescribed nerve tonics. I never prescribed arsenic for him in any shape or form, but I remember having a conversation with him some years ago about it. My impression of the conversation is that he told me that he knew it as an anti-periodic. When he returned from America, I think he said he had been taking quinine, and as he said that quinine did not suit him, I suppose I suggested arsenic... The nerve tonics which I prescribed were very ordinary ones, nux vomica and phosphoric acid.*'

Hopper said Florence had visited him the day after the Grand National. The following day he had gone to Battlecrease and had spoken to both James and Florence in an effort to reconcile their differences. In his cross-examination, Russell asked Hopper if James was a man given to dosing himself; he replied '*Yes... distinctly.*' Hopper said James had told him that '*finding no effect from his medicine, he had doubled the dose... I said to him it was a dangerous habit.*' Russell asked whether James had given him a bundle of prescriptions written by a Dr Séguard in America. Hopper replied, '*Yes,*' but admitted he had destroyed them some months ago. He said they were principally prescriptions of the aphrodisiac kind, and contained strychnine and nux vomica. He said that, as far as he could recollect, they did not contain arsenic, though he did agree that arsenic was a nerve tonic of the aphrodisiac kind. Hopper said that, sometime around mid-1888, Florence had told him that James '*was in the habit of taking some very strong medicine which had a bad influence on him.*' Hopper said the next time he visited the house he looked in James' dressing-room for bottles but did not find any. Russell asked Hopper if James knew arsenic was used as a nerve tonic, and that it had similar properties to nux vomica and strychnine. He replied, '*Yes, I believe so [and] that he had taken it in America as an antiperiodic, and knew all about its properties.*' Russell asked Hopper if he was sure he had not prescribed arsenic for James, and he replied, '*I am morally certain.*'

In his cross-examination, Russell had been able to demonstrate that James was not quite as healthy as the prosecution was trying to make out. Further, Hopper admitted James frequently took medicines in large quantities and it was a potentially fatal habit.

Dr Hopper was followed into the witness box by Mrs Matilda Briggs. Her evidence followed the pattern of the previous prosecution witnesses, in that she claimed that James' '*general health was that of a man always quite well.*'[908] She said the only time that Florence had made a complaint to her about her husband was after the Grand National, and she had '*heard of no quarrel of any consequence before that.*' Mrs Briggs also gave evidence about the numerous items that had been found around the house after James' death that contained arsenic. She said, '*I made a search of the house along with my sister and the two Mr Maybricks.*' As she referred to the various items and bottles found in the hat boxes, they were produced in court so the jury could see them.[909]

In his cross-examination, Russell asked Mrs Briggs if she knew that on the Wednesday before James' death Florence had telegraphed for a nurse. She replied, '*I know now. I did not know then.*' Russell asked Mrs Briggs if Florence's writing table, wardrobe and the hat boxes were locked or secured, and she answered, '*No.*' Russell questioned her about the letter to Brierley which Florence had written after James had died. He asked, '*Is it not a fact that you suggested the writing of it?*' She replied, '*I did in sarcasm.*' Russell asked if Mrs Briggs had observed a large number of medicine bottles in the house, being told, '*Yes.*' He asked if there were as many as 50 in one room. She replied, '*I could not tell, but I know there were a good many.*' Russell asked if she knew about James' habit of dosing himself with medicines and things suggested by his friends, to which she replied, '*Yes.*' He then asked how she came to know it. She replied, '*He used to recommend me medicines.*'

Russell's gentle but relentless prodding of Mrs Briggs had again undermined the testimony of one of the Crown's witnesses. For example, it was one of the main tenets of the prosecution's case that Florence had not provided adequate health care for her seriously ill husband and, more seriously, had prevented professional nurses being called to assist with his care. Russell had shown that this was not the case and that Florence had telegraphed to Hale for a nurse before Mrs Briggs had insisted that she did so. Russell also managed to get Mrs Briggs to make some other important admissions; firstly, that none of the objects found in Battlecrease were in any way secured or locked. Secondly, that the house contained a very large number of medicine bottles. Importantly, she said she knew James

---

908 Ibid., page 39.
909 Ibid., page 39.

was in the habit of dosing himself with different medicines. Finally, she admitted she recommended to Florence that she should write to Brierley for help, though she said it was just a sarcastic suggestion. When Mrs Briggs left the witness box a hiss of disapproval was heard in the courtroom.

Mrs Briggs was followed by her sister, Mrs Martha Louisa Hughes. She was present in Battlecrease at the time of James' death and had helped her sister search the house. Mrs Hughes made a short statement and was not questioned by the prosecution team. She told the court: '*I am a sister of Mrs Briggs. I live in Sefton Park, Liverpool, and was acquainted with the late Mr Maybrick for a considerable time. We met several times at Battlecrease House, where I went with my sister. I was at the house the day after his death. I found some letters (produced) in the middle drawer of the dressing-table, and handed them to Mr Michael Maybrick. The dressing-table was in Mrs Maybrick's bedroom.*'[910]

In his cross-examination, Russell asked her if the circumstances of James' death were the subject of a conversation between her, her sister and the nurse. She replied, '*Yes.*' He asked if she recollected hearing that arsenic had been found in a bottle of Valentine's meat juice. Again, she replied, '*Yes.*' Russell asked her when she learnt about the Valentine's meat juice and she replied, '*I heard it on the Saturday.*' Russell asked her from whom had she heard that news and she replied, '*Mr Michael Maybrick.*'

Mrs Hughes's admission that Michael had told her about the arsenic in the meat juice on Saturday evening is intriguing. Michael gave the bottle to Dr Carter on Friday 10th May, and he analysed its contents when he arrived home. Although these tests did show the presence of a metallic deposit, he had not yet ascertained the exact nature of the deposit. Alexander MacDougall asked how Michael knew about the arsenic in the meat juice when its presence had not yet been established by Carter. [911] MacDougall does not answer his own question, but both Paul Feldman and Bruce Robinson suggest that Michael knew about the arsenic as he had added it. Although there is no evidence to support this view, Robinson does make an interesting point when writing that both Michael and Edwin '*were constantly in and out of the sickroom, with as much opportunity to poison James as anyone else. The only difference is that they weren't suspected, and Florence was.*'[912]

There are other more realistic answers to MacDougall's question. While Carter had not conclusively established that the metallic deposit was arsenic in his tests on Friday night, on the basis of the colouring of the deposit he had found in his tests, he must have considered it likely that the deposit was arsenic. At 10:30am on Saturday morning, Carter had arrived at Battlecrease and told Dr Humphreys the results of his tests from the previous night, saying, '*if the matter turned out to be so bad as I feared it was, it would be taken out of our [the doctors'] hand entirely.*'[913] Carter then examined James and concluded he was dying. Such a view must have confirmed his suspicion that the metallic deposit he had found was arsenic. It is quite likely that Carter told Michael on Saturday that he believed the meat juice contained arsenic. Michael in turn passed on this information to Mrs Hughes.

Edwin Maybrick was next in the witness box. Under examination from Addison, he said he had returned from America '*on 25th April, and on the following day I saw my brother in his office. I dined with him that evening. He appeared to be in his usual health. So far as I knew my brother on the whole enjoyed very good health. From time to time he took ordinary liver medicine.*' Addison asked if James took arsenic and Edwin replied, '*No.*'

Edwin then answered questions about James' condition on Sunday 28th April, the day after the Wirral races. He said, '*I went to his house and found him lying on a sofa, apparently ill. He said he had been taken ill on the previous morning, but that feeling somewhat better, he had gone out to the Wirral races, where he had not felt himself the whole day. He also said that he had numbness in the legs and in the hands.*' Edwin said James recovered from this illness, and returned to work on Wednesday 1st May. On that day: '*Mrs Maybrick gave me a parcel to take to his office. I afterwards learned that it contained a brown jug in which there was some farinaceous food in liquid form. My brother poured the liquid into a saucepan and heated it over the fire, and he then poured it into a basin and partook of it. He remarked, "The cook has put some of that-... sherry into it, and she knows I don't like it." Sometime after that I asked him how he was, and he said that he had not felt so well since his lunch.*'[914]

Edwin's statement implies, though he doesn't explicitly state it, that James' second and more serious bout of illness came after he had eaten this lunch at his office.

In his cross-examination Russell asked Edwin if Florence seemed attentive to her husband. He replied, '*Yes.*' Russell also asked Edwin if he could recollect Mrs Maybrick suggesting on the Tuesday that he should send for his own doctor. Edwin replied, '*She telegraphed to me suggesting that Dr McCheyne... should be sent for.*'

Russell moved on to tackle another prosecution assertion; the notion that James was essentially a healthy man. He asked Edwin if he had found a bundle of prescriptions amongst his brother's papers. He replied: '*There were several*

---

910 Ibid., page 45.
911 MacDougall A.W., (1896) op cit., pages 113-114.
912 Robinson, B., op cit., page 665.
913 Irving H.B., op cit., page 116.
914 Ibid., page 47.

prescriptions found in the room on its being searched by Mr Baxendale.' When asked if among the prescriptions were there any from Dr Ward, of Norfolk, Virginia, Edwin answered, '*Not that I am aware of. I should have noticed them at once, knowing the gentleman, if I had seen anything of the kind.*' Russell asked Edwin if a large number of bottles had been found at James' office. He replied, '*Yes, I believe so. I am told as many as twenty-eight. There was no arsenic in these.*' Russell then asked Edwin if he could look at the prescriptions that night to see if there were any from Dr Ward, of Virginia. Edwin answered, '*Certainly, if they are handed to me.*'

Russell had again managed to get a prosecution witness to make important admissions that helped his client. Edwin had admitted that Florence was very attentive to James during his illness and she had asked him to arrange for his own doctor to visit. Edwin was forced to admit that, during the final stage of James' illness, Florence had no responsibility for providing her husband with his food and medicine. If that was the case, then how was she possibly able to administer poison to him? Russell clearly suspected that Edwin was not telling the truth about James taking arsenic. Of all the prosecution's witnesses, Edwin is the one who was the least truthful. He knew his brother was not in the best of health, and he also knew that James was in the habit of taking strychnine.

The next two witnesses were the owners of the chemist shops in which Florence had purchased the flypapers. Thomas Wokes testified he remembered '*an occasion when Mrs Maybrick called upon me, somewhere about the 24th April last, and purchased from me a dozen flypapers... She made a remark to me at the time that the flies were beginning to get troublesome in the kitchen. I had sold only one lot of flypapers before that during the present year. I had an account against the deceased, but Mrs Maybrick paid for the flypapers.*'[915] Under cross-examination by Russell, Wokes admitted he had sold flypapers on another occasion when it hadn't been hot and flies weren't in season. He was followed by Christopher Hanson, the owner of the chemists in Cressington, who said: '*Mrs Maybrick was a customer at my shop. On the 29th April last she came to my shop for a lotion and purchased two dozen flypapers, which cost one shilling. The flypapers were similar to those produced. She had an account running, and did not usually pay at the time of ordering. Upon this occasion she paid for the flypapers, but not for the lotion.*'[916] During his cross-examination, Russell asked Hanson if arsenic was a common ingredient in many cosmetics. He replied, '*It is, sir, quite common.*'[917]

The last witnesses of the day worked in James' office. The first was George Smith, his bookkeeper, who testified that James' health was '*generally good,*' though he '*sometimes complained of his liver.*'[918] He also said that on Wednesday 1st May, he had seen James '*warming food in a pan for his lunch.*'

Smith was followed by Thomas Lowry, the clerk, who told the court:

> '*I recollect Mr Maybrick coming to the office on the 1st May, about eleven o'clock. He sent me out to buy a saucepan, a basin, and a spoon. The articles produced are something like those I purchased. Upon giving the articles to Mr Maybrick, he poured some liquid into the saucepan out of a jug, and put it on the fire, and he afterwards partook of it. The vessels were afterwards left in the office.*'

He also testified that before James' final illness, his general health '*had been good.*'[919] Although both Smith and Lowry claimed James' health was good, they both admitted that his complexion was very pale.

The final witness was Mrs Eliza Busher. She said: '*I cleaned the offices of the late Mr James Maybrick. On the morning of 2nd May I washed the pan and other vessels produced. On the following morning I saw the vessels had been used again, and that particles of food were left adhering to them, some white and some black. I cleaned the vessels, and put them on the mantelpiece.*'[920]

There can be no doubt that, at the start of the trial, the prosecution team were confident they could secure a guilty verdict. In large part, this was due to the fact that Florence's lawyers had, at the inquest and the magisterial hearing, reserved much of her defence and had barely challenged the prosecution's assertions. This inaction created a perception that the prosecution's case was unanswerable.

In this context, the first day of the trial has to be viewed in a positive light for Florence's defence. From virtually every one of the prosecution witnesses, Russell had managed to get admissions that were '*nearly all in favour of the innocence of Mrs Maybrick*' and, as a result, '*the whole cloud of suspicious circumstances seemed to be gently blown away before the insinuating manner of Sir Charles who trifled with the bottles and the handkerchief from the chocolate box as if they were matters of small moment.*'[921] For the first time the prosecution's arguments were being tested and challenged, and a clear line of defence was beginning to emerge.

---

915 Ibid., page 53.
916 Ibid., page 53.
917 Ibid., page 54.
918 Ibid., page 55.
919 Ibid., page 85.
920 Ibid., page 57.
921 *Liverpool Echo*, 31st July 1889.

LINKS TO THE RIPPER DIARY: DOES JAMES MAYBRICK FIT THE PROFILE OF A SERIAL KILLER?

Much of the debate about James Maybrick being a credible candidate to be Jack the Ripper centres around scientific and technical arguments surrounding the nature and the construction of the Diary. Not everyone agrees with this approach. Professor Rubinstein wrote the '*case that James Maybrick was the Ripper is strong even without the diary.*'[922]

He suggests the '*most striking evidence*' to support his bold statement were a number of communications found by Paul Feldman and his research team. One of these was a postcard of particular significance, and a transcript appeared in the *Liverpool Echo* of 10th October 1888, the day after the newspaper ran a story that the Ripper was about to strike in Dublin. The postcard stated:

> '*I beg to state the letters published in yours of yesterday are lies. It is somebody gulling the public. I am the Whitechapel purger. On 13th, at 3pm, will be on Stage, as am going to New York. But will have some business before I go. Yours Truly, Jack the Ripper DIEGO LAURENZ (Genuine).*'

Rubinstein felt this was the most important clue to the Ripper's identity. because '*Diego*' is Spanish for '*James,*' while '*Laurenz*' is meant to rhyme with '*Florence.*' To Rubinstein, this was an example of the word games that permeated the Diary. The author of the letter was stating that his name, and therefore the name of the Ripper himself, was none other than James Maybrick.

Rubinstein also suggests that the reason why there were no Ripper killings in October 1888 was because James may have been in New York on a business trip. Rubinstein asks why did the Ripper killings stop – if indeed they did – after the brutal murder of Mary Kelly on 9th November? He answers his question by pointing to the fact that, on 19th November, James started having medical consultations with Dr Drysdale, who successfully treated him with homeopathic remedies and, as a result, he lost interest in further killings.

Rubinstein's proposition is extremely tenuous, and lacks any supporting evidence. For example, there are no records that show James travelled to New York or anywhere else abroad in October 1888. Nevertheless, there are some parts of Rubinstein's hypothesis that are worthy of further discussion. Rubinstein suggested there are aspects of James' behavioural patterns that match the profile of a serial killer, writing:

> '*All five murders were committed on Friday, Saturday or Sunday. The idea of weekend slaughter is itself strange: prostitutes walked the streets of Whitechapel every night, but there were more potential witnesses around on weekends. This pattern, however, is consistent with the lifestyle of a Liverpool cotton broker who spent the weekdays at the Liverpool Cotton Exchange but was free to travel on weekends (as Maybrick was). All the murders took place late at night or early in the morning. Few men can be about at that hour without attracting attention from their family, neighbours, servants, land-ladies, or fellow tenants, let alone covered in blood and carrying a knife and the organs of their victims. But Maybrick went to London alone and lived alone in the centre of the Ripper district, coming and going as he pleased.*'

The fact that James did visit London frequently is undisputed. In his opening address at Florence's trial, Sir Charles Russell said: '*You cannot follow closely the habits of a man who is in Liverpool, London, and other places going about his business.*'[923] James not only visited London frequently, he also probably had a clear knowledge of the Whitechapel area, where the murders took place, as he had moved to London in 1858 to work. His workplace was off Fenchurch Street which was close to where Catherine Eddowes was murdered. While he was in London, he started a long-term relationship with Sarah Ann Robertson. Records have been discovered that show Sarah lived at 40 Mark Lane and later at 55 Bromley Street, two streets close to the East End of London. If James did live with Sarah during certain periods in his life, then he would have acquired a familiarity with the area where the Ripper murders were later to have been committed.

Although James did visit London at the weekends, it is unlikely he stayed by himself on these trips to the capital. It is more likely he stayed with his brother Michael or with other business associates, or in hotels that were popular with the cotton merchants. For the Ripper to have remained undiscovered, it was vital that the killer returned to a base where he would be completely alone. This would have allowed for his movements to go unnoticed and provided him with the opportunity to clean himself and remove any blood-soaked clothes without detection.

---

[922] Rubinstein, W. D., 'Hunt for Jack the Ripper' in *History Today*, Vol. 50, May 2000.
[923] Irving H.B., op cit., page 179.

James Maybrick (*Weekly News*, 9th June 1889)

The author of the Diary wrote, '*I have taken a small room in Middlesex Street... It is indeed an ideal location. I have walked the streets and have become more than familiar with them.*' Although there is no evidence to prove that James rented a room in Middlesex Street, the address provided is suggestive. Professor Canter developed geographical profiling, a technique that uses crime locations to help understand the offender and also to help identify where the offender might be living. Canter wrote the movements of serial killers are not random; they need to know the area of their criminal activities extremely well if they are to avoid capture.[924]

With all five canonical murders being committed in a relatively small area, coupled with the fact that they all occurred in the early hours of the morning, suggests that the murderer had a base somewhere in a circle marked out by the five crime scenes. Canter fed the known details of the murders into a special computer programme developed under his guidance at Liverpool University. The result suggested that the murderer lived somewhere between Mitre Square and Miller's Court, in the vicinity of Middlesex Street. As Professor Canter put it, if the Diary is a fraud, then the diarist made a '*remarkably good guess*' and if it is genuine, then it fits in with what we know about the '*activities and movements of many, but certainly not all, serial killers.*'[925]

While certain aspects of James' life do fit some of the circumstantial aspects of profiling, the key question is whether he had the mindset of a serial killer who brutally and savagely murdered prostitutes. It is true that James regularly visited prostitutes. Mary Hogwood, a brothel-keeper in Norfolk, Virginia stated in an affidavit she provided after Florence's trial that James frequented her brothel when he was in America. William T. Stead, the editor of the Victorian journal the *Review of Reviews*, visited Liverpool in the early 1890s to try to establish the truth about Florence's guilt. He was scathing about James' character, writing that he maintained '*relations with loose women.*'[926]

One of the features of the Diary is that its author appears to have a knowledge of the symptoms and effects of long-term arsenic abuse. There is a great deal of evidence to support the view that James was an arsenic addict. It is the view of those who think the Diary might be genuine, that James' arsenic addiction had a powerful and an adverse effect on his demeanour and personality, and this in turn may have caused him to have become a brutal murderer. Dr Hopper, James' doctor, said that although he was generally a healthy man he did complain from time to time of various symptoms, such as dyspepsia and nervousness. After June 1888, '*he complained more than formerly*', and between June and September 1888 he saw James very frequently, '*perhaps twenty*' times.[927]

At Florence's trial, Sir Charles Russell stated that James '*had been ordered to Harrogate for his health*' in 1888.[928] It was around about this time that Florence told Dr Hopper that James was '*taking some very strong medicine which had a bad influence on him; for he always seemed worse after each dose.*' Therefore, at the time of the Ripper murders, James' long-term addiction to arsenic was clearly having a detrimental effect on his health.

Shirley Harrison argued that James' work and lifestyle provided a public profile of a person who was outwardly sociable and genial, but behind '*the well-groomed facade there was a darker side. Rumours spread during Florie's trial that he had killed his neighbour's dogs; there was a strange packet marked 'poison for cats' and the known outbursts of violent temper resulting in blows.*'[929]

Dr Forshaw, a specialist consultant in addiction at the Maudsley Psychiatric Hospital in London, spent several months examining the Diary. He produced a lengthy report in which he concluded that if you had to rely on the content of the Diary, then '*on the balance of probabilities from a psychiatric perspective, it is authentic.*'[930] Forshaw told Harrison serial killers are nearly all male, and they are often hypochondriacs. They may appear on the outside to be mild-mannered, but deep down they '*seethe with pent-up anger.*' They often '*dream of power and are preoccupied with their masculinity and sexual potency.*'[931]

One of the major problems with the analyses provided by Professor Canter and Dr Forshaw is that they rest on the hypothesis that the Diary is an authentic document written by James Maybrick. If that is not the case, then both are

[924] Canter D., *Mapping Murder*, (Virgin, London, 2003) page 86.
[925] Ibid., page 94.
[926] Stead W. T., 'Ought Mrs Maybrick to be Tortured to Death?' In *The Review of Reviews*, (vol. VI, October, 1892) pp. 390-396.
[927] Irving H.B., op cit., pages 32-33.
[928] Ibid., page 69.
[929] Harrison S., op cit., page 341.
[930] Ibid., page 19.
[931] Ibid., page 344.

of little help in identifying the real Whitechapel killer. For example, the only evidence that James had a base in Middlesex Street comes from the Diary; there is no other collaborating evidence to support such a statement. The two experts also rely on information about James' personality that came from Shirley Harrison, and some of that had been selectively chosen. For example, Harrison suggests James was involved in the mysterious death of two dogs belonging to his neighbour. In fact, there is no evidence to support such a view. Also, James was not viewed as a particularly violent man. He did have a temper and on at least one occasion he did hit Florence, but most people seemed to have enjoyed his company and he had many long-standing male and female friends.

Any detailed profiling analysis of James must move away from using information from the Diary, and instead take a holistic and not a selective view of his personality traits. One such profiling exercise has been undertaken by John Douglas, who was a leading expert on criminal investigative analysis during his 25 years at the FBI. He was part of the team that investigated the Unabomber and the JonBenét Ramsey cases.

In his book, *The Cases That Haunt Us*, written with the novelist and filmmaker Mark Olshaker, Douglas dealt with the Ripper murders and with James Maybrick as a potential suspect. He started by examining details of the murders of the five canonical killings to see if any behavioural clues could be ascertained from the way in which the victims were killed. For example, in the case of the first assumed victim, Polly Nichols, she had severe bruising to the face. Douglas wrote that this suggested an initial '*blitz-style attack*' to quickly neutralise any defence that she could pose to try and ward off the attack. Douglas argued this suggested an offender who was '*unsure of himself*,' someone with an inadequate personality who lacked the confidence to think they could easily dominate women.

On a couple of occasions it appeared that an attempt had been made to decapitate the corpse. To Douglas, this meant that the killer was a person who '*both hates women and has a bizarre and perverse curiosity about the human body*.' All of the victims had been savagely cut and, with the exception of Elizabeth Stride, all had body parts cut or removed. In contrast to these acts of sheer brutality, some of the victims' personal possessions had been purposely and carefully placed around their bodies. In the case of Annie Chapman, the second victim, her belly had been sliced open and her intestines had been ripped out and placed over her shoulder, but personal items had apparently been placed with some care around the body. Douglas wrote such behaviour was not uncommon amongst offenders who committed this type of brutal and frenzied style of attack. The careful and ritualistic elements indicated the need to '*control or master small, discrete components of the crime scene or victim*.' The removal of body parts, especially genitalia, showed that the victim had '*real problems with normal sexual functioning*.' Douglas used this information, and more, to provide a list of offender traits and characteristics of the killer. Such a list can then be compared to the known facts about James Maybrick.

OFFENDER TRAITS

(John Douglas and Mark Olshaker, 2000)[932]

Profile Feature of the Whitechapel Serial Killer

The killer was a white male, aged between around 25 to 35 (though his age is a '*difficult characteristic to categorise*'), who did '*not look out of the ordinary*.'

Does James Maybrick match the Profile Feature?

James does *not* match the age profile, being almost twice the suggested age. He was also physically unwell at the time of the killings.

Profile Feature

The killer came from a home with a '*domineering mother and weak, passive and/or absent father. In all likelihood, the mother drank heavily and enjoyed the company of many men*.'

James Maybrick

Although little is known about James' mother, it is extremely unlikely that she drank heavily or cavorted with many men. James' father was certainly not a weak or passive figure.

Profile Feature

As a result of his childhood, the killer would have become '*asocial, preferring to be alone. His anger became internalised, and in his younger years, he expressed his pent-up destructive emotions by setting fires and mistreating or torturing animals*.'

James Maybrick

Little is known of James' childhood, but there is no evidence to suggest that either James or his brothers had anything other than a normal homelife. All of them grew up to be responsible citizens and held respectable jobs. James also became a loving father.

[932] Douglas J. and Olshaker M., *The Cases that Haunt Us*, (Pocket books, London, 2000) pages 64-66.

Profile Feature

The killer would be employed, hence the murders taking place at the weekend. He would have '*sought a position where he could work alone and vicariously experience his destructive fantasies… this might include employment as a butcher, mortician's helper.*'

James Maybrick

James was employed, though in Liverpool and not London. His work involved constant interactions with others. The essence of being a successful cotton merchant was the ability to work with and be trusted by others. A loner could not have functioned in the cotton trade. James was a member of many clubs.

Profile Feature

The killer would be '*paranoid,*' with a poor self-image. There could possibly be some type of '*physical abnormality, scarring or speech impediment that he perceived as psychologically crippling.*'

James Maybrick

There is no evidence that James was paranoid or suffering from a poor self-image, though he did suffer from bouts of pessimism over his company's business prospects.

Profile Feature

The killer would '*not be adept at meeting people socially, and most of his relationships would have been with prostitutes.*' This type of offender is unlikely to have been married '*or to have carried on a normal relationship with a woman.*'

James Maybrick

James did have relationships with prostitutes; however, he was very adept at meeting people, and had many long-standing male and female friends. He was also married with children, and the early years of his marriage seem to have been happy ones.

Profile Feature

The killer would have been perceived as a '*quiet, shy, loner, slightly withdrawn, obedient and fairly neat and orderly in appearance.*'

James Maybrick

James did like to be neat and properly attired, but he was not in any way shy or withdrawn, or a loner. If anything, he craved company.

Profile Feature

The killer was '*disorganised,*' not sophisticated enough to commit a well-planned crime. He would not have wanted to communicate with the police through the use of cleverly constructed letters and write about future crimes as he would only be thinking about the present. That means the *Dear Boss* letter and *Saucy Jacky* postcard are '*fakes*'

James Maybrick

The diarist clearly implies that he wrote some letters to the police, including the *Dear Boss* letter. Another problem here is the handwriting of the letter does not match that of James. Also, it is widely accepted that the *Dear Boss* letter is a fake written by a journalist. If this letter is a fake, then the Diary must also be a fake.

In the autumn of 1888, James Maybrick was suffering from the long-term effects of drug abuse, and his marriage was getting close to breaking point. Nevertheless, if one strips the Diary away from the profiling process, one is left with a picture of a man who does not, in the least, resemble a psychopathic murderer. James had his faults; he had a temper, could be jealous and aggressive, but he was not a savage and sexually depraved serial killer. As Douglas wrote, '*How does a fifty-year-old man with a family, children, and no sociopathology suddenly blossom into a disorganised serial killer? He can't, and doesn't.*'

On top of that, James lived for another six months after the murder of Mary Kelly, yet no more Ripper murders are recorded. Professor Rubinstein's view that James – supposedly Britain's most notorious serial killer – was somehow magically cured after a few courses of treatment with a homeopathic medicine is not in the least bit credible.

The American Psychiatric Association defines personality as: '*The characteristic way in which a person thinks, feels, and behaves; the ingrained pattern of behaviour that each person evolves, both consciously and unconsciously, as the style of life or way of being in adapting to the environment.*'[933] These behaviour patterns are relatively stable throughout an individual's life, barring highly unusual circumstances. From a psychological perspective, childhood is the critical period in the formation of a sociopathic personality, and therefore the objective of any profiling analysis must be to find evidence of aberrant behaviour during James' upbringing. Of particular interest, is there any

[933] American Psychiatric Association. (2013). *Diagnostic and statistical manual of mental disorders* (5th ed.). Arlington, VA, page 103.

documentation of violent or aggressive behaviour from James, when he was a child or adolescent? To date, there is no significant indication that James' conduct was disordered as a child or as an adolescent. Furthermore, his upbringing was not an impoverished one and he appears to have lived in a stable and loving household.

With regard to his personality profile, it is apparent that James was drug dependent. Colleagues commented on his '*morose and pessimistic nature*' and quick temper. Today these symptoms would be consistent with a diagnosis of mild to moderate depression, likely associated with his drug abuse. In younger days, James was generally a strong and healthy man, yet he was a hypochondriac and a chronic user of both prescribed and non-prescribed drugs.

By 1888, James was keenly aware of his physical decline, adding to his feelings of depression. His spouse and significant others further reminded him of the aging process. An anti-depressant and/or cognitive-behavioural therapy may have worked wonders had they been available. James' answer to all this was to increase dosing himself. Such was his cognitive and physical decline it is difficult imagining the physically ill and cognitively dysfunctional James of 1888, travelling to London, viciously killing prostitutes and evading detection.

If James was Jack the Ripper, a diagnosis of sociopathic disorder would be justified. Without murder and harm to others, James' psychological diagnosis, based on Diagnostic and Statistical Manual (DSM-5) criteria, would likely be: (1) Major depressive disorder, recurrent. (2) Substance abuse disorder. (3) Gambling disorder, possible. (4) Illness anxiety disorder. (5) Major neurocognitive disorder due to another medical condition, possible.[934]

In other words, James did have health issues and he would have benefited from a course of drug therapy and/or cognitive therapy. However, he was in general a well-balanced and psychologically stable individual; he simply does not fit the profile of a profoundly brutal and inhuman serial killer.

[934] Psychological Assessment with the MMPI-2, (2001). Lawrence Erlbaum Associates, Inc., Publishers, Mahwah, New Jersey, London.

15

SCIENCE AND SUSPICION

Compared to what had happened at the coroner's inquest, when Florence's defence team had done little to resist the onslaught of attacks on her character, the first day of the trial had gone well for her. Despite these early positive steps, Florence was finding the court proceedings emotionally draining, but she still managed to remain relatively calm as she entered the courtroom on the second day of her trial. A local Liverpool newspaper commented, '*Mrs Maybrick looked more haggard today. Her attitude in the dock – patient, motionless, and modest – is, I feel sure, breaking down prejudice and winning her sympathy.*'[935] The reporter from the *Liverpool Echo* also remarked on Florence's calm composure in the dock, commenting that she '*sat in her accustomed attitude, her hands folded on her lap, her head slightly bent forward, and her eyes half closed, as if she were dozing.*'

It was not only Florence who was feeling the pressure of the occasion; even her defence counsel, Sir Charles Russell, '*looked somewhat fagged, but was alert as usual. He refreshed himself with large pinches of snuff and frequently flourished the famous bandana handkerchief which was a signal of attack at the Parnell Commission.*'[936]

The first witness on the second day of the trial was Dr Fuller, Michael Maybrick's doctor. He had examined James twice in April 1889 when he visited London to pay Florence's debts. The *Liverpool Daily Post* described him as a '*dapper little gentleman, self-confident and experienced – and he answered both Mr Addison and Sir Charles Russell with easy sang-froid, but added very little information before the court.*'[937]

Dr Fuller said the first time he examined James he had '*complained of pains in his head and of numbness, and said he was apprehensive of being paralysed.*'[938] After examining him, Dr Fuller could not find anything the matter with James apart from indigestion. He prescribed two medicines, one an aperient and the other a tonic, with liver pills. On Saturday, 20th April, James visited Fuller at his house; the doctor examined James again and found him better: '*The dyspeptic symptoms of which he complained had partially disappeared. I thereupon slightly altered the prescriptions and wrote another... None of the three prescriptions contained arsenic.*'[939]

The next two witnesses were employees at Clay and Abraham's chemist in Liverpool, where Fuller's medicine for James had been compounded. Christopher Robinson, a chemist's assistant, and Frederick Tozer, a chemist and druggist, both confirmed that '*there was no arsenic in the ingredients.*'[940]

The next four witnesses were the servants from Battlecrease. It must have been a painful experience for Florence to have to listen to all the minutiae of her personal life dragged out in court for all to hear.

Nurse Yapp was the first to give evidence, entering the witness box just after 11:00am. A local reporter wrote: '*the nurse in a spruce-looking black gown and sprightly fashionable hat, liberally adorned with pale pink flowers, stepped into the box amid the very pronounced interest and curiosity of the court.*'[941] Some of the criticisms of her actions had clearly affected her since the inquest, and she gave her evidence in a quiet voice and in a very subdued manner. The reporter from the *Liverpool Daily Post* noticed the change in her attitude, writing she was '*a good-looking girl of about two and twenty, with a painfully diffident manner – somewhat in contrast to her demeanour at the inquest when the whole affair seemed to be treated in a light-hearted and somewhat frivolous manner.*'[942]

Yapp gave her evidence so quietly that at one point Addison had to ask her to speak more loudly. She recalled the details of the argument between James and Florence that had occurred on the evening of the Grand National. She said about two or three weeks later Bessie Brierley, the housemaid, drew her attention to some flypapers that were soaking in a washbasin covered with a towel in Florence's bedroom. Addison asked her if she had ever seen flypapers being used for killing flies in the house, to which she answered, '*No, sir.*'[943] The nurse said on Tuesday, 7th May she had seen Florence pouring something out of one medicine bottle into another. After James' death, Bessie Brierley

[935] *Liverpool Review*, 3rd August 1889.
[936] *Liverpool Echo*, 1st August 1889.
[937] *Liverpool Daily Post*, 2nd August 1889.
[938] Irving H.B., op cit., page 58.
[939] Ibid., page 58.
[940] Ibid., page 63.
[941] *Liverpool Review*, 3rd August 1889.
[942] *Liverpool Daily Post*, 2nd August 1889.
[943] Irving H.B., op cit., page 65.

and herself – following instructions from Michael Maybrick – had gone to the linen closet; they '*did not find anything there but in the night nursery we found a chocolate box and packet. They were in a tray inside a trunk belonging to Mrs Maybrick. I opened the chocolate box in the presence of Nurse Wilson. I noticed the label, Arsenic - Poison for Cats.*'[944]

During his cross-examination of Yapp, Sir Charles Russell asked her about the incident when Florence was transferring medicine from one bottle to another. He established that it happened on the landing outside the main bedroom and was not done in a covert manner. Yapp admitted she had not attached any importance to the incident at the time. Russell then focused on the nurse's behaviour in opening the letter intended for Brierley. He asked her repeatedly why she opened it, and said if she was concerned the envelope had become dirty, then she could have placed the letter unopened into a clean envelope. Yapp replied, '*I never thought of that.*' Russell's questioning upset Yapp, and many observers felt she had betrayed her mistress.

Elizabeth Brierley, the housemaid at Battlecrease, was examined by Mr McConnell. She too recounted the details of the row between James and Florence on the night of the Grand National, saying that the following day she had found some flypapers soaking in a small sponge basin on the washstand in the bedroom and called the attention of Nurse Yapp to them. The next day she found more flypapers in the slop pail. She said flypapers had never been used for killing flies, and on top of that they '*were not troublesome at that time.*' Brierley had clearly made a mistake when she claimed she had first seen the flypapers, as Florence did not purchase them until three weeks after the Grand National. The housemaid said that before his final illness James had '*seemed to be a healthy man.*' On Friday, 3rd May, he had come '*home from business and was seized with vomiting.*'[945] This was an important admission, as Dr Carter was to suggest this was the day that James had been given the fatal dose of poison by Florence.

Mary Cadwallader, the waitress at Battlecrease, told the court that up to the time James attended the Wirral races he appeared to '*enjoy good health.*' On Friday morning, 26th April, a bottle of medicine had arrived in the post for James from London. On the morning of 28th April, Florence sent her to fetch Dr Humphreys as James was ill. Cadwallader said: '*Mr Maybrick said to me that he had had an overdose of medicine from London... Mr Maybrick said he felt very dizzy.*' She said on Tuesday 30th April, the cook had prepared food for James to take to his office; she had given it to Cadwallader, who in turn passed it to Florence. Florence wrapped the food in paper and string and gave it to James. Cadwallader said James' lunch was prepared this way two or three times.

Cadwallader was questioned quite extensively about the flypapers. She recalled '*some flypapers being brought to the house by the chemist's boy, but up to the time the master died no flypapers had been used. I did not notice the flies to be troublesome.*' She had burnt the flypapers around about the time James died.

Russell asked Cadwallader whether Florence was '*very attentive*' to James during his final illness; she answered '*Yes.*' He then asked her if she thought there was '*anything suspicious about what was done or not done*' by Florence at that time, and was told '*No, I did not.*'[946]

Elizabeth Humphreys, the cook, was the last of the servants to give evidence. The *Liverpool Daily Post* described her as the '*best and kindliest friend Mrs Maybrick had got amid these extraordinary surroundings.*'[947] She told the court that soon after her appointment she found about half dozen flypapers on the window sill in the kitchen. They lay there a long time and she only destroyed them just before James' death. Humphreys said the last time she prepared food for James was Saturday, the week before he died. After that she made nothing for him, apart from one glass of lemonade. She said Florence blamed her husband's illness on an overdose of his London medicine. Florence had thrown this medicine down the sink. The cook recalled an incident that had taken place on the evening of Thursday, 9th May. Florence said to her she was getting '*blamed for all this,*' and when Humphreys asked her in what way, she replied: '*In not getting other nurses and doctors.*' Humphreys said Florence subsequently went into the servants' hall and started to cry.

When Russell cross-examined Humphreys, he asked if she thought Florence's behaviour had appeared suspicious. She answered, '*No, it did not.*' Russell then asked her if Florence seemed to be attending to her husband, and was told: '*She seemed very kind to him, and spent all her time with him.*' He then asked her if she sympathised with Florence, to which Humphreys replied: '*I did, certainly.*' Humphreys said Florence was '*very much grieved over it and was very sorry. She was crying.*'[948]

Humphreys had a little taste of the pressure that Florence was under at the adjournment of the trial at the end of the sixth day, on Tuesday 6th August. As she left the court with Mary Cadwallader and some male friends from Warrington, they found themselves surrounded by an angry crowd of several hundred who rushed towards them. The *Liverpool Daily Post* reported: '*The crowd appeared to be under the impression that the females were the nurse,*

---

944 Ibid., page 67.
945 Ibid., pages 72-74.
946 Ibid., pages 74-79.
947 *Liverpool Daily Post*, 2nd August 1889.
948 Irving H.B., op cit., pages 79-87.

Alice Yapp, and Brierley, the housemaid. They hooted and groaned, and used every objectionable language with respect to these two women.'[949] The women were only saved by the intervention of their male friends, a burly Bold Street tradesman who struck out with his fists, and the deployment of half a dozen constables.

Dr Richard Humphreys was the final witness of the second day. According to one newspaper report, he spoke '*in a particularly loud, formal tone but with remarkable clearness.*'[950] He told the court that while he was treating the Maybrick children in March 1889, he had a conversation with Florence about her husband's health. She told him James '*was taking some white powder, which she thought was strychnine, and she asked what was likely to be the result.*'[951] Humphreys told her that, if James took a large enough dose, he could die.

Dr Humphreys said the first time he treated James was on Sunday 28th April, the day after the Wirral races. James complained about his chest, his heart and his fear of becoming paralysed. After examining him, Humphreys did not think there was too much wrong with him. He gave James some dilute prussic acid and advised him to drink nothing but soda water and milk for a day. Humphreys returned to Battlecrease that evening and found James much improved. He called again at 10:00am the next day, Monday, 29th April. All the symptoms had disappeared apart from a furred tongue. Humphreys examined him again, and concluded he was a chronic dyspeptic and prescribed a special diet. Humphreys said he next visited James on the evening on Wednesday, 1st May and found him much improved.

On Friday 3rd May, Humphreys received a request to visit James, who was ill again. Humphreys couldn't find anything wrong with him, and advised him to continue with the prescribed diet. At midnight, the doctor was back again at Battlecrease as James had become very ill. He was in bed and in great pain. James said that he had been sick twice since he arrived home, and thought it was due to some '*inferior sherry having been put in Du Barry's Revalenta food,*' which he had eaten at lunchtime.[952] Humphreys gave James a morphine suppository. He was there again the next morning and gave instructions that the patient was to drink nothing at all.

Humphreys told the court about his repeated visits to Battlecrease over the next few days and the different remedies he prescribed for James, though nothing seemed to improve the condition of the patient. One of the things he gave James was Fowler's solution, a mixture of white arsenic, carbonate of potash and lavender water. He gave James three doses, which he estimated would contain about 1/250th of a grain. On the afternoon of the same day – Tuesday, 7th May – Humphreys accompanied Dr Carter as he examined James. The two of them agreed that James was suffering from dyspepsia. Humphreys returned on Wednesday 8th May, and found James better, though he had endured a restless night. Following a request from Florence, Humphreys telegraphed a nursing agency for help. When he returned to Battlecrease that night at 7:00pm, he found Nurse Gore had arrived. Humphreys said that later in the evening Michael Maybrick had visited his house, and they had a lengthy discussion about James' health.

The next morning, Thursday 9th May, Humphreys again visited James. He found that the patient's condition had worsened, and he was in great pain. Humphreys returned later in the day, this time with Dr Carter. Following a conversation with Michael Maybrick, Humphreys carried out a test for a metallic irritant on James' faeces. The result was negative. He later tested James' urine, which again returned a negative result. Michael told Drs Humphreys and Carter he had serious grounds for believing that something was not right. Although both doctors were sceptical of his accusations, they agreed to keep a closer watch on events and Florence's actions.

On the afternoon of Friday 10th May. Humphreys considered James' condition had deteriorated, and that he was now in a '*serious condition.*' It was at this point he began to think that the accusations made by Michael '*might have some grounds.*'[953] The same day, Dr Carter took away the bottle of meat juice that Nurse Gore had seen Florence move. McConnell finished his examination by asking, '*From what you saw during his life and from the post-mortem examination, what do you say was the cause of death?*' Humphreys replied, '*Arsenic. Arsenical poisoning.*'[954]

It was late in the day when McConnell had finished questioning Dr Humphreys, leaving just a short time for Sir Charles Russell to start his cross-examination of the witness. Nevertheless, he did manage to get Humphreys to admit that, prior to James Maybrick, he had never previously assisted at a post-mortem examination of any person supposed to have died from arsenical poison, or at a post-mortem where it was alleged that death had been due to irritant poisoning. Humphreys also admitted that he did not suspect James' illness was a case of arsenical poisoning until Michael Maybrick had suggested it to him. These were important admissions that revealed the inexperience of the doctor in dealing with arsenic poisoning. One American newspaper commented that Russell had put in some '*sledge-hammer work in way of cross-examination,*' and this had '*caused a great rebound of popular opinion in Mrs Maybrick's favour.*'[955] Although such a view was an exaggeration of the situation, Russell had made inroads into the prosecution's case.

---

[949] *Liverpool Daily Post*, 7th June 1889.
[950] *Liverpool Review*, 3rd August 1889.
[951] Irving H.B., op cit., page 87.
[952] Ibid., page 90.
[953] Ibid., page 94.
[954] Ibid., page 97.
[955] *The World* (New York), 2nd August 1889.

Florence in the dock at St George's Hall (© Chronicle/Alamy)

When Florence entered the dock on the third day of the trial, the reporter from the *Liverpool Daily Post* thought she looked '*extremely jaded.*' He wrote that her '*face was perfectly white and thin, and although she still maintained generally her perfect repose, there were occasional movements of the head indicating that she was struggling against weakness and illness.*' The female warder, who had been sitting some yards away at the side of the dock, moved her chair so she was sitting right next to Florence in order to be ready to '*render instant assistance in case it should be required.*'[956] Despite her warder's concerns, Florence may have felt the trial was beginning to go her way. At lunchtime, unlike the first two days, she ate the sandwiches provided for her by the Bee Hotel in St John's Lane. She even managed a small glass of claret.

The third day of the trial started with Dr Humphreys back in the witness box. As he had with the earlier witnesses, Sir Charles Russell managed to score a series of points in favour of the defence's case. He asked Humphreys if he had noticed whether James had any redness of the eyes or the eyelids. He replied, '*I did not.*' Russell pressed the point, and Humphreys said he was positive there had not been any redness of James' eyes. Humphreys also admitted that up until Thursday, 8th May James had not suffered from any excessive purging or diarrhoea. Both of these admissions were important because they were typical symptoms of an acute case of arsenical poisoning. Russell then quizzed Humphreys at some length about the tests he conducted on James' faeces and urine. The doctor had to embarrassingly admit that he was '*not skilled in the details of testing,*' and that his tests might have '*been inefficient.*' Although Russell had scored an important point, he did not want to press it too far because Humphreys' tests had failed to detect any arsenic. This was an important issue for the defence, because previously Addison had argued that the arsenic that killed passed quickly out of the victim's system. If this was the case, then one would have expected James' urine and faeces to have contained arsenic.

Russell then moved on to a series of questions about the cause of death and managed to obtain '*two astounding admissions.*' He asked Humphreys, '*had it not been for the suggestion of arsenic, were you prepared to give a certificate of death if he had died on Wednesday?*' Humphreys replied, '*Yes.*' Russell then asked Humphreys what he believed had been the cause of death and he replied, '*Acute congestion of the stomach.*'

Russell, in a very calm and deliberate manner, told Humphreys to consider the next question very carefully before answering it. He then paused for effect, and there was dead silence in the courtroom. He asked Humphreys if he could mention any post-mortem symptom which is distinctive of arsenical poisoning which is not also distinctive of gastro-enteritis? Humphreys replied, '*I can't give you any.*'[957] The reporter from the *Liverpool Echo* wrote that, following Humphreys' reply, Russell '*looked triumphantly at his junior counsel [Mr Pickford] and those who closely followed the medical evidence and understood the value of this admission cast meaningful looks around.*'[958] Before he had finished, Russell also got Humphreys to state that Florence had done '*everything*' he had requested her to do with regard to James' treatment.

The questioning of Dr Humphreys had lasted over one hour and thirty minutes, and as he left the witness box, there was a general movement in the courtroom as people stretched their legs. At 11:45am, Dr Carter was called to give his evidence. As an experienced physician, he gave his evidence in a resolute and clear manner. During his testimony, Florence showed signs of exhaustion and the female warder beside her handed her a glass of water. Carter ran through the course of events during his visits to Battlecrease on Tuesday 7th and Thursday 9th May. He said on his visit on the 9th, both he and Dr Humphreys started to believe that James was in a serious condition and they decided to double the doses of his medicine. On that day, Michael Maybrick informed him of his suspicions that Florence may have administered some form of poison to James. Although he was doubtful about such a view, he did carry out tests on some Neave's food and brandy that Michael had given him. In both cases he found nothing wrong with them. On Friday 10th, Carter again saw James in the presence of Dr Humphreys. It was at this point that Michael gave Carter the bottle of Valentine's meat juice for testing. Carter told the court that he had '*examined the meat juice by Reinsch's test, and discovered a marked deposit on the copper foil introduced upon boiling it in hydrochloric acid. That meant there was some metallic substance in the sample.*'[959] Carter told Dr Humphreys the result of the test at 10:30am the next morning, when he arrived at Battlecrease. He examined James, and came to the opinion he was going to die. After he left Battlecrease he carried out more tests on the meat juice, finding traces of arsenious acid. Addison asked Carter what he thought had killed James. He replied, '*Arsenical poisoning.*'[960] Addison then asked Carter questions about James' post-mortem, at which he had been present. Carter said: '*From the post-mortem examination I came to the conclusion that there had been an irritant of some kind, and now, since I have heard the evidence given by Mr Davies, I have no doubt whatever that arsenical poisoning was the cause of death. I judge the fatal dose had been given on Friday 3rd, but a dose might have been given after that.*'[961]

---

956 *Liverpool Daily Post*, 3rd August 1889.
957 Irving H.B., op cit., page 109.
958 *Liverpool Echo,* 2nd August 1889.
959 Irving H.B., op cit., page 115.
960 Ibid., page 116.
961 Ibid., page 117.

Carter told the court that, in his opinion, James died after being given a series of small doses of arsenic spread over a period of time, commencing on 27th April, when he first became ill. As it normally takes two grains of arsenic to kill a person, Carter speculated that James may have been given that amount in five successive doses of ⅖ of a grain.

Russell started his questioning of Carter in an extremely courteous manner, an indication of how important he considered the witness to be. Although Carter had earlier told Addison he had experience of '*cases of overdosing medicinally with arsenic*,' Russell quickly established that, prior to James, he had not assisted at a post-mortem of a person whose death had been caused by arsenic. Russell also got Carter to admit that some of his knowledge on arsenic had come not from practical experience but from '*reading up*' on the subject. Russell managed to get Carter to agree that redness of the eyes and an itching sensation in the eyelids, both commonly found in cases of arsenic poisoning, were not present in James' case.[962]

Russell then asked Carter about the onset of diarrhoea. He put it to Carter that diarrhoea typically sets in within two hours of the administration of arsenic, but in James' case it did not appear, according to Dr Humphreys, until Thursday 9th May. This was important, as Carter had suggested James had received the fatal dose around 3rd May. Carter responded by saying he had noticed diarrhoea starting to appear earlier on the 7th. When Russell asked if he was therefore taking a different view to Humphreys, Carter said he took Humphreys '*to be correct.*'

After a break for lunch, Dr Barron entered the witness box. He had attended James' post-mortem and exhumation. He told the court that he '*attended the post-mortem on Mrs Maybrick's behalf.*' He said he had concluded that '*death was due to acute inflammation of the stomach, probably caused by some irritant poison*.'[963]

During his cross-examination, Russell tried to establish that although death was caused by some irritant poison, that poison could have been impure food rather than arsenic. He asked the doctor if impure food might have caused gastritis or gastro-enteritis. He answered that it might have. A little later, he asked the doctor if he would be able to '*differentiate the symptoms*' of food poisoning from arsenic poisoning, to which Barron replied: '*I should not be able to do so myself.*'[964] Russell then asked Barron about James' post-mortem and the condition of his stomach, and whether there were marks of any kind that were characteristic of arsenic. Barron said, '*No, I have no mention of such on my notes*.' This answer from such a respected and experienced medical man had the potential to completely derail the whole prosecution's case, and for the first time in three days Addison got to his feet to object to the use of Barron's notes from the post-mortem.

When he was re-examined by Addison, Barron told the court he knew people to have had gastritis or inflammation of the stomach after eating a leg of mutton which had gone off and, in another case, after eating grouse meat that was tainted. In both cases, those infected had recovered. Addison asked him if he remembered a death from poisoned meat, to which he replied '*No.*'[965]

The next three witnesses were the police officers who had been directly involved in the case. Their contributions were largely perfunctory, outlining the actions they had taken and when they had taken them. After they made their statements they were barely questioned by either prosecution or defence counsels. Under cross-examination, Inspector Baxendale said none of the objects removed from Battlecrease had been '*locked or sealed.*'[966] Christie believes this to be significant, as it suggests that whoever brought the arsenic into the house had not tried to hide it.[967]

Mr Edward Davies was the next witness. He was the county analytical chemist who had carried out the tests to ascertain whether arsenic could be found in James' body or in the numerous other items removed from Battlecrease and James' office. The reporter from the *Liverpool Daily Post* described Davies as a man of '*decided character and great ability, an enthusiast in his profession, with steely-grey hair and beard and spectacles*.'[968] When he was called to give his evidence, he was sitting in the body of the court and had to push his way through the crowded room while holding a huge yellow tin travelling trunk that contained the various bottles and items in which he had found traces of arsenic. As he stood in the witness box surrounded by all these bottles, he '*lent a dramatic colour to the scene.*' It was not long before Davies became confused when identifying items and Mr Justice Stephen directed Inspector Baxendale to stand by him to help in the process. Davies told the court his first involvement in the case came on Saturday, 11th May, when Dr Carter had asked him to test the bottle of meat juice. He tested the bottle on 12th May, and found the presence of arsenic. He said he thought it had been added to the meat juice in solution form, as there was no solid arsenic in the sample tested. This was an important point, but neither the prosecution nor the defence teams followed up on Davies' comment.

Davies continued by methodically working his way through the items he had tested in which arsenic had been found. His ponderous style did not play well with the spectators. One reporter commented: '*Mr Davies is a painfully*

[962] Ibid., page 120.
[963] Ibid., page 124.
[964] Ibid., page 125.
[965] Ibid., page 127.
[966] Ibid., page 128.
[967] Christie T.L., op cit., page 102.
[968] *Liverpool Daily Post*, 3rd August 1889.

slow, excruciatingly accurate, elderly gentleman, who describes inch by inch and step by step every process he has adopted in connection with his analysis. His accuracy, though perhaps necessary, is desolation to all forms of human patience.'[969] Davies said he found arsenic in various parts of James' body including the intestines (an amount too small to determine), the kidneys (estimated to be $^{1}/_{100}$ of a grain) and the liver (a distinct amount). He found no arsenic in either the spleen or the stomach. He then mentioned the other items in which arsenic had been found, including samples from the sinks and lavatories from Battlecrease, various medicine bottles, the contents of the bottles from James' hat boxes, the packet labelled *Arsenic - Poison for Cats*, cooking utensils from James' office, the flypapers and Florence's dressing gown, handkerchief and apron. The moment when Davies produced Florence's fashionable dressing gown from his large tin box of exhibits and held it up for all to see was described by one newspaper as the '*sensation of the day.*' As he pointed to the pocket where he had found traces of arsenic, his words and actions were '*followed by the audience with intense interest.*'[970]

When Russell cross-examined Davies, he focused much of his attention on the small amount of the arsenic found in James' body. He established that the liver was the only organ in which arsenic had been found in any weighable amount. Russell asked Davies to show the test tube to the court that contained the arsenic crystals he had obtained from James' liver; Davies retrieved the item and passed it to the judge, telling him the arsenic appeared as a minute film on the pieces of copper foil in the tube. Mr Justice Stephen, despite employing two different magnifying glasses, could not identify the film. He asked the chaplain if he could use his slate hat so he could examine the test tube against a dark background, but still struggled to see the film. After a lengthy pause, the judge passed the test tube and magnifying glasses to the jury who searched for the film using the black coats of their fellow jurymen as a dark background. Russell then asked to see the test tube that contained the traces of arsenic that had been found in the kidneys. Once again, the test tube was inspected by the judge before it was passed to the jury.

Russell's strategy with the test tubes was clear; he wanted the jury to understand, in a very simple and practical manner, how little arsenic had been found in James' body. Russell continued by asking Davies about the parts of the body in which no arsenic had been found. Davies had to admit that none had been found in the stomach, the contents of the stomach, the spleen, the bile, the fluid that escaped from the body when it was turned over, the heart, the lungs, as well as none in the bedding or the clothing. Russell asked Davies about the small round unlabelled bottle that contained a weak solution of arsenic and some scent. He suggested that, as it was scented, it could have been used for '*toilet purposes.*' Davies replied, '*It might have suggested that.*'[971] This was important for the defence, as it supported Florence's claim the flypapers had been bought purely for cosmetic purposes. Russell then suggested the arsenic stain was on the handkerchief as it had been used to apply this solution to Florence's face, and the arsenic stain in the pocket of the dressing gown was there because the handkerchief had been placed in the pocket. Davies replied, '*I believe what was found in the pocket [of the dressing gown] did come from the handkerchief.*'[972]

Russell finished his cross-examination by questioning Davies once again about the amount of arsenic he had found in the liver. Russell asked, '*In this case you only found half the arsenic you have found in any case which ended fatally*?' Davies replied: '*Yes; it was one-half of what I found in the case of Margaret Jennings [one of the women murdered by Mrs Flanagan], and that was half of the smallest amount I have ever known.*'[973] *This evidence again reiterated the point that only small amounts of arsenic had been found in James' body and it 'scored well for the defence.*'[974]

Sometime after the trial, Davies was approached by MacDougall, the Scottish lawyer who campaigned for Florence's release, as he wanted to try and ascertain the exact specific gravities for the meat juices he had tested. Davies refused, saying that: '*Being perfectly satisfied of the justice of the verdict, I decline to enter upon any discussion, as that is not my duty in the matter*.'[975]

It had been another long and tiring day for Florence, and on a couple of occasions she looked as though she was about to faint. The reporters felt that, for much of the trial, she had a '*very languid interest in the proceedings*;' however, during the cross-examination of Mr Davies she seemed to take a real interest in what was happening. As Russell quizzed the analyst, Florence followed every question with '*undisguised anxiety*' and appeared to be in a state of '*nervous excitement.*' At the rising of the court at the end of the day, for the first time during the trial she '*had to be assisted down the stairs by one of the warders.*'[976] Although Florence was feeling the pressures of the trial, the momentum was continuing to shift slowly in her favour.

During the break for lunch, Alfred Brierley had been spotted by some in the crowd outside the court and he had been loudly hissed. In contrast, as Florence left in the prison van to return to Walton Gaol the jeers that had greeted

---

[969] *Liverpool Review*, 10th August 1889.
[970] *Liverpool Weekly Courier*, 3rd August 1889.
[971] Irving H.B., op cit., page 137.
[972] Ibid., page 138.
[973] Ibid., page 141.
[974] Ryan B., op cit., page 150.
[975] MacDougall A.W., (1891) op. cit., page 604.
[976] *Pall Mall Gazette*, 3rd August 1889.

her on the first day of the trial had now turned to cheers. A little later, when Russell left the court, he was warmly applauded by the crowd who had waited outside hoping to catch a glimpse of him.

Saturday 4th August, was the fourth day of the trial, and the final prosecution witnesses gave their evidence in the morning session. Interest in the case was as high as ever, and the crowds outside and inside the court remained large. As the use of opera glasses had upset many of the witnesses they had been banned by the court officials. Some of the ladies attempted to get around the ban by using very powerful hand eye-glasses.

Just before 10:00am, Florence walked up the stairs into the dock. She was '*pale and there was a wearied look about her eyes, a thoughtful wrinkle on her brows; yet she continued to seem fairly composed.*'[977] The first three witnesses of the day were the professional nurses who had been at Battlecrease during the final stage of James' illness. Nurse Gore said she first arrived at Battlecrease on Wednesday 8th May, and described James' condition as '*very ill indeed.*'[978] Gore said she was relieved by Nurse Callery on Thursday morning, but was back on duty at the house on Thursday night. She then told the court the story about how Florence moved a bottle of Valentine's meat juice into the inner-dressing room before returning into the bedroom and placing it on the round table.

In his cross-examination, Russell asked if '*anything injurious*' was given to James while she was on duty. She replied, '*Not that I am aware of.*' He then asked Gore if she, or any of the other nurses, had given any extract from the meat juice bottle to James after Florence had moved it. She replied, '*No.*'

In his re-examination of the witness, Addison asked Gore if her suspicions had been aroused by the manner in which Florence had taken the meat juice bottle into the inner-dressing room. Russell immediately rose to his feet and objected to the question. Mr Justice Stephen intervened in this spat between the counsels, and asked Gore if Florence had taken the bottle openly. She replied that Florence '*did not take it openly... She took it from the table in her left hand, and covered it with her right hand.*'[979]

Nurse Callery was the next professional nurse to be questioned. Under examination from McConnell, she said that while she cared for James, he was '*very much exhausted, and complained of a burning sensation in his throat and pains in his abdomen.*'[980] Florence had remained in the bedroom with James most of the time, but only she and the other nurses had administered food and medicine to him. At one point James said to Florence, '*You have given me the wrong medicine again.*'[981] The suspicious nature of the remark was undercut when Callery said it had been made by James when Florence was trying to get him to take some medicine being administered by the nurse.

Under cross-examination from Russell, Callery said James had not been given any Valentine's meat juice during the day. Russell asked Callery what James did when Florence left the room. She replied, '*He asked for her when she went out of the room.*' Russell then asked if Florence appeared to be very anxious about her husband. She replied, '*Yes, very much so,*'[982] and added that Florence used to sit on the bed talking to him.

Nurse Wilson followed Callery into the witness box and was questioned by Mr Swift. Like the other nurses, she also confirmed it was she and not Florence who administered all the medicine and food to James. The nurse said that at about 6:00pm on Friday evening, James said to Florence on three occasions: '*Oh Bunny, Bunny, how could you do it? I did not think it of you.*'[983] Wilson said James '*appeared quite conscious*' when he made his remarks to Florence.

Wilson told the court she was present in the house when James died, and she was still there when Nurse Yapp opened the trunk that contained the chocolate box with the package *Arsenic - Poison for Cats*. In his cross-examination Russell asked if James had experienced delirious turns on the day that he made the '*Oh Bunny*' remark. She replied, '*After then he was delirious.*' Russell asked, '*The same evening*?' and received the reply, '*Yes, sir.*' During this line of questioning Florence became noticeably affected, and tears were clearly visible in her eyes.[984]

The next witness was Alfred Schweisso, the head waiter at Flatman's Hotel in London. He identified Florence as the woman who arrived at the hotel around lunchtime on Thursday, 21st March and occupied a bedroom suite with adjoining dining room. He testified that Florence went out Thursday evening with a gentleman. He said that when he took a single breakfast to her sitting room at 9:30am on Friday morning he saw a different man in the room with her. This must have been a mistake, as Brierley did not arrive in London until Friday evening. Schweisso said that on '*Friday, the 22nd, I saw Mrs Maybrick with Mr Brierley.*' The two of them had '*occupied the same bedroom up to Sunday, when they left between twelve and one o'clock. Mrs Maybrick paid the bill.*'[985] At the inquest, he had said Brierley had paid the bill. Schweisso's evidence at the trial, as it had done at the inquest, sent shock waves across the court and the mutterings became even louder when Russell declined the opportunity to cross-examine him, thereby

---

977 *Lloyd's Weekly Newspaper*, 4th August 1889.
978 Irving H.B., op cit., page 141.
979 Ibid., page 150.
980 Ibid., page 151.
981 Ibid., page 152.
982 Ibid., page 154.
983 Ibid., page 155.
984 *Lloyd's Weekly Newspaper*, 4th August 1889.
985 Irving H.B., op cit., page 157.

admitting the adulterous affair of his client. After the trial, as Schweisso waited at Lime Street Station for his train back to London, an Irishman who presumably had sympathies for Florence's plight knocked out three of his teeth.[986]

The final witness for the prosecution was Dr Thomas Stevenson, a leading toxicologist whom the prosecution believed would be their '*star witness*' and help deliver a guilty verdict.[987] Stevenson was born in Rainton in Yorkshire, entering Guy's Hospital in London as a medical student in 1859. His great ability was soon recognised, and after qualifying as a doctor he rapidly rose through the hospital's medical hierarchy. He became demonstrator in practical chemistry at Guy's in 1864, lecturer in chemistry between 1870 and 1898 and lecturer in forensic medicine between 1878 and 1908. He also served as the President of the Institute of Chemistry and of the Society of Public Analysts. In 1872, he became scientific analyst to the Home Office, rising to the position of senior analyst in 1881. In his latter role, he came to be involved in many of the leading poisoning trials for the next 25 years. His evidence, delivered in his strong Yorkshire accent, carried great weight, and he was rarely knocked out of his stride while under cross-examination.

Dr Thomas Stevenson (1838-1908)

Addison asked Stevenson about the articles he received from Inspector Baxendale on 22nd July. Stevenson said he received eleven vessels, and had analysed five of them in a very thorough and scientific manner. His testimony was highly technical, and many in the court found it hard to follow. He testified that one of the vessels contained the content of James' stomach, which he analysed but found no arsenic. Another jar was labelled intestines and spleen, but Stevenson said he could not find the spleen. He said he took some of the intestines and found they contained '*arsenic and bismuth.*' He concluded that in the intestines as a whole there '*would probably be* $^{1}/_{11}$ *part of a grain of white arsenic*' and '*1½ grains of bismuth.*' Analysing another jar labelled '*Kidney,*' he found the presence of arsenic but not enough to '*admit to accurate weighing.*' The whole of the liver was contained in two vessels. He carried out an analysis on just one of the vessels and found there would have been about ⅓ of a grain of arsenic for the whole liver. He also found a grain of bismuth for the whole liver.

Addison asked Stevenson what the results indicated. He answered, '*that the body at the time of death probably contained a fatal dose of arsenic.*' Addison then asked Stevenson in which organs of the body would you usually find arsenic after death. He replied, '*The liver is the chief organ one finds it in cases of arsenic poisoning, and, I may add, in large quantities.*' Stevenson told the court, with an air of complete confidence and authority, that as far as James' death was concerned, '*I have no doubt that this man died from the effects of arsenic.*' Addison asked what were the '*general grounds*' he had for forming that opinion, to which Stevenson replied that James' main symptoms were those attributable to irritant poisoning,

Some of the toxicological exhibits from Florence's trial, including the meat juice bottle, stored at New Scotland Yard (Chris Jones collection)

[986] Ryan B., op cit., page 228.
[987] Christie T.L., op. cit., page 107.

and they more closely resembled arsenic 'than any other irritant.' Addison then asked, '*In what respect is that so*?' Stevenson replied, '*The dryness of the throat, glazed appearance, the whole character of the sickness*.'[988]

Addison's next line of questioning was to try and show James' symptoms and death had been caused by a succession of small doses of arsenic. The analyst told the court that '*two grains or thereabouts*' constituted a fatal dose of arsenic, and such a dose would kill a person anywhere between '*six to twenty-four hours*.' Addison asked him what would be the effect of repeated, smaller doses of arsenic, to which Stevenson replied that the normal symptoms of arsenic poisoning would be '*much the same, but more spread out*.' Symptoms such as vomiting and purging would still occur, but may be '*less severe*.' With smaller doses the symptoms may subside, but would '*recur with another dose, and again subside, and so on*.' Addison questioned Stevenson about the symptoms that James complained about when he first became ill on 27th April. Stevenson said James' sickness, foulness of the tongue – a sign of a congested stomach – and nausea were all signs that he had consumed some irritant. Addison asked about the feeling of '*numbness*' that James complained of during that period. Stevenson replied that '*numbness is a symptom of arsenical poisoning, which usually comes on not at the beginning, but later on, when the patient is recovering, if he does recover*.' Stevenson's reply suggested that if James was suffering from numbness on 27th April he could not have been given arsenic on those dates. His comment surprised Addison and he quickly moved on to other questions. More surprising, is that the defence team did not pick up on this comment and use it to their advantage. Addison finished by tackling Stevenson on three lines of argument that he knew would be raised by Russell. He asked Stevenson if the gastro-enteritis that killed James could have been brought on after eating '*improper food*' rather than arsenic. The analyst said he had seen many such cases and had examined the organs of people who had died after eating impure food and that '*from post-mortem appearances gastro-enteritis is lower down in the bowels in the case of injurious food*.' Addison asked Stevenson if the deceased had taken arsenic as an antiperiodic in America years earlier, might it have contributed to his death. Stevenson replied, '*I do not think so*.' Finally, Addison asked whether arsenic was used as a cosmetic. Stevenson said it is '*very rarely used as a cosmetic; it irritates the skin*.'

As Russell rose to begin his cross-examination there was a feeling of great anticipation in the courtroom. It was a clash of two titans. Russell was considered one of the most *formidable* advocates of his generation, '*powerful in analysis and exposition, forceful in polemic and charming in persuasion*,' while Stevenson was considered the '*greatest toxicologist of the time*.'[989] The two men were known to one another. In 1886, Russell had been the prosecuting counsel in the trial of Adelaide Bartlett. It was a trial that had similarities with the Maybrick case, in that a young woman was accused of murdering her older husband after having an affair, though the alleged murder weapon in the Bartlett case was chloroform rather than arsenic. To help secure a guilty verdict, the Crown had called upon the services of Stevenson, whose expertise had proved decisive in the past. Although the case against Bartlett was strong, her counsel, Sir Edward Clarke, had managed to unsettle Stevenson and got him to contradict some of the important statements he made earlier in his testimony. This caused the case against Bartlett to collapse, and a not guilty verdict was secured. The lesson of the trial was not lost on Russell. He realised that if he too could unsettle Stevenson and undermine his conclusions, then he would be able to put a real dent in the prosecution's case.

During his examination by Addison, Stevenson had confidently asserted his conclusions were based on his '*own very extensive experience*.' Russell started his cross-examination by trying to show that Stevenson's experience in the field of arsenical poisoning was not as great as he had claimed. He asked Stevenson when was the last time he had assisted at a post-mortem of a person said to have died for arsenic. After Stevenson had given a series of vague answers, Russell pointedly asked him to '*fix one date*.' Stevenson started to refer to a case in 1858, but his answer was disdainfully dismissed by Russell as being '*too long ago*.' Stevenson said he was involved in a case '*a few years ago*,' but could provide no details or date. The sparring between the two men continued a little longer, until Russell put it to Stevenson that he could not give a single example of a case in which he had been involved where death had followed from the administration of arsenic and he had assisted with the post-mortem and analysis. Stevenson was forced to admit '*not where any definite known quantity was given*.' It was not a decisive victory, but it was a minor victory for the defence.

Russell then asked Stevenson if the symptoms of gastro-enteritis were '*substantially similar*' to arsenical poisoning. Stevenson replied they were '*substantially similar, but there are differences*.' Russell asked him to provide an example of a symptom that was different but he was unable to do so. Instead, he said '*there is no distinctive symptom of arsenical poisoning; the diagnostic thing is finding the arsenic*.' Russell then asked about the general symptoms a person would typically have if they were suffering from arsenical poisoning. Stevenson said diarrhoea usually affected a patient an hour or two after vomiting. This had not been the case with James, although Russell did not specifically make that point. He then asked about the symptoms of severe abdominal pain, redness of the eyelids and

---

[988] Irving H.B., op cit., pages 157-160.
[989] Moiseiwitsch M., op cit., page 195.

the bloodshot appearance of the eyeballs, presumably as these were all symptoms that had not been experienced by James. Stevenson agreed they were all usually found, though '*not necessarily so.*'

Finally, Russell tackled Stevenson about the arsenic in James' body. Although he could not get him to move from his belief that James had been poisoned by arsenic, he did get him to admit that in total he had found only $^{76}/_{1000}$ of a grain of arsenic in the liver and $^{15}/_{1000}$ of a grain in the intestines.[990] As two grains of arsenic was normally needed to kill a man, Stevenson had, by his own admission, only found an amount that was less than $^{1}/_{20}$ of what was considered to be a fatal dose. Not surprisingly, despite Stevenson's acknowledged expertise, not everyone was convinced by his testimony that James had been murdered by arsenic.

After Stevenson left the witness box, Addison indicated that the case for the prosecution had closed. It has been claimed that Russell's questioning of Stevenson had '*succeeded in reducing the prosecution's case to tatters.*'[991] This view is an overstatement. Russell had certainly made holes in the Crown's case, but it had not disintegrated beyond all recognition. The circumstantial evidence against Florence remained strong, and the prosecution had shown she had the motive, means and opportunity to have committed the crime. The Flatman's Hotel affair and Florence's letter to Brierley had provided a powerful motive. When Russell had not cross-examined Schweisso, Florence's affair with Brierley had been admitted to in all but name. The Crown had also proven that Florence had purchased flypapers and soaked them in water to extract arsenic. Traces of arsenic were found on her dressing gown and her handkerchief. Florence also had the opportunity to commit murder. She had packaged some of James' food that he had eaten in his office. When the jug was tested by Mr Davies, it showed traces of arsenic. She alone, at first, provided James with food and medication when he was ill. Some of the servants at Battlecrease commented that the food tasted differently to how it had been prepared by the cook. There was also the incident that was crucial to the prosecution's case, when Florence had tampered with the meat juice bottle that was found to have contained half a grain of arsenic in it. Nurse Gore's testimony that Florence had tried to conceal her actions had given the behaviour a decidedly criminal flavour.

The trial had moved in Florence's favour but there was still a lot of work for her defence team to do if they were to secure a not guilty verdict.

LINKS TO THE RIPPER DIARY:
ARE THERE ANY HISTORICAL INACCURACIES OR MISTAKES IN THE DIARY?

The credibility and authenticity of the Diary as a historical document written in the 1880s, has been seriously undermined by historical inaccuracies and mistakes identified within the narrative of the journal. These mistakes have been made despite the author's attempts to avoid such errors by being vague about the details of key events. Indeed, the only specific date that can be found in the whole document comes at the end of it, when its author supposedly makes final entry as 3rd May 1889. Why would the author otherwise be so vague, especially as he had provided enough details so as to identify the person who claimed to write it as being James Maybrick? The answer is simple; he wanted to avoid writing something that could be shown to be false, or place James in a situation when a historical record might later be unearthed to show he was elsewhere at that particular time.

Despite the author's attempts to avoid errors, some important and significant historical inaccuracies can be found within the text of the document. Some of the simplest mistakes are evident when the author of the Diary refers to named people, and gets the name slightly or completely wrong. For example, the diarist refers to one of James' brothers as '*Thomas*' when everyone in the family always called him '*Tom*' other than on formal occasions, such as in the writing of a will. The diarist mentions a Mrs Hammersmith in a much-debated section of the journal, writing: '*Strolled by the drive, encountered Mrs Hamersmith, she enquired of Bobo and Gladys and much to my astonishment about my health. What has that whore said? Mrs Hammersmith is a bitch.*' (NB the diarist spells Hammersmith the first time with only one *m*, and the second time *mm*.)

It is assumed by most commentators that the '*drive*' referred to is Aigburth Drive, the road that circles Sefton Park in South Liverpool. The question is, who was Mrs Hammersmith? To some pro-diarists she may not exist at all, but is just the product of the imagination of the diarist. If that is the case, why can't the rest of the Diary just be the product of imagination and fantasy? Shirley Harrison spent a great deal of effort trying to track down the elusive Mrs Hammersmith, with little success. An early possibility she identified in the 1881 Census was Mrs Margaret Ann Hamersmith, the 17-year-old wife of Benjamin Hamersmith, a labourer living in Prescot, a small town near Liverpool. However, she never looked like a real possibility for someone who knew James Maybrick and his family.

In her presentation to the Trial of James Maybrick event held at Liverpool in May 2007, Shirley Harrison said that after ten years of research she had found another possible candidate to be Mrs Hammersmith. She had discovered the

[990] Irving H.B., op cit., page 174.
[991] Colquhoun K., op cit., page 253.

Poste House in Cumberland Street, Liverpool (Chris Jones collection)

marriage certificate from 1856 in the Parish records of St Thomas's Church, Stepney in London's East End of Emma Orbell and George William Hammersmith. He was a shipwright at a time when James was himself working in a shipping office somewhere in the East End. If ten years of research can produce only this sole, rather unlikely candidate to be the elusive Mrs Hammersmith, one has to conclude the diarist made a mistake in mentioning a person who did not exist.

One of the entries in the Diary that causes its authenticity to be questioned is the sentence, '*I took refreshment at the Poste House it was there I finally decided London it shall be.*' The problem with the entry is that there is no record of any public house in Liverpool having such a name in the 1880s. Indeed, by Shirley Harrison's own admission, despite '*hours of trawling*' she could not find a pub with such a name in either Liverpool or London.[992]

The pub that is usually identified as the most likely candidate is the Poste House in Cumberland Street, Liverpool. It was certainly in existence at the time, and is situated between James' offices in Tithebarn Street and the railway station at which he caught the train back to Aigburth. However, records show it was known as the Wrexham House in 1882 and the Muck Midden in 1888; it was officially named the New Post Office Hotel in 1894. It was not until the 1960s that it was given the name Poste House.

A sketched picture of part of Cumberland Street *drawn* in the 1880s has been found. In it, the public house is clearly labelled as '*The old MM.*' Supporters of the Diary try to overcome this problem by suggesting the term '*post house*' could be applied to any premises where mail was delivered, and therefore any number of inns or public houses could have been referred to as post houses.

Sketch of Cumberland Street in the 1880s showing '*The old M.M.*' (Muck Midden) public house (Chris Jones collection)

Another suggestion, put forward by Robert Smith, is that the diarist may have been referring to the '*Post Office Tavern,*' which was a public house in existence in 1888 and was so named as it was situated next to Liverpool's General Post Office.[993] It was also close to Central Railway Station, the Liverpool terminus of the line to Aigburth, where James was living in 1888. The problem with Smith's suggestion is that the Post Office Tavern was located extremely close to Church Alley where James grew up, and he would have been fully aware of the name of this public house. Therefore, if James had written the Diary he would have referred to it by its proper name. The fact that the diarist uses a name of a public house that didn't exist in 1888, but was so named much later, is proof that the Diary is a modern fraud.

The Diary contains a line of poetry written by Richard Crashaw, a little-known early seventeenth century poet. The line is: '*Oh costly intercourse of death,*' and is taken from a poem called *The Mother of Sorrows*. In many ways the words of the poem, with its phrases of blood and death, fits comfortably with the rest of the writings of the Diary; however, those who consider the Diary to be a modern forgery believe it is unlikely James would have read Crashaw's works.

992 Harrison S., (2003) op cit., page 101.
993 Smith R., (2017) op cit., page 31.

Such critics became even more sceptical about the Diary's authenticity when Michael Barrett became the first person to correctly identify the origin of the line, when he found it in a modern poetry book in Liverpool's main library. When he later announced he had the same poetry book at home, opponents of the Diary were jubilant as they saw this as conclusive proof that Barrett had been involved, in some capacity, in forging the document. Barrett's poetry book, with the poem from Crashaw, is currently owned by Keith Skinner, who bought it from Alan Gray in 2004. Although it is possible that James could have accessed the works of an obscure poet from a different century as some limited editions of Crashaw's poetry did appear during his lifetime, it is extremely unlikely to have occurred. It is much more feasible that Mike Barrett, or someone known to him, copied the line from the poetry book that Barrett actually owned.

Another problem with the Diary is that some of the words or phrases found in it did not exist in the late 1880s. An example of this was the term '*one-off*' used by the diarist, which does not appear in dictionaries until the early twentieth century. Research by Shirley Harrison did find the term being used by a building company in Kent in the 1860s; however, as the term was not widely used, it is unlikely it would feature in a document supposedly written in 1888/1889.[994]

Another phrase that has been identified as more modern than Victorian is '*top myself*.' The diarist wrote, '*Perhaps I should top myself and save the hangman a job*.' The problem is that the term '*top myself*' doesn't become associated with committing suicide until the mid-twentieth century. Robert Smith tries to overcome this issue by pointing out that in the 1971 edition of *The Oxford English Dictionary* the term '*to top*' was defined specifically as: '*To put to death by hanging*' and was in use between 1811 and 1851.[995] This period is 30 years before the Diary was dated, and is thus a very unlikely phrase to be found in the document.

Author William Beadle has gone further than just focusing on particular words and phrases, and argued that the overall style of writing in the Diary appears to be '*more in tune with the twentieth century that the nineteenth*.'[996] He believes that while words and phrases that weren't in use in Victorian times have not necessarily been found, the Diary lacks the overly elaborative style of writing that one would expect in a nineteenth century journal. Caroline Morris disagreed with this view, and pointed out that the diarist consistently avoided modern contractions such as '*isn't*,' and did tend to favour '*longwinded constructions*' in the journal.[997] Morris' interpretation is interesting, but the fact is the Diary is awash with short and simple sentences, and it lacks the true feel of the typical language that is found in a genuine Victorian document.

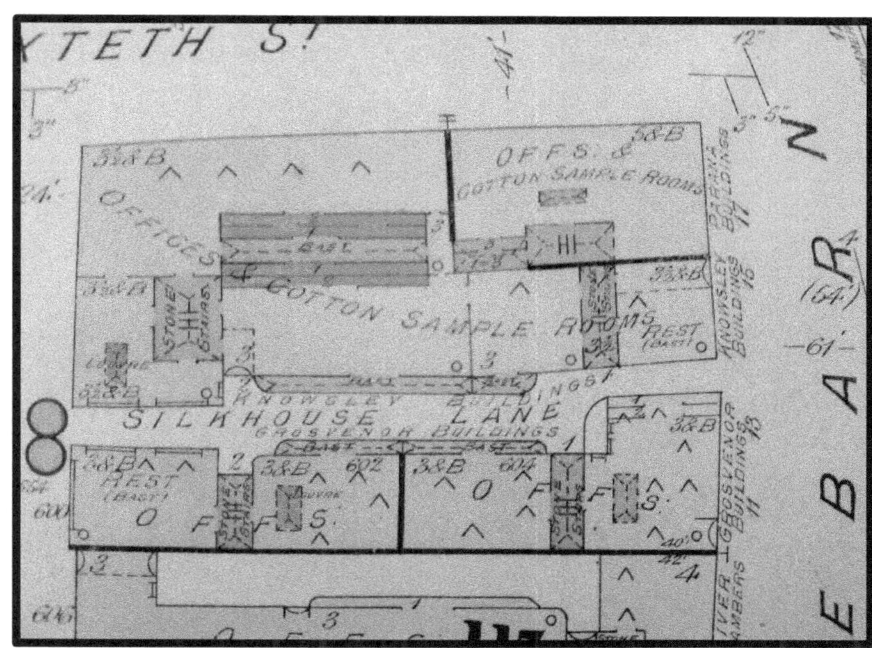

Goad's fire insurance plans for 1888 showing Silkhouse Lane to the south of the Knowsley Buildings where James Maybrick had his offices. (Chris Jones collection)

At the beginning of December 1888, James Maybrick was one of 19 local men who were called up to serve on the Grand Jury in Liverpool. He was to spend five days in the service, from the 3rd to 7th December. The report on the meeting of the Liverpool City Sessions in December 1888 is referred to in a few local papers. They all actually spell James' surname incorrectly as '*Meybrick*,' obviously a mistranscription of what they heard as the name was called out. Nevertheless, the reference to his place of work in Silkhouse Lane, which was the narrow street next to the Knowsley Buildings, does imply that it should have been written as '*Maybrick*.' The recorder, in his charge to the Grand Jury, said they were assembled again to '*contribute their part in the administration of justice. People sometimes argued that the duties of the grand juries were not so useful as to necessitate the maintenance of such an old institution. He must say respectfully that he did not agree with that contention. He thought the enormous advantage given to gentlemen of their station to view the state of crime in a great city like Liverpool, and to have*

[994] Harrison S., op cit., page 352.
[995] Smith R., (2017) op cit., page 31.
[996] Beadle W., 'Revisiting the Maybrick Diary' in *The Journal of the Whitechapel Society*, Edition 20, June 2008.
[997] Morris C., 'Response to Bill Beadle' in *The Journal of the Whitechapel Society*, Edition 22, October 2008.

their minds awakened to any mode by which that might be obviated and improved, was of itself an essential service to the public.'[998]

The diarist, who continually ridicules the police for their failure to catch him, does not mention this event in the journal. If James had written the journal, surely he would have mentioned his time on the jury; the irony of the situation would not have been lost on him. He would have loved the idea that the most sought-after person in the whole country was now serving on a body that had the job of deciding whether sufficient evidence existed to put a person on trial. So why isn't it mentioned? The obvious explanation is that the author of the Diary simply did not know about it. If he had he would have definitely referred to it, probably in a vicious and sarcastic verse.

There are other numerous, but much smaller errors contained within the Diary. For example, the diarist writes: '*Encountered an old friend on the Exchange floor.*' Everyone in Liverpool, especially the people who worked there, always called the Cotton Exchange by the abbreviated phrase '*Change*.

Near the end of the journal, the diarist claims that he '*no longer*' takes the '*dreaded stuff*,' which presumably means he is claiming he had stopped taking arsenic and/or strychnine. That is an inaccurate statement, as we know James took these drugs right up to his death. Only a couple of days before he died he was imploring Florence to give him some white powder.

There also factual errors in the Diary concerning the death of the last Ripper victim, Mary Kelly. The diarist wrote he cut off her breasts and '*left them on the table with some of the other stuff.*' According to the police surgeon's report, the breasts had been left '*one under the head and the other by the right foot.*' All these smaller errors are not by themselves overly significant but, looked at in total and combined with the more serious errors, one is left with the unmistakable conclusion that the Diary is a forgery.

[998] *Liverpool Courier*, 4th December 1888.

16

THE CASE FOR THE DEFENCE

After lunch on Saturday a hush of anticipation settled over the court as Sir Charles Russell rose to give the opening speech for the defence, '*grasping the lapels of his robe, as his wont when about to make a supreme effort, he began in low and measured tones,*' and spoke about the great responsibility he faced defending Florence, whom he referred to as '*the friendless lady in the dock.*'[999]

In a solemn tone, he told the jury there were two main questions they had to consider: '*Was it death by arsenical poisoning? If it were, was that poison administered by his wife*?'[1000] He emphasised that their answers to these two questions must not be based on suspicions or probabilities, unless the strength of the evidence be strong enough to dispel from their minds any reasonable doubt and would justify them in pronouncing a verdict, which he said, pointing to the defendant, would '*snap the thread of this poor woman's life.*'

Russell's words were more than just a touch of theatre; he wanted to remind the jury, in the starkest of terms, that a guilty verdict would send his client to the scaffold. In the dock, tears started to run down Florence's face and, for a second or two, it looked as though she was about to collapse with emotion.

Having set the parameters of the case, Russell began to run through some of the key facts. He reminded the jurors that neither Dr Humphreys nor Dr Carter had any suspicion that James' death had been caused by arsenic until others had planted that thought in their minds. He added that neither doctor had any idea what the irritant poison was that killed James until the '*analysis had shown the presence of arsenic in the stomach.*' It was therefore the presence of arsenic in James' body that was the '*determining factor*' in shaping the mind of these men. Russell said that while he did not dispute that a '*minute quantity*' of arsenic had been found in the deceased's system, there were many ways in which its presence could be explained other than through the criminal intent of his wife. He said he would produce witnesses from America to testify that when James was in that country, up to at least 1881 or 1882, he had '*unquestionably been in the habit of taking arsenic.*' Russell said he would also call a Liverpool chemist who would state that in 1888 he provided James with a '*pick-me-up*' tonic between two and five times a day. He said that the difference between him and the others who came for this tonic was that James required his dose to contain the additional ingredient of liquor arsenicalis.

Russell paused and, looking directly at the jury, said '*I think you at once will see the bearing it has on the matter.*' He added that James had been keen to try and '*conceal*' his arsenic habit from his friends. Russell drew the jury's attention to the fact that, in the summer of 1888, Florence had spoken to Dr Hopper about her husband's '*habit of drugging himself with something that was pernicious and she invited his aid to stop the habit.*' She had made the same request to Dr Humphreys in March 1889, and a little later to Michael Maybrick.

Russell was attempting to show that, rather than wanting to kill her husband, Florence was in fact the only person trying to save him. Russell said it was an extraordinary thing to his mind that '*an anxious inquiry was not made into this matter*' during James' lifetime, especially while he was on his sick bed. He criticised those who had been in Battlecrease when James was dying, because they had not been '*manly enough, friendly enough, honest enough,*' to tell Florence that she was under suspicion and ask her if she had any explanation to offer.[1001]

After speaking about James as an arsenic eater, Russell returned to the first of the two questions he had posed the jury. He said that although James had suffered from symptoms, some of which were consistent with arsenical poisoning, when the medical witnesses for the prosecution were asked to identify a symptom that would not also have existed in gastro-enteritis, they failed to mention a single one. Further, it was a '*peculiarity of this case*' that some of the more typical symptoms of arsenical poisoning, such as pain at the pit of the stomach and redness of the eyelids, simply did not exist in James' case. Russell, looking directly at the jury said, '*perhaps most important of all,*' there was an '*absence of diarrhoea at any time in what one might call an excessive degree*' until Dr Humphreys said it started on Thursday, 8th May. Russell said Dr Tidy, '*a gentleman as eminent in his profession as Dr Stevenson,*' would be called to show that this was not a case of arsenical poisoning; instead, it was a case of gastro-enteritis. James' illness probably began on the day of the Wirral races when he got very wet, followed by an '*error of diet, not unassisted by the strange course of treatment*' which was pursued in the later stage of his illness.

---

[999] *Liverpool Mercury*, 5th August 1889.
[1000] Irving H.B., op cit., page 176.
[1001] Ibid., page 180.

Russell then moved on to the second of his questions. He told the jury that even if they did believe that James died from arsenical poisoning, it did not prove it was Florence who administered the poison. The only evidence that she had obtained any substances which contained arsenic came from the chemists, Wokes and Hanson, who testified she had purchased flypapers. Russell asked the jury if it was likely – if she was truly a '*wicked woman contriving an ill thing*' – that she would make the purchases in a shop where she was well known?[1002] He finished by telling the jury that they must not allow '*any repugnance*' they may feel for Florence because of her unfaithfulness to her husband to therefore assume that she would have '*deliberately and wickedly*' killed him.[1003]

After completing his opening remarks, Russell asked the judge's permission for Florence to make a statement to the court. He said it was his client's desire to make such a statement, and she had expressed a similar wish to her solicitors prior to the inquest hearing. Mr Justice Stephen said he would '*allow the prisoner to make any statement she wishes,*' though he was disappointed that Russell had not mentioned it to him earlier. He said that under the legal guidelines as they currently existed, Florence could make a statement, but she could not be sworn in or questioned on it. The judge also insisted that Florence could not write down what she intended to say, though she could use notes to help her deliver the points she wished to make to the court.

The first four witness for the defence had all been summoned to demonstrate that James was an arsenic eater. Nicholas Bateson had been brought over from Memphis, Tennessee, where he worked in the cotton business. He said he had shared a house with James in Norfolk, Virginia from 1877 until 1881, when James married. Under examination from Pickford, he said James had '*chills and fever in the autumn of 1877, or what is commonly known as malaria fever.*' He took quinine, the ordinary remedy for the fever, but it had no effect. As a result, '*he took arsenic and strychnine, by order of Dr Wood.*' When Pickford asked him how long James had continued with these prescriptions, Bateson replied, '*about three months, so far as I know.*' Bateson also said that James was a man who was nervous about his health; '*he constantly rubbed the back of his hands in the morning, and complained of numbness in his hands and limbs... He was very much afraid of being paralysed.*'

Under cross-examination by Addison, Bateson said James had taken arsenic under medical advice, and that it was in a '*bottle in solution with something.*' He said he took it for three months, and '*it cured him.*' He did not afterwards complain of malarial symptoms. Addison asked when was the last time he had seen James, and was told '*last year, in July.*'[1004] Bateson's evidence was useful for the defence, in that it established James had taken arsenic in America. However, it only showed he had used it for a period of three months, more than ten years before his death.

Captain Richard Thompson, a master mariner, said in 1880 he had been second officer on the steamship *Plantain* and had sailed from Liverpool to Norfolk, Virginia taking two dogs for Mr Bateson. During his stay in Norfolk he had met James almost every day for a meal or drink, and had become '*intimate with him.*' On one occasion he accompanied James into a druggist on Main Street, and an assistant handed him two powders saying, '*Now Mr Maybrick, be careful.*' Thompson said a day or two later he had been sent to the same druggist on a message by the ship's captain, and the assistant had told him about the nature of the powders he had given James. Thompson said later, when James had come into his cabin, he asked him about his habit of '*taking a dangerous and noxious drug.*' James replied, '*What is that*?' Thompson said, '*arsenic.*' James responded, '*Who the devil told you that*?' Thompson told James what the assistant had told him, to which he replied, '*Damn his impudence.*'[1005]

Russell asked Thompson if he had any further conversations with James about arsenic, to which he replied, 'No.' He said James was '*very touchy on the subject.*' Thompson's testimony showed that James had not just taken arsenic for a three-month period in 1877, as Bateson had suggested, and was still taking it some three years later. It also appeared, from Thompson's evidence, that James was trying to hide his arsenic use from his friends.

Thomas Stansell, the servant of James and Bateson between 1878 and 1880, followed Thompson into the witness box. His appearance added greatly to the drama of the occasion. A reporter for a contemporary newspaper wrote, in an age well before political correctness, that his '*ebony skin and woolly head, standing in the witness box on the bench, was a direct contrast to the ruddy faced judge in his scarlet robes. Answering the questions put to him with a simple "Iss, Sar," he conjured up a host of recollections in one's mind. One thought of distant cotton plantations, of sultry climes, of piccaninnies, of wide-spreading Panama hats, of buckwheat and hominy, of the hunted slave and the planter's whip.*'[1006] Stansell told the court that on three or four occasions James had given him half a dollar to buy arsenic from local drugstores. Russell asked what James did with the drug, to which Stansell replied: '*he told me to go and make him some beef tea. I went and filled a cup and brought it to him. He asked me to give him a spoon and taking the spoon opened the package and took a small bit out. This he put in the tea and stirred it up.*'[1007]

[1002] Ibid., page 182.
[1003] Ibid., page 185.
[1004] Ibid., pages 185-7.
[1005] Ibid., page 189.
[1006] *Liverpool Review*, 10th August 1889.
[1007] Irving H.B., op cit., page 190.

Addison, in his cross-examination, asked when this had happened. Stansell said it was in 1878, and had occurred '*about four times in the season.*' Stansell's evidence was useful to the defence, but, like Bateson's, it only fixed James' arsenic use to a limited period some ten years before his death. His answers were also at odds with an interview he gave to an American newspaper before the trial, in which he said he had bought arsenic on other occasions for James, and that he had continued to use it after his marriage. Such information, if it had been given in court, would have added extra significance to Stansell's evidence.

Having established that James used arsenic in America, Russell now wanted to show that he continued to use the drug on his return to Liverpool. Edwin Heaton, a retired chemist who had run a chemist shop in Exchange Street East, Liverpool for 17 years until April 1888, told the court that James had been a customer at his shop '*for about ten years; it might be more.*' Heaton said James regularly purchased a '*pick-me-up*' tonic. When he had first asked for it, he had given Heaton a prescription that added *liquor arsenicalis* to the ingredients. Russell asked if Heaton had dispensed the same quantity of *liquor arsenicalis* '*at the beginning as at the end,*' to which Heaton replied that, by the end, it was '*75% greater in quantity*' compared to the beginning, an increase from four drops to seven drops. He had supplied James with the tonic between '*two and five times a day*' for 18 months prior to April 1888.

In his cross-examination, Addison tried to undermine the impact of Heaton's evidence. First, he suggested that the person Heaton identified may not have been James. He asked him if the name of Maybrick appeared in any of his books. Heaton said it didn't; however, he had recognised James' likeness '*at once*' from a portrait of him in the *Liverpool Echo.* Addison then tried a different approach, asking Heaton how many gentlemen from the Cotton Exchange visited his shop for the tonic, being told '*as many as sixteen.*' Addison asked what was its effects, and was answered, '*to improve digestion.*' Then, importantly, Addison asked Heaton if, as far as he knew, had the tonic harmed anyone; he replied '*No.*'

Russell, in his re-examination, asked the chemist if most of his customers who bought the tonic also wanted *liquor arsenicalis* in it. Heaton replied that '*Not many had that.*' In his final question, Russell asked Heaton if seven drops of this pick-me-up, James' usual amount, was taken five times a day, would it contain $^{1}/_{3}$ of a grain of white arsenic? Heaton replied: '*Pretty near it.*'[1008]

After the trial, Michael Maybrick gave an interview in which he denied that James had used arsenic, and said Heaton had been mistaken in identifying James as the man who had regularly bought the *pick-me-ups.* He told the reporter that Heaton did not know James' name, '*but recognised him from a newspaper cut. That cut was unrecognisable as a likeness. When shown my brother's photograph Heaton said "Yes; he looked like that, only whiter." Now my brother was scarcely grey at all, and he did not have the pale complexion arsenic-users are understood to have.*'[1009]

The next witness was Dr Drysdale, the homoeopathic doctor who had treated James on six occasions between November 1888 and March 1889. A local newspaper provided a graphic description of his testimony: '*What an ideal witness! A neat old gentleman, with white hair and sharp clear features, looking through his glasses with calm keen eyes, and reminding one of the late John Stuart Mill. How sparing of words he was. How characteristic of the cautious, methodical, philosophical Scotchman it was to see him read from his diary the careful notes he had taken on the dates when Mr Maybrick called on him for advice.*'[1010]

Drysdale said James had told him that for three months he had endured pains in his head.[1011] If he smoked or drank too much he experienced a numbness on the left side of his hand and his leg, and was liable to suffer from an eruption of the skin on his hands. Russell asked Drysdale if James had been in the '*habit of doctoring himself,*' being told: '*He did not say anything about that. I asked him what medication he had been in the habit of taking, and he said nitro-hydrochloric acid, strychnine, hydrate of potash and several others.*' Russell asked if James understood the various drugs, to which Drysdale replied, '*Oh, yes, he understood them.*' The doctor told the court that James seemed to be suffering from '*nervous dyspepsia,*' and that he was a hypochondriac.[1012]

Addison, in his cross-examination, asked if James had ever discussed using arsenic; Drysdale replied, '*He made no mention of it.*' On being asked if he had ever prescribed arsenic in any form for James, Drysdale answered, '*No.*'

William J. Thomson, an old friend of James, said that he had seen him riding at the racecourse on the day of the Wirral races. He said it had been raining during the day. He described James as '*shaking about,*' and having problems riding his horse. When he asked him what was wrong, James replied he was not feeling well. A little later James told him he had taken a '*double dose*' of his medicine that morning.[1013]

Thomson was in the witness box for only a very short time, and was not cross-examined. Although brief, his evidence was important as it suggested the start of James' illness coincided with him overdosing on his own medicine

---

[1008] Ibid., page 195.
[1009] *Evening Express*, 21st August 1889.
[1010] *Liverpool Review*, 10th August 1889.
[1011] Irving H.B., op cit., page 195.
[1012] Ibid., page 196.
[1013] Ibid., page 197.

rather than due to anything that Florence may have done. One thing Thomson didn't mention, was the exact nature of the medicine taken by James; a reference to strychnine would have added extra importance to his evidence.

John Thompson's evidence was as brief as the previous witness. He said he was a Liverpool wholesale druggist of some 17 years standing. He knew James, as he had employed his cousin [William Maybrick] as his assistant between 1884 and 1886. After William had been sacked, James had visited Thompson to try and get his relative reinstated. Thompson told the court: '*As my assistant he had access to all the drugs. I believe Mr Maybrick was at my place three or four times. I think that I saw him every time that he had called.*'[1014]

James' concern for his cousin was probably one of self-interest. As a hypochondriac and drug user, it would have suited him to have an insider who could help supply him with the drugs that he craved. James' self-concern in intervening on behalf of his cousin is confirmed by the fact that he seems to have abandoned him when he could not get him reinstated. William died in October 1888 in a Liverpool Workhouse.

The case for the defence had got off to a solid rather than a strong start. Three witnesses said James had taken arsenic in America, but two of them – Bateson and Stansell – had implied it had only been for a short period, and had occurred more than ten years before his death. Edwin Heaton's evidence had been more valuable, as it had shown that James continued to use arsenic up until at least April 1888. But the impact of his evidence had been partially undermined when Addison had managed to get the chemist to admit he did not know a single person who had been harmed by consuming his tonic.

Dr Drysdale's evidence had shown that James knew a lot about various medicines and had taken strychnine, but its importance had been weakened when the doctor said he had never prescribed arsenic for James. William Thomson's evidence had been important in showing that James' first illness appeared to have been brought on by him overdosing on his own medicine, although Thomson failed to mention whether it had contained strychnine.

The useful but limited impact from these early witnesses meant the defence team needed a strong witness to put them back on track to help win the case. They must have hoped that their final witness of the day, Dr Charles Tidy, would provide the necessary firepower required.

Dr Tidy's credentials as an expert witness were impressive. He was a Bachelor of Medicine and a Master of Surgery, and had been an Examiner of Forensic Medicine at London University for more than twenty years. Like Dr Stevenson, he was an official analyst for the Home Office. Importantly, he had assisted at more than 1,000 post-mortems, including – crucially – assisting at some 40 cases of people who had died as a result of arsenical poisoning.[1015] Tidy was described as a '*little over medium height*' and, like Dr Stevenson, stooped slightly. He had dark curly hair, '*carefully arranged, but wears neither beard or moustache, and the absence of these may account for the semi-boyish aspects of his pronounced features. His eyes are keen and restless, and he has the curious habit – most probably involuntary habit – of twitching the muscles of his face at the end of almost every utterance he delivers. Decisive in manner, he gave his evidence admirably.*'[1016]

Dr Charles Meymott Tidy (1843-1892)

Sir Charles Russell started his questioning of Dr Tidy by asking him to list the most distinctive symptoms of arsenical poisoning. He replied that the four most prominent symptoms were '*first the sickness; violent and incessant vomiting, very often with blood, frequently mixed with bile; the diarrhoea; and the pain in the stomach and the eyes.*'[1017]

Russell then asked one of the most important questions in the whole trial; did Tidy know a single case of arsenical poisoning in which all four of these distinctive symptoms had been missing? He replied: '*Personally, I have known cases where each one of the four symptoms have been absent in the case, but I have never known a case in which all the four symptoms have been absent.*' Russell asked if the doctor had been following the case, receiving the reply '*every detail,*' so far as he could, including all the dispositions before the coroner and the magistrates.

Russell then dealt with each of the four main symptoms of arsenical poisoning in turn to find out if they were evident in James' illness. He started with his sickness, and asked if it met the key criteria of excessive and persistent

---

1014 Ibid., page 198.
1015 Irving H.B., op cit., page 198.
1016 *Liverpool Mercury*, 5th August 1889.
1017 Irving H.B., op cit., pages 199-210.

vomiting. Tidy answered, '*certainly not... the peculiarity of the vomiting in arsenic cases is that it does not relieve; but the patient, as soon as he has vomited, begins to vomit again immediately.*' Russell next asked about the diarrhoea James' had experienced, which Dr Humphreys said first appeared on 9th May. Tidy said he would have expected James to have suffered diarrhoea long before that date if arsenic had been administered around 27th or 28th April and 5th or 6th May. He added, agreeing with the view that had been expressed earlier by Dr Stevenson, that diarrhoea normally occurs within two hours of a person taking arsenic.

Russell questioned Tidy about the fact that there was no mention of James experiencing a severe pain in his stomach until the eve of his death, which Dr Tidy called a '*toxicological curiosity.*' Russell asked Tidy if he had ever experienced a case in which there was an absence of discomfort to the eyes: '*No; no case has ever come before me.*' Russell asked if James' symptoms pointed to arsenical poisoning; Tidy replied decisively, '*Certainly not.*'

Russell's next set of questions concerned the post-mortem appearance of James' body. Tidy said that one of the most important post-mortem characteristics of someone who had died from arsenical poisoning was '*redness, more or less, over the entire stomach.*' He said this redness was unique in cases of death by arsenic, in that there were '*minute petechiae* [Italian for fleabites] *over the surface of the redness.*' Russell handed Tidy a drawing that the witness had himself made of the stomach of a person who had died in 1863 from arsenical poisoning. The doctor said the drawing illustrated the condition of the stomach, and the small blots denoted the appearance of the petechiae. The diagram was given to Mr Justice Stephen, who scrutinised it carefully and then passed it on to the jury to examine. Tidy said that, from the notes he had seen of the post-mortem, the condition of James' stomach did not at all convey the view he had suffered from arsenical poisoning. Russell asked him to explain the areas of redness that did appear in some parts of James' stomach. Tidy replied that they were '*perfectly consistent with death from gastro-enteritis,*' and were not caused by arsenical poisoning at all.

When Russell moved the questioning on to the arsenic levels in James' body, one of Tidy's answers took direct aim at Dr Stevenson's methodology. He said the quantity of arsenic in the intestines or the liver should not be estimated by just '*cutting off a bit here and there,*' as arsenic is not equally distributed over these organs. Russell then suggested that Stevenson's figures were therefore '*not a reliable datum to go on.*' '*Certainly not,*' replied Tidy. Russell said that the total quantity of arsenic found in James' liver, using the figures provided by both Drs Davies and Stevenson, was some 83/1000 of a grain, and asked if such a quantity proved '*the evil administration, criminally, or otherwise, of arsenic.*' Tidy answered '*No.*' Russell's final question to Tidy enquired as to his conclusion about the cause of James' death. The doctor answered that it was '*due to gastro-enteritis of some kind or another, but that the symptoms of the post-mortem distinctly point away from arsenic.*'

Addison realised that Tidy's evidence had undermined the prosecution's case and, as a result, was more confrontational in his questioning of him than he had been with previous defence witnesses. He put it to Tidy that gastro-enteritis meant inflammation caused by an irritant poison. Tidy responded that James died from an irritant, but it did not necessarily mean it was a poison. He had known impure food, such as sausages, cheese and even a small piece of lobster to produce symptoms of acute irritant poisoning that might be mistaken for arsenical poisoning. Addison asked Tidy if knew cases in which sausages and cheese had killed people, and was told he did. Addison retorted, '*But in those cases there were no traces of arsenic in the stomach or the liver*?' Tidy replied, '*Oh no, no.*' Addison asked whether James' symptoms were caused by an irritant of some kind; Tidy answered, '*Yes, I think so.*' He then asked Tidy if the irritant poison had killed James. The doctor answered, '*Possibly.*'

Addison moved on to tackling Tidy's assertion that James' symptoms pointed away from the irritant being arsenic. He focused his questions on the doctor's assertion that James' sickness was neither persistent nor excessive. Addison pointed out that, during the whole of 4th and 5th May, James could not retain anything in his stomach, and that Dr Humphreys had found the patient '*straining and vomiting*' all day and had to give him morphia to relieve him. [In fact, Humphreys had given James a morphine suppository on the evening of 3rd May.] Addison then rather pointedly asked Tidy if, given all this information about James' condition, would he change his opinion. Tidy replied, '*No; it is only one of the symptoms, and was not associated, as arsenic invariably is, with diarrhoea.*' Addison, remaining on the offensive, asked Tidy if James' '*excessive straining all night*' wasn't an obvious sign of diarrhoea. '*No, certainly not,*' was the reply.

Addison then dealt with Tidy's interpretation of the post-mortem findings. He asked if he had viewed any of James' body parts. Tidy admitted that he hadn't seen them. Addison said that although Tidy had stated there was no mention of *petechiae*, Dr Humphreys – who had been at the post-mortem and who had seen the body parts – said he observed *petechiae* on the stomach. Tidy responded by arguing that what Humphreys had seen was something different, and the markings were not the *petechiae* of a linear dotted appearance that were associated with arsenical poisoning. Addison disagreed, saying Humphreys had described them as *petechiae*. Tidy answered, '*Well, my recollection is very different.*' Addison asked Tidy if he found a person who had undoubtedly died from some irritant poisoning, and arsenic had been found in that person's body, wouldn't it lead him to think that the irritant poison must have been arsenic? Tidy responded, '*No it does not.*'

In his re-examination, Russell returned to the question of whether *petechiae* had been observed during the post-mortem. He said that in Dr Carter's notes placed before the coroner there was no mention of *petechiae*; however, he did refer to '*spots of bright absorbent vascularity*.' He asked Tidy if these spots met his description of *petechiae*. Tidy replied, '*No, not at all*.' Russell finished by asking Tidy if some of the symptoms that James had, such as dryness and thirst in the throat and gullet, were peculiar only to arsenical poisoning. Tidy replied: '*Not at all*.'

It had been a strong performance from Dr Tidy, and one newspaper commented that his evidence had '*proved a pillar of strength to the defence*.'[1018] Although Addison had caused Tidy some discomfort with his abrasive style of questioning, the doctor had stuck firmly to his belief that the symptoms of James' illness and the appearance of his stomach at the post-mortem pointed to his death being caused by gastro-enteritis, and not arsenical poisoning.

The court did not sit on Sunday 4th August. While Florence remained alone in her cell at Walton Gaol, lost in her thoughts, the jury were treated to an afternoon's sailing on the River Mersey. One of the jurors, Mr R.G. Brook, said in a post-trial interview they had requested a river trip and it had been allowed. The authorities had chartered the tug *Dispatch*, and between 2:00pm and 6:00pm, the jury had sailed up to the lighthouse at the mouth of the river and then back again, up as far as the Ship Canal and Eastham.[1019]

The break in the trial's proceedings did little to diminish interest in the case. One Liverpool newspaper commented that between Saturday evening and Monday morning the interest in the trial '*grew to boiling point*.'[1020]

Monday 5th August was a Bank Holiday. The shops of Liverpool were shut, but the streets were busy with people heading down to the waterfront, hoping to spend an enjoyable day away from the daily grind of work. At St George's Hall it was no holiday. The crowds trying to get into the building remained as large as ever. People were aware that the drama was getting close to a conclusion, and they were desperate to catch some of the excitement before it finished. As the doors to the court opened the onlookers poured into the chamber, hoping to find a seat as close to the front as possible.

At around 10:30am, the first witness of the day entered the witness box. Dr Rawdon Macnamara was another medical expert with impressive credentials. He was a Fellow of the Royal College of Surgeons of Ireland, an organisation of which he had been President and was, at that time, its representative on the General Medical Council of the UK. He was Professor of Materia Medica at the Royal College. He was Senior Surgeon at the Lock Hospital in Dublin, a Doctor of Medicine at the University of London, and an expert on arsenical poisoning. A Liverpool newspaper commented that he was a '*most distinguished medical and scientific expert from Dublin. Dr Macnamara was an elderly gentleman, who occupied a seat during the trial in front of Sir Charles Russell, and has frequently joined his confrere*' advising him on technical scientific points.[1021]

Macnamara started his testimony by telling Russell he had administered arsenic in a large number of cases. In some of them, due to accident, the idiosyncrasies of the patient or the necessities of the case, a patient had received a dangerous dose of the poison. Russell asked, when this point was reached, what the effects were. Macnamara replied that the strongest symptom was '*redness of the eyelid, where the lashes come out upon the eyelid*.'[1022] He said there was a burning hot pain in the pit of the stomach that gradually spread downwards until the arsenic was eliminated. Russell asked Macnamara to describe the nature of the purging and vomiting in the patient. He replied that vomiting is '*copious, violent and persistent; the purging is of a severe character at first, but of course, it passes into ineffectual effort eventually*.' Russell, referring to Dr Humphreys' description of James' sickness, asked if the deceased had suffered arsenical poisoning. Macnamara said the nature of his sickness pointed towards inflammation of the stomach or bowels rather than arsenical poisoning. He added that the blister that Humphreys had applied to James' stomach would not have stopped arsenical vomiting, but would have stopped vomiting in the case of gastro-enteritis. Russell asked the witness if he had ever known cramps in the calves of the legs to be a symptom of arsenical poisoning, and was told '*Never*.' Russell then asked Macnamara if he believed James' death was caused by arsenical poisoning; he replied, '*Certainly not*.'

Addison started his cross-examination by asking the witness what he thought the cause of James' death had been. Macnamara replied, '*To the best of my judgement and belief, he died of gastro-enteritis not connected with arsenical poisoning*.' Addison next wanted to know if the witness agreed with Dr Tidy's view that gastro-enteritis was caused by the deceased ingesting some '*foreign substance*.' The medical expert replied, '*I agree with Dr Tidy, but I go beyond Dr Tidy in my experience, in my belief*.' Macnamara said that although ingesting a foreign substance could lead to gastro-enteritis, there were other circumstances that could cause it to develop. For example, a person with a weak stomach, suppose dyspepsia, exposed to wet for some time without taking proper precautions and then committing a '*trifle error of diet, the result would be gastro-enteritis*.'

[1018] *Liverpool Mercury*, 5th August 1889.
[1019] *Garston and Woolton Reporter*, 10th August 1889.
[1020] *Liverpool Review*, 10th August 1889.
[1021] *Liverpool Review*, 10th August 1889.
[1022] Irving H.B., op cit., pages 211-215.

In his re-examination, Russell asked him to '*assume a case where there was a chronic weakness or derangement of the stomach, in the case of a man who had been taking various drugs, and who in that condition gets a wetting, such as that described, is a man in that condition the more liable from a slight cause to have set up in his system this gastro-enteritis*?' Macnamara replied, '*Yes.*' Russell continued: '*The weaker from whatever cause, the patient is, the more likely is disease to be set up*?' Macnamara answered, '*Yes, the weakest spot invariably suffers.*'

The next witness was another medical expert. Dr Frank Thomas Paul was a pathologist, a skilled chemist and Professor of Medical Jurisprudence at University College, Liverpool. He was also Examiner in Forensic Medicine and Toxicology to the Victoria University. According to a local newspaper:

> '*his manner and style were faultless. Though apparently quite a young man, considerably under forty, Dr Paul possesses many academic honours and has had an experience which includes the making of no fewer than from two to three thousand post-mortem examinations. A fine doomed forehead, regular features, clear voice, and a modest, but perfectly confident, opinion were characteristic of this witness. His answers were brief, to the point, sufficient, without being scant, and with a degree of accuracy and moderation which carried home conviction as strongly as the answers of any witness I have ever seen in a court of law.*'[1023]

Dr Paul said he had tested four pans identical to the one taken from James' office and found arsenic in the glazing of all of them. This meant that the arsenic found by Mr Davies in his tests on the pan might have been there naturally and therefore had nothing to do with any food in the pan. Russell moved on to the tests that Dr Humphreys had conducted on James' urine and faeces on Thursday, 8th May which had failed to find arsenic. He asked Paul if, had James had received a fatal dose of arsenic around that period, would there have been a deposit indicating the presence of a metallic element in the tests, and was told '*Yes, in my judgement.*'

Dr Frank Thomas Paul (1851-1941)

Dr Paul stated that, as a pathologist at the Royal Infirmary, he had assisted at between 2,000 and 3,000 post-mortems, including many for people who had died of gastro-enteritis. Russell asked Paul if the symptoms experienced by James were similar to those found in gastro-enteritis. He answered, '*They agree with cases of gastro-enteritis pure and simple.*' Russell then asked what post-mortem appearances were missing, if it had been a case of arsenical poisoning. Dr Paul said he would have expected the stomach to have been more affected, and to '*show the characteristics of petechiae spots.*' Russell asked Paul if it was a case of arsenic poisoning. He replied, '*I think it is a case of gastro-enteritis. The post-mortem appearances do not show that it was set up by arsenic.*' Russell then asked '*if, in the case of a man who had been complaining for a considerable number of years of what you would call chronic dyspepsia, who had been drugging himself or had been drugged, following the occurrences we heard of on the day of the Wirral races – take the case of such a man – would a slighter cause be sufficient to set up gastro-enteritis than in a man perfectly well*?' Paul replied: '*Certainly. Such a case in such a man would be more likely to be fatal.*'[1024]

Addison tried to undermine the expert credentials of the witness in his cross-examination by asking him about his experience of cases in which arsenic had been found in the liver. Paul replied that his knowledge came from '*reading,*' and he had '*not been engaged in any arsenical case before this.*'

It was a significant admission, and it dented his credibility as an expert witness. Addison then questioned Paul whether James suffered from inflammation of the stomach. The doctor said he didn't think the condition of the stomach was '*at all unusual.*' Addison then asked if that meant he didn't think James died from it, to which Paul replied: '*I presume that he died from exhaustion, produced by gastro-enteritis, I do not call this a severe case.*' Addison asked how it could not possibly be a severe case, since the patient had died. Paul responded, '*Some people are more easily killed than others. He merely had to get into a condition of exhaustion. I don't think there was pain in this case.*'[1025]

In his re-examination of the witness, Russell said James had told both Dr Humphreys and Mr Thomson that he had taken a double dose of his medicine on the day of the Wirral races. He asked Paul if that would be sufficient to account for his sickness, to which the witness replied '*Yes.*'

The next two witnesses were called to show that arsenic-based solutions were used by some women for cosmetic purposes. Mr Hugh Lloyd Jones told the court he was '*a chemist and a druggist, carrying on business at Bangor. I*

1023 *Liverpool Review*, 10th August 1889.
1024 Irving H.B., op cit., pages 219-220.
1025 Ibid., page 222.

was for some time assistant to Mr Lathbury, a chemist, of Liverpool.'[1026] He testified he sold flypapers to ladies when there were no flies about. He said there was an impression in the trade that arsenic was used as a cosmetic.

Jones was followed by James Bioletti, a hairdresser and perfumer of Dale Street, Liverpool, of some 30 years standing. In reply to a question by Russell, Bioletti said arsenic '*is used a good deal in the hair for some purposes, and I have used it as a wash for the face on being asked for it by ladies. There is an impression among ladies that it is good for the complexion.*' He added that he had used it on a few occasions, but only when it had been requested.[1027] When asked if Florence was a customer of his, he replied '*Not to my knowledge.*'

In his cross-examination, Addison asked Bioletti for what purpose did he use arsenic. He replied it was largely used to remove hair, principally from under the arms. He said that ¼ yellow arsenic was mixed with ¾ slaked lime and placed in a two-ounce bottle, labelled '*Depilatory.*' Each bottle would contain about ½ ounce of arsenic. The customer would mix the powder with water to make the consistency of cream. Addison produced such a bottle and read to the court, '*Depilatory, to remove superfluous hair.*' He asked Bioletti if he knew whether arsenic was used as a cosmetic, to which he replied: '*Not as a rule… I have been asked for it a very few times in my life. I have been spoken to on the subject by ladies, asking as to its value as a cosmetic. It is generally supposed to be a good thing for improving the complexion.*' Addison then asked, '*But when do you prepare it*?' Bioletti answered, '*I only prepare it just for the occasion, and only in small quantity. I only remember distinctly one occasion.*'

During his re-examination Russell held up the Depilatory bottle and asked, '*Although you do not have it for sale, are you sometimes asked for it for the purpose of cosmetics*?' '*Yes*,' came the reply.[1028]

After Bioletti's testimony was complete, Russell produced a pill box and said he would like someone to speak to the item. It was labelled '*Taylor Brothers, pharmaceutical chemists, Norfolk, Virginia*,' and carried the description: '*Iron, quinine and arsenic, one capsule every three or four hours; to be taken with food.*' At the bottom of the label was the name '*Mr Maybrick.*'

Edwin Maybrick was recalled and asked by Addison where the pill box had been found. He said it had been in the drawer of the wash-hand stand of James' bedroom. He added that the last time James had been to Norfolk was in 1884. Russell asked Edwin when he found the item. He said when the furniture was being removed from the house, a week or two after James had died. Russell asked him if he knew Mr Cleaver was acting on behalf of Florence and, if he did, did he hand the box to him. Edwin said he knew Cleaver was acting for Florence, but he had not told him about the pills. He handed the box in on 1st August.

Edwin then rather sheepishly left the witness box. Surprisingly, Russell did not quiz him any further about his motivation in trying to keep the pill box a secret.

Sir James Poole (1827-1903)

The final witness for the defence was Sir James Poole. He was one of Liverpool's best-known merchants and was a former Lord Mayor of the city. He testified he had met James and several others as he left the underwriter's room in April 1889. He said they had a casual conversation, in which someone remarked that it was becoming a common practice to take poisonous medicines. Poole testified that James, whom he described as having '*an impetuous way*,' had '*blurted out, "I take poisonous medicines.*"' Poole said he replied, '*How horrid. Don't you know, my dear friend, that the more you take of these things the more you require, and you will go on till they carry you off.*' James shrugged his shoulders and moved on.[1029] After the trial, Poole was interviewed by a reporter from the *Liverpool Daily Post*, who wanted to know if he interpreted James' remarks to mean he was taking poisonous medicines under '*doctor's orders.*' He replied: '*I never gave it a thought whether he was taking it by doctor's orders. I look with supreme contempt upon a man who doses himself.*' The reporter then asked if he knew of James' alleged habit of taking arsenic. He replied, '*Oh dear no. I only knew him slightly as a member of the Palatine Club.*'[1030]

In 1898, Russell wrote a letter to the then Home Secretary in which he mentioned the evidence given at the trial by Sir James Poole. He said his evidence had highlighted the '*notorious arsenic-eating habits*' of James Maybrick. He

[1026] Ibid., page 224.
[1027] Ibid., page 224.
[1028] Ibid., page 225.
[1029] Ibid., pages 226-227.
[1030] *Liverpool Daily Post*, 16th August 1889.

also wrote that it was one of '*the faults of the summing-up that the judge failed to give due weight to this entirely reliable evidence.*'[1031]

The case for the defence was now complete, but before Russell made his closing speech there was to be one more dramatic twist. At a few minutes past noon, Russell said Florence was now ready to make her statement. He looked at her and she gently nodded back. Mr Justice Stephen then gave her permission to speak.

The attendant next to Florence handed her a glass of water and she took a sip. She stood up, and with her hands tightly clasped, holding a pocket handkerchief and a piece of paper, she started to speak in a '*low, tremulous voice, but in perfectly coherent and elegant phraseology. She had to stop several times for a moment or two, and with great effort controlled her emotion so as to allow herself to proceed.*'[1032]

Florence Maybrick, paper in hand, makes her statement to the court

Florence's statement was perhaps the defining moment of the trial. A local reporter wrote that '*the court now audibly pulled itself together to witness one of the most remarkable incidents in the history of criminal inquiries, I mean the speech made by Mrs Maybrick, as she stood at the rail of the dock with the angel of death hovering overhead. It was an incident almost unique in its dramatic intensity.*'[1033]

In her statement, Florence said that she wished to '*principally refer to the use of flypapers and to the bottle of meat essence.*' She said that the flypapers, which the prosecution had made so much of, had been bought with the intention of her '*using as a cosmetic.*' For many years she had been in the habit of using a face wash that had originally been prescribed for her by Dr Greggs of Brooklyn. It consisted primarily of arsenic, tincture of benzoin, elderflower water and some other ingredients. Florence said that, as she had lost Dr Greggs' prescription, she had decided to make a '*substitute*' facewash solution. While she had lived in Germany she had seen many of her young friends using a solution derived from flypapers plus elder water and lavender water. She said that once she had prepared the solution, she applied it to her face using her handkerchief.

Florence moved on to the meat juice and, crucially, admitted to adding some white powder to it. She said she had only done so because her husband had implored her to do it, having assured her that the powder was perfectly harmless. She later moved the bottle to a spot where James could not see it. Florence said she only became aware of the exact nature of the white powder much later, when Mrs Briggs alluded to the presence of arsenic in the meat juice. She finished by saying that for the love of the children and for their future, a '*perfect reconciliation*' had taken place between her and her husband.

If the statement was an attempt by Florence to convince the jury that some of the prosecution's charges against her were untrue, then it was to fail miserably. Instead, her statement undid much of the good work that had been completed by her counsel during the trial. The defence team had been trying desperately to provide an alternative narrative for how James had died. In so doing, they wanted to draw the jury's attention away from the circumstantial evidence that pointed towards Florence's guilt and replace it with an account that focused on James' destructive and ill-advised lifestyle. Florence's statement played straight into the prosecution's hands, as it put their view of events back into the very centre of the minds of the jurors. The admission that Florence had put a dangerous white powder in her husband's meat juice was undoubtedly a great mistake.

1031 O'Brien R. Barry, op. cit., pages 262-263.
1032 *Liverpool Echo*, 5th August 1889.
1033 *Liverpool Review*, 10th August 1889.

LINKS TO THE RIPPER DIARY: WAS FLORENCE'S TRIAL RIGGED BY THE FREEMASONS?

Bruce Robinson has argued that Michael Maybrick was Jack the Ripper, and his supposed hatred of Freemasonry motivated him not only to kill, but also to kill in a manner that linked in with Masonic rituals and beliefs. He suggests that the mutilated bodies of all the Ripper's victims showed signs of Masonic rituals. Robinson also argues that many of the letters sent to Scotland Yard purported to have been penned and sent by Jack the Ripper contained phrases and drawings that were linked to Masonic rituals. For example, the *From Brum* letter received by the CID at Scotland Yard on 9th October 1888 was headed by a skull and crossbones, complete with a halo, crossed daggers, coffin and a skeleton, all drawn in black ink. Posted in Birmingham on 8th October, the letter itself was written in red ink and signed '*Jack the Ripper*'. According to Robinson, '*out of all the Ripper correspondence it is the most fastidious in its artwork. He sat down and bothered with it, using different coloured inks. This macabre assembly meant something to its author, and was designed to mean something to its recipient. In my philosophy, it had to mean something to Charles Warren.*'[1034]

Robinson argues that important Masonic figures, including Warren, the Commissioner of Policing in London, and many members of the British Government and Establishment, recognised these rituals and became determined to cover-up key incidents. They were alarmed at the potential reaction from the general public if it emerged that the most notorious killer in British criminal history was actually one of their very own Masonic brothers.

It is a key element of Robinson's hypothesis that Michael framed his brother James as the Ripper, and murdered him with the assistance of brother Edwin, Mrs Briggs and Nurse Yapp. He then arranged for Florence to be made the scapegoat for the crime. Robinson wrote: '*I am certain Michael murdered James, and framed James's wife Florence for the deed.*'[1035] For this plan to be successful, it was vital that Florence was found guilty of James' murder and sentenced to be hanged. Michael was worried that if news of his brother's arsenic use emerged in court, doubt might appear in the mind of the jury and Florence might be acquitted. To ensure a conviction, Sir Charles Russell was enlisted to be a part of the Freemasonry conspiracy. Robinson wrote that while Warren was '*required to pretend he was hunting the Ripper,*' Russell was '*entrusted to put up a show of defending Florence Maybrick.*'[1036] Robinson savages Russell, calling him among other things the '*Belfast Judas*' and arguing that he displayed '*energetic courtroom wizardry*' to actually get her convicted.[1037]

Russell places great store on an incident that happened at the start of the trial when Russell leaned over and whispered something to Addison during his opening speech. Irving referred to it in his account of the trial, stating that Addison responded by saying: '*It has been suggested to me, and probably it is right, that, except the scientific witnesses, all the witnesses should be requested to leave the court.*'[1038] That is exactly what happened next, though curiously Michael Maybrick was allowed to stay in the courtroom. There is no conspiracy; it is merely a sensible attempt by Russell to prevent the witnesses' responses being influenced by listening to the prosecution's case.

Robinson asserts that a '*huddle formed*' of the '*men in robes,*' at which Russell called for the suppression of the *Dear Blucher* letter that James had written to Michael on 29th April – although Bruce believes it had actually been forged by Michael.[1039] What huddle? It is not mentioned in the Irving or Levy accounts of the trial, and it is not mentioned in any of the reports in the Liverpool press. Robinson refers to an article in a New York newspaper, *The World*, but that report has no mention of a '*huddle.*' It does state that the production of the letter was the '*most important thing during the day,*' but it does not say when or how in appeared. Therefore, it is likely that the journalist from *The World* saw the letter in the same manner that everyone else did. Moreover, if it had been secretly suppressed, then how could the correspondent have found out about it? *The World* article also states that their correspondent had been told the '*defence will be prepared to go to any expense' to secure the expert medical testimony necessary to secure Florence's acquittal.*[1040] A full reading of the article paints a picture of Russell's team beginning to put together a credible set of arguments for Florence's defence. This view is supported by the following day's article in the same newspaper, which states that Russell had put in some '*sledge-hammer work in way of cross-examination,*' and this had '*caused a great rebound of popular opinion in Mrs Maybrick's favour.*' The article also said that Russell had taken a much lower fee due to the sympathy he felt for Florence, and that he was the '*hero*' of Liverpool.[1041]

Robinson makes other inaccurate assertions about the manner in which Russell handled the defence in order to try and produce a guilty verdict. He suggests Russell deliberately '*sabotaged*' the evidence of Dr Paul, one of the

---

1034 Robinson B., op. cit., page 555.
1035 Ibid., page 177.
1036 Ibid., page 634.
1037 Ibid., page 633.
1038 Ibid., page 3.
1039 Ibid., page 692.
1040 *The World* (New York), 1st August 1889.
1041 *The World* (New York), 2nd August 1889.

defence's scientific witnesses, by '*dragging back the glazed pan from which James had eaten his office lunch.*' This had the effect of '*replanting the virus of arsenic in the jurors' mind.*'[1042] This is an interpretation that simply does not stand up to scrutiny. Dr Paul said he tested four pans identical to the one taken from James' office, and had found arsenic in the glazing of all the pans. This piece of evidence was important, as it was part of the Crown's case that this was one of the occasions in which Florence had administered arsenic to her husband. Dr Paul's testimony meant that the arsenic found by Mr Edward Davies in his tests on the pan might have been there naturally. Christie called this a '*small gain for the defence.*'[1043] Russell then asked Dr Paul if it was a case of arsenic poisoning, to which he replied: '*I think it is a case of gastro-enteritis. The post-mortem appearances do not show that it was set up by arsenic.*'[1044] Therefore, rather than sabotaging Florence's defence, Russell was actually doing the complete reverse.

Robinson questions why Russell didn't bring in witnesses to testify that flypapers were ingredients of a widely used cosmetic. He implies that Russell's actions were deliberately undermining the case for the defence.[1045] In fact, Russell *did* try to explain that arsenic obtained from flypapers was used for cosmetic reasons, in both the evidence of Hugh Lloyd Jones and James Bioletti and in his final summing-up. Russell's questioning of Bioletti was clearly an attempt by him to counter the accusation that Florence had bought the flypapers with the intention of extracting arsenic to poison her husband. In reply to a question by Russell, Bioletti told the court that '*arsenic is used a good deal in the hair for some purposes, and I have used it as a wash for the face on being asked for it by ladies. There is an impression among ladies that it is good for the complexion.*' During his re-examination of Bioletti, Russell asked him if he was sometimes asked for an arsenic-based solution for '*the purpose of cosmetics*?' Bioletti replied '*yes.*'[1046]

Robinson suggests that while Russell did bring some witnesses from overseas, he failed to bring witnesses from Liverpool to show that James Maybrick was a user of powerful drugs. This is simply not the case. Edwin Heaton, a Liverpool chemist, testified that James visited his shop between '*two and five times a day*' for 18 months prior to April 1888 to drink a '*pick-me-up*'. The latter was a preparation that contained a small amount of arsenic. Russell asked Heaton if seven drops of this pick-me-up – James' usual amount – was taken five times a day, would it contain one-third of a grain of white arsenic? Heaton replied: '*Pretty near it.*'[1047] He also called Sir James Poole, a former Lord Mayor of Liverpool, who testified he met James and several others in April 1889 and that they had held a casual conversation in which someone had remarked that it was becoming a common practice to take poisonous medicines. He testified that, in response, James had blurted out that he took poisonous medicines.[1048]

Robinson's assault on Russell is lengthy and brutal. It is also unfair, inaccurate and unsustainable. Although Russell did make mistakes in his handling of Florence's trial – such as allowing her to make a statement to the court – he was to become one of her most ardent supporters, and devoted much time and effort trying to get her death sentence commuted and later to secure her release from prison. While Home Secretary Henry Matthews was pondering whether to go ahead with Florence's execution, Russell sent him a detailed and powerfully worded seven-page memorandum in which he implored the minister to carry out an '*independent examination*' of the case.

Russell was especially harsh in his condemnation of the manner in which Mr Justice Stephen conducted the case, and the negative tone he adopted towards Florence in his final summing-up. He wrote that, '*the verdict cannot be regarded as satisfactory and the irrevocable penalty ought not to be inflicted.*'[1049] These are not the words of a man who, as Robinson asserts, had deliberately set out to have Florence found guilty and executed. They are, in fact, the words of a man who is intent on doing the exact opposite; Russell is doing all he can to save his client from the gallows. Even after Russell was appointed Lord Chief Justice, he still continued to champion Florence's cause. In November 1895, he wrote to Sir Matthew White Ridley, the Home Secretary, that Florence Maybrick '*ought never to have been convicted, and that her continued imprisonment is an injustice which ought promptly to be ended.*' He criticised Henry Matthews, the Home Secretary at the time of the trial, who had commuted the sentence to life imprisonment on the grounds that Florence was guilty of attempting to administer arsenic with intent to murder. Russell continued that this was '*a most serious state of things. It is manifestly unjust that Florence Maybrick should suffer for a crime in regard to which she has never been called upon to answer before any lawful tribunal.*' He added that her continued imprisonment was an injustice as the '*foundation on which the whole case rested was rotten, for in fact there was no murder; that on the contrary, the deceased had died from natural causes.*'[1050] Florence herself wrote that Russell was '*the noblest, truest friend that a woman ever had: the champion of the weak and oppressed.*'[1051]

[1042] Robinson B., op. cit., page 707.
[1043] Christie T.L., op cit., page 117.
[1044] Irving, H. B., op. cit., pages 219-220.
[1045] Robinson B., op. cit., page 703.
[1046] Irving H.B., op. cit., page 225.
[1047] Ibid., page 195.
[1048] Ibid., page 227.
[1049] HO 144/1638/A50678.
[1050] Irving H.B., op cit. pages 260-261.
[1051] Maybrick F., op. cit. page 43.

17

TRIAL BY JUDGE

At 12:13pm on the fifth day of the trial, Sir Charles Russell rose to give his closing speech. As he did so, he knew the fate of his client lay in the balance. The defence had mounted a strong challenge to the prosecution's case, but Russell must have been aware that some of the defence witnesses had not been as convincing as he would have liked. The defence had paid a lot of money to bring Bateson and Stansell from America to testify, yet both of them had only fixed James' arsenic use to a brief period of three months, some 12 years before he died. When Bateson had been asked if James had become increasingly addicted to different medicines when they had shared a house together, he answered '*No.*'[1052]

On the other hand, some testimonies had boosted the defence's arguments that James was a serial user of dangerous drugs and had been the architect of his own death. Dr Tidy had impressed with his expertise and his firm conviction that James had died from gastro-enteritis rather than arsenical poisoning. Heaton was certain that the man he had regularly served with an arsenic-laden tonic was James Maybrick. The testimony of Sir James Poole, a pillar of Liverpool's commercial and political communities, would have also carried weight with the jury. Just one month before James' death, Poole had heard James say that he took '*poisonous medicines.*'

Despite these positives, Russell realised that Florence's statement in court had been rash and had damaged her cause. He knew it would take all of his abilities if he was to convince the jury of her innocence. As he got to his feet, everyone in the courtroom fixed their eyes on him; could '*this chieftain and pride of the English bar,*' with his persuasive arguments and eloquence, save the '*friendless lady*' from the gallows? The reporter from *The Liverpool Review* wrote that although Russell looked '*worn,*' he opened his speech with '*great deliberation, speaking 70 words to the minute.*' The same reporter compared Russell's closing remarks with his opening statement, saying that on '*Saturday his speech contained more sentiment than argument; on Monday it displayed more argument than sentiment.*'[1053]

Russell started his address by saying Florence had '*elected to take her trial in Liverpool before a Liverpool jury, in the community with which her husband lived.*'[1054] This wasn't completely true, as Florence had originally asked her lawyers to get the trial moved elsewhere. Russell described James as '*a man who appears to have been liked by his friends, and not without a kindly or generous nature.*' He said that while James was not a man who was frequently ill, in the sense he was unable to go to work, he did at least as far back as 1878 suffer chronically from '*derangement of the stomach.*' He added that it was a '*peculiar feature of the case*' that the symptoms James suffered from in his final illness, such as '*coldness and numbness in the extremities,*' were the very same symptoms he had experienced whilst living in America in the late 1870s. Russell said James had a '*dyspeptic tendency*' and a '*hypochondriacal nature*'. He was used to '*dosing himself*' and he '*displayed a familiarity with the properties and uses of poisonous drugs and medicines.*'

Russell described the Maybrick marriage between 1881 and 1889 as a happy one. He said this was important, because in June or September 1888 Florence had called Dr Hopper's attention to the fact that her husband was in the habit of using certain powders that were making him '*irritable*' and '*doing him mischief.*' She made the same observations in March 1889 to Dr Humphreys, and later to Michael Maybrick. Russell said James' brother had questioned him about the allegation, but had meekly accepted his denial that he took such powders. He asked the jury if they thought Michael's lack of action was a '*satisfactory course to pursue in such a case,*' especially as James had been in the '*habit of visiting constantly, several times a day, the shop of Mr Heaton.*'

Russell then moved on to Florence's affair with Brierley, admitting: '*This lady fell. She forgot her self-respect. She forgot her duty to her husband.*' He said James did not find out the full '*gravity*' of her fault until it was told him on his deathbed; however, he did complain about her '*conduct*' at the Grand National, and a '*stormy scene*' followed back at Battlecrease. Russell claimed that this was the first such angry row their servants had witnessed between the couple. The next day, in the company of Mrs Briggs, Florence visited the former's solicitors in order to enquire about separating from her husband due to the black eye she had suffered, and because of '*a woman, concerned in the matter.*'

1052 Irving H.B., op cit., page 186.
1053 *Liverpool Review*, 10th August 1889.
1054 Irving H.B., op cit., pages 229-256.

Under Florence's insistence, Russell did not say anything else about James' long-term mistress or the fact that she had considered divorcing him in 1887. He has been criticised for this, but it could be argued that knowledge of this fact may have caused the jury to think that Florence had an even stronger motive for murdering her husband. Russell said that, due to the intervention of Dr Hopper, a reconciliation had taken place between James and Florence. He said that without Florence's infidelity, there would be '*no motive assigned in this case*' and surely there was a '*wide chasm*' between '*moral guilt*' and '*criminal guilt.*' Florence may have '*sinned once,*' but was she to be '*misjudged always*?' Russell then pointed out the double standards that existed in Victorian England; when a man had an illicit sexual liaison it was often regarded with '*toleration,*' but if a woman did it was seen as '*an unforgiveable sin.*'

Russell said the only event of significance between March 1889 and the Wirral races was Florence's purchase of the flypapers. He poured scorn on the idea that Florence, if she had murder on her mind, would have bought these items in chemists where she was known and then have them delivered to her house. Russell agreed with the prosecution that James' illness dated from the Wirral races of 27th April, but said that the cause was the double dose of medicine James had taken that morning, coupled with the soaking he received after being caught in heavy rain. He said the fact that James had taken a double dose was proven by statements from both Dr Humphreys and Mr Thomson. The next day James was '*taken ill*' and complained of vomiting. Florence's response was to call a doctor to get treatment for his husband. Later, she was to send a telegraph to the nurse, Mrs Howell in Hale, asking her to attend James. She also sent a telegraph to James' brother Edwin, asking him to get a second doctor to visit the house.

Russell ridiculed the notion that Florence had put poison in the food that James had taken to his office. He pointed out that if James had eaten this food on 1st and 2nd of May, why, on 3rd May, had Dr Humphreys found his condition much improved? He also underlined that from Wednesday, 8th May until his death, Florence was '*not allowed to administer the smallest thing*' to her husband. Russell said there would not have been a trial at all if it had not been for the letter intercepted by Nurse Yapp that Florence had sent to Brierley. He said that the letter contained '*exaggerated language*' that was '*scanned by jealous and even suspicious eyes*' and was used against his client. Florence had written her husband was in a serious condition, but that was also the opinion of Mrs Briggs and her sister when they visited Battlecrease, and it was a view endorsed by Nurse Gore when she first saw the patient. Russell then turned to the '*medical aspect*' of the case. He emphasised the fact that, according to Dr Humphreys, James did not suffer from diarrhoea until Thursday 9th May. He asked the jury why, if Florence had been coldly planning murder, didn't she remove all traces of evidence that could point to her guilt?

After a break for lunch, Russell resumed his address by reminding the jurors of the two questions he had posed in his opening address. The first question had been: Did James Maybrick die of arsenical poisoning? He said the possibility that arsenical poisoning was the cause of death did not occur to either Dr Humphreys or Dr Carter until after the suggestion had been made to them. The crucial factor in determining whether it had been death by arsenic was the discovery of a very small quantity of the poison in James' body. Russell recalled the evidence of Dr Tidy, who described with '*great correctness*' the typical symptoms of arsenical poisoning: excessive and persistent vomiting, excessive diarrhoea, pains in the stomach, affection of the eyes and cramps in the calves of the legs. Such symptoms were largely absent in James' case. Russell referred to the evidence of Dr Macnamara, who said he had never seen an example of arsenical poisoning in which there was '*an absence in a marked degree,*' as there had been in the case of James, of at least three of these main symptoms.

Russell moved on to the small amount of arsenic found in James' body. He said that if the prosecution was correct in their theory that James had received '*repeated doses*' of arsenic, then one would have expected there to have been a '*large or serious quantity of arsenic*' in his body on analysis. But, according to the combined figures from Dr Stevenson and Mr Davies, '*less than one-tenth of a grain*' was actually found to be present. No arsenic was discovered at all in the stomach, spleen, bile, heart, lungs or portions of the bones which were tested. Dr Tidy's experience had shown that when repeated doses of arsenic are administrated to a person, there was a direct action on the kidneys '*which lessens their power as eliminating agents.*' This causes arsenic to be stored in the liver, yet only tiny traces of arsenic were found in James' liver. Russell said that the lack of *petechiae* or flea-bitten appearance of the condition of the stomach at the post-mortem also pointed away from arsenic being the cause of death. He asked the jury if, on reviewing this evidence, could they really be satisfied, '*as reasonable men, beyond reasonable doubt, that this was a case of arsenical poisoning*?'

Russell then dealt with the second of his two questions: Did Florence administer arsenic to her husband? He said that while a large quantity of arsenic had been found in Battlecrease, the only part that could be directly traced to his client were the flypapers. He asked why, if Florence had criminal intent and access to this vast store of arsenic in the house, did she resort '*to the clumsy, the stupid contrivance of trying to steep flypapers in water*?' Russell admitted a trace of arsenic had been found in the vessels used to heat up the Du Barry's food that James had eaten in his office, but he said that a small amount of arsenic was naturally '*let free in the usage*' of such vessels when they are heated. Russell asked why, if James had eaten from a '*poisoned dish,*' had Dr Humphreys on Wednesday, 1st May, found him '*better. He had no headache. His tongue was cleaner and he appeared to be making progress.*'

THE MAYBRICK MURDER TRIAL.

Pall Mall Budget, 8th August 1889

Russell said a trace of arsenic had been found on Florence's gown and handkerchief, but that was perfectly consistent with her '*dipping her handkerchief for cosmetic purposes and for purposes of rubbing her face*' and then placing the handkerchief in the pocket of her gown.[1055] He referred to Florence's statement to the court, and reminded the jury that none of the meat juice from the bottle moved by Florence had been given to James. He said he would '*not enlarge*' on the rest of the statement.[1056]

Russell then went through all the evidence that showed James was a regular user of arsenic, both in America and more recently in Liverpool. He referred to Captain Thompson's testimony, who described how in Norfolk, Virginia, a '*shopman*' in a local drug store had told him that James was in the '*dangerous habit of taking arsenic.*' He described how Heaton, the Liverpool chemist, had for many years prepared a pick-me-up for James that contained arsenic. He said that over time James had required an increasingly stronger arsenic content and, instead of once a day, James had started to partake of it five times a day. He mentioned James' remark to Sir James Poole that he had a '*pernicious habit of taking poisonous drugs*' and asked if anyone could possibly doubt that such a respectable Liverpool man was not telling the truth. Russell told the jury the fact that James had taken arsenic in one form or another over such a sustained period of time helped explain why traces of the substance were found in his body.

Russell finished by telling the jury he was not making an appeal for mercy, as it was the law itself which was merciful. He told the jurors: '*You are administering a law which forbids you to pronounce a verdict of Guilty unless all other reasonable hypotheses can be excluded.*'[1057]

As Russell sat down murmurs of approval quietly, but distinctly, echoed around the chamber. The reporter from *The Liverpool Review* had been impressed, and wrote: '*Sir Charles manipulated his facts not only with masterly skill, but also with remarkable resource of memory. He made no attempt to use the ordinary common-place addresses to juries. Even his peroration was more argumentative than rhetorical. His closing sentences were impressively eloquent and delivered with remarkable oratorical power.*'[1058]

Modern writers on the case have also tended to praise the power and the scope of Russell's final statement. Moiseiwitsch described it as a '*long, closely reasoned and brilliant final speech,*' and that Russell '*dealt with everything fully except the statement of Mrs Maybrick.*'[1059] Colquhoun called it a '*master-class in legal oratory, tunnelling effectively under the prosecution's case, reminding them repeatedly of the uncertainty that existed and the moral importance of deciding fairly.*'[1060]

The question is this: if Russell had been so brilliant and so persuasive, why did the jury find Florence guilty? Perhaps, given the composition of the jury, an '*ordinary common-place*' address might have been a more suitable style to have employed. He could have made more of the mismatch between James' symptoms and those of a typical victim of arsenical poisoning. His failure to address the issues raised by Florence's statement was another error on his part. After the trial had finished, all the jurors who gave interviews to the press spoke about the negative impact her statement had made on them.

When Addison rose to make his own final address he was also aware that the trial was in the balance. He knew that Russell had seriously undermined some of the prosecution's key pieces of evidence, so he employed a simple but effective strategy to try and counteract the defence counsel's arguments. He said that while Russell had sought to undermine the Crown's case by examining each piece of evidence separately, he would take all the circumstances and '*put them together.*'[1061] He told the jury that, while it was possible to explain away one suspicious matter or see two as a coincidence, when it came to three, four or, in fact, many suspicious events, they could only be understood when examined holistically as part of '*one theory.*'

Such a line of argument caused Addison to take a more chronological and narrative approach to his address. While such a style did not have the oratorial brilliance of Russell, it was a clever tactic as his address was easy to follow and allowed him to argue that while some individual items of evidence might appear weak, collectively they pointed with some certainty towards the defendant's guilt.

Addison began his chronological approach by agreeing with the defence that James had taken an arsenic-based medicine while he was in Norfolk, Virginia, prior to his marriage. However, he said that he had only done so on the advice of his doctor who had prescribed it as a treatment for malarial fever. Addison cleverly latched on to the evidence of Stansell, James' servant, and said that in the '*whole of the three or four years' from 1877-1881, James 'had only taken it four times.*' Addison said that from 1881 onwards, James had been under the medical care of Dr Hopper, who was '*morally certain*' that from the '*first to the last*' he never prescribed arsenic for his patient. He then

[1055] Ibid., page 251.
[1056] Ibid., page 252.
[1057] Ibid., page 256.
[1058] *Liverpool Review*, 10th August 1889.
[1059] Moiseiwitsch M., op cit., page 62.
[1060] Colquhoun K., op cit., page 270.
[1061] For a full account of Addison's address, see Irving H.B., op cit., pages 256-273.

dismissed Heaton's important testimony in just two sentences, arguing that while James may have taken a pick-me-up due to his nervousness and numbness, he had provided Heaton with a doctor's prescription for the preparation because he was a '*careful man, priding himself upon his knowledge of medicine.*' Addison said that James had not mentioned taking arsenic during his consultations with Dr Drysdale, and Dr Fuller's prescriptions had '*contained no arsenic whatever.*' Addison's picture of James' arsenic use was in total contrast to the one provided by Russell. Although he admitted James did have hypochondriacal tendencies, Addison suggested he was a '*strong and healthy man*' who was careful about his health and avoided taking medicines in a '*reckless or foolish manner.*' As to Florence's remarks to Dr Hopper and Michael Maybrick that her husband was taking some white powder, Addison told the jury they had to decide whether to accept James' denial to his brother or accept the word of a woman who had been '*unfaithful to her husband.*'

Addison next focused on Florence's affair with Brierley. He wanted to blur Russell's assertion that there was a difference between moral and criminal guilt, so outlined the lengths that Florence had gone to, and the lies she had told, in order to book the rooms at Flatman's Hotel. He told the jurors that '*it was impossible to treat it as an ordinary case of adultery, and not treat it as having any actual connection with the alleged crime. We cannot help remembering that on the 16th, 17th, 18th of March last it was shown she was a woman capable of duplicity, deceit, and falsehood.*'

Addison moved on to the flypapers, and told the jury that James had become ill on 27th April and that Florence had purchased the flypapers on 25th and 29th April. He said the timing of the purchases was '*extraordinary*' and mirrored the onset of James' illness. He questioned Florence's statement that she claimed the flypapers were purchased for cosmetic purposes, and asked why she had not told such a story to the police at the time of her arrest. His implication was clear – Florence's claim was just a ruse, developed later, to mask her real intentions for buying the flypapers.

Addison then tackled the key issue of the start of James' illness dating from the day of the Wirral races. He said James had told both Mr Thomson and Nurse Yapp he had become sick after taking a double dose of the medicine from London. Addison said arsenic had been found in one of the medicine bottles prepared by Clay and Abraham's from Dr Fuller's prescription, and asked who put it there. This statement was misleading, for although Davies, the analyst, had found distinct evidence of arsenic in one of the Clay and Abraham's bottles, that particular medicine had been compounded in Liverpool and therefore could not have been the medicine that James received in the post from London.[1062] Addison continued his skewed account by saying James '*clearly*' did not know that arsenic was in the Clay and Abraham's bottle because, if he had, '*the first thing he would have done would have been to see that he should not receive an overdose*'. Addison next spoke about the food James had taken to his office. He said arsenic had not been found in the pan or the basin used to reheat the food, but it had been found in the jug. That was incorrect; the arsenic had been found in the washings that had come from all three items. Addison continued by saying the inference to be made from Mr Davies' analysis of the items was '*there was arsenic*' in the food to begin with.

The prosecutor moved on to the cause of James' death, knowing he had to counter the defence's case that he died of gastro-enteritis. His arguments here were simple but effective; all the doctors agreed James had died from the effects of an irritant poisoning, and the post-mortem and various other analyses after his death all revealed the presence of arsenic in his body. As to the fact that James' symptoms did not appear to have followed the regular sequence or intensity normally associated with arsenical poisoning, Addison said this was simply because such symptoms may vary depending upon the '*idiosyncrasy of the patient, of his treatment, and his habit.*' With regard to the lack of *petechiae* found in James' body in the post-mortem examination, Addison said these were '*niceties and disputes' upon which the jury would find it difficult to 'come to a right conclusion.*' As a result, he said, they could ignore these issues as '*theories which are started to explain away facts.*' In other words, Addison was saying to the jury they didn't need to consider the detailed medical evidence that suggested James' death had not been caused by arsenical poisoning.

Although Addison wanted the jury to ignore key pieces of the medical evidence, he did not want them to ignore the letter Florence had written to Brierley. He read out sections of it, commenting on Florence's words with his own interpretations of her thinking at the time. For example, after he had read out the sentence '*M has been delirious since Sunday,*' he stopped and repeated out loud the word '*delirious*!' He suggested that, as James had not been delirious up to that point, Florence must have been '*preparing the way for what was going to happen.*' Addison said the person who wrote such a letter could only be described as '*consummately cunning.*' He then linked this implied criminal intent with the meat juice episode. While Russell had ignored Florence's statement to the court, Addison was not going to make the same mistake. He focused in-depth on Florence's words, and when he did his argument '*became rejuvenated in direction and force.*'[1063] Addison seized on Florence's admission that she had put a powder in her husband's meat juice and Nurse Gore's testimony that the juice had not been fed to the patient. This, as the jurors later confirmed, was probably the most significant piece of evidence in the whole trial and Addison was going to

[1062] Irving H.B., op cit., page 132.
[1063] Moiseiwitsch M., op cit. pages 62-63.

make the most of it. He said: '*But why was it not administered? Not by the will or act of this woman. She left it to be administered by the first nurse who would come on duty, and in that food was half a grain of arsenic, such a dose as being repeated would kill.*'[1064]

Addison also attacked another part of Florence's statement, in which she said she had made a full confession to her husband and the two of them had been reconciled. Addison asked why, if that was the case, had she sent a second letter to Brierley appealing for his assistance?

He finished his address by telling the jury that they had to '*disregard all those feelings of sympathy which the age and sex and the position of this unhappy woman would naturally create in your bosoms and deal out to her the same justice as you would deal out to a poor and ill-favoured person who might be found guilty of this terrible crime.*' He told the jurors that if they were satisfied Florence was guilty of murder, then she had carried out the act with '*hypocrisy and a cunning which have been rarely equalled in the annals of crime.*'[1065]

At 5:30pm, Addison concluded his speech and sat down. He had spoken with '*solid ability, if not with brilliancy*' for two hours, one hour less than Russell.[1066]

Addison's address has been attacked by some commentators on the trial. Ryan suggests he had made '*many small errors*' in his summing up. He had '*oversimplified, for this ordinary jury, the detailed medical evidence on gastro-enteritis and inflammation. He had confused London medicine and Clay and Abrahams' medicine. He had ignored or discredited the evidence of several witnesses on Maybrick's reckless use of medicines.*'[1067] Graham and Emmas wrote that Addison's summing up '*did not do him credit. He made a considerable number of errors, was vague with the facts and wild with the evidence. Sir Charles Russell found himself jumping up and down to correct him.*'[1068]

While Addison did make mistakes, it was not true that Russell was continually jumping up and down to correct his errors. If anything, he allowed some of Addison's more questionable remarks to go unchallenged. Addison's role was to secure a conviction, and therefore he was bound to focus on those parts of the evidence which were the most damaging to Florence. His strategy in telling the jury to ignore parts of the medical evidence and take a holistic view of events was particularly effective. He wanted to steer the jury away from considering whether James' symptoms were characteristic of arsenical poisoning, and he did not want them to get involved in a debate about whether or not *petechiae* could be found in his post-mortem analysis, because neither of these areas were helpful to the prosecution.

His aim was to construct a picture of Florence as a cunning criminal who was intent on murdering her husband so that she could be with her lover. He wanted the jury to focus their minds on a few key incidents: Florence's adultery and her letter to Brierley, the fact that arsenic had been found in James' body, Florence's purchase of the flypapers, and her admission that she had added a white powder – later found to be arsenic – to the meat juice bottle.

In so doing, Addison provided a misleading picture of James, minimising his chronic drug use. He also provided inaccurate information on the source of the London medicine that precipitated James' illness. While it is possible to criticise Addison, perhaps the real fault lies with the defence team for their failure to rebuff these narratives. Few contemporary newspaper accounts were critical of Addison, and some even praised him for his even-handedness. There were occasions when he intervened to correct the judge's statements that were inaccurate. For example, he corrected Mr Justice Stephen when he mistakenly said Florence had slept with Brierley after her reconciliation with her husband. The *Liverpool Review* wrote: '*It is known that Mr Addison himself, the prosecuting counsel, who performed his painful task so chivalrously and so generously, believed that the prisoner would escape.*'[1069]

Tuesday, 6th August, was the sixth and penultimate day of the trial. Heavy rain prevented the usual crowds from gathering outside St George's Hall, and the sightseers who were present were huddled together under the colonnade of the building. Inside, there was no fanfare of trumpets as the judge took his seat just after 10:00am and began his summing-up. Mr Justice Stephen's address was to last 12 hours and was spread over two days. He started by telling the jury that, due to the importance of the trial, he felt obliged to '*go through the whole of the evidence which has been given.*'[1070] He said this would involve a great deal of '*repetition,*' which might be '*tedious*' for them to hear.

According to one reporter, '*The judge spoke in very low, almost inaudible tones, reading over the evidence from his voluminous notes and commenting on it as he went along. Mrs Maybrick who seemed more animated and watchful than usual, kept her eyes fixed on the judge, trying hard to catch the whole of his observations.*'[1071]

[1064] Irving H. B.., page 269.
[1065] Ibid., page 273.
[1066] *Liverpool Review*, 10th August 1889.
[1067] Ryan B., op cit., page 280.
[1068] Graham A. and Emmas C., op cit., page 189.
[1069] *Liverpool Review*, 10th August 1889.
[1070] For a full account of Justice Stephen's summing up, see Irving H.B., op cit., pages 274-355.
[1071] *Liverpool Daily Post*, 7th August, 1889.

'Judges, No. 14' (*Vanity Fair*, 7th March 1885)

The judge's summing-up was so ponderous and difficult to hear that, after a heavy lunch, Addison, '*who had a newspaper spread out before him, fell fast asleep, with his head lying on the desk before him.*'[1072] Sir Charles Russell may have anticipated the lengthy and repetitive approach the judge was going to adopt, as he decided not to attend the trial that day but instead was engaged in another case in the building. Pickford, his second, kept a watching brief for the defence team on the day and was soon on his feet correcting the judge who, very early on in his summing-up, made the basic mistake in fixing Florence's purchases of the flypapers as being in March instead of April.

Mr Justice Stephen ran through the evidence provided by all the witnesses in the order they had appeared in the trial, and highlighted the areas he deemed to be significant. For example, in dealing with Dr Fuller's evidence the judge said that '*one of the most remarkable points of this case*' was that one of the bottles of medicine the doctor had prescribed, which had been made up in Clay and Abraham's Chemist in Liverpool, contained arsenic, even though Fuller – and the chemist who compounded it – both said they had put no arsenic in it. The judge told the jury they would have to draw their '*own conclusions*' as to who put arsenic in the bottle.

When discussing the evidence provided by the servants at Battlecrease, Stephen said Elizabeth Brierley, the housemaid, had taken Nurse Yapp into Mrs Maybrick's room and shown her some flypapers in a basin. Although the judge had drawn the attention of the jury to the fact that Florence had purchased the flypapers at around the same time as her husband had become ill, he also noted that they had been left on the washstand in the main bedroom, so there had been '*no concealment*.' When discussing Nurse Yapp's evidence, the judge described Thursday, 8th May as a '*date of the utmost importance, and one which contains the whole history of the case.*' He said on this day Nurse Yapp had overheard Florence refusing to rub her husband's hands, saying it didn't do them any good. Stephen commented that while the remark didn't reveal a '*criminal mind*,' it was an '*unkind thing.*' On Thursday afternoon, Florence had given the nurse a letter to Brierley to post. Stephen described the letter as '*of the greatest importance*' and '*one of the critical points of the case.*'

Mr Justice Stephen would have undoubtedly claimed that his process of running through the key points from the witnesses' testimonies was designed to be helpful to the jury, highlighting what he considered to be important and indicating elements that they could ignore. For example, he said that the reason why Nurse Yapp opened Florence's letter to Brierley didn't make the '*smallest difference as to Mrs Maybrick's innocence or guilt*' – it was the content of the letter rather than Nurse Yapp's actions that was the critical issue.

He would also have claimed to have been even-handed in his approach. According to his brother, who was also his biographer, one of Stephen's core aims during his time on the bench was to be '*thoroughly fair*' in the manner in which he conducted the trial.[1073] In his mind, justice implied '*fair play*' to the accused, and he always tried to speak to the defendant in a '*friendly manner.*'[1074] It is the case that not everything that Stephen said was harmful to Florence's cause. When he was discussing Edwin's evidence, the judge told the jury that, during her husband's illness, Florence did:

> '*seem to have sent for nurses. I don't see anything upon which you can ground a suggestion that she kept people away from her husband, or prevented the medical men or nurses seeing him on every occasion when they could be of use to him.' He also pointed out when discussing Nurse Yapp's evidence, that when James became sick after taking an overdose of his medicine, Florence had given him an emetic. He described the act as something which would have 'likely' done 'him good' and 'no doubt was the best thing to do.*'

As Mr Justice Stephen made his address he was surrounded by an array of papers, and he moved from his own notes to court reports to newspaper accounts in a seemingly random and often confusing manner. Levy is particularly critical of the manner in which the judge delivered his summing-up, describing it as '*disjointed.*'[1075] His main source

[1072] *Liverpool Review*, 3rd August 1889.
[1073] Stephen L., *The Life of Sir James Fitzjames Stephen, bart., KCSI., a judge of the High Court of Justice*, (Smith Elder and Co., London, 1895) page 439.
[1074] Ibid., page 442.
[1075] Levy J.H., op cit., page 323.

of information was a diary he kept throughout the trial. Stephen was '*proud of his power of rapid writing,*' and in all his cases he took copious notes of the witnesses' testimony.[1076] According to one newspaper report, what he '*appeared to do' was 'take his diary of the trial and read a page of it, or the statement of a witness, and then offer his comments thereon.*'[1077] This is illustrated by the manner in which he covered the evidence of Dr Humphreys. He read out a newspaper account which provided a verbatim report of what the doctor told the court, stopping on occasions to add his own personal comments. For example, when he read out a section from Humphreys' evidence for Wednesday 8th May, he noted that the doctor had said the patient was '*getting on favourably*'. He stopped and commented that this was important, because on this day '*the letter was sent by the prisoner to Brierley, in which she used the words "He is sick unto death."*'[1078]

Stephen's approach was not only lengthy and uninspiring, it also led him to make numerous errors over dates, places, people and even factual errors about some of the witnesses' statements, all of which cast a very real doubt on his competence. One serious error came when he was reviewing the evidence of Dr Carter, quoting the doctor as saying that during his initial examination of James, '*I saw a great deal of vomiting.*' In fact, Carter did not say those words, but had instead asked to examine any vomited material that had come from the patient, though no such material was available for his inspection. This error is important, because excessive vomiting was a symptom of arsenical poisoning and the judge, by misquoting Carter, had given the impression that James was suffering from such a symptom. Also when reviewing Carter's evidence, Stephen said the doctor claimed that two grains of arsenic given in successive days '*would have killed him.*' The judge implied the doctor was speaking specifically about James' death, but Carter had been speaking about another case in which he had been involved. Dr Paul, in his evidence, referenced the same case, and said the person involved was a woman. Dr Paul also stated it would take '*not less than three grains of arsenic*' to kill a man of the age and habits of James Maybrick.[1079]

Another important error made by Mr Justice Stephen came when he went through the evidence given by Sir James Poole. The judge said that in January 1889, James had told Poole he was in the habit of taking poisonous medicines. This was a serious mistake, as James had made this remark in April and not January. This date is significant, because if the dangerous medicine taken by James in April had been arsenic it would explain why its presence had been detected in his body during his post-mortem. The judge did admit while discussing Poole's evidence that '*it tends to explain what is certainly the strongest part for the case of the Crown, namely, that arsenic was found in this man at his death.*' He did not develop this point any further, as he said he would '*feel some kind of delicacy*' about advancing such a line of argument. If the judge had been acting in an even-handed manner, this was a point that needed to be developed as it went right to the heart of the case against Florence.

The judge's selection of what he considered to be the important pieces of evidence led him on several occasions to omit some significant items that would have been very helpful to the defence's arguments. Levy describes the summary of Mary Cadwallader's evidence as '*strangely defective.*'[1080] Stephen referred to some of her testimony, such as when she spoke to the chemists' boy who delivered the flypapers to the house, but completely ignored other parts of her evidence that were extremely relevant to the case. He failed to mention the fact it was Mary Cadwallader who had taken in the London medicine that arrived in the post for James on Friday 26th April. Even more importantly, he did not refer at all to James' statement to her that he had become ill after taking a double dose of this medicine. This point is relevant, as the defence had argued that James had become ill on the day of the Wirral races after taking the medicine received in the post from London, while the prosecution had argued that James' illness was caused by him taking the Clay and Abraham's medicine which had arsenic added to it. When discussing Elizabeth Humphreys' evidence, Stephen refers to a statement that Florence made to the cook that if James had taken much more of the London medicine it would have killed him; yet he did not mention that Florence had told the cook she had thrown away what remained of the medicine. That he failed to mention such an important action by Florence, and one that had been designed to save her husband's life, again casts doubt on his impartiality and competence.

The largest part of Mr Justice Stephen's summing-up was devoted to the conflicting medical evidence. He began this process after lunch on the sixth day of the trial, and continued with it when the court resumed on Wednesday morning. After running through the evidence provided by Drs Humphreys and Carter the judge told the jury that he was not '*disposed*' to go '*through the evidence of the doctors to have been called merely to give an opinion.*' Although he did in fact deal with the evidence provided by these other doctors, his statement is alarming as he seems to be telling the jury they could ignore the views of the medical experts and limit their analysis to the two doctors, Humphreys and Carter, who had been witnesses for the Crown, stating James died of arsenical poisoning. Neither of these doctors, prior to the Maybrick case, had never been involved in a case of death by arsenical poisoning.

1076 Stephen L., op cit., page 440.
1077 *Liverpool Review*, 10th August 1889.
1078 Levy J.H., op cit., page 333.
1079 Irving H.B., op. cit., page 218.
1080 Levy J.H., op cit., page 331.

As to the question of whether minute *petechiae* spots had been visible during James' post-mortem, the judge said Dr Humphreys had said they were present and, as he was an '*intelligent and observant doctor*,' he was '*very apt to believe him*.' This is a troubling remark, as the judge was seemingly advising the jury to accept Dr Humphreys' assertion that *petechiae* were visible, and to disregard the view of Dr Barron – who was also present at the post-mortem – who said that their presence was '*doubtful*.' What makes this comment even more concerning is that Dr Barron was by far the more experienced medical practitioner, having attended more than 500 post-mortems. As they are one of the key characteristics of arsenical poisoning, the lack of *petechiae* visible at James' post-mortem is a clear indicator that his death was not caused by arsenic.

One of the reasons why Mr Justice Stephen seemed to place such great store on the evidence of Drs Humphreys and Carter was because he believed the medical experts to be '*advocates rather than witnesses*.' His advice to the jury on the medical evidence has been described as '*a curious mixture of adroitly concealed cynicism about the capacity of the jury to form a valid opinion about this part of the evidence and an exposition of it so dilatory that it could have only aggravated the confusion in the jury's mind*.'[1081]

Before the court rose at the end of day six of the trial, Mr Justice Stephen drew attention to the marked differences of opinion between Dr Stevenson and Drs Tidy and Macnamara over whether James had died from arsenical poison. He said it was an issue of '*great importance*,' and then told the jury: '*I fear that we are there getting amongst questions which I have already warned you are really, speaking quite plainly, too difficult for us. At all events, they are too difficult for me*.' He later told the jury it was a great relief it was they, rather him, that had to determine the verdict.

If we accept Stephen's analysis that the medical evidence was confusing, contradictory and impossible to understand by a layman, then that would seem to imply that a genuine doubt existed over whether James died as a result of arsenical poisoning. If that is the case, he should have directed the jury to have cleared Florence of the charge of murder. That, of course, did not happen. Instead, the judge said a '*subtle partisanship*' between the experts diminished the value of their evidence, and he told the jury that they should be '*free from all unnecessary respect for the opinions and special knowledge of men especially acquainted with these things*.' In other words, the judge was telling the jury they could ignore the statements of the experts and instead reach their own conclusions about the cause of death.

Mr Justice Stephen's summing-up on day six had lasted more than six hours. Although it contained many minor errors and some serious mistakes, many observers still believed he had attempted to be balanced. While he had not always met that high standard, no serious damage had been done to the defendant's cause.

The next day, the judge's tone and words took on a much darker complexion as far as the defence was concerned. Something must have happened overnight to have changed his mood.

A clue to what occurred is provided in the memoirs of Sir Henry Dickens. He recounts a story told to him by a fellow judge, who was sharing lodgings with Stephen at the time of the Maybrick trial. That judge claimed that early in the morning of the final day of the trial he was awakened by Stephen, who was walking up and down his room in his dressing gown repeatedly saying, '*That woman is guilty*.'[1082]

Although this recollection is from an unnamed source, there are reasons to believe it provides a reliable account of what happened. In his memoirs, Sir Henry Dickens writes favourably of Stephen as a judge. He refers specifically to a case before him in which, as a young lawyer, Dickens had represented a fish porter who had brought an action of slander to clear his name of a charge he had been stealing fish. Dickens said at the trial he had directed his final remarks at the judge more than the jury, and had managed to convince him of his client's case. As a result, Justice Stephen had '*summed up very strongly in my favour*.'[1083] It is therefore probable that, overnight, Mr Justice Stephen had come to believe in Florence's guilt and set about shaping his remarks on the final day to secure such a verdict.

Wednesday 7th August, was the seventh and final day of the trial. Outside the court there was a large police presence, partly because it was envisaged the trial would end that day, but also because some of the witnesses had been jostled by the crowd as they had left the building on the previous evening. For the first time, Florence had to be helped by her attendants as she climbed the steps into the dock.

At just after 10:00am, Mr Justice Stephen resumed his summing-up by returning to the evidence provided by the medical experts. Almost immediately he made yet another mistake, stating that Dr Stevenson had analysed James' intestines and found '*one 53-thousand part of a grain*', when in fact the actual quantity was 15 thousandths of a grain. After going through the differences in opinion between Dr Stevenson and Dr Tidy over whether James suffered from the symptoms of arsenical poisoning, he added that '*poison was present*,' and to his mind that meant '*a great deal to consider*.' When the judge moved on to the evidence given by Dr Paul, he said when Mr Davies conducted his tests on the pan and vessels that James had used to heat up his food in his office, '*nothing was found to contain*

1081 Moiseiwitsch M., op. cit., page 47.

1082 Dickens H., *The Recollections of Sir Henry Dickens, K.C.*, (Heinemann, London, 1937) page 171.

1083 Ibid., pages 170-171.

arsenic except in the food.' This was yet another inaccurate statement as the food had not been examined separately; instead, the content of all the items had been mixed together and then analysed.

It was when Mr Justice Stephen moved on to the issue of motive that his verbal onslaught on Florence's character truly took shape. As a judge, he had come to view the criminal court as a '*school of morality*,' and he was '*animated and directed to work by strenuous moral convictions.*'[1084] In his mind, Florence was morally guilty and that meant she was also likely to have been criminally guilty. Florence's statement to the court and the presence of arsenic, albeit a very small amount in James' body, had helped confirm this judgement.

Stephen started his attack on Florence's character by stating there was no need to '*determine any moral question*,' but then proceeded to explore the moral issues in some depth. He said there could be '*no doubt*' that in late March she had carried on an '*adulterous intercourse with this man Brierley.*' He added the '*most remarkable feature*' about her conduct was that Brierley was '*not the first person who appeared at the hotel in London.*' The implication of the judge's remark was clear, but the man in question had been John Baillie Knight, an old family friend, who had taken Florence out for the evening and no improper behaviour had occurred. The judge then read out Baillie Knight's letter to Florence in which he had criticised her behaviour during her stay in London. Stephen commented the letter showed '*her relations seem to have complained bitterly of the mass of falsehoods which she told them.*'

He then moved to the letter Brierley had sent Florence that had been found in Battlecrease. As he did, a great excitement erupted in the court as the judge seemed about to call Brierley to verify that he was the author of the letter. The judge said the letters showed '*wicked falsehoods*' and that Florence's behaviour was '*very grave and great disgrace.*' The judge then read out the letter Florence had written to Brierley in reply, pausing occasionally to comment on some of its content. For example, he noted that at the time when Florence had written about James being '*sick unto death*,' Dr Humphreys still believed the patient would recover. He looked at the all-male jury and described it as a '*sad and terrible case*' and one in '*which in many ways appeals to the feelings of every man who has a heart.*' The judge then made a serious error in stating that Florence had continued her adulterous relationship with Brierley after the attempt at reconciliation following the quarrel at the Grand National. Addison rose to his feet to correct the judge, who was forced to admit that he had made a mistake.

Having attacked Florence's character and motives Mr Justice Stephen turned his fire on her statement to the court, which he read out from a newspaper report of the trial. He asked why the defence had not produced any witnesses, such as Florence's mother, to support her statement she had previously bought flypapers in order to produce a cosmetic solution. Levy has strongly attacked the views expressed by Stephen over this particular issue, calling them '*quite indefensible.*' He points out that a judge has '*no right to call upon an accused person to call witnesses.*'[1085]

Mr Justice Stephen next focused his attention on Florence's admission she had added a white powder to the meat juice. He said that as she had spoken to Drs Hopper and Humphreys, plus Michael Maybrick, about the detrimental impact consuming such powders had on her husband's health, why then would she do '*so extraordinary a thing as to put an unknown white powder into her husband's meat juice*?' He added it was a point '*which presses very hard upon her.*' He questioned why Florence had not explained her actions over the flypapers and the meat juice when she had first been charged by the police, but had decided to reserve her defence. After lunch, Mr Pickford rose and told the judge that the decision to reserve Florence's defence had been made by him, and he took the entire responsibility for the action.

When the judge dealt with the evidence from Nurse Gore he read a verbatim account of what she had told the court from a report in the *Liverpool Daily Post*. Coming to the section in which Florence had asked the nurse to leave the room to fetch some ice, he commented: '*That certainly did suggest to my mind that Mrs Maybrick made an excuse, and tried by sending Nurse Gore out of the room, to get an opportunity of putting arsenic into her husband's meat juice.*' Apart from the fact that his statement was factually incorrect, as Florence had already put the white powder into the meat juice before she asked the nurse to leave the room, the judge was clearly leading the jury down a path that pointed towards Florence's guilt.

He did something similar when he spoke about the large quantity of arsenic that was discovered in Battlecrease. Although he did not say that all of it was in Florence's possession, he did say that she '*undoubtedly had access*' to the drug. As the judge went through the various places, bottles and items in which traces of arsenic had been found he made a whole series of mistakes, some of which definitely counted against the defendant. For example, he said that arsenic had been found in the wooden box in the inner-dressing room that '*Mrs Maybrick used, and which was packed up for the children.*' In fact, the wooden box was kept in an entirely different room, one which everyone in the house had access to. He finished his misleading summary of all the arsenic found in Battlecrease by saying that the house was '*infected*' with arsenic, and it was in '*places where Mrs Maybrick continually was.*' It was also, of course, in places everyone else – including James – had continually used as well.

[1084] Stephen L., op cit., pages 441 and 481.
[1085] Levy J.H., op cit., page 323.

Mr Justice Stephen concluded his remarks by telling the jury they '*must not consider it as a medical case*' in which they merely decided whether or not James died from arsenical poisoning, but as a '*highly important moral question.*' He said that if Florence was guilty, then she had been '*deliberately administering poison to a poor, helpless sick man upon whom she had already inflicted a dreadful injury... the person who could do such a thing as that must indeed be destitute of the least trace of human feeling.*'

He continued his moral tirade against Florence by telling the jury they had to take into account the '*whole story,*' something Addison had also urged them to do, and '*must remember the intrigue which she carried on with this man Brierley, and the feelings – it seems horrible to comparatively ordinary, innocent people a horrible and incredible thought that a woman should be plotting the death of her husband in order that she might be left at liberty to follow her own degrading vices.*' Although the judge added that the jury should not convict Florence '*unless you are sure in your own mind*' that she '*really committed*' the murder, he did nevertheless add that it was '*easy enough to conceive how a horrible woman, in so terrible a position, might be assailed by some fearful and terrible temptation.*'

Mr Justice Stephen's summing-up on the last day of the trial was undoubtedly biased against Florence. He emphasised the evidence against her, told the jury she had lied to her husband and her friends, and condemned at length her affair with Brierley. Crucially, on all the most important issues in the trial he had sided with the arguments put forward by the prosecution team. For example, he had poured scorn on Florence's claim she had purchased the flypapers for cosmetic purposes, and had openly rejected her statement she had only added the white powder to the meat juice because her husband had urged her to do so. Although the judge's biographer was later to contend that during the Maybrick trial Stephen had '*kept his mind open to the last,*' the veracity of this claim is not supported by the judge's sustained verbal assault on Florence's character and behaviour, and his skewed analysis of the pivotal points of contention in the case.[1086]

[1086] Stephen L., op cit., page 447.

Despite the judge's hostile summing-up, at 3:08pm, when the jury went out to consider their decision, many people in the courtroom still believed that the defence team had done enough to put doubt in the jury's mind and an innocent verdict was widely expected. In anticipation of such a result, a group of women approached court officials to see if they could present Florence with flowers as soon as the jury's decision was announced.

In the holding cell below the courtroom, Florence sat in a dazed condition. The worry of the trial, lack of sleep and the judge's harsh words had hit her hard. She was painfully aware that her life was very much in the balance. A guilty verdict would mean a death sentence. Although she had asked to be left alone, William Potter, an agent of Armstrong, her American lawyer, and Thomas Sherman, the US consul in Liverpool, entered her cell and told her she needed to sign some legal documents. These were the papers that related to the agreement made some years earlier, in which the Baroness had agreed to sell all interests in her American properties in Kentucky to David Armstrong in return for a one-off payment of $10,000. Potter said her signature was urgently required, as a guilty verdict would invalidate the agreement. How much Florence understood about the documents she was told to sign was later to be a matter of contention. She was later to state that, as she sat waiting the jury's deliberations, she was '*utterly incapable of comprehending anything or caring about anything beyond the fact that my life was at stake.*'

It took the jury only 35 minutes to reach a verdict. The quick decision was seen as a positive sign for the defendant. McConnell, the junior counsel for the Crown, said the thing that shocked him the most at the trial was the short time the jury took to arrive at its decision. He said he was washing his hands when his clerk came in with the news that the jury had returned, and exclaimed, '*Oh then, they have acquitted her.*'[1087] It was just after 4:00pm when the court reassembled and Florence entered the dock for the final time. As she did so, she had an intuition the verdict was unfavourable. She later wrote in her autobiography that '*everyone looked away from me, and there was a stillness in the court that could be felt.*'[1088] A Liverpool journalist recorded what happened next:

> '*The jury returned at four minutes to four, and the whole of the persons in court rose and stood in silence. The silence and the tension of the moment was most impressive. After being asked by the Clerk of Arraigns whether they found the prisoner Guilty or Not Guilty, the foreman of the jury pronounced the verdict in a low voice, "Guilty." After an instant's hush there was a loud murmur – half a groan and half an ejaculation of astonishment; but it was most decidedly expressed and felt throughout the court, and during the following few minutes of the pronouncement of the dread sentence there were few who were not shaken with the pain and agitation of the terrible scene. At the moment of the verdict, the prisoner – who had been looking up confidently towards the jury box (though she might have guessed by the averted faces of the jurymen what was to happen) – dropped her head down on one hand, resting it almost on her knee, and sat in that attitude for about fifteen seconds amid the profoundest silence. At this moment a second female warder came up and stood behind her in order to be ready in case of the prisoner requiring assistance.*'[1089]

The Clerk of Arraigns then addressed Florence saying: '*You have been found Guilty of wilful murder; have you anything to say why the Court should not pronounce sentence upon you?*' She replied, '*Although I have been found Guilty, with the exception of my intimacy with Mr Brierley, I am not guilty of this crime.*'[1090]

After the verdict was pronounced Mr Justice Stephen placed his black cloth on his head, and said: '*Prisoner at the bar, I am no further able to treat you as being innocent of the dreadful crime laid to your charge. You have been convicted by a jury of this city [in fact the jury was made up of men drawn from Lancashire and not Liverpool] after a lengthy and most painful investigation, followed by a defence which was in every respect worthy of the case.*'

The judge then sentenced Florence to be hanged. The guilty verdict and sentence were greeted with anger outside St George's Hall. One newspaper stated that '*a great angry howl (for nothing else could describe it) went up from the crowd.*' As the prosecution barristers and witnesses left the court, they were '*treated to uncomplimentary and forcible remarks, and altogether there was no mistaking how the popular sympathy lay.*' It was when the judge appeared at the door of the Hall that anger of the crowd really erupted. He was '*hooted most determinedly and loudly, and indeed at one moment there were not wanting symptoms that an attack might be made on the judicial carriage. The large number of policemen who were on duty kept the people at bay as well as they could until Mr Justice Stephen had driven away, followed by storms of howling and cries of "Shame."*'[1091]

If there was such a public outcry at the verdict, the obvious question to be addressed is why was Florence found Guilty? Some writers, shocked at the verdict and the conduct of the judge, have sought to minimise the strength of

---

1087 *Liverpool Daily Post*, 22nd December 1906.
1088 Maybrick F., op cit., pages 54-55.
1089 *Liverpool Daily Post*, 8th August 1889.
1090 Irving H.B., op. cit., page 355.
1091 *Halfpenny Weekly*, 10th August 1889.

the prosecution's case and the evidence against her. That is a mistake. Moiseiwitsch has called the case against Florence '*very formidable*' and '*one which appeared, on the face of it, all but impossible to answer.*'[1092]

There were three key factors that helped produce a Guilty verdict. The first of these was Florence's affair with Brierley. Without this liaison, there would not have even been a trial. When Nurse Yapp opened and read Florence's letter to Brierley and then passed it to James' brothers, she unleashed a wave of suspicion that almost took Florence to the gallows. There can be no doubt that Florence's affair with Brierley counted against her. It allowed the judge to attack both her behaviour and her character, and gave the prosecution the motive needed for murder. To the modern mind, such attacks appear hypocritical. Florence had only the briefest of affairs with Brierley; there is no evidence that she stayed with him on any occasion other than at Flatman's Hotel. James, on the other hand, had a longstanding mistress; even Michael Maybrick in his evidence at Florence's trial admitted there were complaints on both sides.

The second factor was Florence's statement in court. When she admitted adding powder to the meat juice, she reinvigorated the prosecution's case and brought new life to the argument that she had poisoned her husband. Moiseiwitsch has written: '*In a few seconds the whole of the admirable and wellnigh irrefutable part of the defence dealing with the medical evidence and Maybrick's private history of addiction to arsenic, suggesting that, had he died from it, he had poisoned himself, was cast into doubt.*'[1093] The statement was an error of judgement, and it was an error made even worse because Russell did not tackle its implications in his final address. Addison, on the other hand, used the statement to dramatic effect. He asked the jury if Florence had put the white powder in the meat juice with an innocent intent, '*why then did she not tell the nurse*?' What made his attack even more powerful was the defence no longer had the opportunity to respond to it. The only person who could still respond was the judge, and he was in no mood to excuse Florence's behaviour.

Mr Justice Stephen's summing-up was the third factor that produced the guilty verdict. His review of the medical evidence had been long and confusing, yet his criticism of Florence's affair was concise and brutal. While Russell had made the distinction between moral and criminal guilt, the judge had seemed to blur the two. There is no doubt that Stephen, as a strict moralist, was shocked by Florence's behaviour. He was a man who felt that a wife should obey her husband in the same manner as a '*seaman should give way to his captain.*'[1094] He told the jury that when Florence went to London to stay with Brierley she not only lied to her husband, but she also told a '*mass of falsehoods*' to her friends and relations who lived there. He went on to say: '*It is not my business to speak as a moralist, but there is one horrible and lamentable result of a connection of that sort which renders it almost a moral necessity, it furnishes the strongest possible provocation, the strongest possible inducement, for entering upon a system of the most disgraceful intrigue, and telling a great number of lies.*'[1095] The implication was clear; a woman who committed adultery and was prepared to lie to her own family was a woman who was capable of murder.

One person who felt that the judge's summing-up had been unfair to Florence was Sir Charles Russell. After the trial, he sent a memorandum to the Home Secretary in which he wrote that:

> '*It is no exaggeration to say that every point made by the prosecution was put by the learned judge, and with greater insistence as well as other points which the prosecution had not made – while at the same time he does not seemed to have realised the importance of many of the points made on the part of the prisoner, and did not put some of them at all and those which he did put he minimised and discounted.*'

He continued, saying that the judge had '*taken the view that the woman was guilty,*' and that there was '*little to be said for her.*' He '*impressed*' that view on the jury during the course of the two days of his summing-up in a 'manner which would justify the trial being described as a trial by judge rather than by jury.'[1096]

It wasn't just Russell who felt that the judge's hostile attitude to Florence had been very influential in producing the verdict. In her autobiography, Florence wrote the '*main element*' in her conviction was Mr Justice Stephen, whose mind she claimed, due to '*incipient insanity,*' was '*incapable of dealing with so intricate a case.*'[1097]

Although the judge was not insane at the time of the trial, it is clear that he was no longer at the peak of his powers. Even his own brother felt he had taken a '*step downwards*' after his illness in 1885.[1098] McConnell, Addison's junior, wrote the judge '*never fully mastered the facts of the case*'.[1099] The *Liverpool Review,* stunned by the decision of the jury, felt '*that the judge's summing-up was the real cause of the result.*'[1100] It described it as a '*formidable battering ram*' that virtually drove the jury to produce a guilty verdict.

[1092] Moiseiwitsch M., op cit., page 42.
[1093] Ibid., page 62.
[1094] Stephen L., op cit., page 329.
[1095] Irving H.B., op. cit., page 328.
[1096] HO 144/1638/A50678.
[1097] Maybrick F., op. cit. page 237.
[1098] Stephen L., op cit., page 436.
[1099] *Liverpool Daily Post*, 22nd December 1906.
[1100] *Liverpool Review*, 10th August 1889.

Not everyone agreed with the *Liverpool Review*. The *Garston and Woolton Reporter* stated:

> *'Very much has been said as to the unfairness of the judge's summing up; but we venture to state that from the summing up nobody could positively say whether, if the judge had been a juryman, he would have been in favour of a verdict of guilty or not. He did not even follow a very customary practice with the bench, and express approval of the jury's verdict, as he most certainly might have done if he had thoroughly concurred in it.'*[1101]

Apart from these key factors, there were other things that Florence's defence team could have done to have helped clear their client of the murder charge. For example, they could have made more efforts to definitely prove that women commonly used arsenic-based solutions for cosmetic purposes. Although Bioletti did tell the court that the drug was used in cosmetic preparations as a '*wash for the face*,' he also said that, to his knowledge, Florence had never been one of his customers.[1102] It wasn't until some years later that Florence's lost prescription by Dr Bray of New York for a face wash using an arsenic base was found, and affidavits were produced that supported her statement.

The defence team also needed to tackle the damage caused by Florence's use of the phrase '*sick unto death*' in her letter to Brierley. Russell tried to deal with it by saying Florence was simply '*speaking in exaggerated language*;' he also pointed out that Mrs Briggs, who saw James on the day that the letter was written, believed that he was in a very serious condition.[1103] It was an insufficient explanation, and the jury were left with the lingering impression that if Florence knew James was about to die, then she could be poisoning him.

The outcry at the end of the trial and the harsh criticism of the judge caused it to be one of Mr Justice Stephen's final trials. Within two years he was in an asylum for the insane, where he died in 1894. Before he entered the facility he did seem to be having second thoughts about his handling of the trial. He wrote that, of the 1,216 criminal cases that had come before him, the trial of Florence Maybrick was the '*only case in which there could be any doubt about the facts*.'[1104] Hostettler has argued the Maybrick case '*worried him to the end*'.[1105]

Many of the legal appeals on Florence's behalf that followed the trial referred directly to the performance of the judge. In 1892, the legal brief of Lumley and Lumley included a section on the Stephen summing-up, which they said was prejudiced and unbalanced against Florence. A memorandum from Richard Cleaver, Florence's solicitor, to the Home Secretary in November 1895 made a similar point. He argued that not only did he make numerous mistakes, there was also a '*change in the demeanour of the judge on the second day*' of the summing up that was '*most remarkable*.'[1106] It is clear that this once strong and formidable judge was no longer at his best, and the trial did much damage to his reputation. After his death, the *Liverpool Daily Post* commented that '*it was shocking to think that a human life depended upon the direction of this wreck of what was once a great judge*.'[1107]

LINKS TO THE RIPPER DIARY: DID JAMES MAYBRICK MATCH THE LIKENESS PROVIDED BY RIPPER WITNESSES?

Like many of the details concerning the events surrounding the Ripper murders, the information from potential witnesses about the physical appearance of the murderer is confusing and often contradictory. Despite this, Ripperologists have tried to produce a picture of the killer from the people who possibly saw him.

Philip Sugden suggested that by examining the six '*best*' witnesses – whom he identified as Elizabeth Long, PC Smith, Joseph Lawende, Joseph Hyam Levy, Israel Schwartz and George Hutchinson – it appears that the murderer was '*a white male of average or below average height in his twenties or thirties*.'[1108] If we narrow down this group even further – as Elizabeth Long did not see the man's face, and Hyam Levy said he paid no attention to him – we are left with four witnesses who provide descriptions that are not too dissimilar.

PC William Smith described the murder suspect as being aged 28 (the youngest age provided by the four); both Israel Schwartz and Joseph Lawende described him as being around 30, while George Hutchinson said he was aged 34 or 35. This provides an average age of 30 to 31. When it comes to the issue of height there are once again similar views expressed by the four witnesses, with the suspect's height varying over the relatively narrow range from 5 feet 5 inches to 5 feet 8 inches. This provides an average height of around 5 feet 6 inches.

Schwartz, Lawende and Hutchinson all said the suspect was of fair complexion and had a moustache, though Hutchinson said that the moustache was curled at each end. All the witnesses described the killer as being quite

---

1101 *Garston and Woolton Reporter*, 17th August 1889.
1102 Irving H.B., op. cit., page 224.
1103 Ibid., page 238.
1104 Maybrick F., op cit., page 394.
1105 Hostettler J., op. cit., page 245.
1106 HO 144/1639/A50678/A264.
1107 *Liverpool Daily Post*, 13th August 1894.
1108 Sugden P., op cit., page 367.

respectable in both dress and appearance, which would indicate that he was in paid employment and not poor. Elizabeth Long used the term '*shabby genteel*' in her description, which tends to indicate the person was trying to affect an appearance of gentility even though they may have fallen on hard times.

Interestingly, there is only one eyewitness of Jack the Ripper after he killed a victim. PC George Ellis was running to the aid of a police officer who was frantically blowing his whistle when he bumped into a '*gentleman*' running the other way. PC Ellis apologised to the man and carried on to his colleague, who was at the scene of a recently committed Ripper murder (probably Polly Nichols). Although one has to be careful with this evidence as it is based on a third-hand account, it does lend support to the view that the killer could well have been a man from a relatively affluent background.[1109]

The witness who provided the most detailed description was George Hutchinson. He claimed to have seen Mary Kelly with a man, presumed to be the murderer, just prior to her death. According to the description he gave to the police, the Ripper suspect was aged '*about 34 or 35. Height 5ft 6 complexion pale, dark eye and eye lashes... slight moustache, curled up each end, and hair dark... respectable appearance walked very sharp.*'[1110] The detailed nature of the description, plus the fact that Hutchinson provided it three days after the murder and only after the inquest into Mary Kelly had been completed, has caused some observers to doubt its truth and accuracy. Inspector Frederick Abberline interviewed Hutchinson and he was satisfied that his statement was true. Author Stewart Evans, a former police officer who had a great deal of personal experience of obtaining statements from witnesses, is critical of the statement Hutchinson provided to the police, arguing that it is '*too short and lacks much detail and clarification of facts.*' For example, Hutchinson failed to provide the police with a clear reason for why he followed Kelly and the unknown man, and then watched them for so long. Some have speculated that Hutchinson may have acted in such a manner as he intended to rob the man after he left Miller's Court. That may have also been the reason for him '*taking particular note*' of the thick gold chain he described the man as wearing underneath his coat.[1111]

Witness

Mrs Elizabeth Long, the wife of a cart owner. She left her home very early on the morning of 8th September to go to Spitalfields Market. At 5:30am, she saw a man talking to a woman (whom she later identified in the mortuary as being Annie Chapman) near 29 Hanbury Street. The man had his back to Mrs Long as she walked near the couple.

Description of Murderer

At the inquest, Mrs Long described the man as '*dark complexioned and was wearing a brown deerstalker hat... he was a man over 40, as far as I could tell... he seemed to be a little taller than the deceased [Chapman's height was 5 feet.] He looked to me like a foreigner, as well as I could make out... He looked what I should call shabby genteel.*'

Witness

PC William Smith, whose beat included Berner Street. At 12:30am on the night of 30th September, he passed a man with a woman who was wearing a red rose, talking near the spot where Elizabeth Stride's body was later discovered. As a policeman on duty, he was '*probably more observant than most.*'[1112] PC Smith later identified Stride as the woman wearing the red rose.

Description of Murderer

According to PC Smith, the man was '*about 5ft 7in, clean-shaven, aged about 28 and respectable-looking. He was wearing dark clothes and a dark-coloured hard felt deerstalker.*'[1113] Intriguingly, the man carried in one of his hands a parcel wrapped in newspaper. It was eighteen inches long and six to eight inches broad. Did it contain a knife?

Witness

Israel Schwartz, a Jewish immigrant who lived very close to Berner Street. On 30th September, he witnessed a man assaulting Elizabeth Stride. The man threw her down on the footpath and she cried out three times, '*but not very loudly.*' He also saw a second man who was standing on the other side of the road, though he was uncertain if the two men knew each other and were acting together. He later identified Stride's body at the mortuary.

Description of Murderer

According to a report from Chief Inspector Swanson, Schwartz said the man who assaulted Stride was aged about 30. He was around 5ft 5in tall, with a fair complexion, dark hair, a small brown moustache, full face, broad

---

[1109] For a fuller discussion on this incident see Moody F., 'P.C. George: An Update' in *The Journal of the Whitechapel Society*, Edition 15, August 2007, pp 8-10.
[1110] Evans S.P. and Skinner K., *The Ultimate Jack the Ripper Source Book*, (Robinson, London, 2000) page 377.
[1111] Evans S.P., 'Suspect and Witness: The Police Viewpoint' available to view at www.casebook.org
[1112] Sugden P., op cit., page 201.
[1113] Begg P., Fido M. and Skinner K., op cit., page 479.

shoulders. He wore a dark jacket, trousers and a black cap with a peak.[1114] The second man was aged about 35; height around 5ft 11in; fresh complexion and light brown hair. He was wearing a dark overcoat and an old black, hard felt hat that had a wide brim.

Artist's impression of the man described by George Hutchinson

Witness

Joseph Lawende, a commercial traveller who lived on Fenchurch Street. With two companions (Harris and Hyam Levy) he left the club in which he had spent the evening at 1:30am on 30th September and saw a man and a woman standing near Mitre Square. He later identified Catherine Eddowes as the woman he had seen from her clothes, when he viewed her body in the mortuary.

Description of Murderer

Lawende's description is recorded in a memorandum from Chief Inspector Swanson. It describes the man he saw as: '*Age 30, height 5ft 7in or 8in, complexion fair, fair moustache, medium build; dress, pepper and salt colour loose jacket, grey cloth cap with peak of same colour, reddish neckerchief tied in a knot, round neck, appearance of a sailor.*'[1115] Harris and Hyam Levy said they paid no attention to the man.

Witness

George Hutchinson, an unemployed labourer who lived in Commercial Street. Hutchinson knew Mary Kelly, and claimed he sometimes gave her money. He said he saw Kelly at about 2:00am on the morning of 9th November, when she asked him for sixpence. He told her he had no money. She was then almost immediately approached by another man, with whom she went off. Hutchinson followed the couple as they headed for Miller's Court. He said he paid particular attention to the man because he had a foreign appearance, and was well dressed. Of all the witnesses, he provided the police with the most detailed description of the killer.

Description of Murderer

Hutchinson went to the police three days after Kelly's murder. He was questioned extensively by Inspector Abberline, who found him a credible witness. He said the man was of Jewish appearance, aged 34 or 35, between 5ft 5in and 5ft 6in tall, with pale complexion, dark hair and eyes and had a slight moustache curled up at each end. He was wearing a dark felt hat, a long dark coat with the collars and cuffs trimmed with Astrakhan. Underneath he wore a dark jacket, light waistcoat, dark trousers, a thick gold chain with a large seal and red stone set into it. He was holding a dark parcel about eight inches long wrapped in a sturdy cloth with a strap around it.[1116]

Shirley Harrison and Paul Feldman have both pointed to a composite sketch of a Ripper suspect with a moustache that appeared in the *Daily Telegraph* on 6th October 1888, and argued that it resembles James Maybrick. Bruce Robinson, in his book on the Ripper murders, claimed the picture depicts Michael Maybrick rather than James.

In fact, in the accompanying *Daily Telegraph* article, there were two different pictures of Ripper suspects, both based on descriptions provided to the police by Matthew Packer and others who had seen a man talking to Elizabeth Stride in Berner Street on the night she was murdered. When Packer was shown both sketches he identified the portrait of the man without the moustache and wearing the soft felt or American hat as the one that most looked like the man he had seen that night. He said he had served him grapes and described him as 5 feet 7 inches in height, well built, and wearing dark clothes and a '*wideawake*' hat. Although Packer's account of events on the night of the murder was at first given great importance by both the police and the newspapers, interest in his story quickly deteriorated when he started to change key details about what he had witnessed.

What is also interesting about the two pictures is that they were reprinted in the *Liverpool Echo* on Monday 8th October. The newspaper said they were not '*authentic portraits*' but a '*likeness*,' based on descriptions provided to the police by an '*important witness*' who had seen a man with Elizabeth Stride in Berner Street on the night of her murder.[1117]

[1114] Evans S.P. and Skinner K., (2000) op cit., page 123

[1115] Wood A. and Souden D., 'The Man Who Saw: The Face of Joseph Lawende Revealed' in *Ripperologist*, 87, January 2008 via www.casebook.org

[1116] Begg P. and Bennett J., op cit., page 182.

[1117] *Liverpool Echo*, 8th October 1888.

Two sketches of Jack the Ripper based on descriptions provided by Matthew Packer, which appeared in the *Daily Telegraph* on 6th October 1888 and the *Liverpool Echo* two days later.

As the picture of the suspect with the moustache had been printed in the *Liverpool Echo*, it would have almost certainly been viewed by James Maybrick. Why didn't he, if he really was Jack the Ripper and had penned the Ripper Diary, refer to the picture in his journal? It is a situation the diarist would have revelled in and found greatly amusing. The author of the journal continually pokes fun at the police, and if James had truly been the author of the document he would have jumped at the opportunity to pour yet more scorn on the hapless authorities who couldn't catch him despite having a picture of his likeness. One is drawn yet again to the obvious conclusion that James Maybrick was not Jack the Ripper, and he did not write the Ripper Diary.

From the witnesses' descriptions, could James Maybrick have been Jack the Ripper? Although there are a few details that do vaguely match his description, including that he had a moustache and was of respectable appearance, the clear and obvious fact is that James was far too old to be seriously considered as a realistic suspect based on the witnesses' testimonies. In 1888, he was almost 50 and only one witness – Elizabeth Long – described the killer as being over 40.[1118] Every other witness described a man who was around 20 years younger than James would have been at the time of the killings.

Not only that, we know that around the time of the murders James' physical health was beginning to deteriorate, and he was showing his age. Therefore, not only did he not look like the serial killer, he would have also been incapable of showing the fleetness of the foot that the real murderer demonstrated in carrying out his heinous crimes and evading detection from the police on the streets of Whitechapel.

[1118] Begg P., *Jack the Ripper: The Facts*, (Robson, London, 2004) page 76.

18

VERDICT TO COMMUTATION

At the end of trial and the return of the guilty verdict, Florence was returned to Walton Gaol where her life was to change dramatically. She was no longer a prisoner on remand entitled to special privileges; she was now a convicted felon, in prison clothing, facing the death penalty. As prescribed by law, the High Sheriff of Lancashire, Colonel Clement Molyneux Royds, fixed the date for the execution to be 8:00am on Monday 26th August, the first day after the third Sunday from the day of sentencing.

In her autobiography, Florence wrote a short but vivid passage about her feelings at this time, stating that for '*nearly three weeks I was confined in this cell of the condemned, to taste the bitterness of death under its most appalling and shameful aspect.*' As to her state of mind, she wrote that she was '*too overwhelmed for either analytic or collective thought.*' Her strong religious convictions and the certainty of her innocence meant she had '*no fear of physical death,*' but '*petitioned for a reconsideration of the verdict... for the sake of my mother and my children.*' She said she knew '*nothing of any public efforts for my relief. I was held fast on the wheels of a slow-moving machine, hypnotised by the striking hours and the flight of my numbered minutes, with the gallows staring me in the face.*'[1119]

The only visitor Florence was now allowed was her mother. The Baroness described one of her visits to the prison to a reporter from the *Liverpool Echo*: '*I was not allowed to approach Florie. A table was between us as we talked. I could not kiss her or touch her hand; since the very first day I arrived here from Paris and the very first moment we met, I have not been allowed to kiss my child. Florie was crying.*'[1120]

(*Illustrated Police News*, 17th August 1889

As Florence waited in the cell for her execution or possible reprieve, a reporter from the *Liverpool Citizen* somehow managed to get into the prison to see the conditions under which she was held. Although he did not interview Florence, he did claim to visit her prison cell, writing:

> '*The cell in which Mrs Maybrick is held prisoner is about fourteen feet by thirteen feet. There was originally no condemned cell on the female side in Walton Gaol, and the division wall between two of the ordinary cells had to be removed in order to make the more roomy cell in which the prisoner is now confined. It has two windows inside of the ordinary prison type, the outlook being towards the front gate. In fact, the cell itself can only be about twenty to thirty feet from the entrance to the gaol. It is a grim and ghastly fact that they have already brought Mrs Maybrick almost as near the gallows as they can do, for the scaffold if erected will be close to – indeed, only just outside the walls of the condemned cell within which she will have passed such hours of agony. Of course, as you all know, she is watched continually night and day. From the instant that the sentence was pronounced to the moment of its execution, or reprieve, there will be one pair of wakeful, watchful eyes upon her unceasingly, careful lest by any suicidal stroke the law might be robbed of its victim and the scaffold of its prey! Accordingly, there are two beds in the cell. One of these for a warder and the other for the prisoner. There are two female warders who watch her turn and turn about the whole time.*'

1119 Maybrick F., op cit., pages 58-59.
1120 *Liverpool Echo*, 22nd August 1889.

The reporter said he had one last revelation that would astonish the readers of the newspaper. The door to her toilet, which was some 30 feet down the corridor, had been removed. Therefore, '*not merely should Mrs Maybrick be followed even there by the watchful eyes of the female warder, but that any passing officials of the gaol should have a full inspection of the interior of the closet even at a time when the natural modesty which is common to all of us must make such a position, to a person habituated to the refinements of society, shocking to the last degree and almost unbearable.*'[1121]

As Florence sat in her cell listening to the scaffold being constructed just outside, the debate about her verdict and sentence gripped the whole country. The editorials of the Liverpool and national newspapers were sharply divided over whether justice had been served. The general opinion in Liverpool during the trial was that Florence would be acquitted, or the jury would fail to reach a unanimous verdict. Therefore, when the guilty verdict was announced, it sent shockwaves across the city. The *Liverpool Mercury* wrote that although there was '*an uneasy feeling abroad as to the prisoner's guilt,*' hardly anyone believed the prisoner's guilt would be legally established and that she would not be acquitted on the medical evidence.'[1122] The *Birkenhead News* wrote that the verdict in the Maybrick case was '*received with universal astonishment and dismay.*' The newspaper felt the case was so full of '*uncertainty and perplexity*' that the '*ordinary observer*' would '*shrink from horror from the idea of consigning the hapless inmate of the condemned cell in Walton Gaol to the gallows.*' It pointed out that James had been a '*habitual taker of arsenic,*' and that '*no amount of suspicious circumstances*' could shake that fact. It described the judge's summing-up as a '*deplorable mistake,*' and to hang Florence on the basis of circumstantial evidence was a '*catastrophe*' that was '*too awful to be contemplated calmly.*'[1123]

In total contrast, the *Liverpool Courier* argued that as the jury had heard the whole of the evidence, they were the '*one body of men competent to give a verdict*' and they had found the defendant guilty. The newspaper added it was '*monstrous to suppose that, as intelligent and responsible men, they would have given such a deliverance without feeling compelled to do so, or that the judge would have passed the dreaded sentence upon a decision which he did not consider to be justified by the evidence.*'[1124]

Another Liverpool newspaper that supported the verdict was Florence's local Liverpool paper, *The Garston and Woolton Reporter*. It described her trial as '*singularly fair and favourable,*' and added that if she had been a poor woman '*she would have been sentenced to death and hanged with little ceremony.*'[1125] The newspaper was critical of the abuse the jury and the judge had received following the verdict, writing there was not the '*slightest reason to suppose that the jury underestimated the awful character of duty thrust upon them.*' It finished by boldly stating '*we have no reasonable doubt as to Mrs Maybrick's guilt.*'[1126]

The diversity of opinion in the Liverpool newspapers was replicated in the national press. The *Northern Echo* wrote there was '*no denying the terrible truths*' that Florence had been convicted in the '*face of testimony which did raise a certain amount of reasonable doubt in the minds of many*', and that '*multitudes are horror-struck at the possibility of doing a woman to death where any particle of doubt exists to her guilt.*'[1127] The newspaper took a critical view of Mr Justice Stephen's role, arguing that he '*far exceeded his duty when he volunteered evidence of his own during the summing-up.*' It also criticised his belittling of the testimony of the chemical experts, describing these actions as '*grave errors of judgment.*'[1128]

On the other hand, the *Manchester Times* wrote it could '*hardly be expected that the jury, having heard the whole of the evidence, and especially having heard Mrs Maybrick's own statement, should believe her other than guilty.*' Despite this, the newspaper felt that while there was no room for doubting the verdict, there was '*slight*' room for doubting the '*accuracy of reasoning*' behind the decision, and therefore hoped the Home Secretary might commutate the sentence.[1129] The *Glasgow Herald* commented that while it must have been a '*painful thing for the jury to agree to a verdict which consigns Florence Maybrick to a painful death,*' the circumstances of the case meant '*they had no alternative. They found it impossible to doubt that this unhappy woman has been guilty of a deep-laid, cunning and successful plot to compass the death of her husband.*'[1130]

One influential publication that provided a strong critique of the Maybrick case was the respected medical journal, *The Lancet*. In the edition that appeared ten days after the trial, it included a three-page article that selectively examined some of the medical evidence. It concluded that James Maybrick had been the victim of arsenical poisoning administered by his wife and, as a result, supported the guilty verdict which it claimed was '*warranted by the*

1121 *Liverpool Citizen*, 21st August 1889.
1122 *Liverpool Mercury*, 8th August 1889.
1123 *Birkenhead News*, 10th August 1889.
1124 *Liverpool Courier*, 8th August 1889.
1125 *Garston and Woolton Reporter*, 10th August 1889.
1126 *Garston and Woolton Reporter*, 17th August 1889.
1127 *Northern Echo*, 9th August 1889.
1128 *Northern Echo*, 10th August 1889.
1129 *Manchester Times*, 10th August 1889.
1130 *Glasgow Herald*, 8th August 1889.

evidence.'[1131] Disappointingly for such a prestigious publication, the article contained significant errors, suggesting the journal did not have an observer in court but instead relied for its details on newspaper reports of Mr Justice Stephen's summing-up. The article totally underplayed James' use of arsenic, implying he may have taken it no more than '*on two occasions*;' once in America as a malarial treatment and once as a pick-me-up tonic from a Liverpool chemist. It ignored the testimony of the Liverpool chemist, Heaton, who told the court that James visited his store up to five times a day over a period of more than six months to purchase a tonic containing arsenic. There was no mention of Sir James Poole's evidence, in which he said he heard James openly admit to using poisonous medicines. The article said the total amount of arsenic found in James' body at post-mortem was calculated to be '*something under two grains, or in itself nearly a fatal dose.*' In fact, Dr Stevenson admitted at the trial he found only 76/1000 of a grain of arsenic in the liver and 15/1000 of a grain in the intestines, an amount that was less than one-twentieth of what was considered to be a fatal dose. *The Lancet* article stated it was '*evident*' the flypapers Florence bought were '*not put to the use for which they were intended.*' In fact, the evidence pointed towards them being used to make a cosmetic solution for Florence's own personal use.

The journal claimed James overdosed on the medicine prescribed by Dr Fuller into which arsenic had been added. That was not the case. Mary Cadwallader testified the medicine which James had overdosed on had come in the post from London, and James himself told two witnesses that it contained strychnine and not arsenic.

The Lancet article repeated the serious mistake Mr Justice Stephen had made in his summing-up, in that James had told Dr Carter on 7th May that he had complained of '*vomiting and diarrhoea for several days.*' This was something that Dr Carter had said at the inquest but withdrawn at the trial as not being true. The article referred to Florence's handkerchief in Hatbox B, which was in the tumbler of milk and arsenic, and stated that the handkerchief contained '*twenty grains of arsenic*' when in fact it contained just 2.94 grains. The journal finished with the untrue claim that Florence was '*proved to have recently purchased arsenic, to the extent of seventy grains or more.*'

The timing of the article was important, as it was published just as the Home Secretary was considering whether to commute Florence's sentence. Its inaccurate nature had the potential to send the prisoner to the gallows.

In its next edition *The Lancet* carried a short piece from an unnamed Liverpool correspondent, in which the author wrote that many who had watched the Maybrick case from the start and taken a '*dispassionate view of it*' viewed the guilty verdict to be '*a foregone conclusion.*'[1132] This was simply not the case. Most of the leading barristers at the trial believed Florence would be found not guilty. It was yet another inaccurate statement from the medical journal, whose post-trial commentary can only be described as inadequate, misleading and error-strewn.

The American newspapers, as to be expected, tended to be more favourable to Florence's plight than their British counterparts. The *New York Times* was especially harsh in its criticism of the trial process and the British legal system. It described English law practice in murder cases, especially the lack of an appeal process, as '*simply shocking.*' It wrote that the character of Mr Justice Stephen and other English judges had been '*incredibly hardened*' by the influence of '*aristocratic power*' and, as a result, were the '*most conceited, dogmatic body of men probably existing in the whole English-speaking world.*'[1133]

Not all of the American press was sympathetic to Florence. The *New York World* wrote there was a '*strong probability*' that Florence was guilty, though it did also suggest the case against her had not been fully proved and sufficient '*reasonable doubt*' existed to have led to an innocent verdict.

Perhaps the American view was best summed up by the editorial in the *Norfolk Virginian*, which wrote the '*conviction of Mrs Maybrick surprises and disappoints the majority of Americans. Those who have followed the testimony do not regard the case as made out against her, beyond a reasonable doubt. While her character has been destroyed there is much sympathy for her.*' The newspaper went on to hope that Florence would be '*more leniently dealt with by the executive authorities than she has been by the courts.*'[1134]

As was to be expected given the nationwide interest in Florence's trial, the newspapers were inundated with letters following the end of the trial. The wide range of opinions expressed in these communications reflected the national mood. Many sharply criticised the verdict and the role of the judge, whilst others supported the jury's decision by arguing that Florence had been found guilty after a lengthy trial in which she had been stoutly defended by eminent barristers. One of the most hotly debated aspects of the trial was the conflicting medical evidence. An important letter on this topic was sent to the *Liverpool Daily Post* from Ewing Whittle, MD, who had held the chair for forensic medicine for 22 years in the Liverpool School of Medicine. He wrote that he had dealt with several cases of arsenical poisoning, and '*thoroughly endorsed the opinion of Drs Tidy and Macnamara and Paul, that neither the history of the case nor the post-mortem appearances are consistent with the theory of arsenical poisoning.*'[1135]

1131 'The Maybrick Case' in *The Lancet*, Vol. 134. Issue 3442, 17th August 1889, pages 318-320.
1132 'The Maybrick Trial' in *The Lancet*, Vol. 134. Issue 3443, 24th August 1889, page 407.
1133 *New York Times*, 11th August 1889.
1134 *Norfolk Virginian*, 14th August 1889.
1135 *Liverpool Daily Post*, 13th August 1889.

Another significant letter was sent to the same newspaper by Albert Blackburn, a chemist who lived in Eccles, near Manchester, who wrote he had worked for some time at the Grassendale Post Office and saw Florence '*almost daily.*' He said it was very common for people, especially those from the '*higher ranks of society,*' to use dangerous drugs both internally and externally for cosmetic purposes and not tell the full truth about why they purchased them. He added that, in Florence's case, the fact that the arsenic had been '*found in combination with oxide of zinc and perfume, the former of which is so largely used for skin eruptions and excoriations, is itself proof that it was used for that purpose.*' Blackburn finished by saying that while Florence may have broken the law of God due to her adultery, she was innocent of the charge of murder and only a reprieve and a complete restoration to her two children would rectify the situation.[1136]

Some of the letters and newspaper articles proposed interesting new theories about the possible cause of James' death, many of which revolved around the widespread use and potential dangers of taking arsenic. The *Liverpool Echo* reported that in some countries, especially Austria, arsenic was given to horses and cattle to '*render their skin bright and glossy.*' In parts of Austria, such as Styria, arsenic was taken by peasant girls to '*increase their attractions*;' and arsenic-eating was secretly conducted by men who lived to a healthy old age. These men believed that arsenic '*improves the complexion, increases the digestive powers, and so strengthens the respiratory organs as to enable the bearers of heavy burdens to climb mountains with ease.*'[1137] Closer to home, Mr David Cummins of Liverpool wrote to the *Times* that he had regularly used arsenic for many years as a means of treating a very severe skin disease. He felt the jury in Florence's case may have dismissed the idea that James used arsenic as too '*incredible,*' and come to the false conclusion that '*no man could consume such quantities of the poison and survive.*' He wanted to draw attention to the fact that using arsenic as a form of medication was much more widespread than many would have assumed to be the case.[1138]

One hypothesis suggested that James died not from taken arsenic but '*for the want of it.*' A letter to the *Liverpool Mercury* referred to the case of a man who had been '*accustomed to arsenic eating for some years*' and suffered from the symptoms of arsenical poisoning, albeit in a '*modified form*' when he was deprived of the drug. This lack of arsenic produced gastro-enteritis from which he died.[1139] Yet another theory was proposed by Mr William Burton, a skin specialist in London, who said James' death may have been accelerated by taking antimony and bismuth, two medicines he had been prescribed during his final illness. He pointed out that antimony, bismuth and arsenic were three metal elements with similar physiological actions. A large dose of any one of these elements would set up gastro-enteritis, but taking all three together was potentially lethal.[1140]

One of the most unusual letters was sent to the *Daily Telegraph* by Pauline Cranstoun of South Kensington, London. She wrote that James Maybrick had replied to one of her advertisements, in which she claimed she '*ruled the planets, cast horoscopes,*' and therefore was able to discover '*intricate diseases incurable by medical men.*' She said James had written a '*strange account of his aliments,*' and that he was in the habit of taking '*large doses of arsenic,*' often in his food, as it '*aided his digestion*' and '*helped to calm his nerves.*'[1141] Although many of the books on James and Florence Maybrick accept Cranstoun's statement as a truthful account, there are serious reasons for doubting its validity. First, and most importantly, when she was asked by reporters to produce the correspondence from James she was unable to do so, and claimed she '*must have destroyed them.*'[1142] Secondly, Cranstoun (1854-1929) was an eccentric and self-publicist; even her own mother said that her daughter was '*inclined to spiritualist ideas*', and she did not understand her.[1143] Cranstoun's interest in Florence's case may have been piqued by the fact that she was a relative of William Henry Cranstoun, who had figured in a famous poisoning case from the eighteenth century. Thirdly, it is unlikely that James – a very private man who usually denied his drug-taking habits – would tell his innermost thoughts to a woman with such unconventional views whom he didn't even know.

A more believable letter was penned by Henry Bliss, the former steward to the Duke of Sutherland and once proprietor of the Sefton Club and Chambers in Liverpool, of which James had been a member. During the coroner's inquest into James' death, Bliss wrote a letter from his home in Waltham Green in London to a gentleman friend in Liverpool. He reminded him of their acquaintances with James, and their knowledge of his drug-taking habits during the time he was a member of the club. He sent a second letter after the trial on 10th August, in which he wrote:

> '*Mr Maybrick lived in the chambers on and off for several months, and was in the habit of dosing himself. On one occasion he asked me to leave a prescription at a well-known Liverpool chemist's to be made up by the time he left the 'Change. The chemist remarked: "he ought to be very careful and not take an overdose*

1136 *Liverpool Daily Post*, 13th August 1889.
1137 *Liverpool Echo*, 10th August 1889.
1138 *Liverpool Daily Post*, 13th August 1889.
1139 *Liverpool Mercury*, 13th August 1889.
1140 *Liverpool Echo*, 17th August 1889.
1141 *Liverpool Echo*, 17th August 1889.
1142 *Lancashire Evening Post*, 19th August 1889.
1143 *St James's Gazette*, 3rd April 1894.

of it." I wrote to Sir Charles Russell on the subject during the trial, knowing full well Maybrick took anything he was advised to, when ailing by his friends.'[1144]

The enormous coverage in the press of the verdict in Florence's trial resulted in *Maybrick mania* taking a firm hold of the entire country. In London, Madame Tussaud's was quick to realise the commercial potential of the situation and within just three days of the verdict had produced a waxwork display of Florence, heavily-veiled and dressed in a black cape, as she had appeared in the courtroom. The effigy was placed in its own viewing-room and attracted thousands of interested spectators, mainly women.[1145]

The *Liverpool Echo* carried a story of two men doing a '*roaring trade*' selling songs about Florence, one singing in favour of the prisoner and one '*rather sarcastically against her.*' Each ballad was illustrated by '*Penny Dreadful woodcuts representing a woman on her knees before a chaplain, and a tomb overshadowed by a weeping willow.*'[1146]

A considerable number of people travelled to Walton Gaol to stand outside the prison where Florence was confined.

Walton Prison, Liverpool, with its original Victorian building still visible behind the modern walls (Chris Jones collection)

A large number of meetings were held up and down the country, organised with the specific purpose of trying to get the sentence commuted. At Liverpool, one such meeting took place on the evening of Monday 12th August, in front of St George's Hall. It attracted a crowd of about 3,000 angry protestors, principally drawn from a working-class background, and including many women.[1147]

The following day another well-attended meeting took place in the large hall of the Cannon Street Hotel in London. It was organised by a Scottish lawyer, Mr Alexander W. MacDougall, who was to campaign tirelessly for Florence Maybrick's reprieve and later for her release from prison. MacDougall said he had called the meeting to elect a chairman and then pass the following resolution:

> '*To the Secretary of State for the Home Department – Your petitioners having anxiously considered the evidence adduced at the trial of Florence Elizabeth Maybrick for the murder, and also the summing-up of, and especially his comments upon, the evidence by Mr Justice Stephen, and also the verdict of the jury, are clearly convinced that the law of England, that an accused person is entitled to the benefit of any reasonable doubt, has not been observed by either the judge or the jury. Your petitioners, therefore, pray that the sentence of death passed upon Florence Elizabeth Maybrick be remitted, and that the verdict of the Jury be quashed.*'[1148]

The meeting quickly adopted MacDougall as chairman, and he said that he was authorised to announce that Thomas Maybrick, one of James' brothers, was willing to sign a memorial asking for a reprieve. He also said he wanted to know why facts about another woman in the case [presumably James' long-term mistress] were withheld from the jury. He said Florence had no motive to poison her husband as she had sufficient information to arrange a divorce. Other speakers in favour of the resolution included Professor H. Brougham, Regius Professor of Law in the University of Dublin and Dr Forbes Winslow, who said that, during his illness, James had put 21 pellets of poison into his stomach, each one of which was sufficient to have caused his death. The resolution was then put to the meeting and carried by great applause, with only a few dissenting voices.

As well as large meetings, other important means of supporting Florence's cause were petitions and memorials. The first of these was started almost immediately after Mr Justice Stephen pronounced his sentence on Florence. According to one report, Sir Charles Russell hurriedly left the court followed by Mr Cleaver, Florence's solicitor, and others, and they all went into a private room. Once inside, a proposal was immediately put forward for a petition from members of the Bar in favour of a commutation.[1149] The petition, which was placed in the barristers' library at

---

1144 *Evening Express*, 13th June 1889 and *Pall Mall Gazette*, 14th August 1889.
1145 *Pall Mall Gazette*, 13th August 1889.
1146 *Liverpool Echo*, 19th August 1889.
1147 *Liverpool Mercury*, 13th August 1889.
1148 *London Evening Standard*, 14th August 1889.
1149 *Liverpool Echo*, 8th August 1889.

St George's Hall, asked the Home Secretary to recommend to the Queen that the sentence be commuted on the grounds that there was a '*great conflict of medical evidence*' as to the cause of death.

Another petition was started by traders at the Liverpool Cotton Exchange. It also referred to the conflicting medical evidence and included the lines that there was '*no direct evidence of administration of arsenic by the prisoner*,' and that there was a '*strong body of medical testimony*' that James' death '*was ascribable to natural causes.*'[1150] This was telling, because the men who launched the petition would have known James well, and some of them may have been aware of his habit of taking dangerous powders. The petition obtained up to 800 signatures, including '*many well-known men in the Liverpool commercial circles.*'[1151]

Yet another significant petition was put forward by members of the medical profession in Liverpool. One of the signatories was Dr Barron, who had been at James' post-mortem and had given evidence for the Crown in court. After the trial he made a statement to the press saying he had signed the petition because he certainly did not '*consider that in this case it was proved that death was due to arsenical poisoning.*' He did admit that it was a '*possible*' case of arsenical poisoning, but added that there was '*strong evidence*' to show that arsenic might have been present in Mr Maybrick's body on '*account of his habits of self-administration.*'[1152] Other medical men who signed it included Dr Paul, who had also given evidence, and Mr Henry Churton, Coroner for South Cheshire and Birkenhead.

The various petitions from Liverpool included nearly 70,000 signatures. One petition that failed to attract many signatures was the one placed in the House of Commons Library. It was signed by only 88 MPs, and the ones who did sign it tended to be those members who followed the Irish Nationalist MP Charles Stewart Parnell, and Liberal MPs who were opposed on principle to the death penalty.[1153]

It is estimated that in total, about 5,000 petitions – containing nearly half a million signatures – were sent to the Home Secretary in an effort to get Florence's death sentence commuted. Such was the passion and clamour for a reprieve the Cleaver brothers were forced to keep their offices open late, and their entire office staff were '*engaged in dealing with an extraordinary mass of correspondence relating to the Maybrick verdict and the agitation for reprieve.*' The Cleavers, who were receiving in excess of 2,000 letters a week, asked the newspapers to pass on to their readers the fact that it was a '*physical impossibility*' for them '*to comply with all the demands made upon them from all parts of the country*' with regard to organising meetings and petitions in support of their condemned client.[1154] They asked that any memorials should not be sent to them, but instead directly to their own MPs or the Home Secretary. Both Cleaver brothers made affidavits in support of Florence that were presented to the Home Secretary. The affidavit of Richard Cleaver was the longer of the two; in it, he outlined how he came to represent Florence and what she had told him about the discovery of the arsenic in the meat juice bottle. Richard Cleaver was summoned to the Home Office and interviewed by the Home Secretary to ascertain exactly what Florence told him about putting the white powder in the meat juice.

As well as the affidavits of the Cleaver brothers, several other important statements and affidavits were considered by the Home Secretary as he pondered whether to commute Florence's sentence. One of these was from Morden Rigg, the cotton merchant friend of James who had known him when he had lived and worked in Norfolk, Virginia, and had continued their friendship when both of them lived in Liverpool. Rigg made a statement in which he said that he and his wife had met James at the Wirral races on 27th April 1889. According to Rigg, James '*turned around to my wife's carriage and told her he had taken an overdose of strychnine that morning and that his limbs were quite rigid. She is prepared to testify to this if necessary.*'[1155] This is a significant statement, as it makes clear that the medicine that James overdosed on the morning of the races was not the contents of the Clay and Abraham's bottle, as suggested by both Addison and Mr Justice Stephen, but the medicine he had received in the post from London. The statement also supported the testimony of Mary Cadwallader, the maid at Battlecrease, who said James had told her that he had overdosed on the London medicine.

The fact that it was strychnine and not arsenic that James overdosed on was further substantiated by an affidavit from Captain Irving of the Royal Mail steamship *Germanic*. On Wednesday, 1st May 1889 Irving had dined at Battlecrease with James and Florence, as well as Edwin Maybrick. In his affidavit, Irving wrote that he '*remarked in the course of the evening how unwell the deceased then appeared, and mentioned the circumstances afterwards to his brother Edwin, who, in reply, stated to me that he believed it was in consequence of the poison he was taking. I inquired what poison he was taking, and he replied strychnine.*'[1156] What makes Irving's statement highly credible is that he had known James since 1878 and was a good friend of his, describing James as a '*mighty good fellow*'. In September 1889, a reporter from the *Liverpool Daily Post* interviewed Captain Irving, who told him he had met

1150 *Liverpool Mercury*, 9th August 1889.
1151 *Liverpool Weekly Courier*, 10th August 1889.
1152 *Liverpool Echo*, 14th August 1889.
1153 *St James's Gazette*, 16th August 1889.
1154 *Liverpool Mercury*, 12th August 1889.
1155 Levy J.H., op cit., pages 436- 437.
1156 Ibid., pages 439-440.

James and Edwin Maybrick at their office in the Knowsley Buildings on Wednesday 1st May. James remarked that he was feeling unwell after having eaten his lunch. He blamed this on some bad wine in the soup that had been sent to him by his wife. Later, Irving saw James take a small packet from his breast pocket and empty the contents of it into a glass of water and drink it. Edwin asked James what the '*stuff*' was that he had put in the glass, and he replied it was a prescription made up for him by the chemists Clay and Abraham's.

Captain Peter John Irving

Captain Irving said it was well known that James had been in the habit of taking strychnine for years. He said when he had first heard about James' death he had been '*astonished*,' but he also said he knew about the matter long before '*you newspaper chaps got hold of it*.' He claimed that a mutual friend of his and the Maybricks had kept him informed of events at Battlecrease, and of the suspicions that had been aroused even before James had died. Although Irving spoke well of James, when he spoke about Florence the reporter found he was '*by no means so laudatory*.' The reporter also wrote that Captain Irving led him to understand that '*he quite coincided with the verdict returned by the jury*.'[1157]

Further evidence that James was a regular user of dangerous drugs was provided by an affidavit from Mary Hogwood (Howard), the woman who kept the brothel in Norfolk, Virginia, frequented by James prior to his marriage. She said James Maybrick visited her brothel at least three times a week before his wedding, and that he kept arsenic in a cigarette case. She said he would take arsenic two or three times a night, usually with a sip of wine. She added that while she didn't know all the facts of Florence's trial, she always believed that James' habit of '*arsenic-eating would carry him off*.' She finished by saying she knew James well and was familiar with his habits and, as a result, she was not surprised by his sudden death. She said: '*I often feared that his habit of using drugs would take him off suddenly. I regret to hear that his poor wife is charged with his murder, and knowing Maybrick as well as I did, I do not hesitate to say that his wife, in my opinion, had nothing more to do with his death than I had*.' [1158]

Alfred Brierley signed an affidavit in which he tried to clarify his relationship with Florence. He said he first met her at a dinner two years ago, and that he had only met her once or twice between that date and a dance at Battlecrease in November 1888. He wrote he '*subsequently met her at various dances, and became on intimate terms with her and her husband*.' He added James was at home on every occasion that he called at the house. Brierley said he was never '*improperly intimate with her until our meeting in London on 22nd March last*', and added that after the stay in the hotel he only saw Florence on two further occasions, at the Grand National meeting and on 6th April, when he met her in Liverpool. He finished by stating he '*verily*' believed that Florence's stay in Flaman's Hotel was '*the only occasion on which Mrs Maybrick was unfaithful to her husband*.'[1159]

Brierley also gave an interview to a reporter from the *New York Herald*. He repeated the points he made in the affidavit, but added some additional details about his relationship with Florence. He described the meeting with her as a '*grave wrong*,' but said during the trial it had been '*magnified greatly to her injury and mine and assumptions have been based upon it which are entirely unwarranted by the actual facts*.'[1160] He said it had led to the breakup of his business and caused him to leave Liverpool. At the end of the interview, he said he had two things which he was '*inclined to say*;' the first being he felt that the judge had '*laid unnecessary and unfair stress on the motive*.' He described the letter from John Baillie Knight as a '*perfectly innocent letter from a perfectly innocent party*,' but the view the judge had taken of it had told '*heavily on the jury*.' Brierley also blamed the judge for his '*unauthorised and stated assumption that the intimacy between Mrs Maybrick and myself, which ended on March 21 last, was in progress during all the period which the trial covered*.'

Another man who was upset and angry by the judge's references to the *Dear John* letter was the man himself. Mr Justice Stephen had implied in his final remarks to the jury that Florence and John Baillie Knight (he did not use his surname in court) had conducted an intimate relationship at Flatman's Hotel in March 1889 before Brierley arrived at the establishment. Although Knight did not sign a formal affidavit, he did send a letter to the judge making his position absolutely clear. He told him that he was a longstanding friend of Florence, and nothing at all improper happened between the two of them. The *Dear John* issue was also mentioned in a letter to the press from Mr J. Treeve

---

1157 *Liverpool Daily Post*, 9th September 1889.
1158 *Norfolk Virginian*, 16th August 1889 and *Liverpool Echo*, 15th August 1889.
1159 Levy J.H., op cit., pages 438-439.
1160 *Liverpool Mercury*, 14th August 1889.

Edgcombe, who held a '*watching brief*' on behalf of the Baroness. He said he would not '*pander to morbid tastes of the unbelievers in Mrs Maybrick's innocence*' by providing '*John's*' surname, but he wanted to point out that Mr Maybrick was well aware that the person in question was going to accompany Florence to dinner, and that he had '*no objection*' to the arrangement.[1161]

After the trial, the newspapers were desperate to interview as many of the leading players as possible, and top of their list were the jurors. In an editorial, *The Garston and Woolton Reporter* argued that although the jury's verdict had '*surprised the vast majority of people,*' Florence had experienced a fair trial. The *Reporter* praised the jury for not shirking from their public duty, and reminded its readers that Florence had been '*unhesitatingly convicted by twelve of her countrymen.*'[1162] The same paper carried an interview with Mr R.G. Brook and Mr G.H. Welsby of St Helens, two of the jury, in which they gave their version of events. Brook described the jury as '*men of as good average intelligence as you could find. Now they are calling us "duffers" because we have found her guilty.*' The reporter asked him if the verdict reflected his honest conviction. Brook replied: '*We could have come to no other conclusion. We would have been glad to acquit her if we could. The foreman told us if we could find a pinhead's worth in her favour to give her the benefit of it, but we couldn't... We were unanimous.*' Brook said Russell's speech had very little effect on the jury, and they had all agreed upon the verdict within a few minutes.

Mr Welsby added that '*up to the time of Mrs Maybrick's statement he felt there was a possibility of the jury being able to acquit her; but the statement did away with that. The jury followed the case with the utmost care, some of the jurymen taking 13 or 14 folios of notes in one day.*'

Timothy Wainwright, the foreman of the jury, said something similar to a journalist from the *New York Herald.* He said that at the start of the trial a few of the members of the jury believed Florence to be innocent, but her personal statement to the court turned them against her. In particular, they found her admission that she was prepared to add some white powder to James' food in his final illness to be very damning.[1163]

One of the main criticisms levelled at the jury was that they were not kept apart from the general public during the course of the trial. Afterwards, a rumour surfaced that because the hotel in which they were staying did not have a billiard table, some of the jurors walked to a nearby hotel so they could play the game. A Liverpool newspaper did investigate this rumour but could find no evidence to substantiate the claim.[1164] A section of the legal brief produced by Lumley and Lumley in 1892 making the case for a retrial was based on evidence they claimed proved that the jury were not properly secluded from the general public. It stated the jury '*went into a public billiard room where the case was the subject of general conversation, and that all had access to and read the newspapers containing ex parte accounts of the trial and any comments thereon which were published.*'[1165]

Brooks, in his newspaper interview, paints a very different picture of events. His account provides a fascinating glimpse into life for the members of the jury during the trial. They had lunch about half past one each day in the room reserved for the jury, where they were given bread and butter and a bottle of beer. In the evening they were taken to the Victoria Hotel where they had a '*knife and fork tea.*' On Sunday, they had a '*better meal.*' Every night and morning, if it was fine, they had '*a drive in a waggonette, which accommodated twelve, with one keeper at front and one behind.*' Amongst the places they visited were Newsham and Sefton Parks, and on Sunday they even had a four-hour cruise on the Mersey. The reporter asked them specifically if they had been allowed downstairs in the hotel to play billiards or visit the bar. Brook answered: '*Oh, no.*' He said that if a juryman tried to go downstairs an official followed him to see what he wanted. All they could do was play cards amongst themselves and read the newspapers about the trial. Brooks said they cut out the reports and marked the important sections. They did discuss the case, and tried to keep up to pace with all the evidence.[1166]

Perhaps the most important interview given at this time was the one by Baroness von Roques to the London edition of the *New York Herald.*[1167] It was a direct attempt by her to counter the negative stories being written about her daughter. The Baroness said Florence had no motive for poisoning her husband, as '*she had plenty of evidence upon which she could have obtained separation from him had she desired.*' She said James died a '*natural death,*' and the idea he had been poisoned by arsenic was '*simply absurd*' as it would have been impossible to '*poison a man with arsenic who has been using arsenic for eleven years without his knowing or suspecting it.*' The Baroness agreed that Florence had put some white powder in James' meat juice, but had only done so at his request. She said her daughter admitted the act in '*her first interview with her solicitor. She said the same thing to me. She has said it all the time, and she has never varied, and there will be no difficulty in proving this to anybody's satisfaction. She also said to me, "Why, mamma, if they had only told me what they suspected – if I could only have taken them over my own house*

1161 *Pall Mall Gazette*, 13th August 1889.
1162 *Garston and Woolton Reporter*, 10th August 1889.
1163 *Liverpool Daily Post*, 9th August 1889.
1164 *Liverpool Weekly Courier*, 10th August 1889.
1165 HO 144/1639/A50678/104.
1166 *Garston and Woolton Reporter*, 10th August 1889.
1167 *Liverpool Echo*, 14th August 1889.

and shown them everything, there would have been nothing needed to be explained but they would not let me do this. They did all the searching, and I was already prisoner and in bed.'"

In the interview, the Baroness focused much of her wrath on Mrs Briggs, whom she described as a '*very intimate friend of Mr Maybrick,*' who from '*the outset was a potent factor in the household. She kept a general eye upon affairs.*' She said that after listening to Nurse Yapp and seeing James ill in bed, Mrs Briggs sent a telegram to Michael Maybrick which said: '"*Come up at once. Strange things are going on here...*" *All of Michael Maybrick's actions were based upon Mrs Briggs' information. He was simply the expression of her convictions. It was she who actually made the charge. She set everything in motion which has placed my daughter in Walton Gaol condemned to death.*'

Baroness von Roques (1839-1910)

After James' death, the Baroness said Mrs Briggs and her sister, Mrs Hughes:

> '*ransacked drawers, boxes, everything that belonged to Mrs Maybrick. They even broke the lock of the wardrobe. It was in this search, before any charge had been made, before any suspicion had been made public, that these two women and these two brothers [Michael and Edwin] violated the bedroom of Mrs Maybrick. It was during this search that Mrs Hughes found the Brierley letter under the paper lining of the drawer. It was my daughter's concealment of her one sin, a sin that the world might look on with different eyes if it knew all. But Mrs Hughes found it. The search which the women conducted while the brothers looked on, lasted for days. The search was scarcely finished when everything was taken away. My daughter, lying prostrate, was robbed of everything she might have needed to substantiate her case if she had had the mental grasp to understand her position. The pillbox containing Mr Maybrick's private store of arsenic only turned up at the trial. It had been kept back. Who knows what else had been kept back? Does the judge know? Do the jury know? Where are Mr Maybrick's clothes? Have they been examined for arsenic? Have the pockets been examined? Of all that belonged to my daughter, of all the presents that had been given her, of all that she needed to save her life, all that she got back was a dressing wrapper, which was valuable because it was stained with arsenic.*'

At the end of the interview, the Baroness said she wished to say something about the story in a New York newspaper which suggested that she might have been responsible for her first husband's death. She said her:

> '*solicitor in New York promptly asked me by cable if he should begin action for libel, and I directed him to wait until the case was over. I could not fight for my own reputation when my daughter's life was hanging the balance. With reference to it, however, permit me to say this. Mr Chandler died. I probated his will, and I was there for three months after his last words, which I have ready at hand, describing me as "my beloved wife, a perfect woman, and a perfect wife." I have married and lived and been about the world for thirty years from that time up to now, and I am perfectly willing to state in the most sacred way that I have never heard any statement, suggestion, intimation, or hint of such a horrible thing until it came out of this trial. I have tried to trace it from Liverpool to Mobile, but I have not succeeded. I may be wrong, but I cannot help believing that it came from here.*'

Not long after the Baroness' interview was published, a reporter spoke to Mrs Briggs about the accusation that she had done everything she could to build up the case against Florence. Mrs Briggs responded by saying: '*That is not true. We knew nothing but what we were told; and the suggestion that either my sister or myself were animated by malice is perfectly false. We did what we conceived to be our duty under painful circumstances.*'[1168] The reporter also asked her to comment on another allegation made by the Baroness, that the '*charge itself*' was made by her. Once again, Mrs Briggs denied the allegation, saying that the '*charge arose out of the refusal of the doctors to sign a death certificate, even though they were earnestly pressed to do so by the brothers Maybrick.*' When asked if she knew James was in the habit of taking arsenic, she replied: '*I never heard a word of it mentioned to my recollection.*' The reporter finished the article by stating: '*Mrs Briggs' earnestness of manner, and the straightforwardness with which she answered every question put to her, deeply impressed her interviewer. The lamentable affair with which she has been so prominently mixed up has caused her much annoyance and anxiety, from the effects of which she is now suffering. Mrs Briggs is known by her friends to have acted all through from the best motives, although for her own peace of mind it might have been well if she had not allowed her sympathetic nature to carry her so far.*'

[1168] *Evening Express*, 15th August, 1889.

The anxiety that the reporter is referring to was probably the result of the adverse criticism Mrs Briggs received during and after the trial. For example, after the verdict was announced and people were leaving the court, an angry mob surrounded a woman who was mistaken for Mrs Briggs. The police had to intervene, and after '*hard struggling*' managed to get her into the North Western Hotel and relative safety.[1169]

The Baroness' interview, in addition to the public outcry at the verdict, forced Michael Maybrick to publicly justify his actions. He told a journalist from the *New York Herald* that he completely denied reports he placed Nurse Yapp in his brother's household in order to spy on Florence. He said there was '*not a shadow of truth in such a report.*'[1170] He described his relationship with Florence as '*always pleasant*' and that he had only spoken to her harshly on one occasion – when he accused her of poisoning James – and he had only done that because he was '*excited at the moment.*' He said his: '*sole desire was to save my brother's life, not to get her or anyone else into trouble. Since his death my chief desire has been to save his good name for the sake of his children. For their sake I hoped she would not be convicted, and am now anxious for her release. I have no enmity against her, and do not want to be understood as making any charges against her.*' He also said that nothing would please him more than '*to hear the Home Secretary's decision is that Mrs Maybrick shall go free.*'

Michael made several surprising claims in the interview. He said he '*thought that no one connected with the case tried very hard to have Mrs Maybrick convicted.*' He also claimed that he tried his best to '*have the physician give a death certificate that would have prevented the trial entirely, but he refused to do so, and when the trial came I assure you I was a most unwilling witness.*' When asked if he thought James used arsenic, he replied: '*No, I do not. I am sure he didn't as I am of almost anything. If he had used it I would have been certain to know of it.*'

Michael also claimed that the sale of the furniture from Battlecrease had the consent of Mrs Maybrick and her counsel. He said he had '*nothing to do with the search*' of Battlecrease after James' death; the police carried it out. He also said he was positive that James died in '*absolute ignorance*' of Florence '*having been unfaithful, and without a suspicion that he was poisoned.*'

Michael's interview was clearly an attempt by him to salvage his reputation after the attacks on his actions and character in the press. Some of his claims are difficult to accept. Drs Humphreys and Carter, as they testified at Florence's trial, had no inkling that James' illness might have been caused by arsenic poisoning until Michael suggested it to them. He was certainly involved in the various searches that took place at Battlecrease. His denial that James used arsenic is questionable; even if he hadn't known before James' death, he must have found out after his death. An article in the *Manchester Courier* suggested that Michael might have had something to do with administering the poison to James. He responded by threatening the newspaper with a libel action, although in the end he never followed through on his threat.

Another person who tried to salvage her reputation was Nurse Yapp. Some newspapers, such as the *Liverpool Citizen*, had been sympathetic to her, calling her '*one of those simple-minded innocent girls.*' Other newspapers were far more critical of her behaviour, especially her opening of Florence's letter to Brierley.[1171] One said that, in opening the letter, Yapp had been '*guilty of a gross abuse of trust*' and hoped that she '*will never again obtain a situation in a private home.*'[1172]

After the trial Yapp gave an interview to a journalist from the *Liverpool Courier* in response to an article about her the same newspaper had carried in their edition two days earlier. She completely denied the assertion that she had 'been in the habit of prying about her mistress's room.'[1173] She had always found Mrs Maybrick to be '*an exceedingly nice woman*' and couldn't say a word against her. Yapp stated the Maybricks were on '*affectionate terms*' and the first quarrel she had ever witnessed between the couple came on the day of the Grand National. At that time, all the servants '*thought it was money matters*' that caused the quarrel because a money-lender had come to the house to see Florence. As to the opening of the letter, Nurse Yapp told the reporter that if she '*had only known that my doing would have placed Mrs Maybrick where she is today, I would have torn it up, burned it, or done anything with it.*' If the latter remark had been designed to salvage her reputation, it was too little, too late. If anything, she further angered Florence's supporters when she made a '*startling statement*' that, on the Saturday before James died, Florence had sent Mary Cadwallader to the local chemists with a prescription that the chemist had refused to makeup '*on the grounds that it contained a poisonous drug.*' It was a statement that Cadwallader later clarified had just been the result of a simple error; the prescription had not been signed by the doctor. When it was signed, it was duly compounded.

The hangman, James Berry (1852-1913), was also interviewed. From Heckmondwike in Yorkshire, Berry was the public executioner from 1884 to 1891. During that time he carried out 131 hangings, including those of five women.

[1169] *Liverpool Daily Post*, 8th August, 1889.
[1170] *Evening Express*, 21st August, 1889.
[1171] *Liverpool Citizen*, 21st August 1889.
[1172] *Truth*, 15th August 1889.
[1173] *Liverpool Courier*, 21st August 1889.

He was proud of his work, and became the first British executioner to write his memoirs. In his newspaper interview, Berry denied a rumour that he had refused to hang Florence due to the public outcry at her sentence. He said he had '*made all the arrangements for the execution and unless Mrs Maybrick be reprieved I shall carry them out. I have no business with the guilt or innocence of a condemned prisoner. I have simply to carry out the sentence of the law and if the sentence is wrong the blame will not be with me.*'[1174] As Florence's sentence was later commuted, Berry wrote the word '*Reprieved*' in his appointments book and received his £5 fee for the cancellation. Florence's reprieve, and James Berry, were both mentioned in a street ballad that became very popular at the time:

But Mrs Maybrick will not have to climb the golden stairs;
The Jury found her guilty so she nearly said her prayers;
She's at another kind of mashing and at it she must stop,
Old Berry is took down a peg with his long drop.[1175]

As Maybrick mania gripped the whole of the nation, Florence remained locked and isolated in her cell in Walton Gaol, listening to the noise of the scaffold being built close to where she was incarcerated. During her time in the prison she received an average of 18 letters a day.[1176] According to *Vanity Fair*, during the course of her trial Florence received seven marriage proposals.[1177] All of Florence's letters had to pass through the hands of the prison governor before reaching her, but the ones she did read would have given her an idea of the scale of the agitation that was taking place across the country to try and get her sentence commuted. One thing that didn't reach Florence was the numerous bouquets of flowers sent to her at the prison and, even if they had, she would have been largely oblivious to them as she spent much of her time lying prostrate on her bed. On 14th August the *Liverpool Echo* reported that Florence was '*very weak and ill*', and was confined to her bed unable to rise. Her illness meant she was eating very little, and was no longer able to take '*short periods of exercise in the gaol yard.*' It stated that Florence's weak condition was causing the '*utmost anxiety*' to her friends.[1178] Another newspaper reported that the greatest source of Florence's distress was the thought of her children, which '*frequently causes her to give way to the most painful emotion.*'[1179]

On Sunday, 18th August Florence attended a service in the prison's chapel conducted by the chaplain, the Rev D. Morris. Due to her extremely weak state, she had to be helped to and from the chapel by the two female warders who attended her. Rev Morris, who was described as an '*elderly man, if not an old man,*' who was '*very gentle in his manner,*' visited Florence every day. Although, as an officer of the prison, he was unable to answer all the questions of the reporters who waited every day outside the gaol, he did appear genuinely sympathetic and concerned at Florence's plight. One thing he did tell the reporters was that Florence had '*always declared her innocence and always had since he had first visited her.*' He also said that as every day passed without a reprieve, she was '*growing more nervous' and that 'the strain is telling upon her, as it naturally would.*'[1180]

On Wednesday, 21st August the London correspondent of the *New York Herald* interviewed the Baroness after she had visited her daughter that morning. The Baroness said Florence was sitting in a chair crying almost uncontrollably. There were two female warders in the cell, whom she said had been '*exceedingly kind*' to her daughter. During her visit, the Baroness was not allowed to approach Florence or hold her hand, but had to sit with a table between them as they spoke to one another. The Baroness said she had urged Florence to try and control herself and '*don't give way;*' but she only shook her head and said that her strength was all gone. The Baroness told the reporter that Florence had '*two attacks of light-headedness since Saturday night.*' She was very weak, and any more suspense could '*throw her into a brain fever.*' She said Florence had quizzed her about the whereabouts and condition of her children, and the Baroness replied that, while she did not know where they currently lived, she had been assured they were well. The Baroness said she had asked Florence about some of the key incidents in the case, including her letter to Brierley and whether she knew that James used arsenic. Florence said that she '*never had the slightest idea*' that her husband was in the habit of taking arsenic. As for the letter, she said that she wrote it when she was '*very miserable*' and tired having had no sleep for four days and nights.[1181]

On Thursday 22nd August, the prison governor, had the difficult job of telling Florence that her sentence stood and she should prepare herself for death. She thanked him and said her conscience was clear. All that day, just six yards from Florence's cell, the final preparations were made to complete the scaffold. The uprights were fixed, the cross-beam placed and the trap door was laid.

1174 *Liverpool Echo*, 15th August 1889.
1175 Evans S.P., *Executioner: The Chronicles of a Victorian Hangman*, (Sutton Publishing, Thrupp, 2004) page 312.
1176 *Liverpool Echo*, 19th August 1889.
1177 *Liverpool Echo*, 14th August 1889.
1178 *Liverpool Echo*, 14th August 1889.
1179 *Runcorn Examiner*, 17th August 1889.
1180 *Liverpool Echo*, 22nd August 1889.
1181 *Liverpool Echo*, 22nd August 1889.

Henry Matthews, Home Secretary
(*The Graphic*, 14th August 1886)

As there was not a Court of Appeal in Britain at that time, the man who held Florence's life entirely in his hands was the Home Secretary, Henry Matthews, QC, MP (1826-1913). He had been educated at Paris University and University College, London, becoming a barrister in 1850 and a QC in 1868. He served as Conservative MP between 1868-74 and 1886-95. In 1886, Lord Salisbury appointed him Home Secretary in his Second Ministry (1886-92), in so doing making him the first Roman Catholic cabinet minister since the reign of Elizabeth I.

Although he could be charming on a personal level, he was not a successful Home Secretary. The *Liverpool Review* described Matthews as a '*stubborn man entirely out-of-touch with the opinions of the country and with public feeling generally.*'[1182] Ensor wrote of him that he did '*more, perhaps, to render the government unpopular than any other minister.*'[1183]

One of the reasons for his unpopularity – both in Parliament and in the country as a whole – was his role in causing the resignation of two Metropolitan Police Commissioners, Warren and Monro, in a period of just two years. Matthews was Home Secretary during the time of the Jack the Ripper murders, and both he and the police were severely criticised for not offering a reward for information leading to a conviction. As Matthews '*reacted badly to criticism,*' the '*resolution of the Ripper scare became a matter of prime importance since Salisbury refused to let him resign under fire.*'[1184]

After the verdict and death sentence at Florence's trial, Matthews became so absorbed in the case that many of his ordinary duties at the Home Office had to be discharged by his under-secretary.[1185] He received numerous letters, memorials and petitions from those who supported the verdict and those who sympathised with Florence's plight. He summoned Mr Justice Stephen, Mr Addison, Richard Cleaver and several medical witnesses from both sides of the case to meetings in the Home Office.

Sir Charles Russell submitted a seven-page memorandum outlining the case in favour of his client. In it, he wrote:

> '*I am sorry to say it will be necessary for you to consider this case. Against her there was a strong case, undoubtedly, of the means being within her reach to poison her husband; but there was no direct evidence of administration by her. But further: but a small quantity of arsenic was discovered in the body after death, and none in the stomach, bile, heart, spleen, &c. The symptoms, all were agreed, were those of gastro-enteritis; but while witnesses for the prosecution attributed it to arsenical poisoning, a very strong body of evidence was given for the defence that it was not so.*'[1186]

Russell's memorandum included a powerful critique of the role of Mr Justice Stephen, whom he accused of placing '*greater insistence*' on the prosecution's arguments and minimising – and even discounting – the defence's case. He finished by saying that the verdict '*came as a surprise upon the trained minds of the Bar of the Northern Circuit,*' and even Addison felt that, due to the conflicting medical evidence, the jury could not find '*a verdict of guilty.*'[1187]

Behind the scenes, the Home Office also received some private lobbying on behalf of some ministers in the American Government who urged clemency. It is said that the issue was even discussed by the British Cabinet, and that two ministers stopped speaking to one another after arguing about the decision.[1188]

The meeting between Matthews and Mr Justice Stephen was especially important, as Home Secretaries tended to rely heavily on the view of the judge who had presided over the case when it came to reviewing the sentence. After the conclusion of the trial, Stephen sent all his notes to Matthews and, on 12th August, the Home Secretary summoned him to the Home Office to discuss them and his views on the trial. Following a meeting which lasted over one hour, it was reported that Stephen '*expressed not only his concurrence with the verdict, but also his appreciation of the careful way in which the jury performed their arduous duties.*'[1189]

A different view of the judge's mind-set at that time was expressed by his biographer, who wrote that Stephen suggested to the Home Secretary that the sentence be commuted to one of penal servitude, because although he felt

[1182] *Liverpool Review*, 17th August 1889.
[1183] Ensor R., *England 1870-1914*, (Clarendon Press, Oxford, 1987) page 173.
[1184] Begg P., Fido M. and Skinner K., op. cit., page 298.
[1185] *Liverpool Echo*, 16th August 1889.
[1186] O'Brien R. Barry, *The Life of Lord Russell of Killowen*, (Smith, Elder and Co., London, 1901) pages 259-260.
[1187] HO 144/1638/A50678.
[1188] Christie T.L., op. cit., page 156.
[1189] *Liverpool Echo*, 14th August 1889.

that there was '*no doubt*' that Florence had administered poison, it was 'possible that her husband had died from other causes.'[1190] It is possible, therefore, that while Stephen *did* tell Matthews he supported the guilty verdict, he may have also conveyed the view that there were elements of the evidence that troubled him and this prompted the Home Secretary to obtain additional information.

On 16th August, Matthews convened a special meeting at the Home Office to discuss the case. Present were Mr Justice Stephen, Lord Halsbury (Lord Chancellor), Sir Godfrey Lushington (Permanent Under-Secretary of State at the Home Office), and Drs Stevenson and Tidy. Also there was Dr Poore, Professor of Forensic Medicine at University College, London, and private doctor to the Prince of Wales.

At the start of the meeting, Matthews said his main aim in bringing them all together was to try and get the doctors to reconcile their differences.[1191] It proved to be a fruitless exercise, as both Stevenson and Tidy stuck rigidly to the views they had expressed in the trial. In a further effort to try and resolve this issue, Matthews asked Dr Poore to personally review the conflicting medical evidence. On 19th August, Poore's detailed report was delivered to Matthews, but once again it failed to provide the definitive answer that the Home Secretary was desperately looking for. Although Poore wrote it was impossible to '*avoid the conclusion that arsenic was the cause of death,*' he also wrote that, from the post-mortem appearances alone, it was not possible to state that '*arsenic was the poison.*'[1192]

As Matthews reviewed Florence's sentence, one Liverpool newspaper commented that while the Home Office should '*carefully consider every point that is urged in Mrs Maybrick's favour,*' it should not allow the '*clamour of the mob to influence them in any degree.*' Intriguingly, the newspaper then went on to suggest that if Mrs Maybrick had been found innocent there would have been another outcry of public sentiment, this time '*ready to denounce the favouritism displayed towards a woman who happened to be of good circumstances.*'[1193]

Finally, just four days before the execution was due to be carried out, Matthews decided to commute the sentence. The messenger carrying the news reached Walton Gaol just after 1:00am on the night of the 22nd/23rd August. Governor Anderson was roused from his bed. He read the message, and then went to Florence's cell. He told her: '*It is well, it is good news, I have just received a message from the Home Office which states that he advised the Queen to commute your sentence to imprisonment for life.*' Florence, not too surprisingly, fainted on hearing the news. She later wrote, '*When I opened my eyes once more, I was lying in the bed in the hospital, and I remained there until I was taken to Woking Convict Prison.*'[1194] The official text of the commutation released by the Home Office stated:

> '*The Home Secretary, after fullest consideration, and after taking the best legal advice that could be obtained, has advised Her Majesty to respite the capital sentence on Florence Maybrick and to commute the punishment to penal servitude for life in as much as, although the evidence leads clearly to the conclusion that the prisoner attempted to administer arsenic to her husband with intent to murder, yet it does not wholly exclude a reasonable doubt whether his death was in fact caused by the administration of arsenic. This decision is understood not to imply the slightest reflection on the able and experienced practitioners who gave evidence or on the tribunal by which the prisoner was tried. We understand the course adopted has the concurrence of the learned judge.*'

The decision was well received by most of the British public. *The Times* welcomed the decision commenting, '*The case against Mrs Maybrick was and remains a case of terribly strong suspicion, but suspicion which, after all is said, just misses moral certainty.*' The decision was also welcomed in Liverpool, by those who thought that Florence was innocent and even by those who thought that she was guilty. The *Garston and Woolton Reporter*, a newspaper that had agreed with the verdict of the jury, commented:

> '*The fact that the Home Secretary has at last been able to give decisive advice to Her Majesty in the Maybrick case will be read with general satisfaction... Although we have felt no reasonable doubt as to the prisoner's guilt, we have also expressed our wish that she should not be executed unless the evidence was sufficient to prove her crime. We are pleased to find that the Home Secretary has been able to arrive at the conclusion that there is some doubt in the case, at least from a legal point of view. There need have been no delay over the matter, and no hesitation about letting Mrs Maybrick off, if the crime with which she was charged had not been of such a serious nature that the law and humanity demanded that every effort should be made to bring a prisoner alleged to be guilty of such an abominable sin to justice.*'[1195]

1190 Stephen L., op cit., page 447.
1191 HO 144/1638/A50678.
1192 HO 144/1638/A50678.
1193 *Garston and Woolton Reporter*, 17th August 1889
1194 Maybrick F., op cit., page 60.
1195 *Garston and Woolton Reporter*, 24th August 1889.

On the Liverpool Cotton Exchange, the attitude to the Home Secretary's decision was '*eminently satisfactory, all things considered.*' Even those who believed Florence to be guilty had '*come round to the opinion that there was an element of doubt*' and that the interests of justice were better served by commuting the sentence to one of penal servitude for life.[1196]

In reaching his decision, the Home Secretary had decided that while there was reasonable doubt that James died of arsenical poisoning, he still believed that Florence had attempted to administer arsenic to her husband. In other words, while Florence may not have been guilty of murder, she was guilty of attempted murder and therefore a life sentence was appropriate. The problem with this view is that it was not the offence for which Florence was tried and convicted. If there was reasonable doubt that James died from arsenical poisoning, as the Home Secretary said in his statement, then Florence should have been found not guilty and released.

Florence's reaction to the Home Secretary's decision was mixed, and aroused '*conflicting emotions.*' Although she was clearly relieved not to be executed, she was still angry at the verdict and worried by the thought of a life sentence. She had anticipated a free pardon, and the '*gloomy prospect of passing the rest of her life in prison had caused her the most intense and excruciating agony.*' One of the female warders supposedly heard Florence say that had it '*not been for the disgrace of dying on the scaffold, she would have preferred death to penal servitude.*'[1197]

A friend of the Baroness travelled to the house in which she was staying in Blundellsands, to the north of Liverpool, and told her the news of her daughter's reprieve. When the Baroness heard her daughter was to be saved she jumped up, overjoyed at the decision, before falling back strengthless on to the couch. Her friend felt the Baroness had aged greatly since the verdict and had grown thinner and paler, but news of the reprieve '*seemed to bring all the freshness and brightness back again.*'

The Baroness wanted to go immediately to Walton Gaol to see her daughter, but that was not possible as Florence's prison status had changed. The visiting rules granted to a felon facing the death penalty no longer applied. Florence was now a prisoner with a life sentence and subject to the strict rules that applied to prison life. For the Baroness to now visit her daughter, she had to formally apply to the prison governor for permission.

1196 *Liverpool Echo*, 23rd August 1889.
1197 *Liverpool Echo*, 23rd August 1889.

One person who was not happy that Florence's sentence had been commuted was Queen Victoria. Influenced by Florence's admission of adultery in court, the monarch believed her to be guilty of the murder of her husband. However, following the intervention of the Home Secretary she reluctantly agreed to commute the sentence to one of life in prison. Victoria later wrote to Matthews, saying '*the only regret that she feels about the decision is that so wicked a woman should escape by a mere legal quibble! The law is not a moral profession, she must say. But she must never be further commuted.*'[1198]

LINKS TO THE RIPPER DIARY: DID FLORENCE BELIEVE THAT JAMES MAYBRICK WAS JACK THE RIPPER?

One of the final entries in the Diary of Jack the Ripper reads as follows: '*The pain is unbearable. My dear Bunny knows all. I do not know if she has the strength to kill me. I pray to God she finds it. It would be simple, she knows of my medicine, and for an extra dose or two it would all be over.*'

If you believe the Diary was written by James Maybrick, and the journal provides a truthful account of his actions, then you have to accept the diarist's statement that Florence had knowledge of James' murderous deeds. The main justification for the assertion that Florence '*knows all*' comes from a few lines in the letter she wrote to Brierley which was intercepted by Nurse Yapp. In the letter, Florence wrote: '*The tale he told me was pure fabrication, and only intended to frighten the truth out of me. In fact he believes my statement although he will not admit it. You need not therefore go abroad on this account dearest, but in any case, please don't leave England until I have seen you again.*'

Paul Feldman directly referred to these lines in his book that argues James Maybrick was the notorious Whitechapel serial killer, stating that while Florence may or may not have believed her husband's tale, '*Alfred Brierley had taken it most seriously.*' Feldman added, '*Whatever the tale was, it was most certainly intended to frighten. Alfred Brierley clearly was frightened.*'[1199] The problem with Feldman's view is that he just quotes three sentences from the letter, and as a result ignores the context in which they were written.

To fully understand the three sentences, it is important to examine the circumstances in which the letter was written. Florence was replying to Brierley's letter, which she had received on 6th May. His letter was a response to an earlier telegram from Florence, in which she had warned him that her husband was threatening to place adverts in newspapers asking for information about her movements in London when she had stayed in Flatman's Hotel with him. As no such adverts have been found, it is unlikely that James did place them. Brierley describes Florence's telegram as '*a staggerer,*' and states he '*cannot find an advertisement in any London papers.*' Brierley informed Florence he was: '*going to try and get away in about a fortnight and think I should take a round trip to the Mediterranean, which will take six or seven weeks, unless you wish me to stay in England. Supposing the rooms are found, I think both you and I would be better away as the man's memory would be doubted after three months.*'

In other words, Brierley *was* frightened – not by the possibility that James was Jack the Ripper – but by the prospect of James discovering that he and Florence had spent two nights together in a hotel in London. Such a discovery would have almost inevitably led to a violent confrontation with James; it also had the potential to completely destroy his personal and business reputation. In that context, it is relatively straightforward to decode Florence's response in her letter to Brierley. She did not want Brierley to travel to Europe and for him to be away for two months, so she was trying to reassure him that her husband was '*perfectly ignorant*' of their affair, and therefore there was no need for him to travel abroad. James had questioned her about the London trip and, in order to try and extract the truth, he had threatened to place adverts in newspapers. It was an empty threat, as he did not place any adverts.

In his book on the Ripper murders Philip Sugden posed the question: '*If Maybrick was the killer and, as the diary alleges, confessed everything to his wife, why didn't Florence mention it in her defence at her trial*?'[1200]

Feldman responded to Sugden's question by providing two reasons why Florence might not have mentioned she was the wife of Jack the Ripper at her trial. The first was a '*legal one*;' it would have provided her with a clear motive for killing her husband. Feldman asserts that the Crown were struggling to provide a strong motive for why Florence might have wanted to kill James. They could not use money, as James' will had left her '*nothing to speak of,*' and they could not use her love affair as she was '*seeking a separation through legal means.*'[1201]

Feldman's argument is clearly flawed. While Florence may have had the necessary information to file for a divorce, the prosecuting counsel and the judge repeatedly emphasised Florence's affair as her motive to commit murder. Mr Justice Stephen finished his summing-up at the end of the trial by telling the jury that they must remember the intrigue

[1198] Quoted in Graham A. and Emmas C., op. cit., page 215.
[1199] Feldman P., op cit., page 299.
[1200] Sugden P., op cit., page 10.
[1201] Feldman P., op cit., page 300.

that Florence had '*carried on with this man Brierley, and the feelings – it seems horrible to comparatively ordinary innocent people a horrible and incredible thought that a woman should be plotting the death of her husband in order that she might be left at liberty to follow her own degrading vices.*'

The second reason Feldman provides as to why Florence might have wanted to keep quiet about her husband's evil deeds concerned her children. He wrote that if it became public knowledge that James was Jack the Ripper, it would have '*ruined all the Maybricks, including the children she loved and cherished so much.*' While the first reason Feldman provides has no credibility, his second reason does have some credence to it. It is the case that prior to her trial, Florence had implored her solicitors not to present the evidence they had acquired to demonstrate that James had been involved in an adulterous relationship as she wanted to protect his reputation. It is therefore feasible that if Florence had known that James was the Ripper she might have decided not to tell the police, for the sake of her children's future. One can only imagine the long-lasting damage such information could have caused them on every level, from social to psychological, if they had become publicly branded as the offspring of Britain's most infamous serial killer. On the other hand, even if Florence had chosen not to go public with the information she could have still used it as a bargaining-chip with the authorities. Feldman suggests that if she had pursued such a course of action then she could have faced the serious charge of withholding evidence; however, this could have easily been answered by Florence telling the police she only learnt of James' guilty secret in the last few days of his life.

The biggest reason for rejecting the view that Florence believed her husband to be Jack the Ripper is that it is entirely unlikely that, as a very religiously-minded woman, she would have wanted to have lived with and protected such an evil person, both before and after his death. Right to the very end of his life, Florence appeared to care for her husband. When the cook, Elizabeth Humphreys, was asked by Sir Charles Russell at the trial whether Florence had seemed to be attending to her husband, she replied, '*She seemed very kind to him, and spent all her time with him.*' Even after he died and Florence had been cautioned by Superintendent Bryning, she insisted on seeing James' coffin before it left the house on the day of his funeral. She knelt by the coffin, prayed and then began to cry. None of these things would have happened if Florence believed James was Jack the Ripper.

As she approached the end of her life, when her son was dead and she was estranged from her daughter, Florence had many opportunities to have told the truth about her husband, had he been Jack the Ripper, but she never provided even the slightest hint that she believed James to be the killer. One is therefore drawn to the obvious conclusion that Florence did not believe her husband was the Whitechapel fiend, or have the remotest suspicion. The diarist is wrong, and it is yet another example of a mistake in the Diary that demonstrates its fraudulent nature.

An alternative view of whether Florence knew that her husband was Ripper is provided by Bruce Robinson, who argued the Diary was actually written by Michael Maybrick rather than by his brother James. He suggests Michael wrote the document as a means of framing James to be the serial killer, and therefore removing any suspicion from himself being considered the actual murderer.

Robinson proposes the hypothesis that Michael successfully managed to get the authorities to believe that James was the Ripper and, as a result, after his death they had '*reason enough to believe that the nightmare who had been terrorising Whitechapel was in his grave.*' Although this was a welcome development, one problem still remained: '*It was believed [by the authorities] that Florence Maybrick had discovered the truth of a terrible secret.*'[1202]

When Robinson refers to the '*authorities*' what he means is the Freemasons who dominated many of the top positions of power in the country. They were determined to protect Freemasonry from any scandal, and that therefore required them to remove any trace of James from their records and have his wife '*permanently shut up.*' To that end, it was determined that Florence would be charged with James' murder and her trial would be rigged to ensure that she would be found guilty and hanged. Robinson suggests that '*in reality Florence knew nothing, because there was nothing to know. It was a lie within a lie.*'[1203]

Like many of Robinson's ideas, the hypothesis is strong on speculation and weak on supporting evidence. To accept his view, one has to accept the notion that a large number of powerful people, drawn from the top echelons of government, had to secretly conspire to have a high-profile trial rigged and an innocent woman found convicted and executed. It is not a very believable proposition, and is totally undermined by the fact that, despite the verdict, Florence was saved from the gallows by the Home Secretary who commuted her sentence. Florence was not '*permanently shut up*' and one of the so-called insiders of the conspiracy, Sir Charles Russell, was to spend a great deal of time and effort to try and get her released from prison. The only thing about Robinson's hypothesis that is true is his view that '*Florence knew nothing*' about her husband being Jack the Ripper – and the reason she knew nothing was because James was not the serial killer.

[1202] Robinson B., op cit., page 619.
[1203] Ibid., page 620.

19

WOKING PRISON

On Wednesday 28th August 1889, Florence's solicitor, Mr Cleaver, visited Walton Gaol and spent a considerable amount of time with Florence sorting out her estate and drawing up her will, which was said to be entirely in favour of her children.[1204] At 9:00am the following day, Thursday 29th, Florence was taken by a cab from Walton Gaol to Liverpool Lime Street Station, and then transferred by train to Woking Female Prison. She was accompanied by one male warder and two female attendants.

A reporter from the *Liverpool Courier* claimed to have seen Florence's departure from Lime Street Station. He reported that at the station, the door to the cab was opened by a senior railway official and then Florence and her female attendants made their way across the platform into a reserved compartment that had blinds drawn across the window.[1205] Another report said that while Florence '*looked in fairly good health,*' it did appear as though she had '*shrunk much in size. She wore the convict dress with the broad arrow.*'[1206]

After Florence's arrival at Woking, she had to remove the prison clothes she had travelled in as they were to be sent back to Walton Gaol, and instead had to put on the prison costume of a new arrival at Woking. A warder then cut her hair to the nape of her neck, an act which Florence later described as filling her with a sense of '*degradation*' and '*utter hopelessness.*' Her weight was recorded as eight stone, and her height as 5 feet 3 inches. Her clothing was marked with a red star – meaning first time offender – and her prison identification, '*L.P. 29*'. '*L*' stood for lifer, '*P*' for the year of imprisonment, and '*29*' as the 29th prisoner of the year. Florence was then escorted to a cell in the prison's infirmary.

In an adjoining cell an insane woman spent the night '*raving and weeping*' and Florence wondered whether in the years to come would she suffer the same fate. The next day she was visited by the governor and then the prison doctor, who gave her a medical inspection and ordered her to be '*detained in the infirmary until further orders.*'[1207]

Prisons in the mid-nineteenth century have been described as '*a man's world; made for men by men. Women in prison were seen as somehow anomalous; not foreseen and therefore not legislated for.*'[1208] Women were housed in male prisons, but in separate wings and with female warders. Prison governors tended to see women prisoners as '*troublesome*' and treated them '*rather like difficult men,*' although they were largely excluded from the more physical measures of discipline that were deemed appropriate for male inmates.

Mary Gordon (1861-1941), the first woman to be appointed as a prison inspector in Britain, said most female prisoners had short sentences and very high rates of recidivism. This was mainly due to poverty, their lifestyle and the stigma they faced after leaving prison. Women who committed crimes were judged against the prevailing social construct that saw the *ideal* woman as performing maternal and domestic roles, and acting in a pure and submissive manner. Therefore, women who committed a criminal act not only broke the law, they also deviated from social norms. This made them doubly-deviant in the eyes of respectable society. As a result, once a woman '*fell from virtue she found it almost impossible to regain it, and consequently was precluded from pursuing an honest career.*'[1209]

Although there were fewer female than male offenders, they still made up between 20 to 25% of those prosecuted by the criminal courts. Women tended to be over-represented in certain offence categories, including thefts, offences under the Pawnbroker's Acts, drunk and disorderly, lower-level assaults and public disorder, and offences relating to prostitution. For those women sentenced to imprisonment, '*the most common experience was a short sentence in a local prison, usually just a few days or weeks for petty offences.*' In the 1880s, the average number of women given a custodial sentence in a local prison was 46,000 per year; however, the average daily female prison population was 3,400 demonstrating the high turnover of women on short sentences.[1210]

Compared to modern prisons, Woking Female Prison appeared grim, oppressive and highly regulated; but by Victorian standards it was considered one of the more enlightened penal institutions. It was located at Knaphill in

---

[1204] *Liverpool Echo*, 30th August 1889.
[1205] *Liverpool Review*, 7th September, 1889.
[1206] *Garston and Woolton Reporter*, 31st August 1889.
[1207] Maybrick F., op cit., pages 63-65.
[1208] Priestley P., *Victorian Prison Lives*, (Pimlico, London, 1999) page 69.
[1209] Zedner L., found at 'Review of: Women, Crime, and Custody in Victorian England' by Lucia Zedner (pugetsound.edu)
[1210] Turner Dr J. and Johnston Dr H., 'Female Prisoners, Aftercare and Release: Residential Provision and Support in Late Nineteenth-Century England' in *British Journal of Community Justice*, Vol 13(3) pages 36-37.

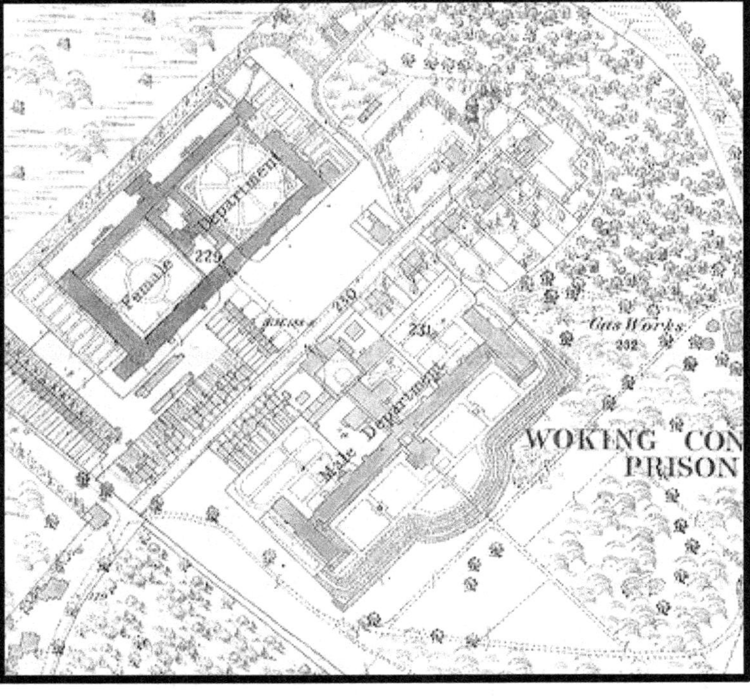

The layout of Woking Prison

Woking, Surrey, a fifty-minute train journey from London Waterloo Railway Station. It was built next to Woking Convict Invalid Prison for men, and was surrounded by beautiful countryside. When it opened in 1869, it was the first purpose-built female prison in England. Although constructed to hold just over 700 women, in its earlier years it regularly exceeded that total. The 1881 Census showed there were 715 male inmates in the Invalid Prison and 798 female inmates in Woking Female Prison.[1211]

Like the men's prison next door, the female prison was built to hold convicts who had been sentenced for a term of five years or more, but were elderly and infirm and thus deemed unable to complete the heavy labour tasks that prisoners were typically expected to undertake.

The prison was built in a series of blocks, standing at right-angles to one another. There were eight long and narrow halls or wards, the largest of which had 150 cells. On either side of the halls were four floors of cells, each measuring eight by five feet. Most cells had a floor of blue slate, though some of the slightly larger cells had wooden floors. An iron rod was attached to the cell wall so that a hammock could be fastened to it at night.[1212]

The female inmates at Woking were divided into different classes, each with its own style of prison-wear for identification purposes and a clearly defined set of rules that prescribed exactly how they were expected to behave. For the first nine months of imprisonment, prisoners were in the probationary class and wore dark brown dresses. In the second nine months, they were in the third-class and wore dark green dresses. In the third period of nine months, they became prisoners of the second-class. They wore dark blue dresses. In the fourth period of nine months, female convicts became prisoners of first-class. There was little distinction between prisoners of second-class and first-class, though the latter got slightly better food.

When a convict had only nine months of her sentence left, she was dubbed to be a prisoner of Special Class. At this point she wore a light-striped dress, and was allowed a '*Princess*' robe of dark grey striped flannel. Movement between stages was dependent upon the good conduct of the prisoners who were '*very proud of distinguishing marks and higher grades of service, and do their best, as a rule to secure them.*'[1213] Convicts who had never been to prison before were distinguished by a red star on their right arm. This was done to keep them apart from the habitual prisoners, who were said to be '*easily identified by their degraded, evil-looking countenances.*'[1214]

As female prisoners were not usually thought to have the strength to carry out arduous physical labour beyond the prison walls, they were set tasks that centred around the notion of domesticity that could be completed within the prison itself such as sewing and garment production, and working in the laundrettes and kitchens.

Farming was the one work activity that allowed the women to move beyond the prison walls. The prison stood on five acres of land but there was a further two and half acres of farmland surrounding it, and some of the female inmates were allocated agricultural work.

In 1889, around the time that Florence moved to Woking, the novelist Frederick William Robinson (1830-1901) visited the prison, and an account of his experiences were published in *The Graphic* newspaper. He reported that when he visited the Woking it was not much more than half full, with 409 female convicts – all of whom were serving long sentences. He said that many of the women were '*busy at twine-making – a new feature of convict labour that is progressing very satisfactorily – at post office bags, at making clothing for Greenwich boys [at the Royal Naval College].*' He described the tailor's room as an '*imposing scene,*' with the '*clicking of innumerable sewing-machines.*'[1215]

[1211] *Surrey Advertiser*, 27th October 1888.
[1212] *Liverpool Echo*, 3rd September 1889.
[1213] *The Graphic*, 7th September 1889.
[1214] *Liverpool Echo*, 3rd September 1889.
[1215] *The Graphic*, 31st August 1889.

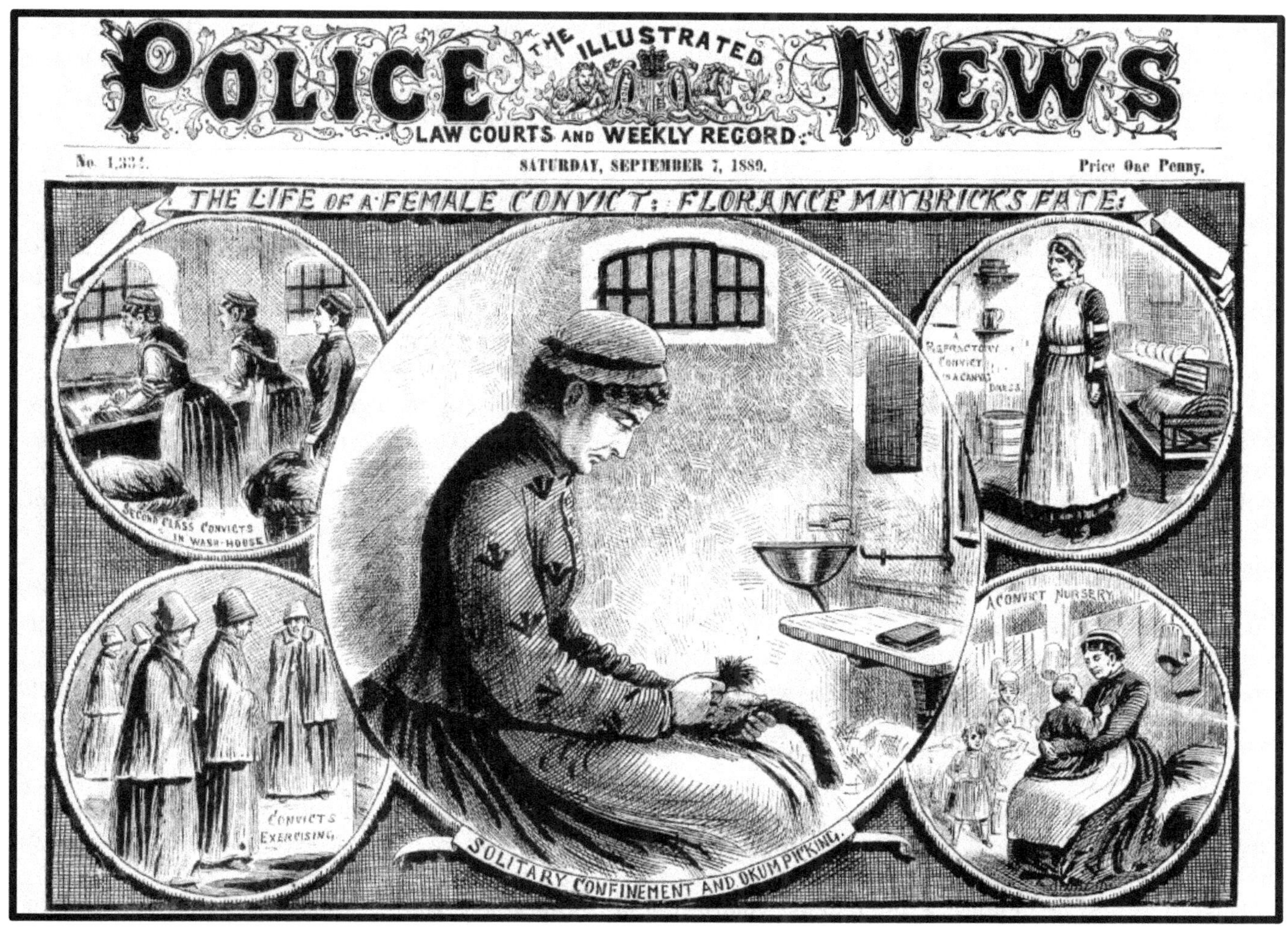

Florence must have been in a complete state of shock when she arrived at Woking. Nothing in her life would have adequately prepared her for the ordeal she was to face. The first nine months of Florence's sentence were a period of solitary confinement in her tiny cell. The furniture was only a hammock and the three simple shelves. The hammock was a '*legacy of the hulks,*' the old rotting ships that were used as prisons.[1216] For a seat, Florence had to place her bedclothes on the floor.

When she first saw the cell, Florence cried out in despair to her gaolers: '*Oh don't put me in there! I can't bear it.*'[1217] Inside the locked cell she was instantly hit by the smell and the darkness. The gloom in the cell was only relieved by '*the dim light of a window that was never cleaned.*'[1218]

Prison life followed the same routine every day. At 6:00am, the bell rang and the prisoners got dressed. In winter, this meant getting dressed in the dark. The hammock was neatly folded and put to one side. Slopping-out followed; the inmates had two buckets, one served as their toilet and the other had cold water for washing themselves, their plate and jug, and their cell. The prisoners then waited by their cell door until it was opened, and they were given a breakfast of a six-ounce whole-meal loaf and three-quarters of a pint of gruel.

At 8:30am, the bell rang again, and the cell door opened. The prisoners, in single-file – three paces behind the person in front – walked to the chapel for the daily religious service. Florence called this '*an oasis in a weary desert.*'[1219]

At 9:00am, the prisoners returned to the cell and began their work. Florence was given the task of making a shirt every day. At 10:00am the Governor inspected the cell. It had to be neat and tidy, and very clean. This was followed by the exercise hour. In a yard some 40 feet square, 35 convicts walked in single file around the yard in a circle without speaking. Florence said that although the experience was '*dull,*' it was the '*only opportunity for a glimpse of the sky and for a taste of outdoor life, and affords our only relief from an otherwise almost unbearable day.*'[1220]

[1216] Priestley P., op cit., page 32.
[1217] Maybrick F., op cit., page 67.
[1218] Ibid., page 67.
[1219] Ibid., page 69.
[1220] Ibid., page 72.

Lunch was at noon, and between then and 2:00pm, the inmates were allowed to rest or work. After 2:00pm, there was another three hours of work, until tea at 5:00pm. The food served at tea was the same as breakfast. At 5:30pm, work resumed again, and continued for one and a half hours. At 7:00pm, work finished, the cell door was locked, and a long, cold, lonely night began. Throughout the whole of the day, Florence was not allowed to speak to any other inmate. Years later, she wrote: '*no one can realise the horror of solitary confinement who has not experienced it.*'[1221]

In the second nine months of her sentence Florence was moved to a larger cell, that had a floor made of wood instead of slate. She had a camp-bed with a mattress rather than a hammock, and she was given two coarse sheets and blankets. Although the cell changed, prison routine didn't and Florence still faced severe restrictions on movement and speaking. In her autobiography, Florence wrote: '*There is no rule of prison discipline so productive of trouble and disaster as the "silent system", and the tyrannous and rigorous method with which it is enforced is the cause of two-thirds of all the misconduct and disturbance that occurs in prison.*'[1222]

She continued: '*The torture of continually enforced silence is known to produce insanity or nervous breakdown more than any other feature connected with prison discipline.*'[1223] Two other problems that Florence suffered were the bitter cold nights of winter, and insomnia. She wrote: '*During all the fifteen years of my imprisonment, insomnia was (and alas! is still) my constant companion.*'[1224]

After 18 months, Florence moved to the next stage of prison life, '*hard labour.*' She was given back-breaking work in the prison's kitchens, but the tasks did help break the monotony of prison life and she was now able to talk to other inmates.

To a woman who had led a pampered existence, prison life must have been a major shock. Although Florence was reduced to tears and despair on numerous occasions, time was to show she had both the character and the resilience to survive the ordeal. As Christie so aptly puts it, '*the frivolous girl had been transferred into a resolute woman almost overnight.*'[1225] In her autobiography, Florence claimed that '*by the exercise of great self-control and restraint I had maintained a perfect good conduct record at Woking for a period of years*!'[1226] She implied that only once was she involved in any trouble, and that was a fairly minor affair which was not really her own fault.

In 1892, a prisoner gave Florence some wool so she could knit a warm pair of socks. Unfortunately, the wool had been stolen, and when it was discovered in her cell Florence found herself in trouble with the prison authorities. Florence said her punishment was to be '*degraded for a month to a lower stage, with a loss of 26 marks, and had 6 days added to my original sentence.*'[1227]

One early break in Florence's monotonous daily routine came at the end of October 1889, when she was interviewed by a Mr Hood. He was a solicitor who was acting on behalf of Mrs Briggs, who was pursuing a libel action against the satirical Liverpool newspaper *Porcupine* following an article it had published about the evidence Mrs Briggs had given at Florence's trial. Although the libel action was to be dropped by Mrs Briggs following the unexpected death of her sister Mrs Hughes, reports of Hood's interview with Florence did reach the press.

Hood said Florence '*appeared in extremely good health, did not seem to be overcome with any sense of the terrible nature of her position, but was, on the contrary, as calm, cool, and collected as possible. It was, indeed, somewhat a matter of surprise to find her in such good spirits.*' He went on to say that Florence was '*of course, attired in prison dress, which consists of a chocolate-coloured costume of rough woollen material. The gown was gathered in at the waist, whilst round the shoulders, and falling down as far as the waist, was a shawl, of the same material and colour as the dress, and pinned at the throat.*'[1228] Hood attributed Florence's cheerfulness to be the result of the kind and considerate attention she was receiving from the prison staff. What he didn't realise was that any lack of co-operation on Florence's part, or any criticism of the prison regime, would have resulted in her losing good conduct marks and access to privileges.

As Florence suffered the hardships of a Victorian prison regime, Alfred Brierley, his reputation in ruins and his business destroyed, left England for America. He was never to see Florence again. On 7th September 1889, *The Garston and Woolton Reporter* carried two separate stories about Florence and Brierley that showed the marked difference between the two in terms of their future lives. The newspaper reported that Florence was in '*a serious condition*' in the infirmary at Woking Gaol. It said the '*strain of the last few weeks has told terribly upon a system already weakened by weeks of suspense.*' The next story reported that Brierley had recently arrived on the Cunarder *Scythia* at Boston Harbour, USA, stating: '*He was accompanied by his brother, Frederick. During the voyage across*

[1221] Ibid., page 68.
[1222] Ibid., page 78.
[1223] Ibid., page 81.
[1224] Ibid., page 85.
[1225] Christie T.L., op cit., page 177.
[1226] Maybrick F., op cit., page 111.
[1227] Ibid., page 114.
[1228] *Cardiff Times*, 9th November 1889.

the sea Brierley was reserved, and appeared to feel the delicacy of his position; but he was on friendly terms with several of the passengers, including Judge Oliver Wendell Holmes, the son of the octogenarian poet.'[1229]

The main reason Brierley travelled to America was to rebuild his life and career. He gave a brief statement to a persistent reporter from the *Boston Globe*, saying he was sailing to America to '*escape notoriety*,' as he no longer wanted to feature in the daily journals. He claimed he had spent £6,000 on Florence's defence, but in fact he had spent a lot less. He said he had heard of her reprieve at Queenstown, whilst travelling to America. He closed the interview by saying: '*I have figured more prominently in the case than my real connection with it warranted. Besides this I have nothing to say as to where I am going in Boston, or after I leave there. I have nothing to say regarding anything, and you will oblige me by bringing your questions to a close.*'[1230]

In response to a series of articles about her daughter, the Baroness had a letter published in which she sought to '*contradict many of the foolish statements which appear in the Public Press.*'[1231] She wrote the total amount that Brierley actually contributed was '*one cheque of £100.*' She ridiculed a report that Florence's diary, supposedly three small volumes tied together with blue silken cord, had been taken by a family relative and put up for sale, and that she had agreed to pay a large price for it in order to suppress it. The Baroness wrote that '*there is no truth whatever in this statement. My daughter did not keep a diary. It is quite true that some books are missing; it is supposed that they have been taken away by someone interested in my daughter's downfall.*'

By far the largest portion of the Baroness' letter was devoted to Florence's children. She was especially angered by a report that she had consented to the children being adopted '*by a lady and gentleman in London.*'[1232] She complained bitterly that the Maybrick brothers declined to '*furnish any information as to the whereabouts of the children.*' She commented:

> '*Do they belong to the Maybrick brothers more than to my daughter, or to me? The anxious thoughts and doubts about these poor children have caused my daughter greater pain than anything else in this dreadful ordeal she has gone through. Her heart is breaking for some scrap of information about them. I assured the Messrs. Maybrick that if I was permitted to give the children a home I would remain in England and keep a home for them in England, and that from me they would never hear anything but good of both parents. Surely this latter condition cannot be their reason for sending them away among strangers.*'

The Baroness' pleas with regard to her grandchildren were to fall on deaf ears. Michael Maybrick, in particular, was determined that young James and Gladys were to have as little contact with their mother and the Baroness as possible. He arranged for the children to live in London with Dr Fuller and his wife, who were paid £100 a year to look after them. James Chandler Maybrick (Bobo/Sonny) was to take the surname Fuller, though neither of the children were to be formally adopted by the Fullers.

In January 1890, after a short break from the limelight, Michael made his first public appearance since the trial at a ballad concert at St James's Hall in London. According to a review in a Liverpool newspaper, he was '*given a hearty reception by the audience, which included a large number of personal friends.*' He was in '*hearty voice*' and his own songs, such as *They All Love Jack* were '*enthusiastically received.*'[1233] In its next edition, the same newspaper wrote of Michael that '*Liverpudlians are justly proud of their fellow citizen,*' and he was always '*sure of an uproarious reception in his native city.*'[1234]

In the early months of her daughter's imprisonment at Woking, the Baroness set up a temporary home in England so she would be close to Florence, and be more able to lobby the authorities on her behalf. The Baroness was prepared to speak to anyone and everyone in an effort to get Florence released. She wrote that she had been advised by certain '*honourable men*' – whom she didn't name – '*to bring private and direct powerful influence in England and America to induce the Home Secretary to recognise the importance, for the sake of a generous use of his power*' and pardon her daughter. She said that in America, all of Florence's relatives – even her '*most distant cousins*' – had written to the Home Secretary to try and get him to change his stance on Florence's imprisonment. The Baroness wrote that Colonel Andrew H. Dawson was helping to raise funds to pay for the legal costs of the trial. She described him as '*intimate friend*' of Daniel Chandler, who was her father-in-law and Florence's grandfather. If that is the case, then perhaps some of the old antagonisms directed towards her from her husband's family and friends had diminished or, at least, been set aside in the effort to help Florence.[1235] Although Dawson was then in his seventies, he was said to have an '*erect, elastic figure of a man of 30.*' He was described as being '*active and energetic as the typical*

[1229] *Garston and Woolton Reporter*, 7th September 1889.
[1230] *Garston and Woolton Reporter*, 21st September 1889.
[1231] *Liverpool Echo*, 30th September 1889.
[1232] *Liverpool Echo*, 17th September 1889.
[1233] *Liverpool Weekly Courier*, 11th January 1890.
[1234] *Liverpool Weekly Courier*, 18th January 1890.
[1235] *Manchester Courier and Lancashire General Advertiser*, 6th October 1891.

Kentuckian.' He was strongly committed to Florence's cause, as he believed she had been '*unjustly imprisoned*' and '*held for a murder she never committed.*'[1236]

In 1890, the Baroness sent a long, rambling and barely readable letter to Queen Victoria asking her to pardon her daughter. She described Florence as a '*good religious woman, dedicated quiet and dignified, a good daughter, a devoted mother and a patient wife.*'[1237] Some of the more ill-advised passages in the letter were her criticisms of Mr Justice Stephen, the British legal system and the Home Secretary. It is extremely unlikely that the Queen even read the letter before it was sent by one of her secretaries to the Home Office and lodged in a file.

The Baroness' letter to the Queen, like many of her efforts on behalf of her daughter, have been roundly criticised. Graham and Emmas wrote that the Baroness was prepared to use '*every crooked trick in the book,*' and as a result '*she probably put more years on Florence's sentence than anyone could possibly have foreseen.*'[1238]

While it is undoubtedly the case that some of the Baroness' actions were to prove counter-productive and antagonised some of the influential people who had the power to reduce Florence's sentence, the fact is the usual prison tariff for a person convicted of murder at that time was between fifteen and twenty years. The Baroness made mistakes, but she must be praised for the undying commitment and abundant energy she devoted to her daughter's cause. Ultimately, the reason why Florence remained as long as she did in prison was purely down to the intransigence of the authorities; by their desire to protect a flawed judicial process over the claims of a convicted woman whom many believed had suffered a miscarriage of justice.

Although the Baroness was to fight an uphill battle on Florence's behalf, she did score the occasional minor victory. One of these came very early on, when she managed to secure a special pass to visit her daughter after less than three months into her prison sentence, the usual period being a minimum of six months after a person's conviction.

On Wednesday 20th November 1889, the Baroness, accompanied by a family friend, Rev Mr Long, visited Florence at Woking. The purpose of the visit was '*family matters of business,*' as the Baroness needed to resolve some issues relating to her daughter's finances and assets.[1239] While Florence had been waiting for the verdict at the end of her trial she had signed a document put in front of her by Mr Potter, who was acting on behalf of the Baroness' American lawyer. The document related to the agreement made some years earlier in which the Baroness had agreed to sell all interests in her American properties in Kentucky in return for a one-off payment of $10,000. The Baroness had recently received that money, minus Potter's quite substantial fee. Potter sent the money, with a letter in which he advised the Baroness to be '*prudent with this little sum*' as it might be all she would have '*hereafter.*'[1240]

Following the Baroness' visit, one newspaper report stated that Florence was in '*excellent health,*' and she had received the previous Saturday a '*kind message*' from the Home Secretary that had come via her solicitor Mr Cleaver.[1241] Mr Frank Richards, a friend of the family, wrote to the Baroness and drew her attention to the article. This prompted the Baroness to release a letter saying she knew nothing of any such message from the Home Secretary, and that her daughter's health was anything but excellent. She said she barely recognised Florence, as she was '*deadly pale, dark under the eyes, weak.*' She added that, during the interview, Florence had '*laid her head against the stone wall and wept bitterly.*' Florence had been especially hard hit by the news that, despite her mother's efforts, she had been unable to locate the whereabouts of her children.

The Baroness next saw Florence on 24th January 1890. It was one of the regular visits that were allowed under prison rules. Every six months or so over the next seven years the Baroness would make the arduous journey from her home in Rouen, France, to visit her daughter at Woking. Florence later wrote that '*neither heat nor cold*' could deter her mother from making this '*fatiguing journey*' in order to '*cheer, comfort and console.*'[1242] The regulations governing these visits were detailed and strict. A prisoner was allowed a thirty-minute visit by up to three friends at one time, at intervals of six, four and two months, depending upon their prison stage. An inmate might lose the right to receive a visitor through any action they committed that was deemed to be bad conduct. A potential visitor had to formally apply to the prison governor for permission to visit an inmate, and he had the right to deny any request. The prisoner was banned from making any reference to prison life during a visit; any attempt to break this rule would lead to the meeting being immediately stopped by the matron in charge. To make matters even worse, Florence was separated from her mother by two grilled barriers. Sitting between the two barriers was a prison matron, who closely monitored all that was said. Florence was unable to hold her mother's hand, let alone give her a kiss, something which she described as the '*very depth of humiliation.*'

One of the things that Florence's mother was able to do was to keep her daughter informed about the activities that were taking place to get her released from prison. Florence was especially pleased by the efforts being made by her

---

[1236] *Sioux City Journal*, 30th December 1892 and the *Canton Sentinel*, 29th December 1892.
[1237] HO 144/1639/A50678/D47.
[1238] Graham A. and Emmas C., op cit., page 227.
[1239] *Liverpool Weekly Courier*, 11th January 1890.
[1240] Letter from Potter to the Baroness, dated 2nd September 1889, stored in Richmond Chancery, Virginia, USA.
[1241] *Pall Mall Gazette*, 21st November 1889.
[1242] Maybrick F., op cit., pages 108-110.

supporters in America. She wrote in her autobiography that while '*their efforts proved all in vain,*' it was '*knowledge of their belief in my innocence, and of their sympathy comforted, cheered, and strengthened me to tread bravely the thorny path of my daily life.*'

The campaign to get Florence released started immediately she began her sentence at Woking Prison. The Maybrick Committee, led with great energy and passion by Alexander MacDougall, the Scottish lawyer based in London, was at the forefront of these efforts. In a circular printed in the *Liverpool Mercury* of 6th September 1889, the Committee invited '*cooperation in taking every legitimate step, whether by legal process or public agitation, which may be open to them*' to challenge and quash Florence's guilty verdict and '*let her go free.*' It said subscriptions were urgently needed '*for engaging counsel, employing detectives and conducting the necessary public agitation.*'[1243]

In Liverpool, the committee came to be seen as the '*London*' Maybrick Society. The *Liverpool Echo* wrote that while the committee had the right to seek new evidence, it should not go down the path of re-examining the existing evidence which had already been tested and refuted. The newspaper also commented that Mr Cleaver had declined to cooperate with the committee, as he believed '*the operations*' of MacDougall '*will injure rather than benefit whatever shadow of a case Mrs Maybrick may possess.*'[1244]

Despite criticisms of his approach, MacDougall never wavered from his belief in Florence's innocence. In 1891, he published a book in which he castigated all those who had prosecuted Florence, and he ridiculed the evidence against her. Christie called the book '*highly bombastic, endlessly repetitious... in which the barrister glorified the defendant and blackened all her accusers.*'[1245]

MacDougall targeted much of his criticism on Michael and Edwin Maybrick, Mrs Briggs, Mrs Hughes and Nurse Yapp, whom he came close to accusing of planting the arsenic to incriminate Florence. Although MacDougall does make some telling points, his crusading zeal caused him at times to lose his objectivity. One of the more effective points that MacDougall made was in response to the Home Office's statement issued when Florence's sentence was commuted. The official statement included the line: '*The evidence leads clearly to the conclusion that the prisoner administered and attempted to administer arsenic to her husband with intent to murder.*' The problem was, as MacDougall pointed out, '*intent to murder*' was a different charge to the one that Florence had been put on trial for and found guilty. On that basis alone, he argued, the charges against her should be quashed.

MacDougall contacted many of the witnesses at the trial to try to get them to change their evidence. He had some success here with Alfred Schweisso, the head waiter at Flatman's Hotel, who stated he had only been able to recognise Florence at the inquest after a police inspector had twice pointed her out. When the Baroness found a prescription from a Parisian chemist for a face wash that contained arsenic while unpacking Florence's possessions, she immediately took it to MacDougall. He obtained a copy of the prescription from the chemists' records. This issue was to form an important part of the campaign to secure Florence's release, as it supported the statement she had made in court about extracting arsenic from flypapers to use as a cosmetic. MacDougall later fell out with the other members of the Maybrick Committee, though he continued his campaign to get her released.

Apart from the publicity generated by the committee, the case was also kept at the forefront of the public's attention due to articles written by the medical experts who testified at the trial. One of these was by Dr Carter. The Maybrick case had '*brought Carter unwelcome publicity*' and some public criticism.[1246] As a result, in January 1890, he vigorously defended his actions in an article published in a Liverpool medical journal.[1247] After outlining James' symptoms, he wrote that both he and Dr Humphreys had agreed that the patient's irritation had '*most likely been originally caused by some grave indiscretion of diet away from home.*' He felt the key moment in the case came when he tested the bottle of Valentine's meat juice on the evening of 10th May, and detected '*some metallic irritant in the juice.*' This discovery made it impossible for him to issue a certificate as to the cause of death. Carter wrote the symptoms and post-mortem appearances were '*believed by all who witnessed them, to be those of an irritant poison, and arsenic was found in his liver, intestines and kidneys in such an amount as to warrant Dr Stevenson in his belief that the whole body contained nearly a fatal dose at the time of death.*' Carter spent much of his article dealing with the conflicting opinions of the experts. He admitted that James' symptoms, such as the lateness in the onset of diarrhoea and the slightness of abdominal pain, were '*in some respects anomalous;*' however, he argued that '*anomalies are much commoner in arsenical than in other kinds of poisoning.*' He provided explanations why they might have occurred, for example the use of morphia may have reduced the level of abdominal pain.

One point made by Carter was to be an issue later raised by Florence's supporters. He said he was '*very sceptical*' that Florence had been able to dissolve arsenic powder in the meat juice. He had conducted his own tests and found, '*even with the aid of frequent and violent shaking, one-quarter of a grain was the outside amount that I could dissolve*

[1243] *Liverpool Mercury*, 6th September 1889.
[1244] *Liverpool Echo*, 28th January 1890.
[1245] Christie T.L., op cit., pages 208-209.
[1246] Sykes A. H., 'Dr William Carter: A Medical Life in Victorian Liverpool' in *Medical Historian*, No. 21, 2009-2010, page 57.
[1247] Carter W., 'Notes on the Maybrick Trial' in *Liverpool Medico-Chirurgical Journal*, (no.18, Jan 1890) pages 118-145.

in a bottle of undiluted juice in twenty-four hours.' Dr Carter's tests provided support for the view of Mr Davies, the analyst, who had testified that the arsenic had been added in the form of a solution rather than a powder. If Dr Carter and Mr Davies were correct, and Florence just added a powder to the bottle, then the meat juice bottle which had been the key exhibit at the trial could not have been the one that Nurse Gore had seen Florence '*suspiciously*' move.

Another medical expert who agreed with Florence's guilty verdict was the Home Office pathologist, Dr Stevenson. In an article published in *Guy's Hospital Reports* he outlined the inferences that could be drawn from the chemical analysis of James' viscera. He was of the '*opinion that the results of the analysis were in entire accordance with death from arsenic,*' as he stated in the witness box.[1248] According to Levy, Stevenson's objective in writing the article was '*to defend the evidence of the medical witnesses of the Crown.*'[1249] Levy was critical of some of the statements made by Stevenson concerning James' illness, such as his contention that '*diarrhoea was in fact present at a period when it seems to me that all the evidence implies to the contrary.*'[1250]

There can be no doubt that Stevenson's article contained misleading statements. For example, he wrote that James attributed his illness on the day of the Wirral races to '*an overdose of Dr Fuller's medicine.*' This was something that both Addison and Mr Justice Stephen had also said at the trial, but it was untrue. James told the servants at Battlecrease that his illness had been brought on not by Dr Fuller's medicine, but by the medicine he had received in the post. Stevenson downplayed James' habit of taking arsenic and other dangerous drugs, saying there was no evidence that he had taken arsenic '*within six months of his decease.*' This ignored the testimony of Sir James Poole, who had heard James say he took poisonous substances just one month prior to his death. Stevenson also wrote that the soaking flypapers had been '*carefully covered up*' by Florence, and that '*no proof*' was provided to show that she was in the habit of using arsenical face washes. Once again, these were not accurate remarks. Even Mr Justice Stephen stated in his summing-up that no attempt had been made by Florence to hide the flypapers, and two witnesses had been put forward by the defence to testify to use of arsenical solutions as a cosmetic treatment.

Stevenson's article referenced some of the evidence provided by the defence medical experts at Florence's trial and, as a result, Drs Tidy and Macnamara felt they had to respond. In 1890, they produced a pamphlet entitled *The Maybrick Trial: A Toxicological Study*. In it, they listed 20 principles of arsenical poisoning and said that only one or two were present in James' final illness and then only in the closing stages.[1251] In James' body, only one-tenth of a grain of arsenic was discovered, which was '*only one-twentieth part of the smallest recorded fatal dose.*'[1252] As a result, the doctors wrote that the arsenic found in James' body may have been taken in merely medical doses, and secondly, that the arsenic may have been taken a considerable time before either his death or illness.

The two doctors wrote: '*Our toxicological studies led us to the three following conclusions: 1. That the symptoms from which Maybrick suffered are consistent with any form of acute dyspepsia, but that they absolutely point away from, rather than towards, arsenic as the cause of such dyspeptic condition. 2. That the post-mortem appearances are indicative of inflammation, but that they emphatically point away from arsenic as the cause of death. 3. That the analysis fails to find more than one-twentieth part of a fatal dose of arsenic, and that the quantity so found is perfectly consistent with its medicinal ingestion.*'[1253]

Arsenical Poisoning Symptoms
Countenance tells of severe suffering.

James Maybrick's Case
Not so described.

Arsenical Poisoning
Very great depression an early symptom.

Maybrick
Not present until towards the end.

Arsenical Poisoning
Fire-burning pain in the stomach.

Maybrick
Not present.

Arsenical Poisoning
Pain in stomach increased on pressure.

1248 Stevenson T., 'The Maybrick Trial and Arsenical Poisoning' in *Guy's Hospital Reports*, Vol. XLVI, (J & A. Churchill, London, 1889) pages 307-328.
1249 Levy J.H., op cit., page 452.
1250 Ibid., page 455.
1251 Tidy C. M. and Macnamara R., *The Maybrick Trial: A Toxicological Study*, (Bailliere, Tindall and Cox, London, 1890) pages 6-7.
1252 Ibid., page 29.
1253 Ibid., page 30.

Maybrick
Pressure produced no pain.

Arsenical Poisoning
Violent and uncontrollable vomiting, independent of ingesta.

Maybrick
'Hawking rather than vomiting'; irritability of stomach increased by ingesta.

Arsenical Poisoning
Vomiting not relieved by such treatment as was used in Mr Maybrick's case.

Maybrick
Vomiting controlled by treatment.

Arsenical Poisoning
During vomiting burning heat and constriction felt in throat.

Maybrick
Not present.

Arsenical Poisoning
Blood frequently present in vomited and purged matter.

Maybrick
Not present.

Arsenical Poisoning
Intensely painful cramps in calves of the legs.

Maybrick
Not present.

Arsenical Poisoning
Pain in urinating.

Maybrick
Not present.

Arsenical Poisoning
Purging and tenesmus an early symptom.

Maybrick
Not present.

Arsenical Poisoning
Great intolerance of light.

Maybrick
Not present.

Arsenical Poisoning
Eyes suffused and smarting.

Maybrick
Not present.

Arsenical Poisoning
Eyeballs inflamed and reddened.

Maybrick
Not present.

Arsenical Poisoning
Eye-lids intensely itchy.

Maybrick
Not present.

Arsenical Poisoning
Pulse small, frequent, irregular and imperceptible from the outset.

Maybrick

Not so described until approach of death.

Arsenical Poisoning
Arsenic easily detected in urine and faeces.

Maybrick
Not detected, although looked for.

Arsenical Poisoning
Tongue fiery red at tip in its entirety, or fiery red at tip and margins, and foul towards base.

Maybrick
Tongue not red; '*simply filthy.*'

Arsenical Poisoning
Early and remarkable reduction of temperature generally.

Maybrick
Temperature normal up to day preceding death.

While the articles of the medical experts had created renewed interest in the Maybrick case, their impact was far eclipsed by an article written by William Stead. Stead (1849-1912), one of the most colourful journalists of the late Victorian period, was the editor of the *Review of Reviews*, a newspaper he had founded and largely wrote. In August 1892, he claimed to have received a letter from a Mr Neuberg in South Africa who alleged that in January 1892, a man called Henry Wilson confessed to him on his death-bed that he, along with an unnamed woman, had tampered with the medicine intended for James Maybrick by adding arsenic. Neuberg said that in March 1892, he had sent the details of the confession to Sir Charles Russell, but as he hadn't received a reply he was informing Stead so he could tell the story in his newspaper. In October 1892, Stead published Neuberg's letter, as well as the confession that Henry Wilson had supposedly told Neuberg.

It is important to note that there are some differences in content between the copies of the confessions received by Russell and Stead. In both, Neuberg stated that Wilson admitted to adding arsenic to James' medicine with the assistance of an unnamed woman; however, in the letter sent to Russell he specified that this woman was a servant girl. There was also some additional information in the confession sent to Stead. Wilson stated that the motivation for his actions was a grudge he had against Florence, so presumably he believed his actions would make it appear as though she had murdered James. Wilson also said there was another person involved called Sarah, but he didn't specify how she was involved or provide her last name.

Although Stead used the letters as a basis for his article on the Maybrick case, questions have been asked about the provenance and authenticity of the documents. Bruce Robinson labelled the Neuberg letter '*South African Fraudulence*,' and is surprised that Stead gave it '*a moment's credibility.*'[1254] He suggests the letter was written by Michael Maybrick as he '*had a grudge against Florence*' and because he would have known that James' mistress was named Sarah; while Henry Wilson, even if he was a real person, would not have known her name.

Although Robinson's view has little credibility, it does seem certain that the letter is forgery. One obvious reason is that if a person named Henry Wilson did exist, and he really had a grudge against Florence, then surely the person he would have tried to poison would have been her, rather than her husband.

In December 1892, the *Liverpool Weekly Courier* labelled the Neuberg letter a '*mischievous hoax*'.[1255] It said that a search by '*special commissioners*' had found '*no man of the name of Neuberg has been known at or near Rietfontein, whence he is alleged to dispatched his letters.*' The newspaper added that it was very strange that such a person, if he existed, would have decided to have sent the details to Stead in London rather than approaching an editor of a local newspaper in the Transvaal.

If Neuberg didn't write the letter, who did? The obvious answer is Stead himself. As a pioneer of investigative journalism, the Maybrick case would have been very appealing to him, and by forging the letter he was providing himself with an opportunity to pursue the story. A modern biographer of Stead wrote that he '*twisted facts, invented stories, lied, betrayed confidences; but always with a genuine desire to reform the world.*'[1256] The fact the letter came from South Africa is suggestive, as Stead was a man who '*almost from boyhood*' had '*been keenly observant of South African affairs.*'[1257] He had a great knowledge of the country and the Afrikaan language, and it would have been easy for him to have written a letter purporting to have come from that part of the world. The research he completed prior to writing his story would have provided him with the name of James' mistress.

[1254] Robinson B., op cit., page 793.
[1255] *Liverpool Weekly Courier*, 10th December 1892.
[1256] Sydney Robinson W., *Muckraker – The Scandalous Life and Times of W.T. Stead*, (The Robson Press, London, 2013) page 256.
[1257] Whyte F., *The Life of W. T. Stead Vol, 1*, (Jonathon Cape, London, 1925) page 269

Stead was also hostile to Lord Salisbury's Government and its Home Secretary, Matthews. He had written an article defending Israel Lipski, a Polish Jewish immigrant accused of the murder of Miriam Angel in 1887, principally as means of attacking the Government.[1258] He was also a man who had a fondness for the opposite sex. A feature of his office was that it was '*staffed almost exclusively by attractive young women.*'[1259] In that sense, one can understand how the case of Florence would have appealed to him. Finally, in the closing months of 1892, Stead's psychological health was beginning to fail. The strain of producing and writing the newspaper, plus his financial difficulties, meant he was '*approaching the borderland of insanity.*'[1260] He was increasingly drawn to eccentric storylines, and it is easy to understand how such a man could have written the Neuberg letter.

In his article, Stead wrote – probably to hide the fact he had written the letter – that he was initially sceptical about the validity of Neuberg's claims, but nevertheless decided to find out if there was any substance to his story. He travelled to Liverpool to investigate the evidence. While there, he received help from another colourful character, William Le Couteur (1858-1905), who was then living in the Broad Green area of the city. Originally trained as a surgeon, Le Couteur was a past president of Liverpool Science Club and a former secretary of the Liverpool Choral and Orchestral Union. As a result of his research, Stead said he found two points on which everyone agreed: firstly, that James was a habitual adulterer; and secondly, he regularly used arsenic as an aphrodisiac '*in the hope of restoring his exhausted vitality.*' He said James kept arsenic everywhere: in his pocket, in his house, in capsules and powders and solutions. Stead labelled James a '*seducer, an adulterer and a debauchee.*' He said before he married Florence, James had a long-term relationship with a young woman who had given birth to five children. Even after his marriage he had continued occasionally to visit this woman. On top of that, James had maintained '*relations with loose women.*'

Stead wrote that Florence's case was not decided by the evidence, but '*solely upon the prejudice imported into the case by the judge on the last day of his summing-up. Sir Fitzjames Stephen, who was much prejudiced against wives suspected of misbehaviour, had worked himself up into a kind of frenzy at the thought of Mrs Maybrick becoming a popular heroine.*' Stead also criticised the actions of the Home Secretary, Henry Matthews, who decided that although there was '*reasonable doubt*' that James actually died of arsenical poison, he still felt that Florence had attempted to administer arsenic to her husband. As Stead pointed out: '*Although the Home Secretary thus summarily destroys the foundation of the verdict of the jury, he refuses to alter the decision that she is guilty of wilfully murdering a man who, he admits, may never have been murdered at all.*' Stead wrote: '*The capital sentence was not inflicted; but penal servitude for life is, under present conditions, a sentence of death. Surely, considering all the circumstances, the time has come for that sentence to be revoked.*'

Whatever the truth about the origins of the Neuberg letter, Stead passionately believed that Florence had suffered a miscarriage of justice. He wrote: '*I cannot resist the conclusion that the case is so scandalous an illustration of the very worst sides of the British judicial system and of the British character, that, if only to give us a chance of burying the matter in oblivion, Mrs Maybrick should be released. I do not care how prejudiced anyone may be against Mrs Maybrick. No Englishman can feel otherwise than ashamed of having to defend the manner in which she has been dealt with by our Courts and our Governments.*'

Although the Neuberg letter is a forgery, Stead's article is significant in a number of ways. Firstly, as he went to Liverpool to examine the facts of the Maybrick case, we have independent verification of some of the more controversial details concerning James and Florence's relationship. Stead's investigations make it clear that James was a regular user of arsenic and that he had a long-term relationship with a woman who wasn't his wife, presumably Sarah Ann Robertson. The fact that Stead had spoken directly to the woman gives his assertions great credibility. Secondly, Stead's article helped paint Florence in a more sensitive and positive light. It broke with the portrayal of her as the immoral woman that Mr Justice Stephen and some newspapers had made her out to be. Therefore, whatever dubious actions Stead may have taken in the process of writing his story, there can be no doubt that his article provided a boost for those who were campaigning to get Florence released from prison.

While Florence's supporters in Britain had succeeded in keeping her cause alive and prominent, they had achieved very little in the way of getting her released from prison. The campaign was given a new lease of life by the determined and energetic actions of Florence's supporters in America. Although she had lost her American citizenship when she married James, to many Americans she remained a citizen of their country and they were determined to rally to her cause. The campaign in America was led by Mary Dodge (1838-1896), an American writer and campaigner who became the '*unchallenged captain of the crusade*' for Florence's release.[1261] Mary Dodge was a woman of great intelligence who, after a short career in teaching, became a successful author, writing under the pen name '*Gail Hamilton*' to avoid personal publicity. As well as her intellectual ability, she was also a woman of

[1258] Sydney Robinson W., op cit., page 138.
[1259] Ibid., page 198.
[1260] Ibid., page 214.
[1261] Christie T.L., op. cit., page 190.

great personal courage and she was prepared to fight long and hard for the causes in which she believed. One of these was Florence Maybrick's plight. As well as her personal qualities, Mary Dodge also had the advantage of being the cousin of Mrs James Blaine, the wife of the Secretary of State in the Benjamin Harrison Presidency, and she was fully prepared to use this connection to the advantage of the Maybrick campaign.

In April 1891, Secretary of State Blaine took the first of a series of '*extraordinary personal measures*' in his efforts to try and secure the release of Florence.[1262] He sent an instruction to Robert Lincoln, son of Abraham Lincoln and the American Ambassador in London, to take up the Maybrick case with the British Prime Minister, Lord Salisbury. Despite his best efforts, Lincoln found the door had been firmly shut on the case by the British Government. He informed Blaine he had spoken to the Home Secretary, Henry Matthews, at a dinner party, and he was '*very firm in his conviction of her [Florence's] criminality, and that if any mistake had been made it was in commuting the sentence at all.*' In August 1891, Mary Dodge persuaded the First Lady, Caroline Harrison, to send a petition to Queen Victoria, who was the one person, in theory, who had the powers to overrule her Home Secretary. Caroline Harrison admitted that she had '*not studied the case carefully,*' but said that she trusted Mary Dodge's views on the subject because she had '*perfect confidence in her ability to get at the truth of the question.*'[1263] The petition stated:

> '*There seems to be the very highest medical and scientific authority in support of the proposition that Mr Maybrick's symptoms were not compatible with the arsenical poisoning. There was, it is understood, an entire absence of proof that Mrs Maybrick administered or attempted to administer arsenic to her husband with intent to kill; while evidence that Mr Maybrick had been in the habit of taking arsenic as medicine was present in the case.*'

It ended, '*In view of all these facts we earnestly, respectfully, and trustfully entreat of your Most Gracious Majesty a pardon and release for Mrs Maybrick.*' The petition was signed by Caroline Harrison, Harriet Blaine (wife of James Blaine) and by the wives of two other American cabinet ministers.

The Baroness referred to the petition in a letter to a Manchester newspaper, optimistically writing that Her Majesty, who was the '*highest type of a mother and a woman, will show mercy*' to Florence and '*restore her to her little children.*' The Baroness rejected the idea that the petition was '*impertinent interference,*' but instead described it as '*an appeal for an American, who has not by the verdict of all England received the fair play so venerated in your honest country.*'[1264] Sadly for Florence, her mother's optimism was not well founded. The petition was badly received by Queen Victoria, who greatly resented being approached directly on the issue. It also angered Salisbury's Government, who saw it as an American attack on the British judicial system.

After these failures to win a reprieve for Florence through diplomatic lobbying at the highest level, her supporters decided to adopt a different strategy. Instead of concentrating their efforts on trying to obtain a pardon, the new approach centred on trying to get a retrial on the basis that the manner in which the trial had been conducted was seriously flawed. For example, the summing-up of Mr Justice Stephen was deeply prejudicial to the defendant's case. There were also criticisms directed at the wording of the commutation of the death sentence by the Home Secretary, who said that while Florence may not have *committed* murder, she was guilty of attempted murder. As one of Florence's supporters wrote: '*The basis of the argument on which we are trying to open the case is that there has been a breach of constitutional law. The thirty-ninth article of the Magna Carta, which is contained in the coronation oath, states that no subject shall be imprisoned on any charge for which he has not been indicted or tried.*'[1265]

In October 1891, the Baroness engaged the highly-respected British law firm Lumley and Lumley to make the case for a new trial.[1266] In order to pay the costs of this new legal challenge the Maybrick Defence Fund was launched, which aimed to raise money in both Britain and America. An account was opened at the Union Bank in Manchester and a target figure of £295 was set, the money to be raised by public subscription. One of the earliest donations came from the Baroness herself, who gave 300 francs to the cause.

In America, Mary Dodge started a public fund-raising appeal with a letter to the *New York World*. The newspaper responded by writing: '*Gail Hamilton [Mary Dodge] is convinced that Americans, especially American women, will generously furnish the needed means and she has asked The World to become the agent through which subscriptions may be made.*' The newspaper said it would '*gladly receive and transmit whatever sums of money Americans may contribute for the purpose of securing for Mrs Maybrick such aid as legal ability in England can furnish. Hers is a cry of innocence against cruel oppression.*'[1267]

[1262] Hamilton G., *Biography of James G. Blaine*, (Henry Bill Publishing Co., Norwich, Conn., 1895) page 695.
[1263] *New York World*, 20th October 1891.
[1264] *Manchester Courier and Lancashire General Advertiser*, 6th October 1891.
[1265] Letter from Albert Kenyon published in the *Manchester Courier and Lancashire General Advertiser*, 6th October 1891
[1266] *Pall Mall Gazette*, 20th November 1891.
[1267] *New York World*, 13th October 1891.

As a result of Mary Dodge's letter and her high public contacts, the money started to pour in. Just two weeks later the *New York World* reported that $1,500 had been raised, and that no more money was currently required. The newspaper listed the names of people who had made donations, including Mrs James G. Blaine and Dr Helen Densmore, who had both donated $100 dollars. The largest amount donated was $456, which came from a fund-raising event given by Clara Morris, a leading American actress, at the Grand Opera House.

Florence showed her appreciation in June 1892, by sending Mary Dodge a letter from prison. This was a real sign of appreciation, as she was only allowed to send one letter every two months. In it, she wrote: '*I feel that I owe you a debt of gratitude for the truly noble, beautiful and womanly manner in which you have used that glorious gift of God – your genius – in the cause of a helpless and sorely afflicted sister.*'[1268]

Although the amount of money raised – especially in America – had been substantial, it appears it was still not sufficient to meet the costs involved in the case. In January 1892, the *New York World* reported that all the money raised from public donations had been exhausted, yet the case was still not ready.[1269] Where all the money had gone is not clear, though it is likely that much of it had been used to pay the arrears for legal services claimed by Florence's solicitors. In a letter to Mary Dodge in September 1891, the Baroness wrote that although Mr Cleaver had been paid between £3,000 and £4,000, he still required an additional £1,000 to cover his costs.[1270]

Attempts to attract new income sources were a never-ending activity for the Baroness. She was not helped in that quest by the suggestion that because she and her daughter owned property in New York, they were actually richer than they made themselves out to be, and therefore should contribute more of their own money to meet the legal costs. To tackle such stories, the Baroness's American lawyers, Roe and Macklin, issued a statement in which they said in the twenty years that they had dealings with the family, they '*never had any reason to doubt their honesty, integrity and trustworthiness.*' They added that the '*position of Mrs Maybrick is a very sad one. Her mother has expended nearly all her resources in her behalf. She has barely enough left to support herself in the simplest manner. Mrs Maybrick would be penniless if she were released today.*'[1271]

One way the Maybrick Campaign attempted to raise money was through a legal case against New York Mutual Reserve Fund Life Insurance Company. Florence assigned all her interests in Britain to her solicitor, Richard Cleaver, and he commenced a legal action against the company as it had only paid half the amount due on James' life insurance policy on the grounds that a convicted felon should not benefit from her criminal act. Although Cleaver was not to be successful, the claim was taken up by Michael and Thomas Maybrick as the executors of James' will. In December 1891, the case was resolved in the Court of Appeal. In a landmark judgement, the judges ruled that '*public policy required that a criminal should not benefit by a contract, but that the crime should not be allowed to interfere with the rights of third parties. Therefore, though the executors could not recover for Florence Maybrick, they could for the state of the deceased.*'[1272] Thus, although the initial action had been started to realise funds for Florence, in the end the money the insurance company did eventually pay out went to pay off James' creditors and then, if any money still remained, it would have gone to his children.

Despite the ongoing financial problems faced by the Baroness, the efforts to secure a retrial for Florence continued with increased momentum. In February 1892, a Liverpool newspaper reported that Mr Walter Lumley and Mr Alexander MacDougall, who were staying in the North Western Hotel, were in the city attempting to gather '*fresh facts*' that could be presented as part of the legal brief.[1273] By April, Lumley and Lumley had finalised their brief. It was a substantial and persuasive document that provided a detailed review of all the evidence that supported Florence's innocence. It placed great emphasis on the negative and prejudicial role the judge played in the trial, and it stressed the contradictory nature of the medical evidence.

One of the most important issues dealt with by the Lumley and Lumley brief related to all the arsenic found in Battlecrease after James' death. Although the purchase of the flypapers was the only direct evidence of Florence having possession of arsenic, Mr Justice Stephen told the jury that Florence '*undoubtedly had access to considerable quantities of arsenic.*' The brief argued that this was a serious misdirection by the judge to the jury. Mr Justice Stephen's comments had been referring to the items containing arsenic discovered in Florence's trunk and in James' hatboxes by Nurse Yapp and Mrs Briggs. The brief stated that both women '*exhibited the most unfriendly feeling' towards Florence, and described the circumstances in which they produced the arsenic as 'so suspicious as to justify the suggestion that the arsenic was not there before his [James'] death.*' According to the brief, Florence '*never had any access to it or knowledge of it at all. There was no evidence as to where or by whom this arsenic was obtained.*' In contrast, the wholesale druggist William Thompson testified at the trial that James had frequently visited his cousin who was employed at Thompson's store and who could have obtained white arsenic from him '*without any difficulty.*'

1268 Maybrick F., op. cit., page 139.
1269 *New York World*, 31st January 1892.
1270 *New York World*, 18th October 1891.
1271 *New York World*, 19th October 1891.
1272 See articles in the *Pall Mall Gazette*, 8th December 1891 and the *Liverpool Mercury*, 9th December 1891.
1273 *Garston and Woolton Reporter*, 27th February 1892.

The flypapers purchased by Florence could not have been the source of arsenic with which certain items were infected, as Mr Davies, the analyst, searched them for the fibres of the flypapers and for charcoal and '*could not find any traces of either.*'

The Lumley and Lumley brief also dealt at some length with the bottle of Valentine meat juice tested by Dr Carter and found to contain half a grain of arsenic. It had been assumed by both the prosecution and defence teams at the trial that this was the bottle that Nurse Gore witnessed Florence handling on the night of 9/10th May. This was an assumption that was never '*proved.*' There was, in the house, another half-used bottle of meat juice from which James had partaken on Monday 6th May. As the meat juice had not agreed with James and made him vomit, Dr Humphreys told James to stop taking the mixture. This bottle did not appear on the list of trial exhibits. A third bottle of half-used Valentine's meat juice was found by Mrs Briggs in one of the hat boxes in the inner-dressing room; this was tested and found to be free of arsenic.

The Lumley and Lumley brief argued the various bottles of meat juice had become confused, and the bottle of meat juice which Florence handled was *not* the one Dr Carter tested and found arsenic. The brief provided two reasons to support its view that the meat juice bottle had become misidentified. Firstly, it provided scientific proof to show that it was '*a physical impossibility for any person to dissolve half a grain of solid arsenic in 411 grains of Valentine's meat juice, which was all the liquid that was in the bottle when it was handed to Mr Davies.*' Florence was clear that she added a white powder to the bottle. There is no reason to doubt her statement, as in making it she was leaving herself open to the charge that she had added a potentially dangerous substance to her husband's food. If Florence hadn't volunteered this information, then there would have been no evidence that she had put anything in the bottle. In his evidence at trial Mr Davies, the analyst, stated that the arsenic in the meat juice bottle must have been introduced in the form of a solution. The only way that could have happened based on the items found in Battlecrease was from a bottle found in the hatbox, Trial Exhibit no. 10, which contained a saturated solution of arsenic. There was, in total, around two grains of arsenic in that bottle. No evidence was provided to show that Florence had any knowledge of that bottle, or any other items found in the hat boxes.

The second reason lies in the contradictory statements allegedly made by Michael Maybrick about from exactly where in James' bedroom he had removed the meat juice bottle. The brief suggested: '*Mr Michael's evidence at the inquest is the true account of where he got the bottle, and that his evidence at the trial is cooked, to suit the evidence of Gore, and that the identity of the bottle is not established.*'[1274]

In her court statement, Florence said that when she left the inner-dressing room she placed the bottle on the small table by the window in the bedroom, before later moving it to the washstand. At the inquest, when Michael was asked by the coroner where he had found the bottle, he answered, '*I found it on the table mixed up with several other bottles.*'[1275] Nurse Gore, who spoke after him at the inquest, said she left the bottle '*on the washstand where Mrs Maybrick had placed it.*' When Michael testified at the magistrates' hearing he said he had taken possession of the meat juice bottle, '*which was lying on the washhand-stand amongst some other bottles.*'[1276] At Florence's trial, he said he had taken it '*from the washstand in the bedroom.*'[1277]

It was the view of the Lumley and Lumley brief that Michael had '*concocted*' his account at the magistrates' hearing and at the trial, in order to fit-in with Nurse Gore's account. At the inquest he had told the truth, and he had therefore removed the wrong bottle which he subsequently gave to Dr Carter for testing. One of the problems with the suggestion that Michael may have removed the wrong bottle of meat juice is that contemporary newspapers provide different accounts for the words he spoke at the inquest. While the *Liverpool Echo* stated he '*found it on the table*' as opposed to the washstand, both the *Liverpool Courier* and *The Times* state he said the bottle was placed '*between two washing basins in the centre of the table.*'[1278]

Elizabeth Brierley, the housemaid, told the inquest that on Thursday 9th May, she had seen Michael '*standing near to the washing stand*' and '*saw him take up something and put it into his pocket.*'[1279] This is usually considered to have taken place earlier in the day, when Michael removed the bottle of Neave's food. Nevertheless, the fact he removed it from the washstand does suggest he was aware some medicine bottles were located at that spot. He had also spent time in the bedroom, and would have observed nurses administering medicines to his brother. What might have confused Michael was the possibility there had been more than one meat juice bottle on the table or washstand. The bottles were all identical, and they were all approximately half-full. It is conceivable that the bottle he removed could have been the one used on 6th May, to which arsenic in solution had been added. If that happened, then the question is who added arsenic to the meat juice bottle? If it had come from the bottle now labelled '*Trial Exhibit no. 10*', found in the hatbox, then the obvious answer is that it was James himself who put it in the bottle.

1274 Maybrick F., op cit., page 305.
1275 *Liverpool Echo*, 28th May 1889.
1276 *Liverpool Daily Courier*, 14th June 1889.
1277 Irving H.B., op cit., page 44.
1278 *Liverpool Courier*, 29th May 1889.
1279 *Liverpool Mercury*, 29th May 1889.

Although this is by no means conclusive, there remains a genuine doubt that the bottle Dr Carter tested and found half a grain of arsenic was the same bottle that Nurse Gore had seen Florence move. The fact that the arsenic had been added in solution, and not a powder, makes it almost certain that it was a different bottle.

Before it was sent to the Home Secretary, the brief was submitted to Sir Charles Russell and three other eminent Queen's Counsel. They unanimously decided that because the verdict had been decided upon by a jury in a properly constituted court of law there were no grounds for a retrial. Crucially, they also added that, had a Court of Criminal Appeal been in existence, there would have been matters for its '*grave consideration.*'[1280]

The views of Russell and the other judges were attached to the brief before it was sent to the Home Secretary, along with an opinion from Alexander MacDougall. He wrote that if the issues raised by Lumley and Lumley regarding '*irregularities of procedure both by judge and jury... can be conclusively proved, the court should be invited, ex debito justitiae [a remedy that the court has no discretion to refuse], to set aside the verdict and order a new trial.*' He again mentioned the fact that, when the Home Secretary had commuted Florence's sentence, he had done so on the grounds that the evidence '*left a reasonable doubt as to whether his death was in fact caused by the administration of arsenic.*' MacDougall argued that her continued imprisonment was unconstitutional, and therefore illegal.[1281]

To support the brief, Mary Dodge organised a petition that contained the signatures of many high-ranking officials in the American Government, including Vice President Levi P. Morton and all the members of the Cabinet. The petition referenced some of the issues raised by Lumley and Lumley, such as the manner in which the trial had been conducted had '*resulted in a profound impression of a miscarriage of justice,*' and that the case would be '*proper for the grave consideration of a court of criminal appeal, if such tribunal existed.*' The petition also referred to Florence's delicate health, and that she was frequently in the infirmary of the prison. It added that her family had a '*strong tendency*' to tuberculosis and, if Florence was not released, she would suffer the same fate as her deceased brother. It concluded by '*earnestly*' asking the Home Secretary to advise the Queen to '*pardon and release*' the prisoner.[1282]

Disappointingly for Florence and her supporters, the legal brief was to be rejected by Matthews. Once again, a petition signed by influential and important American politicians was to have no effect on the British Government. Lord Salisbury informed Lincoln, the American ambassador, that Florence was an adulteress who had attempted to poison her husband when she was supposed to be nursing him back to health.

On 4th August 1892, the Baroness sent an eight-page letter to the Home Secretary from her home in Rouen, France which was received at the Home Office on 15th August. The Baroness wrote in response to a '*communication*' she received on 28th (presumably July) in which Matthews had stated he would '*carefully consider any representations*' from her on the subject of her daughter.[1283] Unlike the Baroness' earlier letters, this one was written on a typewriter and was well-constructed. She raised new issues, such as the fact that no arsenic had been found in Battlecrease in '*lockfast places*' for which only Florence held the key. She questioned what happened to James' clothing, and asked why none of it was ever checked or tested. She was critical of the role of Mrs Briggs, whom she claimed was '*formerly engaged to marry James.*' She also criticised James' brothers, whom she alleged '*lived at a feud with him.*' She was especially critical of Mr Justice Stephen, and wrote that the jury came to the wrong verdict as a result of a '*biased charge from the judge, whose peculiar hatred of women and Americans was an unrealised (or unconscious) motive for his injustice and the colour he gave to motive.*'

The Baroness addressed her letter to Henry Matthews, but on the day it was received at the Home Office there was a change of Government. In the General Election of July 1892, Lord Salisbury's Conservative Party lost its majority in the House of Commons and, on 15th August, Gladstone's Liberal Party formed a minority Government with the support of the Irish Nationalist MPs. The change of Government also meant a change of Home Secretary; Henry Matthews, who had been so opposed to Florence's release from prison, was replaced at the Home Office on 18th August by the more liberally-minded Herbert Asquith, who was pro-social reform.

Most of Florence's supporters were delighted by the change of Home Secretary, and were optimistic that Asquith would be much more open to their pleas for her release. Their hopes were soon dashed. On 26th August, Asquith discussed Florence's case at a meeting with Queen Victoria. Two weeks later, on 9th September, a letter was released by the Home Office stating that a '*petition praying for the release of Mrs Maybrick*' had been received; however, '*the Secretary of State had not been able to recommend her Majesty to comply with the prayer.*'[1284]

Asquith's decision produced a furious response from the Baroness. In a letter to the *Liverpool Weekly Courier*, she wondered how the Home Secretary, who was a supporter of a court of appeal, could have turned down the petition to hold a retrial for her daughter. She wrote it was not possible for a great and powerful country like Great Britain to take any pride '*in retaining a young, delicate woman a prisoner.*'[1285]

1280 *Liverpool Weekly Mercury*, 21st May 1892.
1281 *Liverpool Weekly Mercury*, 21st May 1892.
1282 *Liverpool Mercury*, 22nd June 1892.
1283 HO 144/1639/A50678/D92.
1284 *Liverpool Echo*, 12th September 1892.
1285 *Liverpool Weekly Courier*, 24th September 1892.

Although Asquith's decision was bitterly disappointing to Florence's supporters, it was not unexpected. In a period before the existence of a criminal court of appeal his scope for action was limited, especially when the Queen remained unsympathetic to Florence's plight. It was also the case that many people still believed Florence to be guilty of the crime for which she had been convicted. The *Garston and Woolton Reporter*, in an editorial, commented on the opinion given by the eminent counsel, stating: '*The pitiful death poor Maybrick suffered, and the atrocious and unfeeling manner in which it was brought about by the woman who should have been the first to protect him, appear to have been quite lost sight of now.*'[1286] One positive outcome of the *brief* for Florence was that it helped to increase support for her in the United States. Secretary of State James Blaine wrote that the Brief was '*unanswerable*' and he increased his efforts to try and secure Florence's release from prison.[1287]

The rejection of the petition put forward by the leading American politicians and the unwillingness of the Home Secretary to accept the arguments put forward by Lumley and Lumley, were devastating blows to Florence. She had started her life sentence in Woking Prison in a state of complete despair. Her spirits had been gradually lifted by the knowledge that so many people in Britain and America were rallying to her cause. In 1892, she must have had real hope that there was an end in sight to her prison nightmare. The comprehensive case presented by Lumley and Lumley had provided an effective challenge to all the arguments that had been presented at her trial by the prosecution. She had received support from both the President and the Vice President of the United States. In Britain, Sir Charles Russell was just one of the many influential people who publicly stated she had suffered a miscarriage of justice. Numerous books and pamphlets had been written in her defence. Florence must have thought that this tidal wave of support would have secured her freedom, especially when a new Home Secretary came to review her case.

In a letter written in May 1892, Florence gave some instructions on what clothes she would need when she left prison. She also asked which of her London friends '*would be willing to receive her for a couple of days in the event of her release.*'[1288] Therefore, when Asquith announced that he was not prepared to alter her sentence, all of Florence's hopes were in ruins and she fell back into utter despondency and despair.

Such a desperate mood prompted the most desperate of actions. On 18th December 1892, the *Liverpool Echo* carried a dramatic story about Florence's health and condition in Woking prison, stating that she was: '*lying seriously ill in the hospital of that establishment. Her mother, the Baroness von Roques, has been summoned to see her, and is at present residing near the prison at the village of St John's. She has paid frequent visits to her daughter, who is still in a critical condition, but is gradually recovering. The vicar of the village, Rev W. F. Hamilton, has administered the Sacrament to her. Owing to the reticence of the upper officials the nature of the illness cannot at present be ascertained, but rumour has it that it was a haemorrhage.*'[1289]

In the village of St John's a rumour circulated that Florence had attempted suicide. The Baroness, in an interview to a reporter, admitted that Florence was suffering from insomnia, and was '*terribly depressed in spirits.*' She revealed that her daughter had told her that very day, "*Mama, really I don't wish to live if I have to remain here, I am in a state of exhaustion.*"[1290] Despite this, the Baroness completely denied that Florence had attempted suicide. She said Florence's brother had died of consumption (tuberculosis), and Florence's symptoms were the same. A different version of events was provided by the prison authorities, who briefed the press that Florence had suffered an '*internal haemorrhage*' caused by '*her own carelessness.*' The National Archives files contain a report dated 5th December 1892 by Dr Glover, Medical Inspector, who said he had examined Florence that very day and '*found her in a state of syncope due to sudden and extensive haemorrhage from the vagina.*'[1291] The doctor wrote that Florence had for some weeks '*complained of spitting blood*', and had shown the medical officer every day '*some blood sometimes mixed with mucus.*' She told the doctor that '*this mixture came from her lungs.*' Dr Guy wrote that the hospital's medical officer had inspected Florence, and concluded that her lungs were '*perfectly sound.*'

On 28th November Florence had been secretly observed through a hospital window by the Principal Infirmary Matron, who claimed she had seen Florence get out of bed and place the spitting cup on the floor. She had obtained a dinner knife and then '*introduced this knife so far as the matron could see, into the vagina and withdrew it covered in blood.*' Florence, '*in her manipulation of the knife,*' had '*unintentionally divided the vaginal artery.*'

Florence's supporters were to empathetically deny that her illness was self-inflicted; however, it is noticeable that Florence does not refer to it in her autobiography. One person who provided an alternative account of the events was an ex-prisoner at Woking who said she spent some time talking with Florence while the two of them were in the prison infirmary. She said that one Monday morning the bell in Florence's cell began to ring '*violently.*' When officials went to see what was wrong, they '*found Mrs Maybrick lying prostrate in her cell completely saturated with blood and almost unconscious.*' They wrapped her in a blanket and took her to the infirmary, where they tried to stop

[1286] *Garston and Woolton Reporter*, 21st May 1892.
[1287] Christie T.L., op. cit., page 198.
[1288] *Barmouth and County Advertiser*, 13th July 1892.
[1289] *Liverpool Echo*, 8th December 1892.
[1290] *Liverpool Weekly Courier*, 17th December 1892.
[1291] HO 144/1639/A50678/D133.

the flow of blood. She was to remain in bed for the next three months, with two warders '*constantly attending her day and night, and a doctor going to see her at all hours. She was terribly ill.*' At one point she was in a '*dying condition,*' and an extra chaplain had to be summoned to '*administer the Holy Communion to her. I believe that plenty in the prison now don't know how near a squeak she had.*'[1292]

This version of events sounds more plausible than the story of a prison matron covertly watching Florence through one of the small prison windows. What it does not explain is the cause of the bleeding. If Florence did suffer a haemorrhage of the vaginal artery, then the illness may well have been caused by her own actions. Florence's intention had probably been to obtain blood, which could be placed in the spittoon in an effort to show that her health was deteriorating in prison. Her actions were the product of despair. She had been in prison for three years, and the legal brief by Lumley and Lumley making the case for a retrial had been rejected by the Government.

Florence did gradually recover from her illness, but the incident caused her to lose her visiting rights. Her mother, Baroness von Roques, who had been summoned from France when it was feared that Florence might die, returned home. Florence returned to her cell and slowly settled back into the prison routine.

LINKS TO THE RIPPER DIARY: DID JAMES MAYBRICK WRITE THE *DEAR BOSS* LETTER?

In a passage after he supposedly describes the murders of Elizabeth Stride and Catherine Eddowes on the night of 29th/30th September 1888, the author of the Ripper Diary wrote: '*Before my next will send Central another to remember me by.*' It is a typical line from the journal in that the diarist, interspersed between accounts of his murderous deeds, mentions events that are known to have occurred and are directly linked to Jack the Ripper. The author's aim is to try and provide some historical credibility and authenticity to the Diary. In this particular case, the diarist is clearly alluding to a letter received by the Central News Agency a few days prior to the double killing of Stride and Eddowes. The letter, referred to as the *Dear Boss* letter, is arguably the most infamous and important of all the correspondence sent to the police about the Ripper murders. Its greatest significance was that it was signed *Jack the Ripper* and, following its publication in the press, that was to be the *nom de plume* by which the serial killer was always to be remembered. The same signature (though in different handwriting) was also to be found at the end of the Diary.

The letter also contains the words '*ha ha,*' a phrase which was to feature on several occasions in the Ripper Diary. Another point of interest about the *Dear Boss* letter is that some of the words used in it, such as '*Boss,*' '*fix me*' and '*quit,*' are considered as Americanisms, suggesting that Jack the Ripper could have been an American, or someone like James Maybrick, who had lived there for a while. Paul Feldman wrote '*there could be no denying*' that the author of the Diary, whom he believed to be James Maybrick, was claiming he had sent the *Dear Boss* letter and the *Saucy Jacky* postcard to the police. He added, '*If the letters were a hoax then the diary must be a hoax as well.*'[1293]

The *Dear Boss* letter contains the sentence, '*You will soon hear of me with my funny little games.*' Although it is not entirely clear what the author of the letter means, it does suggest he is hinting at future murderous deeds. The author of the Diary of Jack the Ripper picked up on this line, and used it in the document. While he (supposedly James) was speaking to his friend, George Davidson, about a recent Whitechapel murder, Davidson commented that Liverpool had the finest police force and therefore women could safely walk the streets of the city. The diarist then writes, '*And indeed they can for I will not play my funny little games on my own doorstep ha ha.*' The implication is clear: the diarist is saying that he is killing women in London and not in his home city of Liverpool. On several occasions the diarist refers not to '*funny little games,*' but instead to the altered form of words, '*funny little rhyme(s).*' The justification for these funny little rhymes is that the author, supposedly James Maybrick, is trying to outdo his brother Michael, who was a successful singer and composer. The major problem with this assertion is that Michael did not write the words for his songs and therefore could not be said to be proficient in the art of verse.

25 Sept. 1888

Dear Boss

I keep on hearing the police have caught me but they wont fix me just yet. I have laughed when they look so clever and talk about being on the right track. That joke about Leather Apron gave me real fits. I am down on whores and I shant quit ripping them till I do get buckled. Grand work the last job was. I gave the lady no time to squeal.

1292 *Liverpool Mercury*, 4th October 1895.

1293 Feldman P., op cit., page 244.

How can they catch me now. I love my work and want to start again. You will soon hear of me with my funny little games. I saved some of the proper red stuff in a ginger beer bottle over the last job to write with but it went thick like glue and I cant use it. Red ink is fit enough I hope ha ha. The next job I do I shall clip the ladys ears off and send to the police officers just for jolly wouldn't you. Keep this letter back till I do a bit more work, then give it out straight.

My knife's so nice and sharp I want to get to work right away if I get a chance. Good Luck.

Yours truly

Jack the Ripper

Dont mind me giving the trade name.

Wasnt good enough to post this before I got all the red ink off my hands curse it No luck yet. They say I'm a doctor now. ha ha" [These final lines were written at right angles compared to the rest of the text]

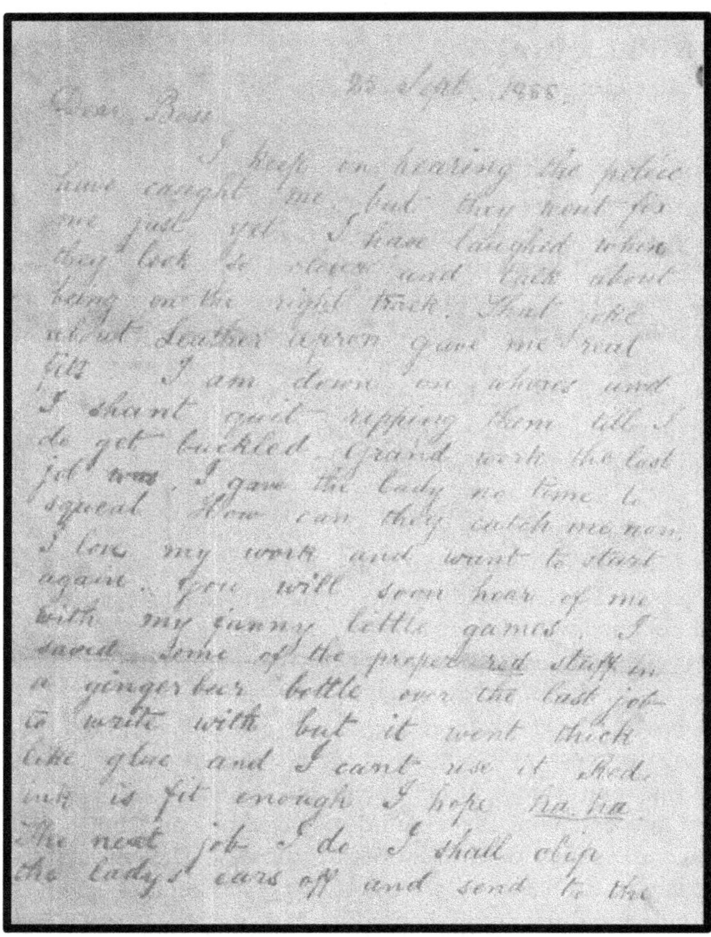

25 Sept. 1888.

Dear Boss

I keep on hearing the police have caught me but they wont fix me just yet. I have laughed when they look so clever and talk about being on the right track. That joke about Leather Apron gave me real fits. I am down on whores and I shant quit ripping them till I do get buckled. Grand work the last job was. I gave the lady no time to squeal. How can they catch me now. I love my work and want to start again. You will soon hear of me with my funny little games. I saved some of the proper red stuff in a ginger beer bottle over the last job to write with but it went thick like glue and I cant use it. Red ink is fit enough I hope ha. ha. The next job I do I shall clip the ladys ears off and send to the

The *Dear Boss* letter which gave Jack the Ripper his name

The *Dear Boss* letter was addressed to '*The Boss, Central News Office, London City.*' The envelope bore a penny lilac stamp, and had on it a London East Central postmark dated 27th September (the letter itself was dated 25th September). It was written in red ink in a mocking tone, starting with the phrase '*Dear Boss*' and ending with the signature '*Jack the Ripper.*'

The Central News Agency was located in Ludgate Circus in London. It was a '*media service that collected reports by telegraph from correspondents throughout the United Kingdom and abroad.*' It had a reputation for '*securing scoops*' and also '*enjoyed a good relationship with the London police forces.*'[1294] The company said they initially thought the letter was a hoax and delayed for two days before passing it on to the police.

The letter referred to a previous murder, presumably that of Annie Chapman, who had been murdered on the 8th September. It also contained the threat to '*clip the lady's ears off*' in the next murder. The police received the letter from the Central News Agency on 29th September. The timing was to prove crucial, as in the early hours of Sunday, 30th September the murders of Stride and Eddowes were to occur. Both the murder victims were found to have cuts to their ears.

A few days later, a second message – known as the *Saucy Jacky* postcard – was sent to the Central News Agency. It was in similar handwriting to the *Dear Boss* letter, but this time it was written on a postcard. Again, it had an East London postmark, dated 1st October 1888. Some of the phrases on the postcard – '*Boss,*' '*Squeal*' and of course '*Jack the Ripper,*' were also found on the *Dear Boss* letter, making it possible that both messages were written by the same person.

I was not codding dear old Boss when I gave you the tip. You'll hear about Saucy Jack's work tomorrow. Double event this time. Number one squealed a bit. Couldn't finish straight off. Had not time to get ears off for police. Thanks for keeping last letter back till I got to work again. Jack the Ripper.

The postcard was passed to the police, who put the two documents together and thought they may have come from the actual murderer. As a result, they released facsimiles copies to the press and asked if anyone recognised the handwriting. This action only added to the hysteria surrounding the murders and provided the killer with the infamous name of Jack the Ripper. According to Sugden, the results of the police action were '*disastrous.*' The publicity about

1294 Evans S.P. and Skinner K., *Jack the Ripper: Letters from Hell*, (Sutton Publishing, Stroud, 2001) page 14.

the letter and card '*did nothing to unmask the killer, or even the letter writer, it did inspire a host of imitative pranksters to deluge police and press in a tide of bogus Ripper letters.*'[1295]

The *Saucy Jack* postcard

Although the police initially believed the letter and the postcard may have been written by the killer, they soon came to view the documents as forgeries. Both Robert Anderson and Melville Macnaghten, two senior police officers at Scotland Yard, believed they had been written by a journalist. Anderson later even claimed to know who the journalist was. There are some clues in the letter that point to the author being literate. For example, all the full stops are in the correct place; there isn't a single spelling mistake, and there are no crossings out. The letter was also addressed to the Central News Agency rather than the police. Some of the language of the letter, such as '*ripping*' and planning to '*clip the ladys ears off*' also points more to a journalist trying to milk a story rather than a real murderer glorying in his crimes.

The police's scepticism about the authenticity of the two documents has been shared by most modern Ripperologists. Rumbelow points out that details of the double murders did appear in the Sunday newspapers of 30th September, and the *Dear Boss* letter was published in a Monday newspaper the next day. Therefore, a clever forger could have produced an '*imitative hoax.*'[1296] Sugden agrees. He also points out that neither of the victims had their ears severed, which the writer of the *Dear Boss* letter had threatened to do. This was despite the fact that he would have had the time to have carried out such an act. Eddowes did have an ear lobe detached, but considering the extensive mutilation to her face and body that was hardly significant. Stride had no marks on her ear apart from an old wound. Sugden concludes: '*In short there is no reason to believe that the Jack the Ripper letter and postcard were anything more than hoaxes.*'[1297]

Another letter that has been directly linked to the *Dear Boss* and *Saucy Jacky* correspondence is the *Moab and Midian* letter. On 5th October 1888, Thomas J. Bulling (1847-1934), a journalist employed by the Central News Agency, sent a transcript of a letter he claimed to have received to Chief Constable Williamson at Scotland Yard. This so-called *Moab and Midian* letter shows some similar features to the two earlier messages, including the author's hatred of prostitutes and some of the words contained within it, such as '*Boss*,' '*ha ha ha*' and '*Jack the Ripper*.' In addition, the letter also contains a reference to a murdered woman whose body had been found in the basement of the building which was part of the construction works for New Scotland Yard. It also referenced certain biblical texts from the Old Testament, suggesting that the person who wrote it, may have had a real knowledge of these religious texts.

Despite its similarities to the earlier messages, there are some very odd features about this particular letter. Firstly, and most importantly, is the question of why Bulling decided to transcribe the letter rather than just sending the original copy to the police. Secondly, what happened to the original copy? It is not in the police files, so they may never have requested the document. All of this is suggestive that the police may have already had doubts about the provenance and authenticity of the letters being passed to them from the Central News Agency.

A recent study into these and other Ripper letters by Dr Andrea Nini has provided valuable new insights into these documents. Dr Nini is the Senior Lecturer and Associate Professor in Linguistics and English Language at the University of Manchester. His areas of teaching and research are forensic linguistics, corpus linguistics, register variation and sociolinguistics.[1298] He made a close examination of the letters whose authors claimed to have been Jack the Ripper. He said that there were four such letters prior to the publication of the *Dear Boss* and *Saucy Jack* correspondence, and some 130 letters after the publication of these letters up until the death of Mary Kelly in November 1888. The fact that so many letters came after the *Dear Boss* letter was made public by the police indicates that many of them were copycat hoaxes.

Dr Nini had two research questions: (1) Was there any linguistic evidence that any of the four pre-publication texts were written by the same person? (2) If there is such evidence, is there any evidence that connects any of the post-publication texts to this person?

Although his methodology was highly scientific, Dr Nini's main aim was to try and identify if there were any words or phrases that could only be found in one or more of the letters, and whether these words were unique to these and

[1295] Sugden P., op cit., page 263.
[1296] Rumbelow D., op cit., page 118.
[1297] Sugden P., op cit., page 270.
[1298] For full details of Dr Andrea Nini, his academic profile and his research into the Ripper letters, visit andreanini.com

could not be found in any other letters – or indeed, any other contemporary written texts. As a result of his research, he concluded that: '*There is very solid linguistic evidence that Dear Boss and Saucy Jacky were written by the same person.*' For example, the phrase '*letter back till I*' is virtually unique to these two texts. He also concluded that: '*there is some evidence that Moab and Midian was also written by this same person.*'

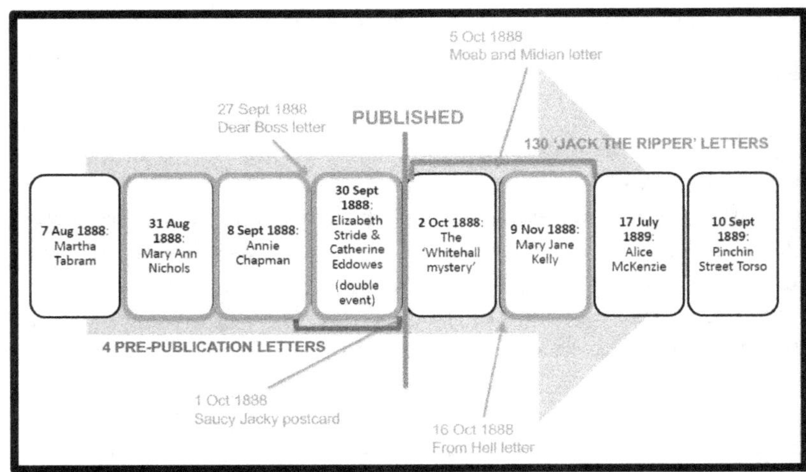

Dr Nini's research into the Ripper letters

Dr Nini's research is groundbreaking in that it suggests that the *Dear Boss* letter, the *Saucy Jack* postcard and the *Moab and Midian* letter were all written by the same person, while the other pre-publication and post-publication letters appear to have been written by different people.

Evans and Skinner wrote that the *Moab and Midian* letter, if '*correctly attributed*' to the same source as the *Dear Boss* and *Saucy Jack* messages, '*certainly tends to detract from the apparent veracity of its predecessors.*'[1299] Therefore, one can say that Dr Nini's findings add weight to the arguments of those who believe that the *Dear Boss* letter is a forgery. His findings also undermine those writers, such as Feldman and Robinson, who feel that their own favoured suspect to be Jack the Ripper penned the *Dear Boss* letter and numerous other letters.

What conclusions can be drawn from examining the three Ripper communications – the *Dear Boss* letter, the *Saucy Jacky* postcard and the *Moab and Midian* letter?

1) All three letters came to be viewed as hoaxes by the senior police officers who were investigating the Ripper murders. In September 1913, Chief Inspector John Littlechild wrote in a letter: '*With regard to the term 'Jack the Ripper' it was generally believed at the Yard that Tom Bullen [sic: Bulling] was the originator, but it is probably Moore, who was his chief, was the inventor. It was a smart piece of journalistic work.*'[1300]

2) The author of these three letters was very likely a journalist from the Central News Agency. The company had a lot to gain financially from the publication of the letters. Evans and Skinner wrote: '*There can be no doubt that the Central News Agency was wringing every last drop of sensation from the [Ripper] communications and selling good copy as a result. These were lucrative and sensational times for the company and many newspapers were buying the stories.*'[1301]

3) The majority of Ripperologists share the view that these three *Dear Boss* messages are hoaxes. Both Rumbelow and Sugden have demonstrated how a clever forger could have constructed the letters.

4) The letters contain certain errors, such as references to the cuts to the ear of Elizabeth Stride that suggest that the author was not in fact the perpetrator of the murderous deeds.

5) The linguistic forensic research of Dr Nini has suggested that the three documents were produced by the same hand, which in turn undermines the credibility of the documents as being authentic and produced by the killer.

6) A major problem for those who suggest that James Maybrick could have written the *Dear Boss* and *From Hell* letters is that the handwriting, as Shirley Harrison admits, does '*not appear to be compatible*' with the handwriting of the author of the Diary.[1302] The handwriting also does not match that of Michael Maybrick.

Examining the Ripper letters can be a highly subjective process. Those who support a particular Ripper suspect tend to cherry-pick the bits of the letters that support their hypothesis and ignore the bits that undermine their hypothesis. Such a process led Feldman to conclusively write that James Maybrick wrote many of the letters, Robinson to write that Michael Maybrick wrote many of the letters, and Patricia Cornwell to write that Walter Sickert wrote many of the letters. They all cannot be correct in their assertions, and it is highly likely that they are all incorrect in their skewered analyses of the Ripper letters. Paul Feldman wrote that if the *Dear Boss* letter was a hoax, then the Diary must also be a hoax. As it is clear that the *Dear Boss* letter *is* a hoax, using Feldman's own criteria, one must conclude the Diary is a hoax as well.

1299 Evans S. and Skinner K., op cit., page 38.
1300 Begg., Fido M. and Skinner K., op cit., page 301.
1301 Evans S. and Skinner K., op cit., page 38.
1302 Harrison S., op. cit., page 130.

20

HOPE AND DESPAIR

The year 1893 began with Florence still seriously ill in hospital and with continued controversy over the cause of her illness. A report in the *St James's Gazette* stated that she had become ill by swallowing needles in order to cause an effusion of blood from her stomach, as she wanted to give the impression she was in the final stages of consumption.[1303]

This report provoked a fierce response from Mary Dodge. In a letter to Prime Minister William Gladstone, Miss Dodge wrote:

> '*I am horrified to find a gross libel in the St James's Gazette on Mrs Maybrick. I ask you to contradict entirely, on my authority, this infamous charge against a defenceless woman, who is powerless to speak, or even to know what is said against her. It is unworthy of the English. Every word is false.*[1304]

Another person concerned by the newspaper report was Henry White (1850-1927), the First Secretary of the U.S. Legation in London. He was an experienced official who had been connected with the embassy in London since 1884, and before that had served at the U.S. Legation in Vienna. Although White was technically outranked by Robert T. Lincoln, the U.S. Ambassador in Britain, he was an influential figure whose role was to liaise with governmental figures below the rank of Head of State and Prime Minister.

White had received a letter from the Baroness informing him that her daughter was seriously ill in a prison hospital, '*transparent, without blood, unable to lift a hand or turn her head.*'[1305] He had also received a communication from John W. Foster (1836-1917), who had replaced James Blaine as Secretary of State for the final months of Harrison's Presidency from June 1892 to February 1893.

Foster instructed White to act promptly to secure Florence's release. White spoke to Asquith about Florence and accepted the Home Office's explanation of her illness. He cabled Foster to inform him that Florence's haemorrhages '*did not emanate from the lungs but were caused by self-inflicted injuries.*' In another dispatch, he wrote that her '*attempt to deceive the authorities has not improved her chance for release.*'

In an unusual move to try and ascertain the true extent of Florence's condition, White sent his wife into Woking Prison to interview her. He subsequently wrote to Foster that his wife had spoken to Florence in her hospital bed, and she had '*looked pale and weary as from loss of blood. She said she was perfectly comfortable and could not possibly be better cared for. All concerned had been most kind to her during her illness – which was not discussed.*' He added the prison governor had told his wife that Florence was '*very reticent and has never portrayed emotions or feelings of any kind, save a great depression at times.*'[1306]

As Mrs White did not discuss Florence's illness with her, it is unlikely she was able to establish the full truth about the cause of her ill-health. Nevertheless, irrespective of whether Florence's condition had been self-inflicted or not, it is clear she had been seriously ill. When the Baroness regained visiting rights in May 1893, she found her daughter still physically weak and still in an infirmary bed.[1307]

Mary Dodge's letter to Gladstone was to be one of the last acts she contributed to Florence's cause. In 1893, whilst she was working on a biography of James Blaine, she suffered a stroke that left her unconscious for weeks. She was to only partially recover from the stroke and she died in Hamilton, Massachusetts, in August 1896. After her death, *The New York Times* carried a rather bitter story that criticised her actions in support of Florence. The newspaper suggested that if she had not presented the case in her '*own brusque and characteristic way, as if she were handling a political question, Mrs Maybrick would have been a free woman today.*' The article argued that the undiplomatic language of the petition she had '*induced*' all the wives of President Harrison's Cabinet to sign soured relations with the British Government, and made it impossible for the United States to '*resume friendly*

[1303] *St James's Gazette*, 31st December 1892 and 2nd January 1893.
[1304] *New York Times*, 6th January 1893.
[1305] Christie T.L., op. cit., page 179.
[1306] Ibid., page 180.
[1307] *Berkshire Chronicle*, 13th May 1893.

Mary Abigail Dodge (1838-1896)

intercession on behalf of Mrs Maybrick because of this unfortunate incident.'[1308] The newspaper report is partially correct in that the petition was probably counter-productive; however, both Queen Victoria and Home Secretary Henry Matthews would have almost certainly denied a pardon for Florence no matter how diplomatically the request had been made. The article also failed to mention all the other work that Mary Dodge had done over many years in support of Florence.

A real understanding of the energy and determination that Mary Dodge expended campaigning on Florence's behalf can be gained by reading the memoirs of John W. Foster. He wrote that while he was Secretary of State: '*Miss Dodge, with her impetuous temperament, gave me little rest in the consideration of the case... Besides her formal communications to the Department of State, Miss Dodge poured in upon me long personal letters.*'

In one four-page letter to him, Mary wrote: '*May I beg another favour. It is for the most wronged and wretched women in the world... It is the crime of the Nineteenth Century.*' Not long after that, she sent him an eight-page letter, in which she commented:

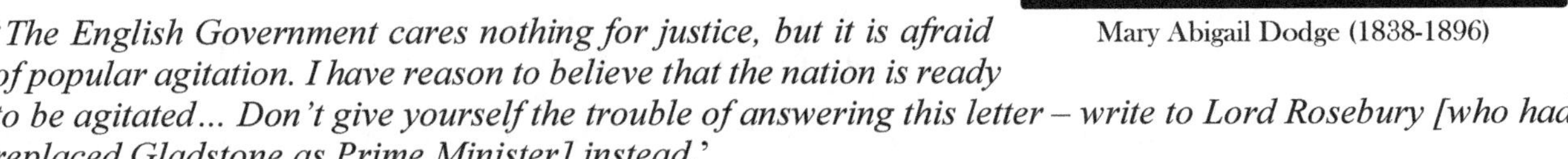

> '*The English Government cares nothing for justice, but it is afraid of popular agitation. I have reason to believe that the nation is ready to be agitated... Don't give yourself the trouble of answering this letter – write to Lord Rosebury [who had replaced Gladstone as Prime Minister] instead.*'

A few weeks later, she sent Foster a sixteen-page letter with a new line of argument. She said the President had demanded that the British Government release Irish-American male prisoners, so why, therefore, could he not do the same for one American woman who was '*an innocent prisoner – the victim of rapacity and tyranny*'?

In one of her final letters to Foster, she included a telegram from Mrs Blaine who said that there was '*hardly anything in life I myself desire so much as to give Mrs Maybrick back to her mother.*' Mrs Blaine added that her husband, who was close to death at the time, was '*anxious that an effort should be made*' to secure Florence's release. Foster said he had been so '*influenced by these appeals*' that he '*instructed our Minister in London to make some verbal and unofficial representations to Lord Rosebury.*' Foster added that Mary Dodge's '*untiring efforts*' and his own '*feeble intervention*' were to no avail; Florence remained '*languished in prison.*'[1309]

In 1893, President Cleveland (1837-1908) replaced President Harrison in the White House, and in October of that year the new Secretary of State, Walter Gresham, wrote a letter to Thomas F. Bayard, the newly-appointed American Ambassador in London, instructing him to take up the Maybrick issue again with the British Government. In the letter, he wrote:

> '*It is the President's desire that without resorting to criticism of the judicial aspects of the matter and avoiding the beaten paths of argument heretofore unavailing followed, you make discreet representation in the proper quarters with view to ascertaining whether, after this lapse of time, a disposition may not now exist to bring about the release of Mrs Maybrick on condition that she leave England.*'[1310]

The communication is interesting as it shows the new administration was trying to adopt a much more informal and conciliatory approach to dealing with the Maybrick issue. President Cleveland was of the view that previous American interventions, such as the petition sent by Caroline Harrison, had only created hostility and hardened attitudes in Britain. Despite this change of tack by the new American Administration, the efforts ended yet again in failure.

Although Mary Dodge's illness was to remove her from the forefront of the campaign to secure Florence's release from prison, other women soon took her place. One of these was Dr Helen Densmore (1833-1904), the American physician who had already served a term as President of the Women's International Maybrick Association which she had helped to found.

In 1881, she had married Dr Emmet Densmore (1837-1911), a physician and prominent American businessman, who advocated a diet that consisted of fruit, meat, nuts, fish, eggs and milk, which he believed were the natural foods

1308 *New York Times*, 13th September 1896.
1309 Foster J. W., *Diplomatic Memoirs Vol 2*, (Houghton Mifflin Co., Boston and New York, 1909) pages 310-313.
1310 Christie T.L., op. cit., page 202.

of primal man. Helen Densmore attended medical school in America, though she did not graduate.[1311] She shared many of her husband's views and was a notable advocate of the benefits of eating nuts, mingled with fruits.[1312] In the late 1880s, the Densmores moved to Britain and in 1890 they founded the Natural Food Society of London.

Dr Helen Densmore (1833-1904)

In 1893, Helen Densmore published a lengthy pamphlet entitled *The Maybrick Case: English Criminal Law*. In it, she wrote: '*Can those who love justice rest until she is free, and until the only restitution has been made that is now possible for so frightful a miscarriage of justice.*'[1313]

The pamphlet was particularly effective in its attack on the contradictory medical evidence presented at Florence's trial. Here one can see echoes of the Densmores' general criticisms of the medical profession, and the use of conventional drugs to treat a seriously ill patient. They viewed the drug regime that James was exposed to by Drs Humphreys and Carter as the prime cause of his death. Helen Densmore savaged Mr Justice Stephen's role in the trial in a very powerful attack on his character and actions. She wrote his conduct '*was a disgraceful disregard of the true functions of his office. He displayed prejudice and settled disapproval of Mrs Maybrick as a woman from the first.*'[1314]

The partisan nature of the pamphlet is evident in the section where Helen Densmore denied that Florence and Alfred Brierley were intimate. She suggests that Brierley only met Florence in Flatman's Hotel '*for the purpose of giving evidence*,' so as to help Florence get a divorce.[1315] This is clearly inaccurate, but no doubt she was trying to maximise support for Florence by denying her adulterous relationship with Brierley.

The *Liverpool Mercury* was harsh in its criticism of the book, describing it as a '*futile attempt to secure sympathy*' for Florence. The newspaper wrote that Dr Densmore's central argument was that James had not died from arsenical poisoning, but instead his death had been the direct result of him taking a series of deadly and poisonous medicines. The article said that Dr Densmore '*obviously knows very little or nothing of the facts of the case.*'[1316]

Despite some criticisms directed at her booklet, Helen Densmore never wavered in her support for Florence and campaigned vigorously to get her released from prison. In May 1893, she gave a talk on the case at the Pioneer Club in Regent Street, London, telling the audience that if Morden Rigg's statement outlining what James had said to him on the day of the Wirral races had been given in court as evidence, it '*would have gone far to destroy the theory of arsenic poisoning.*'[1317]

As Florence lay ill in Woking Prison infirmary, life for the Maybricks had returned to normal. Michael Maybrick was back touring on a full-time basis. In January 1893, he performed at the first London Ballad Concert of the new year, with his rendition of a nautical song was '*favourably received*' by the audience.[1318]

Edwin Maybrick was again immersed in the volatile world of the cotton trade. In October 1889, he had assumed control of the company he had jointly run with James, when all his dead brother's shares were transferred to him.[1319] He retained the company's offices in the Knowsley Buildings, Tithebarn Street and continued trading for almost the rest of his life.

In January 1893, Thomas Maybrick was elected on to the management committee of Manchester Athenaeum.[1320] He and his wife Julie were very active in the Athenaeum Dramatic Society. In February 1893, they were both involved in a performance of the Gilbert and Sullivan opera *The Pirates of Penzance*. Julie played the part of Edith, while Thomas was praised for the '*careful and satisfactory manner in which the opera was produced.*' Thomas was also credited with a dramatic sketch, *A Gentle Reminder*, which preceded the show, in which a '*homely moral was*

1311 *New York Times*, 27th November 1904.
1312 *The Queen*, 27th September 1890.
1313 Densmore H., *The Maybrick Case: English Criminal Law*, (Swan Sonnenschein & Co., London, 1892) page 30.
1314 Ibid., page 16.
1315 Ibid., page 26.
1316 *Liverpool Mercury*, 29th March 1893.
1317 *Eastern Daily Press*, 8th May 1893.
1318 *The Queen*, 21st January 1893.
1319 Records of Liverpool Cotton Association Limited, Board Meeting Book Vol 2. (1888-1894)
1320 *Manchester Courier and Lancashire General Advertiser*, 30th January 1891.

pleasantly interpreted' by the performers, who included his wife.[1321] Thomas was also successful is his business life. In 1882, he had bought shares in the newly-launched firm of H. Atwood Beaver in Manchester.[1322] Michael Maybrick also bought shares in the company that appears to have been an offshoot of R. Atwood Beaver and Co, cotton brokers and general produce brokers, of Old Hall Street, Liverpool. They had a Manchester office at 40 Dickenson Street, which was the address at which Thomas was listed. Beaver had been one of the mourners at James' funeral. H. Atwood Beaver were the '*makers-up and packers*' of goods '*by means of steam, hydraulics or other motive power.*'

The year 1893 also saw the tragic death of George Davidson, James' closest friend. In February that year, the *Liverpool Echo* carried a '*police notice*' with a £10 reward for any information concerning the disappearance of Davidson. He was described as a '*cotton merchant, about 55 years of age, height 5ft. 7in., stout build, grey hair, reddish moustache with little side whiskers, dark coat, striped trousers, and dark overcoat, black felt hat with flat top.*' The same edition also carried a story about the missing man, stating that his friends feared he might have committed suicide. After dinner on 10th February, he left his apartments in Chatham Street, saying he had been suffering from insomnia of late and was going to take a walk around the square, but never returned. When his office was searched, letters were found in his clothes '*relating to a loan of some £200 for which the lender was pressing in his demands, intimating that if the money was not repaid by a certain date, it would be necessary to apply to some of his friends in Scotland. As Mr Davidson was not at that moment in a position to meet the debt it is believed that this preyed upon his mind and drove him to desperation.*'[1323] Two weeks later, the *Liverpool Echo* reported that George Davidson's body had been found at Millom in Cumbria, where it had been '*cast on the shore. A very great friend of the deceased recognised the body, and at the inquest held yesterday a verdict of "Found Drowned" was returned.*'[1324]

If money troubles had led to the sad demise of Davidson, they were also the perennial problem of the Baroness. In August 1893, a bill was filed in the Chancery Court in Richmond, Virginia by L.D. Yarrell, her legal counsel, charging David W. Armstrong, the Baroness' former attorney, with defrauding her out of her rightful share of the income derived from the sale of over 2,500,000 acres of land in Virginia, West Virginia and Kentucky. The Baroness had entered into an agreement with Armstrong in 1879, by which he was employed to recover any land and properties to which he could show she was entitled. Armstrong was to receive half the value of any money raised by the sale of these lands. In 1887, Armstrong informed the Baroness he had found a buyer, Mr Harrison T. Groom, for the only part of the Kentucky lands which was of any value. He said she could expect only $5,000 or $10,000 from her share of the sale if it was successfully completed. Sometime later Armstrong told the Baroness that the negotiations with Groom had broken down, and several difficulties needed to be overcome before he would agree to purchase the land.

In 1889, when Florence was on trial, the Baroness urged Armstrong to quickly close the Kentucky negotiations so she would have the money to fund her daughter's defence. In the bill filed in Richmond, the Baroness claimed that during a lull in the trial when the jury were considering their verdict – a time when both Florence and herself were totally distracted by events in court – they were asked to sign documents they had not read and had not been properly explained to them. The Baroness said in signing the deeds she was not made aware that she was in fact agreeing to sell all the land she claimed in Kentucky, as well as millions of acres in Virginia. She was told the Kentucky properties were to be sold for $20,000, of which half the money would be accredited to Armstrong. The $10,000 accredited to her was received long after the execution of the deed, and one-third of that sum was retained by William Potter for services he claimed to have performed in connection with the sale, such as discovering the whereabouts of Baron von Roques.[1325] In the bill, the Baroness charged Armstrong with receiving far more money from the land sale than he actually declared to her. The Baroness alleged that Armstrong had in fact received $85,000 for the sale, plus an additional $20,000 from an English syndicate for other parts of her estate. As a result, the primary object of the Baroness' legal action against Armstrong was to have the court decree the deeds which she had signed during the trial in Liverpool in August 1889 null and void. The further object of the suit was to have Armstrong render an account of all the moneys received by him while he acted as the Baroness' attorney from the land sales and transfers, a figure which was estimated in some quarters to be in excess of $300,000.[1326]

Armstrong responded by filing a denial of the charges made by the Baroness in the court at Richmond. He stated he had never deceived the Baroness in any way, and declared he had paid her far more than she was really entitled to for her interests in the land, which he said he had purchased himself. Armstrong told a reporter from the *New York Times* that the '*whole affair is a great piece of scoundrelly misrepresentation. I have papers and letters from the Baroness von Roques, and from other persons connected with her, which clearly show that my dealings with her are*

1321 *Manchester Courier and Lancashire General Advertiser*, 20th February 1893.
1322 *Liverpool Daily Post*, 10th April, 1882.
1323 *Liverpool Echo*, 23rd February 1893.
1324 *Liverpool Echo*, 10th March 1893.
1325 *The Times* (Richmond, Virginia), 2nd August 1893.
1326 *Boston Daily Globe*, 26th August 1893.

of the most honourable character.' He said that in his own bill presented to the court he had shown '*conclusively that every one of her allegations is false.*'[1327]

Armstrong's counter-allegations were fully supported by William Potter, who offered to provide Armstrong with all his correspondence with the Baroness, although he warned him that reading the letters might '*upset your Christian patience and destroy your respect for the ten commandments.*'[1328]

In mid-November 1893, the Baroness had to temporarily abandon her case against Armstrong. The following month, Armstrong successfully moved a motion in the Chancery Court to dismiss the case.[1329] The reason behind the Baroness' decision to halt legal proceedings was she had received news that Florence was '*dying*' in Woking Prison.[1330] The Baroness explained what happened in a letter to Rev John Philips Thurston Ingraham (1817-1906), who was the Episcopal Rector of Grace Church in St. Louis, Missouri.

The Rev John Ingraham was the brother to the Baroness' mother and also to Rev. Joseph Holt Ingraham, who had been the rector in Mobile, when Caroline Holbrook (as the Baroness was then called) arrived in the city. He was therefore an uncle to the Baroness, and a great uncle to Florence. He was also one of the three trustees of the Baroness' and Florence's estate. Rev John Ingraham was to become one of Florence's most ardent supporters in America, believing firmly that his great-niece had suffered a terrible miscarriage of justice. He told a reporter that while he did '*not want to say anything that will offend English people,*' it did seem to him that '*English justice overreaches itself.*'

In her letter to Rev Ingraham, the Baroness wrote that when she had last seen her daughter, about four weeks earlier, she had been '*cheerful, resigned and seemed determined to bear her fate with Christian fortitude.*' Florence was employed in the kitchens in the prison, and '*save when she is too ill to work, has little time to reflect upon the wretchedness of her condition.*' The Baroness believed that Florence's confinement in prison was '*killing her,*' and the British authorities '*will surely liberate her; when they know that she is dying.*' The Baroness said she didn't think her daughter would receive a pardon, but did believe she might be '*quietly liberated.*' Although the Baroness claimed her daughter was dying, this was not the case, though it is likely she had fallen ill again.

In her autobiography, Florence described her work in the prison kitchen writing that her duties were '*to wash ten cans, each holding four quarts; to scrub one table, twenty feet in length; two dressers, twelve feet in length; to wash five hundred dinner-tins; to clean knives; to wash a sack of potatoes; to assist in serving the dinners, and to scrub a piece of floor twenty by ten feet.*'

Florence said that besides herself, there were eight other women on hard labour in the kitchen. Their day: '*commenced at 6am and continued until 5:30pm. A half hour at breakfast time, twenty minutes at chapel, one hour and a half after the midday meal, and half an hour after tea summed up our leisure. The work was hard and rough. The combined heat of the coppers, the stove, and the steamers was overpowering, especially on hot summer days; but I struggled on, doing this work preferably to some other, because the kitchen was the only place where the monotony of prison life was broken.*'[1331]

Florence described the kitchen as the '*show place*' that was inspected by all the visitors to the prison. She wrote that during the four years she worked there she saw many people, including '*the Duke of Connaught, Sir Evelyn Wood and his staff, Lord Alverston, Sir Edward du Cane, the late Lord Rothschild, and Sir Evelyn Ruggles-Brise, besides judges, magistrates, authors, philanthropists and others of an inquiring turn of mind, who had obtained the necessary permit to make the tour of the prison under the escort of the governor or one or two of his satellites.*'

As Florence toiled away in the kitchens at Woking, new evidence started to appear that cast doubt on her conviction. In November 1893, a newspaper reported that Mr Bird, the head of the wholesale chemical works of Messrs A. Bird and Sons of Birmingham, had recently informed *Food and Sanitation* that a short time prior to the death of James Maybrick, a lot of glycerine was offered to his firm by a German manufacturer. When Bird's company analysed a sample of the product, they found it contained a large proportion of arsenic. Although Bird rejected the German batch, he said it was likely to have been sold in large cities like Birmingham, Manchester and Liverpool by other companies who may not have tested the glycerine for impurities. Evidence to support Bird's view came from a report by Mr T. Fairley, the public analyst for Leeds. In December 1893, he analysed eight samples of commercial glycerine on sale to the public, and found that five of them contained appreciable quantities of arsenic.[1332]

This new information was directly relevant to Florence's case as one of the items found in Battlecrease that had been tested by Mr Davies and found to contain arsenic, was a blue bottle of Price's Glycerine. At Florence's trial, both Nurse Gore and Nurse Callery said they had refreshed James' mouth with glycerine and borax, though it was never clear whether the glycerine used by the nurses had actually come from the blue bottle containing arsenic. Even if it had, the dosage would have been so low that it would not have caused James any harm. Mr Justice Stephen

[1327] *New York Times*, 26th August 1893.
[1328] Graham A. and Emmas C., op cit., page 248.
[1329] *Altoona Mirror*, 8th December 1893.
[1330] *Saint Joseph Herald* (St Joseph, Missouri), 15th November 1893.
[1331] Maybrick F., op. cit. pages 97-101.
[1332] *Liverpool Mercury*, 16th January 1894.

mentioned the bottle in his summing-up, saying if James' mouth had been moistened with poisoned glycerine, then '*it is certainly a very shocking result to arrive at.*'[1333]

MacDougall in his 1891 book, quoted from a pharmaceutical journal which stated the arsenic in the bottle may not have been put there by Florence, or anyone else; instead, the action of glycerine on the glass may have caused the arsenic to be extracted out of the glass bottle.[1334] Levy noted that the sulphuric acid used in preparing glycerine was often obtained from iron pyrites, which contains arsenic. Therefore, arsenic was frequently found in glycerine, and in similar quantities to the amount discovered in the blue bottle.[1335]

While Bird's statement about arsenic in the glycerine had provided a positive lift to the Maybrick campaign, it was soon to be over-shadowed by the new evidence compiled by Mr Jonathan E. Harris, the solicitor of the Baroness, who was based at 69 Leadenhall Street, London. On 11th April 1894, Harris submitted this evidence, which was essentially a series of signed declarations, to Asquith at the Home Office. He coupled the declarations with a covering letter from himself, in which he confidentially asserted that once Asquith had read the new evidence, Florence's detention would '*be a thing of the past.*' He added, rather ominously, that he had other evidence in his possession, which on '*grounds of public policy and respect for our legal system*' he was '*anxious to suppress.*'[1336] Whether he did have any suppressed evidence is unknown, but it is doubtful because he never released this into the public domain.

The first four of Harris' declarations were designed to support Florence's assertion at the trial that she bought the flypapers in order to make a cosmetic solution. The Baroness wrote that in 1890 she was opening up a box of items that had belonged to her daughter and found the Bible that had originally belonged to Florence's father. As she turned its pages, a piece of paper fell out which was picked up by her servant, Marie Salome Meyer. When the Baroness read the paper, she identified '*the earliest of several prescriptions for face wash*' that Florence possessed which included arsenic in the list of ingredients. The prescription was marked with the name '*Brouant,*' a chemist and perfumer in Paris. The Baroness said she communicated with Monsieur Brouant to ask him if he had a copy of an entry in his books showing he had dispensed such a prescription. He replied affirmatively, and sent a copy of it to the Baroness who attached to it her declaration along with a copy of the prescription.

The second declaration was from the Baroness' servant, Marie Salome Meyer, who confirmed the details the Baroness had outlined in her own declaration. The third declaration came from Edouard Bourgeois, who was clerk to a company of Parisian solicitors. He confirmed he had inspected Monsieur Brouant's books, and had seen the entry relating to the prescription purchased by Florence in July 1878.

A fourth declaration was made by Anna Ruppert, of Regent Street, London, who described herself as an '*expert in the treatment of human skin.*' She had treated more than 125,000 people, including '*members of the English Royal Family.*' In more than 10,000 cases, she had found that her lady clients '*practised the use of arsenic.*' The majority of those were '*acquainted with the fact*' that arsenic '*could be obtained from flypapers*' and they occasionally purchased them in order to extract arsenic. The other five declarations were all linked to Harris' attempts to show that James was an '*arsenic-eater.*' One of them was from Harris himself, who said that one of his representatives had called at the factory of Alfred Bird and Sons, and he had confirmed Bird's statement that a batch of glycerine had gone on sale which had contained high levels of arsenic. Two declarations were from people who knew James, and who had witnessed him put arsenic in his food or drink. Franklin G. Bancroft stated that between the years 1874 and 1876, when James had lived in Norfolk, Virginia, he had frequently been in his company. He stated that:

> '*from time to time I have seen him take from his vest pocket a case resembling a cigarette case, which contained a packet of white powders, and placed the contents of one such powder on several occasions into the glass of wine (usually Chablis, claret or champagne) he was at the time drinking, and swallow the same. Seeing him take this powder, I did on one occasion, ask him what it was, and the said James Maybrick replied, "Longevity and fair complexion, my boy!" and he subsequently informed me that the said white powders were composed of arsenic among other ingredients.*'[1337]

Captain John Fleming, a master mariner from Halifax, Ontario said he had known James when he lived in Norfolk sometime between 1882 and 1884. He recalled seeing him putting a grey powder on his food. When he asked James what it was, he replied '*arsenic.*' Fleming said he had been shocked, and had said to James, '*Good God, man, that is a deadly poison.*' He replied, '*We all take some poison more or less; for instance, I am now taking enough arsenic to kill you.*' James said he took arsenic '*once in a while*' because it strengthened him. Fleming added that after that

---

[1333] Irving H.B., op cit., page 349.
[1334] MacDougall A.W., (1891), op cit., page 488.
[1335] Levy J.H., op cit., page 395.
[1336] For Harris' letter and details of the seven declarations, see: *Evidence in the Maybrick Case, 1894*, (King, Bell and Railton, London, 1894).
[1337] The affidavit is printed in Maybrick F., op. cit., pages 391-392.

event he had frequently seen James putting a similar powder on his food. Unfortunately for Florence, Fleming had been in the Dutch East Indies at the time of her trial and therefore had been unable to give evidence.[1338]

Although all the declarations were important, the most significant one came from Valentine Blake, whose statement was confirmed by another declaration from his then employer, Mr W.D. Nation. Blake recalled the time in January 1889 when he had met James in Liverpool. He said James had agreed to help Nation's company in the campaign to launch Ramie Grass as a substitute for cotton on the British market. In return, Blake agreed to provide James with arsenic, which was used in the manufacture of the product. A month later Blake returned to Liverpool and gave James about 150 grains of arsenic in three packets: one packet of white and two packets of black arsenic, mixed with charcoal. Blake's affidavit helped explain why there was so much arsenic in Battlecrease.[1339]

One person whom Harris could not get to sign an affidavit was Nurse Yapp. The Home Office records contain a request from a Mr Murrin in 1894, who was asking for police protection for his wife, formerly Nurse Yapp, who had worked at Battlecrease. He accused Harris, the Baroness' solicitor, of harassing his wife. He alleged that Harris got into their house under false pretences, and then accused his wife of '*having worked up the case against Mrs Maybrick.*'[1340] Harris wanted Alice Murrin to change her evidence, but she refused and Harris was thrown out of the house.

Within weeks of Harris submitting the new evidence in the Maybrick case, the Central News Agency in London was reporting that the Home Office had not acceded to the declarations presented for the release of Florence.[1341] Harris responded by turning the submission into a pamphlet and sending it to as many news agencies as possible. The pamphlet was accompanied by a letter from the Baroness, in which she wrote:

> '*I have been told, although I have not been able to establish the truth of the rumour, that the repeated refusals received from the Home Office officials to give me the attention I ask is due to their having secret adverse evidence. If such is the case, and the nature thereof made known to me, I am certain of being able to refute it as I am also certain of my daughter's innocence of the crime, either of murder or the attempt.*'[1342]

The release of the pamphlet provided new impetus to the campaign, and newspapers reported there was '*something like a Maybrick cult in London.*'[1343]

In early June 1894, MacDougall announced he was planning to send a '*form of requisition*' to the Home Secretary calling '*for a public reinvestigation*' into the Maybrick case. He was keen to stress that the requisition was not a '*petition for mercy*' from the prisoner's friends, but was instead a '*requisition on behalf of the public for a public reinvestigation*' to ascertain '*whether a miscarriage of justice has occurred, and, if so, who is responsible for it.*' He said such a process would meet the beliefs of both those who believed that Florence was proved guilty at a '*properly conducted trial,*' and those who believed '*there may be an innocent woman passing a life-death in our midst.*' MacDougall said the requisition had already received some 500 signatures, and when 1,000 signatures are '*attached to it*', it would be presented to the Home Secretary.[1344]

In July 1894, the Baroness visited Liverpool '*for the purpose of seeing some influential people on behalf of her daughter.*'[1345] During her stay in the city, she was the guest of Mrs Louisa Rigg and her husband. The Riggs' domestic servant was Mary Cadwallader. The publication of the pamphlet containing the new evidence and the demand for a reinvestigation of the case stirred public opinion, but singularly failed to move the Home Office. The latest setback had some negative repercussions, including a falling-out between MacDougall and the rest of the campaign leaders.

One person who remained true to Florence's cause was Sir Charles Russell. In April 1894, he had become a member of the Privy Council, and in May 1895 he was raised to the peerage as Lord Russell of Killowen, his native village in County Down, Ireland. In July 1894, he had been appointed Lord Chief Justice of England, a role that made him Head of the Judiciary in England and Wales. It was a post he was to hold until August 1900, being the first Roman Catholic to occupy the position since the Reformation. Despite Russell's elevation to the highest ranks of British society, he continued to devote time and effort in trying to secure Florence's release from prison. In June 1895, in a letter to her in prison, he wrote: '*I beg to assure you that I have never relaxed my efforts where any suitable opportunity offered to urge your release ought to be granted. I feel as strongly as I have felt from the first that you ought never to be convicted, and this opinion I have very clearly expressed to Mr Asquith, but I am sorry to say hitherto without effect.*'[1346]

[1338] Irving H.B., op cit., page xlii.
[1339] HO 144/1639/A50678D/702.
[1340] HO 144/1639/A50678D/192.
[1341] *Eastern Evening News*, 12th May 1894.
[1342] *Wells Journal*, 31st May 1894.
[1343] *Halifax Evening Courier*, 21st May 1894.
[1344] *Hastings and St Leonards Observer*, 2nd June 1894.
[1345] *Liverpool Daily Post*, 17th July 1894.
[1346] Maybrick F., op. cit. page 240.

The Petitioner not to write on this margin.

To the Right Honourable Her Majesty's Principal Secretary of State for the Home Department.

THE PETITION OF THE ABOVE-NAMED PRISONER

HUMBLY SHEWETH—

I wish respectfully to submit to your Lordship's kind consideration, the question — whether it is not possible in order to meet the exigencies of my case, to make some exception to the Rule which prohibits a prisoner from writing to a Judge, or any person, holding office under Government. This Rule not only precludes all direct communication with the Counsel of my case, Lord Russell, but has also proved a serious hindrance to the proper expression of my wishes & sentiments, to friends & relatives who happen to hold official appointments in England & the United States, & who are desirous to receive some direct word from me.

I shall also feel deeply grateful to your Lordship, for an extension of time, as my mother — the Baroness de Roques — future visits, on the ground of her failing health & inability to take the long journey from France every 3 months as hitherto. I have not seen her since October, but the love & unexampled devotion which can triumph over pain & weakness to come & comfort me, pleads for itself.

I beg to subscribe myself your Lordship's humble & obedient Servant

23rd April 1895. Florence E. Maybrick

Prays that the Rule which prohibits prisoners writing to a Judge or any person holding Office under Govern^t. may be relaxed in her case, as it prevents her holding direct communication with her Counsel Lord Russell & certain friends & relatives who hold Official Appointments in England & the United States and who

LAG

(4621)

Petition sent by Florence Maybrick in April 1895 to the Home Office requesting permission to be able to write directly to Lord Russell (Chris Jones collection)

In June 1895, Lord Salisbury, the leader of the Conservative Party, became British Prime Minister for the third time and Sir Matthew White Ridley (1842-1904) replaced Asquith at the Home Office. A change of Home Secretary was always welcomed by Florence's supporters as they hoped the new incumbent would be more open to their pleas for clemency than the previous office holder. On hearing the news that White Ridley had replaced Asquith, the Baroness returned from America where she '*been making exertions to secure petitions*' in support of her daughter, and took up residence in England.[1347] With the help of Messrs Cleaver of Liverpool, she set about providing White Ridley with information that might persuade him to release Florence. According to Ralph Blumenfeld (1864-1948), the London correspondent of the *New York Herald* and later editor of the *Daily Express*, the Baroness '*bombarded incessantly*' the new Home Secretary with petitions and applications and for a period, '*came every morning to the Home Office.*'[1348]

On 20th August 1895, an Irish Nationalist MP, Mr T.P. O'Connor, raised Florence's case in a question to White Ridley in Parliament. He asked him to '*consider the whole of the evidence and the circumstances of the case and see whether or not he could come to a more favourable judgement than had been arrived at hitherto.*' White Ridley replied that he '*knew nothing whatever of the case*'; however, he did '*promise the best attention he could give to it.*'[1349] Christie refers to O'Connor's question, and suggests that in his answer the Home Secretary alluded to a '*secret dossier*' possessed by the Home Office that proved the prisoner's guilt.[1350] Some years later White Ridley did admit there was a '*Maybrick dossier pigeon-holed at the Home Office,*' but that can hardly be considered surprising as the case was frequently discussed, and civil servants would not have been doing their job properly if they didn't have information and advice readily available for the person in post.[1351]

1347 *Worcester Journal*, 28th September 1895.
1348 Blumenfeld R., *RDB's Diary*, (Heinemann, London, 1930) page 136.
1349 *Liverpool Weekly Courier*, 24th August 1895.
1350 Christie T.L., op cit., page 219.
1351 *Sheffield Evening Telegraph*, 2nd February 1899.

In November 1895, Lord Russell, formerly Sir Charles Russell, wrote to White Ridley saying that Florence *'ought never to have been convicted, and that her continued imprisonment is an injustice which ought promptly to be ended.'* He added he had '*never wavered in this opinion.*' He criticised Henry Matthews, the Home Secretary at the time of her trial, who had commuted the sentence to life imprisonment on the grounds that Florence was guilty of attempting to administer arsenic with intent to murder. Russell continued that it would be seen:

> *'(1) that such a doubt existed as to the commission of the offence for which Florence Maybrick was tried as rendered it improper, in the opinion of the Home Secretary and his advisers, that the capital sentence should be carried out, and (2) that for more than six years Florence Maybrick has been suffering imprisonment on the assumption of Mr Matthews that she committed an offence for which she was never tried by the constitutional authority, and of which she has never been adjudged guilty. This is a most serious state of things. It is manifestly unjust that Florence Maybrick should suffer for a crime in regard to which she has never been called upon to answer before any lawful tribunal. It is not obvious that, if the attempt to murder had been the offence for which she was arraigned, the course of the defence would have been different? I speak as her counsel of what I know. Read the report of the defence and you will see that I devoted my whole strength to, and massed the evidence upon, the point that the prosecution had misconceived the facts; that the foundation on which the whole case rested was rotten,* ***for that in fact there was no murder****; that on the contrary, the deceased had died from natural causes.*' [Authors' emphasis]

Russell finished his letter by stating that if he was '*called upon to advise in my character of Head of the Criminal Judicature of the country, I should advise you that Florence Maybrick ought to be allowed to go free.*'[1352]

It was an extremely powerful statement from a man in his position. It deserved a detailed response from the Home Office, but that was not to happen. Yet again, a well-argued and heart-felt appeal from a person whose knowledge of the case could not be faulted was rejected by the Home Secretary.

Another person who saw the change of Home Secretary as an opportunity to renew the campaign on Florence's behalf was MacDougall. He wrote to White Ridley, requesting an interview to discuss the Maybrick case. On 30th November 1895, Kenelm E. Digby, who had replaced Godfrey Lushington as permanent under-secretary at the Home Office, replied to MacDougall informing him that the Home Secretary could not grant a personal interview. However, he did say he would be '*ready to consider any new representations which her friends decide to forward in her favour.*'

Although MacDougall was disappointed by the reply, he decided to issue a written statement of the case as a whole as it would '*form a record of the event, and serve for her [Florence's] children, as a vindication of their mother from the charge of having murdered their father.*'[1353] In December 1895, he submitted his statement to the Home Secretary in the form of three very detailed letters. Early in 1896, he published the statement in a new book on the case. Like his earlier book of 1891, it lacked structure and had a tendency to be repetitious; nevertheless, it provided a well-argued critique of the key issues and controversies. Significantly, MacDougall argued that the irresistible conclusion to be drawn by examining the facts was that '*strychnine self-administered was the originating cause of James Maybrick's illness.*'[1354] Important new evidence in the case came in an appendix at the end of the book. Dr Coates, Fellow of the Chemical Society, had carried out new experiments on the flypapers, the *Arsenic - Poison for Cats* package and the Valentine's meat juice. He reached clear conclusions on each of these items. They were: '*(1) It is, I believe, a fact beyond contradiction that in the Maybrick case flypapers could not have been used. It is almost impossible for anyone not skilled in analysis to have got rid of the woollen fibres, a few of which would have been proof positive, especially as they are so uniformly stained. (2) The rat or cat poison could not have been used, for the charcoal blocks the way, and could not have been got rid of without filtration, and it is unwarrantable to assume that non-professional persons have such technical knowledge. (3) As to the Valentines' juice, my experiments prove beyond the shadow of an argument that arsenic was not put into it in the form of powder. The failure to dissolve the whole of the arsenic introduced in the above experiments is a very important fact bearing on this case.*'[1355] Coates' conclusions were corroborated by similar experiments made by another scientist, Mr E. Godwin Clayton.

On 22nd February 1896, MacDougall received another letter from Kenelm E. Digby, in which he said: '*I am directed by the Secretary of State to inform you that, having now given fresh consideration to the case in all its aspects, he regrets that he feels himself unable, consistently with his public duty, to advise any further interference with the sentence.*'[1356]

The reply marked yet another dead-end in the Maybrick campaign. The failure of the Home Office in 1892 to take into consideration the points made by Lumley and Lumley had marked a real low in the campaign to release Florence.

1352 O'Brien R. Barry., op cit., pages 261-262.
1353 MacDougall A.W., (1896) op cit., pages 11-12.
1354 Ibid., page 33.
1355 Ibid., pages 249-250.
1356 *London Evening Standard*, 2nd April 1896.

Rather than just meekly accepting that decision, her supporters had fought back with further submissions to successive Home Secretaries. Lord Russell, the Chief Justice of England, had lent his support to the campaign. Yet it was all to no avail; the Home Office remained resolutely opposed to pardoning Florence or allowing her to leave prison early.

The new evidence sourced by Jonathan Harris in 1894, the support of Lord Russell in 1895 and the on-going efforts of MacDougall would have put Florence on an emotional roller-coaster. There would have been times when she must have felt her release was imminent, and times when she lapsed into despair and depression. We get some idea of her fluctuating moods from the reports of prison doctors and from interviews with former prisoners at Woking.

One such interview featured in the *South Wales Daily Post* in October 1895. A former female prisoner at Woking said she had slept for some weeks in the infirmary at the prison in a bed next to Florence, and had a '*great number*' of conversations with her.[1357] She described Florence as a '*splendid talker*;' she was '*very clever and could talk both French and German*.' She said that sometimes Florence could be '*very lively*' and would '*dance about the room before getting into bed*.' When Florence discussed her trial she '*always declared her innocence of the crime for which she was committed*.' The ex-prisoner said she would never forget '*the bitter and utterly despondent way*' in which Florence used to exclaim that her '*life had been sworn away, and how troubled she used to be about her children*.' She said she often heard Florence exclaim that if she could only hear from her children she would feel '*so much happier*.'

In her autobiography, Florence wrote a moving and poignant passage about the pain she felt about not being able to see her children. She wrote:

> '*The innocents – my children – one a baby of three years, the other a boy of seven, I had left behind in the world. They had been taught to believe that their mother was guilty, and, like their father, was to them dead. They have grown up to years of understanding under another name. I know nothing about them. When the pathos of all this touches the reader's heart, he will realise the tragedy of my case.*

Florence's mental turmoil over her children became even worse towards the end of 1895, when she stopped receiving photographs and information about their health and progress. Again, her autobiographical account graphical reveals her raw emotions over this unexpected development:

> '*During the early years of my imprisonment, I received my children's photographs once a year; also, several friendly letters from Mr Thomas Maybrick, with information about them. But as time passed on, these ceased altogether. When I could endure the silence no longer, I instructed Mr R.S. Cleaver, of Liverpool — who had been the solicitor in my case, and to whose unwavering faith and kindness I owe a debt I can never hope to repay — to write to Mr Michael Maybrick to forward fresh photographs of my boy and girl. To this request Mr Thomas Maybrick replied that Mr Michael Maybrick refused to permit it. When the matter was further urged Mr Michael Maybrick himself wrote to the governor to inform me that my son, who had been made acquainted with the history of the case, did not wish either his own or his sister's photograph to be sent to me*.'[1358]

Another source of anguish for Florence would have been the publication in some newspapers in September 1895 of a sensational and simply absurd rumour that she had recently given birth to a child in prison, the father supposedly being a senior prison official. From her home in France, the Baroness responded to the story by calling it the '*grossest libel*.' She said it was '*absolutely false, and all the more infamous that it entirely sets aside all humanity, chivalry, and good and decent feeling*.' The Baroness claimed the story emanated from a well-known member of the British Parliament, who told the story as '*an item of news to an American journalist*.' She added prison rules establish that at no time was any male officer allowed to be alone with a female prisoner, and that a lady matron was always present whenever the governor or the doctor, the only male officers in a female prison, have occasion to see one of the prisoners.[1359]

It is not a surprise that such stories and the setbacks of the year were to damage Florence's health, and she was again to spend time in the prison infirmary. In November 1895, she was to be transferred from Woking Prison to Aylesbury Prison. She later wrote: '*I arrived at Woking ill, and I left Woking ill*.'[1360]

[1357] *Liverpool Mercury*, 4th October 1895.
[1358] Maybrick F., op cit., page 223.
[1359] *Manchester Times*, 27th September 1895.
[1360] Maybrick F., op cit., page 126.

LINKS TO THE RIPPER DIARY: JAMES MAYBRICK AND THE RIPPER LETTERS FROM HELL

The *Dear Boss* letter is the most infamous of the Jack the Ripper letters; however, it was just one of many letters received by the police, the press and various other groups and individuals about the murders. According to Rumbelow, '*at the peak of the murders, the police were being bombarded with an estimated one thousand letters per week.*'[1361] Although many letters were sent at this time, the ones that are of most interest to Ripperologists are those, such as the *Dear Boss* letter, that claim to have been written by the murderer himself. In their study of the Ripper letters, Evans and Skinner list around 220 such missives that are held in the National Archives and in the City of London Record Office.[1362]

After the *Dear Boss* letter, the second most well-known Ripper correspondence is the *From Hell* letter, which was sent to George Lusk, the Chairman of the Mile End Vigilance Committee. He received it through the post on the evening of Tuesday, 16th October 1888. It consisted of a small brown parcel wrapped in brown paper; inside was part of a kidney and a note addressed '*From Hell.*' It read:

> '*Mr Lusk, Sor I send you half the Kidne I took from one woman prasarved it for you. tother piece I fried and ate it was very nise. I may send you the bloody knif that took it out if you wate a whil longer. Signed Catch me when you can Mishter Lusk.*'

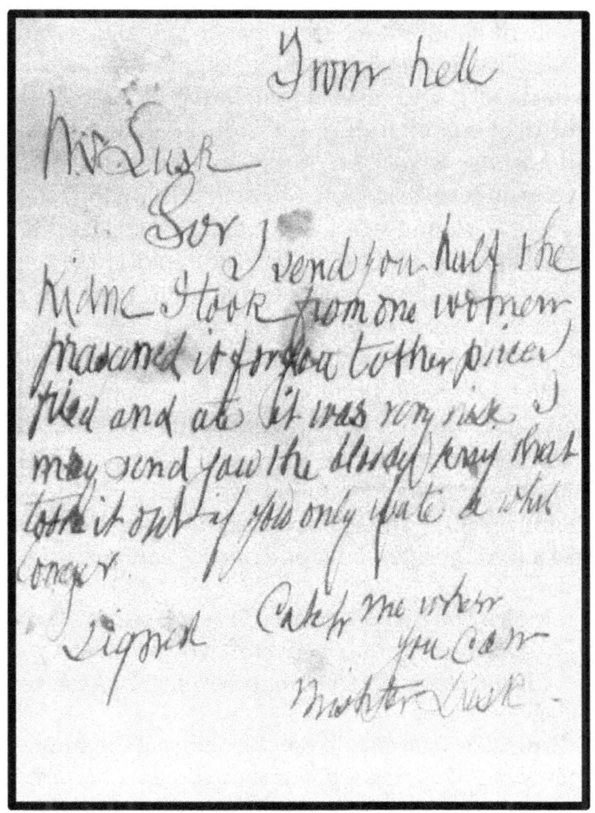

From hell

Mr Lusk

Sor

I send you half the Kidne I took from one women prasarved it for you tother piece I fried and ate it was very nise I may send you the bloody knif that took it out if you only wate a whil longer.

Signed Catch me when you Can Mishter Lusk.

The *From Hell* letter

The kidney was sent to Dr Openshaw, the Pathologist Curator of the London Hospital Museum. He described it as a '*ginny*' kidney, and said it came from an alcoholic woman of about 45 who suffered from Bright's disease and who had died within the last three weeks. As the kidney was felt to be very similar to the one that had been left in Catherine Eddowes' body, it was believed the letter might have actually come from her killer. Openshaw's opinion about the kidney was later disputed by Dr Sedgwick Saunders, the City's Public Analyst, who felt the whole thing was just a hoax by a medical student. Rumbelow has written that opinion is still divided over the Lusk letter, but if it was indeed genuine '*it would be the only letter that we could say, with any certainty, came from Jack the Ripper.*'[1363]

The author of the Diary of Jack the Ripper makes no specific reference to the *From Hell* letter; however, he does imply he removed a kidney from the victim. After describing the murder of Catherine Eddowes, he writes, '*I took all I could away with me. I am saving it for a rainy day ha ha.*' A little later in the document, as part of a verse, he wrote, '*A kidney for supper.*'

If the diarist had taken away one of Eddowes' kidneys, then that must also make him the author of the *From Hell* letter. As the diarist had earlier implied he had written the *Dear Boss* letter, that would make him the author of the two most infamous letters in the history of the Ripper murders.

The problem here is that the two letters are dramatically different in terms of style, punctuation, language and handwriting. The letters are also very different to the handwriting of both James and Michael Maybrick, as well as to the handwriting of the diarist. The usual solution to this problem for those who argue that either James or Michael was Jack the Ripper is to argue that they disguised their handwriting. Bruce Robinson wrote that Michael '*had many styles of handwriting, and used many different pens – his table was littered with quill pens.*'[1364]

Robinson is missing the point. Having many different pens does not equate with having many styles of handwriting. Only a small number of Michael's letters have survived, but what is noticeable about them is that the handwriting is remarkably similar on all of them. James' handwriting is also consistent in its structure and style. There is simply no evidence to suggest that either James or Michael Maybrick wrote the *Dear Boss* or the *From Hell* letters, and the

1361 Rumbelow D., op cit., page 105.
1362 Evans S. and Skinner K., op cit., pages 217-298.
1363 Rumbelow D., op cit., page 121.
1364 Robinson B., op cit., page 383.

evidence that does exist, such as an analysis of the handwriting, points away from them being the authors of these letters.

Although we can easily dismiss James Maybrick as being the author of the *Dear Boss* and *From Hell* letters, is it possible he may have been the author of any of the other 220 or so letters that have been purported to have come from the serial killer? Although most of these letters are usually dismissed by Ripperologists as bogus, Robinson has argued that '*a substantial number of these so-called hoaxes were in fact penned by the Ripper.*'[1365] He points out that many psychopaths believe they are '*cleverer than anyone else and usually they are of high intelligence.*' They like to boast about their superiority, and their ability to escape punishment. They like to poke fun at those who are trying to capture them; '*virtually everything he [the Ripper] wrote was intended to ridicule the authorities, most especially senior policemen.*'[1366]

One of the problems in suggesting a large number of the Ripper letters are genuine is that they vary enormously in terms of handwriting style, paper, ink and geography, being mailed from all around the country. Robinson attempts to get around this difficulty by suggesting the changing locations reflects the movements of a man who was travelling extensively, such as a singing artist like Michael Maybrick. He also suggests that, as Michael was constantly in and out of the capital during October 1888, he was unable to kill prostitutes in London. As he '*very much enjoyed murdering, he took advantage of his engagements to keep the fun alive*' by writing mocking letters to the police. He even suggests that some of postmarks on the letters '*synchronise*' with the towns and cities on Michael's concert tour dates.[1367] He provided an example to substantiate this statement: an advert stating that Michael would be performing in Bromley on 30th October 1888 and a letter sent to an Inspector Reilly at Bromley Police Station, in which the writer says if he doesn't receive money for information on the whereabouts of the Whitechapel murderer, the killer '*will start work on some of the hores of Bromley.*' The problems with this letter are it is undated and no '*hores*' were murdered in Bromley. It is also the case that letters claiming to be from the killer, listed numerous other places he could be found in London, including Clapham Junction, Kentish Town, Hackney, Clerkenwell, Hampstead, Waltham and Battersea. It is therefore not the strongest piece of evidence and, it is linked to Michael and not James Maybrick.

Although most of the letters are almost certainly hoaxes some have been linked to James Maybrick, although these links are extremely tenuous. One letter of note was sent to the *Liverpool Echo*, and printed in the newspaper on 10th October 1888. The letter was in response to one printed the previous day, which claimed the Ripper was about to kill in Dublin. Written on a postcard, it said:

> '*Strafford Street. Dear Sir, – I beg to state the letters published in yours of yesterday are lies. It is somebody gulling the public. I am the Whitechapel purger. On 13th, at 3pm, will be on Stage, as am going to New York. But will have some business before I go. Yours Truly, Jack the Ripper DIEGO LAURENZ (Genuine).*'

Professor Rubinstein has argued that the message is '*arguably the most important clue that we have.*' He suggests that '*Diego*' is Spanish for James, while '*Laurenz*' is meant to rhyme with Florence. He therefore argues this could be seen as '*virtual proof that James Maybrick was Jack the Ripper.*'[1368] Although it is an interesting letter, the notion that it is virtual proof is absurd.

On 12th October the *Liverpool Echo* reported that two days earlier a young lady had been walking along Shiel Road in Liverpool when an elderly lady, in an agitated state, warned her not to go into the nearby park. She explained that '*a few minutes previously she had been resting on one of the seats in the park when she was accosted by a respectable looking man dressed in a black coat, light trousers and a soft felt hat, who inquired if there were any loose women about the neighbourhood, and immediately afterwards he produced a knife with a long thin blade and stated that he intended to kill as many women in Liverpool as in London.*'[1369] As this incident occurred on the same day that the Diego Laurenz letter was published in the *Liverpool Echo*, some, such as Robinson, have suggested that the two events were linked and that Jack the Ripper may have been in Liverpool at that time. A London detective was sent to Liverpool to investigate the incident in Shiel Road, but no new evidence was unearthed. It was just one incident in a long list of similar incidents that occurred up and down the country. Such reports are not really surprising, when one remembers that the whole country had been gripped with fear following the double murder in Whitechapel on 30th September.

Another letter of interest is the so-called '*Liverpool letter.*' This letter was headed '*Liverpool, 29th inst. [presumed to be September 1888]*' and said: '*BEWARE I shall be at work on the 1st and 2nd inst. in the Minories at 12 midnight, and I give the authorities a good chance, but there is never a Policeman near when I am at work. Yours Jack the*

1365 Ibid., page 359.
1366 Ibid., page 391.
1367 Ibid., page 368.
1368 Rubinstein W.D., 'Hunt for Jack the Ripper' in *History Today*, Vol. 50, May 2000.
1369 *Liverpool Echo*, 12th October 1888.

Ripper Prince William St., Liverpool. P.S. What fools the police are I even give them the name of the street where I am living.'

Shirley Harrison made the point that Prince William Street is just off the main road from Aigburth to Liverpool city centre, and James may have passed it on the way to work. Paul Feldman made a more telling point when he focused on the Minories, the London address mentioned in the letter. This was a street relatively close to where Gustavus Witt had his offices when James worked for him in the 1860s and 1870s. In his book, Feldman wrote he had shown that James had lived in Whitechapel, and had worked only a short distance from the scene of the murders; crucially, both of these facts were unknown when the Diary surfaced in 1992. He wrote, '*No self-respecting forger could even contemplate that sort of luck, particularly when his chosen subject was believed to live and work in Liverpool.*'[1370] Feldman is only partially correct in his assertion as James never lived or worked in Whitechapel, although it is the case that at certain points in his life he did live and work relatively close to the area where the murders were much later to be committed. Gustavus Witt, who knew James well, had the highest regard for him as a person and business partner. He would have rejected out of hand the idea that he was a psychopathic killer. Finally, although the Liverpool letter does have its interesting points, the original letter has long disappeared. It is therefore very difficult, if not impossible, to draw any real conclusions from it. Like so much else about Ripper speculation, it interests and tantalises the observer, but fails to deliver anything of substance.

A more recent theory, proposed by Carl Davies, sees some of the Ripper letters being carefully constructed to conceal messages within the text as a result of codes, ciphers and cryptograms.[1371] One such cipher is the Caesar shift cipher, named after Julius Caesar, who employed it when sending messages to his subordinates. It involves substituting a letter by another letter some fixed positions up or down the alphabet. Davies suggests that *Maybrick* is the key word to be employed when deciphering the letters. In one example, he applies this process to a letter which reads: '*Dear Boss, I am living in 129 C Rd... and I mean to do another murder tonight in Pen Rd to night. Yours truly Jack the ripper.*'

M		A	Y	B		R	I	C		K
N	↑	B	Z	C	↑	S	J	D	↑	L
O		C	A	D		T	K	E		M
P		D	B	E		U	L	F		N
Q		E	C	F		V	M	G		O

Davies argues that the word Pen is an important clue; if you employ a three letter upward shift, the P becomes M, E becomes B, and N becomes K. He uses the '*129 C Rd*' as a route to get the letters: A, Y, R, I, C. When he adds these letters with M, B and K, he is able to produce the word '*Maybrick.*' Davies' theory is interesting, but far from convincing. He selects certain Ripper letters and ignores others; he selects certain words from those letters but ignores others. In one bizarre example, using a somewhat arbitrary process, he manages to squeeze out the letters L, B and W from a rhyme in the Diary and writes '*L.B.W. – leg before wicket, a default in the game of cricket which occurs on the "crease" and results in the batsman being declared out.*' He then pointed out that James lived in Battlecrease. Apart from the fact that the house was not named after anything to do with cricket, it is a highly contrived link in which the facts are seemingly designed to fit the theory, rather than the theory being fashioned out of the facts.

Although it is unlikely that any of the letters sent to the police claiming to come from the murderer were actually genuine, there are examples of serial killers who have written letters to the police. For example, Peter Kürten, the Dusseldorf murderer who partly modelled himself on Jack the Ripper, wrote letters to the newspapers in the same manner that he believed the Whitechapel killer had done. He was able to avoid capture for a long period of time as he successfully disguised his style of handwriting. Therefore, it is possible that one or more of the letters from the person claiming to be Jack the Ripper, such as the infamous *From Hell* letter, were penned by the killer.

As far as linking any of the letters to James Maybrick is concerned, there is no evidence of any real merit. There are some vague and tenuous connections, such as in the letter signed *Diego Laurenz*, but none of these amount to anything other than interesting coincidences. Proof of guilt, even in the vaguest of forms, they certainly are not. Although it is not known if the murderer wrote any of the Ripper letters, one thing that is clear; the only group to benefit from them were the newspapers, who used them to sensationalise storylines and boost sales. In truth, the main contributions of the letters – especially the anonymous ones, were essentially negative – wasting a great deal of police time and stirring up public opinion and hatreds, especially against minority groups such as the Jews and foreigners.

[1370] Feldman P., op cit., page 265.

[1371] Davies S.C., *The Funny Little Games of Jack the Ripper: Cryptic Clues from the Whitechapel Killer* (Amazon, Great Britain).

21

AYLESBURY PRISON

When Woking Prison first opened in 1869, almost 800 women were incarcerated within its walls; by September 1895, there were only just over 200 women in the prison. The decline in numbers was felt to be the result of women receiving shorter sentences rather than any real decrease in female crime.[1372] As a result of the changing circumstances, it was decided to convert the prison into an army barracks and transfer the remaining prisoners to the newly-refurbished, all-female Aylesbury Prison.

In early November 1895, 206 female convicts were transferred from Woking to Aylesbury in groups of around 35 per day over six days. The journey took five hours, travelling via London on the North Western Railway, and from Aylesbury Station to the prison in a covered horse-drawn carriage.[1373]

Florence was one of the first group of convicts to be moved on Monday, 4th November. A female warder entered her cell and gave her a '*long, dark cloak covered with broad arrows, the insignia of the convict.*' She was then taken to the chief matron's office, where the other prisoners of Star Class were waiting, and handcuffed. Florence wrote:

> '*A male warder stepped forward and told me to hold out my hands, where-upon he fastened on a pair of handcuffs and chained me to the rest of the gang. This was done by means of a chain which ran through an outer ring attached to each pair of handcuffs, thus uniting ten women in a literal chain-gang. This was to me the last straw of degradation – the parting indignity of hateful Woking; but happily, this was a painful prelude to a more merciful regime at Aylesbury.*'

Florence remembered the special train, with its male warders, and the crowds who lined the road to the station, despite it being bitterly cold and raining heavily:

> '*We were objects of morbid curiosity to the idle and curious people, who may or may not have felt sorry for us. But to be stared at was most distressing to all... When we got out at Aylesbury it was with difficulty that a passage was made for us. The prison-vans were in readiness, and we were rapidly driven away. I felt weak and faint and cold.*'

Aylesbury Prison

When inside Aylesbury Gaol, Florence's handcuffs were removed, leaving her wrists '*bruised and sore.*' The chain which bound her to her fellow prisoners was unclasped. The prisoners were then taken up two flights of stairs and, each one in turn, was locked into a cell. Florence later recalled, '*thus ended my second journey as a prisoner.*'[1374]

With the closure of Woking Prison, Aylesbury became the only female penal institution in England. Until October 1895, it had been used for male prisoners, but they had been either released or moved to other prisons. A reporter from a local newspaper visited the facility in August 1896 and described the surroundings as '*not being very terrible. Large elm trees spread their foliage around the red pile of buildings which constitute the prison for women – and a plentiful disposition of shrubs would not indicate the approach to a convict establishment; but then women are not subject to so rigid a discipline as the sterner sex, and there is nothing to appal*

[1372] *Manchester Times*, 25th September 1895.
[1373] *Buckinghamshire Advertiser*, 9th November 1895.
[1374] Maybrick F., op. cit. pages 129-132. Florence mistakenly gives the year she was transferred as 1896 rather than 1895.

when one enters the precincts of Aylesbury Prison.'[1375] The reporter said he'd not been permitted to see Florence, but he had heard that the '*years of her servitude have told severely on her health and constitution. She is a very well-behaved prisoner, and often exercises a very good effect upon the other convicts.*'

The prison regime at Aylesbury was more relaxed than Woking, with the prisoners even allowed to talk to one another for one hour every day. Florence appreciated the softening of some of the more severe prison regulations, later writing: '*Six months after our arrival, there came a change of authorities, and with the passing of the years a more enlightened regime was instituted by the Home Office.*' The prisoners were allowed to receive three photographs of near relatives and keep them in their cells. Previously, these had to be returned within 24 hours.

Florence believed the best rule change was the one that reduced the intervals between letters and visits by one month. The number of letters permitted to be sent by a prisoner varied according to their stage in prison life. In the fourth stage, a letter was allowed every two months, with an additional occasional letter if the prisoner's conduct had been good. The time of solitary confinement at the beginning of the prison sentence was reduced from nine months to four, and when it was completed the prisoners were able to work in '*association*' with other inmates in one or other of the prison workshops.[1376]

Another change welcomed by Florence was the introduction of the Board of Visitors. Their role was to '*act as a guaranty to the public that everything is honest and above board, and that there can be no possibility of inhuman treatment.*' Florence believed that they did:

> '*much to ameliorate the prisoners' condition. Whereas, at one time the women slept in their clothes, they are now provided with nightdresses; instead of sitting with their feet always on the stone floor, they are now allowed a small mat, as well as a wooden stool; and, as the result of many complaints regarding the rapid decay of teeth, toothbrushes are allowed, a concession which I much appreciated. For a short time felt slippers were granted us, but these have been discontinued on the ground of expense. The same beneficent influence also secured wide-brimmed hats for the women. Formerly they had nothing to protect their eyes, and the reflected glare from the stone walls was the cause of much weakness and inflammation.*'

The Home Office appointed Lady Battersea and Adeline, Duchess of Bedford, to be the Lady Visitors for Aylesbury Prison, and both women assumed the responsibility with the '*deepest sense of consciousness and zeal.*'[1377] The Duchess of Bedford, a woman renown for her philanthropic work, was a regular visitor to the prison and she tried to find gainful employment for the female convicts once their sentence was completed. The Duchess met Florence on numerous occasions and it was claimed that, over time, she became sympathetic to Florence's cause and was one of her '*champions.*'[1378]

Although the Duchess in private may have supported Florence, as a result of her role as Lady Visitor, she never publicly expressed any opinion about her guilt or innocence.[1379] Florence told an American reporter who visited Aylesbury Prison, that the Duchess of Bedford came to the prison once a fortnight, while Lady Battersea came at least once a month. Florence said both women were '*so kind, and I can talk to them alone, and say to them a great many things that I could not say to anyone else, and you do not know what it is to be for a little while alone in the presence of refined, cultured women.*'[1380]

Despite these positive changes, life in a Victorian prison remained harsh. The cells were still very Spartan by modern standards, having no heating or gas lighting.

In September 1896, Dr George Walker, who was both prison governor and medical-officer, issued his report for the year ending 31st March 1896.[1381] He said the total number of prisoners for the year had been 191 males (now all moved) and 305 females, including the 206 moved from Woking Prison. He said that although the behaviour of the prisoners '*had been on the whole good,*' with 253 out of the 305 women incurring '*no report whatever*', some had committed offences against prison regulations. During the year, 33 female inmates were guilty of violence, and there had been 108 other breaches of prison regulations by women, with some offending more than once. The punishments for these offences had included dietary punishment, loss of stage, class and privilege. Walker commented that the '*industry of the prisoners had been undoubtedly good.*' In total, 21,436 lbs of twine had been manufactured; 17,088 mail bags had been made for the use of the Post Office, and a large quantity of clothing had been made – including all the uniforms worn by the female officers.

1375 *Bucks Herald*, 15th August 1896.
1376 Maybrick F., op cit., pages 132-137.
1377 *Bucks Herald*, 9th January 1897.
1378 *Halifax Evening Courier*, 15th December 1900.
1379 *New York Times*, 23rd December 1900.
1380 *Sunday Inter Ocean* (Chicago), 26th September 1897.
1381 *Bucks Herald*, 26th September 1896.

After a few months at Aylesbury, Florence petitioned the Home Secretary to reconsider her case, with a view to an early release. In April 1896, after she heard the Home Secretary had refused to reopen her case, she wrote a defiant letter to her mother. She asked her to thank Lord Russell and Judge Yarrell, the family's attorney in America, on her behalf as she was not allowed under prison rules to write to them personally. She told her mother to assure Lord Russell that he would have '*no cause to be disappointed*' in her as she had '*inherited indomitable courage and tenacity.*' She would '*not yield to wrong or be conquered by circumstances, or be overwhelmed by outward events be they what they may.*' She described her life in prison as '*long and dreary,*' but said her spirit was still '*strong,*' although the '*flesh must and does suffer grievously under the strain.*' Near the end of the letter she made some heartfelt and emotional comments to her mother, saying her visits were always so '*pleasant and sweet.*' She added, '*never was there a mother like unto my own dear mother, so devoted and so loving.*' She finished by writing that she was '*not feeling either strong nor well,*' but she still had faith in God, who '*has never failed us yet.*'[1382]

In the early years of her imprisonment in Aylesbury, Florence worked in the prison officers' mess. Each officer had a small bedroom in a separate building within the prison precincts, in which they slept and spent their off-duty time. Florence described her duties as follows: '*All meals are served in the mess-room, and consist of breakfast at seven o'clock, lunch on turn between nine and eleven, dinner at twelve-thirty, tea at five, and supper whenever they are off duty. The cooking is excellent and varied. A matron is in charge of the commissariat department, and has four prisoners of the "Star Class" working under her. I did scullery work, which consisted of washing up all the crockery, glass, knives, forks, and spoons used at these five meals, besides all the pots and pans required in their preparation. As a staff of twenty-five sat down to these frequent meals daily, the work was very hard and quite beyond my strength.*'[1383]

Florence's stint in the officers' mess ended abruptly when she had a nervous breakdown. She blamed her illness partly on insomnia, and partly on the '*unrelieved strain and stress of years of hard labour.*' Her mother visited Florence in August 1896 and was shocked by her physical condition. She described her appearance as '*weak, emaciated, grey in colour, like a dead person.*'[1384] A week later, a report by the Medical Officer stated that Florence '*sits listlessly in her chair all day, appears to take no interest in her surroundings, and makes no effort to arouse herself, either by reading, or employing herself at needlework, or in any other way.*'[1385]

Gradually, Florence's health began to improve. A couple of months later, the same Medical Officer found her '*less despondent,*' and reported that '*she no longer says that she has no wish to live, and from my own observation, I am of the opinion she is endeavouring to free herself from the mental depression from which she has suffered during the past few months.*'[1386] Florence was to remain in one of the infirmary cells for about 18 months. She wrote that, during her years of imprisonment, she: '*learned many lessons I needed, perhaps, to have learned during my earlier life; but, thank God, I was no criminal! I was being punished for that of which I was innocent. I believe it is God's task to judge and ours to endure, but I could not understand what his plans and his purposes were. I believed they were good, although I could not see how eternity itself could make up for my sufferings.' During her years in prison, Florence's Christian faith remained strong and she believed that she would not have been able to have endured prison life without 'God's sustaining grace.*'[1387]

In all three prisons in which she was incarcerated, the prison chaplains were a source of strength to Florence. She described them as '*the only friend of the prisoner,*' as they were the '*only one within the walls to whom she may turn for sympathy and advice.*'[1388] Attending the weekly religious services was important to Florence. The services provided far more than spiritual comfort; they were also a welcome break from the dull monotony of prison life, and allowed the prisoners to associate with one another, albeit in a limited way. When Florence arrived at Aylesbury, it had no chapel and the daily twenty-minute service was held in one of the prison halls. With the help and financial support of the two Lady Visitors, a new chapel was constructed in the prison. It was consecrated by the Bishop of Reading in a special service in March 1897. Florence at that time was in the prison infirmary, but the day before the consecration service she was asked to assist in decorating the chapel with flowers that had been donated by Lady Rothschild. Florence later said that Lady Rothschild was '*deeply affected*' when she told her how '*profoundly the women appreciated her recognition of a common humanity.*' Florence was also given permission to attend the special service along with about 120 other prisoners. Before the Bishop of Reading left the prison, he went into the infirmary and, as he passed Florence's cell, he spoke a few '*words of hope and encouragement.*'

When Florence finally left the prison hospital she was given light duties in the prison library. This involved repairing old books and assisting the schoolmistress by changing the prisoners' library books twice a week. Florence

---

[1382] *Indianapolis Sun*, 27th April 1896.
[1383] Maybrick F., op. cit., pages 190-191.
[1384] HO 144/1640/A50678D/313.
[1385] HO 144/1640/A50678D/312.
[1386] HO 144/1640/A50678D/315.
[1387] Maybrick F., op. cit., pages 192-193.
[1388] Ibid., page 96.

described the library as a '*very good one,*' containing '*not only the latest novels, but philosophical works and books for study; also, a limited number in French and German. To these were added religious works, especially poetry, and sermons for Sunday reading.*'

Reading was Florence's '*only solace*' and, later in prison life after her health improved, she read every moment she was allowed. She wrote that she had '*always been fond of reading, and during my leisure hours I got through a large number of books. This was between noon and half-past one, and seven and eight in the evening, when my light had to be put out.*' One thing that wasn't allowed in the library was newspapers. Prison rules forbid any national or international news being conveyed to the prisoners, either by letters or from visitors. Florence considered this a very short-sighted policy, and felt that '*no harm can possibly come of allowing information regarding public affairs of national interest to be conveyed through the legitimate channels of letters and visits.*' These strict rules were relaxed on just two occasions: Jubilee and Coronation days, and that was tinged with disappointment because instead of '*a mitigation of our sentences, as was the case in India, they gave us extra meat and plum pudding.*'

Postcard depicting Florence Maybrick in Aylesbury Prison (Chris Jones collection)

In March 1897, President William McKinley (1843-1901) was sworn into office as the 25th President of the United States. As she had done with his predecessors, the Baroness was soon sending letters asking him to intervene on behalf of her daughter. Both President McKinley and Colonel John Hay (1838-1905), the American Ambassador in London, were to take a personal interest in the case.

In July 1897, Ambassador Hay formally petitioned the British Crown for a pardon for Florence. The petition did not refer to her guilt or innocence; it was just a simple request '*on the part of many American people, through their accredited representative, for her release.*'[1389] Ambassador Hay handed the petition to Lord Salisbury, the Foreign Secretary, who in turned passed it on to Home Secretary, White Ridley, who within a month '*regretfully stated that he was unable, in view of the conclusion reached by himself and his predecessors as to Mrs Maybrick's guilt, to recommend to Her Majesty any exceptional treatment should be accorded to her.*'[1390]

As Florence received no details on how the Home Office review had been conducted, one of her friends asked Ambassador Hay to look into the case. Hay replied he had been informed by the Home Office that Florence had been a '*disobedient and troublesome prisoner.*' When she was told this by one of her visitors, Florence immediately asked to see the prison governor. At that meeting, the governor looked through her prison record but could find no such entry, so told her she must have been misinformed. He said that, quite the reverse was true: her '*conduct was good, and that he had never made any report to the contrary.*'

Florence concluded that the report from the Home Office to Colonel Hay was due to '*an adverse influence, of which I have still no knowledge.*' She complained, quite justly, that '*statements are made against a prisoner, of the nature of which she is entirely ignorant. Being ignorant, she has no way of refuting them. Worse still, they are retained in the Home Office to her dying day, and the unfortunate woman knows nothing of them or their effect.*'[1391]

In September 1897, the Baroness was accompanied on her visit to see her daughter by Mrs Rigg from Liverpool, one of Florence's most ardent supporters, and Mary Krout (1851-1927), an influential American author and journalist for the *Chicago Inter Ocean*. The women were taken into a small office inside the prison in which a table, four feet wide, ran across the entire width of the room. The door opened and in walked Miss Russell, a prison attendant, who was escorting '*a pale woman in a grey gown, with a tiny snow-white cap of transparent book muslin, its borders prettily frilled, upon her head, and a little dark-blue shawl covering her shoulders.*'[1392] It was not until the woman

---

[1389] *New Albany Weekly Tribune* (Indiana), 9th July 1897.
[1390] *Andura Courier* (Indiana), 5th August 1897.
[1391] Maybrick F., op cit., pages 146-148.
[1392] *Sunday Inter Ocean* (Chicago), 26th September 1897.

called the Baroness '*Mamma*' that Mary Krout realised she was Florence. The Baroness and Florence approached each other and stretched their hands across the table.

Krout wrote:

> '*I do not know which was the most painful to witness, the simulated cheerfulness and animation of the poor mother, who had but one desire, to revive the failing heart of the child, or the fixed despair of the face turned towards us.' Krout described Florence as: 'slight and somewhat below medium stature; her face has the waxen pallor of the prison; the ears were as white and transparent as the ears of the dead and the lips were bloodless. The eyes were fixed and staring – the expression one of terror and suffering.*'

The Baroness introduced Mrs Rigg and Mary Krout to Florence, and she said she was glad to see any friend of Miss Dodge. Florence said she was '*not up to much today*' as she could not sleep. She suffered continually with headaches, despite trying remedies such as opiates and spirits. It was quickly apparent to Krout that Florence was '*suffering from profound melancholia,*' which had seriously affected her general health.

As the Baroness was concerned that Florence's condition may lead her to contemplate suicide, she always greeted her daughter with '*a smiling face and a semblance of courage and hopefulness that she assuredly cannot feel.*' The Baroness told her daughter that President McKinley was her friend, and that he had written in his own hand a '*most touching*' letter about her case. So far, it had not achieved anything, '*but we are certain that it will in time.*' Florence replied that it was very kind of the President, but it '*is of no use; I have ceased to hope for anything... I once used to like the English, but I like them no longer. They are as hard as stone.*'

Florence's position in the infirmary meant she did not have to observe all the prison rules and she was entitled to better fare; however, she had no real appetite. Krout wrote that for months Florence '*suffered torture with toothache... the decaying teeth were never attended to. Finally, they had to be removed, but not until chronic indigestion had set in. "Now that I have proper food, I cannot eat it," she said. "It's too late."*'

The Baroness asked Florence if she read; she answered, '*No*,' as 15 minutes of reading would cause terrible headaches. For the same reason, she could neither knit nor sew. Florence said she did '*nothing but sit in my chair and think.*' She had seen pictures of her children, and with a '*burst of inextinguishable maternal pride*' said her son, who was now aged 15, was 5 feet 4 inches tall, and her daughter was a talented and charming girl of 12. Their photographs had been sent to the prison governor and they had been '*lent to her for a time until she could fix their features in her memory; then they were returned. Photographs had been sent in this manner once a year, with news of their progress in school and of their general welfare.*' Florence said her son had been sent to the Isle of Wight [where Michael Maybrick lived] to be with his cousins, '*because he was somewhat delicate from too rapid growth.*'

The time allowed for the meeting between Florence and her visitors had been extended to one hour following appeals from personal friends to the Home Office. When the time elapsed, there was a rap on the door, and mother and daughter rose and held out their arms again. The Baroness said, '*Consider that I have embraced you, Florence, and given you a thousand kisses.*' The visitors then left the prison.

Mary Krout wrote that three things had profoundly impressed her about the visit to meet Florence. Firstly, the '*affection and pity*' shown towards Florence by the prison official, Miss Russell. Secondly, the '*dignity*' with which Florence bore her suffering. Thirdly, the '*brilliancy and strength*' of Florence's mental powers. Krout finished her report of the meeting by saying she would never forget Florence's '*inscrutable smile.*' She had seen a similar expression before upon the face of a woman who was about to die, and who listened to the '*cheerful reassurances of those about her as though they were voices in a dream. She had no more to do with this life, and felt neither fear nor regret to quit a world in which she had only suffered.*'

In 1898, President McKinley decided to use the occasion of Queen Victoria's Diamond Jubilee to again ask for a pardon. A dispatch from Secretary of State John Sherman, to Ambassador Hay stated:

> '*Moved by the sympathy manifested by the people of the United States in favour of Mrs Florence Maybrick, the President suggests that if brought to the attention of Her Majesty she might welcome the present as a most fitting opportunity to express mercy in Mrs Maybrick's behalf.*'[1393]

Unfortunately for Florence, although many prisoners did receive a Royal Pardon, she was not one of them. White Ridley stood by the view of his predecessors at the Home Office; that Florence was guilty.

A couple of years later, the American Ambassador in London, Joseph H. Choate, had a very frank and angry meeting with White Ridley over Florence's case. According to Choate, White Ridley told him that he:

[1393] Christie T.L., op cit., page 204.

> *'and his whole official staff had no doubt of her guilt and that his predecessors had made a mistake in considering it doubtful; that they had all examined the record of the trial with great care and were absolutely convinced that she was guilty of murder and not merely of an attempt.'*[1394]

Further efforts were made on Florence's behalf by McKinley's Administration, but to no avail.

In April 1901, Henry White, who was still the Secretary of the U.S. Embassy in London, was introduced to President McKinley whilst on his annual visit to America. He told a reporter from the *Evening Star* in Washington DC that:

> *'Mrs Maybrick is in the Aylesbury prison and is as kindly treated as is possible. I hear from her about once a week from two distinguished ladies [presumably the Duchess of Bedford and Lady Battersea] who do charitable work in the prison. Her health is not seriously affected, although she has never been in the best of health. She is not strong and is put in the infirmary whenever there is any indication of declining health. She is fairly cheerful and has a good prison record.'*
>
> *'...the worst thing that could happen for Mrs Maybrick is for someone to resume the agitation of her case in this country... I have been working on the case ever since Mrs Maybrick was sent to prison, and at every opportunity do something for the unfortunate woman. I have seen every Home Secretary in the British cabinet for many years and have talked with everyone connected with the case.*[1395]

Gentlemen,

In accordance with the instructions contained in the accompanying letter No.16203/216 dated the 23rd inst: asking for a full report upon the condition of the above-named Prisoner, I beg to state that at the present time her health is fairly good, and she is free from any organic disease. Her weight - 112 lbs - is exactly the same as on her reception into Prison.

Although imprisonment does not appear to have had any injurious effect upon her general health, it appears to have had the effect of making her, at times, morose and bad tempered, and inclined to make herself very disagreeable to her fellow Prisoners. Her mental condition has, however, decidedly improved during the past twelve months, for whereas she then professed inability to employ herself in any way, either by doing needle-work or reading, she now not only amuses herself by reading, but is fairly industrious both at knitting and needle-work.

I am of opinion that she will not be injuriously affected by further imprisonment.

I have the honour to be,
Gentlemen,
Your obedient Servant,
(sd) George E. Walker
Governor & M.O.

Report on Florence Maybrick by Mr George Walker, Governor and Medical Officer of Aylesbury Prison (Chris Jones collection)

Although it was certainly the case that White did speak to every British Home Secretary, his harsh remarks about the campaign to get Florence released are undeserved. While some of the campaign efforts had been counter-productive, three different American Presidents had tried a wide range of strategies, including both public petitions and private deferential messages, and all had met with failure.

Christie questioned why successive British Governments were so resolute in their opposition to Florence's release, and wondered if they had some undisclosed evidence that pointed to her guilt. Or was it the '*majestic force*' of the Queen who stood in Florence's way?[1396] It is likely the Home Office were always going to stick to their default position that, as a prisoner found guilty in a court of law, her sentence should be enforced. This was especially the case when Queen Victoria so ardently supported the guilty verdict. In these circumstances, it was inevitable that Florence would spend a minimum of 10 years and a maximum of 20 years in prison.

Florence wrote that a life sentence usually meant '*twenty years and three months is taken off each year as a reward for good behaviour,*' and that her '*unbroken record of good conduct*' resulted in her sentence being reduced to 15 years.[1397] Florence may have had special friends, but she did not receive special treatment. McKinley was re-elected in the 1900 Presidential election, but his second term came to a tragic end when he was assassinated by a deranged anarchist in September 1901; he was succeeded by Theodore Roosevelt. It was Roosevelt who was President when Florence was finally released from prison in 1904.

As well as the occasion when Mary Krout and Mrs Rigg visited the prison, Florence did occasionally receive letters and visits from people other than her mother. In August 1897, she sent a letter to Florence Aunspaugh, the young girl who had stayed in Battlecrease in the summer of 1888, in reply to one she had received from the younger woman. Florence wrote that she remembered the visit of the '*vivacious, pert little miss, with big brown eyes and long brown*

[1394] Ibid., page 206.

[1395] *Evening Star* (Washington D.C), 19th April 1901.

[1396] Christie T.L., op cit., page 207.

[1397] Maybrick F., op. cit. pages 211-212.

curls, who kept the entire household in an uproar of laughter.'[1398] She said that those were '*happy days, never to come back to me again in this life. Now I am a deserted, lonely woman, with nothing to look forward to in the future. I labour hard all through the day; and at night I lay awake thinking, until physical exhaustion carries me to unconsciousness. It is hard and cruel to be imprisoned for a crime of which I am not guilty.*' Florence added that if the '*old happy days were still in existence, I would most assuredly have you visit me this summer and would give you the largest ball Battlecrease ever witnessed.*'

In the same letter, Florence revealed that '*all the cotton men of Liverpool and London and their wives have been so kind and thoughtful of me. Especially Mr and Mrs Ratcliffe. If it were not for them, I feel that it would not be possible for me to exist. They never come to see me without bringing me some remembrance. When Mr Ratcliffe leaves he always says, "Cheer up Mrs Maybrick, and don't lose heart, you will yet be outside the prison bars."*'

Florence also referred to an application made by John Aunspaugh to visit her in prison, but permission only came through after he had already sailed back to the United States. Some years later, John Aunspaugh did manage to visit Florence. When he finally saw her – with her grey hair, sunken eyes and pale complexion – he remembered how beautiful she once looked and started to cry. Florence said, '*I do not wonder at your tears, but mine have ceased to flow.*'[1399] It is noteworthy that some of James' closest friends never abandoned Florence. George Davidson wrote to her when she was awaiting trial in Liverpool; John Aunspaugh, James' great American friend, actually visited her in Aylesbury. These are actions that would not have taken place if either man was convinced of Florence's guilt.

In February 1900, Florence received a surprise visit from Lord Russell. She later wrote she was sitting in her cell '*one day feeling very weak and ill. I was recovering from an attack of influenza, and the cold comfort of my surroundings increased the physical and mental depression which accompanies this complaint.*' She heard an old familiar voice in the corridor and thought she must be dreaming and then, standing right in front of her, was the '*noblest, truest friend that woman ever had: the champion of the weak and the oppressed; the brave upholder of justice and law in the face of prejudice and public hostility — Lord Russell of Killowen, Lord Chief Justice of England.*' Russell walked into Florence's cell while the prison governor waited outside. He greeted Florence with a friendly smile, sat down on a stool, and spoke to her for 30 minutes. As he rose to leave, he took Florence's hand and said, '*Be brave, be strong; I believe you to be an innocent woman. I have done and will continue to do all I can for you.*'[1400] The two never met again; Russell died six months later after a short illness. Although Russell was to fail in his efforts to get Florence released from prison, he never wavered in his support for her. In 1898, he protested yet again to the Home Secretary writing: '*I consider the history of this case reflects discredit on the administration of the criminal law... The prisoner has already undergone imprisonment for a period four times as long as the minimum punishment fixed by law for the commission of a crime of which she has never been convicted, or for which, indeed, she has never been tried, but of which she has been adjudged guilty by your predecessor in the office of Home Secretary.*'[1401]

Just before his death he penned one final letter to the Home Secretary, writing:

> '*I saw the wretched woman last week while at Aylesbury, looking wretched, although I believe she is not ill in the ordinary sense... You say you regard her as a properly convicted murderer undergoing a commuted sentence. Is this so? Your predecessor Llandaff, after inquiry, in which the Lord Chancellor and the Government chemist assisted, publicly stated there was room for doubt whether any murder had at all had been committed; but that he came to the conclusion that the accused had attempted to commit murder.*'[1402]

After Russell's death, some expressed doubts over whether he really believed Florence to be innocent. His own son, in a letter to Christie, wrote: '*My father never held her up as an innocent woman deserving of sympathy. He only thought that the conviction for murder was not justified by the evidence and on that ground pressed Home Secretaries for her release.*'[1403] In contrast, his grandson wrote: '*I think it improbable that my grandfather was moved, when he was Lord Chief Justice, to visit Mrs Maybrick in prison because of illogicality in the Home Secretary's grounds.*'[1404] Russell would not have championed Florence's cause over the length of time that he did if he had doubts about Florence's guilt.

During her early years in Aylesbury, Florence spent a great deal of time in the infirmary prison cells. Her physical ill-health was mirrored by her mental ill-health. She was often despondent and depressed. In January 1898, the Baroness spoke to a newspaper reporter after visiting her in prison, saying:

1398 Letter from Florence Maybrick to Florence Aunspaugh, dated 10th August 1897; in the Trevor Christie Collection.
1399 Christie T.L., op cit., page 184.
1400 Maybrick F., op. cit., pages 142-144.
1401 O'Brien R. Barry, op. cit., page 262.
1402 Ibid., page 262.
1403 Christie T.L., op cit., page 272.
1404 Ryan B., op cit., page 7.

'My daughter is merely existing, and that is all. She is still in the infirmary, where she has spent six of the eight years imprisonment. She has grown so thin that it would be hard to recognise her. There are great black rings under her eyes, and she can barely drag herself about... She is unable to do any work, whatever, even the taking care of her cell, which is expected of prisoners. Her greatest trouble is insomnia... In addition to other troubles, her sight is failing.'[1405]

In 1898, the Governor of the Prison wrote that imprisonment had the effect of making Florence occasionally '*morose and bad tempered,*' and also '*very disagreeable to her fellow prisoners.*'[1406] Thankfully, over time both her physical and mental health saw an improvement.

At the beginning of the new century, Florence had become Aylesbury's longest serving prisoner. This is not too surprising, as the '*prostitute was the typical woman prisoner of the later nineteenth century.*'[1407] Within the prison walls Florence had acquired a level of status and respect amongst her fellow inmates. In her autobiography, Florence tells of a tragic incident involving a young female prisoner, aged 24, who was serving a five-year sentence for a violent offence. The woman had a poor prison record, and was in a very '*depressed state of mind.*' One day she asked to speak to Florence, and although permission was initially denied, following the intervention of the chaplain she was allowed to have a few minutes' conversation.

Florence told her: '*The people of God have a promise of a Comforter from heaven to come to them and abide with them, even in tribulation and in prison.*' The woman seemed to be in better spirits, and told Florence she would try to be less confrontational. Sadly, several days later she was found hanged in her cell. When word of her death got out, there was a great deal of resentment amongst the female prisoners who felt she had been driven to her death by the prison officials. Soon anger in the prison had grown to such an extent that the prison warders feared they were losing control of the situation. Florence said at this point the Chief Matron was so alarmed she asked her to speak to the women, to try and calm the situation. Florence wrote: '*Accompanied by an officer, I did so, and in a few minutes the uproar calmed down and the women returned quietly to their cells. I have reason to believe that I always had the full confidence of my fellow prisoners; they were quick to know and appreciate that I had their welfare at heart, and that I never countenanced any disobedience or breach of the rules.*'[1408]

Although it is difficult to ascertain the truth of Florence's account of the incident, there is evidence to support her assertion that she had the respect of her fellow inmates. In 1896, Mary Campbell, a former prisoner at Aylesbury, was interviewed by a newspaper reporter who was anxious to hear her opinion on Florence.[1409] Campbell said that in 1892 she had been given a four-year prison sentence and, as a result, had spent time with Florence in both Woking and Aylesbury Prisons. Campbell said she had first met Florence in August 1893, when then they were both in the infirmary at Woking. She said at that time Florence was not well liked by her fellow prisoners due to her attitude, which Campbell described as a '*haughty disdain.*' The other prisoners were jealous of Florence, as they believed she received '*many favours*' during her time in the infirmary, such as more opportunities to see her friends and relatives.

After her move to Aylesbury, Florence had become '*exceedingly popular amongst her fellow prisoners, whom she was always willing to help in their work and for whom she gladly did a favour whenever she possibly could.*' Campbell added that although it was obvious that Florence was from a '*superior station in life, she was always kind and courteous to the others and particularly to the younger women.*'

In September 1898, Ambassador Hay was appointed the new US Secretary of State, and Joseph Choate (1832-1917) took over his former role as the US Ambassador to Britain. In January 1901 the Baroness had two interviews with Ambassador Choate, and received a '*polite assurance*' that her daughter's case would be presented to the new Home Secretary '*when an opportunity arises.*'[1410] Although the phrase '*polite assurance*' does not appear very inspiring, a dramatic change was about to take place in the British political landscape.

In January 1901, Queen Victoria died, and so ended one of the major stumbling blocks to Florence's release. Two months earlier there had been a change at the Home Office, when Charles Ritchie (1838-1906) replaced White Ridley as Home Secretary. In July 1901, Joseph Choate met Ritchie, who told him that Florence would be released from prison on 25th July 1904. The Home Secretary added he had personally informed Florence of the decision in her cell at Aylesbury. In her autobiography, Florence recalled the moment when three gentlemen from the Home Office stopped by her cell and spent several minutes talking to her, though she mistakenly identifies one of the men as Sir Matthew White Ridley rather than his successor, Charles Ritchie.

She wrote: '*One morning, a week later, I was summoned to appear before the governor.' When Florence arrived at his office, he shuffled some papers and said to her: 'Florence E. Maybrick, is to be informed that the Secretary of*

[1405] *New York Times*, 9th January 1898.
[1406] HO 144/1640/A50678D/320.
[1407] Priestley P., op cit., page 72.
[1408] Maybrick F., op. cit., pages 172-175.
[1409] *Sheffield Independent*, 5th August 1896.
[1410] *New York Times*, 6th January 1901.

State has decided to grant her discharge from prison when she has completed fifteen years of her sentence, conditional upon her conduct.'

Florence recalled how she felt upon hearing these words: '*For a moment I failed to grasp the full meaning of these words, but when I did – how shall I describe the mingled feelings of joy and thankfulness, of relief and hope, with which I was overwhelmed.*'[1411]

In the summer of 1902, another American journalist, Harriet Hubbard Ayer (1849-1903), managed to visit Florence in Aylesbury Prison by disguising her true reason for visiting the institution. She described Florence as '*a little over five feet in height. She cannot hardly weigh over ninety pounds. Her face has the deadly waxen look which long deprivation of sunlight and fresh air inevitably produce. Her features are not regular, but very pleasing – very gentle. Her eyes are blue and large, and excepting when she looks one directly in the face, they are expressionless as to make one wonder if there is any sight in them.*'[1412]

Harriet Ayer asked Florence how she lived. Florence replied: '*I cannot tell. I often wonder how it is that I have lived. I think it must be because my belief has never died that one day, sooner or later, my innocence will be proved. I am willing to die when that time comes.*' When Ayer asked Florence about her children, she started to cry and said: '*I know nothing of them for the past seven years... I have never seen them since they were taken away from me all those years ago.*' When Florence discussed the prison routine, she said she was '*glad*' she always ate her meals alone in her cell as many of the prisoners were of a '*terrible class,*' and it would be '*very dreadful to eat with some of them.*' Later during her visit, Ayers said she was told that Florence had been a '*model prisoner*' and had an '*unparalleled influence for good on the other prisoners who adore her.*'

After returning to London, Harriet Ayers decided to travel to Rouen, France to visit the Baroness. She found her living in '*abject poverty,*' all her money having been spent on the campaign to release her daughter. The Baroness told her:

> '*I have grown into an old woman, and I am I know, in a very serious state of health, but I will not die until my child is free. I have worked thirteen years, day and night, for my Florrie, the innocent victim of an unheard-of wrong. I will never give up until she is released and back again in the land of our birth. My child is innocent. She was foolish, indiscreet, driven to one mad act of folly by a man who to the grossest marital infidelity added physical brutality. Has she not atoned for her single lapse by thirteen years of hideous torture in an English gaol?*'

The Baroness' commitment to Florence's cause is further demonstrated by the fact that she was even prepared to send a '*piteous letter*' to Michael Maybrick, '*asking him to help her in her appeal for her daughter's release from prison.*'[1413] The Christmas of 1903 was to be Florence's last in prison. She helped decorate the chapel with evergreens, which she described as the only way the event was marked inside the prison. Despite the lack of festive spirit, Florence later wrote that her heart

> '*felt the dawning of a brighter day. Only four weeks more and I would have passed out of its grim gates forever. How I counted those days, and yet how I shrank from going once more into the world that had been so cruel, so hostile, so unmerciful, in spite of the fact that there was no proof that I was the guilty woman they assumed me to be! But kind friends and loving hearts were waiting to greet me, to give me refuge and comfort.*'

On Saturday, 23rd January 1904, her mother visited Aylesbury for the last time and they discussed Florence's leaving arrangements. Beside the governor, chief matron and her escort, no-one else in the prison was told the day or the time when Florence was to be released. Florence said she would have liked to have said goodbye to her fellow prisoners, and even to some of the guards, but in the end she '*thought it best to pass into my new life as quietly as possible.*'[1414]

Florence was to spend the last six months of her sentence under the care and supervision of the Anglican Sisters of the Epiphany in their convent in Truro in Cornwall. In April 1903, she had petitioned the Home Office '*to grant a change of confinement for a few months previous to my anticipated release... to go to private retreat.*'[1415] Her petition was supported by the prison doctor, who wrote that Florence '*feared the sudden change with the unaccustomed excitement might be prejudicial to her health and mental condition.*'

[1411] Maybrick F., op. cit., page 214.
[1412] *Bucks Herald*, 6th September 1902.
[1413] Blumenfeld R., op cit., page 164.
[1414] Maybrick F., op. cit., pages 217-220.
[1415] HO 144/1640/A50678D/350.

The Home Office gave permission for the move, so that Florence could be physically and mentally prepared for the outside world. It wasn't easy to find a convent that was prepared to accept a convicted murderer; however, the Mother Superior of the Truro convent agreed to take on the responsibility. At 6:30am on Monday 25th January 1904, Florence left Aylesbury Prison. Wearing a new set of clothes sent by her mother and accompanied by Miss Stewart, the principal matron, she took a cab to Aylesbury Station and then caught a train to London. She travelled across London to Paddington Station, where she was to catch the train to Cornwall.

It was an exciting yet frightening experience. She later wrote that '*the noise and the crowds of people everywhere bewildered me.*'[1416] *After almost twelve hours of travelling she arrived at Truro at 6:00pm and made her way to the convent, where she was met by Mother Julian who introduced her to the other nuns as 'Mrs Graham.'*

Florence later wrote: '*I look back upon the six months spent within those sacred walls as the most peaceful and the happiest in the true sense of my life. The life there is so calm, so holy and yet so cheerful that one becomes infected, so that the sad thoughts flee away.*'[1417] She spent her days working in the sewing room with the other nuns, and read a lot; when the weather was fine she took long walks through the grounds, though she never ventured beyond its walls. Living there allowed Florence to regain '*her vitality, weight and the colour of her cheeks.*'[1418] Despite the efforts of the authorities, the press soon found out about Florence's stay in the convent and it wasn't long before reporters were camped outside.

On 20th July 1904, Florence left the convent a free woman. Her release had been brought forward by five days in an effort to avoid the attention of the newspapers. She travelled to London, where she received her release papers from the Home Office. These papers included a list of stipulations, including the clauses she must not write a book or give interviews to the press. She then went to the American Embassy, where she was met by her mother. The two women kissed and embraced for the first time in 15 years. They then travelled to her mother's home in Rouen, France, accompanied by an escort provided by Ambassador Choate.

In Rouen, the Baroness lived under the assumed name of Mme. de Moremont. Her house, on the Rue de Tannery, was '*surrounded by high walls, completely shutting off the neighbouring residences.*'[1419] Despite this, it wasn't long before British and French reporters discovered Florence's location and became so annoying that an appeal had to be made to the French authorities. General Horace Porter, the American Ambassador to France, arranged for French police officers to be placed outside the house to prevent any harassment.[1420]

In an effort to placate the press, Florence agreed to be interviewed by a reporter from the *Daily Chronicle*. He found her to be a '*clear-witted and outspoken, mildly robust, perfectly calm and pleasing-looking little lady.*' Although her eyes were '*listless,*' there was still a '*confidence of demeanour, an entire absence of nervousness or embarrassment, and a quiet deliberation in answering questions or waving them aside.*' He wrote that Florence still possessed an '*instinctive tact and grace*' that her prison years had not killed. She had '*delicate hands, good features and above the pallid but kindly face, a mass of dark hair neatly dressed with a great bow of black velvet.*'[1421]

Florence spoke about the '*horror*' of her prison experience, saying that for the first part of her sentence she was '*too stunned to do more than bear my burden,*' and it was only for her '*mother's sake*' that she '*wished to live at all.*' She described herself as a '*broken woman,*' but although she was a convict, she was not a criminal.

After a three week stay in Rouen, Florence prepared herself for her return to America. She told the *Daily Chronicle* reporter she was going there to give testimony in a law suit. She said that just before the verdict in her trial, she was '*told to sign certain documents by my then solicitor and I did so. Afterwards I found that I had unknowingly signed my property away and I am claiming them again.*' The Baroness was unable to travel with Florence to America due to ill health and was to remain in Rouen. The *Liverpool Echo* reported that Florence was expected to arrive in New York sometime in August; '*Her friends are prepared to welcome her something of a martyr.*'[1422]

LINKS TO THE RIPPER DIARY: THE GOULSTON STREET GRAFFITO

In one passage in the Diary of Jack the Ripper, the author of the document wrote: '*I wondered if they enjoyed my funny little Jewish Joke.*' The placement and wording of this sentence suggests that the author was directly referring to the graffito found written on a wall in Goulston Street on the night of the *Double Event*; the murders of Elizabeth Stride and Catherine Eddowes, which both took place in the early hours of Sunday, 30th September 1888.

1416 Maybrick F., op. cit., page 217.
1417 Ibid., page 219.
1418 Graham A. and Emmas C., op cit., page 272.
1419 *New York Times*, 22nd July 1904.
1420 *The World Evening Edition*, 23rd August 1904.
1421 Florence's interview with the *Daily Chronicle*, reported in the *Stockton Herald, South Durham and Cleveland Advertiser*, 29th August 1904.
1422 *Liverpool Echo*, 21st July 1904.

Eddowes was the second victim. Her body was found at 1:45am by P.C. Edward Watkins in Mitre Square. As the murderer fled the scene, it is very possible that he dropped a bloodstained portion of the victim's apron in Goulston Street, which may have been used by the killer to wipe blood off his hands or his knife.

The piece of apron was discovered by PC Alfred Long at 2:55am. He later said he had passed through the same street earlier, at around 2:20am, and seen neither the apron or the graffito. On the wall, above the scrap of apron, he spotted writing on the wall. Written in chalk, just one inch high, were the words: '*The Juwes are the men That Will not be Blamed for nothing.*'

It was on the right-hand side of the entry leading to 108-119 Wentworth Model Dwellings. The buildings were five storeys high and contained 222 apartments. At the time of the Ripper murders they were '*predominately occupied by Jews, and certainly by 1900, the residents of the buildings were 95-100% Jewish.*'[1423] In 1982, the buildings were cleared of occupants and earmarked for demolition; however, in 1990, the buildings were refurbished, renamed Merchant House, and once again became apartments.

After discovering the piece of apron and the writing on the wall, PC Long searched the stairwell, but found nothing else of note. Leaving another constable to guard the writing, and to make sure nobody entered or left the building, Long took the piece of apron to Commercial Street Police Station and reported his findings. Soon a number of police officers were in Goulston Street inspecting the writing, though they failed to agree on its significance or whether it was linked to the murder of Catherine Eddowes.

Inspector McWilliam of the City of London Police, felt the writing was important and gave orders for it be photographed. Superintendent Arnold of the Metropolitan Police didn't agree; he felt it had nothing to do with the murder, and was worried that it would soon be seen by people coming to Petticoat Lane market and stir up anti-Semitism in the area. Arnold ordered a police officer to be ready with a sponge to clear the writing, but decided he needed the authority of a more senior officer before taking such action. At 5:00am, Sir Charles Warren, Metropolitan Police Commissioner, arrived at Leman Street Police Station and spoke to Arnold. He immediately went to Goulston Street, had a copy of the writing taken, and then – in one of the most controversial decisions during the whole of the Ripper murders – gave the order for the writing to be cleaned away before the photographer arrived.

Warren was to be heavily criticised for his actions. In a report to the Home Office dated 6th November 1888, he tried to justify his decision: '*I do not hesitate myself to say that if the writing had been left, there would have been an onslaught upon the Jews, property would have been wrecked, and lives would probably have been lost.*'[1424]

As Warren had the graffiti removed before it was photographed, the exact wording of what was written on the wall is disputed. The official police version reads: '*The Juwes are the men That Will not be Blamed for nothing.*' Inspector McWilliam, who saw the writing, agreed with the word order but believed that the word '*Juwes*' was spelt '*Jewes.*' DC Halse, who also saw the writing, claimed it actually read: '*The Juwes are not The men That Will be Blamed for nothing.*' A further spelling '*Juews*' was suggested at the inquest.[1425]

The meaning of these words has been interpreted in many different ways. If the official police version of the words is accepted then, according to Paul Begg, they seem to mean:

[1423] Begg P. and Bennett J., op. cit., page 161.
[1424] Sugden P., op. cit., pages 185-186.
[1425] Begg P., Fido M. and Skinner K., op cit., page 186.

'that the Jews were not the people who would tolerate being blamed for something they didn't do. If written by the murderer he may have intended it to indicate that he was responding to some real or imagined offence to his race or religion – i.e. that the murders were being committed in response to false accusations.'[1426]

Warren's order to have the writing cleaned away can only be described as shocking. As details of what he had done emerged at the inquest into Eddowes' death, the *Pall Mall Gazette* asked: *'Who was the infatuated person who... in defiance of the protests of the City detective and the sensible suggestion of the Metropolitan police, persisted in rubbing it out? It was none other than Sir Charles Warren himself.'*[1427]

If the chalk writing on the wall had been left by the killer, then it was one of the most important pieces of evidence in the whole case. If Warren was concerned it might unleash anti-Jewish riots, then he could have taken some obvious alternative actions, such as having the area cordoned off, covering the writing with a sheet or a cloth, or simply wiping away the word '*Juwes*.' The latter action was suggested to him by a Metropolitan police officer at the time.[1428] If that had occurred, then the writing could have been photographed early that morning and then removed.

Stephen Knight wrote: '*Until the discovery of the writing on the wall, Sir Charles Warren had not ventured into the East End. The news of the message brought him scurrying from Whitehall as fast as a carriage could convey him.*' Knight argues there was only one reason why a senior police officer would go to such great lengths to destroy evidence, and that is '*when the officer owes allegiance to a master higher than justice.*' Warren, a senior Freemason, had recognised the significance of the word '*Juwes,*' which was not a misspelling of the word Jews. Knight wrote, '*The Juwes were the three apprentice Masons who killed Hiram Abiff and who are the basis of Masonic ritual.*'[1429] Therefore, when Warren saw the writing he became concerned that it implicated Freemasons in the murders and, even worse, Jack the Ripper himself might be a Freemason. His loyalty to Freemasonry took precedence over his loyalty to the police force and he felt he had no alternative but to destroy the evidence.

Knight's views on this issue are controversial and they are certainly not shared by all Ripperologists. One person who did agree with him was Bruce Robinson, who suggested that Michael Maybrick was the Whitechapel serial killer. He wrote that nothing was more important than the '*Masonic taunting*' of Warren at Goulston Street; the '*mocking on the wall is the sum of the whole of Jack the Ripper, a key to his psyche – and, by the insanity of his reaction, Bro Sir Charles Warren's too.*'[1430]

Alternatively, Paul Begg wrote the word '*Juwes is not and never has been a Masonic word, nor has Juwes or any word approximating to it ever appeared in Masonic ritual.*'[1431] Begg and Bennett say something very similar in a more recent book. They argue that, in Britain and the United States, the collective name for the three apprentices who murdered Hiram Abiff was not Juwes but Ruffians. They also point out that though the writing was washed off the wall, there was never any attempt to prevent it from becoming known. They conclude that '*all the reasons given for Warren attempting to erase it on the basis of any Masonic connection therefore amount to nothing.*'[1432]

The Goulston graffito, despite some vague suggestions from the author of the Ripper Diary, cannot be linked to James Maybrick or, for that matter, to his brother Michael.

Firstly, it is not clear if the chalk writing on the wall was written by the man who murdered Catherine Eddowes. Superintendent Arnold, one of the first police officers on the scene, immediately concluded the writing had nothing to do with the murder. Walter Dew, who later found fame as being the officer credited with the capture of Crippen, also believed it had nothing to do with the murder. He remarked the graffito was one among many such scrawlings in the area, and he did not believe any of them to be genuinely written by the Whitechapel killer.[1433]

Secondly, even if the writing had been penned by the murderer, as many believe, it still cannot be linked to James Maybrick. Philip Sugden wrote: '*Although it seems likely that the graffito was written by the murderer it yields little clue to his identity.*'[1434] As the precise wording of the writing is uncertain, there can be no definitive explanation of the meaning behind them. The words can be subjectively interpreted as meaning anything from a cryptic clue from the murderer himself to an angry rebuttal from a Jewish resident of Wentworth Model Dwellings, denying Jewish people were involved in the murders.

As to the possible Masonic links to the graffito, it is an interesting theory – but ultimately, just a theory with no real evidence to substantiate it other than the fact that Sir Charles Warren ordered the writing to be removed. If Warren had desperately wanted to hide the word '*Juwes*' from the public's attention he could have simply agreed with PC Long's statement, as recorded in Long's notebook, that the word was '*Jews*' and not '*Juwes*.' That one

---

[1426] Begg P., (2005) op cit., page 244.
[1427] *Pall Mall Gazette*, 12th October 1888.
[1428] Ibid.
[1429] Knight S., op cit., pages 178-179.
[1430] Robinson B., op cit., page 143.
[1431] Begg P., op. cit., page 183.
[1432] Begg P. and Bennett J., op cit., page 163.
[1433] Begg P., Fido M. and Skinner K., op cit., page 187.
[1434] Sugden P., op. cit., page 256.

simple step would have effectively ended any talk of a possible Freemason link. As it was, his order to clean away the writing spectacularly backfired, as it put him – and therefore the graffito – at the forefront of public scrutiny.

One has to also question why James Maybrick, a longstanding Freemason, would possibly want to draw adverse attention to the organisation of which he proudly belonged. Linking Freemasonry to Jack the Ripper would have only done the organisation irreparable harm. Robinson suggests that Michael Maybrick did have a motive, in that he hated Freemasonry and wanted it to be publicly ridiculed. Unfortunately for Robinson, this assertion clashes with all the known facts, which singularly point to Michael being a highly active and devoted Freemason.

Another reason for believing that the graffito had nothing to do with James Maybrick comes from some recent research carried out on a shawl that allegedly belonged to Catherine Eddowes. In 2007, businessman Russell Edwards bought the shawl at an auction. Its owners claimed it had been in the family's possession since Eddowes' death.

Their story was that one of their ancestors had been a policeman on duty at the time of the murders, and when her body was being taken to the mortuary he asked a senior police officer if he could have the silk shawl for his wife, who was a dressmaker. As the shawl would have probably just been destroyed, the senior police officer agreed to the request. When the policeman showed the shawl to his wife she was horrified as it contained bloodstains and, as a result, the item was stowed away without ever being washed.

Although it was impossible for Edwards to fully verify these claims, he nevertheless bought the shawl and paid for it to undergo extensive forensic testing. DNA results suggested the blood on the shawl had a positive match with both descendants of Catherine Eddowes, the victim, and also Aaron Kosminski, one of the leading Ripper suspects.

Although many Ripperologists were less than impressed with either the provenance of the shawl or the robustness of the scientific tests, Edwards was confident he had finally unearthed the identity of the Ripper. In his book, Edwards writes little about the Goulston Street graffito, other than he thought its author was actually Eddowes' murderer. He points out that the writing was found directly above where the apron had been left, and also that '*it was not in a prominent site where an agitator would have chosen to splash their incendiary message.*'[1435]

If James Maybrick had been Jack the Ripper and the author of the Ripper Diary, he would have taken the opportunity to have explained and rationalised the words he had scrawled on the wall in Goulston Street. He would have added some catchy rhyme or some poignant text. None of this happens. Instead, we get just a short throw-away line that merely states it was a '*funny Jewish joke.*' Why is this? There is an obvious explanation – the person who wrote the Diary was not the serial killer and only had a basic knowledge of the murders. He barely mentions the Graffito, because he had not been the person who had written the words on the wall and did not know what they meant. As he had done on every other occasion when he lacked detailed knowledge, the person who penned the Diary resorted to brevity and vagueness. All the Diary entry concerning the Goulston Street Graffito provides is yet another reason for reaching the conclusion that the document is a forgery.

[1435] Edwards R., *Naming Jack the Ripper*, (Sidgwick and Jackson, London, 2014) page 97.

22

HOMEWARD BOUND

While Florence was in the convent in Truro, Mr T.W. Sargent, American Commissioner General of Immigration, wrote to the Baroness in Rouen, stating: '*The Commissioner of Immigration at New York has been instructed to facilitate Florence Maybrick's landing... she is recognised as an American citizen, with every right as such.*'[1436]

This was a statement of the utmost importance to Florence. When she married James Maybrick, Florence had lost her American citizenship and became a British citizen. Under American immigration regulations, a British citizen with a criminal record would have been barred entry to the country. By regaining her American citizenship, Florence was free to return to the land of her birth.

Florence Maybrick arrives in America

The move to America also put Florence beyond the reach of British law, and that meant she would not have to comply with the strict terms of the licence issued by the Home Office when she was released from prison. Under Condition Six, the Home Office could forfeit or revoke the licence at any time if Florence broke any of the terms, or was convicted of another offence. This meant she could be returned to prison and be '*liable to undergo a term of penal servitude for life.*' The return of her American citizenship gave Florence both hope for the future and the chance to escape the nightmare scenario of a possible return to a British prison.

Florence was booked on to the Red Star line steamship SS *Vaderland* for her return journey to America, sailing on 13th August 1904 from Antwerp in Belgium to New York.

Two days before the sailing, Florence left her mother's house and headed for Brussels, followed by at least five English reporters. In Brussels, she managed to evade the journalists and travelled to a hotel in Antwerp, where she met up with her solicitor, Mr Samuel V. Hayden, and his wife, who were going to accompany her on the voyage home.

When the time came for the ship to sail, Mr and Mrs Hayden left the hotel followed by the reporters who mistook Mrs Hayden for Florence. Florence was then able to slip out of the hotel unnoticed and board the steamer under the name of '*Rose Ingraham*' (a surname from her mother's side of the family). For the first three days of the voyage, Florence's identity remained a secret to all but her travelling companions and the ship's captain, and she was able to walk the decks without anyone bothering her.

Then, somehow, her fellow passengers found out her true identity and she became the focus of curious, though mostly polite, attention. One of the passengers, Dr W.H. Wilmer, a noted eye specialist of Philadelphia, agreed to examine Florence's eyesight. After the ship berthed in New York, he said reports that Florence was going blind were all '*nonsense.*' Her eyes had been '*weakened by long confinement and by reading in insufficient light,*' but with '*plenty of rest*' there was no reason why her eyes '*should ultimately be as good as they ever were.*'[1437]

Shortly before midnight on Monday, 22nd August, after a nine-day voyage, the SS *Vaderland* sailed passed Sandy Hook into Lower New York Bay. The passengers were not to disembark until Tuesday morning after the required quarantine arrangements had been completed.

1436 Morland N., op cit., page 228.

1437 *New World, Evening Edition*, (New York), 23rd August 1904.

Florence wrote: '*When I first caught sight of the Statue of Liberty, I, perhaps more than anyone on board, realised the full meaning of what it typifies, and I felt my heart stirred to its depths at the memory of what all my countrymen and countrywomen had done for me during the dark days of my past, to prove that they still carried me in their hearts, though the great ocean rolled between, and that I had not been robbed of the high privilege of being an American citizen.*'[1438]

On Tuesday morning as the passengers disembarked, Florence and Mrs Hayden remained in their cabins, which were guarded by custom officials. Florence's baggage, which consisted of three trunks, was inspected by custom officials inside her room. Finally, as the last passengers left the ship, Florence emerged on to the largely empty decks. She was met by Judge Yarrell, Hayden's legal partner, and some of her long-standing supporters including Dr Emmet Densmore and Margaret Hubbard Ayer, the daughter of Harriet Hubbard Ayer, who had visited her in prison. Florence walked off the ship on the arm of Hayden, followed by Mrs Hayden and Judge Yarrell. She was wearing a white silk gown with fine black stripes and a hat to match; her face was covered by a white veil. Florence was greeted by a large crowd of reporters and sightseers who closely followed her every move. It took the '*strenuous efforts of two detective sergeants*' to clear a space to allow her to get to her carriage.[1439] Once inside, the vehicle sped rapidly away to Holland House, a resplendent hotel located on Fifth Avenue, where Florence was to spend the next two days. As she left, Hayden answered questions from reporters and then issued a specially-prepared statement from Florence:

> '*I regret that the state of my health as well as business reasons prevent my talking to my friends of the American press at this time as I should like. To them and to my fellow countrymen and women I am deeply indebted. For their effort in my behalf, I take this means for expressing my everlasting gratitude as well as words can and also to thank them for their congratulations on my release which I regret I have not been able personally to acknowledge. As my mother was not able to accompany me, I came over under the protection of Mr Hayden of Hayden & Yarrell, my attorney and his wife. I am assured by my English physician and by Dr Wilmer of Washington D. C., who prescribed for me during the voyage, that quiet and mental rest will in time restore my health. It is on the advice of my counsel and my physician that I have travelled incognito. I cannot express the feelings of deep joy and thankfulness with which I return to my native land. At the earliest opportunity I shall visit my birthplace, Mobile, Ala., and also Norfolk, Va., my home during my married life. I now believe, as I have always, that God will in his own time right the great wrong that I have suffered. For further information concerning my plans, I must refer you to my counsel. Most sincerely, Florence Elizabeth Maybrick.*'[1440]

One reason for Florence's early return to the United States was the upcoming court case in Richmond, Virginia, between the Baroness and her former attorney, David Armstrong. The day before Florence landed in New York, Armstrong gave an interview in which he claimed Florence's release from prison '*had been secured by a sharp trick on the British Government by her friends.*' Armstrong said Florence only got released so she could '*defend certain interests she claims in the state of her father [actually her grandfather] Darius Blake Holbrook.*'[1441] Hayden angrily denounced Armstrong's remarks, calling them '*absolutely false and coming at this time is even more cruel than Armstrong's treatment of Mrs Maybrick and the Baroness von Roques themselves.*'[1442]

Whilst her current and former attorneys traded barbs in the press, Florence was having problems of her own coming to grips with the every-day conveniences of modern life in the upmarket hotel, Holland House. Although her friends had done their best to enlighten Florence on operating all the '*strange devices,*' she was still mystified by how they worked. After pressing a button several times to get some ice-water she found, after a procession of waiters had arrived at her room, that she had mistakenly ordered '*about all the hotel cuisine afforded.*' Later in the evening when trying to adjust the brightness of the light, she was plunged into darkness and proceeded to lose her key. She therefore decided, with a '*quaking heart,*' to seek refuge in her bed to escape from her '*accumulated troubles.*'[1443]

After spending two nights in Holland House, Florence left New York to join Dr Helen Densmore and her husband, Dr Emmet Densmore, in their summer retreat of Cragsmoor, in the south-eastern part of New York State, approximately 100 miles from New York City. Cragsmoor was a '*hamlet of a few homes and small farms*' on a narrow plateau called the Shawangunk Ridge.[1444] Its isolation and unspoilt beauty attracted artists from all over America to paint the stunning scenery of rocky outcrops, waterfalls and spectacular views of the Catskill Mountains.

1438 Maybrick F., op cit., pages 221-222.
1439 *Hagerstown Mail* (Maryland), 26th August 1904.
1440 *New York Times*, 24th August, 1904.
1441 *New York Times*, 23rd August, 1904.
1442 *New York Times*, 24th August, 1904.
1443 Taken from an article written by Florence that featured in the *Sunday Magazine*, 19th November 1905.
1444 Radl M., 'Early Cragsmoor: The Beginning of an Art Colony' in *About Town Magazine*, (2007).

Emmet Densmore's niece, Austa Densmore Sturdevant (1855-1936), the well-known American painter, owned and managed the Cragsmoor Inn, which had become something of an artists' colony. Florence loved the beauty and tranquility of the area, writing: '*beautiful Cragsmoor, with its wide reaches of inspiring scenery*' is a '*greater antithesis to prison walls*' than could possibly be imagined.[1445]

Florence Maybrick photographed shortly after her arrival in America

The *New York Times* reported that the Densmores had taken charge of Florence when she arrived in America, even though '*Mrs Maybrick had never seen Mrs Densmore until she returned to this country.*' Although Florence had never met Helen Densmore, she '*knew her well through her letters and her efforts for her pardon during the fourteen years she had spent in English prisons after the death of her husband.*' The report added: '*The two women have become strongly attached to each other, and Mrs Densmore had aided Mrs Maybrick in the preparation of the story of her experiences in the course of her trial and imprisonment.*'[1446]

In September 1904, Florence accompanied the Densmores when they returned to their home in Brooklyn. Florence was still living with the couple when Helen Densmore died unexpectedly of heart failure two months later. In April 1905, *The New York Times* reported that in her will, Helen Densmore had '*authorised to set aside a sufficient amount of money to provide for 150f. quarterly to Baroness de Roques and her daughter, Mrs Florence E. Maybrick, the American woman who was incarcerated recently in a British prison.*'[1447]

Whilst Florence was staying with the Densmores, several American newspapers reported she had become estranged from her mother. The disagreement between the two women was said to have developed after Percy Lindon-Howard, the leading figure in the Central News Agency in London, published an article based on a number of letters written by the Baroness, in which she stated: '*The relations existing between the Maybrick children and their mother... are not of the best.*'[1448] The Baroness wrote that Florence's children knew where their mother is, but have failed to communicate with her. She said if the attitude of the boy doesn't change, he '*will never get a cent of her money.*' The Baroness was also critical of Michael Maybrick, whom she claimed was '*holding the Maybrick children and managing the Maybrick estate under what she considered a doubtful will.*'

Although there *was* no estrangement between Florence and her mother, Florence would have been irritated by the Baroness' comments. The timing of the article was unfortunate as Florence still hoped for a reconciliation with her children and knew that antagonising them and Michael would not be helpful in that process. As a result, she publicly contradicted some of her mother's statements. For example, she said: '*The decision that my children should neither visit me nor receive visits from my mother was a necessity under the conditions of their custody, and my consent.*' She spoke positively about Edwin and Michael, saying her relationship with the brothers had been '*friendly until their minds were influenced against me by false imputations of my enemies.*'

During Florence's stay in Cragsmoor she was introduced to Cora Griffin, an American writer who had campaigned for her release. She and Florence quickly became friends. After Florence left the Densmores' house in Brooklyn, Griffin found her a six-room apartment at 175 West 78th Street at the corner of Amsterdam Avenue in Manhattan, which had a monthly rental of between 50 and 60 dollars. Florence was to live there for a number of years.

The Densmores encouraged Florence to write a book about her prison experiences. It was not a task she wanted to take on as it meant a '*mental return to the dread past.*' However, she was persuaded that some good might come from her recollections, especially for '*those whom a dire fate shall compel to follow in my steps, with bruised spirits and bleeding feet.*'[1449] Another reason for writing the book was Florence's '*desire to vindicate her character from all reproach not only in the eyes of the world, but in the eyes of her two children.*'[1450] The book took around two months to write and, when published, Florence dedicated it to '*those friends in America and England*' who had '*worked steadfastly*' for her freedom. It was divided into two main parts. The first half dealt with the period from when she was arrested until her return to America. The second half provided an analysis of her case. Florence also suggested a range of penal reforms, emphasising the view that '*punishment should be carried out in a humane and*

[1445] Maybrick F., op cit., pages 12-13.
[1446] *New York Times*, 27th November 1904.
[1447] *New York Times*, 9th April 1905.
[1448] *Atlanta Constitution* (Atlanta, Georgia), 20th November 1904.
[1449] Maybrick F., op cit., pages 9-15.
[1450] *Alton Evening Telegraph* (Alton, Illinois), 19th January 1905.

sympathetic spirit and not in a dehumanising or tyrannous manner.' The latter parts of her book were generally well received, and helped *'foster the steadily growing movement for their adoption.'*[1451]

Although the book did receive some favourable reviews, Christie was highly critical of it, writing that it was *'so badly written, so mawkishly phrased, so poorly organised'* that Florence must have produced it *'in haste without a ghost writer and with little direction from her editors.'*[1452] One of the things which was most noticeable about the memoir was what was not included. There were no details of her early married life, and no reference at all to Alfred Brierley. Florence wanted to steer well away from any discussion of her involvement with him in case it would offend the moral sensitivities of her American audience. She also wanted to minimise the notion that she was in any way a poor mother and a less than dutiful wife. She wrote about kneeling at her husband's coffin, and claimed they had become reconciled for the sake of the children. Her trial was barely mentioned, covering just a handful of pages. The most powerful part of Florence's book came when she wrote about her experiences in Woking and Aylesbury Prisons. Sadly, these emotive passages were interspersed with turgid sections on topics such as prison regulations which were devoid of references as to how they impacted on her own situation.

The second half of the book is, as Christie suggests, poorly organised, and one can understand why it only had a limited appeal to the casual reader. Perhaps the most interesting section of the book is the 14 pages at the end, in which she provided her own analysis of the case. She tackled some of the key issues, such as the phrase *'sick unto death,'* which she described as an American colloquialism with no sinister connotations. She also dealt at length with the Valentine's meat juice bottle which Mr Davies tested and found to contain half a grain of arsenic. Florence stuck firmly to her account that she had put a powder in the bottle and had not added arsenic in a state of a solution. Florence wrote: *'It is absolutely clear that the bottle of Valentine's meat juice which Mr Michael Maybrick took possession of and handed to Dr Carter is not the same bottle which Nurse Gore saw me place on the washstand.'*[1453] It was an important point, but one that was rather lost in a book that failed to deliver the impact Florence had hoped for when she started on the project.

Florence's memoir was to be neither a critical nor a commercial success. She later admitted she had been *'greatly disappointed'* by the way it had been received by the American people. She said she had *'hoped to go to Europe'*

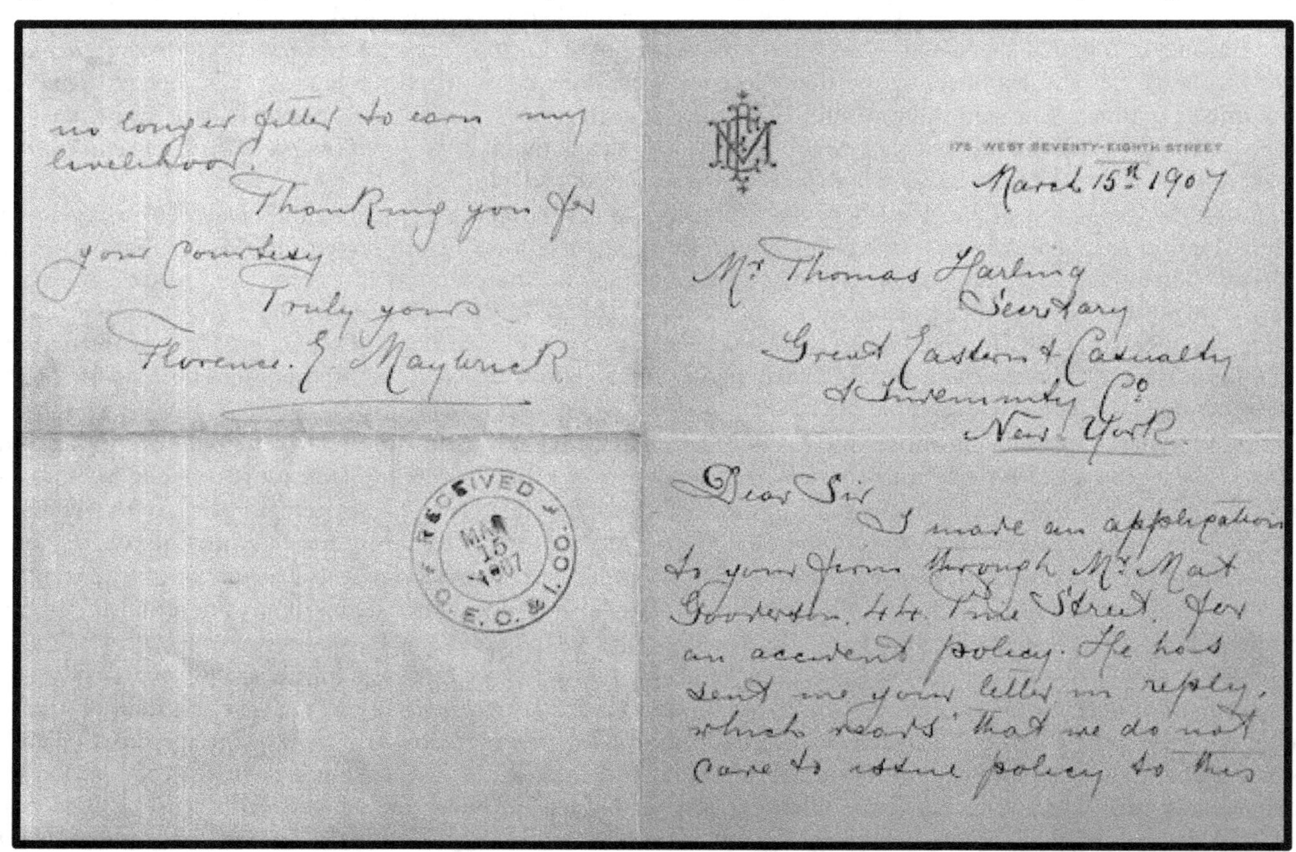

175 WEST SEVENTY-EIGHTH STREET

March 15th 1907

Mr Thomas Harling
Secretary
Great Eastern & Casualty
& Indemnity Co.
New York.

Dear Sir
I made an application to your firm through Mr Mat Goodstein, 44 Pine Street, for an accident policy. He has sent me your letter in reply, which reads that we do not care to issue policy to this

no longer fitted to earn my livelihood.
Thanking you for your courtesy
Truly yours
Florence E. Maybrick

RECEIVED MAR 15 1907 G.E.C.&I.CO.

Front and back page of a letter of application for an accident policy sent by Florence Maybrick in 1907. The letter-headed paper shows her New York address. (Chris Jones collection)

[1451] *Manchester Courier and Lancashire General Advertiser*, 20th January 1905.
[1452] Christie T.L., op cit., page 235.
[1453] Maybrick F., op cit., page 379.

with her lawyer, Mr Hayden, but on '*account of the small sale*' of the book she said she could not afford it.[1454] Florence wanted to accompany the launch of the book with a lecture tour of the country, that was scheduled to open at Hartford, Connecticut, in the middle of January 1905. It was said she had signed a lucrative contract with a theatrical agent, and intended to '*devote her lectures to a discussion of the abuses of British prisons.*'[1455] The lectures were never to take place as the British Government contacted the American State Department to object to the planned tour. They said that Florence, as a ticket-of-leave prisoner, was not supposed to express such views on a public platform, and also the tour might harm friendly relations between the two countries. Florence later overcame this problem by focusing her lectures on penal reform in America, and providing only a limited account of her experiences in British prisons.

As well as writing her memoir, Florence also wrote an article comparing criminal court procedures in England and America. Unlike the book, the article was extremely well-structured and written. She described herself as '*a helpless victim of unreasoning prejudice and mental incapacity, in the case of both judge and jury.*' She wrote that, in England, '*everything possible has been done to magnify the position of the judge, and at the same time to degrade and reduce to utter ignominy the unfortunate wretch in the dock.*' She said the only possible aim of such a process was the conviction of the defendant for it is a '*stigma on the police if a person once brought into court for trial by any chance slips through their meshes.*' As well as being critical of the judge in her trial, Florence also savaged the jury, writing that some of its members were '*so incapacitated for duty by reason of physical or mental disabilities that they could not keep off evident drowsiness during even the most exciting moments, and at least one of its members has made public confession that he did not hear a considerable part of the testimony.*'[1456]

One positive result from writing the book was that Florence was asked to visit a range of penal institutions in America. She was invited by Mr Cornelius V. Collins, Superintendent of Prisons for New York State, to visit the leading prisons in his state. She also received an invitation from Mr Francis J. Lantry, Commissioner for Corrections for Greater New York, to visit the prisons and workhouses under his jurisdiction. Florence wrote that both officials '*seemed deeply imbued with the reformatory spirit,*' and were keen to hear her observations of the prisons under their control, how they compared to British penal institutions and in what ways they could be improved.[1457]

One of the most infamous penal institutions that Florence visited was Sing Sing Prison in Ossining, New York State, about 30 miles north of New York City. In January 1905, she was shown around the facility by Superintendent Collins and Prison Warden Addison Johnson. She praised certain features of the prison, including the free conversations which were allowed between inmates and their visitors, and the fact that prisoners were provided with uniforms that actually fitted them. She also liked the fact that in the prison hospital wards '*every room was flooded with light and sunshine.*' On the other hand, she was highly critical of the cell blocks, which she described as a '*scandal and a disgrace.*' She said prisoners were being kept in '*kennels 3½ by 5 feet, without a window, without any means of ventilation other than by the grated door with the foul air of the corridor, with no sanitary provisions whatever, with a minimum of light.*'[1458]

Another well-known prison Florence visited in February 1905, was New York's municipal jail, better known as The Tombs. She was escorted around the prison by Dr McGuire, the prison physician. Florence found the condition of the female wards in The Tombs to be in marked contrast to the conditions she had endured in England, and said: '*When I saw those women in large airy rooms, cheerfully engaged in their work, talking to one another, I thought of my own miserable conditions in Woking and Aylesbury, where I was in solitary confinement during the first four months of my incarceration. The awful contrast made me cry.*' As well as the cells being larger in The Tombs, Florence also liked the fact that female prisoners were allowed books on shelves, and mementoes and pictures decorating the wall. Whilst visiting the women's wards, Florence was introduced to Miss Nan Patterson, a young American dancer and actress who had been charged with murdering her English-born lover, Frank (Caesar) Young, in June 1904. Florence said to Miss Patterson, '*I want to express to you my deep sympathy. I hope the end for you will be happier that it has been for me.*'[1459] Patterson was to endure three trials before finally being released as the jury was unable to reach a verdict.

In December 1906, Florence spoke on the topic of prison reform at a meeting of the Young Men's Club of Dr Parkhurst's Church in Madison Square, New York. She told the audience that since her return to America she had visited 24 prisons. She said the worst was the Eastern Penitentiary of Philadelphia, where '*prisoners were virtually buried alive.*' At Trenton Prison in New Jersey, she found strange contradictions; the prison still had appalling underground dungeons, yet at the same time it provided apple dumplings as part of the prisoners' diet.

1454 *Washington Post*, 30th March 1905.
1455 *Minneapolis Journal* (Minnesota) 3rd January 1905 and *Cayuga Herald* (Indiana) 14th January 1905.
1456 Maybrick F. E., '*Criminal Court Procedure in England and America*' in *St Louis Republic*, 22nd January 1905.
1457 *Boston Sunday Globe*, 5th March 1905.
1458 *Boston Sunday Globe*, 5th March 1905.
1459 *The Newark Advocate*, 16th February 1904.

Florence was critical of the fact that one-half of the inmates in American prisons were under the age of 25. She said there were 10,000 boys under the age of 16 in jail for '*misdemeanours, not for crimes*', and commented that it was a terrible mistake to lock-up these youngsters with hardened criminals; they needed a special penitentiary for themselves. Florence also described her visit to Sing Sing Prison, declaring '*prisoners must have more sunshine.*'[1460]

Florence's comments about her visits to American prisons, expressed at both public meetings and in newspaper articles, were to be far more influential than she is usually given credit for. She raised public awareness of an issue that went largely undiscussed by polite society. She cleverly shaped her views so they appealed to the Americans' sense of morality as well as to their financial prudence, by arguing that bad prisons meant higher taxes. She recommended that men in prisons be put on paid work, and the money earned beyond paying for their keep should be given to their families. Florence argued that if prisons were merely seen as instruments of punitive revenge, then there would be no change in prisoners' behaviours and re-offending rates would remain high. She focused on prison conditions and the need for light and airy cells. Florence was to have some very real and tangible successes as a result of her campaign. In Trenton, legislation was passed to abolish the '*underground dungeons at the state prison.*' A local newspaper wrote that '*the bill is the result of a movement started by Mrs Florence Maybrick, who visited the prison recently. Mrs Maybrick declared that New Jersey is the only state in the union which retains this relic of barbarism.*'[1461]

In March 1905, the lawsuit between the Baroness and David Armstrong recommenced, with hearings in the law offices of Hayden and Yarell in Washington DC. The proceedings had originally begun in August 1893 when a bill had been filed in the Chancery Court in Richmond, Virginia by L.D. Yarrell, legal counsel to the Baroness. The filing charged David W. Armstrong, the Baroness' former attorney, with defrauding her out of her rightful share of the income derived from the sale of over 2,500,000 acres of land in Virginia, West Virginia and Kentucky. The case had stalled on a couple of occasions, primarily when Florence was ill in prison and her mother returned to England.

On 28th March 1905, Florence appeared as a witness at the hearing, although she also claimed a direct interest as her mother had allocated her one-third of the property at the time of her wedding. Florence stated: '*I am a journalist at present and earn my living to support myself and my mother until I secure my legal rights by the help of God.*' She outlined the events of 7th August 1889, when she was waiting for the jury to reach its verdict at her trial. She said Mr Potter, an agent for Armstrong, entered her '*underground cell beneath the courtroom*' and demanded she sign some legal papers as her signature would be illegal if the jury found her guilty.

When asked about her mental condition at that time, Florence replied: '*It was the condition of a woman who had had no sleep for eight days, under the most fearful strain, terrible agony of mind and utterly unable of counterbalancing anything or caring for anything beyond the fact that her life was at stake.*' She added that she neither read nor understood the documents she was asked to sign.[1462]

Florence's testimony was challenged by Armstrong on numerous occasions. Some of his objections were petty, such as criticising her statement that she was a journalist, and was trying to restore her legal rights with the help of God. Other objections were more serious, such as his rejection of Florence's claim of right of ownership to one-third of the property. During one series of heated exchanges with Armstrong, in an evasive manner Florence said she was unable to identify the handwriting on certain letters, including some which Armstrong said were from her deceased husband and others which he said were from her mother. Florence said she could not identify her mother's handwriting as she had only received typewritten letters from her during her imprisonment.

At the end of his questioning, Armstrong attacked the right of Florence to give evidence as she was a convicted felon. He asked her if she had received a pardon from the British Government, to which she replied that she had papers in her possession given to her by the Government. When Armstrong asked her to produce the papers, she replied they were not permitted to be produced except at the request of the British Government. Although the cross-examination was a '*trying ordeal*' for Florence, the reporter from the *Washington Post* wrote she had '*stood it well.*'

Armstrong's line of questioning over whether Florence had received a formal pardon must have concerned her. Accompanied by her counsel, on 31st March she called at the State Department in Washington DC and had a long meeting with the U.S. Second Assistant Secretary of State, Mr Alvey A. Adee (1842-1924). Adee, a long-time official at the State Department, served under eight presidents. Florence asked him if the State Department could '*procure from the British Government the papers necessary to completely rehabilitate her in the eyes of the law.*'[1463] The issue was taken up by U.S. officials, but with no success. In May 1905, Ambassador Choate cabled the State Department to inform them that the British Government had '*refused to grant any further clemency in the case of Mrs Florence E. Maybrick.*'[1464] The following year the Baroness petitioned King Edward VII in a further attempt to get a pardon

[1460] *New York Times*, 21st December 1906.
[1461] *Perth Amboy Evening News* (New Jersey), 20th February 1907.
[1462] *Washington Post*, 29th and 30th March 1905.
[1463] *The Evening Star*, (Washington D. C.), 1st April 1905.
[1464] *Muskogee Democrat*, 11th May 1905.

for her daughter. Once again it met with failure, the British Secretary of State informing her that he '*regrets that is unable to advise his Majesty to take any action thereon.*'[1465]

On Saturday 6th May 1905, the Baroness sailed into New York on the French steamer *La Touraine* after a seven-day voyage from Le Havre. Florence was at the quayside to meet her. It was the first time the two of them had met since Florence left her mother's home in Rouen in August 1904. The Baroness was described as being '*broken in health,*' and had only left her cabin twice during the crossing of the ocean.[1466]

Florence and her mother spent a night in New York before heading to Richmond, Virginia where the Baroness was to give testimony in her suit against Armstrong. On 10th May, they appeared in the city's Chancery Court. Florence was described as being in '*good health,*' but has the '*appearance of a woman who has suffered much.*' The Baroness was described as an '*aged woman,*' but '*still possessed of much vitality and unclouded intellectual powers.*'[1467]

If Florence and her mother thought their presence together in America would help bring a swift and successful conclusion to the legal wrangling over the disputed land sale, they were to be disappointed. They did achieve a partial victory when Judge Grinnan, the man who was charged with overseeing the case, instructed Armstrong to provide a full account of all the lands and money handled by him while he was the Baroness' attorney. However, the judge also ordered dispositions to be taken from a range of interested parties in several states, including Kentucky, West Virginia, Virginia, New York, Massachusetts and Pennsylvania. All of this took a great deal of time.

In December 1906, Florence and her mother were back in the Chancery Court to listen to further arguments on their behalf from their counsel, Samuel Hayden. They followed proceedings with '*considerable interest,*' watched by a large crowd of '*curious people*' who had been attracted to the court '*by reason of the appearance there of Mrs Maybrick.*'[1468]

As the court case dragged on with no conclusion in sight, Florence gradually became accustomed to life in early twentieth century America, though she found it difficult to throw off the '*mechanical habits acquired under the repressive English prison regime.*' For example, on the hot nights of her first summer back in America she would awake and want to get up, but would feel the '*constraint of the old prison rule*' that made it a punishable offence to leave one's bed before the '*early-morning summons.*'[1469] Another problem Florence encountered was the simple act of shopping, which caused her '*bewildering perplexity*' and '*filled her 'with dread.*' She found herself so out-of-touch with current fashions, coupled with the fact she was more acquainted with their English names, that she found it advisable to do her shopping in '*friendly company or by proxy.*'

Two things Florence did enjoy were music and children. She wrote that one of the '*chief delights*' of her regained liberty was that she was able to mix with young children. In her memoir she asked, '*robbed of my own little ones when they were at an age when child life is at its liveliest, is it cause for wonder that I now seek hungrily the companionship of these darlings of other loving mothers.*' Something else she enjoyed and felt distinguished her countrymen was their '*love of fun,*' which was in '*marked contrast to English modes of enjoyment.*' She said that although the English do have a '*jolly time,*' it was nothing like the '*heart-whole fun*' of Americans.

In April 1906, Florence applied for an American passport. She described herself on the official application as aged 44 (born on 3rd September 1861); height 5 feet 2 inches tall, blue eyes, brown hair and fair complexion. She classified her occupation as '*literary work.*' She said she intended to go abroad for a period of two months. The passport was issued on 2nd May. It is not known where Florence travelled to, though it is possible it was just a trip to Europe to visit old friends. It is unlikely she visited Britain as she was still legally obliged to meet the conditions of her ticket of release issued by the Home Office if she had. What is known, is that Florence travelled incognito, under the assumed name of '*Mme F. Cheney,*' to avoid being identified.

She arrived back in America on 5th August 1906, after a stay of three months abroad, sailing into New York on the French liner *La Gascogne* without anyone recognising her. Florence's true identity was only discovered when a custom inspector recognised her as he was checking her bag. Florence was asked if she had visited England, but would only answer, with a smile, '*it stands to reason that I did not stay in the same place all the time.*' Later that night, a *New York Times* reporter called at her house. He wrote that he found a '*short, slim, grey-haired woman, was standing on the steps while a hackdriver carried in four steamer trunks.*' The woman, who did not admit to being Florence, said '*How can I be interviewed dressed like this?*'[1470]

Towards the end of 1906, Florence's finances were said to be in a desperate state. One of her American friends, Mrs Manuel Jamet, claimed that when Florence had first returned to America she was greeted with the '*wildest enthusiasm,*' and many promises were made of financial support. Sadly, Mrs Jamet continued:

[1465] HO 1654/7/A50678D/861.

[1466] *Los Angeles Herald*, 8th May 1905.

[1467] *The Times-Dispatch* (Richmond, Virginia) 11th May 1905.

[1468] *Harrisonburg Evening News* (Virginia), 6th December 1906.

[1469] Taken from an article written by Florence Maybrick that featured in the *Sunday Magazine*, 19th November 1905.

[1470] *New York Times*, 6th August 1906.

'With the exception of a few, promises made with impetuous haste were forgotten and good intentions died a natural death... I have witnessed some most pathetic scenes in the little flat occupied by Mrs Maybrick and her aged, sad-eyed mother, the Baroness von Roques, I have heard plans discussed, and accounts gone over and over again so that every cent might be accounted for. To use Mrs Maybrick's own words, "It is one bitter struggle to live; was liberty worth having?"[1471]

It is difficult to ascertain the true state of Florence's finances. It is likely they were stretched, rather than broken. She had, after all, recently been able to finance a trip to Europe. A short-term solution to Florence's financial plight came in early 1907 after Alden Freeman – a New Jersey philanthropist and political radical – invited her to speak at a public meeting on penal reform in New Jersey. In the audience was Charles L. Wagner (1869-1956), the secretary of Slayton Lyceum Bureau of Chicago and the manager of several well-known celebrities and opera stars. His offices were at 511 Fifth Avenue in New York and, rather flamboyantly, his desk was a converted piano. He wrote:

'I went to Orange, New Jersey, to hear and meet Mrs Maybrick before her lecture. She had entered the room before I knew it. Prison life had taught her the humble art of self-effacement. Her face was the stillest I have ever gazed upon. It was as isolated from the real meaning of life as a white sheet of paper before it receives the printed impression. It had no cry, no need, no desire, no hunger, but it looked just to me. It stood for what fifteen years of life in an English prison can do to sterilize a human countenance. And it was this deadly unemotional quiet that controlled her audience with as great power as the rounded eloquent of Ingersoll. [Robert Ingersoll was a renowned speaker.] Mrs Maybrick gave her audiences tamed, unadorned facts about English laws and prisons, and her lectures were a cog in the wheel which moved towards the establishment of a Court of Criminal Appeal in England, instituted some years later.'[1472]

Charles L. Wagner at his converted piano desk

Although Florence was very different to Wagner's other clients, and he had doubts about her potential to attract the crowds, he nevertheless decided to offer her a contract. Florence claimed her prime reason for going on the lecture tours was that they provided her with an opportunity to *'expose prison brutalities and to plead for sympathy for those so unfortunate as to get in to the clutches of the law;'* however, it is more likely that her motives were mainly financial.[1473] She needed to support herself and working under Wagner's direction gave her the opportunity to be better paid and to speak to audiences across the country.

Public speaking at that time could be a very lucrative business as most American towns and cities had venues that provided a full calendar of public speaking events. Wagner's most successful client was Mr William Jennings Bryan (1860-1925), a former Secretary of State and a leading figure in the Democratic Party. Bryan earned around $50,000 a year from his lectures. Although Florence was never to be as popular or as well-paid as Bryan, Wagner described her as a *'very successful platform speaker,'* who was *'winning great popularity.'* He said Florence *'made a good impression everywhere. She is a woman of remarkable talents and character. She has a fine stage presence, an admirable delivery and has a message to the American people which is intensely interesting.'*[1474] He wrote that during Florence's time with his company he had arranged approximately 100 lectures for her. As she was paid an average of $50 for each lecture, he estimated she earned around $5,000 from her tours.

As Wagner was Florence's manager, it is easy to understand why he was so fulsome in his praise of her speaking abilities; however, there are also a large number of newspaper accounts that echo his sentiments. One, from Indiana, said the *'great curiosity to see Florence Maybrick was evidenced by the immense audience attracted by the announcement of her appearance.'* When Florence spoke, a *'shiver ran through the audience when this slender*

1471 *Mobile Daily Item*, 30th December 1906.
1472 Wagner C.L., *Seeing Stars*, (Arno Press, New York, 1940) page 84.
1473 *Saturday Spectator* (Terre-Haute, Indiana), 27th July 1907.
1474 *Evening Star* (Washington D.C.), 29th December 1907.

woman' spoke of her prison hardships.[1475] A report from Iowa stated: '*Mrs Maybrick spoke for over an hour, yet all the time the very large audience hung with a tragic interest upon her words which were the sublimity of heart-touching pathos.*'[1476]

On 3rd December 1908, Florence spoke to an audience of 700 in the Athenaeum in New Orleans. According to one report, she '*talked for over an hour, steadily, but not bitterly of her prison experiences.*' Those present listened with '*perfect attention and frequent applause attested the agreement of the audience with some of the noble sentiments she expressed.*' Florence said, since her return to America, she had visited prisons and jails in 30 states and conditions in some prisons were so bad that humans wouldn't keep their animals in them. She said crime was increasing in America, but the methods used for dealing with the problem were obsolete, as they were '*punitive,*' when they should have been '*corrective.*'

Most of Florence's talk was serious in tone. The only joke she made was when she described prison tea as being so weak it would not run out of the spout. Near the end of the talk, Florence spoke sorrowfully about her two children, whom she had not seen since the day she was arrested. She finished her lecture, as she had begun, '*with expressions of gratitude for the interest Americans had taken in her case.*'[1477]

An advert for one of Florence's prison lectures in Hannibal, Chautauqua, August 1909 (Chris Jones collection)

On Wednesday 9th December, Florence gave a lecture in Mobile, the town of her birth. It was probably the first time she had visited the city since her return to America. The address took place in the auditorium of Battle House, an 800 seated venue that was comfortably filled when she commenced her talk promptly at 8:30pm. Florence was introduced by Mr John C. O'Connell, the Associate Editor of the *Mobile Register*, who by coincidence had been employed by the *Liverpool Daily Post* at the time of her trial.

O'Connell said '*no case in the entire legal annals of the nations had created such a wave of worldwide sympathy as the trial of Mrs Maybrick.*' He added that if a Court of Appeal existed in England, then '*without a doubt*' the guilty verdict would have been reversed. As in her previous talks, Florence devoted only a '*short time to her own prison sufferings,*' instead spending most of her time on '*an earnest plea*' for reform of the criminal justice system in America. The address was described as '*deeply interesting and exhibited Mrs Maybrick as a woman of deep thought and practical ideas.*' Throughout the talk there were '*ripples*' of applause, but when Florence finished '*applause broke out in a storm,*' and there was '*no mistaking that she had the full sympathy of her audience.*' The majority of those in the auditorium, including members of her extended family, waited patiently at the end to shake Florence's hand and '*bid her God's speed in the work she had undertaken.*'[1478]

In January 1909, a rumour circulated that Florence had become engaged to Charles Wagner. The *Chicago Examiner* even printed a large picture of Florence with a head insert of Wagner. The *New York Times* reported that an announcement had been made by Mr J.H. McCracken, the Southern Representative of the Bureau, that '*the wedding would take place within a few weeks. The marriage according to Mr McCracken, will be the culmination of a romance extending over a period of several months.*'[1479] The report stated that Mrs Maybrick had at first turned down Charles Wagner's offer of marriage, '*because her unfortunate past might cloud his future,*' but he persisted until she finally consented to become his wife.

Both Florence and Wagner immediately denied the report. Wagner told the newspapers: '*Mrs Maybrick is a charming woman whom I know, however, in a purely business way. The report that we are to marry is an injustice to both of us.*'[1480] In his autobiography, Wagner blamed the rumour on an '*innocent exchange of shoptalk*' which was

[1475] *Saturday Spectator* (Terre-Haute, Indiana), 27th July 1907.
[1476] *Atlantic Daily Telegraph* (Atlantic, Iowa), 11th August 1908.
[1477] *Times-Democrat* (New Orleans), 4th December 1908.
[1478] *Mobile Register*, 10th December 1908.
[1479] *New York Times* 6th January 1909.
[1480] Christie T.L., op. cit., page 240.

misinterpreted by the '*ever-present eavesdropper.*'[1481] Whatever the truth of the story, it ended Florence's association with Wagner. Florence continued her talks for another couple of years, but she did so without the assistance of the Slayton Lyceum Bureau.

Florence's lecture tours organised by Wagner were financially rewarding; nevertheless, the Baroness and Florence continued to pin their long-term hopes for financial prosperity on a resolution to the legal dispute over the ownership of the land originally purchased by Darius Blake Holbrook. In February 1909, it appeared all their hopes had finally been realised. In the Chancery Court in Richmond, Judge Daniel Grinnan entered his formal decree in the long-running case between the Baroness and David Armstrong. It stated that while Armstrong was '*not shown to have been guilty of intentional wrongdoing in respect to the matters alleged against him in the complaint's bill,*' he must abide by the terms of the contract of 1879 and not the contract of 1887, which Florence had signed during the latter stage of her trial in August 1889. That meant that the Baroness was entitled to half of the money that Armstrong had realised from the sale of the lands since 1879, and not just the $10,000 she had received as a result of the 1887 agreement. The judge determined that the '*aggregate amount received by Armstrong from these sales was $131,025.*' The Baroness was entitled to half of that sum – $65,512.50 – minus the £13,000 that Armstrong had already paid the Baroness and the other trustees under the will of Darius Holbrook, $52,512.50, plus interest of 6% on that money from September 1889 – producing a final total owed by Armstrong to the Baroness and her associates of $52,912.50.[1482]

After many years of bitter wrangling, the court decision appeared to be a massive victory for the Baroness, Florence and their legal team. Armstrong, though angry and frustrated by the decision, decided not to appeal the judgement.

If Florence and her mother believed their financial future was finally secured, they were soon to receive yet another setback. In June 1910 Armstrong filed a voluntary petition for bankruptcy in a Federal Court in Kentucky. His liabilities were given as $210,769 and his assets as only $1,500. His two biggest creditors were listed as Gilbert Ray Hawes of New York, whom he owed $137,520, and Baroness von Roques, whom he owed almost $53,000.[1483] Although Florence and her mother did not yet know it, they had been at the centre of one of the longest running court cases in American legal history and, at the end of it, while they had come out with a legal judgement in their favour they were never to receive a single cent of compensation.

In 1909, on one of her lecture tours, Florence stayed in Moraine Hotel in Highland Park, a small but wealthy suburb of Chicago located about 30 miles north of the city on the west shoreline of Lake Michigan. Florence loved the tranquil setting of Highland Park so much that she made it her base, and later – between 1910 and 1915 – decided to live permanently in the hotel. The owner of the Moraine was Frederick William Cushing (1856-1941). As well as being a hotel proprietor, he was a scientist, inventor and entrepreneur. He moved to Highland Park in 1886 from Wisconsin, and was employed as secretary to Elisha Gray, one of Highland Park's most well-known luminaries.

Moraine Hotel, Highland Park

Gray had given the first ever public exhibition of the telephone at his local Presbyterian church in December 1874, but he was to lose the battle to patent the invention to Alexander Graham Bell. Despite this setback, Gray did manage to patent several other inventions including the stock printer, burglar and fire alarms, and the telautograph, an early version of the fax machine. In 1894, Cushing travelled to London and demonstrated the telautograph, which Professor Gray had invented, for the Princess of Wales and her daughters. Cushing worked for Gray for more than ten years, but when Gray moved away from Highland Park Cushing decided to stay in the area, quickly becoming a leading citizen of the community.

In the late 1890s, Cushing decided to build a grand hotel in Highland Park. He selected thirteen acres of land on the bluffs overlooking the lake and, in 1898, purchased the land for the sum of $20,000. The title to the land was placed in his wife's name to protect the investment and because much of the money for the purchase came from her wealthy family. Cushing had married Cassie M. Scott, the daughter of the lumber king Thomas B. Scott, from Merrill, Wisconsin in 1883. The couple were to have two daughters.

[1481] Wagner C. L., op. cit., page 85.
[1482] *Washington Post*, 4th February 1909.
[1483] *New York Tribune*, 14th June 1910.

Work on the hotel began in October 1899, when one of Cushing's daughters helped cut down the first tree and the other turned over a spadeful of earth. The hotel took its name from a large granite boulder that was dug up some fifteen feet below the surface. From the start, Cushing had a grand vision for the hotel and was '*determined to make the building as good as possible.*'[1484]

The hotel opened on 1st June 1900 in a blaze of publicity and with all its rooms fully reserved. It was built in colonial style, with its main building measuring 266 x 45 feet and with a wing of 40 x 70 feet. It had nearly 140 bedrooms, which were either singles or suites, and some 50 bathrooms. There was a main dining hall that could seat 300 hundred people, and some smaller private, more intimate dining rooms. Near the main dining room was a large ballroom, with a stage and outside veranda. The hotel also had a library, a terrace room, a beach club, a number of parlours and other rooms for the guests to relax in or be entertained.

The hotel enjoyed the latest in all modern conveniences, including steam heat and electric lights. Huge expense and effort were made to ensure the internal décor of the hotel met the highest standards. '*The floors were all Georgia pine... The dining room was said to be elegant, with solid mahogany tables made exclusively for the hotel. The smaller dining rooms were furnished in European decors. The kitchens and pantries were set apart from the main building in the L-shaped wing.*'[1485] The hotel buildings were surrounded by beautifully landscaped gardens, through which the guests could walk or ride horses. The hotel also had its own private beach.

In a letter to Trevor Christie in 1933, Cushing stated that Florence first visited his hotel in the summer of 1910. He wrote that he had received a telegram from Lake Geneva, Wisconsin, signed by F.E. Maybrick asking for accommodation for herself and her secretary for a coming weekend. He said he recognised her immediately upon her arrival, because at one time she had been the '*most advertised woman in the world.*' In fact, the hotel's register for 1909 shows that between June and August 1909, Florence stayed at the hotel on at least five occasions, with the earliest date being 23rd June 1909. The register also shows that Florence's mother, Baroness Von Roques, stayed in the hotel without her daughter in October 1909.

When Florence first stayed at the Moraine she was still travelling the country on her lecture tours; however, the hotel so '*suited*' her that she decided to make it her '*headquarters*' and go on her tours from it. As soon as she became '*settled, her secretary, a Miss Carruthers, left as her services were no longer needed.*'[1486]

It is not hard to understand why Florence liked the hotel so much. The register of 1909 shows she stayed in Room 141 on most of the occasions she visited. Plans of the hotel reveal that this room was the last one at the west-end of the main building. It measured 17 feet by 12 feet, had its own bathroom and a private porch. One can only assume the room perfectly suited Florence's needs. It was part of the main building, yet nevertheless provided her with both quietness and privacy.

As well as excellent rooms, the hotel was also renowned for its culinary excellence. Florence would have loved the beautiful grounds where the hotel was situated and the abundance of walks available in the local countryside and along the shores of Lake Michigan. As well as its fine comforts, the hotel also offered a wide range of diverse activities designed to keep the guests interested and entertained. The local paper commented that '*scarcely a day or evening goes by that does not offer some interesting diversion, pleasantly planned by the management for its guests. The beautiful new ballroom is the scene of a brilliant dance every Tuesday and Saturday evening; there are lectures and recitals, regattas, ping-pong and tennis tournaments, card parties and coaching parties.*'[1487]

According to Christie, Florence's time at the hotel was '*the most placid time of her life since leaving the Cornwall convent, rising about noon, going for walks in the countryside, and sitting of an evening on the wide porch with her fellow-guests.*' One of these was Grace N. Veeder who remembered Florence as a '*fascinating character and always something of a mystery. Slender, of medium height, alert with a bit too much of white powder and an evident transformation [wig], she yet carried herself with dignity.*'[1488] Cushing himself said he found Florence to be a '*very well educated and refined little woman, but she had the prison pallor that came for her long confinement and which she could never get rid of. She spoke excellent French, and while not attractive physically, was a most interesting conversationalist and attracted much attention from the guests in the house.*'[1489]

Whilst staying at the Moraine Hotel Florence was informed of her mother's death in Paris on 10th April 1910. The Baroness had been travelling in France under the name Mme Maumont, and had died in the nunnery in the Avenue Des Ternes which was run by an English order. She was buried next to her son Holbrook in a Paris graveyard. Some newspapers suggested that Florence did not know her mother had gone to Paris, that the Baroness died in poverty and non-relatives paid for her burial.[1490]

1484 *Sheridan Road News-Letter*, 1st August, 1902
1485 Crooks E.M., *The Moraine Hotel of Highland Park, Illinois 1900-1972* (January 1977)
1486 Trevor Christie Collection.
1487 *Sheridan Road News-Letter*, 1st August 1902.
1488 Christie T.L., op. cit., page 243.
1489 Trevor Christie Collection.
1490 *Boston Globe* (Massachusetts), 13th April 1910.

Like many stories about Florence, these reports were only partially true. Florence was shocked by the news of her mother's death as she did not think she was seriously ill. When she first heard it, she asked her attorney to contact the American Consul in Paris to ascertain whether the reports were accurate. It is also likely that some of the Baroness' friends *did* contribute towards the cost of the funeral as it took place in one of the city's more exclusive cemeteries. Florence said the stories of her mother dying in want were '*false*.' She said she had '*taken care of her*' ever since they had been together in America. Florence said her mother had been staying with her at the Moraine Hotel, but had '*been in poor health and believed that if she returned to France, she would get stronger*.' She said she persuaded her mother '*to wait until April or May*', when she could accompany her on the trip to Paris, '*but because of the rigors of the Chicago spring climate, sent her south with friends a month ago*.'

While travelling down south, the Baroness decided to change her plans and left her companions, going to New York and taking the boat to France. Although the Baroness sailed without notifying her daughter, she did write to Florence after her arrival in the country. Florence said her mother had '*been in Paris about a fortnight and I have received three letters from her, all telling how well she was getting along. The last one I received only this morning. I had intended going to her just as soon as my lecture engagements would allow me*.' [1491]

Christie wrote that if Florence did not know her mother had travelled to Paris, this suggested there had been a '*partial estrangement between mother and daughter in the closing years*.' He also wrote that Florence '*bore a long-time resentment over her mother's style of life, and her capricious methods of bringing up her child*.' [1492]

Although they did have disagreements – for example, when Florence publicly contradicted some of her mother's statements in November 1904 – the evidence suggests there was no partial estrangement. Mother and daughter maintained a strong bond right to the end. A true reflection of Florence's view of the Baroness comes in a glowing tribute she paid her in an interview she gave many years later to the *Liverpool Daily Post,* whilst visiting Europe in 1927:

> '*In all my troubles I have had one loyal friend only – my mother. She beggared herself to defend me when I was arrested, and she never lost faith in my innocence. When the shadow of the scaffold was over my head and it seemed certain that I should go to a shameful death, it was my mother who worked until the last minute and wrung a respite from the authorities for her unhappy child. While others who called themselves friends cast stones at me, my mother was the true Christian who had nothing but love and pity for the sinner*.' [1493]

Exactly one year after the death of the Baroness, Florence's son, James Chandler Maybrick, known as James Chandler Fuller, died on 10th April 1911 in a tragic accident in British Columbia, Canada. Shortly after their mother's trial, James and his sister Gladys had been taken to London where they had been cared for by Dr Fuller and his wife.

In the 1891 Census, the two siblings are listed as living with the Fullers in their house in Albany Street, London. Their surname is recorded as '*Fuller*;' however, there is no evidence they were ever formally adopted by the doctor and his wife. When James was old enough to be told the details about his father's death, he took it badly and decided to have no further contact with his mother.

At some point in the late 1890s, the two children left the Fuller household and went to live with Michael Maybrick in his palatial home, '*Lynthorpe*', in Ryde on the Isle of Wight. This happened sometime after Michael married his housekeeper, Laura Withers, on 9th March 1893. The wedding was a low-key affair in the register office at Marylebone, with Dr Fuller and his wife as the witnesses.

Florence was furious when she eventually found out that her children had left the Fuller household. In October 1899, she wrote to the Home Office to complain that Laura Maybrick was not a suitable person '*by birth, education, previous life or association*' to be Gladys' guardian.[1494]

In the 1901 Census, Gladys is recorded as living with Michael and his wife. Her surname is listed as '*Maybrick*.' Over the next few years, newspaper reports reveal she was a regular attendee at the Royal Victoria Yacht Club Garden Party, with her uncle and aunt. Michael was President of the club.[1495]

In 1907, she assisted on a stall in Ryde bazaar, organised to raise money for the county hospital building fund. Michael was then Mayor of Ryde.[1496]

In the 1901 Census, James is recorded as being a boarder in a household in Camborne in Cornwall, where he was a student in the Camborne School of Mines. His surname is listed as being Fuller, and his birthplace incorrectly shown as America. Records reveal that James was a popular and successful student. He obtained a first-class

---

[1491] *Chicago Tribune*, 13th April 1904 and *Washington Post*, (Washington D.C.), 15th April 1910.
[1492] Christie T.L., op. cit., page 244.
[1493] *Liverpool Daily Post*, 2nd May, 1927.
[1494] HO 144/1640/A50678D/331.
[1495] *Isle of Wight Observer*, 20th August 1904.
[1496] *Isle of Wight Observer*, 20th April 1907.

examination pass in assaying,[1497] and was the honorary secretary of the school's student committee.[1498] He was also an extremely talented athlete and rugby player, being awarded his rugby colours and playing at least two seasons on the mining school's rugby team. One rugby match report stated that Fuller was one of three players who '*led every movement*' in the game.[1499]

Gladys Maybrick (front) with Michael Maybrick standing behind her, at the 'Old Madrid Fancy Fair' in Ryde, 1907. Taken from a postcard sent by Gladys to Amy (Doris) Maybrick, 9th May 1907. (Derek Warman collection)

In 1904, James graduated as a mining engineer and left Cornwall to work in Canada. Passenger lists show that he arrived in New York on 14th August 1904, aboard the *SS Etruria* from Liverpool. He was certified as being in good health, having more than $50 in his possession, had never previously been to the United States, and was in transit to Rossland, British Columbia. Also on board the *SS Etruria* was Anthony J. McMillan, the managing director of the Le Roi Gold Mine in Rossland.[1500] By coincidence, Florence was on her return voyage to New York when her son arrived in the city; however, when she landed on 23rd August James was probably already in Canada.

With the exception of short periods abroad, working in Rhodesia (Zimbabwe) and Mexico, James was employed at the Le Roi Mine for the rest of his short working life. Passenger lists show him sailing into Quebec from Liverpool in July 1909, on board the *Empress of Ireland*. He is recorded as a '*returning Canadian*,' and his occupation as a '*mining engineer.*'[1501] This voyage was possibly after his short time working in Africa, or maybe after a holiday in Britain.

James was employed in various capacities at Le Roi Mine, including several years as chief mining engineer. In the period before his death, operations at the mine had been reduced and it was up for sale.[1502] James had been assigned the task of assaying, a key role that involved testing the purity of the metal extracted from the mine. He appears to be both successful and popular at work, with one source stating, '*He was held in high regard by all with whom he came in contact, and the management bears testimony to his ability as an engineer.*'[1503] He also appeared to be happy in his personal life and was engaged to Marion Martin, a local Canadian woman, whom he was due to marry the following June.

On 10th April 1911, James was sitting alone at his desk in the laboratory. At 1:30pm, Frederick Peters, the mine superintendent, phoned him and he '*seemed very cheerful.*'[1504] Fifteen minutes later, James rang Peters and told him to '*come quick.*' He seemed to Peters to be in trouble and was breathing as though in '*great distress.*' Peters rang James twice but, as he got no reply, ran to the assay office and found him lying on the steps, about 75 yards from the office. He had an asbestos mitt on one hand and a pair of tongs and a sandwich were beside him. James would not answer Peters' questions. He was frothing at the mouth, breathing hard and his pulse was beating faintly. Peters realised that James was seriously ill. He sent another work colleague to look after him while he ran for help and called the doctor. He returned two or three minutes later and the two of them carried James to the office, but he died on the way. When James' desk was checked, there was a beaker of water on the table and also an upset beaker of potassium cyanide.

The manner of James' death has provoked some debate. For example, Graham and Emmas wrote '*many of the newspapers hinted at suicide*' and suggested he might have been suffering from depression.[1505] In fact, nearly every newspaper covering the case uses the word '*accident*' in their report, and there is no evidence that James was suffering

1497 *Royal Cornwall Gazette*, 29th August 1901.
1498 The Camborne School of Mines Magazine, stored in Exeter University archives.
1499 *Royal Cornwell Gazette*, 3rd October 1901.
1500 Ellis Island and other New York Passenger Lists, 1820-1957; accessed at myheritage.com
1501 Canada, Incoming Passenger Lists, 1865-1935; accessed at ancestry.com
1502 *Vancouver World*, 22nd April 1911.
1503 Obituary in *The Engineering and Mining Journal*, Vol. 91, 13th May 1911, page 976.
1504 Inquest Report into the Death of James Fuller, 11th April 1911 (Rossland, British Columbia, 138/11)
1505 Graham A. and Emmas C., op cit., page 282.

James Chandler Fuller (far right on the back row) in Camborne School of Mines Rugby XV 1900/01 (Chris Jones collection)

from depression. William Hannay, an assayer who gave evidence at James' inquest and had known him since 1904, described him as '*one of the most cheerful men I ever knew.*' Alexander MacDougall, one of James' co-workers at Le Roi Mine who had known him for two years, said he '*was always very cheerful.*'

The coroner's jury examined the case and concluded that '*from the evidence produced the deceased came to his death... through accidentally drinking or otherwise partaking of a solution of Cyanide Potassium.*' The fact that James had a sandwich in one hand and there was a beaker of water on his desk, and that he struggled about 75 yards desperately trying to get help, all supports the view that it was an accident. Peters testified he had known James to use a similar beaker to the one that contained potassium cyanide for drinking purposes, though not in the laboratory. Hannay said a solution of potassium cyanide cannot be told from water without conducting a test.

Two days after his death James' body was taken to Vancouver and, on Saturday 15th April, he was buried in a grave belonging to the family of his fiancée, Marion Martin. She sent pictures of him to Gladys, and they were to become lifelong correspondents. Florence was told about the death of her son by some of her friends as she stepped downstairs and into the office of the Moraine Hotel. One report stated she '*gasped, lifted her hands as if overcome by a momentary faintness and sank into a nearby seat.*'[1506] Florence quickly regained her composure, and said: '*The past is dead. This boy has been dead to me for than twenty years. Why should these words affect me? I have not had a son since my imprisonment began.*'[1507]

A short obituary appeared in the *Times* newspaper in Britain stating: '*Maybrick – On April 10th, at Rossland, B.C., James Chandler Maybrick, only son of the late James Maybrick of Liverpool, aged twenty-nine.*'[1508] That James was referred to as *Maybrick* and not *Fuller* is confirmation he never legally changed his surname, and that he only used *Fuller* to avoid being linked to his mother. Although the obituary was short, it wasn't long before stories started to

[1506] *Chicago Tribune*, 10th May 1911.
[1507] *The Province* (Vancouver, Canada), 10th May 1911 and *Seattle Star* (Washington, USA), 10th May 1911.
[1508] *The Times*, 22nd April 1911.

appear in the newspapers about Florence's trial. One stated: '*The simple announcement in the death column of the Times on Saturday recalls one of the most sensational trials of the last three decades.*'[1509] Most of the reports referred to the letter that Florence had written to Brierley, and incorrectly stated that its contents only came to light because James, rather than Gladys, had dropped it in the mud in his eagerness to place it in the letter-box. After years of trying to hide his connection to his mother, it was a terrible irony that the report of his death made James a headline story in rehashed accounts of Florence's trial in newspapers across the world.

Evidence of James' successful career as a mine engineer is the sizeable estate he left in Britain after his death, which was valued for probate at £4,775 9s 2d. Under the terms of his will, dated 5th July 1903, the two executors were Michael and Thomas Maybrick, his uncles, who had also been the executors of his father's will. James left his entire estate in trust to his sister Gladys, or for the benefit of her children if she had already died. Interestingly, if his sister died unmarried before attaining the age of 21, then his whole estate passed to Michael Maybrick. The fact that Florence was not mentioned in the will, and that James was prepared to leave his whole estate to Michael, confirms the view that he had come to believe his mother was guilty of murdering – or at least attempting to murder – his father.

Although the death of her brother must have shocked and saddened Gladys, the money she inherited from him would have helped her when she got married the following year. On 3rd August 1912, aged 26, Gladys married Frederick James Harold Corbyn, aged 28, at St Mary the Virgin Church in Hampstead. Corbyn was listed on the marriage licence as being a '*merchant*' who lived in Morpeth Mansions, London. He also had a naval connection and, as a lieutenant in the Royal Naval Reserve, was to be awarded a military OBE at the end of the First World War. Corbyn's deceased father was listed on the marriage certificate as having been a doctor of medicine. Gladys was listed as having no work or profession, and her surname was given as Maybrick, further confirmation that both she and her brother had never actually changed their name to Fuller. Gladys was recorded as living at 3 Elsworthy Terrace, London. This was the home of Mrs Fuller, who had moved there after the death of her husband, Dr Fuller, in November 1902, aged 72. Mrs Gertrude Mary Fuller was shown on the marriage licence as one of the witnesses to the wedding. The fact that no announcement or report of the wedding featured in any of the newspapers suggests that Gladys, like her brother, had been very keen to avoid any connection being made to her mother, and wanted to deliberately hold a low-key event. It was also possibly a reflection of the fact that her husband's family were less than pleased he had married the daughter of such an infamous convicted murderer and had, as a result, supposedly disowned him. If this was the case, then the money Gladys inherited from her brother would have been invaluable.

It is not known if Michael Maybrick attended the wedding of his niece. He perhaps didn't, if the desire was to keep it a quiet affair, as although he was no longer a public performer, he was still a person of considerable note. On the Isle of Wight he had left behind his musical career and become a high-profile civic figure. He became Chairman of the Isle of Wight Hospital, a justice of the peace for both the county and the borough of Ryde, and was elected Mayor of Ryde on no less than five occasions. As Michael was mayor in the Coronation years of Edward VII and George V, he had the distinction of representing Ryde in Westminster Abbey at both coronations.

On 26th August 1913, while convalescing from periodic gout at St Anne's Hotel in Buxton, he died suddenly from heart failure. He was buried four days later at All Saints' Church in Ryde, in one of the biggest funerals ever seen on the island. Both Thomas and Edwin Maybrick attended the funeral. The local newspaper wrote about Michael that '*to the people of Ryde the loss will be irreparable, and to very many of them life cannot be exactly the same again since so true a friend, so strikingly endowed and so unique a man has gone where beyond these voices there is peace.*'[1510]

It is unknown when, if at all, Florence received any news about her daughter's wedding; however, she was informed over the telephone of the death of Michael Maybrick in August 1913. On hearing it, she supposedly said it did not come as a surprise as he had been ill for some time.[1511] By this time Florence had stopped her lectures tours and was living permanently in retirement in the Moraine Hotel. Her last big lectures had taken place in 1911. The newspapers carry several adverts and reports for events at which she spoke in states such as Indiana and Ohio, from July 1911 to October 1911. The biggest of these was probably a nine-day event in Tipton, Indiana, in July 1911, when she shared the bill with several other speakers including Dr Frederick Cook, the Arctic Explorer.[1512]

At the end of October 1911, Florence called a halt to her tours. There were probably a few contributing factors to this decision, including a breakdown in her health and the delayed impact from hearing about the deaths of her mother and her son. Although Florence's relationship with her mother had not always been smooth, and she was totally estranged from her son, the combined effect of these two deaths must have affected her both mentally and physically.

[1509] *Dundee Courier*, 19th April 1911.
[1510] *Isle of Wight County Press*, 30th August, 1913.
[1511] *Cincinnati Commercial Tribune*, 27th August 1913.
[1512] *Tipton Tribune* (Tipton, Indiana), 29th June 1911.

The major consequence of Florence halting her lecture tours was had insufficient funds coming in to pay for her stay at the Moraine Hotel. She told Cushing she had inherited more than two million acres of land in Virginia from her grandfather. She also told him about the successful verdict in her case against David Armstrong in the Richmond Chancery. Cushing agreed to allow Florence to stay in his hotel at no charge, while he pursued her claim to the land. Although his act was not without its generosity, he did hope to obtain a sizeable commission if he could successfully regain some of Florence's lands or money for her. Unfortunately, after years of trips to Washington and Virginia and endless meetings with lawyers, Cushing had to admit defeat and he informed Florence that she would receive no money from the lands. He told her the taxes had not been paid on the land, and as a result some of it had reverted to the government. In other parts, coal mining companies and squatters had occupied the land for so long that they had established legal rights of ownership.

Florence was effectively broke. In 1915, she left the hotel and Cushing never saw her again, although he did receive a card from her a few years later saying she was going to make one more effort to succeed. She said if she wrote to him again she had been successful; if he didn't hear from her, then she was probably dead. In the 1930s, Cushing received further news of Florence from one of her relatives, who told him that she was living in Connecticut.

LINKS TO THE RIPPER DIARY: DID JACK THE RIPPER'S INFAMOUS PSEUDONYM HAVE A LIVERPOOL ORIGIN?

Those who believe that James Maybrick was the Whitechapel serial killer and the author of the Diary, suggest he could have constructed the name Jack the Ripper by amalgamating words taken from the High Rip criminal gangs who plagued Liverpool and the mythical Spring-Heeled Jack, who was said to have paid occasional visits to Liverpool.

In his article advocating James as the infamous murderer, Professor Rubinstein wrote the name Jack the Ripper '*may itself have had a Liverpool origin.*' He said that between 1884 and 1886, '*Liverpool's local newspapers made great play over the alleged existence of a murderous "High Rip Gang" which, it was claimed, terrorised passers-by in the Scotland Road slums. There was considerable debate about whether such a gang actually existed, and mention of the "High Rip" seems to have ceased in early 1887. However, the "High Rip" and its association with street violence would have been well-known to any Liverpudlian in 1888.*'[1513]

Rubinstein is correct in his assertion that James, as a Liverpool resident, would have known about the *Rippers*, the members of the High Rip gangs who spread fear in the city. Victorian Liverpool, thanks to its great port, was widely recognised as the Second City of the British Empire; however, underneath its increasing wealth and prosperity lay great poverty and much human misery.

Nowhere was this disparity of riches more evident than in Tithebarn Street, the street in Liverpool in which James had his office. In the 1880s, it was one Liverpool's busiest streets. It was also '*a place where two worlds met, a microcosm of the city itself.*'[1514] At the western end of the street could be found the Liverpool Docks. As one moved down the street you passed some of Liverpool's finest buildings, including the Clarendon Building and the Knowsley Buildings, while at the eastern end of Tithebarn Street were some of the most deprived slums in the whole of Britain.

In the 1870s, the area was the scene of high levels of crime, much of it associated with Liverpool gangs known as the Cornermen. These gangs were so named as they comprised youths who loitered outside public houses, many of which were situated on street corners, and threatened passers-by to give them money to buy drinks. The Cornermen achieved national notoriety in the Tithebarn Street Outrage of 1874, when an innocent man was savagely beaten to death by a street gang.

In 1884, when James and Florence settled in Liverpool, the city was again plagued by street violence, much of it orchestrated by the notorious High Rip Gang. The gang first came to prominence with the Blackstone Street murder of January 1884, when Nunez, a Spanish sailor, was kicked and stabbed to death in Liverpool. A seventeen-year-old local, unemployed labourer of Irish descent, Michael McLean, was hung in Kirkdale Prison after being found guilty of the crime. The murder of Nunez had some similarities with the so-called Tithebarn Street Outrage of 1874; however, while the Cornermen had mainly been a loose group of unemployed youths who stood outside pubs trying to beg or steal money from passers-by, the High Rip Gang members more closely resembled '*ruthless, organised criminals.*'[1515]

Members of the gang were usually referred to as '*High Rippers*' and they habitually carried a knife called the *bleeder*. They also wore a belt that had been adapted so it could be turned into a vicious weapon.[1516] Gang members

[1513] Rubinstein W D., 'Hunt for Jack the Ripper' in *History Today*, Vol. 50, May 2000.
[1514] Macilwee, *The Gangs of Liverpool*, (Milo Books, Lancs., 2007) page 15.
[1515] Ibid., page 146.
[1516] Ibid., pages 152-153.

were often better armed than the police, and local people were usually too terrified to testify against them. The gang was at its worst between October and November 1886, though it was still active in 1888 when the Jack the Ripper murders took place in London. In June 1888, a Liverpool newspaper referred to a gang of youths that attacked a police constable as '*high rippers*'.[1517]

Spring-Heeled Jack was a mythical character from English folklore who supposedly existed during the Victorian period, and was capable of extraordinary leaps. He was said to be tall and thin, with a frightening and devil-like appearance. He wore a tight-fitting helmet, and skin-tight clothing that looked something like an oil skin. The first claimed sighting of him occurred in London in September 1837. A businessman returning home late at night saw a mysterious figure leap effortlessly over ten foot high railings.

A short time later, Spring-Heeled Jack was said to have attacked a group of people, three women and one man, who all ran, but one of the women, Polly Adams, was caught and sexually assaulted. Further strange attacks occurred in Lavender Hill and Clapham. In January 1838, London's Lord Mayor, Sir John Cowan, declared Spring-Heeled Jack a '*public menace*'. In so doing, he unintentionally gave a degree of credibility to '*the first Victorian urban legend.*'[1518] A posse of men, including the aged Duke of Wellington, was formed to search for the individual responsible for the attacks.

Spring-Heeled Jack was never found, and further attacks occurred in the East End of London, including one on Commercial Road, close to where the Ripper murders were to occur in 1888. After 1839, there were only occasional sightings of Spring-Heeled Jack. One well-documented sighting was in 1877, when he was spotted by a group of soldiers in an army camp in Aldershot.

In the 1880s, Spring-Heeled Jack allegedly made a series of appearances in Liverpool. He was first seen in High Park Street, Toxteth. A few years later, he was supposedly seen jumping over garden walls in St Michaels-in-the-Hamlet, very close to Aigburth and the Maybricks' home. Next he appeared in Childwall, close to where the Janions lived. In 1888, he appeared in Shaw Street, where the Liverpool Collegiate School was situated.[1519]

Whether Spring-Heeled Jack really existed – and if he did, who or what he actually was – is a matter of great speculation. The character has been linked to Jack the Ripper in certain respects, such as his name, his tendency to sexually assault women, and the fact that some of the alleged incidents involving him took place in the East End of London.

James Maybrick would have been aware of the mythical character from stories about him in Liverpool in the 1880s. A newspaper report in the *Liverpool Citizen* in 1887 makes it clear that '*everyone*' in Liverpool was talking about Spring-Heeled Jack. The report even suggests that the character may have even been a young '*buck*' from the Cotton Exchange where James worked, who was acting in the manner of the mythical demon to win '*a bet of a thousand pounds.*'[1520] Whether the story is true or not, James would have certainly heard the rumours at the 'Change.

Although it is the case that James would have known about the High Rip gangs and also some of the stories concerning Spring-Heeled Jack, that does not mean that he coined the name Jack the Ripper, or indeed was the notorious serial killer. It is widely accepted that the name originates from the *Dear Boss* letter received at the Central News Agency on 27th September 1888. The author of the letter signed off '*Yours truly, Jack the Ripper.*' Prior to this letter, the name did not feature in any earlier communication received by the police, or in any newspaper reports of the murders. In reports on the early murders, the person responsible for the killings is simply referred to as '*the Whitechapel Murderer*' or '*Leather Apron.*' The latter name first appeared when the police were making enquiries following the death of Polly Nichols. Their enquiries revealed that '*a man named Jack Pizer, nicknamed Leather Apron, had been ill-treating prostitutes*' in Whitechapel and in other parts of London for some time. Although there was little else to connect him with the murder, the police made extensive enquiries to try and find him. Suspicion that Pizer was the killer '*hardened into near certainty when a second body was discovered [Annie Chapman] eight days later with a piece of leather apron close by.*'[1521]

On 10th September 1888, the police arrested John Pizer, who was hiding in his family home. When they questioned him he was able to provide a cast-iron alibi for the night of Polly Nichols' murder and, as a result, was set free. After Pizer's release the public panic over '*Leather Apron*' quickly evaporated, and the name no longer featured prominently in newspaper stories. Pizer's release caused great concern at the *Star,* as they had been the newspaper that had most ardently pursued the Leather Apron angle in their reporting of the murders. They were concerned at the prospect of having to pay him substantial damages. In order to avoid this, they called Pizer into the newspaper's offices and he '*accepted a nominal amount in full settlement of any claims he might have against the paper.*'[1522] As the Leather Apron storyline was '*no longer of any use in selling newspapers and promoting the story of the unsolved*

[1517] *Liverpool Weekly Mercury*, 2nd June 1888.
[1518] Bell K., *The Legend of Spring-Heeled Jack*, (The Bodywell Press, Woodbridge, 2017) pages 1-2.
[1519] Whittington-Egan R., *Tales of Liverpool: Murder, Mayhem & Mystery*, (Gallery Press, Parkgate, 1987) page 187.
[1520] *Liverpool Citizen*, 29th October 1887.
[1521] Rumbelow D., op cit., pages 34-35.
[1522] Begg P., Fido M. and Skinner K., op cit., pages 287-289.

murders,' most newspapers '*reverted to calling the unknown killer the Whitechapel Murderer, but this seemed altogether too mundane and lacked the impact of a catchy sobriquet.*'

The newspapers required a '*telling name to give the story an edge. What was needed was a nom de guerre for the unknown and phantom-like stalker of East End prostitutes.*'[1523] *The nom de guerre* was to be provided by the infamous signature '*Jack the Ripper*' at the end of the *Dear Boss* letter.

Both Robert Anderson and Melville Macnaghten, two senior police officers at Scotland Yard, believed that the *Dear Boss* letter was a forgery and that it had been written by a journalist. In 1913, Chief Inspector John Littlechild wrote that the author of the letter had probably been either Tom Bulling or John Moore, both of whom were journalists at the Central News Agency. Littlechild called it a '*smart piece of journalistic work.*'

The new name for the killer provided the edge that the newspapers were desperately seeking. It enabled them to further sensationalise their articles, sell even more copies and make even more money. The pseudonym Jack the Ripper had nothing to do with James Maybrick; it appeared for the first time in the *Dear Boss* letter, which caught the public's imagination following its publication in newspapers, and thereafter became indelibly linked with the serial killer. The name itself was probably crafted by a clever and enterprising journalist who cynically realised that the dreadful nature of the murders provided a golden opportunity for the newspapers to make a lot of money.

[1523] Evans S.P. and Skinner K., op cit., page 13.

23

FINAL YEARS

It is not easy to track down Florence's exact movements for the first two years after she left the Moraine Hotel as she changed location on a number of occasions. In 1916, she is listed as living at 318 E. Park Ave., in Highland Park.[1524] Florence found employment with the George L. Schuman Publishing Company based in Chicago.

Schuman was a long-time resident of Highland Park and his house on Michigan Avenue was near Florence's new home. Schuman's company often employed middle-aged, educated women, especially teachers, to help them sell their products. One of their adverts in 1915 stated: '*Old established firm desires services of a cultured woman of good appearance; personality main requisite; will make attractive offer to right party: must be over 28 and free to travel.*'[1525] On paper, Florence made the ideal candidate for the post; she was cultured and educated, and had already travelled over much of America on her lecture tours. In reality, Florence found the extensive travelling too demanding for her health. After only a relatively short period of time she was forced to resign. That meant she was no longer able to afford the rent for her home in Highland Park.

For a while, Florence was forced to live in a homeless shelter in Chicago run by the Salvation Army. Some reports state that she then moved to Florida, though there are no official records of her living in the state at that time. She did live for a while in a cottage on the Mississippi near Cairo, Illinois, the town her grandfather had helped develop many years earlier.

These must have been desperate times for Florence. She was in her mid-fifties, not in the strongest of health, with no permanent home and chronically short of money. As she had done in the past, Florence contacted friends and relatives and asked to borrow money to help rebuild her life. These were loans she would never repay. As a result of her efforts, Florence managed to deposit $2,000 in her bank account.

Armed with these new funds, she travelled in late 1917 to the small rural village of South Kent in Litchfield County, Connecticut, close to the New York border. She moved there on the recommendation of a teacher friend of Henrietta M. Banwell to take up the appointment of housekeeper to Miss Banwell, who ran a chicken farm.[1526] Before her arrival in South Kent Florence decided she was no longer going to use the surname *Maybrick*, but instead, would revert back to her maiden name of *Chandler*. Although this meant she would not be able to cash in on her famous name, it did provide her with the opportunity to escape her past and live a life of relative obscurity. Miss Banwell wrote that, during the time she knew Florence, her '*ruling obsession was to obscure her identity.*'[1527]

Although Florence immediately took a liking to South Kent, it was soon apparent to both her and her new employer that she was not suited to the role of housekeeper. This was hardly surprising since Florence had not been in the best of health and had never shown an aptitude for physical work. Her unsuitability was also obvious to Mr and Mrs Austin, neighbours of Miss Banwell, who first met Florence when they visited her house. They described Florence as wearing good clothes, speaking excellent English and being an interesting talker, but having too many frills. More importantly, they knew Miss Banwell to be an '*exacting boss*' and it was clear that Florence was somewhat '*irked at her duties.*'[1528] After just one winter, Florence decided to leave the household. Miss Banwell was not surprised as Florence had already made it clear she '*had a very strong desire to be in a house of her own, by herself.*'

In April 1918, Florence rented a house belonging to the Austins. In June that year, she moved into rented rooms in the home of a local family named the Grissells. Miss Banwell saw Florence occasionally after she left her employment and their relationship remained '*friendly,*' however, as she was so absorbed in her business she had little time to socialise with her.

In 1919, after several months of living with the Grissell family, Florence bought a plot of land in nearby Gaylordsville and had a small house built. The house was on a quiet road named Old Stone Road, which wound its way gradually upwards from South Kent Road in the village of Gaylordsville to Bull's Bridge Road, close to South Kent School. The area was sloped and thickly wooded, and the road lined on both sides by old stone walls.

[1524] Highland Park Directory, in *Bumstead's Waukegan City and Lake County Directory, 1916-1917*, page 850.
[1525] *Chicago Daily Tribune*, 3rd July 1915.
[1526] *New Milford Times* (Connecticut), 29th October 1941.
[1527] Letter from H.M. Banwell to Trevor Christie, dated 3rd December 1941, in the Trevor Christie Collection.
[1528] Comments made by Mr and Mrs Thomas Austin to Trevor Christie, in the Trevor Christie Collection.

Old Stone Road, South Kent, Connecticut (Chris Jones collection)

Today, at the Gaylordsville end of the road there are some grand modern houses, many of them second homes of rich New York families. At the other end of the road there is a new golf course. Close to the golf course end of the road, there is a section of Old Stone Road that has remained unchanged over the years, and has retained its rustic charm and unspoilt beauty. This stretch is '*downright primordial – more path than road, no cars or dress shoes allowed. Strolling along the scenic route is a delight. Crows call in the distance, dry leaves rustle in the wind, a colourful, ring-necked pheasant scampers by.*'[1529]

It was on this section of the road that Florence had her new home built. It was a small three-room house, twenty feet by twelve, with a simple porch and fitted with three cat-flaps. It was built by the C.M. Beach Company of New Milford at the cost of $1,200. The house had no electricity or running water. Heat came from a wood-burning stove in the living room; there was a kerosene stove in the kitchen, and kerosene also provided the power for light. Water came from a nearby stream.

During the early years Florence lived in the house, the Austins said she took '*fine care*' of the grounds, and had an attractive flower garden but no vegetable plot. The condition of the house and garden gradually deteriorated as Florence grew older, more eccentric and had less money.

Although nothing of the house now remains, one can still gain a clear impression of how simple Florence's life must have been by walking down the road. At the point where her house stood, the road is little more than a rough and muddy track that must have been almost impassable in winter when the heavy snows carpeted the hillside. Standing at that location makes it abundantly clear that Florence came to South Kent because she wanted to bury her Maybrick past. She chose an isolated spot, one that provided her with the peace and anonymity that she had come to crave. Florence wanted to keep the world at arm's length. She was even reluctant to forge new friendships in her adopted home, lest it should expose her former life.

As Florence spent most of her money on the cottage, for the rest of her life she was largely reliant on financial help from various benefactors. The latter included a wealthy cousin, James Edmundson Ingraham (1850-1924), a Vice President of the Florida East Coast Railway, who provided her with financial help until his death in 1924. Another benefactor was Alden Freeman, the wealthy political reformer from New Jersey. Florence was speaking at one of his meetings in New Jersey when she met Charles Wagner.

Every so often, Freeman's attorney Julian Gregory would arrive outside her home in a chauffeur-driven limousine and present her with a cheque. As well as some rich benefactors, Florence's neighbours in South Kent also provided her with help and support. As a thank you to the Austin family for their assistance, Florence gave Mrs Austin a black silk dress with a lace jacket. When Mrs Austin examined it, she saw that it had a label from a cleaning company that read, '*Mrs Florence E. Maybrick, the Moraine, Highland Park, Illinois.*' Intrigued by the label, Mrs Austin made some inquiries and discovered the identity of her mysterious neighbour. Luckily for Florence, the Austins felt sorry for her and kept the secret to just four people: themselves, Mrs Austin's sister-in-law and Miss Banwell. The Austins said Florence had '*burned her bridges behind her,*' and had come to South Kent to '*bury her past.*' They '*felt sorry for her*' and felt she was '*entitled to her secret and her privacy.*'

Despite supportive neighbours, Florence's erratic behaviour sometimes caused tension in the small community. On occasion, she would take small possessions belonging to other people and keep them for herself. The growing number of cats that lived with her also caused tension. She once stole a cat from one of her neighbours, returned it, took it again and eventually kept it.

Florence developed a reputation for tall tales, once telling the Austins she nursed a sick soldier on a train, that her son was a mining engineer who had died in a mining shaft, and how her daughter died of typhoid at the age of 16. She fell out completely with the Austins in 1926, when she asked Mr Austin to endorse a cheque for $400 so she could get electricity into her home. Austin was understandably reluctant to agree to Florence's request and wrote to Julian Gregory to ask about her finances. Gregory must have informed Florence about Austin's qualms, for she

---

1529 *Litchfield County Times*, 4th December 1998.

Florence Maybrick's house on Old Stone Road (Chris Jones collection)

refused to speak to Mr and Mrs Austin in public ever again. When Mrs Austin went to Florence's house to deliver a basket of food, Florence would not answer the door.[1530]

In 1923, South Kent School, an independent college preparatory school for boys, was founded by the Rev Frederick H. Sill, an Episcopal monk of the Order of the Holy Cross. It was built on Bull's Bridge Road, close to the northern end of Old Stone Road and less than a mile from Florence's home. She had to pass the school on her daily walk to Boyd's grocery store and would sometimes drop in for a visit. Through these visits, she got to know many of the staff and students. On occasion she even attended class day exercises, wearing a '*crepe de chine pink and lavender dress and carrying a small bouquet in one hand and an umbrella in the other.*'[1531]

Florence became friendly with the school chaplain, Rev William Francis Wood, and he often visited her house. He was one of the few people she permitted to enter her home. She became especially friendly with Miss Clara Dulon (1880-1933), a Housemother at the school, and would stop and have tea with her. According to Christie, Miss Dulon took a motherly interest in Florence, even though she was younger than her, and contributed five dollars a week to her upkeep. Florence told her, '*I hope to get some money some day. I'm so tired of begging. I would be too proud to tell anyone else, but you people are my only friends.*'[1532] In 1933, Clara Dulon died from cancer and was buried in the school's small cemetery.

After Miss Dulon's death, Florence continued to visit the school. She became close to the school nurse, Mrs Amy Lyon. She also normally attended the school's prize days, sitting at the back and clapping the winners. Headteacher Samuel Bartlett recalled Florence as a pleasant old lady, '*down in her luck*' but still recognisable as a person from a cultured background. He said she '*wrote beautiful letters. In fact, she used better English than you find in some college classrooms.*'[1533]

[1530] Comments made by Mr and Mrs Thomas Austin to Trevor Christie, in the Trevor Christie Collection.
[1531] *Bridgeport Sunday Post*, 26th October 1941.
[1532] Christie T.L., op. cit., page 250.
[1533] *Bridgeport Sunday Post*, 26th October, 1941.

Final Years

In 1926, Florence's quiet and reclusive existence in South Kent was knocked out of kilter by the publication in England of the autobiography of Sir William Nott-Bower (1849-1939). Nott-Bower had 52 years of service in the police, including acting as Chief Constable of Liverpool between 1881 and 1902, and being elected Commissioner of Police for the City of London from 1902 until his retirement in 1925.

In his book he devoted a chapter to '*Women Poisoners*' and wrote about Flanagan and Higgins, who had been hanged in Liverpool in 1884, and the Maybrick case. One thing he didn't mention in his analysis of Florence's trial, was that his police force was not directly involved in the investigation of James' death. Aigburth came under the jurisdiction of the Lancashire County police force and not the Liverpool force. He wrote he had not kept a diary or even notes of events, and had to rely upon his memory. This, he admitted, might expose him to '*just criticism, in regard to accuracy of detail.*'[1534] His latter statement is apt, because his account of Florence's case contains numerous mistakes. For example, he wrote that in March 1889, Florence and Brierley spent a week living together in a London hotel, rather than just two nights. He wrote that nobody knew what happened to the flypapers Florence purchased, even though the servants at Battlecrease admitted to destroying them. He largely ignored James' use of dangerous drugs, including arsenic, and he failed completely to mention his use of strychnine. Very importantly, he confused the medicine prescribed by Dr Fuller and compounded by Clay and Abraham's in Liverpool with the very different London medicine that James received in the post. This was something Addison had also done at Florence's trial. Nott-Bower wrote Michael Maybrick had '*flatly denied*' being told by Florence that her husband was in the habit of drugging himself. That was not the case – Michael had even questioned James about the accusation.

In one key passage, Nott-Bower said he had details never before revealed to the public. He wrote that '*sometime after the Home Secretary had announced the reprieve of Mrs Maybrick, a highly respected Liverpool chemist*' came to the police with a confession he wanted to '*make known to them.*'[1535] The chemist said in the spring of 1889, Florence had come to his shop and asked for '*powdered arsenic to kill cats.*' He supplied her with a considerable quantity, which she took away. One or two weeks later, Florence returned to his shop and told the chemist she had lost the arsenic and asked for more, which he again supplied her. The chemist said he had not informed the police about this as he '*feared the consequences to himself.*'

Nott-Bower said the police had compared the handwriting of the chemist with the handwriting on the *Arsenic - Poison for Cats* label, and found the two to be identical. Nott-Bower said this supply of arsenic had been known to the defence team at Florence's trial. He had informed the Home Office of the chemist's confession, but by then it was too late as the reprieve had already been granted. The confession had convinced Nott-Bower of Florence's guilt, and he believed it would have been of '*supreme importance*' if presented at her trial. If Nott-Bower's account is accurate and he had given the confession to the Home Office, it is possible that it was the mysterious evidence that was supposedly hidden in their files that proved Florence's guilt.

Nott-Bower's revelation about the chemist's confession provoked a new series of headline stories concerning Florence's case. One Liverpool newspaper led with: '*Famous mystery of crime solved at last – How Florence obtained arsenic to poison her husband.*'[1536] The article stated that if Florence was tried in 1926, instead of 1889, she would be found guilty, sentenced to death and hanged. One of the most important responses to Nott-Bower's claims came in January 1926, in an article in the *Liverpool Daily Post* from John E.J. Holmes (1865-1947). In 1889, Holmes had been a young journalist at the *Liverpool Courier*, and also a special correspondent for the London edition of the *New York Herald.*[1537] Holmes wrote that while he completely agreed with Nott-Bower's opinion that Florence was guilty, it had in fact been him who had obtained the chemist's confession and given it to Nott-Bower. In the second edition of his autobiography, Nott-Bower acknowledged the reporter's version was accurate, and regretted that his memory should have failed him '*even in so small a detail.*'[1538]

According to Holmes, on 20th August 1889 – a few days after the trial finished – he received a letter from Mr James Gordon Bennett, proprietor of the *New York Herald.* Bennett asked him to see a '*certain gentleman who had something of importance to communicate in regard to the Maybrick case.*' Holmes interviewed the '*gentleman,*' who told him he was a friend of a chemist who had supplied arsenic to Florence. The chemist was prepared to confess providing he received full immunity and his friend wished to sell the story to the newspaper which paid the most money. According to the gentleman's account as outlined by Holmes in his article, in the last week of April 1889, an attractive lady – who never gave her name – called into the chemist's shop and made a number of '*small but costly purchases, as she had done on several occasions previously.*' The lady said she was '*dreadfully troubled by the ravages among her fowls of a number of strange cats.*' The lady, who had '*insinuated herself into the good graces*' of the chemist, asked him to supply her with arsenic so she could get rid of the cats.

1534 Nott-Bower W., *Fifty-two years a Policeman*, (Edward Arnold, London, 1926) page v.
1535 Ibid., pages 131-132.
1536 *Liverpool Weekly Courier*, 23rd January 1926.
1537 *Liverpool Daily Post*, 19th January 1926.
1538 Nott-Bower W., op cit., page 131.

The chemist pointed out that under the requirements of the Pharmacy Acts, he could not supply her with the poison unless she signed her name, together with the object for which the poison was intended, in a book kept for that specific purpose. A third party, known to both buyer and seller, also had to sign the book as a witness to the transaction. The lady declined to sign, and said there would be no problems if the chemist made her a present of the arsenic. As she had been such a good customer, the chemist agreed to her request and gave her the arsenic, which he personally labelled *Arsenic - Poison for Cats*. Three of four days later on 1st May, the same lady returned to the shop, made some purchases and then asked for more arsenic as she had lost the packet supplied on the previous visit. Once more, the chemist allowed himself to be convinced by the '*skilful persuasion*' of the woman and gave her another packet of arsenic. As before, she did not sign the book as was required by law. When the chemist handed over the arsenic, he told her to be careful as it contained enough poison to kill a regiment. The lady left the shop and never returned. During '*the police court proceedings*' [James' inquest in Garston], the chemist said he visited the court and recognised the lady who purchased the arsenic as the defendant in the dock. He wanted to inform the authorities, but was afraid he would end up in trouble for breaching the regulations concerning the sale of arsenic.

After the trial, the chemist approached a friend and together they came up with a scheme by which they both could benefit. The friend would arrange immunity for the chemist with the Home Secretary in return for making a full confession; the friend would then sell the story to a newspaper. The plan failed, as the Home Secretary refused to meet the chemist's friend. Four months later, as agitation grew to try and get a reprieve for Florence, the chemist and his friend decided, for the public good, they had to inform the police about the illicit sale of arsenic to Florence. It was at this point that Holmes obtained the confession. With the help of Inspector Bryning, he checked the handwriting of the chemist with the handwriting on the label *Arsenic - Poison for Cats*. He then gave the confession to Nott-Bower so he could pass it on to the Home Secretary. In his article, Holmes identified the chemist as Richard H. Aspinall, whose shop had been at 1 Leece Street, in Liverpool city centre. Aspinall had retired in 1896 and since died. Holmes did not provide the identity of the chemist's friend.

Although the information revealed by Holmes appears to be very damning for Florence, the whole story has to be treated with a great deal of caution. Firstly, it is difficult to believe that a chemist would hand over two large quantities of arsenic to a person he did not know and in a manner that contravened the law. Such an action, if discovered, would get him into serious trouble and cause him to lose his livelihood. Secondly, the chemist said he only recognised Florence when he saw her in the dock at the police proceedings. That cannot be true, as there was no dock in the Reading Room in Garston, the venue for the proceedings; Florence was placed in a separate room away from the spectators. Thirdly, it doesn't appear from Holmes' account that he actually ever talked directly to the chemist. The confession that Holmes gave to Nott-Bower was in his own handwriting, and not that of the chemist. Fourthly, the Liverpool police force, headed by Nott-Bower, was not actually responsible for the investigation, so Holmes gave the confession to the wrong police chief. Fifthly, Holmes' account comes from the chemist's mysterious friend, whom Holmes never named and who had tried to sell the story for a large amount of money. There is also the question of why Holmes sat on the story for so long when he could have made a lot of money by publishing it earlier, when Florence's case was still headline news. Finally, if the police were convinced of the robustness of the confession, why didn't they release this information to the public as a means of vindicating their actions at a time when they faced criticism for the manner in which they had prosecuted the case? One is left with the clear impression that the confession, even if it did exist, lacked credibility and, as a result, the story only appeared in the press long after the chemist had died. One person who was clearly doubtful about the chemist's claim was Richard Webster, the Attorney-General. On 20th February 1890, Webster sent a letter to the Home Secretary informing him that he had '*grave doubts whether there is any foundation in the story.*'[1539]

A further reason for doubting the veracity of the chemist's confession comes from a letter published in the *Liverpool Daily Post* two days after Holmes' article featured in the same newspaper. The letter was from Dr Paul, one of the defence's medical experts at Florence's trial. He said the source of the *Arsenic - Poison for Cats* was only a '*mystery to the prosecution*' and that it was '*quite well known to the defence some time before the trial.*' Paul said he remembered both the name of the chemist and where his shop was situated, and that the chemist's anxiety stemmed from the fact that he '*sold the arsenic without added pigment, which was illegal.*' Paul added '*a man whose confession had apparently been ignored by the defence*' might very well later offer it to the prosecution.[1540]

In some respects, instead of clarity Paul's letter adds another layer of confusion to the purchase of the arsenic. If the chemist first approached the defence, then that implies his information might have been helpful to Florence's cause. If that is the case, why didn't the defence use it? Paul's letter also implies that the chemist, presumably Aspinall, *did* sell arsenic to someone connected with events, but provides no name. If the chemist was prepared to

---

[1539] HO 144/1639/A50678/D54a

[1540] *Liverpool Daily Post*, 21st January 1926.

inform the defence team about the arsenic sale, then who is the mysterious gentleman who was supposedly trying to sell the same story to the highest bidder?

Less than a week after Holmes' article appeared in the *Liverpool Daily Post*, the *News of the World* repeated his claims and ran an even more startling story. They claimed that '*pigeon-holed in the Home Office is a full and complete confession, written by the murderess [Florence] at a time when she believed that she was about to be hanged.*'[1541] They added no further details to support the story, such as who their source was. What they did add was another unsourced story about how '*a friend of a well-known London criminologist once nearly suffered the same fate of Mr Maybrick.*' This friend claimed he had dined with James and Florence after the theatre one night and '*swallowed a glass of claret that unquestionably, had been dosed with arsenic, though he was at a loss then to understand the agitation of his hostess.*' The *Liverpool Daily Post* carried the same story the following day.[1542]

The criminologist who was the source of the story was '*quartered*' in Liverpool during the First World War. One evening he got into conversation with a '*charming member*' of the club at which he was staying. The member said he had been one of James' greatest friends. After attending the theatre with the Maybricks, he went back to Battlecrease for supper. On the table was some cold partridge and a decanter half-filled with claret. He filled a glass with the claret and was about to drink it, when Florence became '*terribly agitated.*' She told him not to touch it as it had been standing for a long time and had gone '*sour.*' Not wanting to cause any trouble, the man swallowed the wine in '*one gulp.*' Florence seized the decanter, left the room and returned with a fresh bottle. On his way home, the unnamed man became seriously ill. Two weeks later, a doctor told him he had been poisoned by arsenic. Not long after this event, the Maybrick poisoning case occurred. He said he had approached a solicitor who had advised him to '*do nothing*' as he would become involved in the case and get no thanks for it.

In his book on the Maybrick case, Morland outlines a very similar story which he said was told to him by a '*professional man of impeccable reputation and honesty*' whose name he knew.[1543] In his version, a '*decent, middle-class friend of James*' had Sunday supper at Battlecrease. During the meal James suggested that they have a glass of claret. Florence '*wished to get a fresh bottle but James said it had only been open at lunchtime when he had taken a glass and insisted on the bottle being used.*' As the friend was walking home, he became violently sick and remained ill for ten days. When a chemist analysed his vomit, it was found to contain arsenic. The family lawyer was approached for advice and told the man to take a voyage to the Mediterranean so he could recover his health. By the time he had returned to Liverpool, the Maybrick case was over.

Despite some differences between the story in the *News of the World* and the account in Morland's book, such as how long the claret bottle had been open and the advice given by the lawyer, it is likely that both are referring to the same event. The major problem with the account provided by the unnamed criminologist, is that the story was told to him during the First World War, at least 25 years after the event supposedly happened, by an unnamed person he happened by chance to be speaking with at his club. He, in turn, did not inform the newspaper until some ten years later. These factors mean the story lacks credibility and is impossible to verify. If the gentleman had been poisoned by arsenic after eating and drinking at Battlecrease and he had been a great friend of James, it is almost certain he would have gone to the police with the information at the time of the trial, but he chose not to. As no name or date are provided in either account, it is impossible to tease out exactly what happened, if anything. It is much more likely that if the claret did contain arsenic it was James, and not Florence who added the poison, because it was something he had done in the past.

The gravity of the various claims made against Florence in the different newspaper articles, forced her to respond to the charges. From her secret location in South Kent, Connecticut, Florence issued a statement through her lawyers in New York angrily denying that she had confessed to murdering her husband. She wrote: '*Do you think I would go before my Maker with a lie on my lips, or so foolish as to destroy my one chance of escaping from the scaffold? At the time when I was supposed to have made this confession friends were working hard to save me from death, and we had high hopes of the prison gates opening for good. How could I have confessed to a crime under such circumstances? I challenge my detractors to produce this alleged confession.*'[1544]

As Florence's alleged confession does not appear in her files in the National Archives, one can assume this particular element of the story is untrue. Florence also denied the story which appeared in the Nott-Bower book and the Holmes' newspaper article concerning the Liverpool chemist supplying her with arsenic, writing: '*The chemist's story of the two packets of arsenic was gone into at the time. The Crown lawyers had it investigated. It was obvious that I could not have been in that part of Liverpool or, indeed in the city at all on one of the occasions sworn to, that the evidence could not be relied upon. On the contrary, it was part of the Crown's case that on this particular day I was in a London hotel with my lover, Mr Brierley. They had to choose between these two conflicting stories and as*

[1541] *News of the World*, 24th January 1926.
[1542] *Liverpool Daily Post*, 25th January 1926.
[1543] Morland N., op cit., page 233.
[1544] *Brisbane Telegraph* (Brisbane, Australia) 6th April 1926.

much as it was to their interest to prove the purchase of arsenic, they could only rely upon the hotel story. That is why this alleged confession was never of any use.'

Although Florence's denial was strongly worded, she was mistaken over the dates. Florence met Brierley in a hotel in London in late March 1889 and she was back in Liverpool for the period of late April and 1st May, when she supposedly purchased the arsenic according to the chemist's alleged confession. Although this part of her denial is rendered ineffectual, it is likely that the Crown did pursue the possibility she had purchased arsenic from a Liverpool chemist. If the police had been able to prove this link they would have had the complete case against her; that they couldn't prove it is an indication that it never happened.

In 1927, Florence somehow raised the money for a brief visit to England. While in Liverpool, she gave an interview to a reporter from the *Liverpool Daily Post.* He wrote: '*Sad-faced, gentle-voiced, with hair turned to silver, the Mrs Maybrick of today is but a shadow of the striking-looking woman who made a lasting impression on those who saw her in the dock at Liverpool, thirty-eight years ago.*' Florence told the reporter she felt '*death's shadow*' over her, and had come to England with '*one object only, to effect a reconciliation with members of my family, if that be possible. To that end I am trying to clear myself of the charge of murder of which I was convicted and sentenced to death.*' She said that despite making '*overtures through friends,*' her '*hopes of reconciliation were dead,*' leaving her with a feeling of '*bitterness worse than death.*' Florence said since the day she had '*heard the verdict of Guilty I have longed for my children who were but babes at the time, and the mother's hunger in my heart was so strong that I felt that I must make this journey now in the hope of seeing them. The knowledge that it has been in vain has almost broken my heart.*'

While Florence was disappointed not to achieve her main object in coming to England, she had arranged with a '*private enquiry agent to go over the ground in the hope of securing corroboration of several points, which it is contended strongly suggest her innocence.*' One area she was examining, with the help of '*expert opinion,*' was the '*possibility of arsenic being taken into the system through inhaling deposits on the walls of the papered room.*' She was also looking at other ways arsenic could have been brought into the house. She said there was evidence from a Liverpool chemist who '*remembers having sold the poison to my husband sometime before his death.*' She said this evidence had come forward after the trial, and was one of the reasons why the Home Secretary had reprieved her death sentence. It is not clear to which chemist Florence was referring. Heaton said he regularly sold James a pick-me-up containing arsenic, but he had made that statement at her trial.

Florence said she was going back to America, where she lived a life of a recluse, and would only return to England if the new inquiries '*bear fruit and produce the evidence necessary to establish*' her innocence. If that happened, she would make *'one last attempt at reconciliation'* with her children and ask them for their forgiveness for all the unhappiness she caused through her *'folly.'* She said there was a time when she thought '*death was the best thing that could happen*' to her, but the longing for reconciliation was so strong in her heart it made her dread death. The reporter asked Florence what she meant by the word '*folly.*' She replied: '*I mean the love affair that played such a big part against me. There were circumstances at home that drove me to the arms of another man and I was foolish enough to think that I could find happiness with that man who offered me the love my husband denied me. Bitterly I have regretted it ever since.*'

Florence said during her prison years she had been buoyed up with the hope that, when released, she would find the man in the case waiting to marry her, in order to make up for what she had suffered. Her feelings were ones of '*bitter, bitter disappointment*' when the man in question, for whom she had sacrificed everything, '*had forgotten me during the years I had been trying to keep my heart young in prison for his sake.*'

At the end of her interview, Florence said she revisited most of the scenes in Liverpool associated with her tragedy, including attending the Grand National meeting and standing outside Walton Gaol. She said the most poignant memories came when she visited places in Liverpool where she used to walk with her children. She said '*tears came thick and fast when I revisited these spots. I should have been the happiest woman could I have wafted back over the years. If only I should have seen what my illicit love would lead me to, I should have acted differently.*'[1545]

Questions have been asked about whether Florence really did visit Liverpool in 1927. It is possible that the interview in the *Liverpool Daily Post* was a work of fiction. The name of the journalist who conducted the interview is not mentioned. There are no pictures of her stay in England, and the story only contains a few simple details about Florence's visit. There is also the factual error when Florence refers to her '*children,*' when she only had one child alive in 1927. Florence would have been in her mid-sixties in 1927, and she was known to be chronically short of money. Significantly, there are no immigration records of her arriving or departing in or out of England at that time. Feldman suggests that Florence may have travelled under an assumed name. He points to a passenger record of a person named '*Eliz. Ingraham,*' who travelled on the Cunard steamship *California* from Liverpool to New York,

[1545] *Liverpool Daily Post*, 2nd May, 1927.

departing Liverpool on 21st May 1927.[1546] Although the date fits, and Florence had previously travelled under the name Ingraham, there are problems linking this passenger with Florence. The woman's age is given as 71, while Florence would have been in her sixties, and the passenger is listed as a '*housewife*.' Her last address in the UK is shown as a cottage in '*W. Livingston, Scotland*,' which is an extremely improbable address for Florence to be staying at during her visit to Britain.[1547] It is more likely that the woman in question is a Mrs Elizabeth H. Ingraham (born in 1856), who appears to have travelled to the UK in 1923 and 1927. She had a permanent address in California, and was definitely not Florence Maybrick travelling under an assumed name. On this issue, as with others, one can see Feldman turning speculation into fact so as to provide support for one of his outlandish hypotheses.

Although this passenger record for Florence is highly doubtful, it is still possible that she did visit Britain at some point in the 1920s. Amy Main, the daughter of Edwin Maybrick, wrote a letter in 1972 in which she claims that '*in about 1920 or perhaps a little earlier*' Florence revisited Liverpool and called in her father's office in the Knowsley Buildings, but he was out at the time.[1548] Amy was in her seventies when she wrote the letter but her memory remained excellent, so it is feasible that Florence did at some point travel to Liverpool, though it may have been earlier than 1927. Perhaps she was interviewed at the time, but the story was of little value to the newspaper until after the Nott-Bower revelations of 1926 had made Florence front page news again.

On her return to South Kent, if Florence did indeed travel to Liverpool, her existence became more reclusive, and her behaviour even more erratic. She earned the nickname of '*cat woman*' due to her habit of looking after a large number of stray felines. These cats became the focal point of her life and she spent much of the little money she had on them. Her appearance gradually became unkempt. She stopped washing, and her clothes became more and more ragged. Local people believed Florence had been educated to be a lady and was therefore unable to perform many of the basic tasks of housekeeping. One of her neighbours told a newspaper after her death that she hardly '*knew how to set a pan of water to boil*.' He said her grocery buying reflected this, as she would buy things which needed little cooking. He said Florence was unused to sewing, and she once tried to mend a long tear in her coat by tacking the cloth together with nails.[1549]

Florence's precarious financial position became even worse in the 1930s when her two main benefactors were no longer able to provide her with funds. In 1924, her cousin James Ingraham died, and Alden Freeman lost heavily on the stock exchange in the Wall Street Crash. By 1935, Florence had failed to pay the taxes on her house for almost two years and was being pursued by tax collectors until the town abated her taxes. In August that year, Florence wrote to Samuel Bartlett, the headteacher at South Kent School, asking for his help. She suggested that, in return for the school helping her with her expenses, she would leave her property to the school in her will. Although Bartlett did not provide Florence with money from the school's funds, he did assist her, in June 1936, in applying for a state pension under Connecticut's old age provision scheme. The pension was granted three months later and Florence received \$6 a week, a sum that later rose to \$7 a week. Bartlett also arranged for her to have a telephone line put in her home. Florence was not particularly grateful for his kind act, telling her neighbours: '*I'm starving and you gave me a telephone*.'[1550]

One of the teachers at South Kent School who got to know Florence well was Samuel A. Woodward, the history master. He would leave newspapers and magazines for her to read. If he and others called at her house, Florence would come outside to greet them; she would never let anyone into her home apart from a few people with whom she was intimate. Woodward found Florence to be mentally alert on current affairs, but she would tell outrageous and unbelievable stories about herself and her life. She once told him that men on the mountain left a sick baby with her. The school sent her food and blankets for the infant, but she refused to show the baby to anyone. Eventually, Mrs Lyon insisted on seeing the baby only to be told by Florence she had sent it to the hospital.[1551]

The only way Florence could maintain her independence was by continually asking friends and acquaintances for money. Miss Cora Griffin, the writer who first met Florence in Cragsmoor in 1904, was one of many who provided her with funds over a lengthy period of time. She frequently gave Florence small sums so she could pay for repairs to her house, such as fixing the roof or chimney. Miss Griffin eventually stopped sending money, because she felt Florence was wasting too much of it on the numerous cats she kept. She was also critical that Florence '*rather thought that the world owed her living*,' and she '*leaned on strangers too much*.' She found Florence too fond of admiration, a little mentally unbalanced and a teller of tall tales. She said Florence once told her that while out West, she received word that the Germans were going to blow up a bridge over a river. Florence said she had managed to frustrate the plot by firing a gun, warning everyone to the danger.[1552]

[1546] Feldman P., op cit., page 184.
[1547] Passenger list, BT27/1155. Images reproduced by nationalarchives.gov.uk and digitalised by findmypast.com
[1548] Derek Warman's private collection of correspondence with Amy (Doris Maybrick) Main.
[1549] *Bridgeport Sunday Post*, 26th October, 1941.
[1550] Christie T.L., op cit., page 258.
[1551] Taken from a letter by Samuel A. Woodward, History Master at South Kent School, to Trevor Christie in the Trevor Christie Collection.
[1552] Taken from a letter written by Cora Griffin to Trevor Christie in the Trevor Christie Collection.

One person whom Florence '*leaned on*' for money was Mrs Laura Lee Robertson. She had known her briefly from September 1931 to June 1932, when her husband had been the chaplain at South Kent School and they lived in a cottage on the school grounds. She was introduced to Florence by Miss Dulon, who described her as '*a lady, well-educated but in dire want,*' prepared to do menial work around the house. Laura Robertson paid Florence to do small jobs for her once or twice a week. Although she enjoyed Florence's company, she described her as having an '*unusual personality, the finest example I had almost ever seen of buoyant courage in the utmost adversity.*' As she did with so many others, Florence told Laura Robertson some '*incredible things to dramatise herself.*' She was tolerant of Florence's tall tales, as she felt them to be a '*natural and excusable psychological development for one in her situation.*'

In 1932, the Robertsons moved from the school. Two years later, Florence sent Mrs Robertson a letter appealing for financial help. She sent Florence a cheque every month, for between 12 and 18 months. She only stopped sending money when she received a letter from the wife of the school's headteacher informing her that Florence was refusing assistance from the school on grounds she knew to be fictitious.[1553]

Another person who provided Florence with money for more than 20 years was Mary E. Calhoun, the founder and headmistress of the Calhoun School for girls and boys in New York. Although she never met Florence and was not aware of her true identity, they maintained a regular correspondence in which Florence wrote of the great hardships she endured. When Miss Calhoun finally found out who Florence really was, she felt no bitterness at the deception. She described Florence as a '*remarkable woman,*' and said she had a '*never-failing courage, her more than human endurance, and her deep gratitude for kindness. If society punished her, whether justly or unjustly, it should not have left her struggle alone.*'[1554]

Although Miss Dulon, the housemother at South Kent School, had died in 1933, Florence still visited the school on a regular basis as she had become close to Mrs Amy Frost Lyon (1879-1974), the school's nurse. She was a widow, originally from Britain, who was to be Florence's last real friend. Mrs Lyon said Florence would visit the school infirmary almost every day to see her and have hot cocoa milk and a sandwich. Florence would often cry, but when she tried to comfort her she would say crying did her good and she felt better afterwards.

When the Second World War broke out in Europe, Florence would visit Mrs Lyon during school vacations and listen to Churchill's speeches on the radio. She regarded Churchill as a '*fine man*' and Hitler as a '*monster.*' When asked to stay for dinner, Florence would say she wasn't hungry but, nevertheless, would stay and eat a hearty meal.[1555]

After Florence's death, Mrs Lyon told a local newspaper that Florence never spoke about her early life, but was often upset and would sometimes break down in tears. She said that if one of the boys appeared, Florence would cheer up and make an effort to say something pleasant. She said: '*The boys would take in wood for her and take food to her from the school. Each time a new boy went, Mrs Maybrick would ask him his name. And you know, she would never forget it. "I always remember boys' names," she would say.*'[1556] Amy Lyon said that '*Wild horses wouldn't drag her to an institution.*' Florence reputedly said: '*If you are going to take me away, I can do without everybody. All of you go away and leave me alone.*'[1557] When ill, she would refuse to go to hospital and insisted on being treated in her own home. She was terrified the doctors might discover her identity and keep her overnight.

By the late 1930s, Florence had become a very reclusive figure, rarely straying far from her cottage apart from trips to the grocery store or visits to the school. She would turn the other way or hide behind a tree or a wall if a strange person or vehicle came down the road. Boys from the school carried provisions to her home. They ensured she had sufficient wood in the bin beside her house to survive the harsh winters. They rarely stayed long; Florence said little to them and wouldn't let them enter. On top of that, the smell from inside the house was almost unbearable. In the summer storms of 1938, Florence said her small house was '*almost blown to pieces.*' She asked Miss Bull, Mr Bartlett's secretary, if she knew of anything that would kill black ants, as she was '*almost eaten up with the insects.*' Florence became ill with food poisoning while trying to make jam. When Mrs Lyon called to see her, she found enough canned cat food to last all winter, yet Florence was lying ill in the living room and her bedroom mattress was crawling with maggots. One of her neighbours, Alexander Hamilton, took it outside and burnt it.[1558]

By 1940, Florence's health was in marked decline. She was unsteady on her feet, and was once found prostrate in the path of her yard. She refused help from the man who found her, insisting he contact Mrs Lyon at the school. The nurse soon arrived with the school doctor. Florence admitted she had suffered from a number of fainting spells. In September 1941, Florence wrote her final letter to Samuel Woodward. In it she said: '*I am sick. I do not know how I will pull through. Mrs Lyon will tell you the emergency things that I have ordered. Perhaps the faculty ladies will help pay for them. In case I cannot write again please continue to care for the interest of my property in conformity*

[1553] Letter from Laura Lee Robertson to Trevor Christie in the Trevor Christie Collection.
[1554] Ryan B., op cit., page 262.
[1555] Letter from Amy Frost Lyon to Trevor Christie in the Trevor Christie Collection.
[1556] *Bridgeport Sunday Post*, 26th October 1941.
[1557] *Bridgeport Sunday Post*, 26th October 1941.
[1558] Ryan B., op. cit., page 260.

with the interest of the school according to the terms of my will which Mr Bartlett has. A small legacy will be coming to me sometime. I have this information from Mr Gregory – before he died. Much gratitude and appreciation of your friendly aid. Florence E. Chandler.'[1559]

Florence's deteriorating health meant she became even more reliant on the goodwill of her neighbours. One of these was Howard Conkrite, known as *Pop*. He was a local farmer who provided two quarts of milk daily to Florence – most of which she fed to her cats. It was an expense which must have taken up a great deal of her weekly pension. Conkrite also ran messages for Florence and checked on her welfare. His wife regularly supplied her with a hot meal.

On the evening of 22nd October 1941, Conkrite and his eleven-year-old granddaughter, Doris Chase, went to Florence's house with a hot meal and found her very weak. The next day, 23rd October, he called again to deliver the milk. When he received no answer he entered the house. He found Florence lying dead, half on her sofa and half on the floor. Her body was surrounded by cats and the bed mattress was crawling with bugs. Conkrite summoned Amy Lyon, who went to the house with another local nurse. They cleaned and dressed Florence, preparing her for the local undertaker, Ralph Bull of Kent.

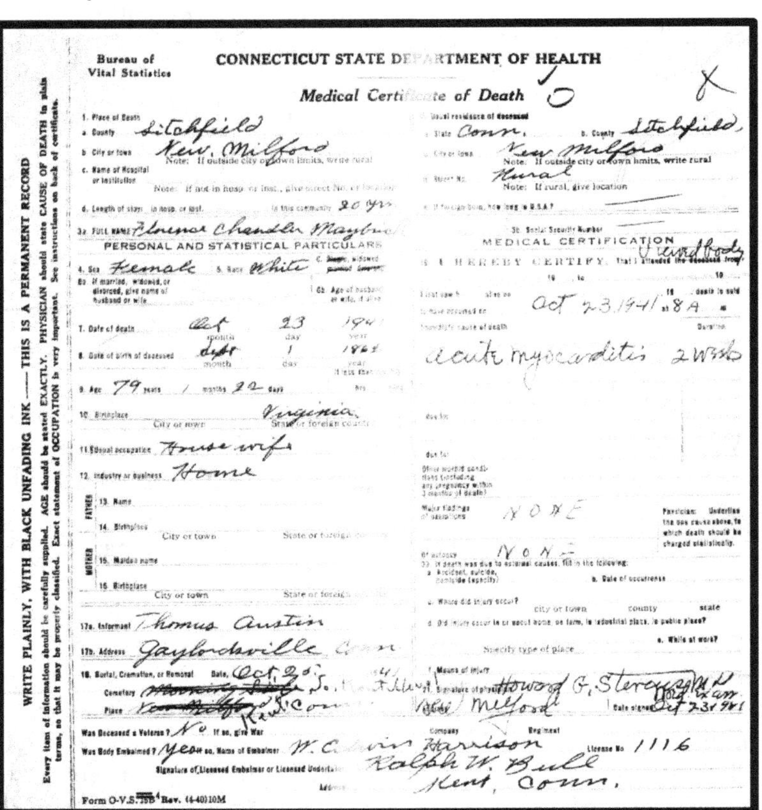
Bureau of Vital Statistics
CONNECTICUT STATE DEPARTMENT OF HEALTH
Medical Certificate of Death
WRITE PLAINLY, WITH BLACK UNFADING INK —— THIS IS A PERMANENT RECORD
1. Place of Death a. County Litchfield b. City or town New Milford
3a. Full name Florence Chandler Maybrick
PERSONAL AND STATISTICAL PARTICULARS
4. Sex Female 5. Race White
7. Date of death Oct 23 1941
8. Date of birth of deceased Sept 1 1862
9. Age 79 years 1 months 22 days
10. Birthplace Virginia
11. Usual occupation Housewife
12. Industry or business Home
17a. Informant Thomas Austin
17b. Address Gaylordsville Conn
18. Burial, Cremation, or Removal Date Oct 26 1941
Was Deceased a Veteran? No
Was Body Embalmed? Yes
License No 1116
Ralph W. Bull, Kent, Conn.
Usual residence of deceased a. State Conn. b. County Litchfield c. City or town New Milford d. Street No. Rural
MEDICAL CERTIFICATION
Oct 23 1941 at 8 A.M.
Immediate cause of death: acute myocarditis 2 Wks
Major findings of operations: NONE
Of autopsy: NONE
Signature of physician: Howard G. Stevens M.D., New Milford
Date signed Oct 23 1941
Form O-V.S. Rev. (4-40)10M

Florence Maybrick's death certificate

A few days after her death, an agent of the Connecticut Humane Society visited her home and killed up to 20 cats. Florence's lonely death, in a derelict cottage, marked a sad end for a woman born into wealth and respectability.[1560]

Florence left behind a few meagre possessions. There was a scrapbook containing old and faded newspaper cuttings from her case. Although worn and battered in appearance, an American journalist described it as a '*human document, unfolding a great heart-breaking drama the like of which no motion picture could duplicate.*' There was a newspaper clipping from 1928 that said Florence was going to receive a large inheritance worth £150,000 from an Englishman named Walter T. Burrell, who had been living in France. It was an untrue story, the product of a journalist's imagination, though it did attract a lot of headlines.[1561] There was an old address book with all the *G*s torn out, and a recipe from the *Cat Review* magazine of 1913 explaining how to cure cats of gastritis. There were some cards and several photographs, including one of her children. There were numerous bills, some pieces of old jewellery and two rosaries. There was also the family Bible, the one in which her mother had discovered the prescription for an arsenical-based cosmetic solution. Florence's will was also found. As promised, she bequeathed her house and property to the school.[1562]

Florence's funeral service was held in the simple but striking chapel at South Kent School. It was led by the Rev Alonzo Wood, the school's chaplain. The mourners, including all the boys from the school, read the 121st Psalm, as requested by Florence. Six students acted as pall bearers: John Garfield, Charles Wreaks, Richard Brown, Harper Payne, Mercer Garrett and Treat Andrew. They carried her coffin from the chapel to the small cemetery that lay behind it. She was laid to rest, at her request, in a plot next to her old friend, Clara Dulon.

Her grave was marked with a simple wooden cross, carved with the letters: '*F.E.C.M. 1862-1941*'. Three simple wreaths of wildflowers were placed on her grave.[1563] A reporter from a local newspaper who witnessed the service wrote:

> '*Thus ended the story of one who had suffered much, and who, in the belief of many thousands, was unjustly declared guilty of a crime under circumstances that made justice a mockery. Doubtless the frail little lady would not have had it any other form than that in which it was conducted. A keen October day, the hillsides*

1559 Ibid., page 262.
1560 *New Milford Times* (Connecticut), 29th October 1941.
1561 *Boston Daily Globe*, 30th November 1928.
1562 Christie T.L., op cit., page 263.
1563 *Sunday Herald Bridgeport*, October 1941.

covered with autumnal beauty, a few fleeting clouds in the blue sky, and not even the usual farm sounds to disturb one who would say: "I will lift up mine eyes unto the hills, from whence cometh my help."[1564]

In December 1956, St Michael's Cemetery at South Kent School was officially consecrated by the Reverend Bishop Walter Gray, Bishop of Hartford. In 1998, the cemetery was re-dedicated, and received a face-lift. The cross on Florence's grave was replaced with a simple stone monument bearing the same inscription.

Florence Maybrick's gravestone (Chris Jones collection)

Florence's death made headlines across the world. For a brief moment, reports about the Second World War were pushed to one side by the death of an old, frail woman. *The Garston and Woolton Reporter* in Liverpool led its edition with the story of her death. The newspaper reported:

> '*There are still a few old residents in the Aigburth and Garston districts of Liverpool who retain personal recollections of the inquest enquiry in the Garston Reading Room in the famous case of Mrs Florence Maybrick. Those recollections have been revived by the news of the death in South Kent, Connecticut, of Mrs Maybrick. Thus passes out the last of the many striking personalities associated with a case that interested two continents.*'[1565]

Connecticut newspaper accounts of Florence's life and death tended to be sympathetic and one can understand why she chose to live her final years in South Kent. In this quiet, rural community she found the peace and tranquillity which had been missing for much of her adult life. Local people treated her with respect and kindness and did not quiz her about her past life. One local paper commented after her death:

> '*Was she innocent or guilty of the charge for which she served 16 years? Well, at South Kent, at least, the question is on the academic side. They never knew Florence Maybrick, but rather a nice cultured old lady who minded her own business.*'[1566]

Florence's death ended a life that was truly an emotional roller-coaster, featuring enormous highs and desperate lows. Her over-riding personality trait was her ability to survive adversity. She outlived her husband by more than 50 years; she outlived her son by more than 30 years.

Edwin, James' brother, died in 1928. He was the last of the Maybrick brothers. He had been emotionally close to Florence, but had let her down badly at her trial when he denied that James used dangerous drugs.

Florence was also badly let down by Alfred Brierley. After her trial, he travelled to the United States and South America, where he was to stay for several years. On his return to Britain, and before Florence's release from prison, Brierley married his first wife, Matilda Agnes Elizabeth Filby (1864-1904). The 1901 Census records that Brierley was living on his '*own means*' in Hillside House at Godstone, Surrey with Matilda and three servants. He was able to live in such fine style as he had inherited around £18,000 (the equivalent of more than £2.5 million today) from his father's estate after his death in February 1896.[1567] After Matilda died in July 1904, Brierley remarried within a year, to Flora Ella Lucas Hemphill (1874-1965), then aged 31. The couple had one son, Patrick Chisholm Brierley (1906-1953). The family moved to a lodging house on the Marine Parade at Brighton, Brierley listing himself as a '*retired merchant*' in the 1911 Census. He died aged 72 on 18th November 1923. He is buried in the village churchyard at Newick on the South Downs.

His wife, Flora, outlived him by 40 years. Their only son Patrick grew up to be a part-time Army officer in the 57th Field Brigade of the Royal Artillery, retiring at the rank of major. He married in 1934, dying childless in Hove in March 1953, 12 years before his mother.

1564 *New Milford Times*, 29th October 1941.
1565 *Garston & Woolton Reporter*, 31st October 1941.
1566 *Sunday News* (USA), 9th November, 1941.
1567 *Liverpool Mercury*, 11th April 1896.

Final Years

Although Florence was released from prison, she never received a pardon for her crime and is therefore, in the eyes of the law, still a convicted murderer. Florence spent the rest of her life proclaiming her innocence, but the Home Office was to continually and resolutely oppose all her efforts – and those of her supporters – to have the verdict overturned.

Florence would have probably accepted this situation if she had just managed to persuade her two children of her innocence. That was never to happen, and it must have been the greatest regret of her life. In 1927, Florence possibly travelled to England to make one last attempt at reconciliation with her daughter. Although some of Florence's friends did make friendly overtures to Gladys, she would not meet or even speak to her mother. The only explanation for this attitude is that she believed Florence murdered her father and she could not forgive her.

According to Commander Kell, the executor of Gladys' will, Gladys and her husband scrupulously avoided having children of their own because of the stigma of the case. Kell added that, in her late seventies, Gladys told him that she never referred to her mother. It was a '*closed book.*'[1568]

LINKS TO THE RIPPER DIARY: DOES THE HANDWRITING OF THE DIARIST MATCH THE HANDWRITING OF JAMES MAYBRICK?

The various analyses of the handwriting of the diarist have been completed with two main aims: firstly, to determine whether it matched the handwriting of James Maybrick; and secondly, to ascertain if it revealed anything about the mind and the personality of the person who wrote the document.

When this process was first carried out by handwriting experts in 1992/93, there were very few documents in existence that were known to be in James' handwriting. The two main ones were his signature on his pre-wedding certificate in 1881, and his final will dated April 1889. Since then, other documents have been found which are in James' handwriting. One of the most important discoveries was made in the Richmond Chancery. It included letters and telegrams sent by James while he was supporting the Baroness in her legal battles over the disputed land she had inherited from her father.

One of the first handwriting experts that Shirley Harrison asked to examine the Diary was Sue Iremonger, who had impressive credentials: she was a member of the World Association of Document Examiners, and a qualified psychotherapist. The British police had asked for her help on a number of fraud investigations as she was considered an expert on false signatures. Sue Iremonger told Harrison that a person's handwriting could be as revealing as their fingerprints. The style might appear to change, but '*the components of every individual's handwriting remain constant.*'[1569]

Iremonger found the handwriting of the diarist to be different from the handwriting on James' pre-wedding certificate and will. She also found it to be different from the handwriting on the *Dear Boss* letter, which the diarist claimed to have written. Iremonger went even further, and examined over 200 of the original Jack the Ripper letters sent to the police and newspapers. She was unable to find a single letter that matched the handwriting of the diarist. Iremonger wrote to Harrison, informing her that the punctuation in the Diary and the *Dear Boss* letter was '*totally different and generally the differences between them far outweigh any slight similarities.*'

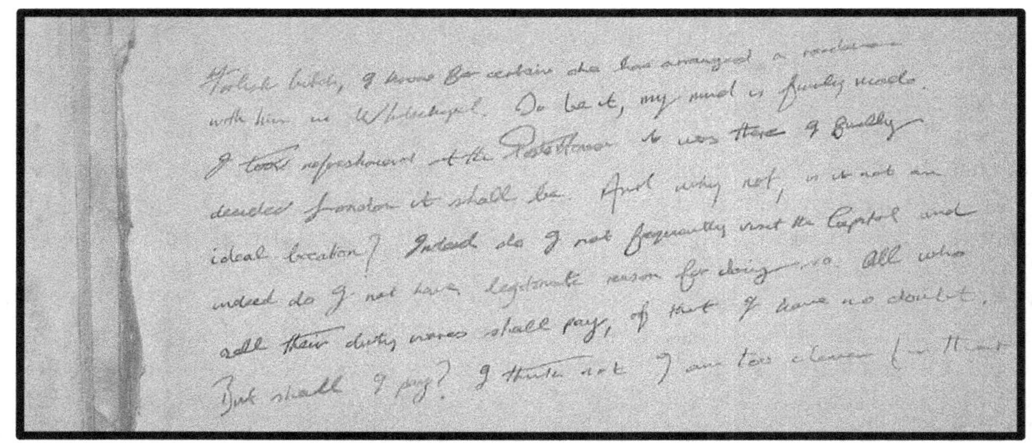
Foolish bitch, I know for certain she has arranged a rendezvous
with him in Whitechapel. So be it, my mind is firmly made.
I took refreshment at the Poste House it was there I finally
decided London it shall be. And why not, is it not an
ideal location? Indeed do I not frequently visit the Capital and
indeed do I not have legitimate reason for doing so. All who
sell their dirty wares shall pay, of that I have no doubt.
But shall I pay? I think not I am too clever for that

Extract from the Diary of Jack the Ripper (Chris Jones collection)

Another expert who compared the handwriting on the documents was Dr Audrey Giles, a former head of the Metropolitan Police Laboratory's Questioned Document Section. She was part of a team of experts employed by the

[1568] Email from Roger Wilkes to Christopher Jones, 23rd October 2021.
[1569] Harrison S., op. cit., page 329.

Sunday Times to examine the Diary. She was certain that James' will was not written by the diarist, noting that the letters '*J*' and '*M*' were very different. She believed this to be extremely significant, as they were James' initials. She agreed with Shirley Harrison and Paul Feldman that the diarist's handwriting could have been affected by his drug use or by his emotional state, but crucially added: '*Although drugs, alcohol and stress can influence the size and proportion of an individuals' handwriting, the fine detail and construction will not be altered.*'[1570]

The reports by the handwriting experts fundamentally undermined the views of those who believed the Diary was a genuine document written by James Maybrick. To overcome this problem, supporters of the Diary argued that handwriting analysis is not an exact science, especially if someone wants to deliberately disguise his handwriting style. Shirley Harrison illustrated this point in her presentation to the Trial of James Maybrick event in May 2007, referring to the handwriting of the German murderer Peter Kürten, known as the Düsseldorf Ripper, who wrote letters to the police after each of his murders. In each letter his handwriting style was different; even his own wife did not recognise his handwriting when shown the letters.

Robert Smith wrote that it was best to leave the handwriting issue as a '*mystery which is unlikely to be solved.*'[1571] The problem with this view is the diarist provided more than enough clues to identify himself as James Maybrick. James, unlike Peter Kürten, had no need to disguise or alter his handwriting. As the diarist's handwriting is so different from James' handwriting, one can only conclude that he did *not* write the Diary. Therefore, rather than the handwriting issue being a mystery, it is an enlightening factor that helps prove the fraudulent nature of the document.

A second line of attack from those who believed the Diary was genuine was to argue that the reason the handwriting of the diarist didn't match the handwriting of James' will was because the will had been written by someone other than James.

Maybrick's final will was dated 25th April 1889, less than three weeks before his death, and was witnessed by his friend George Davidson and his bookkeeper George Smith. The full text of the will was published in the *Liverpool Daily Post* as Florence's trial commenced. The newspaper stated it was a verbatim copy, extracted in due form from the District Registry attached to the Probate Division of her Majesty's High Court of Justice at Liverpool.

Doubts about the validity of this will were first cast in 1891 by Alexander MacDougall, who campaigned to get Florence released from prison. He said it was '*inconceivable' that James could have been in 'sober senses' when he signed the will, as it gave total control of his estate and the well-being of his children to Michael and Thomas Maybrick, while Florence was to have 'neither bed nor blanket.*'[1572]

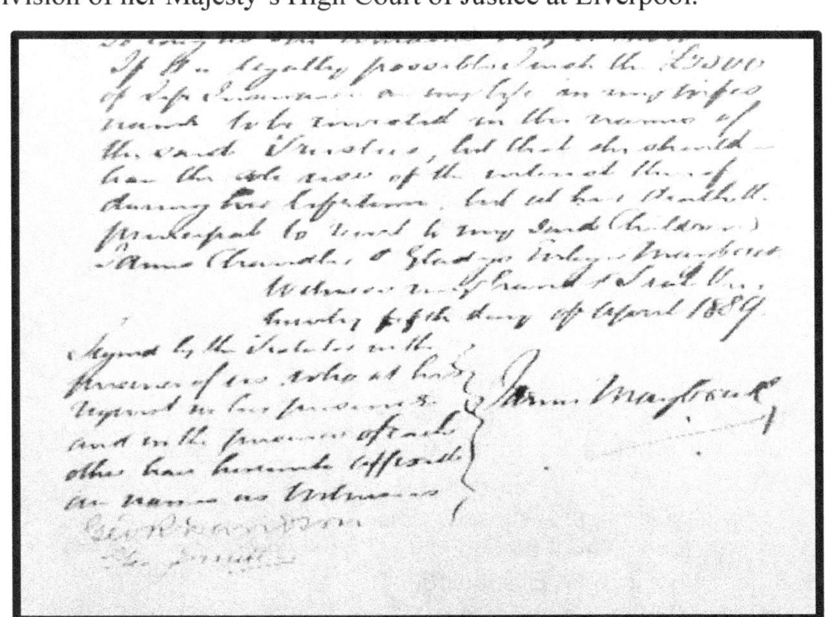

Extract from James Maybrick's will

Paul Feldman has also questioned its validity. He pointed out the will, then lodged in Somerset House, was slightly different in ten respects from the one that MacDougall wrote about. For example, in the actual will Evelyn is possibly spelt incorrectly as '*Eveleyn*,' though that assertion is far from clear. Feldman suggested there were '*two, and arguably three, versions of the will*;'[1573] the first one written in December 1888, after the previous will was torn up by James following a row with Florence; a second will, written on 25th April; and a third will, possibly drafted by Michael and Edwin Maybrick and signed by James the night before he died.

Shirley Harrison also posed questions about the validity of the will. She said it was known that Edwin and Michael Maybrick got James to sign some documents on 10th May, and that these documents – according to Nurse Yapp – included a will.[1574] Harrison also wrote that it was unlikely that MacDougall, a trained lawyer, would have made mistakes when he copied the will.

[1570] Whittington-Egan R., *Jack the Ripper – The Definitive Casebook*, (Amberley Publishing, Stroud, 2013) page 229.
[1571] Smith R., op cit., (2017) page 30.
[1572] MacDougall A.W., (1891) op. cit., page 206.
[1573] Feldman P., op. cit., page 261.
[1574] Harrison S., op cit., page 184.

This latter view is seriously undermined by examining a lengthy document about the Maybrick case that MacDougall submitted to the Home Office in December 1895. This document is littered with mistakes and every page has numerous corrections on it. MacDougall continually refers to Mrs Samuelson by the incorrect name of '*Mrs Saunderson*.' He referred to John Baillie Knight as '*Bailee Knight*,' and his aunts as Misses '*Bailey*' instead of Baillie. He states that Brierley lived on '*Huskison*' Street instead of Huskisson Street.[1575]

It is almost certain that James Maybrick's will is the genuine one signed by James on 25th April and witnessed by Davidson and Smith. James knew he had to make a new will as he had destroyed the old one. This situation had become more urgent in April, as he was worried about his health. He was also angry with his wife after seeing her flirt with Brierley at the Grand National, and possibly finding out about her meeting with Brierley in London. Further, he made the new will just three days after returning from London, where he had repaid Florence's substantial debts to moneylenders. It is known that he consulted his brother Michael about the debts; Michael may have urged James to be stricter in future financial dealings with his wife.

The terms of the will, as published in the *Liverpool Daily Post,* are identical to the one that was originally lodged in Somerset House, with the exception of the possible spelling mistake of Evelyn. It is therefore certain that MacDougall *did* make mistakes when he copied the will. Both George Smith and George Davidson would have seen the will in the newspaper, and if there had been a problem, they would have spoken out at the time. The harsh terms towards Florence reflected James' attitude to her at that moment in time.

Importantly, as further documents written by James have been discovered, they too matched the handwriting found on the will. The handwriting on these documents was also totally different from the handwriting of the diarist. Therefore, it is clear beyond any doubt that the will is a genuine document written by James and the Diary is a forgery written by someone other than James Maybrick.

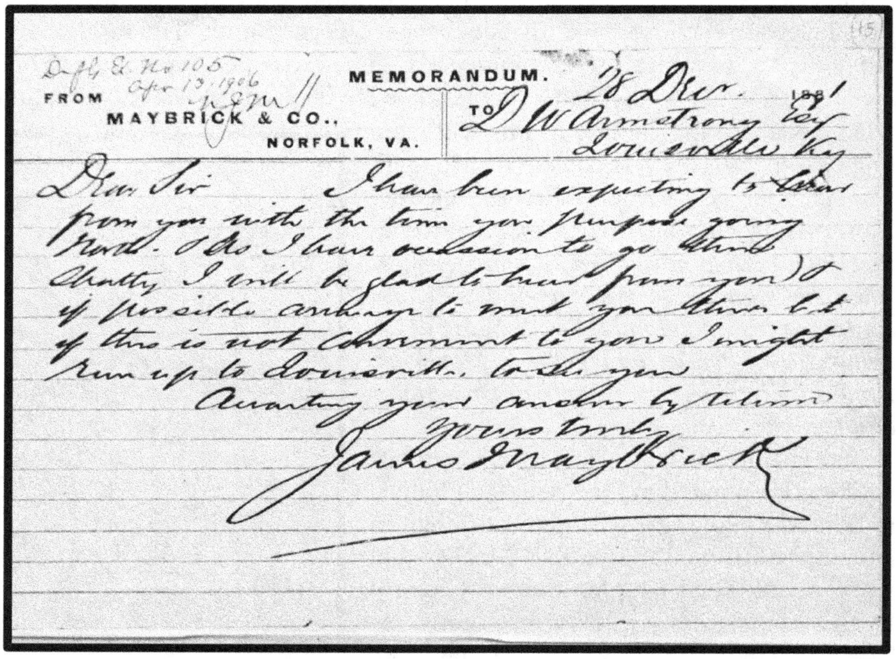
MEMORANDUM. 28 Dec. 1881
FROM MAYBRICK & CO., NORFOLK, VA. TO D W Armstrong Esq Louisville Ky
Dear Sir I have been expecting to hear from you with the time you purpose going North. Also I have occasion to go there shortly I will be glad to hear from you & if possible arrange to meet you there but if this is not convenient to you I might run up to Louisville to see you
Awaiting your answer by return
Yours truly
James Maybrick

Memorandum sent by James Maybrick to David Armstrong in December 1881 (Chris Jones collection)

Analysts have also examined the diarist's style of the writing to see if it reveals anything about the mind of the author of that document, and whether that person could have been a sadistic serial killer. Shirley Harrison asked Dr David Forshaw to examine the Diary for the purpose of providing an insight into the personality of the author. Forshaw was at the time a specialist consultant in addiction at Maudsley Psychiatric Hospital in London, and later became a consultant at Broadmoor Hospital Prison. He examined the Diary for several months and produced a 15,000-word report.

He concluded the provenance of the Diary was the essential component in deciding whether it was authentic. If the provenance could not be determined, then '*on the balance of probabilities from a psychiatric perspective, it is authentic.*'[1576] Forshaw said one of the striking aspects of the Diary was the way in which '*the handwriting changes to reflect the changing emotions of the writer.*'[1577] The handwriting changes from '*the fairly neat school-taught hand to a much larger, uncontrolled scrawl which corresponds to mental deterioration.*'

At the beginning of the Diary, before the murders occur, the writing is '*neat, undemonstrative, restrained even.*' When the murders start, the writing becomes larger, more and more uncontrolled, with an increasing number of crossing-outs and a more aggressive tone. Near the end, after the killings stopped, the writing becomes calmer again. This suggests that either the author did have violent tendencies, or the forger knew about the personality profile of such a person and cleverly interwove those aspects into the Diary narrative.

Paul Feldman asked Hannah Koren, an Israeli Forensic Document Handler, to examine the Diary. In December 1992, she viewed the document and gave her impressions to Feldman and Shirley Harrison, telling them the:

1575 HO 144/1640/A50678D/279 pages 30, 32, 37 and 40.
1576 Harrison S., op cit., page 19.
1577 Ibid., page 347.

> '*Diary shows an unstable personality. Inner conflicts of social adaptability and a tendency to schizophrenia. The author's feelings of inferiority, emotional repression and lack of inner confidence may cause him to explode every now and then and he may explode violently.*

She later said the suggestion the Diary was a forgery was '*impossible*.'[1578] In September 1993, Koren wrote to Feldman, stating that the: '*writer of the Diary was probably schizophrenic. Inside the Diary itself I found a variety of letter formations and features indicating multiple personalities. It is known that writers who suffer from this kind of disturbance 'produce' different handwritings, and this rendered it very difficult to come to an unequivocal conclusion when comparing such handwritings. Thus, I have found both similarities and contradictions in the documents and it is impossible for me to reach a verdict*.'[1579]

Koren's interpretation of the mindset of the diarist was similar to Forshaw's. They both believed the document was written by a person with violent tendencies. Koren went even further, suggesting he might also have schizophrenic tendencies. A primary problem with her analysis is that James Maybrick was not schizophrenic. There is no indication whatsoever that he was psychotic. In addition, his personality traits did not match some of the other characteristics she suggested were possessed by the diarist. His behaviour was not '*unusually bizarre*;' there is no evidence he had '*paranoid suspicions and magic beliefs*' or '*deep-rooted feelings of loneliness*.' He did not in the slightest conform to Koren's view that the diarist's '*perception of sexuality and mating is distracted to the point of a tendency to sadism*.'

If Koren is accurate in her interpretation, and the diarist possessed all these characteristics, then it is yet another reason for concluding that James was not the author of the document.

After the lack of an acceptable provenance for the Diary, the issue of the handwriting is the second most important factor in establishing the Diary as a forgery. The Diarist's handwriting does not match James' handwriting on any existing documents. This includes the limited number of documents available in 1992/93 when the early tests were carried out, as well as all the documents that have come to light since that period.

The most common reasons given by the pro-Diary camp for the difference in handwriting style is that James was either trying to disguise his handwriting or that he was affected by extreme emotional turmoil. Both of these responses can be dismissed. James had no need to disguise his handwriting. The narrative of the document made it abundantly clear who the author was.

As for emotional turmoil, James' personality bears no resemblance to the range of characteristics identified by Hannah Koren. Dr Audrey Giles pointed out that while drug addiction can affect a person's handwriting, the fine detail and construction of the handwriting will remain the same. The handwriting analysis is conclusive proof that James Maybrick was not the author of the Diary.

[1578] Ibid., pages 327-329.

[1579] Feldman P., op cit., page 230.

24

DID FLORENCE MURDER JAMES?

On 11th May 1889, James Maybrick died unexpectedly after a short illness. Only a few weeks earlier, he had been examined by Dr Fuller who had found '*very the little the matter with him*' other than suffering from indigestion. After he died, Drs Humphreys and Carter believed there were suspicious circumstances surrounding his death and refused to sign a death certificate.

All of this made a police investigation inevitable. The problem was not that an investigation was initiated, but the manner in which it was conducted. From the outset, the police believed a murder had been committed and focused all their efforts on just one suspect: Florence. They refused to examine other possible explanations for James' death, or consider other suspects. Florence was cautioned by Superintendent Bryning just three days after James died, and before she had even been interviewed by a police officer. After just one week – still before being formally interviewed – Florence was charged with murder.

There can be no doubt that the police investigation into James' death was deeply flawed. The leading officers – Superintendent Bryning and Inspector Baxendale – believed they were doing their duty, but they were men of limited ability and experience; the early policing of both men had involved tackling agricultural crime.

Influenced by James' brothers and friends, they quickly fixed upon Florence as their only suspect. The presence of Michael Maybrick, a well-known public figure and an associate of the Prince of Wales, would have been especially intimidating. His actions influenced the police's investigation. Some of the key items of evidence, including Florence's letters, the arsenic in her trunk and James' hat boxes, were originally gathered by Michael and Edwin Maybrick, aided by Mrs Briggs and her sister Mrs Hughes, rather than by the police themselves. Items of Florence's clothes such as her dressing-gown were analysed, yet none of James' clothes, other than his bed clothes, were similarly analysed.

A clear example of the police approach is shown by their actions during the inquest into James' death. When Schweisso, the waiter at Flatman's Hotel, arrived at the inquest he was asked by a police inspector if he would be able to recognise Florence or Brierley. He answered, '*No.*' As a result, the inspector took him to a place where he was able to see Florence twice before he was formally asked by the coroner to identify her. The same inspector later pointed Brierley out to him.[1580]

Although the police investigation was inadequate, it is possible to understand why some of Florence's behaviours had aroused suspicion. The police use three criteria – motive, means and opportunity – to identify the perpetrator of a serious crime. Normally, the person who matches all three criteria would be regarded as the prime suspect. According to Morland, '*the case against Florence really began when... Alice Yapp opened a letter she should not have touched.*'[1581] Florence's letter to Brierley was a key piece of evidence. The prosecution claimed it provided the motive for murder: Florence wanted to kill her husband so she could be with her lover. This view was strengthened when it was established that, in March 1889, Florence had spent two nights at a hotel in London with Brierley.

On the other hand, conflicting evidence was surreptitiously removed by the Maybrick brothers; for example, the *love* letters to Florence from Edwin Maybrick and the mysterious Williams, vanished without a trace. The Baroness was to claim that a '*compromising packet of letters written by women*' to James was also among the items which disappeared. She also claimed that Florence's letter to Brierley, which had been written in pencil, had been altered in places to make it appear even more damaging. She said it had originally started, '*Dear A,*' but had been changed to '*Dearest.*'[1582]

Also important in trying to establish motive was the evidence of Christine Samuelson. At the inquest, she testified Florence told her she hated her husband. In her memoir, Florence pointed out there was no incentive to commit murder as she had sufficient evidence to secure a divorce.[1583]

As to having the means to commit murder, there was enough arsenic in Battlecrease to have killed at least 50 people. It was one of the ironies of the case that the only person whom it could be proved had purchased any of this arsenic was Florence, when she bought the two sets of flypapers. This fact, coupled with the unfortunate timing of the purchases, counted heavily against her. At the magistrates' hearing, Bryning told the court: '*It is perhaps*

[1580] MacDougall A.W., (1896) op cit., page 218.
[1581] Morland N., op. cit., page xii.
[1582] Letter from the Baroness to the Home Secretary (August 1892), HO 144/1639/A50678D/99.
[1583] Maybrick F., op. cit., page 268.

significant that these [fly]papers should have been bought at a time when Mr Maybrick's health was becoming worse.'[1584] Although the flypapers generated many of the headlines, arsenic extracted from the papers could not have been the cause of James' death. The analysis of the Valentine's meat juice bottle and other items containing arsenic showed they contained no vegetable fibres from the flypapers.

Mr Justice Stephen in his summing-up at the trial, spoke extensively about the large quantity of arsenic in Battlecrease and, although he did not say it was all in Florence's possession, he did say she '*undoubtedly had access*' to the drug. He added that the arsenic was in '*places where Mrs Maybrick continually was.*' This was a grossly unfair statement, as it seemed to imply only Florence had access to the drug, when everyone else in the house – including James – had access to the places where arsenic was found. The judge's skewed comments were given a degree of resonance by the fact that one of the biggest discoveries of arsenic, the packet labelled *Arsenic - Poison for Cats*, was found inside a trunk marked with Florence's initials, along with one of her handkerchiefs. Another large haul of arsenic was found in James' hat boxes, in the corner of the inner-dressing room – the room in which Florence slept during James' illness. Here too, a handkerchief of Florence's steeped in poison was found. Traces of arsenic were also found on her dressing gown, on her apron and on a handkerchief in the pocket of the gown. This proved Florence must have handled arsenic. Florence's statement, that she had added some white powder, presumably arsenic, to the meat juice also showed she must have had access to the poison.

If it appeared that Florence had the means to poison James, then it was also the case she had the opportunity. She had packaged some of James' food in a jug, which he heated up and ate in his office. James commented that the cook had used some inferior sherry in the making of the gruel. It was a remark interpreted to imply Florence had tampered with the food. When the jug and pan were tested by Mr Davies, the analyst, they showed traces of arsenic. Florence, before the arrival of the professional nurses, handled all of James' food and medication. Some of the servants commented that the food tasted differently to how it had been prepared by the cook. Nurse Callery, one of the professional nurses, said in her testimony at the trial that James had told Florence, '*Don't give me the wrong medicine again.*' Although this sentence appears damning, Florence had simply been encouraging James to take the medicine which was being given to him by the nurse. There was also the incident crucial to the prosecution's case, when Florence had '*suspiciously,*' in Nurse Gore's opinion, moved the meat juice bottle. Mr Davies analysed the bottle and found it contained half a grain of arsenic.

Although Florence was the police's prime suspect, there were fundamental weaknesses in the prosecution's case. Perhaps the most important was the low level of arsenic found in James' body. Mr Davies admitted at Florence's trial that he could only find arsenic in a weighable amount in just one organ; James' liver. He also admitted the arsenic he had found '*would amount to an eight of a grain.*'[1585] Dr Stevenson, the senior analyst at the Home Office, estimated there was one-third of a grain of arsenic in James' liver, and one-eleventh of a grain in his intestines. As around three grains would have been needed to kill someone like James, who was a regular arsenic-user, Stevenson had only found an amount that would not have made James ill, let alone kill him. The prosecution tried to overcome this problem by arguing that the arsenic which killed James, had been eliminated from his body prior to his death. If this was true, traces of arsenic would have been found on his bedding and bedclothes, yet none was found in Mr Davies' tests. It would also have been found in tests on his faeces and urine, which also didn't happen.

On Thursday 9th May, Dr Humphreys tested both James' faeces and his urine for a metallic irritant and found none present. At Florence's trial, Sir Charles Russell asked Dr Paul, one of the defence's medical experts, if a fatal dose of arsenic had been administered within a fortnight of the time when Humphreys carried out his tests, would a metallic deposit have been found. He answered, '*Yes.*' As no such deposits were found, James' death could not have been the result of arsenical poisoning.

FACT FILE ONE: THE LEVELS OF ARSENIC IN JAMES' BODY

Three doctors were involved in James' post-mortem, including **Dr Barron**, who had attended over 500 post-mortems. He was asked at the trial whether there were a number of red spots (*petechiae*) scattered over James' stomach, which were a key characteristic of arsenical poisoning. He replied, '*No, I have no mention of such on my notes.*'[1586] The lack of *petechiae* proves that James could not have died from arsenical poisoning. After the trial, Dr Barron signed a petition which called for Florence's sentence to be commuted. In an interview, he said he did not believe that the symptoms proved James had died from arsenical poisoning.

At Florence's trial, **Mr Davies** said he had found arsenic in James' intestines (though an amount too small to determine); the kidneys (estimated to be 1/100 of a grain), and the liver (a distinct amount). He admitted that no arsenic

1584 *Garston and Woolton Reporter*, 15th June 1889.
1585 Levy J.H., op cit., page 167.
1586 Ibid., page 149.

had been found in the stomach, the contents of the stomach, the spleen, the bile, the fluid that escaped from the body when it was turned over, the heart or the lungs. He also said he had found no traces of arsenic in James' bedding or bedclothes, which should have been present if he had died from arsenical poisoning.

At the trial, Russell questioned **Dr Stevenson** about the symptoms a person would typically have if they were suffering from arsenical poisoning. Stevenson admitted that diarrhoea affected a patient an hour or two after vomiting. This had not been the case with James. Russell then asked about the symptoms of severe abdominal pain, redness of the eyelids and the bloodshot appearance of the eyeballs. Stevenson agreed that they were all usually found, but these too had not been present in James' case. Stevenson said James' body '*probably contained a fatal dose of arsenic*;' however, he also told the court he estimated that there was only one-third of a grain of arsenic in James' liver, and one-eleventh of a grain in his intestines. [1587] These were well below the levels required in a fatal dose.

Further confirmation that James' death could not have been the result of arsenical poisoning comes from the evidence of Dr Tidy at Florence's trial. He said that the four most prominent symptoms of arsenical poisoning were incessant vomiting, diarrhoea, pain in the stomach and redness of the eyelid. He said that these symptoms were entirely absent in James' case, or only present at the end, very close to his death.

In 1890, Drs Tidy and Macnamara produced a pamphlet in which they listed 20 principles of arsenical poisoning and said that only one or two were present in James' final illness, and then only in the closing stages.[1588] In James' body only one-tenth of a grain of arsenic was discovered, which was '*only one-twentieth part of the smallest recorded fatal dose*.'[1589] As a result, they said the arsenic in James' body may have been present from medicinal doses; and secondly, the arsenic may have been taken a considerable time before either his death or illness. They concluded that James' symptoms were consistent with acute dyspepsia, and they '*absolutely point away from, rather than towards, arsenic as the cause of such dyspeptic condition*.' They also wrote that the post-mortem appearances were '*indicative of inflammation, but that they emphatically point away from arsenic as the cause of death*.'[1590]

FACT FILE TWO:
EVIDENCE THAT DEMONSTRATES THAT JAMES USED DANGEROUS DRUGS

Franklin Bancroft (Friend)
Between 1874 and 1876 he saw James put some '*white powder*' into his wine. James told him it was '*composed of arsenic and other ingredients*.'
Signed affidavit, April 1894.

Nicholas Bateson (Friend)
He said that in the Autumn of 1877, James took '*arsenic and strychnine by order of Dr Ward... for about three months*.'
Evidence at Florence's trial.

Thomas Stansell (Valet)
Prior to James' wedding, Stansell said he '*frequently bought arsenic*' for James. He had '*mixed the drug in his soup*.' He said that after his wedding, James continued to use arsenic, and '*his doses grew larger*.'
Norfolk Virginian, 1st August 1889.

Mary Hogwood (Brothel-keeper)
She said '*It was a common thing for him [James] to take arsenic two or three times an evening*.'
Liverpool Echo, 15th August 1889.

Captain R. Thompson (Friend)
In 1880, he saw James collect a powder from a druggist in America. A drug store assistant told Thompson the powder was '*arsenic*.'
Evidence at Florence's trial.

Dr Brown-Séquard (Doctor)
James visited him in New York and was provided with '*prescriptions of an aphrodisiac kind*' that contained strychnine and nux vomica
Dr Hopper's evidence at Florence's trial.

Captain John Fleming (Friend)
Between 1882-84 he saw James put a grey powder in his food. James told him it was '*arsenic*,' and he took it

[1587] Ibid., pages 204-205.
[1588] Tidy C. M. and Macnamara R., op cit., pages 6-7.
[1589] Ibid., page 29.
[1590] Ibid., page 30.

because it '*strengthened him.*'
Signed affidavit, April 1894.

Pauline Cranston (Astrologer)
She told a newspaper James had consulted her about his ailments, and his use of arsenic to '*calm his nerves.*'
Liverpool Daily Post, 17th May 1889.

Florence Aunspaugh (Family friend)
She wrote that James was '*always taking strychnine tablets and was great on beef broth and arsenic.*'
Trevor Christie Collection.

Henry Bliss (Club Proprietor)
He said, '*Mr Maybrick lived in the [Sefton Club and] Chambers on and off for several months, and was in the habit of dosing himself.*'
Evening Express, 13th June 1889.

Edwin Heaton (Chemist)
Up until April 1888 James had visited his shop between two and five times a day, to drink a pick-me-up containing up to seven drops of arsenic, which in total was '*one-third of a grain of white arsenic*'.
Evidence at Florence's trial.

Valentine Blake
In January 1889, James told Blake that arsenic made him '*stronger in mind and body*'. In February, Blake gave him 150 grains of arsenic.
Signed affidavit (April 1894).

Sir James Poole
In April 1889, as he left the underwriter's room James had blurted out, '*I take poisonous medicines*'.
Evidence at Florence's trial.

Thomas Lowry and George Smith (James' employees)
They said that on the day of the Wirral races, James had told them that he had taken '*an overdose of medicine and there was strychnine in it.*' Statement made not at the trial, but at the earlier hearings.
HO 144/1639/A50678/442.

Morden Rigg (Friend)
At the Wirral races James had told Rigg's wife that '*he had taken an overdose of strychnine that morning.*'
Signed statement, MacDougall (1896).

William Thomson (Friend)
At the Wirral races James spoke to Thomson and told him he was unwell, and had taken a '*double dose*' of his medicine that morning.
Evidence at Florence's trial.

Mary Cadwallader (Servant)
On the Sunday morning after the Wirral races, James said to Cadwallader, '*Oh, Mary, I very nearly poisoned myself with an overdose of medicine.*'
Liverpool Echo, 21st August 1889.

Captain Irving (Friend)
On 1st May 1889, Irving saw James put a powder in water. Edwin told him that James was '*killing himself with that damned strychnine.*'
Liverpool Daily Post, 9th September 1889.

Mr Dalgleish (or more likely Daglish) (Original inquest foreman)
Just before the Wirral races, he saw James take powder from a waistcoat jacket. He told him it was '*strychnine.*'
Liverpool Daily Post, 7th June 1889.

Although there was only a small amount of arsenic in James' body, the fact it had been found allowed the prosecution to claim it was arsenic that caused his death. At Florence's trial, the defence did produce witnesses who had seen James take arsenic, but these witnesses were not as effective as they could have been; for example, both Bateson and Stansell said it had happened in America over ten years earlier. It was unfortunate for Florence that Stansell did not repeat in court a statement he made to an American newspaper, in which he said he purchased arsenic for James on numerous occasions. He also did not mention that James had continued to use arsenic after his marriage, and that his doses had grown larger.

The impact of Sir James Poole's evidence was weakened when the judge mistakenly told the jury that James' remark to Poole, that he took poisonous medicines, had occurred in January 1889, when it had in fact been April 1889. If James had taken arsenic in April, that would have explained why arsenic was found in his body during the post-mortem. The defence team also made a mistake by not calling Morden Rigg and Dalgleish to testify, as they could have stated James was taking strychnine at the very time he became ill.

The evidence from numerous witnesses conclusively demonstrates James was a serial consumer of dangerous drugs, including both arsenic and strychnine, and that this habit had persisted over many years. The statements from the two sea captains, Fleming and Irving, are important as they both saw James add a powder into his food. James even told Fleming the powder was arsenic. These statements could help explain why traces of arsenic were found in the pan in James' office which he had used to heat up his food.

As well as the arsenic found in James' body, another factor that counted against Florence was the vast store of arsenic found in Battlecrease after his death. The most important source was the flypapers which she had purchased to make a cosmetic solution. Unfortunately for her, the prescription she possessed for making this solution was not found until 1890 when it fell out of a family Bible.

It was one of the great inconsistencies of the case against Florence that the police argued she purchased the flypapers in order to extract arsenic so she could poison her husband; yet, at the same time, they also argued she had access to a great store of arsenic in her own home. If the latter was true, then there was no need for her to go through the difficult process of extracting arsenic from the flypapers. The flypapers were bought by Florence for the very purpose she said they had been; to make a cosmetic solution. It was something she had done on previous occasions, as acknowledged by a chemist who had worked in Grassendale and had seen Florence '*almost daily.*'[1591]

When Florence purchased the flypapers in April 1889, she did so in two local chemists where she was well known and had them delivered to her house. James even picked up one of the packets. The flypapers were left soaking in the bedroom where anybody could see them. The solution prepared by Florence was found by Sergeant Davenport in an unlabelled small rounded bottle in the linen cupboard. Mr Davies tested it and found it contained a '*very weak solution of arsenic.*' The solution was so weak, that even if James had consumed the whole bottle it would not have affected him. Traces of arsenic were found on Florence's dressing gown, apron and handkerchief in the dressing gown, as she had been wearing these items when she had prepared the solution and applied it to her face.

It was also unfortunate for Florence's defence that Valentine Blake did not provided evidence at her trial. In an affidavit taken in 1894, Blake said he had met James in Liverpool on two occasions in early 1889. In February that year, he had given James about 150 grains of arsenic in three packets: one packet of white and two packets of black arsenic (mixed with charcoal). As he did so, he warned: '*Be careful, you have almost enough to kill a regiment.*'[1592]

Blake's evidence would have explained why there was so much arsenic present in Battlecrease when the house was searched. It would also have explained the presence of the black arsenic, which was found in the *Arsenic - Poison for Cats* package. In another affidavit of 1894, Blake's employer William B. Nation supported his statement, including the fact that some of the arsenic had been mixed with charcoal.

What is noticeable about the major finds of arsenic in Battlecrease, is they were all discovered in places which were unlocked and there had been no attempt at concealment. Florence's wardrobe was the only place in the main bedroom which was locked, and no arsenic was found in it. In fact, no arsenic was found in any cupboard or drawer to which only Florence possessed the keys. The two biggest finds were in Florence's trunk and in James' hat boxes. Florence's trunk was kept in the linen cupboard on the first-floor landing. It was a place that was accessible to everyone, and both Mary Cadwallader and Elizabeth Brierley would go into the cupboard daily to collect bedclothes and towels. Florence's trunk had recently been used to store the children's clothes on a family excursion. Mary Cadwallader said the '*bedroom towels were kept in the trunk, which was not kept locked, and Bessie Brierley was constantly in the linen closet for the linen in use.*'[1593]

It is inconceivable that Florence, if she possessed the arsenic and had murder on her mind, would have placed the poison in her own trunk, which was frequently used by the servants, and located in an area that everyone in the house had access to. The hat boxes are also an unlikely place to hide poison. It is very difficult to believe that Florence, if she was planning on murdering James, would hide the poison in her husband's own hat boxes. These were unlocked and kept in a prominent position in the corner of the inner-dressing room where James frequently slept. He had gone to work on 3rd May, the day Dr Carter said the fatal dose of arsenic was taken, and he would have worn a hat. If arsenic had been hidden in the hat box by Florence, James would have noticed it.

If Florence did not place the items containing arsenic in the trunk and hat boxes, then how did they get there? It is very likely that James himself placed the items in his own hat boxes. The items inside the trunk are more of a mystery. Perhaps James placed the items in the trunk before he became too ill to put them somewhere more secure. An

---

1591 *Liverpool Daily Post*, 13th August 1889.
1592 HO 144/1639/A50678D/702.
1593 MacDougall A.W., (1891) op cit., page 231.

alternative view is that someone other than James placed the arsenic in the trunk. On the night that James died, Nurse Yapp and Elizabeth Brierley removed the trunk from the linen cupboard and placed it unopened in the nursery. It was left there for almost two hours before Nurse Yapp opened it when Nurse Wilson was present. Therefore, almost anyone – except Florence – could have placed the incriminating items in the trunk. Florence is not a possibility, as she was unconsciousness at the time.

If one assumes that the servants and professional nurses did not place the items in the trunk, that can only mean that one, or both, of the Maybrick brothers, with or without the help of the two Janion sisters, were responsible for this action. Perhaps they were trying to hide the fact the arsenic belonged to James, or maybe they had convinced themselves of Florence's guilt and were trying to ensure the police reached the same conclusion.

The random nature of the items in the trunk: – the ant powder, three assorted bottles which did not contain arsenic and one of Florence's handkerchiefs – adds credence to the view that these items had been deliberately placed in the trunk, as there is no other logical reason for them to be found together and seemingly hidden in the linen cupboard.

Even more of a mystery is the bottle of Valentine's meat juice to which Florence admitted adding some powder. Tests conducted by Dr Coates proved that arsenic put into the meat juice in the form of a powder would not have dissolved in the liquid.[1594] That means the arsenic had to be added in the form of a solution. This leaves open two possibilities. Firstly, that Florence was not telling the truth; however, it is unlikely she would have made up such an incriminating statement. Secondly, the bottle to which she added the powder, was not the one Dr Carter tested. If the latter was the case, then Michael Maybrick gave Dr Carter the wrong bottle to test. This could have happened accidently; Michael may have picked up a bottle from the small round table, rather than the washstand. Alternatively, the original bottle had been substituted for one that contained dissolved arsenic. According to the Baroness, the Maybrick brothers told her when she arrived at the house they had '*merely given*' the bottle to Dr Carter to analyse, '*so as to have an excuse*' to send Florence back to her, so they could keep the children. Michael added, the Baroness said, if she '*would prove her daughter mad and have her shut up, they would drop the enquiry.*'[1595]

If Michael had deliberately switched meat juice bottles, he did so as a ploy to incriminate Florence and have the children taken beyond her reach.

FACT FILE THREE:
THE ARSENIC FOUND IN JAMES' HOME AND OFFICE

Drains, sinks and toilets. Mr Davies analysed four jars. Two jars (nos. 1 and 3) from the lavatory and housemaid's closet contained no traces of arsenic. Two jars (nos. 2 and 4) from the water closet and nearby area were found to contain traces of arsenic.

Verdict: Although traces of arsenic were found, few conclusions can be drawn. The fact *no* arsenic was found in the housemaid's sink is significant, as that would have been the sink in which they washed away slops from the bedroom when James was ill.

Unlabelled small round bottle. A white scented solution, found in the linen cupboard by Sergeant Davenport. Mr Davies described it as a '*very weak solution of arsenic... there might have been one-tenth of a grain of arsenic supposing the bottle was full.*'

Verdict: According to Florence's notes at her trial, this was the '*face wash*' she prepared from soaking the flypapers. Even if Florence had used this solution to poison her husband, its weak nature meant it would have been harmless.

Bottle of Clay and Abraham's medicine. Labelled '*Mixture, a sixth part to be taken every morning – James Maybrick, 24th April.*' Found by Inspector Baxendale in the lavatory at Battlecrease. There was a small quantity of thick liquid in bottle, perhaps half a teaspoonful. There was also some thick material adhering to the side. Mr Davies said he '*found very distinct evidence of arsenic... more than a trace.*' Another bottle of Clay and Abraham's medicine (but a different prescription), also made up on 24th April, was found in James' office, but it contained no arsenic.

Verdict: Both Prosecution and Defence agreed that the start of James' illness dated from the day of the Wirral races, when James had taken a double dose of his medicine from London. Addison said arsenic had been found in one of the medicines bottles prepared by Clay and Abraham's from Dr Fuller's prescription. Although Mr Davies found '**distinct evidence**' of arsenic in the bottle, that particular medicine had been compounded in Liverpool and therefore could *not* have been the medicine which James received in the post.

1594 MacDougall A.W., (1896) op cit., pages 249-250.
1595 HO 144/1638/A50678/D99.

A blue bottle of Price's glycerine. At James' inquest, Inspector Baxendale stated he found the blue bottle in the lavatory, but on the official police list it is shown as being found in James' dressing room. Mary Cadwallader and Elizabeth Brierley both said the bottle had been in the house for some time. Mr Davies estimated that if the bottle had been full, it may have contained as much as two-thirds of a grain of arsenic. Glycerine was used by both Nurses Gore and Callery to refresh James' mouth during his illness; however, it is not clear which bottle they used.

Verdict: The glycerine used on James may have come from a different, non-contaminated bottle. Even if it *had* come from the contaminated bottle, the dosage was low and not dangerous. It is likely that any arsenic in the bottle may have been present due to natural processes. Levy pointed out that arsenic is often a by-product when glycerine is prepared. The statement by Mr Bird in 1893 – that glycerine containing arsenic was probably on sale in Liverpool around the time of James' death – further undermined this piece of evidence.

Bottle of Valentine's meat juice. The most important piece of evidence in the trial. This was supposedly the bottle to which Florence admitted adding some powder. Michael Maybrick took it from the bedroom and gave it to Dr Carter. The bottle was later analysed by Mr Davies, who found it contained half a grain of white oxide arsenic.

Verdict: Although this piece of evidence was damaging to Florence, James never drank anything from the bottle, and even if he had, it would not have done him any harm due to the low amount of arsenic in it. The fact the solution in the bottle contained no vegetable fibres means the arsenic cannot have come from the flypapers. Also, it is very possible that Michael Maybrick took the wrong meat juice bottle from the bedroom.

Hat box 1 in the inner dressing room. Four bottles were found: *Bottle with black powder and handkerchief (Exhibit no. 8)*: Mr Davies cut a piece off the handkerchief and found traces of arsenic. *Bottle (Exhibit no. 9)*: Mr Davies found 12 to 15 grains of solid arsenic in the liquid. The bottle also contained powdered charcoal. *Bottle (Exhibit no. 10)*: Mr Davies found the bottle contained a saturated solution of arsenic with a small amount of solid arsenic. *Bottle (Exhibit no. 11)*: A bottle labelled '*Humphreys Jones, Llangollen*'. Mr Davies found several grains of solid arsenic. **Hat box 2 in the inner dressing room.** A *tumbler and handkerchief soaking in a white milk solution (Exhibit no. 12)*: Mr Davies estimated there was between 30 to 40 grains of arsenic in it.

Verdict: The two hat boxes were on the floor in the inner-dressing room. This was the room in which he often slept (used by Florence only during James' illness). The two boxes, one above the other, were in a corner of the room. In the upper hat box was a brown slouch hat that covered a small wooden box that contained some small bottles. In the lower hat box was a tall silk hat, underneath the crown of which was the tumbler containing liquid. Mrs Briggs told the inquest both hat boxes were in a '*prominent place*' in the dressing room. She said nothing was locked in the rooms except Florence's wardrobe, and in that '*none of the bottles or glasses concerned were found.*'

Arsenic - Poison for cats. A package in the chocolate box found in the trunk bearing Florence's initials. Stored in the linen cupboard. Mr Davies found it contained 71 grains, of these 65.2 were arsenic, the remainder being charcoal in a fine powder. In the box were other items including a stained handkerchief, with Florence's name on it.

Verdict: It is extremely unlikely that Florence would have hidden arsenic in an unlocked trunk in a linen cupboard frequently visited by servants. The cupboard was on the landing used by everyone in the house, so the package could have been placed there by anybody. Likely to have been the arsenic provided for James by Valentine Blake.

Florence's dressing-gown. Mr Davies found some stains in the pocket of the gown, and a test showed distinct traces of arsenic.

Verdict: Mr Davies agreed the stain had probably come from a handkerchief soaked in a solution of arsenic.

Florence's handkerchief. Mr Davies tested a handkerchief in the dressing gown. He found a trace of arsenic on a brown stain.

Verdict: Florence would have used handkerchief to apply the cosmetic solution containing arsenic to her face.

An apron. Mr Davies said it was stained a good deal in the front and he found traces of arsenic in the stains.

Verdict: No surprise again. Florence would have worn this apron when preparing the cosmetic solution.

Pan, basin and jug in James' office. Mr Davies said under the ledge of the jug were two little drops of dried skim. He boiled water in the pan and poured it into the jug and basin. He found distinct crystals of arsenic. He estimated there must have been a considerable amount or arsenic in the original food mixture, because the quantity of solid in the test was very small.

Verdict: Dr Paul, at Florence's trial, said he tested four identical pans and found arsenic in the glazing of all of them. That meant the arsenic found by Mr Davies might have been there naturally and have nothing to do with the food. Also, Captain Irving had seen James add a powder to his food, so if arsenic *had* been added, it was probably done by James himself.

Flypapers. Mr Davies tested the flypapers. One of Hanson's sheets contained nearly 2½ grains of arsenic.
Verdict: Arsenic from the papers could not have been added to the food, as no trace of vegetable fibres were found.

If James did not die of arsenical poisoning, what was the real cause of his death? It was the contention of the prosecution at Florence's trial that James was essentially a healthy man who was slowly poisoned to death by his wife. Dr Hopper described James as a '*very healthy man,*' though he said he often complained of symptoms which the doctor did not consider serious.[1596] Mary Cadwallader, the waitress, told the court that up to the time that James attended the Wirral races he appeared, as far as she could tell, to '*enjoy good health.*' Although it is the case that some of James' family, friends and servants *did* believe him to be in good health, there is large amount of evidence to believe the opposite was true.

This evidence strongly suggests that, by early 1889, James' use of drugs, prescribed and non-prescribed had a severely detrimental impact upon his health. John Aunspaugh noticed it, as did Edwin and many of James' colleagues on the 'Change. Therefore, when he took a double dose of the London medicine, almost certainly strychnine, on 27th and 28th April 1889 the general decline in his health meant that his body was unable to cope with the powerful poisonous mixture and he became seriously ill.

James' illness was not brought on by any poison administered by his wife, but was self-inflicted as a result of his long-standing and dangerous use of drugs and other medications.

FACT FILE FOUR:
EVIDENCE THAT DEMONSTRATES THE TRUE STATE OF JAMES' HEALTH IN 1889

Levy wrote: '*after the Ascot races, in June 1888... his health experienced a change for the worse; and he [James] complained among other things, of a constant headache.*' (Source: Levy J.H., 1899, page 6)

In November 1888, James told Dr Drysdale that for about three months he '*was suffering from pains from one side of his head to the other, preceded by pains on the right side of the head and a dull headache. He was never free from pain except in the early morning, and possibly in the forenoon.*' (Source: Dr Drysdale's evidence at Florence's trial)

Florence Aunspaugh wrote: '*In 1888 when I was with my father in England, he said it was very perceptible that Mr Maybrick had again failed very much in that one year. When my father came home he told my mother, "She would hardly know Maybrick, he had aged so much, and he did not believe he would be here very much longer."*' (Source: Trevor Christie Collection)

Sir Charles Russell stated James '*had been ordered to Harrogate for his health*' in 1888. (Source: Question by Russell to Nurse Yapp at Florence's trial)

At Florence's trial, Dr Hopper testified that between June and September 1888 he had seen James '*perhaps twenty times.*' Dr Drysdale testified that James had six consultations with him between November 1888 and March 1889. Dr Fuller examined James twice in April 1889. (Source: Evidence given by the doctors at Florence's trial)

In April 1889, in a letter James wrote to his brother Michael, he said: '*What is the matter with me none of the Doctors so far can make out and I suppose never will until I am stretched out and cold and then future generations may profit by it if they hold a post mortem which I am quite willing they should do.*' (Source: HO 144/1639 A50678/29)

According to a report in a Liverpool newspaper, '*the statement that Mr Maybrick was in the habit of taking doses of medicine in which active poisons were an ingredient is confirmed by the opinions of other friends, and several gentlemen on 'Change say that for several months past he appeared to be ill, and to have something "weighing on his mind."*' (Source: *Liverpool Daily Post*, 20th May 1889) A second report stated: '*It appears that it has been apparent to his friends on 'Change that for many weeks past Mr Maybrick had been seriously ill. He had been petulant in his manner and very delicate in appearance as compared with his usual robust state of health.*' (Source: *Liverpool Daily Post*, 21st May 1889)

At the inquest into James' death, Nurse Yapp was asked if James was in perfect health up to April 1889. She replied, '*No; he did not look well for some time, but I did not hear him complain.*' (Source: *Liverpool Echo*, 28th May 1889)

In May 1889, James' brother Edwin told Captain Irving: '*Oh he's killing himself with that damned strychnine.*' (Source: *Liverpool Daily Post*, 9th September 1889)

[1596] Levy J.H., op. cit., page 52.

Baroness von Roques, in a newspaper interview, said that it was '*simply absurd*' to suggest that her daughter could have poisoned '*a man with arsenic who has been using arsenic for eleven years, without his knowing or suspecting. Mr Maybrick knew his own constitution perfectly well. He had been experimenting on it with drugs ever since I knew him.*' (Source: *Halfpenny Weekly*, 17th August 1889)

At Florence's trial, both the prosecution and the defence argued that James first became seriously ill on the morning of 27th April 1889, the day of the Wirral races, after consuming the infamous London medicine. If this is the case, then identifying the exact nature of the medicine will go a long way to explaining what made James ill, and whether a murder took place.

The prosecution suggested the medicine he took that morning was the bottle of Clay and Abraham's, labelled '*Mixture*,' and dated 24th April. This was the bottle that had been prescribed by Dr Fuller in London, but compounded by the chemists at Clay and Abraham's in Liverpool. When Mr Davies analysed the bottle he found distinct evidence of arsenic, though he was unable to specify the exact amount.

The defence team provided an alternative explanation; they argued that the London medicine was not the medicine compounded at Clay and Abraham's, but was in fact the medicine that had arrived in the post on the morning of Friday, 26th April 1889, and had been taken in by Mary Cadwallader.

FACT FILE FIVE:
WHAT EXACTLY WAS THE LONDON MEDICINE?

At the trial, Mary Cadwallader told Sir Charles Russell that James told her he '*had taken an overdose of London medicine, and it was the same as I had taken in on Friday.*' Russell asked her if it was the medicine that had come from London in the post, and she replied, '*Yes.*'

At the inquest, though not at the trial, James' book-keepers, Lowry and Smith, said they noticed James was unwell on the morning of the Wirral races. They said he told them he had had a '*strange experience that morning*,' and that he had taken '*an overdose of medicine and there was* ***strychnine in it****, that he was on the WC for an hour and all his limbs were stiff and he could not move.*'

At the Wirral races, James told Mr Thomson that he had taken an overdose of medicine that morning. More importantly, James also spoke to Morden Rigg and his wife. Rigg was later to say that James had '*turned around to my wife's carriage and told her he had taken an* ***overdose of strychnine*** *that morning and that his limbs were quite rigid. She is prepared to testify to this if necessary.*'

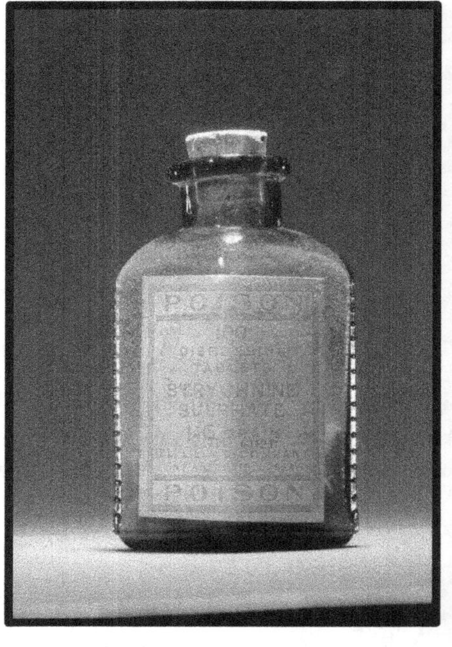

A bottle of strychnine sulphate tablets

Still further proof that the medicine James took was strychnine, rather than arsenic-based, can be seen from the symptoms he suffered after taking the medicine. On Sunday morning, the day after the Wirral races, James told Dr Humphreys he had been in a '*peculiar state*' all day at the Wirral races, his legs felt very stiff and he had been in a '*dazed condition.*' He had trouble riding his horse. He mentioned his unsteadiness, and the **uncontrollable twitching** of his arm at Hobson's house in the evening and how he had knocked over a glass of wine.Any objective analysis of the events surrounding the London medicine conclusively demonstrates the defence's view of the origin of the medicine is the correct one. James became very ill on the morning of the Wirral races, after taking a double dose of the London medicine that had arrived in the post the previous day and which contained a powerful strychnine solution.

It was also part of the defence's case that James' condition became even worse as a result of the soaking he received at the races from the intermittent showers. One would have assumed that the powerful side-effects from his consumption of the London medicine would have warned James of its toxic nature and harmful side-effects; however, such was his craving for strychnine that when he woke on Sunday morning he decided to take another big hit of the medicine. Alexander MacDougall believes that James' reaction to the medicine was even worse on the Sunday morning than it had been on the Saturday morning. The situation must have been serious, as Florence asked the cook to immediately prepare a mustard and water solution, as James '*had taken another dose of that horrid medicine.*' Humphreys said that Florence prepared the first cup herself, mixing it with her finger and '*not waiting for a spoon to be got.*'[1597] Nurse Yapp was present when Florence returned to the bedroom and said to James, '*do take this mustard and water; it will remove the brandy and make you sick again if nothing else.*'[1598]

James took the London medicine on at least three occasions; 27th and 28th April and Saturday 4th May. If the dangers of taking it were not apparent to him, then they were obvious to Florence. She described it to Elizabeth Humphreys as that '*horrid*' medicine, and told her after James had taken it on the 4th May that if he had taken that much more (pointing to her finger) he '*would have been a dead man.*' Florence then threw what remained of it down the sink.[1599]

Florence's actions are highly informative. If she was a woman with murder on her mind, then she would have allowed – even encouraged – her husband to continue taking the medicine. That is not what she did. On 28th April she tried to make her husband vomit in a clear effort to rid him of the poisonous drug. A little later, she instructed Mary Cadwallader to fetch Dr Humphreys. The following week, when James became sick again after taking the medicine, she destroyed what remained of it. These are the actions of a concerned wife, and not a murderer.

If James' final illness did begin on the weekend of the Wirral races, then it was James who caused it through his reckless double-dosing of a powerful strychnine-based medicine, and it was Florence who tried to prevent it getting worse. Dr Carter believed that James suffered from two illnesses, the first one dating from the time of the Wirral races. Carter argued that James partly recovered from this illness before receiving a fatal dose of poison around Friday, 3rd May. What is striking about these dates is that they correspond almost exactly with the dates when James took large doses of the London medicine. Carter got the dates correct, but he got the poison wrong. It was not arsenic that made James ill but strychnine, coupled with the other medications he was taking at that time.

One significant factor that points towards Florence's innocence is the care and attention she paid towards her husband when he was seriously ill. During the trial, Mary Cadwallader was asked by Russell whether Florence was '*very attentive*' to James during his illness. She answered, '*Yes.*' He then asked her if she saw '*anything suspicious about what was done or not done*' by Florence, to which she answered, '*No, I did not.*'

When Russell cross-examined Elizabeth Humphreys, he asked her if she thought Florence's behaviour had appeared suspicious. She answered, '*No, it did not.*' Russell then asked her if Florence seemed to be attending to her husband. Humphreys replied: '*She seemed very kind to him, and spent all her time with him.*'

Michael Maybrick, when questioned by Russell, was forced to admit that Florence had telegraphed Hale for a professional nurse before his brother Edwin had approached the Dover Street Institute and asked them to provide such a nurse. She had also implored Edwin to call an additional doctor. The infamous tampering with the medicine bottle that had so angered Michael had been shown to be an entirely innocent act, designed to remove some sediment. When the bottle was tested, no traces of arsenic were found in it.

At the trial, when Russell asked Nurse Callery what James did when Florence left the room, she replied, '*He asked for her when she went out of the room.*' Russell then asked if Florence appeared to be very anxious about her husband, to which the nurse replied, '*Yes, very much so.*'[1600] She added that Florence used to sit on the bed talking to him. Callery's testimony clearly shows that Florence was concerned and caring towards her husband.

Even Mr Justice Stephen, during his summing-up, referred positively to Florence's support and attention to James. He told the jury that during her husband's illness, she did '*seem to have sent for nurses. I don't see anything upon which you can ground a suggestion that she kept people away from her husband, or prevented the medical men or nurses seeing him on every occasion when they could be of use to him.*' He also pointed out that when James became sick after taking an overdose of his medicine, Florence had given him an emetic. He described the act as something which would have '*likely' done 'him good*' and 'no doubt was the best thing to do.'

Although Florence was attentive to James during his illness, in the hysteria that followed his death certain incidents were given an unfavourable significance they simply didn't deserve. One of these occurred on Sunday 5th May, when Florence told James he could only gargle and not drink a glass of lemonade the cook had prepared for him. Some of Florence's critics suggested she acted in a heartless manner. In fact, she had only been following the instructions of Dr Humphreys, who had told James he should not eat or drink anything, and if he was thirsty he should have a '*wet towel put to his mouth.*' On the same day, Edwin ignored the doctor's advice and gave James a brandy and soda; half an hour later he was sick.

The previous day, Saturday 4th May, had seen an even more important event that was to become badly misconstrued. Florence sent Mary Cadwallader to Wokes' Chemist with a written prescription; however, the chemist said he could not make it up as it had not been signed by the doctor. Cadwallader returned to Battlecrease to find Dr Humphreys, but discovered he had already left. He went to the chemist the following Monday to sign the prescription. Although an innocent mistake had been made, an untrue rumour spread that the chemist had refused to make up the prescription

1597 *Liverpool Mercury*, 29th May 1889.
1598 Irving H.B., op cit., page 66.
1599 Ibid., page 81.
1600 Ibid., page 154.

on the grounds it contained a poisonous drug. The police investigated the matter and concluded nothing untoward happened.

Nurse Yapp heard about the incident in the chemist on Tuesday 7th May, probably from Mrs Grant. She relayed it to Mrs Briggs and Mrs Hughes when they arrived at Battlecrease on Wednesday 8th May. This was the infamous occasion when Nurse Yapp was supposed to have told the two sisters, '*The mistress is poisoning the master.*' She also told them about the flypapers, and James' food being '*tampered with by his wife.*'[1601] In a newspaper interview after the trial, Nurse Yapp denied using the words the '*mistress is poisoning the master*;' however, she did admit telling the sisters about the prescription.[1602]

If the flypapers had been a red herring, then the misinformation about the chemist refusing to make-up a poisonous prescription was yet another red herring in the case. These misleading narratives were given even more impact by stories circulating about the food at Battlecrease tasting differently to how it should taste. Nurse Yapp, in the same newspaper interview, said the other servants in the house told her they had '*tasted things – bread and milk, arrowroot, and so on – and that there was a different taste in them when they came back to the kitchen than when they went up to Mr Maybrick.*' Although it is difficult to assess these accusations, there are some clues to what might have actually occurred in the answers given by the servants at Florence's trial. As far as the arrowroot is concerned, Mary Cadwallader said she had prepared it for James but Florence had finished it. Cadwallader noticed something dark in the food, though she had not put anything dark into it. When questioned by Russell about the incident, she said the cook had told her some vanilla had been put into the arrowroot, and when she looked she found a new bottle of vanilla had been opened.[1603] Elizabeth Humphreys told the court about the time when some bread and milk she had prepared for James' breakfast had been returned. She tasted it and found it had been sweetened, although she had put '*no sweetening mixture in it.*' When Russell questioned the cook, he asked her if she had known James to sometimes use sugar in his bread and milk. She answered, '*Yes.*'[1604] It is clear that the misinformation about the taste of the food was just part of the hysteria that surrounded Florence during James' illness.

The most important of the accusations about the food being tampered with concerns the gruel that was eaten by James in his office on 1st and 2nd May. In both cases, the food had been prepared by the cook but had been packaged by Florence. The food utensils were tested by Mr Davies, and he found distinct crystals of arsenic. Dr Paul, at Florence's trial, said he tested four pans identical to the one taken from James' office and found arsenic in the glazing of all of them. That meant the arsenic found by Mr Davies might have been there naturally. Also, on 1st May, Captain Irving had seen James add a powder to his food in the office; so if arsenic *had* been added to the food, it was probably done by James himself.

Another problem with the arsenic in the office food hypothesis is that Dr Carter stated the fatal dose was given to James on Friday, 3rd May. One of the flaws in this argument is that James did not take his prepared food into work on that day, and therefore he didn't eat any of it in his office as he had done on the Wednesday and Thursday. When Dr Humphreys visited late on Friday night, James blamed his sickness on '*some inferior sherry having been put into Du Barry's Revalenta food*;' however, it is not clear if he was referring to the Revalenta he had eaten the previous day, or to some he had eaten at Battlecrease after his return from the Turkish bath. Whatever he meant, he was sick on a couple of occasions after he returned home.

Therefore, James had hardly eaten anything on Friday, and what he had eaten had been removed from his stomach by vomiting. On Saturday, James had eaten even less, possibly all he had of any substance was a glass of milk late in the evening. If this was the case, how could Florence have given James a fatal dose of arsenic? Although James had eaten very little, he had consumed a wide variety of medicines and drugs, including taking a dangerous dose of his London medicine on 4th May.

The poisoned food hypothesis has no credibility; on the other hand, the strychnine hypothesis fully explains how and why James became seriously ill.

In May 1889, James wasn't just ill, he was seriously ill. Years of drug-taking had weakened his constitution, and the double-dose of the London medicine, certainly strychnine, taken on the Saturday and Sunday, 27th/28th April and again on 4th May, as well as the nux vomica and the other prescribed medications he was also taking, plus the fact that his clothes had become wet at the races, tipped him over the edge.

He needed a knowledgeable doctor and he needed to be honest with that doctor. Neither of these two things happened. Dr Humphreys was concerned and conscientious, but he knew little about the true state of his new patient's health. Florence had told Humphreys earlier in the year her husband was taking some mysterious drug that was making him ill, but Humphreys timidly accepted James' denial of the fact. Even if he had believed James, he was inexperienced and lacked detailed knowledge about the effects of arsenical and strychnine poisoning.

1601 Interview with Mrs Briggs in *Liverpool Echo*, 15th August 1889.
1602 *Liverpool Courier and Commercial Advertiser*, 21st August 1889.
1603 Irving H.B., op cit., page 76.
1604 Ibid., page 87.

James could have told him the truth but decided not to; in that sense, the ultimate responsibility for James' illness, and his failure to properly recover from it, lies squarely on his own head. MacDougall puts his finger right at the heart of the matter when he wrote that James '*deceived Dr Humphreys by attributing [his illness] to the nux vomica in Dr Fuller's tonic medicine; he knew himself perfectly well what was the matter with him, and that his illness was due not to that, but to an overdose of strychnine he had physicked himself with on the previous day before going to the Wirral races and getting drenched through there.*'[1605]

James' illness was his own fault. The failure to get the appropriate treatment for the illness was also James' fault.

Dr Carter was the second doctor to be called in to treat James. He first arrived at Battlecrease on 7th May, accompanied by Dr Humphreys. Prior to the visit, Carter had never seen or treated James. Carter was a distinguished, respected and experienced physician. He made a thorough examination of James. He spoke to all involved in the case, including James, Florence, Edwin and Dr Humphreys. He came to the correct diagnosis that James' illness had been caused by him taking some irritant that had adversely affected his stomach. He changed James' medication, and also gave advice on his diet. Everything should have been perfect and James should have gradually returned to full health; however, that did not happen, and four days later he was dead. Dr Carter was unable to help James, because he did not realise the full extent of his condition. Carter, like Humphreys before him, was not told about James' use of arsenic and strychnine. Another problem faced by Dr Carter was that although he had handled cases of people who had overdosed medicinally with arsenic, he had never previously dealt with anyone who had actually died from arsenical poisoning.[1606] Therefore, despite his vast experience in many fields of medicine, Dr Carter was treating a patient whom he did not know, for a condition about which he had not been provided the full facts and hadn't previously treated.

Bottle of Ipecacuanha wine

The fact that James failed to tell Drs Humphreys and Carter the truth about the real cause of his illness meant that at times they prescribed medications that could only have made his condition worse. For example, on 4th May, James told Humphreys he '*could retain nothing on his stomach.*' Humphreys said the vomiting was a side-effect of taking morphia. As a result, he told James to eat nothing and prescribed ipecacuanha wine to stop the vomiting.

Ipecacuanha wine, in very small doses, could be stimulating to the stomach, exciting appetite and facilitating digestion. In large doses it was an emetic. It was also dangerous when taken in large doses, or when used with certain drugs such as strychnine. As James tended to take large doses, and because he was also taking strychnine, the medicine innocently prescribed by the doctor had the potential to do James great harm.

Between them the doctors prescribed medications for James which, if taken separately in large doses – or even worse, together – were extremely dangerous. He was prescribed medications that contained three metallic elements with a similar physiological action – antimony, bismuth and arsenic – a poisonous dose of any one of these might have set up gastro-enteritis, but the three together, was a highly toxic mixture. Dr Fuller prescribed Plummer's pills, which contained sulphuret of antimony. Dr Humphreys gave James some Fowler's solution, which contained $^{1}/_{25}$th of a grain of white arsenic. Drs Humphreys and Carter prescribed Bismuth. Following James' death, a medical expert commented that the '*stomach and intestines of the habitual arsenic-taker are always more or less inflamed,*' and as a result they have a '*predisposition to gastro-enteritis.*' As a result, '*even a mild irritant might be sufficient to set it up. But neither antimony nor bismuth are mild irritants, but on the contrary are powerful ones.*'[1607]

FACT FILE SIX:
MEDICINES PRESCRIBED FOR JAMES MAYBRICK

Doctor and date	Medicine
Dr Fuller; 14th April.	1. An aperient (cascara sagrada). 2. Plummer's (liver) pills, which contain sulphuret of antimony, a toxic element similar to arsenic.
Dr Fuller; 20th April.	1. Sweet spirits of nitre added to aperient. 2. Pills replaced by sulphur lozenges. 3. Nux vomica – a nerve tonic containing strychnine.

[1605] MacDougall A.W., (1896) op cit., page 19.
[1606] Irving H.B., op cit., page 119.
[1607] *Liverpool Echo*, 17th August 1889.

Did Florence murder James?

27th and 28th April	London medicine – double dose (probably strychnine sulphate) taken by James
Dr Humphreys; 28th April (morning).	1. Humphreys advised James to stop taking Dr Fuller's nux vomica tonic and instead prescribed dilute prussic acid (hydrogen cyanide) and advised him to drink only soda water and milk.
Dr Humphreys; 28th April (evening)	1. Bromide of potassium and tincture of henbane. 2. Advised him to drink plenty of water.
Dr Humphreys; 29th April	1. Seymour's preparation of papaine and iridin. 2. Gave dietary advice, including Du Barry's Ravelenta.
1st May	James adds powder to his lunch. Edwin told Irving that James was killing himself with strychnine.
Dr Humphreys; 3rd May	1. Morphine suppository
4th May	*London medicine – probably strychnine sulphate, taken by James.*
Dr Humphreys; 4th May (morning)	1. Ipecacuanha wine for '*allaying the vomiting*'. (Dangerous when taken with strychnine.) 2. Advised James to take no food or drink. Abate thirst by sucking ice.
Dr Humphreys; 5th May (morning)	1. Prescribed (again) prussic acid from bottle James had not finished. 2. Advised him to take Valentine's beef juice. 3. Wash mouth out with Condy's fluid.
Dr Humphreys; 6th May (morning)	1. Advised James to stop taking the Valentine's meat juice. 2. Stopped the other medicines. 3. Gave James some Fowler's solution (which contained arsenic).
Dr Humphreys; 6th May (evening)	1. Dr Humphreys '*ordered him Brand's beef tea, some chicken broth, Neave's food, and some milk and water.*' 2. Blister to stomach to stop vomiting.
Dr Humphreys; 7th May (morning)	1. Advised to wash his mouth out with Sanitas to clear it. 2. Dr Humphreys throws away the remainder of the Fowler's solution.
Drs Humphreys and Carter; 7th May (afternoon)	1. Prescribed tincture of jaborandi and antipyrine. 2. Given mouth wash of diluted chlorodyne. 3. Continue with foods recommended previous day.
Dr Humphreys; 9th May	1. Introduced an opium suppository to help reduce pain in the rectum. 2. Neave's food, champagne, chicken broth, brandy and Humphrey's medicine.
Drs Humphreys and Carter; 9th May	1. Bismuth (double dose) and if necessary to add diluted brandy. 2. Some Valentine's meat juice. 3. Champagne every 15 minutes.
Dr Humphreys; 9th May	1. Prescribed cocaine to help relieve the pain in James' throat. 2. Glycerine and borax to help clean James' tongue.
Dr Humphreys; 10th May	1. Prescribed sulphonal (a sleep producer) for his restlessness. 2. Nitro-glycerin for his hand. 3. Continue with cocaine. 4. Phosphoric acid for his mouth. 5. Continue brandy and champagne.
Dr Humphreys; 10th May	1. Nutrient suppository.
Dr Humphreys; 11th May	James dies.

When James died, suspicions pointed directly at Florence. The flypapers, the belief that the food tasted differently to how it was prepared, Florence's letter to Brierley and, above all, the meat juice incident, all helped portray her as a woman who was slowly poisoning her husband so she could be with her lover.

Every behaviour by Florence was given a sinister interpretation. For example, when she helped the nurse give James his medicine, she was seen as forcing the wrong medicine down him. When Florence moved some medicine into a bigger bottle to help clear the sediment, she was '*tampering*' with the medicine.

As the clouds of suspicion started to engulf Florence, it is tempting to see those around her as being, as MacDougall wrote, like '*the Witches of Macbeth*' preparing '*their cauldron in their own dark cave.*' However, this is not an accurate picture. Mrs Briggs and Mrs Hughes, longstanding friends of James, would have been shocked when they saw him so ill in bed. Michael Maybrick would have been shocked when he arrived at Battlecrease and saw how ill his brother was, as only a couple of weeks earlier James had stayed with him in London and appeared in good health. While many of the rumours and stories circulating about Florence lacked any substance, the letter to Brierley and the meat juice incident were both serious issues that did appear to cast her as the potential villain in the story. These two factual occurrences helped make the non-factual events appear real.

Was Florence guilty of murder? To answer that we must return to the two questions that Sir Charles Russell asked the jury all those years ago. The first question was: could it be conclusively proved James Maybrick died from arsenical poisoning? The answer to that is definitively ***no***. The amount of arsenic found in his body was insufficient to kill a normal person, let alone someone who was a regular user of the drug. The prosecution tried to counter this problem by arguing that the arsenic that killed passed quickly out of the body. If that was the case, why then was none found in the tests on James' urine and faeces conducted by Dr Humphreys just prior to his death?

As well as that, the defence team called highly-respected medical experts, who testified that James' symptoms were inconsistent with arsenical poisoning. It was the case that there was a large amount of arsenic in Battlecrease, and it was unfortunate for Florence that the packet labelled *Arsenic - Poison for Cats* was found in her trunk. It was even more unfortunate for Florence that Valentine Blake was not called as a witness at her trial, as his testimony would have almost certainly explained its presence.

Sir Charles Russell asked why, if Florence did actually possess all this arsenic, did she need to go and purchase the flypapers to extract arsenic? He said: '*I ask if this was the woman of criminal designs, why with these means at her command if they were hers, should she have resorted to the clumsy, the stupid contrivance of trying to steep flypapers in water?*'[1608]

Florence did not use the arsenic as it did not belong to her, and she did not even know of its existence. As to the flypapers, Florence did not at any point try to conceal their existence. She purchased them to help prepare a cosmetic face solution, as she always claimed.

The second of Russell's questions was: if it was a case of arsenical poisoning, then was the poison administered by Florence? The answer to that question is, again, definitively ***no***. James was a habitual user of arsenic, strychnine and other dangerous drugs. On at least three occasions, Florence warned people of his dangerous drug habit. She had told Dr Hopper sometime in 1888 that her husband was taking some strong medicine. Florence repeated her concerns to Dr Humphreys in March 1889, telling him that James was taking some white powder which she thought was strychnine. In the same month, she had written to Michael Maybrick telling him his brother was taking some white powder that could be the cause of the pains in his head.

As well as taking poisonous medicines, James was also in the habit of taking many prescribed medications as well. Hopper told the court at Florence's trial that James would invariably try all the different remedies suggested to him by his friends. To make matters even worse, he sometimes doubled the recommended dose of his medicines. Hopper said he had warned James about this '*dangerous habit*' and told him he '*would some time do himself a great injury.*'[1609]

When James told Sir James Poole he took poisonous medicines, he was not exaggerating. One of James' associates once said of him, he had a '*dozen drug stores in his stomach.*'[1610] In truth, it was only a matter of time before his lifestyle and drug habit caught up with him and made him seriously ill.

Although Florence quickly became the police's prime suspect, **she did not murder her husband as there was in fact no murder. James was the architect of his own death**. By 1889, his many years of taking dangerous and poisonous drugs had severely weakened his physical constitution. The decline in his health was especially noticeable to those, such as his good friend John Aunspaugh, who only saw him occasionally. His first illness was caused by him taking a double-dose of his strychnine-based London medicine. It was an act of crass stupidity, and one which he was foolish enough to repeat the following day.

All his symptoms are entirely consistent with a strychnine overdose, and he openly admitted taking strychnine to both his friends and the servants at Battlecrease. Just as James was recovering from his self-inflicted illness, he decided to take yet another dose of the London medicine and made himself seriously ill again. Florence, rather than trying to poison her husband, actually tried to prevent him from taking certain drugs and powders. She even poured away the London medicine to prevent James from taking another dose.

The fact that traces of arsenic were found in the items used to prepare James' lunch is hardly surprising, as he had for many years been in the habit of mixing arsenic into his food and drinks. Florence Aunspaugh wrote that James was '*always taking strychnine tablets and was great on beef broth and arsenic.*'[1611]

It is possible that James might have recovered from his second illness if he had been totally honest with the doctors who treated him, but he misled them in the same manner that he had misled his family and close friends over many years. As a result, the doctors prescribed for him a changing array of medications, some of which were so toxic they

---

[1608] Irving H.B., op cit., page 248.
[1609] Ibid., page 34.
[1610] Christie T.L., op. cit., page 35.
[1611] Trevor Christie Collection.

made his condition even worse and finally brought about his demise. While these doctors must share some of the blame for James' death, the ultimate blame must lie with the man himself.

Although some of the evidence that demonstrated Florence's innocence of the crime of murder did not surface until some years after her trial – such as the affidavit of Valentine Blake – the defence had sufficiently undermined and countered the prosecution's arguments that a *Not Guilty* verdict should have been a formality. That it wasn't was primarily down to two main factors: Florence's misguided statement in court, and the grotesquely unfair summing-up of a judge who abandoned impartiality on the altar of misogyny.

Mr Justice Stephen told the Home Secretary, as he was deciding whether or not to commute Florence's death sentence, that one of Florence's expressions had a '*great effect*' upon his mind; '*according to one witness, she said she hated her husband.*'[1612] The only person who used that phrase was Mrs Samuelson, and she did so at the inquest and not the trial. That can only mean that, even before the trial had begun, the judge had taken a prejudicial view of the case and had adopted a hostile attitude towards Florence.

There can be no doubt that Florence suffered a grave miscarriage of justice that led her to spend 15 years in prison for a crime she didn't commit, and this resulted in her losing her home and her family. The injustice of the verdict was to be compounded by the statement of the Home Secretary, Henry Matthews, when he commuted her sentence to life imprisonment. Matthews decided that although there was '*reasonable doubt*' that James Maybrick actually died of arsenical poison, he still felt that Florence Maybrick had attempted to administer arsenic to her husband. The trouble with this view is that this was not the offence for which she had been tried and convicted. If there was reasonable doubt, as the Home Secretary said in his statement, that James died of arsenical poisoning, then Florence should have been reprieved and released.

Florence's understandable anger at her treatment is expressed in a poignant passage in her autobiography that dealt with the personal cost of her imprisonment:

> '*Who shall give back the years I have spent within the prison walls; the friends by whom I am forgotten; the children to whom I am dead; the sunshine; the winds of heaven; my woman's life, and all I have lost by this terrible injustice*?'[1613]

[1612] HO 144/1638/A50678

[1613] Maybrick F., op. cit., pages 222-223.

25

WAS JAMES ACTUALLY JACK THE RIPPER?

Not long after the Diary of Jack the Ripper first appeared in 1992, the *Sunday Times* launched an independent investigation into its authenticity. The newspaper decided there were four possibilities:

It was a **genuine document** written by the killer who identified himself as James Maybrick.
It was a **modern hoax**.
It was a **fantasy document** written by James Maybrick who appeared to be claiming that he was the Whitechapel murderer, but in reality, had nothing to do with the killings.
It was a **Victorian forgery**, perhaps written in an attempt to secure the release of Florence Maybrick from prison, but never used.

The newspaper quickly eliminated the last two possibilities as the Diary contained facts that were not known until 1987. The most obvious example was the reference to the '*tin match box, empty*.' This was not known until 1987, when the police list of Catherine Eddowes' possessions was first published in Martin Fido's book on the Ripper murders. That meant the Diary had to be either a genuine confessional document or a modern hoax.

Since the *Sunday Times* article was printed, Bruce Robinson has proposed a fifth possibility. He suggested the Diary had been written by Michael Maybrick, who was Jack the Ripper, in order to frame James for the murders. This possibility can be dismissed. Why would Michael have wanted to frame his own brother, to whom he was close? The handwriting of the Diary does not match Michael's handwriting. Finally, if he wanted to use the Diary to frame James, why did it not surface for more than 100 years?

One of the problems with examining the idea that James Maybrick was Jack the Ripper is that proponents of this view are often highly selective in their supporting material. They make interpretations that are not always supported by the facts. For example, the death of James' friend George Davidson led Shirley Harrison to speculate he may have suspected James was Jack the Ripper, and that this knowledge was '*too much*' for him, so he committed suicide.[1614] In fact, the evidence suggests that Davidson was driven to suicide by his debts. A creditor was pressing him for money, and he did not have the resources to make good the payment.

Another example of a weak interpretation can be found in the Paul Feldman book. When Florence Maybrick left Aylesbury Prison in 1904, she decided to use the surname *Graham* to try and hide her identity. Feldman pointed out that Graham was the maiden name of Anne Barrett, the wife of Michael Barrett. He used this snippet of information to support his outrageous claim that Florence had an affair when she was aged around 15. An illegitimate child, born in 1879, was supposedly the result of this brief encounter and Florence gave the baby to a couple from Hartlepool in the north of England whom she didn't know. Feldman claimed that this child was the grandfather of Anne Graham. It is an absurd hypothesis, and one without a single shred of evidence to substantiate it.

Florence did briefly use the surname Graham in 1904 to hide her identity. She selected the name – and later Ingraham – because the name was linked to the family of Elizabeth Ingraham, her maternal grandmother.

If one is to decide whether the Diary is a genuine document or a modern forgery, there has to be an objective process that examines all the details. Vague interpretations unsupported by the facts must be discarded. For the Diary to be considered a genuine document, and for James Maybrick to be considered a credible Ripper suspect, there is a need to take a holistic view that critically assesses the evidence in ten key areas of debate.

DOES THE DIARY HAVE AN ACCEPTABLE PROVENANCE THAT LEADS BACK TO JAMES MAYBRICK?

For any historical document to be taken seriously, it must have a clear, direct and verifiable connection back to the time when it was supposedly written and to the person who claims to be its author. The Diary simply does not meet these criteria, and therefore immediately fails the test of credibility.

[1614] Harrison S., op. cit., page 273.

Those who argue the Diary is genuine suggest it is for its detractors to prove it is a forgery. That is not the case. The onus must be on those who believe it to be genuine to demonstrate beyond all reasonable doubt that its authorship can be traced back to James Maybrick. In that task, they have singularly failed.

Every aspect of the varying accounts of how the Diary was discovered is surrounded in controversy. Michael Barrett claimed he had been given it by Tony Devereux in 1991. Devereux died in August 1991, so was unable to substantiate his story. Since 1992, Barrett's account of how he acquired the Diary changed several times, including one version in 1994 in which he claimed he had concocted it himself and had dictated it to his wife. To make matters even more confusing, Anne Graham, Barrett's ex-wife, has also provided a different account of the origins of the Diary. She claimed it had been passed to her by her father, Billy Graham. He would say he had been given it by his step-mother who in turn got it off her mother, Elizabeth Formby, who had supposedly been a friend of Nurse Yapp.

The lack of an acceptable provenance for the Diary has led to the development of several different contradictory hypotheses, all of which rest upon circumstantial evidence. The most established of these is the suggestion that James Maybrick placed the Diary under the floorboards in Battlecrease a week before he died. It was then rediscovered by accident, when some electricians were installing storage heaters on 9th March 1992. This hypothesis assumes one of the electricians took the Diary and sold it to Barrett.

Although it explains how Barrett may have obtained the Diary and why he rang London on that particular day, it does have serious flaws. It is extremely unlikely that James, when he was seriously ill, would have been able to lift heavy floorboards fitted with brass nails. If he had, the noise would have brought attention to his actions. If James had previously lifted the floorboards, then he would not have been able to secure them again without alerting the rest of the household who were constantly in and out of his sick room. In March 1992, the electricians did not lift any floorboards in what had been the Maybricks' bedroom or James' downstairs office. They did lift some floorboards in the corner of the inner-dressing room. This was a room in which the floorboards had previously been lifted by Paul Dodd, the owner of the house. He did not see any hidden items when he carried out the work. All the electricians denied taking anything from the house. Barrett denied buying a Diary off the electricians.

The Diary's lack of a credible provenance is a fundamental and insurmountable problem for those who believe it is a genuine document. All of the hypotheses that have been put forward to try to explain where it might have been for over a 100 years are based on conjecture and circumstantial evidence. Not one of them has definitive proof to substantiate its explanation. As a result, the provenance of the Diary does not go back any further than 1992.

Paul Begg wrote: '*When faced with a possibly forged document the most important thing is provenance: the history or the lack of provenance altogether is highly suspicious. In fact, poor provenance is alone sufficient to brand the diary a forgery.*'[1615]

IS THE DIARY WRITTEN IN A GENUINE VICTORIAN ARTIFACT?

The Diary was originally a scrapbook or a photograph album. The latter possibility is suggested by the presence of some glue stains and the shape of the impressions on the flyleaf. Tests on the paper suggests the Diary does date from the Victorian era. Robert Smith, who owns the Diary, wrote the paper is a '*standard mix of wood pulp and cotton, in general use for the printing of books during the Victorian era and still used to print some books. The scrapbook was of the type in regular use during the latter Victorian period.*'[1616] Smith bought a scrapbook, dated 1871, that is very similar to the Diary.

Although the Diary does appear to be Victorian in origin, that does not mean the writing within it dates from the 1880s. As Smith's own purchase suggests, Victorian scrapbooks can be obtained relatively easily. One person who did try to buy such an item was Michael Barrett. In March 1992, before he first came down to London with the Diary, he placed an advert in the *Bookdealer* in which he attempted to purchase a Victorian diary. A company in Weston-super-Mare responded to his advert, and sent him a small and unused red-coloured appointments diary. Barrett never used this diary, and later sold it. It is not clear why Barrett placed the advert; however, the episode shows how easy it would have been for a potential forger to obtain a Victorian document in which to write a fake confessional account of the Ripper murders.

Questions have been asked about whether a ripped and damaged scrapbook would have been chosen by an affluent gentleman, such as James Maybrick, in order to write down his inner-most thoughts. Dr Kenneth Rendell, an expert in historical documents, was asked by Time-Warner – who had bought the U.S. publication rights to Shirley Harrison's book – to investigate the Diary.

He first viewed the document in August 1993, when Robert Smith took it to Chicago for his team to analyse. His immediate reaction was that the Diary was written '*much more recently than the late 1880s.*' He was struck by the '*uniformity of the writing and the ink, highly unusual in a diary.*' It immediately reminded him of his first viewing

[1615] Begg P., op cit., (2006) page 416.
[1616] Smith R., op cit., page 6.

of the fraudulent Hitler diaries.[1617] Rendell was also '*surprised that the diary was written in a scrapbook, not a normal diary book. Scrapbooks, larger in format and made of very absorbent heavy paper, were used for mounting postcards, photographs, valentines, and other greeting cards.*' He said he had '*not previously encountered one used as a diary. It was possible, but very unlikely.*'[1618]

Rendell was suspicious that the first 48 pages had been torn out. He believed there was '*no logical explanation*' as to why James, a '*man of means,*' would have done this. Rendell argued that if James had wanted to use a scrapbook for a diary he would have bought a new one. He would have been '*unlikely to take one he already had and tear out the contents.*'

On the other hand, Rendell believed it was logical that '*someone wanting to forge a diary, and not knowing the difference between a scrapbook and a diary, would have bought a Victorian scrapbook, torn out the leaves already used, and used those remaining for the fabrication.*'[1619]

Another person who was suspicious of the torn-out pages was Alex Chisholm, who carried out an analysis of the factual content of the Diary. He was struck by the fact that despite the numerous pages missing at the start, the structure of the narrative remained '*intact.*' He wrote that this '*stroke of luck simply beggars belief.*'[1620]

Although the author of the Diary wrote in a scrapbook that is very probably Victorian in origin, there are still reasons for believing the document to be a forgery. Dr David Baxendale, an expert who examined the Diary, discovered a fragment of paper lodged in the binding of the document. As it was of a different material to the document itself and was coated in glue, it indicated the scrapbook had once been used to hold photographs. By examining the stains in the Diary, the photographs were judged to be three-and-a-half inches by two-and-a-half inches. This was a popular size for prints from roll film between the two world wars.[1621]

If the scrapbook had been used as a photograph album decades after James Maybrick died, then it could not have been used by him as a confessional document. Finally, the obvious reason why the diarist selected a scrapbook instead of a real Victorian diary was that he did not want to fix any of his actions against actual dates that could later be checked. The forger needed to be as vague as possible to avoid making mistakes.

IS THE INK USED IN THE DIARY VICTORIAN IN ORIGIN?

Some tests on the ink conducted by Dr David Baxendale of Document Evidence Limited have cast serious doubt on the credibility of the document. One of the most significant of these was a solubility test. This involved dropping a chemical solvent on to the ink. The older the ink, the longer it takes to dissolve because the ink and the paper have started to integrate. In Baxendale's solubility tests, the ink of the Diary started to dissolve in seconds. This indicated the document had only recently been written.[1622]

Rod McNeil, a forensic scientist who was one of Dr Rendell's team, also tried to determine how long the ink had been on the paper, using an ion migration test. Rendell expressed concerns that the nature of the scrapbook, with its more absorbent paper, would make this type of analysis more difficult to accurately complete. McNeil's results gave a median date of 1921, plus or minus 12 years. The unexpected result probably reflected Rendell's concerns about the absorbent nature of the paper in the scrapbook. Although McNeil's results did not prove the Diary to be a modern forgery, it did provide substantial evidence that it was a forgery and the text had been '*written in the twentieth century.*'[1623]

Apart from his tests on the solubility of the ink, other areas of Dr Baxendale's analysis further undermined the credibility of the Diary as a genuine Victorian document. He found the ink to be not iron-based. This was significant, as he believed iron was a key constituent in all inks from the late-Victorian period. He also found a synthetic dye called nigrosine in the ink and, as that had only been in use since the 1940s, concluded the Diary must have been written since 1945.

To counteract the negative findings from Dr Baxendale, Shirley Harrison commissioned a second set of tests, carried out by Dr Nicholas Eastaugh, an independent specialist in dating old manuscripts. His results contradicted two of Dr Baxendale's findings. Firstly, he found that the composition of the ink did not '*appear to be substantially synthetic.*' Secondly, he found the presence of iron in measurable amounts.

Although parts of Eastaugh's report were extensively quoted in Harrison's book, he was not happy with the way in which his findings had been portrayed as he felt the Diary could still be a modern forgery. His concerns led him, in June 1993, to write to the publishers of Harrison's book, warning them:

[1617] Rendell K.W., *Forging History*, (University of Oklahoma Press, Norman and London, 1994) page 150.
[1618] Ibid., pages 150-151.
[1619] Ibid., page 151.
[1620] Whittington-Egan R., op cit., page 239.
[1621] Ibid., page 224.
[1622] Ibid., page 224.
[1623] Rendell K.W., op cit., pages 152-153.

'I think it would be very dangerous to quote [me]... saying I say the ink is Victorian, when I don't – merely that it could be. I also want to underline that I am unwilling to highlight that the ink behaves like the Victorian reference material without the qualifying statement that we cannot actually distinguish it on the basis of solubility from later inks of similar composition, and that the ink of the diary must equally behave like inks applied substantially later than 1889.' [1624]

Tests on the composition of the ink have produced contradictory results. The differences in the results have led many to call for further tests. Even if these occur, the results will probably remain inconclusive as ink chemists in the Victorian era experimented with all sorts of chemicals and kept their recipes secret. As a result, there is no single view of what elements would be found in a typical Victorian ink.

Before he had even viewed the Diary, Melvin Harris predicted that it would be written in a '*simple iron-gall ink.*' He said this type of ink was indistinguishable from those used in the 1880s, '*but is easily made and not difficult to buy.*'[1625] Dr Rendell wrote, '*It is relatively easy today to make ink with the elements that were used in Victorian England.*'[1626]

DOES THE HANDWRITING OF THE DIARIST MATCH THE HANDWRITING OF JAMES MAYBRICK?

For the Diary to be considered authentic, the diarist's handwriting must match the handwriting of James Maybrick. In addition, as the diarist claimed to have written the *Dear Boss* letter, his handwriting must also match the style found on that letter.

The results of handwriting studies have been devastating for those who consider the Diary to be genuine. Sue Iremonger, the expert brought in by Shirley Harrison, found the handwriting of the diarist did not match the handwriting on James' will or that of the *Dear Boss* letter. Dr Audrey Giles, the expert employed by the *Sunday Times*, was equally certain. She stated the handwriting of the diarist did not match the handwriting on James' will. Dr Baxendale, in his analysis, could not accept that the diarist's handwriting was naturally written. He said it was for the most part '*in the looped cursive mode of Victorian copper-plate, but from time to time the penman lapsed into that disconnected-plain-letter script style which did not become common until the mid-twentieth century.*'[1627]

One of Dr Rendell's team who analysed the Diary was Maureen Casey Owens. She was a former president of the American Society of Questioned Document Examiners and, for many years, the Chicago Police Department's expert in document examination. Both Owens and Rendell felt that the writing in the Diary was '*not consistent with letter formations of the late 1880s; there was a uniformity of ink and slant of writing in going from one entry to another (supposedly written at different times) that was unnatural and very indicative of a forger writing multiple entries at one time.*' When they completed their analysis, they felt there was '*sufficient evidence to reach a definite conclusion. The historical facts in the diary so clearly identify the author as James Maybrick that proof that he did not write the diary left only the conclusion that it was a hoax.*'[1628]

Those who believed the Diary to be genuine responded by arguing handwriting analysis was not an exact science. They referred to the handwriting of the German serial murderer Peter Kürten, who wrote letters to the police after each of his murders, and in each letter his handwriting style was different. The problem with this example is that Kürten deliberately tried to disguise his handwriting. That was not the case with the Diary, as the diarist provided plenty of clues to reveal his identity.

The pro-Diary camp also tried to argue away the difference in handwriting styles by saying that the diarist suffered from drug addiction, and had a multiple personality disorder. The renowned FBI profiler John Douglas dismissed this argument as '*bogus.*'[1629] Dr Audrey Giles wrote that, while drug addiction can affect handwriting, the basic construction of the style remains unaltered. In a further attempt to tackle the difference in handwriting styles, Shirley Harrison, Robert Smith and Paul Feldman all suggested it was James' will that was the forgery and not the Diary. They said that the will was different to one that appeared in the MacDougall book of 1891, and that MacDougall, as a lawyer, would not have made any mistakes when he transcribed the will. In fact, some of the submissions that MacDougall made to the Home Office are characterised by their errors and corrections. In one of them, he repeatedly refers to Mrs Samuelson as '*Mrs Saunderson,*' and on one occasion even wrote James' surname as '*Maybric.*'[1630]

All the evidence strongly suggests that James' will is genuine. As Melvin Harris pointed out, a certified copy of James' will was previously stored at Somerset House. The certified copy was made on 29th July 1889, by the firm of

1624 Ibid., page 148.
1625 Harris M., op cit., page 185.
1626 Rendell K.W., op cit., page 152.
1627 Whittington-Egan R., op cit., page 224
1628 Rendell K.W., op cit., page 153.
1629 Douglas J. and Olshaker M., op cit., page 73.
1630 HO 144/1640/A50678D/279 page 36.

Layton, Steel and Springman, the Liverpool solicitors who handled the estate. The text of this certified copy '*agrees in all essentials with the wording of the will in Maybrick's own hand dated and witnessed on 25th April 1889.*' According to Harris, this was '*proof beyond doubt,*' that the will in MacDougall's book was '*flawed.*'[1631]

Harris' view has been strengthened in recent years by the discovery of further documents written by James Maybrick, such as those in the Richmond Chancery. The handwriting on all these documents simply does not match the handwriting of the diarist.

For those who believe that the Diary was written by James Maybrick, the issue of the handwriting is an insurmountable problem. The problem is, as Donald Rumbelow has written: '*The handwriting of the diary did not match the writing and signature on Maybrick's will or on his marriage certificate. Nor does it match a lengthy inscription, in a Bible given by Maybrick to his mistress.*'[1632] The complete failure of the handwriting of the diarist to match the handwriting of James Maybrick, is definitive proof that the Diary is a forgery.

DID THE DIARIST WRITE THE *DEAR BOSS* LETTER?

The *Dear Boss* letter and the *Saucy Jacky* postcard are significant to the debate over whether James Maybrick wrote the Diary in two ways. Firstly, the diarist clearly implies that he was the author of the communications. Secondly, some of the words and phrases that appear in them also appear in the Diary. Although the police in 1888 initially believed the letters may have been written by the killer, they later came to view them as forgeries. The police's scepticism about the authenticity of the two letters is shared by most Ripperologists. Philip Sugden pointed out that neither Stride nor Eddowes had their ears severed, which the writer of the Dear Boss letter had threatened to do. He concluded: '*In short there is no reason to believe that the Jack the Ripper letter and postcard were anything more than hoaxes.*'[1633]

Douglas, the FBI profiler, outlined what he considered to be the likely characteristics of Jack the Ripper. He suggested that the perpetrator was a '*disorganised offender*;' a loner who felt rejected by society. He was also a '*lust murderer.*' A lust murder is one in which '*sex is a key component of the crime*;' the motivation for the act and the psychological needs that it addresses '*give the perpetrator a heightened satisfaction that he does not achieve from anything else in life.*'[1634] Douglas argued that such a person would not have communicated with the police in such a manner as the *Dear Boss* letter. He concluded the letter was forged by someone who '*knew how the game was played,*' and the most likely candidate for that would be a journalist. He pointed out the letter was addressed to a news agency rather than an individual newspaper. This takes a degree of sophistication that would be beyond the intellectual range of a '*largely disorganised, emotionally deficient*' individual.

The language contained in the letter itself also does not fit the mindset of such a killer. According to Douglas, '*psycholinguistically speaking, the "Dear Boss" letter is a performance, a characterisation by a literate, articulate person of what a crazed killer should sound like. It's too organised, too indicative of intelligence and rational thought, and far too "cutesy." I don't believe an offender of this type would ever think of his actions as "funny little games" or say that his "knife's so nice and sharp."*'[1635]

Another serious problem with the suggestion that the *Dear Boss* letter was written by James Maybrick is that the handwriting of the letter does not match his own handwriting. Sue Iremonger, the documents expert consulted by Shirley Harrison, could not link the handwriting of the Diary with the *Dear Boss* letter, or with James' will.[1636]

Dr Rendell and Maureen Owens also concluded that the *Dear Boss* letter was '*definitively not written by the person who wrote the diary.*' They wrote that if Sue Iremonger was correct, there can '*only be one conclusion: the letter is a forgery. If the letter was in fact written by Jack the Ripper, then the diary which copies its language but does not match its handwriting, must be forged. If the letter was a hoax of the time, then the diary must still be a forgery since it copies its language.*'[1637]

The only other consideration is whether it was possible for the diarist to have disguised his handwriting when writing the *Dear Boss* letter. Owens, who was an expert in detecting situations in which a person is attempting to write in a manner to cover up his own handwriting, was absolutely definite; this process had not happened with the *Dear Boss* letter.

1631 Harris M., op cit., page 195.
1632 Rumbelow D., op cit., page 252.
1633 Sugden P., op cit., page 270.
1634 Douglas J. and Olshaker M., op cit., page 37.
1635 Ibid., page 52.
1636 Harrison S., op. cit., page 330.
1637 Rendell K.W., op cit., page 148.

ARE THERE ANY ERRORS OR HISTORICAL INACCURACIES IN THE DIARY?

The credibility of the Diary is seriously undermined by errors and historical inaccuracies contained within the narrative. Some of the simplest errors are evident when the diarist gets the name of a person or a place wrong. The diarist mentions a Mrs Hammersmith. The problem here is that those who argue the Diary is genuine have not found a realistic candidate to be the person mentioned in the document. The diarist wrote that he met a friend on the '*Exchange floor*;' but everyone in Liverpool, especially the people who worked there, always called the Cotton Exchange by the abbreviated phrase '*Change*. Another significant error comes when the diarist wrote that he '*took refreshment at the Poste House*.' The problem with this entry is there is no record of any public house in Liverpool, or London, having such a name in the 1880s. The pub that is identified as the most likely candidate is the Poste House in Cumberland Street, Liverpool. It was in existence at that time, but was then known as the Muck Midden.

The diarist claims near the end of the journal that he had stopped taking the '*dreaded stuff*' or, in other words, had stopped taking drugs such as arsenic. That is an inaccurate statement, as we know that James took dangerous drugs right up until his death. The diarist also claims he confessed to Florence about his murderous deeds just before he died. That cannot be true, as she demonstrated a great desire to protect his memory at her trial and spoke positively about how they had been reconciled. As a devout Christian, she would not have reacted in such a manner if she believed he was a serial murderer. There are also factual errors in the Diary concerning the death of the last Ripper victim, Mary Kelly.

All these smaller errors are not by themselves significant, but when combined with the more serious errors, one is left with the unmistakable conclusion that the Diary is a forgery.

The Diary contains an obscure line of poetry written by Richard Crashaw, a little-known early seventeenth century poet. The line is: '*Oh costly intercourse of death*.' Suspicions were aroused when Michael Barrett became the first person to correctly identify the origin of the line when he found it in a modern poetry book in Liverpool's main library. He later announced that he had the same poetry book at home.

Another problem with the Diary is that some of the words or phrases found in it did not exist in the late 1880s. For example, the diarist wrote, '*Perhaps I should top myself*.' The term '*Top myself*' didn't become associated with committing suicide until the mid-twentieth century. William Beadle has gone further, and argued that the overall style of writing in the Diary appears to be '*more in tune with the twentieth century that the nineteenth*.'[1638] He believes that while words and phrases that weren't in use in Victorian times have not necessarily been found, the Diary lacks the over-elaborate style of writing that one would expect in a nineteenth century journal.

At the beginning of December 1888, James Maybrick was one of 19 local men who were called up to serve on the Grand Jury in Liverpool. The diarist, who continually ridicules the police for their failure to catch him, does not mention this event in the journal. The obvious explanation for this is that the diarist did not know about it. This, in turn, indicates that James cannot have been the author of the Diary.

One of the biggest mistakes is over the issue of chronology. In August 1889, Alfred Brierley wrote in an affidavit that while he had first met Florence about two years earlier at a dinner in her house, he had only met her '*in company once or twice between that occasion and November 1888*.' He subsequently '*met her at various dances, and became on intimate terms with her and her husband*.'[1639] In other words, Florence's affair with Brierley started *after* the Ripper murders had finished (if Mary Kelly had been the last victim), and therefore the relationship could not have been the motive that supposedly started James' killing spree.

DOES THE DIARIST DEMONSTRATE AN INTIMATE AND DETAILED KNOWLEDGE OF THE MAYBRICK FAMILY?

One of the biggest myths about the Diary is that its author had a detailed knowledge of Maybrick family life. This is a view that is completely unfounded. People who propose such a view select an odd line or phrase and suggest it provides an insight that cannot be found in any other source. An obvious example is when the diarist wrote, '*My dearest Gladys is unwell yet again*.' Robert Smith and Shirley Harrison draw attention to this line, especially the word '*again*,' as they claim none of the books suggest that Gladys was often unwell. That is not the case. Ryan, in his 1977 book, wrote that Dr Humphreys was summoned to Battlecrease to treat James. It was a house he knew as '*he had often attended the Maybrick children*.'[1640] If, as Ryan states, Dr Humphreys had *often* attended the children, then it is easy to conclude they must have been frequently ill.

One thing that would have shown an insight into the Maybricks would have been knowledge of the family members' pet-names for one another. The diarist does refer to some of these, such as '*Bunny*' for Florence and '*Bobo*' for young James Chandler. This shows no intimate knowledge, as the names can be easily sourced from books. What

---

[1638] Beadle W., 'Revisiting the Maybrick Diary' in *The Journal of the Whitechapel Society*, Edition 20, June 2008.

[1639] Levy J.H., op cit., page 438.

[1640] Ryan B., op cit., page 32.

would have been significant was if the diarist had used names that did not feature in the books. In 1888, the year of the Ripper murders, Florence Aunspaugh stayed with the Maybricks and spent much of her time playing with young James. In her correspondence with Trevor Christie, she writes about him and uses the nickname '*Sonny*.' This nickname did not appear in books until after 1992. The '*Bobo*' reference in the Diary is not a mistake, but it shows no insight into the Maybricks.

A postcard exists in which Michael Maybrick calls his eldest brother '*Will*,' not William. The diarist called him William. One of the clearest examples that demonstrates the diarist was unaware of family nicknames is when he writes about Thomas, another of James' brothers. When he does, he always calls him Thomas, yet his family and friends called him '*Tom*.' Florence Aunspaugh, who met Thomas, refers to him in her correspondence with Trevor Christie as *Tom*. Charles Ratcliffe, a friend of James, calls him *Tom* in a letter he wrote just after James' death. Amy Main, the daughter of Edwin Maybrick, who frequently met Thomas, refers to him as *Tom* in numerous letters she wrote to a family friend, Derek Warman. Even Thomas called himself *Tom*. At Michael's funeral in 1913, Thomas sent a wreath with a card, which he signed, '*Tom, Julie and Ethel*.'[1641]

Amy Doris Main, the only child of Edwin Maybrick, with her husband, August 1973. (Derek Warman collection)

One of the most powerful examples that demonstrates the diarist had no intimate knowledge of the Maybrick family is the failure to refer to the miscarriage suffered by Florence in Spring 1889. After Florence's conviction, the Home Secretary decided to canvass opinion from a range of people on whether or not he should commute Florence's sentence to life imprisonment.

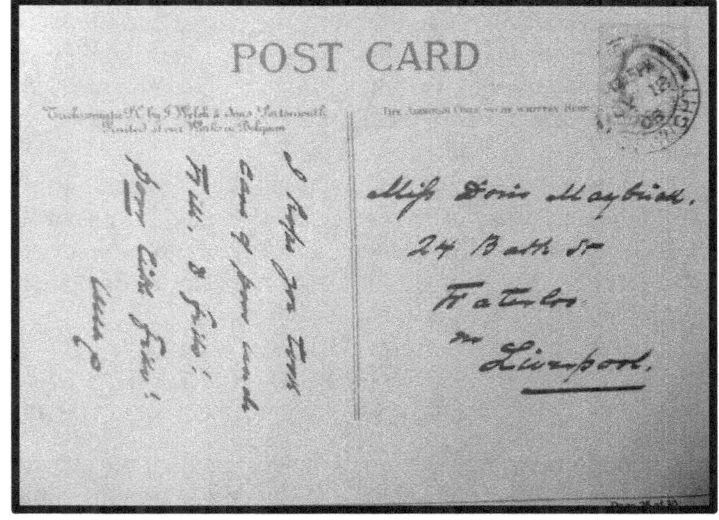

Postcard from Michael Maybrick to Amy (Doris) Maybrick, Edwin's daughter. Michael refers to his brother as 'Will.' The postcard read: 'I hope you took care of poor uncle Will and Fido! Poor little Fido!' The postcard shows Michael's signature. (Derek Warman collection)

As part of this process, in August 1889, Mr Justice Stephen sent him a detailed letter outlining his views on the case. In it, he said that after the trial he had been approached by Dr Humphreys who told him that Florence had suffered a miscarriage in early 1889 and James had expressed doubts about whether or not he was the father of the unborn child. This would have been a truly traumatic event in the Maybrick household. If James had been the diarist, he would have written about it in some detail. He would have launched a viciously-worded assault on his wife, the '*whore*,' and her lover, the '*whoremaster*.' It would have motivated him to have committed further murders.

None of this happens. There is no mention of the miscarriage. There can be only one reason for this gaping omission in the narrative of the Diary – the author of the document did not know about the miscarriage. Therefore, the diarist cannot have been James Maybrick.

The author of the Diary constructed its Maybrick content by sourcing material from books written prior to 1992. When one compares lines in the Diary with lines taken from the Ryan book (1977), one can identify how a clever forger might have written the document, cherry-picking phrases and incorporating them into the Diary's text. For example, Ryan wrote that Dr Fuller could find '*very little the matter with him*' [James]; the diarist wrote, '*Fuller believes there is very little the matter with me*.'

[1641] *Isle of Wight County Press*, 6th September 1913.

DOES THE DIARIST DEMONSTRATE A DETAILED KNOWLEDGE OF THE RIPPER MURDERS?

If the diarist knew little about the Maybrick family, he knew even less about the Ripper murders. There is a lack of in-depth knowledge about the killings, and the details that are provided can be easily sourced from books. The diarist claims his first murder was in Manchester, yet provides no details that would allow the reader to identify whom the victim might have been and when the murder occurred.

The diarist is also vague about the Ripper murders themselves. The killing and mutilation of the first Whitechapel victim, Polly Nichols, is described in only a few short sentences. There is no insight into the killing. The diarist's account of Annie Chapman's murder is almost as brief as the Nichols' murder. There are no details on how he met Chapman, or how he murdered her. Coroner Baxter stated that the dissection of Chapman's body could have only been done by someone with anatomical skill and knowledge, yet there is no information in the Diary on how the mutilation process was carried out.

The murder of Elizabeth Stride is also covered in a short paragraph. Again, no new material is provided. What is also missing is a reference to the murder weapon. The knife used to kill Stride was short and broad, unlike the long narrow-bladed knife used to kill the other victims. This is an area in which the real killer could have provided new information, but it doesn't happen.

The diarist's account of the murder of Catherine Eddowes is a window into how the Diary was constructed. If one compares what the diarist wrote with the account of the murder in Martin Fido's 1987 book, one can identify where the material might have been sourced. One particular sentence is highly suggestive; the diarist's reference to the '*tin match box empty*.' The empty tin match box was not known to the general public until 1987, when a police list of Catherine Eddowes' possessions was first published. The wording in the Diary is almost identical to the wording on the police list, suggesting the author of the Diary simply copied from the list.

In his account of the last Ripper victim, Mary Kelly, the diarist made some obvious factual errors. He wrote that he cut the breasts off and '*left them on the table with some of the other stuff*.' However, according to a report by Dr Thomas Bond, Scotland Yard's police surgeon who conducted an examination of Kelly's dead body, the breasts had been left '*one under the head and the other by the right foot*.' His report was not released until 1987.[1642]

Shirley Harrison recognised that the diarist had made a mistake when referring to the position of Kelly's excised breasts, but argues that nobody who had committed the savage acts of barbarism could have possibly remembered accurately everything that they did that night. The problem with her view is that she argues the exact opposite when it comes to the diarist's recall of the smallest details when recounting what he had done to other mutilated victims, such as Catherine Eddowes.

The Diary exhibits no new material; all the factual information has been taken from books on the murders. Some of this material has been reworked, or turned into rhymes, but none of it shows any insight into the killings. This process is made obvious when factual errors from modern sources are replicated into the narrative of the Diary. It is also obvious when whole lines, such as the reference to the '*tin match box, empty*,' have been copied into the narrative.

DOES JAMES MAYBRICK MATCH THE EYE-WITNESS DESCRIPTIONS OF JACK THE RIPPER?

Although there are issues with the accuracy of the eye-witness descriptions from people who might have seen Jack the Ripper, Ripperologists have used them to produce a picture of the murderer. Philip Sugden suggested they show the murderer to have been '*a white male of average or below average height in his twenties or thirties*.'[1643]

The witness who provided the most detailed description was George Hutchinson.[1644] He said on the night of Mary Kelly's murder, he saw Kelly with a man and followed them as they walked to Miller's Court. Hutchinson described the man as '*about thirty-four or thirty-five years of age, with dark complexion, and dark moustache turned up at the ends... He looked like a foreigner*.' It was not a description that matches James Maybrick.[1645]

In early October 1888, two composite sketches of Ripper suspects appeared in the *Daily Telegraph*. A couple of days later, both pictures were reprinted in the *Liverpool Echo*. The two pictures were different, in that one depicted a man with a moustache and wearing a bowler hat, the other depicted a man without a moustache and wearing a soft felt hat. Shirley Harrison suggested that the picture of the man with the moustache '*seems to bear a resemblance to [James] Maybrick*.'[1646]

[1642] Sugden P., op cit., page 315.
[1643] Ibid., page 367.
[1644] Evans S.P. and Gainey P., *Jack the Ripper – First American Serial Killer*, (Arrow, London, 1996) page 149.
[1645] *St James's Gazette*, 14th November 1888.
[1646] Harrison S., op. cit., page 138.

Both pictures were largely based on information provided by Matthew Packer, who was interviewed by the police after the murder of Elizabeth Stride. The problem with Packer's story is that he changed his account and description of the possible killer so many times that Chief Inspector Swanson felt the information was '*almost valueless as evidence*.'[1647]

It is also significant that the diarist does not refer to these pictures. If James Maybrick had been the diarist, he would have seen the pictures in the *Liverpool Echo* and would have almost certainly referred to them in the Diary, ridiculing the police for failing to identify him from the pictures. None of that happens.

The witnesses' descriptions mean that James Maybrick is far too old to be considered a Ripper suspect. In 1888, James was aged almost 50. Nearly all the witnesses describe a man who was approximately 20 years younger than James was at the time of the killings. James was also suffering from chronic ill-health. As a result, he would have been physically and cognitively unable to have committed the crimes and then successfully evaded detection from the police.

DID JAMES MAYBRICK'S PERSONALITY RESEMBLE THAT OF A PSYCHOPATHIC SERIAL KILLER?

If the diarist is to be believed, a '*gentle man* born' was turned into a serial killer as a result of his wife's affair. He displaces his anger by taking revenge on the prostitutes of London. The simplicity of this motive might suit the narrative of the Diary, but it does not fit the personality of a dangerous psychopath.

Although one has to be careful when constructing a psychological profile of Jack the Ripper, as the killer was never caught, there are some assumptions that can be made by completing a crime analysis. Firstly, the crimes were not just about the murders themselves; if that was the case, then the *Double Event* would not have occurred. The killing of Elizabeth Stride did not satisfy the murderer, as he was disturbed and could not '*rip*' his victim. He needed to commit a second murder, so he could mutilate the body of Eddowes to '*satisfy his psychosexual needs*.'[1648] The mutilation of Mary Kelly was even more horrendous.

The man capable of this level of barbarism was a dangerous psychopath. He was suffering from serious, long-term psychological problems. He was a man who hated and probably feared women. In removing the victims' genitalia, he was attempting to '*neuter*' them, to '*take away what he finds sexually threatening*.'[1649]

Any objective analysis of James Maybrick's personality makes it clear that he does not fit the psychological profile of a serial killer. He appears to have had a normal childhood and lived in a stable home environment. He remained on friendly terms with his brothers all his life. He finished the *Dear Blucher* letter, which he wrote to his brother Michael shortly before his death, with the words, '*With love. Your affectionate brother, Jim*.' He was not a loner or withdrawn from society. He was a very sociable man with a large number of friends and was a member of several clubs and organisations. Sir Charles Russell said of James, '*He was a man who seems to have been liked by his friends – a man not of an unkindly or ungenerous nature*.'

The observations of Florence Aunspaugh, who stayed in Battlecrease in 1888, show that James was a man who could be caring and empathetic. She wrote relations between him and Florence were '*very amicable*.' When he left for work in the morning he '*would always kiss her goodbye*.' After the loud and extremely unpleasant row between James and Florence on the night of the Grand National of 1889, Elizabeth Humphreys, the cook at Battlecrease, saw James walking up and down the hallway, visibly '*upset and crying*.' These are emotional responses unlikely to occur had James been a deranged psychopath or psychotic.

James did not suffer from paranoia or have a poor self-image. He neither hated women nor was afraid of them. He was engaged to be married on possibly four occasions; to Sarah Ann Robertson, Mrs Briggs, Julia Devens Valentine and Florence Chandler. Two of the women, Sarah Ann Robertson and Mrs Briggs, maintained a friendship with him over many years. Sarah Ann Robertson, who despite being abandoned by James, remained loyal to him. Her death certificate even recorded her as '*Sarah Ann Maybrick, otherwise Robertson*.' James was not sexually inadequate, and his marriage produced two well-balanced children. From the evidence that exists, he appears to have been a loving father.

Although James was not a psychopath, he was a flawed character. He had a dangerous drug habit. He had a tendency to be pessimistic, especially in business matters. He could be aggressive and abusive. Mary Cadwallader told MacDougall that James '*was of a violent temper, but it would soon pass off*.'[1650] He was not a man who would have allowed his wife to have had an affair. Florence flirted with Brierley and James hit her. As soon as Brierley heard that James had suspicions about him, he made plans to travel to Europe. He was frightened of James.

[1647] Begg P., Fido M. and Skinner K., op cit., page 395.
[1648] Douglas J. and Olshaker M., op cit., page 47.
[1649] Ibid., page 32.
[1650] MacDougall A.W., (1891) op cit., page 69.

Was James actually Jack the Ripper?

While James was capable of violence, he would not have travelled to London and killed prostitutes as a proxy for his wife. He had never shown any hatred towards prostitutes. During his time in Norfolk, Virginia, before his marriage, he had spent many a night in Mary Hogwood's sporting-house. If James was going to kill anyone, then Brierley would have been top of his list. Just after James died, Charles Ratcliffe sent a letter to John Aunspaugh in which he provided a detailed account of events at Battlecrease at that time. The letter included the sentence that James had found out about events at Flatman's Hotel and he expected him to '*plug Brierley at any time.*'[1651]

There is no aspect of James' personality or life, other than his chronic use of drugs, that makes him remotely resemble a psychopathic killer. Douglas, the FBI profiler, used a crime analysis of the Ripper murders to produce a list of traits and characteristics for the murderer. For example, he wrote that the killer would be '*paranoid,*' with a poor self-image, possibly some '*physical abnormality, scarring or speech impediment that he perceived as psychologically crippling.*' He would: '*not be adept at meeting people socially, and most of his relationships would have been with prostitutes.*' This type of offender is unlikely to have been married '*or to have carried on a normal relationship with a woman.*'

Not a single one of these traits can be applied to James Maybrick. Douglas was scathing about the motive that the diarist provided for starting his brutal killings, writing: '*Love can do a lot of things to a gentle man, but what the Ripper did isn't one of them.*'

There are other serious issues with the notion that James might have been a psychopathic killer. The modus operandi of serial killers evolves as they commit their offences. They learn from their mistakes and become more confident. Both Douglas and David Canter suggest that Jack the Ripper committed other offences in the Whitechapel area before he killed his first victim.

That behavioural pattern is not reflected in the Diary. The diarist wrote that he first killed a woman in Manchester, though provides no details of the killing and, soon after, kills Polly Nichols in Whitechapel. While such a sequence of events is possible, it is unlikely.

On top of that, James Maybrick lived for another six months after the murder of Mary Kelly, yet no more Ripper murders are recorded in the Diary. Professor Rubinstein tried to explain this change in behaviour by suggesting that Britain's most notorious serial killer had somehow been magically cured after a few courses of treatment with a homeopathic medicine. According to Douglas, serial killers do not stop unless they are caught, arrested for another offence, or die. They might get '*scared out of a particular location and move on to another where their previous crimes are not linked.*'[1652]

The diarist, if he is to be believed, abruptly stopped his murderous campaign after supposedly rediscovering his love for his wife. It is an absurd proposition.

CONCLUSION

Robert Smith wrote that the Diary:

> '*weaves together so precisely the previously unconnected lives of James Maybrick and of Jack the Ripper, it would be nothing short of miraculous, were a forger to have created such accurate chronologies for both characters simultaneously, as well as researching a wealth of previously unknown or obscure information to insert into it*'.[1653]

It is a bold statement, and one which reflects Smith's sincere beliefs about the Diary. It is also an inaccurate statement. The Diary fails to provide an accurate chronology of events; for example, the evidence points to Florence's affair with Brierley beginning after the Ripper murders had finished. The affair could not therefore have been the motivation for the murders. The Diary does not provide a wealth of new material. In fact, it provides very little information and what it does provide can be easily sourced from books written before 1992. Indeed, one of the key characteristics of the Diary is its lack of detail. The author is determined to try to avoid writing anything that might later be shown to be incorrect. The murders of Polly Nichols, Annie Chapman and Elizabeth Stride are covered in short paragraphs. Nothing new is to be found in the accounts of the murders. There are no new insights.

Douglas wrote that if the Diary had been authentic, then he would: '*expect it to shed new light on the crimes, or their methodology, which is missing here. In a real killer's diary, I'd expect to see his whole pathological construct laid out, rather than just a simple and breast-beating excuse for why he has to kill these women. All of that is missing from the so-called Maybrick diary, which must be judged an elaborate fake.*'[1654]

[1651] Christie T.L., op. cit., page 50.
[1652] Douglas J. and Olshaker M., op cit., page 61.
[1653] Smith R., op cit., page 2.
[1654] Douglas J. and Olshaker M., op cit., page 74.

The diarist also fails to provide a wealth of new material on James and Florence Maybrick. The details on the Maybrick family found in the Diary are rudimentary and easily sourced from the large number of books that exist on the Florence Maybrick trial. The so-called great insights, such as '*Gladys being ill again*,' are nothing of the kind. The author has simply identified a relevant line in a book and added it into the narrative. The only skill on display is the ability to copy.

If just two books were needed for the Ripper narrative – those by Stephen Knight and Martin Fido – then just one book was needed for background details on the Maybrick family. The book by Bernard Ryan was pivotal in producing the forgery; some of the lines from the book have been copied into the Diary narrative almost word for word. This is where the author of the document has made a fundamental mistake, for although the Ryan book is excellent in many ways, it does contain errors. It is when those errors appear in the Diary's account of events that the fraudulent nature of the document is clearly exposed. For example, the diarist states that his business was flourishing when, at the time, James Maybrick's cotton business was actually struggling. On the other hand, some aspects of his business life were prospering, but none of that is mentioned in the Diary. The failure to refer to Thomas as '*Tom*,' or mention that James Chandler Maybrick's nickname was '*Sonny*,' shows that the diarist did not have access to *obscure* information. Perhaps the most telling fact that reveals the diarist's lack of intimate knowledge of the Maybricks is his complete failure to reference Florence's miscarriage in early 1889. That would have been a traumatic event, especially if James believed he may not have been the father of the child. That can only mean that the diarist was not James Maybrick.

Those who argue that the Diary is genuine point to the fact that it was written in a document that is definitely Victorian in origin. What they fail to answer is why such an infamous murderer would want to write such a powerful confessional account in an old scrapbook that had previously been used as a photograph album. Evidence from the stains in the scrapbook suggest that it might have been used to hold photographs in the 1920s and 1930s. That is many years after the Ripper murders had been committed, and long after the death of James Maybrick.

As a result, the nature and history of the document undermines, rather than strengthens the case for the Diary being genuine. Such scrapbooks are not uncommon and a resourceful forger could have easily obtained one. The ink is more problematic, but once again a resourceful forger could have purchased some old ink, or even produced his own using a Victorian recipe.

Even if one accepts that the paper and the Diary ink are Victorian, there are still two key criteria that the document fails to meet for it to be viewed as a genuine confessional account. Firstly, the handwriting of the diarist does not match the handwriting of James Maybrick. In order to try to overcome this major obstacle, the pro-Diary camp tried to suggest that James' will was a forgery. The weakness of their case was exposed when further documents came to light that provided additional examples of James' handwriting. All of these new documents proved beyond doubt that James' handwriting was very different to the handwriting of the diarist. They also demonstrated a style that was very different to that of the author of the *Dear Boss* letter. Paul Feldman argued that if James Maybrick didn't write the *Dear Boss* letter, then the Diary was a forgery. On this point, Feldman was correct. James did not write the *Dear Boss* letter; therefore, the Diary must be a forgery.

The second major hurdle that the Diary fails to clear is the absolute necessity to provide an acceptable provenance for the document. The Diary can be tracked to 1992, but no further back in time. Anecdotal stories and circumstantial evidence are no substitute for hard facts. All the varying and diverse hypotheses developed to try to explain the Diary's provenance lack substantial evidence to support them.

James Maybrick had his faults. He was addicted to dangerous drugs. He could be violent and abusive, he definitely hit his wife on at least one occasion. He could be pessimistic, and at times he was manipulative.

Nevertheless, despite these undoubted blemishes on his character, he was not a psychopathic serial murderer. He could be kind, considerate, empathetic and generous. He loved his family. He loved his children. He probably loved his wife. Weeks before his death he went to London to pay-off Florence's debts even though he must have had strong suspicions about her relationship with Brierley.

James was popular with his friends, both male and female. He was sociable. He was a man with issues, but he was not Jack the Ripper.

The Diary is, without any doubt, a forgery.

BIBLIOGRAPHY

PRIMARY SOURCES

The National Archives

HO 144/1638/A50678D/11
HO 144/1638/A50678D/13
HO 144/1638/A50678D/24
HO 144/1638/A50678D/629
HO 144/1639/A50678D/29
HO 144.1639 A50678D/47
HO 144/1639/A50678D/72
HO 144/1639/A50678D/99
HO 144/1639/A50678D/103
HO 144/1639/A50678D/104
HO 144/1639/A50678D/192
HO 144/1639/A50678D/264
HO 144/1639 A50678D/442.
HO 144/1639/A50678D/667
HO 144/1639/A50678D/702
HO 144/1640/A50678D/312
HO 144/1640/A50678D/313
HO 144/1640/A50678D/315
HO 144/1640/A50678D/320
HO 144/1640/A50678D/350

Other Primary Sources

American Census Details
Baptism Records, St Peter's Church, Liverpool
British Census Details
Ellis Island and Other New York Passenger Lists 1820-1957, accessed at myheritage.com
Canada In-coming Passenger Lists accessed at ancestry.com
Confederate Army Records of Captain Du Barry accessed in the Records Office in Florida
Presbyterian Church records, Government Street, Mobile, Alabama
Probate Documents in Mobile County Probate Court
Records and minutes of the Liverpool Cotton Association in the Liverpool Public Library
Richmond Chancery documents relating to the Baroness' land claims in America
Sheridan Road Newsletter
Trevor Christie Collection
www.virginiaclub

SECONDARY SOURCES

Newspapers: British

Anglo-American News (London)
Barmouth and County Advertiser
Berkshire Chronicle
Birkenhead and Cheshire Advertiser
Birkenhead News
Bolton Evening News
Cardiff Times
Cheshire Observer
Commercial Gazette (London)
Dundee Courier
Eastern Daily Press
Edinburgh Evening News
Garston and Woolton Reporter
Glasgow Herald

Graphic
Greenock Telegraph and Clyde Shipping Gazette
Halfpenny Weekly
Halifax Evening Courier
Hastings and St Leonards Observer
Isle of Wight County Press
Isle of Wight Observer
Lancashire Evening Post
Liverpool Albion
Liverpool Citizen
Liverpool Courier
Liverpool Daily Courier
Liverpool Daily Post
Liverpool Echo
Liverpool Evening Express
Liverpool General Advertiser
Liverpool Mail
Liverpool Mercury
Liverpool Review
Liverpool Standard & General Advertiser
Liverpool Weekly Courier
Liverpool Weekly Mercury
Liverpool Weekly News
Lloyds Weekly Newspaper
London Evening Standard
Manchester Courier & Lancashire General Advertiser
Manchester Times
Monmouthshire Beacon
Newcastle Journal
News of the World
New York Herald (London edition)
Northampton Mercury
Northern Echo
Northern Times
Pall Mall Gazette
Prescot Reporter
Royal Cornwall Gazette
Runcorn Examiner
Sheffield Evening Telegraph
Southport Visiter
South Wales Echo
Sporting Gazette
St James's Gazette
Surrey Advertiser
The Era
The Graphic
The Porcupine
The Queen
The Times (London)
Truth
Wells Journal
Worcester Journal

Newspapers: Overseas
Adelaide Express & Telegraph (Australia)
Alton Evening Telegraph (Illinois)
Altoona Mirror (Penn)

Atlanta Constitution (Georgia)
Atlantic Daily Telegraph (Iowa)
Austin Daily Statesman (Texas)
Bridgeport Sunday Post (CT)
Brisbane Telegraph (Australia)
Boston Daily Globe
Boston Sunday Globe
Cairo Daily Bulletin
Charleston Daily Courier (South Carolina)
Charleston Mercury (South Carolina)
Chicago Daily Tribune
Chicago Inter Ocean
Chicago Sunday Inter Ocean
Cincinnati Commercial Tribune
Cincinnati Star
Columbus Daily Times (Indiana)
Columbus Enquirer Sun (Georgia)
Connecticut Magazine (CT)
Daily Constitutionalist (Georgia)
Daily Picayune (New Orleans)
Davenport Democrat (Iowa)
Evening Star (Washington DC)
Evening World (NY)
Galveston Daily News (Texas)
Hagerstown Mail (Maryland)
Harrisonburg Evening News (VA)
Indianapolis Star (Indiana)
Litchfield County Times (CT)
Los Angeles Herald
Macon Telegraph (Georgia)
Minneapolis Journal (Minnesota)
Mobile Daily Item
Mobile Register
Morning News (Savanah, Georgia)
Muskogee Democrat (Oklahoma)
Newark Advocate (New Jersey)
New Haven Register
New Milford Times (CT)
New World (New York)
New York Herald
New York Times
New York Tribune
New York World
Norfolk Chronicle (VA)
Norfolk Landmark (VA)
Norfolk Virginian (VA)
Perth Amboy Evening News (New Jersey)
Pittsburgh Dispatch
Pittsburgh Press
Saint Joseph Herald (Missouri)
Sioux City Journal (Iowa)
South Australian Chronicle
Sunday Herald Bridgeport (CT)
Sunday News (USA)
Sunday Oregonian (Portland)
Sunday Spectator (Indiana)
The Province (Vancouver, Canada)

The Times (Richmond, VA)
Times-Democrat (New Orleans)
Times-Dispatch (VA)
Times-Picayune (New Orleans)
Tipton Tribune (Indiana)
Vancouver World (Canada)
Virginian Pilot (VA)
Washington Post

Books
Adkin M., *The Gettysburg Companion,* (Stackpole Books, London, 2008)
American Psychiatric Assoc. (2013). *Diagnostic and statistical manual of mental disorders* (5th ed.). Arlington, V.A.
Amos H.E., *Cotton City,* (University of Alabama Press, Alabama, 1985)
Aughton P., *Liverpool - A People's History,* (Carnegie Press, Preston, 1990)
Baines T., *History of Liverpool,* (Longman, Brown, Green and Longmans, London and Liverpool, 1852)
Belchem J., (ed.) *Liverpool 800,* (Liverpool University Press, Liverpool, 2006)
Bell K., *The Legend of Spring-Heeled Jack,* (The Bodywell Press, Woodbridge, 2017)
Begg P., *Jack the Ripper: The Facts,* (Robson, London, 2004)
Begg P., *Jack the Ripper: The Definitive History,* (Pearson, London, 2005)
Begg P., and Bennett J., *Jack the Ripper,* (Carlton Books, London, 2017)
Begg P., Fido M., Skinner K., *The Jack the Ripper A to Z,* (Headline Books, London, 1991)
Begg P., Fido M., Skinner K., *The Jack the Ripper A to Z,* (John Blake, London, 2010)
Blake V., *Mrs Maybrick,* (National Archives, Kew, 2008)
Blumenfeld R. D., *RDB's Diary,* (Heinemann, London, 1930)
Boumphrey I., *Yesterday's Liverpool: A Pictorial History 1857 to 1957,* (Boumphrey, Preston, 2007)
Brabin A., *The Black Widows of Liverpool,* (Carnegie Publishing Ltd., Lancaster, 2003.)
Brack A., *The Wirral,* (Phillimore, Sussex, 1988)
Burns P., *Grassendale - Birth of a Suburb,* (Green Hey Press, Liverpool, 2021)
Canter D., *Mapping Murder,* (Virgin, London, 2003)
Chataigne, J. H., *Directory of Norfolk and Portsmouth 1882-83,* (Chataigne, Norfolk, 1883)
Christie T.L., *Etched in Arsenic,* (Harrap and Co, London, 1969)
Colquhoun, K., *Did She Kill Him?* (Little Brown, London, 2014)
Cornwell P., *Portrait of a Killer - Jack the Ripper, Case Closed,* (Time Warner, London, 2005)
Crooks E.M., *The Moraine Hotel of Highland Park, Illinois 1900-1972,* (January 1977)
Davies S.C., *The Funny Little Games of Jack the Ripper,* (Amazon, Great Britain)
De Leon T.C., *Belle, Beaux and Brains of the 1860s,* (T. Fisher Unwin, London, 1909)
Delaney C., *The Story of Mobile,* (HB Publications, Mobile, 1994)
Densmore H., *The Maybrick Case: English Criminal Law,* (London, Swan Sonnenschein & Co., 1892)
Dickens H., *The Recollections of Sir Henry Dickens, K.C.,* (Heinemann, London, 1937)
Douglas J., and Olshaker M., *The Cases that Haunt Us,* (Simon and Schuster, London, 2000)
Edwards R., *Naming Jack the Ripper,* (Sidgwick and Jackson, London,2014)
Emsley J., *The Elements of Murder,* (Oxford University Press, Oxford, 2006)
Ensor, R., *England 1870-1914,* (Clarendon Press, Oxford, 1987)
Evans S.P., *Executioner: The Chronicles of a Victorian Hangman,* (Sutton, Thrupp, 2004)
Evans S.P. and Gainey P., *Jack the Ripper: First American Serial Killer,* (Arrow, London, 1995)
Evans S.P., and Skinner K., *Jack the Ripper: Letters from Hell,* (Sutton Publishing, Stroud, 2001)
Evans S.P., and Skinner K., *The Ultimate Jack the Ripper Source Book,* (Robinson, London, 2000)
Farrell M., *Poisons and Poisoners,* (Bantam Books, London,1994)
Feldman P., *Jack the Ripper: The Final Chapter,* (Virgin, London, 1997)
Fido M., *The Crimes, Detection and Death of Jack the Ripper,* (Weidenfeld and Nicholson, London, 1987)
Foster J. W., *Diplomatic Memoirs Vol. 2,* (Houghton Mifflin Co., Boston and New York, 1909)
Gardiner R., *The History of the White Star Line,* (Ian Allan, Surrey, 2001)
George S., *Liverpool Park Estates,* (Liverpool University Press, Liverpool, 2000)
Graham A. and Emmas C., *The Last Victim,* (Headline, London, 1999)
Graysmith R., *Zodiac,* (Titan Books, London, 2007)
Green, R., *National Heroes - The Aintree Legend,* (Mainstream Publishing, Edinburgh, 1999)
Green R., *Race Apart - The History of the Grand National,* (Hodder and Stoughton, London, 1988)

Bibliography

Griffiths, R., *History of the Royal and Ancient Park of Toxteth Liverpool,* (S. Hill, Liverpool, 1923)
Hall, J.G, and Martin D.F., *A Perfect Judge,* (Barry Rose Law Publishers, London, 1999)
Hamilton G., *Biography of James Blaine,* (Henry Bill Publishing, Norwich, 1895)
Harris M., *The True Face of Jack the Ripper,* (Michael O'Mara Books, London, 1994)
Harrison S., *The Diary of Jack the Ripper,* (Blake, London, 1998)
Harrison S., *Jack the Ripper: The American Connection,* (Blake, London, 2003)
Hayes C., *The Changing Face of Merseyside,* (Breedon Books, Trowbridge, 2002)
Hiley R. W., *Memories of Half a Century,* (Longmans, Green and Co., London, 1903)
Hill M., and Griffiths B., *32 CCL,* (published by the Freemasons, 2005)
Horton S., *Street Names of Liverpool* (Countryvise, Birkenhead, 2002
Hostettler J., *Politics and Law in the Life of Sir James Fitzjames Stephen,* (Barry Rose Law, Chichester, 1995)
Hutto R.J., *A Poisoned Life,* (McFarland and Co., Jefferson, 2018)
Ingraham J.H., *The Sunny South or the Southerner at Home,* (G. G. Evans, Philadelphia, 1860)
Irving H.B., *Trial of Mrs Maybrick,* (William Hodge, London, 1927)
Jarvis A., *Docks of the Mersey,* (Ian Allan, London 1988)
Johnas J., *Highland Park: Settlement to the 1920s,* (Arcadia, Chicago, 2007)
Jones C., *The Maybrick A to Z,* (Countywise, Birkenhead, 2008)
Jones F., *Murderous Women,* (Headline, London, 1991)
Jones C. W., *Norfolk as a Business Centre, Its Principal Industries and Trades* (Virginian Press, Norfolk, 1881)
King P., *The Grand National, Anyone's Race,* (Quartet Books, London, 1983)
Knight S., *Jack the Ripper: The Final Solution,* (Chancellor Press, London, 2002)
Lansden J.M., *A History of the City of Cairo, Illinois,* (South Illinois University Press, 2009 reprint)
Levy J.H., *The Necessity of Criminal Appeal,* (P. S. King and Son, London, 1889)
Lewis D., *The Churches of Liverpool,* (Bluecoat Press, Liverpool, 2001
Linder S., Morris C., Skinner K., *Ripper Diary - The Inside Story,* (Sutton, Stroud, 2003)
Liverpool Cotton Association Ltd., *Board Minute Book, Vol.1* (Sept 1882-Dec 1888)
Lloyd-Jones T., *Liverpool Street Names,* (Bluecoat Press, Liverpool, 2005)
Macilwee, M., *The Gangs of Liverpool,* (Milo Books, Lancs., 2007)
MacDougall A.W., *The Maybrick Case: A Treatise,* (Bailliere Tyndall and Cox, London, 1891)
MacDougall A.W., *The Maybrick Case: A Statement of the Case as a Whole,* (Bailliere Tyndall & Cox, London, 1896)
Maybrick F., *My Fifteen Lost Years,* (Funk and Wagnalls, London, 1905)
Moiseiwitsch M., *Five Famous Trials,* (Heinemann, London, 1962)
Morland N., *This Friendless Lady,* (Frederick Muller, London, 1957)
Mortimer W.W., *The History of the Wirral Hundred,* (Wittaker, London, 1847
Nott-Bower W., *Fifty-two years a Policeman,* (Edward Arnold, London, 1926)
O'Brien R. Barry, *The Life of Lord Russell of Killowen,* (Smith, Elder and Co., London, 1901)
O'Mahoney, *Ways and Byeways of Liverpool,* (Daily Post Printers, Liverpool, 1931)
Onslow T. and Sturgeon J., *Dogs and Ladies Not Allowed,* (Countyvise, Birkenhead, 2007)
Parramore, T.C., et al., *Norfolk – the First Four Centuries,* (University Press of Virginia, Charlottesville, 1995)
Parrott K., *Pictorial Liverpool, The Art of W.G. and William Hardman,* (Bluecoat Press, Liverpool, 1992)
Parry D., *Lady Poisoners,* (Bluecoat Press, Liverpool, 2001)
Pearson P., *Neston and Parkgate Remembered,* (Countyvise, Birkenhead, 1998)
Philpott R.A., *Historic Towns of the Merseyside Area,* (Liverpool Museum, Liverpool, 1988)
Picton J.A., (illustrations by Stephen Amer), *Memorials of Liverpool, Historical and Topographical* (Birkenhead, 1873)
Picton J.A., *Municipal Archives and Records 1700-1835,* (Gilbert G. Walmsley, Liverpool, 1886)
Priestley P., *Victorian Prison Lives,* (Pimlico, London, 1999)
Psychological Assessment with the MMPI-2, (2001). Lawrence Erlbaum Associates, Mahwah, New Jersey, London
Pye K., *Discover Liverpool,* (Trinity Mirror, Liverpool, 2007)
Rendell K.W., *Forging History,* University of Oklahoma Press, London, 1994)
Roberts S. J., *Hoylake and Meols Past,* (Phillimore & Co., Chichester, 1992)
Robinson B., *They All Love Jack: Busting the Ripper,* (Fourth Estate, London, 2015)
Rumbelow D., *The Complete Jack the Ripper,* (Penguin, London, 2004)
Ryan B., *The Poisoned Life of Mrs Maybrick,* (toExcel Press, Lincoln, 2000)
Sharples J., *Liverpool,* (Yale University Press, London, 2004)
Smith J., *The Register of Death,* (Countyvise, Birkenhead, 2007)
Smith R., *25 Years of the Diary of Jack the Ripper,* (Mango Books, London, 2017)
Smith R., *The True History of Jack the Ripper,* (Mango Books, London, 2019)

Stephen L., *The Life of Sir James Fitzjames Stephen, bart., KCSI, a Judge of the High Court of Justice*, (Smith Elder and Co., London, 1895)
Sugden P., *The Complete History of Jack the Ripper*, (Robinson, London, 2002)
Sydney Robinson W., *Muckraker*, (The Robson Press, London, 2012)
Taylor S., *Bulls and Bears*, (C. Tinling and Co., London, 1908)
Tidy C.M., and Macnamara R., *The Maybrick Trial: A Toxicological Study*, (Balliere, Tindall & Cox, 1891)
Swift, Rev. J.M., *Garston and its Church*, (Antony Rowe, Chippenham, 1937 – reprinted 2002)
Visitors' Illustrated Guide to Liverpool (D. Maples, Liverpool, 1886)
Twist C., *A History of the Liverpool Parks*, (Hobby Publications, Bristol, 2000)
Wagner C. L., *Seeing Stars*, (Arno Press, New York, 1977)
Wainwright D., *Liverpool Gentlemen*, (Faber and Faber, London, 1960)
Weatherly, F.E., *Piano and Gown*, (G. P. Putnam's Sons, London, 1926)
Whale D.M., *Lost Villages of Liverpool, Part One*, (Stephenson & Sons, Prescot, 1885)
Whale D.M., *Lost Villages of Liverpool, Part Three*, (Stephenson & Sons, Prescot, 1885)
Whittington-Egan R., *Tales of Liverpool: Murder, Mayhem & Mystery*, (Gallery Press, Parkgate, 1987)
Whittington-Egan R., *Jack the Ripper: The Definitive Casebook*, (Amberley Publishing, Stroud, 2013)
Whorton J. C., *The Arsenic Century*, (Oxford University Press, Oxford, 2011)
Whyte F., *The Life of W.T. Stead*, Vo, 1 (Jonathon Cape, London, 1925)
Wolff C., *Who was Jack the Ripper? A Collection of Present-Day Theories and Observations*, (Grey House Books, London, 1995)

Articles

Carter W., 'Notes on the Maybrick Trial' in *Liverpool Medico-Chirurgical Journal*, (no.18, Jan 1890)
Carter W., Post-trial Transcript notes, New Scotland Yard
Davis, R.S., 'A Cotton Kingdom Retooled for War: The Macon Arsenal and the confederate Ordnance Establishment' in *The Georgia Historical Quarterly*, Vol. 91, No. 3, (Fall, 2007)
Dickens C., *Boz in Egypt*, located at www.charlesdickenspage.com
Dolgin D.L., 'Trials of Womanhood: On the Lecture Circuit with Mrs Maybrick in 1908' in *Mobile Bay Monthly*, (December 2001)
Dolgin D.L., 'Jack the Ripper and a Belle from Mobile' in *Alabama Heritage*, (Number 71, Winter 2004)
Dolgin D.L., 'The Babe of Mobile' in *Ripperologist*, No. 32, December 2000.
Dougherty, M.P., *American Diplomats and the Franco-Prussian War: Perceptions from Paris and Berlin*, (University of California, 1980) accessed at core.ac.uk/download/pdf/215552817.pdf
Extract in Mississippi Encyclopedia on John Ingraham at www.ulib.niu.edu/badndp/ingraham_joseph.html
Evans S.P., 'Suspect and Witness – the Police Viewpoint' available to view at www.casebook.org
George C., 'A Coroner for All Seasons: Sir Samuel Brighouse' at casebook.org/press_report/times/18890529.html
George C., in www.yoliverpool.com/forum/showthread.php?t=2593
Goldberg, M.D., 'Southern Honour, Confederate Warfare', (University of Louisville thesis, 2011) accessed via ir.library.louisville.edu
Harris, J.E., 'Evidence in the Maybrick Case, 1894', (King, Bell and Railton, London, 1894)
Hartley, J., https://jayhartley.com/the-writing-on-the-wall//
Highland Park Directory, in *Bumstead's Waukegan City and Lake County Directory, 1916-1917*
Hoffman, W., 'A Narrative of Personal Adventure and Observation During Two Wars, 1861-65, 1870-71', (Sampson Low, London, 1877) accessed at www.gutenberg.org/files/51195/51195-0.txt
Inquest Report into the Death of James Fuller, 11th April 1911 (Rossland, British Columbia, 138/11)
Jones, C.J.M., 'The Diary of Jack the Ripper: A Modern Construct' in *The Journal of the Whitechapel Society*, (Edition 96, February 2021)
Jones C.J.M., 'Did James Maybrick Commit Ripper Style Murders in Austin, Texas?' in *The Journal of the Whitechapel Society*, (Edition 98, June 2021)
Jones C.J.M., 'The Trial of Florence Maybrick' in *The Journal of the Whitechapel Society*, (Edition 100, October 2021)
Katz, P.M., 'From Appomattox to Montmartre: Americans and the Paris Commune', (Harvard UP, 1998)
Kermode M., 'Interview with William Friedkin' at www.film.guardian.co.uk/interview/interviewpages/0,6737,446941,00.html
Maybrick, F.E., 'Criminal Court Procedure in England and America' in *St Louis Republic*, 22nd January 1905
Moody F., 'P.C. George – An Update' in *The Journal of the Whitechapel Society*, Edition 15, August 2007
Morris A., and Griggs I., 'The Anthropologist and the Assassin – The McFarlands of Battlecrease House', in *The Journal of the Whitechapel Society*, Edition 15, August 2007

Bibliography

Morrison and Fourmy's, *General Directory of the City of Galveston, 1886-1887*, accessed at www.ancestry.com

Murray, J., 'Darius Blake Holbrook – Securing a Foundation', in Alexander County Profiles at alexander.illinoisgenweb.org/1968profiles/hist1968e.htm

New Jersey Department of Health and Senior Services, *Hazardous Substance Fact Sheet: Strychnine Sulphate*, (New Jersey, 2002).

Nini A., His academic profile and his research into the Ripper letters, visit andreanini.com

Obituary of James Chandler Fuller in *The Engineering and Mining Journal*, Vol. 91, 13th May 1911

Parry S., 'Valentine's Days' in *The Journal of the Whitechapel Society*, October 2021

Radl M., 'Early Cragsmoor: The Beginning of an Art Colony' in *About Town Magazine*, (2007)

Rubinstein, W.D., 'Hunt for Jack the Ripper' in *History Today*, Vol. 50, May 2000.

'Rules for Female Prisoners – New Prison at Kirkdale' in *Royal Magazine*, No.1, March, 1820

Smith R., *'The Maybrick Diary: A New Edition'* in *The Journal of the Whitechapel Society*, June 2019

Southern Belle Fashion accessed at projects.leadr.msu.edu/uniontodisunion/exhibits/show/the-history-of-the-southern-be/southern-belle-fashion

Stead W.T., 'Ought Mrs. Maybrick be Tortured to Death? An Appeal from North America, and a Confession from South Africa' in *The Review of Reviews*, (Vol. VI, October, 1892) pp. 390-396. Taken from the W.T. Stead Resource Site (www.attackingthedevil.co.uk)

Stevenson T., 'The Maybrick Trial and Arsenical Poisoning' in *Guy's Hospital Reports*, Vol. XLVI, (J & A. Churchill, London, 1889)

Sykes A.H., 'Dr William Carter – a Medical Life in Victorian Liverpool' in *Medical Historian*, No. 21, 2009-2010

'The Maybrick Case' in *The Lancet*, Vol. 134. Issue 3442, 17th August 1889

'The Maybrick Trial' in *The Lancet*, Vol. 134. Issue 3443, 24th August 1889

Turner, Dr J., and Johnston Dr H., 'Female Prisoners, Aftercare and Release: Residential Provision and Support in Late Nineteenth-Century England' in *British Journal of Community Justice*, Vol 13(3)

Wood A. and Souden D., 'The Man Who Saw: The Face of Joseph Lawende Revealed' in *Ripperologist*, 87, January 2008. Also available to view at www.casebook.org

Zedner L., 'Review of: Women, Crime, and Custody in Victorian England' (pugetsound.edu)

INDEX

www.ingramcontent.com/pod-product-compliance
Lightning Source LLC
Chambersburg PA
CBHW080754030726
47592CB00009B/2866